Crown Corporations
in Canada

Crown Corporations in Canada

THE CALCULUS OF INSTRUMENT CHOICE

Edited by

J. ROBERT S. PRICHARD
M.B.A., LL.B., LL.M.
Faculty of Law
University of Toronto

Sponsored by the
Ontario Economic Council

BUTTERWORTHS

Crown Corporations in Canada

Printed and bound in Canada by John Deyell Company

The Butterworth Group of Companies

Canada:
Butterworth & Co. (Canada) Ltd., Toronto and Vancouver

United Kingdom:
Butterworth & Co. (Publishers) Ltd., London

Australia:
Butterworths Pty. Ltd., Sydney

New Zealand:
Butterworths of New Zealand Ltd., Wellington

South Africa:
Butterworth & Co. (South Africa) Ltd., Durban

United States:
Butterworth Legal Publishers, Boston
Butterworth Legal Publishers, Seattle
Butterworth Legal Publishers, Austin
Mason Publishing Company, St. Paul
D & S Publishers, Clearwater

Canadian Cataloguing in Publication Data

Main entry under title:
Crown corporations in Canada

(Studies in law and economics)
Sponsored by the Ontario Economic Council.
ISBN 0-409-85954-0

1. Corporations, Government – Canada.   I. Prichard, J.
Robert S.   II. Ontario Economic Council.   III. Series.

HD4005.C76   338.7′4   C83-098083-0

This report reflects the views of the author and not necessarily those of the Ontario Economic Council or the Ontario government. The Council establishes policy questions to be investigated and commissions research projects, but it does not influence the conclusions or recommendations of authors. The decision to sponsor publication of this study was based on its competence and relevance to public policy and was made with the advice of anonymous referees expert in the area.

STUDIES IN
LAW AND ECONOMICS

Studies in Law and Economics is a new monograph series being published by Butterworth & Co. (Canada) Ltd., in collaboration with the Law and Economics Programme at the University of Toronto Faculty of Law. Volumes in the series attempt to bring the tools of economic analysis to bear on legal doctrines and institutions with a view to illuminating the economic impacts of these doctrines and institutions. The series will range broadly over common law topics such as contracts, torts, and property rights, and legislative and executive activities of government such as government regulation, public enterprise, regulation of utilities, and social security programmes. The series editors are Michael J. Trebilcock and J. Robert S. Prichard (University of Toronto, Faculty of Law). Other titles in this series include:

Lawyers and the Consumer Interest: Regulating the Market for Legal Services, edited by Robert G. Evans and Michael J. Trebilcock

Property Rights and Compensation: Compulsory Acquisition and Other Losses, authored by Jack L. Knetsch

The Regulation of Quality: Products, Services, Workplaces, and the Environment, edited by Donald N. Dewees

PREFACE

This volume of essays was sponsored by the Ontario Economic Council. The Council provided both financial support for the project and peer review of the initial drafts of the essays. John Todd, Douglas Hartle and David Conklin have been unceasingly supportive of this project and on behalf of all the contributors I want to record our thanks.

Elaine Kirsch and Kenneth McCarter worked as research assistants on this project. In particular they prepared detailed background papers on the legal status of Federal and Ontario Crown corporations and a complete descriptive inventory of Ontario's Crown corporations. These background papers formed an invaluable foundation for much of the research which appears in this volume. Copies of these studies are on file with the Ontario Economic Council.

As secretary to the Law and Economics Programme Verna Percival has been responsible for many of the administrative duties associated with this project and for typing the manuscript. As always I am deeply indebted to her for her fine work.

Marie Graham, Linda Kee and Jim Michaud, all of Butterworths, were enormously helpful in converting the manuscript into this book.

While Michael Trebilcock is not formally listed as an editor of this volume, he was, as with all things associated with the Law and Economics Programme at the University of Toronto, its major moving force. From the conception of the project through to the publication of this volume, his energy and talents have been ubiquitous.

This volume is dedicated to Martin Friedland and Frank Iacobucci, respectively the past and current Deans of the Faculty of Law. This dedication reflects the enormous support which they have provided to the Law and Economics Programme during their leadership of the Faculty. That support has made our Programme possible, and this volume, as with others in the series, is a direct result of their work.

CONTENTS

INTRODUCTION

While drawn from a number of disciplines, varied in approach, and rich in detail, the essays in this volume are directed towards a single question: why might governments resort to public ownership through Crown corporations instead of some other policy instrument (*e.g.*, taxation, expenditure policy, or regulation) to accomplish a particular interventionist objective? That is, the focus of this book is on the calculus of instrument choice rather than on the more general question of why governments decide to intervene at all.

The fact that in most policy contexts governments have available to them a range of alternative instruments that can technically be deployed in the promotion of given policy objectives seems uncontroversial. For example, if a government wishes to promote indigenous cultural activity, it can engage in public ownership, as in the case of the Canadian Broadcasting Corporation or the National Film Board; provide direct subsidies to theatre groups; finance granting institutions (*e.g.*, the Canada Council); provide tax incentives, such as a capital cost allowance on films or an expense allowance for advertising; and engage in regulation (*e.g.*, through the Canadian Radio-Television and Telecommunications Commission's broadcasting content rules).

Across the entire landscape of government activities, these kinds of choices are almost always available. In fact, we observe a wide spectrum of instruments being chosen, often in conjunction with one another, by different governments at different times in given policy contexts. The puzzle this presents is understanding why in particular settings one instrument is used instead of another, and the essays in this volume are directed to understanding the place of Crown corporations within this broader puzzle of instrument choice.

The first essay by Trebilcock and Prichard (both lawyers) presents this puzzle more fully and then develops a theory of instrument choice founded upon the critical distinguishing characteristics of Crown corporations as opposed to alternative instruments of intervention. The essay includes a detailed introduction to the legal and institutional attributes of Crown corporations in Canada.

The second essay by Borcherding (an economist) and the third essay by Chandler (a political scientist) approach the puzzle of instrument choice from economic and political perspectives respectively. Borcherding, in a comprehensive review of the literature on public enterprise, examines the

extent to which economic theory offers an explanation for the ubiquitous
presence of public ownership, while Chandler investigates the extent to
which ideology and party politics can account for the patchwork manifestations of public ownership across Canada.

The fourth and fifth essays provide a comprehensive empirical description of the extent of public ownership in Canada. Langford and Huffman
present the federal evidence, while Vining and Botterell do the same at the
provincial level. Together, these two essays provide an original and detailed
picture of the enormous variety of Crown corporations in all Canadian
jurisdictions and of the substantial economic role they occupy. This
evidence emphasizes that at least in the Canadian context, no theory of
government intervention can fail to incorporate the role of Crown corporations.

The final two essays are, in effect, case studies in the use of Crown corporations. Palmer, Quinn and Resendes (an economist and two lawyers)
provide a detailed study of Gray Coach Ltd., a publicly owned inter-city
bus company in Ontario. Somewhat more broadly, Borins (a political scientist) reviews the wartime experience with Crown corporations with particular emphasis on the privatization decisions in the post-war period. Both
case studies provide a good deal of detail not found in the first three essays,
which are more theoretical and structural in approach. Furthermore, they
emphasize the need to examine Crown corporations not only from
theoretical and aggregate empirical perspectives, but also by means of
detailed empirical examination of specific corporations.

The phenomenon of Crown corporations in Canada presents a constantly evolving target for study. New Crown corporations are created
regularly by both the federal and provincial governments; existing Crown
corporations are reorganized, merged or dismantled; new legislation and
controls are proposed and implemented; and new controversies concerning
Crown corporations arise frequently. This activity reflects the prominent
place of Crown corporations in Canadian public policy and emphasizes the
need for attention and analysis. At the same time, the movement of events
makes it impossible for the essays in this volume to remain completely up-
to-date in terms of the empirical data they present and the regulatory processes they analyze. Despite this constraint, however, the essays present an
analytical framework and a background store of knowledge based on the
past and present which permit application to new developments and controversies as they occur.

CHAPTER 1

CROWN CORPORATIONS: THE CALCULUS OF INSTRUMENT CHOICE

M. J. TREBILCOCK*
J. R. S. PRICHARD†

I. INTRODUCTION

(a) The Context

Debates over the appropriate role of public enterprise in the economic, social and cultural life of this nation run very deep into its history. The very conception of Canada as a country constructed on an east-west axis, despite the powerful north-south pulls in terms of trade and culture, have always implied a role for government in nurturing and influencing the direction of economic development that was more activist than that contemplated by the classical free enterprise model. The National Policy Debate, precipitated by Canada's first Prime Minister and periodically revived to the present day, very much embodies the sense of a partnership role for government with business and other economic interests in the process of economic development. Against this back-drop, Canadian history is rich in examples of the utilization of public enterprise as a policy instrument in the pursuit of a wide range of policy objectives.

Recently, public enterprise has forced itself to a high place on the agenda of major political issues. The Federal elections in 1979 and 1980 elicited various proposals regarding the privatization of a number of Federal Crown corporations and the enhanced accountability of Crown corporations both to government and to Parliament.[1] A prelude to some of these proposals were the highly publicized enquiries during the 1970s into the

---

* Professor, Faculty of Law, University of Toronto.
† Associate Professor, Faculty of Law, University of Toronto.
[1] See Canada. *Royal Commission on Financial Management and Accountability: Final Reports, March 1979* (Ottawa: Ministry of Supply and Services, 1979) hereinafter the "Lambert Commission" or "Lambert Report".

business activities of Air Canada,[2] Polysar Ltd.,[3] and Atomic Energy of Canada Ltd.,[4] variously involving allegations of conflicts of interest, kick backs, secret commissions, and ineffective financial oversight. Critiques of various aspects of the activities of Crown corporations by Royal Commissions, Parliamentary Committees, and the Auditor-General[5] have ensured a high political profile for the issues of the role and accountability of Crown corporations.

At the provincial level, over approximately the same time frame, issues relating to public ownership have scarcely been more quiescent. Recent moves by a number of provinces to enter the automobile insurance business have provoked highly spirited public controversies. In British Columbia, the British Columbia Resources Investment Corporation (a major Crown corporation) was recently "privatized" by giving away and selling shares to most of the adult population of British Columbia. In Alberta, a major regional airline (Pacific Western) has been taken over by the provincial government. In Saskatchewan, substantial portions of the potash industry have been taken over by the provincial government. On the other hand, in Manitoba, the recently defeated Conservative government was elected partly on a pledge to liquidate a number of public enterprises which had been created by the prior New Democratic Party government. In Ontario, continuing debates before Select Committees of the legislature, before the legislature at large, and before the Porter Royal Commission,[6] have focussed on the issue of the political and public accountability of Ontario Hydro. In Quebec, the present provincial government has taken over a substantial part of the asbestos industry. In the Maritimes, political commitments to foster and promote economic development in slow-growth areas of the region have often taken the form of direct government involvement in business enter-

---

[2] Canada. Commission to Inquire Into and Report Upon Certain Matters Related to the System of Financial Controls, Accounting Procedures, and Other Matters Relating to Fiscal Management and Control of Air Canada. *Air Canada Inquiry Report* (Ottawa: Information Canada, 1975) Willard Z. Estey, Commissioner.

[3] Canada. Parliament. House of Commons. Standing Committee on Public Accounts. "Report of the Standing Committee on Public Accounts to the House of Commons", in *Minutes of Proceedings and Evidence of the Standing Committee on Public Accounts*, Second Session of the Thirtieth Parliament, 1976-77, Issue No. 39, July 7, 1977 (Ottawa: Queen's Printer for Canada, 1977).

[4] Canada. Parliament. House of Commons. Standing Committee on Public Accounts. "Report of the Standing Committee on Public Accounts to the House of Commons", in *Minutes of Proceedings and Evidence of the Standing Committee on Public Accounts,* Third Session of the Thirtieth Parliament, 1977-78, Issue No. 21, March 17, 1978 (Ottawa: Queen's Printer for Canada, 1978).

[5] See, *e.g.,* Canada. Auditor General of Canada. *Report of the Auditor General of Canada to the House of Commons for the Fiscal Year Ended March 31, 1976* (Ottawa: Ministry of Supply and Services, 1976).

[6] Ontario. *The Report of the Royal Commission on Electric Power Planning* (Toronto: Royal Commission on Electric Power Planning, 1980) Chairman: Arthur Porter.

prises and have in turn fostered continuing debates over the effectiveness of this form of intervention.

At the international level, the issue of public enterprise also seems to be a matter of general public debate. In the United Kingdom, the current Tory government was elected in part on a platform calling for denationalization of a number of government-owned industries and greater political account-ability for those public enterprises which were retained. In Australia, a Royal Commission Enquiry into Government Administration released a report in 1976 containing a number of recommendations directed at the role and accountability of public enterprise.[7] In the United States, major government "bail-outs" of failing or faltering firms, such as Lockheed and Chrysler, have provoked agitated debates about the appropriate role of government in business. Again, the energy crisis has precipitated a number of proposals, some originating with the Carter administration, to create state enterprises to explore and develop alternative sources of energy. Recent comparative surveys suggest that similar debates are ongoing in many countries around the world.[8]

Part of the explanation for the sharp policy focus on public enterprises may be the sheer size of the assets now controlled by public enterprises, and the rapid rate of increase in the utilization of this instrument in many jurisdictions. In Canada, at the federal level, the Comptroller General's 1979 listing of government-owned and controlled corporations shows 19 ("agency") corporations in Schedule C to the *Financial Administration Act*,[9] 23 ("proprietary") corporations in Schedule D to the Act, 27 in the "other government corporations" category, 24 in the "mixed enterprise corporations" category, 150 in the category of subsidiary corporations and their subsidiaries, and 101 in the category of associated corporations, total-ling 344 government-related corporations. The Lambert Commission notes that, assuming the transfer of the Post Office, which employs 68,000 peo-ple, from departmental to Crown corporation status, the total personnel employed by Crown corporations, as defined by the Lambert Commission, comes to well over 200,000 people. This compares to over 300,000 or so employees in government departments. In certain sectors, such as transpor-tation and storage, and communications and utilities, where government enterprises are numerous, employment by Crown corporations represents roughly one quarter of the total labour force. The Lambert Commission also noted that federal Crown corporations command an impressive share of the government's budget. Their expenditures from appropriations in

---

[7] Australia. *Report of the Royal Commission on Australian Government Administration* (Canberra: Australian Government Publishing Service, 1976) Chapter 4.4.

[8] See, *e.g.*, A. Gélinas, ed., *Public Enterprise and the Public Interest: Proceedings of an Inter-national Seminar* (Toronto: The Institute of Public Administration of Canada, 1978).

[9] R.S.C. 1970, c. F-10 [am. Schedule C, SOR/71-404; SOR/76-376; SOR/79-441; Schedule D, 1974-75-76, c. 14, s. 56, c. 61, s. 15, c. 77, s. 8; SOR/78-287].

1977-78 amounted to about one seventh of the $38.9 billion appropriated for all of government's needs. They generated revenues of their own of close to $12 billion, while gross loans and advances to them came to an additional $3 billion. Out of total governmental assets of over $74 billion, the share controlled by Crown corporations amounted to $29 billion.[10]

At the provincial level, Vining and Botterell list a total of 197 provincial Crown corporations, with Alberta owning 18, British Columbia 27, Manitoba 13, New Brunswick 10, Newfoundland 37, Nova Scotia 10, Northwest Territories 2, Ontario 21, Quebec 33, Saskatchewan 24, and the Yukon Territory 2.[11] Vining and Botterell estimate that provincial Crown corporations own almost $59 billion in assets and that 72 percent of all provincial Crown corporations have been created since 1960, 49 percent since 1970 (although the growth in assets controlled by Crown corporations has been much less rapid than the growth in numbers of Crown corporations).[12]

(b) The Puzzle

The puzzle of public enterprise, in terms of analyzing the calculus of instrument choice, is the patchwork pattern of its manifestations to be observed across Canada. In the electric utility field in the last two decades most electric utilities have been taken over by provincial governments, but in Newfoundland, Prince Edward Island and Alberta the electric utilities are either in whole or in part still privately owned. On the other hand, in provinces where the electric utilities are government owned, natural gas distribution systems are privately owned. In the case of the telephone industry, in Newfoundland, Nova Scotia, Prince Edward Island, New Brunswick, Quebec, Ontario and British Columbia we observe privately-owned telephone systems which are subject to government regulation. On the other hand, in Manitoba, Alberta and Saskatchewan, the telephone systems are publicly owned, although in Manitoba and Alberta they remain subject to regulation by public utility boards in contrast to the position obtaining in Saskatchewan where the government-owned telephone system is subject to Cabinet regulation. In the airline industry we observe a major national carrier, Air Canada, a publicly-owned enterprise, in competition with another national carrier, Canadian Pacific Air, a privately owned enterprise, both being subject to extensive regulation by the Canadian Transport Commission; in regional markets, both airlines compete with various regional carriers, some of which, as in the case of Pacific Western Airlines, are owned by provincial governments. In the case of railways, we observe

---

[10] Lambert Report, *supra* note 1, at 328.
[11] Vining and Botterell, Chapter 5 in this volume.
[12] *Ibid.*

the co-existence of Canadian National Railways and Canadian Pacific Railways, the first of which is publicly owned. In the case of intercity bus services, we observe in Ontario, as an essay in this volume by Quinn, Palmer and Rescendes examines in some detail, the co-existence of both privately owned and publicly owned bus lines. In the oil industry, we note the co-existence of a major private sector along with a publicly-owned oil company (Petro-Canada). In the broadcasting field, we note the co-existence of a number of private networks with the Canadian Broadcasting Corporation, a publicly owned enterprise, all subject to various forms of regulation by the Canadian Radio-Television and Telecommunications Commission. In the insurance industry, we note in some provinces, especially a number of western provinces, the existence of publicly-owned automobile insurance corporations, while in other provinces these activities are carried on by privately owned enterprises subject to government regulation. In the case of postal services, we note the Post Office, run now as an executive department of government, competing with various privately owned parcel and courier services; its planned transformation into a Crown corporation occurs at a time when the United States government is planning to convert its Post Office from a corporation to an executive department of government. We note also, in capital markets, the existence of Crown corporations (*e.g.*, the Canadian and Ontario Development Corporations) providing loan or equity capital to private sector firms in co-existence with private sector financial institutions; yet we also, in similar contexts, observe lending functions being performed directly by departments of government for purposes such as regional economic development.

In the face of such a mass of contradictions, it is tempting to resort simply to stochastic factors and ideology as explanations for divergent patterns of public enterprise. However, in a Canadian context, ideology is not a robust explanator of the emergence of public enterprise, at least if party policies are treated as, in some respects, ideological. Subject to the qualifications developed in Chandler's essay, Vining and Botterell have shown, in the case of provincial Crown corporations there does not appear to be a strong correlation between political parties and the creation of public enterprises.[13] At the federal level, Canada has never had a social-democratic government, but nevertheless a very large number of government-related corporations have been created over the years by both Liberal and Tory governments. In Alberta and Ontario, the two provinces with arguably the strongest ideological commitment to free enterprise, we observe that, in the first case, the provincial government has purchased Canada's third largest airline (Pacific Western) and, in the second case, the provincial government owns Canada's largest Crown corporation (Ontario Hydro). On the other hand, to resort to historical accidents as explanations

[13] Chandler, Chapter 3 in this volume.

for the emergence of public enterprise is largely to acknowledge that the factors that bear on instrument choice are incapable of specification. We are reluctant to resign ourselves too quickly to this conclusion.

Much of the Canadian writing on Crown corporations to date has been largely descriptive in character, or has tended to focus, in the case of political science literature, on issues of accountability, and in the case of economic literature, on issues of comparative economic efficiencies. Lawyers, despite a major disciplinary interest in issues of institutional design, have so far not extended this interest to issues of instrument choice, at least in the present context. Major reform proposals presently on the political agenda reflect emphases similar to the literature. For example, both the Privy Council Office's "Blue Paper" on Crown corporations[14] and the Lambert Commission[15] focus heavily on procedures for enhancing the public accountability of Crown corporations. On the other hand, prevailing pressures for the "privatization" of some Crown corporations seem in part to be motivated by assumptions about comparative economic efficiencies of privately and publicly managed enterprises. Our thesis is that these two reform thrusts—greater accountability and privatization—cannot be adequately evaluated without a fuller appreciation of the distinctive characteristics of Crown corporations as a policy instrument and the impact on those characteristics (and, therefore, the utility of the instrument from the perspective of political decision-makers) which these reforms are likely to have. Assuming that political decision-makers in setting up Crown corporations have made judgments about the comparative advantages of this policy instrument over private sector regulation, what are the benefits and the costs associated with returning activities to the private sector, perhaps subject to regulation, under a policy of privatization? Assuming also that policy makers in setting up Crown corporations have made judgments about the appropriateness of "distancing", to some extent, the activities being carried on by Crown corporations from the executive and legislative arms of government, what benefits and costs are likely to be associated with the implementation of reform proposals that would integrate Crown corporations somewhat more closely into the executive and legislative decision-making processes of government?

This essay will attempt to explore the special institutional characteristics of Crown corporations as a policy instrument. These characteristics will be evaluated from both technical and political perspectives. The vantage point that we adopt, for the most part, throughout our analysis is that of the politician facing choices amongst competing policy objectives and competing instruments. We assume that the ultimate calculus he brings to bear

---

[14] Canada. Privy Council Office. *Crown Corporations: Direction, Control, Accountability* (Ottawa: Ministry of Supply and Services, 1977) (hereinafter the "Blue Paper").

[15] *Supra* note 1.

on these choices is dominated by a vote maximization objective.[16] We recognize that other actors in the policy-making process (*e.g.*, bureaucrats, interest groups, media) may bring different considerations to bear on these choices, and that in a derivative or interactive way, these various actors will influence the choices made by politicians. However, while we attempt to indicate how the various institutional characteristics of Crown corporations are likely to be perceived by these various classes of actors, our principal reference point remains that of the politician.

Within this general framework, we emphasize the technical and political substitutability of governing instruments, and, in particular, attempt to develop an appreciation of what makes alternative instruments close or imperfect substitutes for Crown corporations in particular policy contexts. Clearly, at a general level, Crown corporations are a substitute both for public regulation of private sector activity and for direct Departmental conduct of an activity. It is our contention that it is difficult to be confident about the likely impact of reform proposals directed to any portion of this spectrum without evaluating the substitution possibilities which these proposals may induce.

(c) The Essay: An Overview

This essay continues, in Section II, with an examination of the problems entailed in defining the concept of Crown corporation with any degree of precision. The difficulties associated with a formal definition of the Crown corporation which focuses simply on legal notions of "corporation" and "control", are identified; a parallel range of difficulties are identified in attempting to define Crown corporations in a functional way, given the widely diverse range of purposes for which Crown corporations have in the past been invoked as a policy instrument. The essay then, in Section III, proceeds to array the distinctive legal and institutional characteristics of Crown corporations. As to the distinctive legal characteristics, modes of creation, Crown immunity, tax treatment, labour relations, financial and political accountability, and rules relating to sources of funds, are discussed. As to comparative institutional characteristics, an attempt is made to explore two separate boundaries—the boundary between public owner-

---

[16] In this respect, we adopt the economic perspective on the political process developed by authors such as A. Downs, *An Economic Theory of Democracy* (New York: Harper and Row, 1957); R. Bartlett, *The Economic Foundations of Political Power* (New York: Free Press, 1973); J. M. Buchanan and G. Tullock, *The Calculus of Consent: Logical Foundations of Constitutional Democracy* (Ann Arbor: University of Michigan Press, 1962); A. Breton, *The Economic Theory of Representative Government* (Chicago: Aldine Publishing Co., 1974); and D. G. Hartle, *Public Policy Decision Making and Regulation* (Montreal, Institute for Research on Public Policy, 1979).

ship and private sector regulation, on the one hand, and the boundary between departmental bureaucracies and Crown corporations on the other. With respect to both boundaries, substantial attention is paid to the relative monitoring costs facing political decision-makers in specifying and monitoring desired policy outputs under policy instruments falling on each side of these two institutional boundaries.

In Section IV, we proceed to survey the history of the utilization of Crown corporations as policy instruments in Canada, identifying the principal fields or contexts in which we observe them, and attempt to relate their existence to the distinctive legal and institutional characteristics identified in Section III, highlighting issues of institutional choice by examining also the reasons why the characteristics of alternative policy instruments rendered them less attractive in each of these contexts. These contexts include: natural monopoly regulation; nation building and community development; moderating the effects of economic transitions and stabilizing income; the provision of capital funds; the promotion of national security and security of supply; the creation of yard-stick competitors; and the control of externalities.

We conclude the essay, in Section V, with a review of both major reform thrusts now current, by attempting to identify the principal costs and benefits facing political decision-makers in moving activities presently carried on by Crown corporations either closer to bureaucratic and political processes of government under more stringent accountability regimes, or closer to purely private sector enterprise under programmes of privatization.

II. THE PROBLEM OF DEFINITION

While the term "Crown corporation" is often used in popular discourse with the kind of casualness that would suggest little in the way of ambiguity about its content, the opposite is in fact the case.[17] Obviously, in evaluating the appropriate role of Crown corporations amongst our institutions and instruments of government, it is important that the evaluation be directed at a clearly focussed phenomenon. Two levels of definition suggest themselves—formal and functional—although neither is by any means free from difficulty.

---

[17] For discussions of the difficulties entailed in defining Crown corporations, see the Lambert Report, *supra* note 1, at Part IV; the Blue Paper, *supra* note 14, at 13 *et seq.*; Sexty, "Canadian Government Business Corporations: Definition and Categorization" [St. John's: Working Paper 78-7, School of Business Administration, Memorial University, 1978]; Langford, "The Identification and Classification of Federal Public Corporations: A Preface to Regime Building" (1980), 23 *Can. Pub. Admin.* 76.

(a) Formal Definitions

A formal definition would emphasize the most important *legal* characteristics of a Crown corporation. The first, and easiest, element in such a
definition would be the requirement of corporate form on the part of any
enterprise or set of activities sought to be embraced by the definition. For
the most part, the law has little difficulty in recognizing a corporation,
when it exists, or identifying its principal legal attributes. For example, a
corporation is a legal person having a separate legal entity from its incor-
porators, shareholders, and managers, and an ability to sue or be sued and
to hold property in its own right. A corporation typically is created either by
incorporation (by letters patent formerly and currently by articles of incorporation) under general statutes such as the *Canada Business Corporations Act*[18] or the Ontario *Business Corporations Act*[19] or, on the other
hand, by special act of parliament or legislature. In the context of Crown
corporations, the presence of a corporate form would serve to mark off
governmental activities carried on in this form from governmental activities
carried on directly by executive departments of government. But while we
may generally have little difficulty in determining whether a set of activities
is being carried on by a government department or by a corporation, we en-
counter more difficulties in characterizing a corporation as a *Crown* corporation.

In addressing this task, a formal definition would most likely look to
whether a corporation was controlled by the Crown and in this regard look
first to criteria bearing on the dimension of ownership. At one polarity, one
might view as Crown corporations only those corporations which were
wholly owned by government, that is to say, a corporation which in its constituent act is deemed to hold all property on behalf of the Crown or a corporation which is incorporated under a general corporation statute and
whose shares are wholly owned by the Crown. For example, the federal
Financial Administration Act[20] assumes, or appears to assume, such a
definition of a Crown corporation in s. 66(1) and in Schedules B, C, and D
definitions of "departmental corporations", "agency corporations", and
"proprietary corporations" (at least in the light of the corporations listed in
these schedules). Similarly, the Lambert Commission in its suggested definition of Crown corporation offered as one criterion that a Crown corporation must be wholly owned by government[21]. However, a less restrictive
position is adopted in s. 1 of the Ontario *Audit Act*[22] which defines a Crown
controlled corporation as:

---

[18] S.C. 1974-75-76, c. 33.
[19] R.S.O. 1980, c. 54.
[20] *Supra* note 9 [am. Schedule B, SOR/78-285, 378].
[21] *Supra* note 1, at 439.
[22] R.S.O. 1980, c. 35.

. . . a corporation that is not an agency of the crown and having 50 per cent or more of its issued and outstanding shares vested in Her Majesty in right of Ontario or having the appointment of a majority of its Board of Directors made or approved by the Lieutenant Governor in Council.

This definition, quite realistically, recognizes that ownership of 50 percent or more of the shares in a corporation constitutes effective control as, to a large extent, does the power to appoint a majority of the members of the Board of Directors, even where share ownership is less than 50 percent. The definition does not attempt to deal with cases where voting rights attaching to shares are distributed on a basis other than one vote per share or are contingent, as is often the case with preference share issues where voting rights may only be exercisable after dividends are missed; in cases such as this, ownership of shares cannot be unqualifiedly equated with ownership of voting rights.

A less restrictive definition again would be one that recognized a corporation as a Crown corporation where the government owned less than 50 percent of the shares (or less than 50 percent of the voting rights). In many contexts, quite small minority shareholdings by government might still constitute effective control. For example, some recent proposals for "privatizing" Crown corporations have envisaged a few shares *per capita* being made available to most adult residents of a jurisdiction with a strict limit on the number of shares that might thereafter be accumulated by any single shareholder, and retention of a substantial minority interest by the government. One might plausibly argue that this concept of privatization may derogate very little from a government's ability to control the activities of Crown corporations and that they should continue to be regarded as Crown corporations for many policy purposes. The Lambert Commission went some distance towards recognizing the concept of *de facto* control by suggesting the creation of a new category of government-related corporations, classified as "shared enterprises", where, *inter alia*, government has taken a direct equity position in common with other participants.[23] However, as will be seen, the Lambert Commission suggests a substantially different, and more relaxed, accountability regime for shared enterprises compared to Crown corporations.[24]

As one moves along the ownership continuum from 100 percent government ownership through more than 50 percent government ownership through minority government ownership, one begins to reach the other polarity on the continuum where government involvement in particular corporate enterprises, falling short, in formal terms, of any of these degrees of equity ownership might still be thought, in particular cases, to justify viewing an enterprise as a Crown corporation. For example, a formal definition

23 *Supra* note 1, at 443.
24 See Vining and Botterell, Chapter 5, in this volume.

which centers primarily on equity ownership will not be sensitive to the fact that the distinction between equity interests and debt interests in a corporation, in terms of effective control, is often quite blurred. For example, preference shareholders may often have less effective control or influence over the activities of a corporation in which they hold such an interest than secured bond holders or debenture holders with wide powers of intervention in corporate decision-making under covenants in trust indentures pursuant to which their interests have been issued. As the report of the Privy Council Office in 1977 on Crown corporations (the "Blue Paper") points out in the case of the Canadian National Railways:[25]

> The creation of the Canadian National Railways and government ownership of the Company was not really as large a leap as might be supposed. The federal government had been deeply involved in the promotion, financing and regulation of railroads prior to 1919. As a consequence, although the three national railroads which were to be brought together under the umbrella of the CNR were nominally in private hands, the common stock held by the private sector represented a minimal cash investment and the financial responsibility for the railroads rested largely with the federal government and certain provincial governments.

Exactly the same set of definitional problems are thrown up by the ownership dimension when one moves to the consideration of subsidiaries or sub-subsidiaries or affiliates of corporations categorized as Crown corporations by whatever definition one chooses to apply to the parent or holding companies. For example, if one adopts as the ownership criterion for Crown corporation a 100 percent government ownership requirement, does one exclude from the ambit of the activities of a corporation that satisfies such a requirement a subsidiary in which it owns a controlling interest of more than 50 percent of the shares but less than 100 percent? Or, if the subsidiary is wholly owned by the parent Crown corporation, how does one categorize a sub-subsidiary which is more than 50 percent but not wholly owned by the subsidiary? That these definitional issues are not trivial is underscored by the fact that in the Federal Comptroller-General's 1979 list of government-owned and controlled corporations, there are some 25 corporations identified as mixed enterprise corporations (corporations owned or controlled jointly with other governments and/or other organizations to further common objectives), 159 subsidiary corporations and sub-subsidiaries (corporations whose shares are owned on a majority holding basis by other corporations identified in the Comptroller's list) and 101 associated corporations (corporations in which corporations listed in previous schedules hold a minority of the shares and/or their accounts are not consolidated into the accounts of the holding corporation).

---

[25] *Supra* note 14, at 11.

So far, in examining how a formal definition of Crown corporation might be structured we have focussed on the dimension of ownership. Obviously, many of the same considerations would apply if one were to focus on the ability of government to appoint members of the Board of Directors of a corporate enterprise. Independently of equity ownership, one might wish to argue that such a power, in particular cases, could confer on government effective control over an enterprise. But, for the purposes of a formal definition, one would have to settle the question of how many, or what percentage of, the Board of Directors are required to be appointed by the government before one might, on that account, regard the corporation as a Crown corporation. Thus, in short, any formal definition of Crown corporation which proceeds from the premise that a Crown corporation is any corporation which the government controls is far from easy to formulate.

(b) Functional Definitions

Even assuming that these difficulties have been resolved, a formal definition of Crown corporation—even a definition which only regards as a Crown corporation one which is wholly owned by government and whose Board of Directors is wholly appointed by government—will in many contexts be over-inclusive, at least in terms of any attempt at useful and focussed analysis. Again, as the Privy Council Office's Blue Paper on Crown corporations points out:[26]

> When the term Crown corporation is used, the corporations which most often spring to mind are those which provide goods or services directly to the public on a commercial or quasi-commercial basis. Yet federal Crown corporations do much more than provide goods and services or operate on a commercial or quasi-commercial basis. Some, such as the Economic Council of Canada or the Science Council of Canada have as their primary role the provision of expert and objective advice to the public and to the Government of Canada in special fields. Others, such as the Atomic Energy Control Board, perform functions of a regulatory nature. Still others have the objective of stabilizing the prices of certain commodities and ensuring an adequate return to the producer on labour and investment. A list of such corporations would include the Agricultural Stabilization Board, the Canadian Dairy Commission, the Canadian Saltfish Corporation and the Freshwater Fish Marketing Corporation. Some, such as the National Research Council and the Medical Research Council, perform granting functions in support of research and conduct research themselves.
>
> A large number of Crown corporations perform functions that would normally be the responsibility of a department of government, and in fact, a number of such corporations are almost completely integrated within a department. (For example, The Director Veterans' Land Act, Director of

---

[26] *Supra* note 14, at 14, 15.

Soldier Settlement, Uranium Canada Ltd., Canadian Commercial Corporation.)

While we recognize, with the Lambert Commission, that these various institutions, whether formally characterized as Crown Corporations or not, must be fitted into any overall scheme imposing accountability requirements on public institutions, we have chosen, in this paper, for the sake of clarity of focus, to confine our attention to corporations in which the government has a *de facto* controlling interest and which, in the words of the Blue Paper, provide goods or services directly to the public on a commercial or quasi-commercial basis, *i.e.*, sell their output in a market.

Even applying some such functional criterion, one is still likely to end up with a highly heterogeneous range of "Crown corporations". Leaving aside "shared enterprises" for separate treatment, the Lambert Commission incorporated the following criteria into its definition of Crown corporations.[27]

(a) Established by constituent act, letters patent/articles of incorporation under Canada Business Corporations Act, or provincial acts.
(b) Tasks akin to private sector entrepreneurial undertakings in a market setting.
(c) Wholly-owned by government.
(d) Board collectively is assigned care and management of the corporation as in the private sector.
(e) Separate employer, outside Public Service Employment Act.
(f) Minister may give direction.

Having duly applied these criteria, the Lambert Commission arrived at the following polyglot list of Crown corporations:[28]

Air Canada (and subsidiaries)
Atomic Energy of Canada Limited
Bank of Canada
Canada Deposit Insurance Corporation
Canadair (and subsidiaries)
Canadian Broadcasting Corporation (and subsidiaries)
Canadian Commercial Corporation
Canadian National Railways (and subsidiaries)
Cape Breton Development Corporation (and subsidiaries)
Central Mortgage and Housing Corporation
Eldorado Nuclear Limited (and subsidiaries)
Export Development Corporation
Farm Credit Corporation
Federal Business Development Bank

[27] *Supra* note 1, at 439.
[28] *Supra* note 1, at 439, 440-41.

Harbour Commissions
  Belleville
  Fraser River
  Hamilton
  Lakehead
  Nanaimo
  North Fraser
  Oshawa
  Port Alberni
  Toronto
  Windsor
  Winnipeg and St. Boniface
Harbour Front Incorporated (207 Queen's Quay West)
Loto Canada
National Arts Centre Corporation
National Capital Commission
National Film Board
National Harbours Board
National Museums of Canada
National Research Council (and subsidiaries)
Northern Canada Power Commission
Northern Transportation Company Limited (and subsidiaries)
Petro-Canada (and subsidiaries)
Pilotage Authorities
  Atlantic
  Great Lakes
  Laurentian
  Pacific
Royal Canadian Mint
The DeHavilland Aircraft of Canada Limited (and subsidiaries)
Teleglobe Canada (and subsidiaries)
The St. Lawrence Seaway Authority
The Seaway International Bridge Corporation Limited
VIA Rail Canada Incorporated

The diversity of activities reflected in this list, even applying fairly restrictive formal and functional definitions of Crown corporations, suggests how
elusive the phenomenon is in terms of framing a precise subject for analysis.
Part of the difficulty resides in the fact that a "market activity" test is
purely descriptive and does not address itself to *why* a Crown corporation is
engaging in market acvitity, on what terms and to what ends. A fully functional definition might well, depending on its purpose, attempt to discriminate among these variables.

    One lesson that might be derived from these definitional forays is the
difficulty of embarking upon a definition without having determined in ad-

vance the purpose for which it is required. As we will develop more fully later in this paper, the enterprises one might wish to characterize as Crown corporations might vary significantly from policy context to policy context. For example, which government-related enterprises (to use a neutral phrase) should enjoy the general Crown immunity from complying with statutory obligations, or should be subject to liability in tort, contract, or criminal law, and under what conditions, or should be accountable to government in matters of financial administration and on what conditions, or should be politically accountable to government or to parliament etc., may well yield different answers with respect to these different issues. Accordingly, a different definition of "Crown corporations", employing different criteria, may well be appropriate in each context.

We now turn to a review of the major legal and institutional characteristics that attach to various kinds of government-related enterprises with a view, later in the essay, to identifying which of these characteristics appear to have been influential factors in the choice of the corporate form by governments in pursuing particular policy objectives. We will then attempt to evaluate how any changes in these legal and institutional characteristics might affect the calculus faced by governments in selecting policy instruments in the furtherance of these objectives.

III. LEGAL AND INSTITUTIONAL CHARACTERISTICS OF CROWN CORPORATIONS

In this section we attempt to identify major legal and institutional characteristics of Crown corporations by employing as our reference point the position applicable to federal Crown corporations. Several points should be emphasized at the outset.

First, the following legal and institutional characteristics of Crown corporations do not represent a common set of characteristics invariably to be observed with every Crown corporation. While differences in characteristics can be identified *between* Crown corporations and other instruments of government intervention, differences can also be identified *within* this particular class of instrument. Legal characteristics may vary from case to case, accountability regimes may vary depending on choice of legal status (*e.g.*, a Crown corporation scheduled under the *Financial Administration Act*[29] compared to an unscheduled Crown corporation), and institutional factors affecting behaviour may differ depending, for example, on whether a corporation is wholly owned by government or includes a significant percentage of private investors who may wish to maximize interests partially at variance with those of the government. Thus, policy makers in choosing

---

[29] *Supra* note 9.

policy instruments must address both inter and intra instrument variables. In the case of Crown corporations, policy-makers face a three-step choice: (1) should goods or services be produced publicly or should the government rely on regulation or subsidization of, or contractual arrangements with, private sector firms; (2) if goods or services are to be publicly produced, should production be undertaken through the departmental or corporate form; (3) if goods or services are to be produced through the corporate form, what should be the extent of the government's ownership interest, the method of creation, the management and accountability regimes, etc?

A second point to be emphasized is that the characteristics of Crown corporations canvassed in this section are viewed in an instrumental way, abstracting from the substantive policy objectives sought to be advanced by the choice of instrument. In our framework of analysis, political decision-makers have only one ultimate objective in all policy decisions—promoting their prospects of election or re-election (vote maximization) and both the choice of interests or values to be advanced and the choice of instrument by which they are to be advanced will be evaluated by them against this benchmark. In this sense, the distinction between means and ends, instruments and objectives is not a useful one. Thus, our analysis proceeds on the basis that whatever the interests or values political decision-makers may wish to advance in a given context, the characteristics of Crown corporations arrayed below will be the dominant choice variables in any consideration of this instrument. In the following section, we examine a number of "fields of activity" (we avoid the term "objectives") in which public ownership is observed to determine the extent to which the utilization of Crown corporations can be explained in terms of these characteristics.

Finally, while the characteristics below have been evaluated from the perspective of the political decision-maker, clearly his/her perspective will be strongly influenced by the interests of other political actors—voters, interest groups, bureaucrats, regulators, media. Characteristics that one set of actors will view positively will be viewed negatively by another set of actors, depending on how they impact on their interests. Politicians will be influenced by their vote maximizing calculus in mediating these competing views.

(a) Legal Characteristics

(i) Modes of Creation

At the federal level, all Crown corporations are created by one of three methods: a special constituent act of Parliament, letters patent (typically pursuant to the *Canada Corporations Act*),[30] or articles of incorporation

---

[30] R.S.C. 1970, c. C-32.

under the current *Canada Business Corporations Act*.[31] It appears to be the case that both special acts of parliament and incorporation under the prevailing general corporation statutes have been methods widely invoked by the federal government in creating Crown corporations. Apparently, under the old Dominion *Companies Act* (and later under the *Canada Corporations Act*), a Minister could only create a Crown corporation by the latter method if his own Act empowered him to apply to the Governor in Council to seek incorporation of a company.[32] This is not the case under the current *Canada Business Corporations Act* where the government, through a Minister, can apparently incorporate any company without reference to the Governor in Council or Parliament. Similarly, an existing Crown corporation may create a subsidiary under the *Canada Business Corporations Act* without prior government or parliamentary approval.[33]

(ii) Crown Immunity

While a Crown corporation, by virtue of being a corporation, can sue and be sued in its own name and hold property in its own right, the question of its liability for non-compliance with legal obligations to which private sector corporations, or individuals, are subject, is more problematic.

At the federal level, s. 66(3) of the federal *Financial Administration Act* defines both Schedule B and C corporations to be agents of the Crown. The status of Schedule D corporations, as well as government-related corporations not listed in any of the schedules to the *Financial Administration Act*, is somewhat indeterminate. However, the *Government Companies Operation Act*[34] in s. 3 provides that any company to which the Act applies is for all purposes an agent of Her Majesty. Section 2 of the Act defines the word "company" to mean:

> . . . a company incorporated under Part I of the *Canada Corporations Act* or a corporation incorporated under the *Canada Business Corporations Act*, all the issued shares of which are owned by or held in trust for Her Majesty in right of Canada except, in the case of a company incorporated under Part I of the *Canada Corporations Act*, shares necessary to qualify other persons as directors.

This definition has broad application and would appear to include many government-related corporations not otherwise characterized as

---

[31] *Supra* note 18.
[32] Lambert Report, *supra* note 1, at 334.
[33] Elaine Kirsch, "The Legal Environment of Federal Crown Corporations" [Toronto: unpublished manuscript on file with the Ontario Economic Council, 1979].
[34] R.S.C. 1970, c. G-7 [am. 1974-75-76, c. 33, s. 265 (Item 4)].

agents of the Crown by the *Financial Administration Act*. Beyond these two statutes, the constituent Acts of a number of Crown corporations either expressly confer or expressly negate agency status with respect to the corporation constituted by the Act. Beyond these constituent Acts, whether a government-related corporation is an agent of the Crown appears to rest largely on common law criteria of Crown or ministerial *control*.[35]

The principal significance of Crown agency status is that, by virtue of s. 16 of the federal *Interpretation Act*,[36] a Crown agency is not bound by any federal statute unless the statute so expressly declares. It should be noted that in the absence of any express statutory declaration to the contrary, immunity from statutory obligation does not extend to liability in tort. In general, by virtue of the provisions of the *Crown Liability Act*,[37] the Crown may be held vicariously liable for torts committed by Crown corporations possessing agency status. In turn, by virtue of the same Act, Crown corporations are likely to be liable directly for tortious acts committed in the course of activities being carried on for or on behalf of the corporation. This is subject to a qualification, recognized in recent cases,[38] that the Crown or an agent of the Crown may not be liable for tortious acts committed in the course of legislative or quasi-judicial functions as opposed to the exercise of administrative, ministerial, or business powers. To state the distinction another way, liability in tort may not attach to acts which are policy-oriented or discretionary in nature as opposed to tortious acts committed in the practical execution of policy decisions or of an operational character.

In relation to contractual liability, a party complaining of a breach of contract by a Crown corporation which is an agent of the Crown has two potential recourses: he may sue the Crown itself as the principal bound by the contract, provided that the agent (*i.e.*, the Crown Corporation) had the power to bind the Crown under either the provisions of the *Government Companies Operation Act* or the common law rules of agency. He may also sue the corporation directly if it falls within the *Government Companies Operation Act* or if its constituent act contains a "sue and be sued" clause. If the corporation is not specifically rendered liable in contract under these rules, the plaintiff may still be able to maintain a claim under the common law doctrine relating to breach of implied warranty of authority in cases where an agent of the Crown has improperly represented that it has authority to bind the Crown.

---

35 See generally Kirsch, *supra* note 33.
36 R.S.C. 1970, c. I-23.
37 R.S.C. 1970, c. C-38.
38 *Welbridge Holdings Ltd. v. The Metropolitan Corporation of Greater Winnipeg*, [1971] S.C.R. 957, 22 D.L.R. (3d) 470; *Anns and others v. London Borough of Merton*, [1977] 2 All E.R. 492 (H.L.).

(iii) Taxation

Section 149(1)(d) of the federal *Income Tax Act*[39] expressly exempts from tax:

a corporation, commission or association not less than 90 percent of the shares of capital of which was owned by Her Majesty in right of Canada . . . or a wholly owned subsidiary to such a corporation, commission or association. . . .

Department practice apparently extends this exemption to wholly owned sub-subsidiaries of Crown corporations. However, s. 27 of the *Income Tax Act* negates s. 149(1)(d) immunity for corporations listed in Schedule D to the federal *Financial Administration Act*, and expressly declares them to be subject to income tax. Moreover, the section provides that such corporations shall be deemed not to be private corporations and thus not to be entitled to any of the special benefits accruing to private corporations such as the small business tax rate provided in the Act. It should be noted, however, that according to departmental practice, a wholly owned subsidiary of a Schedule D corporation will be entitled to the s. 149(1)(d) immunity, as it is not itself listed in Schedule D. It should also be noted that these provisions apply to both federally imposed income tax and provincial corporate tax for the eight "agreeing provinces" (*i.e.*, not Ontario and Quebec) who collect their taxes through Ottawa.

In Ontario, ss. 49 and 135(1) of the *Corporations Tax Act*[40] create exemptions for all Crown corporations from tax on corporate income and on paid-up capital respectively. However, s. 14(10) denies the tax exemptions to those corporations specifically designated in s. 601 of Ont. Reg. 350/73 under the Act.[41]

In Quebec, s. 985 of the *Taxation Act*[42] provides: "A corporation commission or association, the shares, capital or property of which are at least 90 percent owned by Her Majesty in right of Canada or a province . . . is exempt from tax." However, s. 192 of the Act expressly supercedes s. 985 to tax any corporation "carrying on a business as an agent of Her Majesty or of the government unless otherwise provided by the regulations". The regulations in turn provide:

For the purposes of the first paragraph of section 192 of the Act, section 985 of said act applies to every Québec or Canada Crown Corporation with the exception of the following corporations:[43]

---

[39] R.S.C. 1952, c. 148 [am. 1970-71-72, c. 63, s. 27(2); am. 1979, c. 5, s. 8(1)].

[40] R.S.O. 1980, c. 97 [am. 1981, c. 37; 1982, Bill 114].

[41] See Kirsch, *supra* note 33, at 42.

[42] *Loi sur les impôts*, L.R.Q. 1977, c. I-3, s. 985 [am. 1980, c. 13, s. 100]; s. 192 [am. 1980, c. 13, s. 13].

[43] "Règlement sur les impots", Décret 1981-80 (1980), 112 (33) *Gazette officielle du Québec*

Thus, Schedules B and C corporations are exempt from tax, but the proprietary corporations listed in Schedule D are not exempt if Quebec has listed them in the regulation or its amendments. Similarly Crown corporations controlled by other provincial governments appear also to be liable to tax.

(iv) Labour Relations

At the federal level, employer-employee relations in Crown agencies are subject to the provisions of either the *Public Service Employment Act*[44] or the *Canada Labour Code*.[45] Broadly speaking, the *Public Service Employment Act* applies to departmental employees and employees of designated government agencies. Crown corporations in the sense in which the term has been used in this essay, with very few exceptions, fall under the *Canada Labour Code* (*e.g.*, all of the entities listed in the Lambert Commission's Crown corporation category, with the single exception of the National Museums of Canada are currently separate employers outside the *Public Service Employment Act*). There are several important differences in the two regimes. First, some matters which may be subject to collective bargaining under the *Canada Labour Code* are not subject to collective bargaining under the *Public Service Employment Act* and the *Public Service Staff Relations Act*;[46] these include the setting of classification standards and of certain terms and conditions of employment. Secondly, under the public sector legislation, there is a prohibition against certain designated employees from striking; this includes those employees whose duties are duties the performance of which is or will be necessary in the interest of the safety or security of the public.[47]

(Partie 2) 3609, 25 juin 1980, art. 192R1 [am. "Règlement modifiant de nouveau le Règlement sur les impôts", Décret 3926-80 (1980), 112 (63) *Gazette officielle du Québec (Partie 2)* 7121, 22 décembre 1980, art. 5 (1) at 7123]. The corporations listed are: St. Lawrence Seaway Authority, Atlantic Pilotage Authority, Great Lakes Pilotage Authority, Pacific Pilotage Authority, Air Canada, Federal Mortgage Exchange Corporation, National Railways (as defined in the *Canadian National-Canadian Pacific Act* R.S.C. 1952, c. 39), Seaway International Bridge Corporation Ltd., Eldorado Aviation Ltd., Eldorado Nuclear Ltd., Freshwater Fish Marketing Corporation, Petro-Canada, Canada Mortgage and Housing Corporation, Canada Deposit Insurance Corporation, Farm Credit Corporation, Cape Breton Development Corporation, Northern Transportation Company Ltd., Polysar Corp. Ltd., Export Development Corp., Canada Broadcasting Corporation, Teleglobe Canada, and Via Rail Canada Inc.

44 R.S.C. 1970, c. P-32.
45 R.S.C. 1970, c. L-1.
46 R.S.C. 1970, c. P-35.
47 See Kirsch, *supra* note 33, at 48-53.

(v) Accountability

At the federal level, only those Crown corporations scheduled in the *Financial Administration Act* are subject to a generalized scheme of financial accountability to government and to parliament. For Crown corporations not scheduled under the *Financial Administration Act*, financial accountability is either defined on an *ad hoc*, statute by statute, basis in the case of corporations set up under constituent Acts, or follows from the shareholder/corporation relationship defined in the *Canada Business Corporations Act* in the case of Crown corporations incorporated under, or governed by, the latter Act. In relation to the scheduled corporations, Schedule B, or departmental, corporations operate in budgetary and administrative matters much as do conventional departments of government. Section 2 of the *Financial Administration Act* defines the term department to include any corporation named in Schedule B. With respect to Schedule C and D corporations (agency and proprietary corporations respectively), the appropriate Minister must annually lay before parliament the capital budget of each corporation, approved by the Governor in Council on the recommendation of the appropriate Minister, the President of the Treasury Board, and the Minister of Finance. In addition, each agency corporation must annually submit to the appropriate Minister an operating budget for the next financial year for the approval of the appropriate Minister and the President of the Treasury Board. The Treasury Board, on the recommendation of the President of the Treasury Board and the relevant Minister, may by regulation prescribe the form in which budgets must be prepared. Both agency and proprietary corporations must also submit to the relevant Minister an annual report, including financial statements, this report to be tabled by the Minister in Parliament. The Minister may prescribe the form of the report.

The *Financial Administration Act* provides that where, in respect to a Crown corporation (presumably scheduled Crown corporations under the Act), no provision is made in any constituent Act for the appointment of an auditor, or if the auditor is to be appointed pursuant to the *Canada Business Corporations Act*, the Governor in Council shall appoint the auditor. As of January 1978 the auditor for all agency corporations was the Auditor General; only in the case of Schedule D corporations have private auditors been appointed.

Beyond the realm of financial accountability, in the case of most Crown corporations, the federal government has the power to approve bylaws and to appoint and remove directors, board chairmen, and chief executive officers, either pursuant to powers to that effect in the constituent Act of a corporation or under the provisions of the *Canada Business Corporations Act* where these apply. Sometimes, in addition, constituent Acts confer on the government power to issue, through a Minister, policy directives to a Crown corporation. In the case of companies incorporated under the *Canada Business Corporations Act* or predecessor Acts, the designated Minister, as sole shareholder, would appear to have an equivalent power to issue policy directives in the form of unanimous shareholder agreements.

(vi) Sources of Funds

At the Federal level, Crown corporations seeking access to government funds face first the budget approval requirements outlined above. With respect to grants or loans from the government, no payments may be made out of the Consolidated Revenue Fund without the authority of Parliament.[48] This authority may be contained in a variety of sources, such as a special or general statute, or an appropriation in votes on estimates. With respect to guarantees of private sector borrowings by Crown corporations, a government guarantee can only commit the Consolidated Revenue Fund if it has been authorized by Parliament.[49] By virtue of his role as manager of the Consolidated Revenue Fund,[50] all guarantees both in law and in practice are given only by the Minister of Finance.

In the case where a Crown corporation borrows money from the private sector, it would appear that if it is an agent of the Crown it can commit the Consolidated Revenue Fund with respect to the borrowing,[51] provided that there is Parliamentary authority for the borrowing in the corporation's constituent Act or elsewhere.[52] The status of a guarantee given by a Crown corporation with respect to, *e.g.*, a borrowing by a subsidiary is somewhat less clear; however, provided the Crown corporation is an agent of the Crown and its constituent Act authorizes the granting of guarantees,[53] it seems likely that the Consolidated Revenue Fund would be committed.

Clearly, the ability of Crown corporations to obtain access to government funds is an important quality. Grants, loans on better than market terms, and guarantees permitting private sector borrowings against the government's credit, all represent explicit or implicit forms of state subsidy. We set out below a table for federal Crown corporations indicating the extent to which Crown corporations have availed themselves of government funds. For federal Crown corporations as defined by the Lambert Commission, the table indicates, for 1977-78, total assets of over $40 billion, grants of $2½ billion, loans outstanding of $18½ billion and guarantee commitments of about $500 million.

---

48 *Financial Administration Act, supra* note 9, s. 19.
49 *Ibid.,* s. 22.
50 *Ibid.,* s. 9.
51 *Ibid.,* s. 45.
52 So as to satisfy the requirements of s. 19 of the *Financial Administration Act, supra* note 9.
53 So as to provide a source of Parliamentary authority under s. 22 of the *Financial Administration Act, supra* note 9.

TABLE I
Government of Canada Participation in Crown Corporations for the Year 1977/78
(dollars in 000's)

	Reporting Date	Assets	Grants	Loans Outstanding	Net Change in Loans	Guaranteed Loans	Net Change in Guaranteed Loans
1. Air Canada	Dec 31/77	1,234,604		310,346[1]			
2. Atomic Energy of Canada Ltd.	Mar 31/78	1,520,137	403,849	1,085,631	(331,123)		
3. Bank of Canada	Dec 31/77	13,416,420					
4. Canada Deposit Insurance Corp.	Dec 31/77	133,483					
5. Canadair*	—						
6. Canadian Broadcasting Corp.	Mar 31/78	395,889	464,242	254,093	14,054		
7. Canadian Commercial Corp.	Mar 31/78	197,383	10,272	13,300	(2,500)		
8. Canadian National Railways	Dec 31/77	4,698,221	349,401	1,465,454	53,932	498,399	(75,424)
9. Cape Breton Development Corp.	Mar 31/78	149,778	43,801	25,860	1,217		
10. Central Mortgage and Housing Corp.	Dec 31/77	9,835,191	519,791	9,708,815	599,533		
11. Eldorado Nuclear Ltd.	Dec 31/77	183,775		63,138	3,866		
12. Export Development Corp.	Dec 31/77	1,858,777		1,084,338	40,381		
13. Farm Credit Corp.	Mar 31/78	2,595,620	444	2,494,584	290,216		
14. Federal Business Development Bank	Mar 31/78	1,493,576	14,000	639,599	232,939		
15. Harbour Commission*	—						
16. Harbour Front Incorporated*	—						
17. Loto Canada	Mar 31/78	43,672					
18. National Arts Centre Corp.*	—						
19. National Capital Commission	Mar 31/78	359,247	61,491	97,906	9,142		

TABLE I—*Continued*

Government of Canada Participation in Crown Corporations for the Year 1977/78

(dollars in 000's)

	Reporting Date	Assets	Grants	Loans Outstanding	Net Change in Loans	Guaranteed Loans	Net Change in Guaranteed Loans
20. National Film Board*	—						
21. National Harbours Board	Dec 31/77	539,559	11,635	741,842	30,294		
22. National Museums of Canada*	—						
23. National Research Council*	—						
24. Northern Canada Power Commission	Mar 31/78	194,748		194,931	(2,282)		
25. Northern Transportation Co. Ltd.	Dec 31/77	60,740		40,675	(3,953)		
26. Petro-Canada	Dec 31/77	878,696					
27. Pilotage Authorities:							
Atlantic	Dec 31/77	2,014	1,029	407	151		
Great Lakes	Dec 31/77	1,954	632	84	(259)		
Laurentian	Dec 31/77	4,176	56	0	(275)		
Pacific	Dec 31/77	1,908		0	(100)		
28. Royal Canadian Mint	Dec 31/77	57,903		26,510[2]	(1,587)		
29. The DeHavilland Aircraft of Canada Ltd.*	—						
30. Teleglobe Canada	Mar 31/78	220,081		23,566	(3,086)		
31. The St. Lawrence Seaway Authority	Mar 31/78	667,652	644,265[3]	210,000	(631,357)[3]		
32. Via Rail Inc.	Dec 31/77	560	2,062				
SUBTOTALS		40,755,764	2,526,970	18,481,579	298,901	498,399	(75,424)

Anomalies

33. Agricultural Products Board*	—					
34. Canadian Dairy C'ssion	Mar 31/78	125,008	452,022		85,960	(130,496)
35. Canadian Livestock Feed Board	Mar 31/78	1,123	11,717			
36. Canadian Saltfish Corp.	Mar 31/78	7,506			5,419	(4,262)
37. Fisheries Prices Support Board*	—					
38. Freshwater Fish Marketing Board	Apr 30/77	12,726	1,500[4]		9,726	(30)
39. National Farm Products Marketing Council*	—					
40. Canadian Egg Marketing Agency*	—					
41. Canadian Turkey Marketing Agency*	—					
42. Canadian Wheat Board	Jul 31/77	1,405,791			62,468	62,468
SUBTOTALS		1,552,154	465,239		163,573	(72,320)
TOTALS		42,307,918	2,992,209	18,645,152	226,581 498,399	(75,424)

All figures (except for note 1) are taken from The Public Accounts 1978—Vol. 3 Financial Statements of Crown Corporations. Grants include parliamentary appropriations for operating expenses, specific projects, contributions to capital for asset acquisition, and loan forgiveness and government services provided free of charge. Loans include both principal and accrued interest as well as outstanding parliamentary appropriations.

[1] Loan figure taken from p. 8.91 of The Public Accounts 1978—Vol. I and represents the balance as of March 31, 1978.
[2] Loan does not include liability arising from profit in excess of statutory limit (6691).
[3] Loans converted to contributed capital (624,950).
[4] Grants in respect to losses of prior years 71/72, and 72/73. Figure does not include grants from Ontario, Manitoba, Alberta and the Northwest Territories (1,200).
* Data unavailable.

(b) Institutional Characteristics

In Hodgett's striking phrase, Crown corporations are "structural heretics".[54] In some ways, they resemble private sector enterprises maximizing profits subject to the constraints of applicable regulation or direction. In other ways, they resemble bureaucracies executing public policies designed to promote non-market objectives. In coming to some view as to why politicians choose Crown corporations as a policy instrument in particular settings, it is important to attempt to identify the institutional characteristics which mark off Crown corporations, on the one hand, from private sector enterprises which are subject to government direction and influence through a wide range of policies such as direct regulation, tax policy, subsidy policy, procurement policy, etc., and on the other hand, from bureaucracies, where government takes over, and directly performs, given economic functions. This task poses two major boundary problems, that of differentiating the characteristics of public ownership from private sector regulation, and within the public ownership mode, that of differentiating departmental bureaucracies from Crown corporations. Viewing instrument choice from the perspective of the calculus that faces political decision-makers, a number of characteristics would seem influential in determining the location of these two boundaries.

(i) *Public Ownership vs. Private Sector Regulation*

A number of institutional factors might suggest a policy preference, on occasions, for public ownership over private sector regulation (compendiously defined). Many of them derive from the notion of monitoring and information costs first developed in the economic literature on the theory of the firm. We therefore begin with a discussion of this concept.

a. Monitoring and Information Costs

The economic literature on the theory of the firm[55] has sought to answer the question of why we observe firms internalizing the process of coordinating inputs rather than relying on the price system through independent contracting between entrepreneurs and input owners. Coase suggests

[54] J. E. Hodgetts, *The Canadian Public Service: A Physiology of Government 1867-1970* (Toronto: University of Toronto Press, 1973) Chapter 7.
[55] Especially Coase, "The Nature of the Firm" (1937), 4 *Economica* 386; Alchian and Demsetz, "Production, Information Costs, and Economic Organization" (1972), 62 *Am. Econ. Rev.* 777; McManus, "The Costs of Alternative Economic Organizations" (1975), 8 *Can. J. Econ.* 334.

that the main reason why it is profitable to establish a firm is that there is a cost to using the price mechanism; the most obvious cost of organizing production through the price mechanism is that of discovering what the relevant prices are. He also argues that the cost of negotiating and concluding a separate contract for each exchange transaction which takes place in the market must be taken into account. On the other hand, when a firm internalizes factor co-ordination, the character of the contract into which the owner of a factor enters with the firm is such that for a certain remuneration the factor owner agrees to obey the directions of the owner of the firm (or his agents) within certain limits. Within these limits the owner directs the other factors of production. When the costs associated with this process of direction are less than the costs associated with ascertaining relevant factor prices in the market and the transaction costs associated with negotiating independent contracts with these factors, it will pay a firm to internalize the co-ordination of its factors.

McManus emphasizes the enforcement costs associated with using the price mechanism as a constraint on behaviour: resources must be expended in measuring the activity for which one is paying. In many contexts, pecuniary constraints on behaviour are not perfectly enforced because some changes in the activity of an individual will not be detected to the mutual satisfaction of buyer and seller. Where the buyer cannot perfectly specify, or enforce, desired outputs from independent contracting, pecuniary incentives exist for the seller to chisel, shirk, or cut corners to the point where it pays the buyer to specify the contractual constraints more clearly and enforce them more strictly, or alternatively choose a different and less costly form of economic organization for co-ordinating these factors. In choosing a firm which either owns or employs many of the relevant factors an entrepreneur may be able to reduce his monitoring costs by acquiring (at a price) the right to engage in continuous direction in the allocation of productive activities within the firm.

Alchian and Demsetz suggest that in the classical private sector firm, the entrepreneur becomes a specialized monitor in directing the allocation of resources, and moreover has strong incentives to perform his role efficiently by virtue of his position as residual claimant to the income of the firm after payment of the factors.

These explanations for the emergence of firms in our economy carry a clear analogue with respect to the boundary between public ownership and private sector regulation. A government contemplating regulating or otherwise influencing the behaviour of private sector enterprises faces many of the same kinds of costs faced by an entrepreneur engaging in independent contracting for factors. For example, to the extent that a regulatory fiat imposes costs on a private sector firm, it obviously faces incentives to undertake less than complete compliance with the fiat. Similarly, where the government is contemplating provision of a subsidy to a private sector firm, it faces the costs associated with obtaining and validating information from the firm as to its real subsidy requirements and specifying, and enforcing, the conditions governing use of the subsidy and probably also the conditions determining qualifications for further subsidies.

To take a specific illustration, suppose a government should decide that, in the interest of maintaining employment in a region of high unemployment, it is necessary to save a "failing" private sector enterprise. One possible option open to the government is to provide continuing subsidies. In order to determine appropriate subsidies, the government needs a great deal of information about the firm's costs, about conditions prevailing in the firm's output markets, about the potential for the firm substituting, over the long-run, more efficient technology, about the likely effects of continuing subsidies on the incentives of the owners of the firm to improve the performance of the firm. In addition, if the purpose of the subsidies is to maintain jobs in the firm, presumably some conditions would need to be specified as to the type and level of employment that the firm would need to maintain over time in the region in order to qualify for the subsidies. These conditions may be difficult to specify and to enforce. Because of the firm's superior access to much of this information, the government faces the risk of strategic behaviour on the part of the firm in exaggerating the size of the subsidy required and of exploiting the threat to terminate activities in the region, and thus precipitating the politically costly elimination of jobs and other spill-over activities in the area. These various costs faced by government in administering a subsidy policy in this context, all of which in a general sense can be subsumed under the rubric of monitoring costs, are likely to be substantial and create the same incentives for government to internalize factor co-ordination as those facing entrepreneurs in the private sector in choosing between factor co-ordination through the price system or through the firm.

While we have chosen, in the interest of clarity of exposition, to isolate other characteristics of public ownership which might induce a government to favour this policy instrument over private sector regulation, they are, in several cases, variants of the monitoring cost concept, as Borcherding emphasizes in his companion essay.

b. Policy Co-ordination

In situations involving multiple public programmes or objectives for intervention, the Crown corporation may be a relatively more effective instrument than a regulated private firm for enhancing policy co-ordination. It may be the case that in situations in which the degree of public support for the private enterprise is both substantial and takes the form of a variety of different programmes, the cost of co-ordinating these activities can be reduced by internalizing them to the public sector through public owner-ship. Similarly, where there are multiple public objectives being sought through a particular enterprise, it may be that the cost of co-ordinating and reconciling these different objectives can be reduced by internalizing them through the management of, and accountability mechanisms applicable to, Crown corporations. This effect will be enhanced in situations where there are competing public policies being advanced; a trade-off among the policies which may be difficult to achieve in explicit terms in an external forum can be internalized through public ownership.

c. Industry Structure

The structure and nature of the relevant industry will affect the relative desirability of public versus private ownership. In particular, the absence or presence of a competitive market structure in the relevant part of the private sector will be influential as it will affect the monitoring costs identified above. Where there are numerous private firms available to perform a given function and there is competition among them to undertake this function, the industry structure itself will generate superior information for the government, thus reducing the costs of specifying and monitoring desired outputs. That is, the competition among the private firms will serve as a form of monitoring and information production, making reliance on the private sector relatively more attractive. However, in those cases where there is only a single firm or small number of firms available or where the existing firms are able through anti-competitive practices to behave as a single firm, the monitoring costs are increased by virtue of this market structure and public ownership will become relatively more attractive.

The potential gains from public ownership in this context are an exam-ple of a more general phenomenon identified by Alchian and Demsetz. They argue that firms are a specialized market institution for collecting, col-lating, and selling input information, thus serving as a highly specialized surrogate market. Any person contemplating a joint-input activity must search out and detect the qualities of available joint inputs. The employer, by virtue of monitoring many inputs, acquires superior information about their productive potential. Intelligent government regulation of private sec-tor activities may not be attainable without this information, and the least costly way of obtaining it may be for the government to enter the industry as an employer of factors itself. Only in this way may the government be able to obtain the specialized information and expertise required to improve the quality of public policy-making in the area.

Another context in which market structure may favour public owner-ship is where the government is the primary purchaser of the product of the industry. In these cases, which may display certain attributes of bilateral monopoly, the strategic and gaming costs of contracting with private firms may be high and the attractions of vertical integration for the government are increased. In the result, the government as public purchaser may wish to integrate by becoming public producer in the form of a Crown corporation to achieve the economies available through vertical integration.

d. Legal Limitations on Substitute Instruments

Certain legal factors may limit the effectiveness of the various substitute regulatory instruments as techniques for aligning private sector activity with specified public objectives, thus favouring the choice of public ownership as the instrument of intervention.

In sectors of economic activity where the constitution allocates regulatory authority to the federal government, a provincial government is deprived of the ability to use direct regulation as a technique of intervention and may therefore choose public ownership as the only instrument available to it for participating in public decisions in such sectors. For example, since the regulation of aeronautics is a federal responsibility under the division of powers in the constitution, a provincial government's only opportunity to participate in this sector may be through public ownership of an airline.

Similarly, regulatory constraints on institutional behaviour, which may in general be well justified in terms of the intended policy objectives, may create special situations where public ownership or at least public participation in business activity becomes advantageous.[56] For example, limits on the voting stock of companies that can be held by banks and similar limitations on the voting stock that may be held by life insurance companies, trust and mortgage loan companies, together with usury-type rate ceiling laws applicable in other cases, may create imperfections in capital markets that inhibit the supply of risk capital to certain kinds of ventures which the government wishes to see encouraged. This may create a rationale for the government to provide this capital itself either in the form of loans or equity.

e. Functional Limitations on Substitute Instruments: Uncertainty, Flexibility, Reversibility

The very nature of direct regulation limits in a functional sense its effectiveness as a mechanism for aligning private sector activity with desired public objectives. To the extent that these limitations are substantial in a

---

[56] J. M. Mintz, "Public-Private Mixed Enterprises: The Canadian Example" [Kingston: unpublished Discussion Paper #325, Department of Economics Queen's University, 1979].

given context, the Crown corporation instrument becomes relatively more attractive to decision-makers. Direct regulation relies primarily on explicit legal orders. These orders may appear in the form of decisions of regulatory tribunals, rules and regulations under statutes, terms and conditions under contracts, undertakings given in memoranda of understanding or agreement, and conditions and qualifications attached to the receipt of public assistance. However, regardless of the particular form in which they appear, legal orders require definition and specification of a private firm's future conduct. As a result, in situations where setting such definitions or specifications is difficult or impossible, direct regulation becomes less effective and public ownership relatively more effective. While Crown corporations also require direction, these directions can be constantly evolving, communicated less formally and less openly, stated with less precision and need not anticipate accurately the financial consequences of the required conduct.

The primary situation in which the limitations of legal orders as a regulatory device will become apparent are situations where the regulatory objectives are evolving or uncertain. This will arise most commonly in situations of relative novelty, whether because of new technologies or new environmental considerations. In these cases, the costs of a proposed undertaking are likely to be highly uncertain, and the particular objectives which the firm will be required to attain are likely to be extremely difficult to state. This state of uncertainty will be magnified in cases where the objectives can be stated only in a general way. For example, an objective in a particular building project may be to have the largest possible Canadian participation in the supply of materials, parts and services. The objective "large as possible" cannot be reduced to a percentage or dollar amount in advance because of uncertainty about the availability of suppliers and the terms on which they will be able to supply. To a private firm, faced with the necessity of forecasting the financial consequences in advance in order to assure a profit, this uncertainty may cause unacceptable degrees of risk in its financial projections. A public firm assured of financial support as the actual degree of Canadian participation clarifies over time may not share the same concern regarding this uncertainty.

These considerations may be particularly important in the regulation of enterprises which serve a central economic function such as providing an infra-structure service which the government wishes to use as a vehicle for supplying incentives and disincentives for other economic activities. In these cases, the policies of the firm must vary in response to the continually changing circumstances of the secondary industries, and policy judgments may be required on a virtually continuous basis. In a situation requiring these marginal adjustments in policy on a frequent basis it may be extremely difficult to issue a continuous stream of legal orders to dictate the behaviour of the private firm, to calculate the financial implications of each order for the private firm, and to compensate the firm appropriately. In such a case, a publicly owned firm not constrained in the same way as is a private firm by the financial implications of changes in policy may be relatively more attractive.

More generally, the ability of a government to reverse policy decisions effectuated through a Crown corporation in a low-visibility, informal, incremental way minimizes the political costs associated with more public and determinate acknowledgments of governmental error.

f. Low-Visibility Taxation

By combining in a Crown corporation a set of profitable activities with a set of activities or objectives that are not financially self-sustaining, politicians may be able to realize political advantages through the imposition of a form of tax (cross-subsidization) which has low visibility for the bearers of it (it never appears on the government's books) while at the same time being raised relatively efficiently through "business-like" management of the tax-bearing resources. This strategy will generally require the conferment of a government-sanctioned monopoly of the profitable activities on the Crown corporation to prevent entry and the competitive erosion of the capacity to cross-subsidize.

Even where a government provides direct subsidies to Crown corporations, whether in the form of capital grants, forgivable loans, loans at below-market interest rates or guarantees, these may be perceived by the cost-bearers (taxpayers) as within the normal investment functions of a shareholder and designed to produce a long-term return, rather than to provide a subsidy to employees or customers of the corporations (as may in fact be the case).

As Borcherding argues in a companion essay, public ownership compared to private sector regulation as an instrument of redistribution is less open, more flexible, and more selective. These are important political properties.

g. Symbolism; Ideology

Public ownership is a symbol of philosophical and ideological preferences. Its symbolic connotations appear material in a number of contexts. For example, in situations in which the government is providing very substantial public support to a private firm, the politician may perceive a risk that, if the firm were at some future date to make a profit, the government would be accused of having used public funds to generate private profit. Therefore, in situations where the public support of the industry or firm is so substantial that the residual private contribution to the firm's potential success is minimal, the government may wish to own the enterprise in the form of a Crown corporation so as to capture any potential success of the firm. To put it another way, in situations in which the government assumes virtually the entire downside risk of an enterprise, it may also wish to capture upside risks so as to avoid potentially damaging political criticisms now or in the future of "corporate welfarism". Simply undertaking to tax upside profits in the future may not be perceived by voters as an even "trade". Similarly, issues of foreign ownership may have high symbolic content and in those cases where there are no existing or potentially available Canadian enterprises to provide certain services or goods, the government may have no realistic alternative other than to create a Crown corporation.

Public ownership may also be attractive as a way of symbolizing and dramatizing a government's commitment to a particular cause or set of values. In some situations, even if it were possible for the government to regulate the private sector activity so as to achieve its objectives, it may be too difficult to generate public confidence in, and understanding of, this reality and an assertion of public ownership may be the only way to communicate sufficiently clearly the government's commitment to a particular public objective.

h. National Security; International Relations

A number of other characteristics of public ownership may sway the decision maker's choice of instrument in particular circumstances. First, the opportunity for decision-making with a relative degree of secrecy may make public ownership particularly suitable in situations involving national security and substantial amounts of confidential information. Secondly, in situations in which Canada's international relations will be affected by a firm's conduct and in which Canada's international posture is intimately related to a range of other international objectives, public ownership may offer the only reasonable vehicle for operating in the international sector in order to internalize the decision making and to permit Canada to speak with a single voice.

i. Competing Considerations

While the cost of monitoring private sector activity is a major factor favouring the utilization of public ownership, the concept of monitoring costs is also the source of major factors which militate against the choice of a public ownership policy instrument in many circumstances. First, as the literature on the theory of the firm points out, while a firm may be able to economize on some of the monitoring costs faced by an entrepreneur in purchasing factors through independent contracting, new and different kinds of monitoring costs are created within the firm by virtue of the attenuation of the relationship between a factor's pecuniary income and his productive activities. While, with respect to his pecuniary income, he tends to become indifferent to the allocation of his productive activities and more susceptible to centralized control, the costs of enforcing constraints against consumption on the job in a centralized organization increase. As McManus points out, there are always some opportunities in any organization to direct one's activities to non-pecuniary forms of consumption. Thus, there will be an increase in monitoring costs associated with specifying and enforcing non-pecuniary constraints.[57] Relative monitoring costs within and outside a firm will largely determine the method of economic organization. At the public ownership/private sector regulation boundary, this implies that while the government will face monitoring costs in attempting to regulate or otherwise influence private sector activity, offsetting monitoring costs must be confronted in the event that these activities are internalized.

A related factor militating against the choice of public ownership as a policy instrument derives from the concept of the residual interest maintained by the controlling owners in a private sector firm. It will be recalled that Alchian and Demsetz in part explain the emergence of firms on the basis that the firm structure creates incentives for residual claimants to firm income to develop specialized monitoring skills. In comparing a publicly owned enterprise to a privately owned enterprise, clearly these incentives are attenuated. Where the residual claimant is the government, there is no cohesive set of individuals who stand to be financially advantaged by more efficient, rather than less efficient, monitoring. If one conjectures that designated representatives of government, such as a particular Minister, are assigned responsibility for the oversight of publicly owned firms, such representatives do not possess the financial incentives possessed by owners of private sector firms to ensure efficient monitoring. As Alchian and Demsetz argue in the case of mutual and non-profit firms, future consequences of improved management are not capitalized into present wealth of stockholders and to that extent monitoring incentives are weakened.

This point runs the danger of over-simplifying the incentive structures facing political overseers of publicly-owned activities, because while there may be no economic returns to efficient management, there are presumably political returns. As Becker,[58] and Breton and Wintrobe[59] have pointed out,

---

[57] In this respect, the agency literature in finance theory is highly relevant: see, *e.g.,* Jensen and Meckling, "Theory of the Firm: Managerial Behaviour, Agency Costs, and Ownership Structure" (1976), 3 *J. Fin. Econ.* 305; Fama, "Agency Problems and the Theory of the Firm" [Center for Research on Security Process; Working Paper No. 20; University of Chicago, 1978].

[58] Becker, "Comment" (1976), 19 *J. Law and Econ.* 245.

[59] A. Breton and R. Wintrobe, "An Economic Analysis of Bureaucratic Efficiency" (unpublished Working Paper, Law and Economics Workshop Series, University of Toronto, Faculty of Law, 1979).

politicians derive no returns from waste *per se* and indeed run political risks from acquiescing in it. However, it can probably be accepted that the ultimate "stock holders" in publicly-owned firms; *i.e.*, the voters, have sufficiently small stakes in whether such corporations are well or badly managed and face sufficiently high information costs in ascertaining which is the case that the penalties attaching to weak monitoring in the public sector are significantly less exacting than those obtaining in the private sector. This proposition will not always hold. The strength of the monitoring incentive created by the owner's residual interest in a private sector firm is directly related to the extent to which the magnitude of his residual claim varies with his performance. Therefore, in situations in which government involvement in a private firm in the form of loans, subsidies, grants and the like is extensive, the residual incentive may be severely diminished by the magnitude and pervasiveness of the public involvement. In extreme cases, the private "owner" may become little more than a manager with very severely attenuated concerns for efficiency. In these cases, public ownership may be relatively more attractive as it then permits explicitly bureaucratic forms of incentives to be created for proper performance by the firm's managers.

To this point we have considered only the relative institutional characteristics of public ownership referrable to the public ownership-private sector regulation boundary. Within the public ownership modality, we need now to attempt to identify those characteristics which make a Crown corporation a preferred policy instrument to direct ownership/administration of economic resources by an executive department of government.

(ii) Crown Corporations vs. Departmental Bureaucracies

There would appear to be a number of characteristics of Crown corporations that would favour their utilization over departmental bureaucracies within the definitional ambit that we have ascribed to them, *i.e.*, the provision of goods or services to the public at a per unit price in circumstances closely resembling those under which private sector enterprises operate in the same or similar areas.

a. Valuing Output

As a number of writers, including Von Mises,[60] Downs,[61] and Niskanen[62] have pointed out, bureaus of government typically face no

---

[60] L. Von Mises, *Bureaucracy* (New Haven: Yale University Press, 1946).

[61] A. Downs, *Inside Bureaucracy* (Boston: Little, Brown and Co. 1967).

[62] W. A. Niskanen Jr., *Bureaucracy and Representative Government* (Chicago: Aldine and Atherton, 1971); see also W. A. Niskanen Jr., *Bureaucracy: Servant or Master?* (Great Britain: Institute of Economic Affairs, 1973) at 10.

economic markets on the output side. Therefore, they have no direct way of valuing their output in relation to the costs of the inputs used to make them.[63] On the other hand, in the case of organizations facing markets for their output, the sale of outputs in voluntary *quid pro quo* transactions provides an automatic evaluation of the work of the producer. If he can sell his outputs for more than his inputs cost (including normal returns on capital and entrepreneurship as costs) then he knows his product is valuable to its buyers. On the other hand; if he fails to cover the costs of his inputs by selling his outputs then he knows that his product is not valuable enough.[64] Downs suggests that one of the main reasons why extensive formal rules are necessary in bureaus is because they have no direct measures of the value of their output. On the other hand, "in many cases members of private firms can shape their behaviour on an *ad hoc* basis because they do not need rules to indicate how they can make profits. . . . But whenever there is no clear linkage between the nature of an action and its value or ultimate end, pressure arises for the development of formal rules to help individuals decide their behaviour."[65]

Von Mises makes the same point somewhat more dramatically:[66]

It is not the task of the hospital director to renounce some improvement of the municipal hospital lest it impede the improvement of the subway system or vice versa. It is precisely the efficient and honest manager who will try to make the services of his outfit as good as possible. But as he is not restrained by any considerations of financial success, the costs involved would place a heavy burden on the public funds. He would become a sort of irresponsible spender of the taxpayers' money. As this is out of the question, the government must give attention to many details of the management. It must define in a precise way the quality and the quantity of the services to be rendered and the commodities to be sold, it must issue detailed instructions concerning the methods to be applied in the purchase of material factors of production and in hiring and rewarding labor. As the account of profit or loss is not to be considered the criterion of the management's success or failure, the only means to make the manager responsible to the boss, the treasury, is to limit his discretion by rules and regulations. If he believes that it is expedient to spend more than these instructions allow, he must make an application for a special allotment of money. In this case the decision rests with his boss, the government, or the municipality. At any rate the manager is not a business executive but a bureaucrat, that is an officer bound to abide by various instructions. The criterion of good management is not the approval of the customers resulting in an excess of revenue over costs but the strict obedience to a set of bureaucratic rules. The supreme rule of management is subservience to such rules.

---

63 Downs, *supra* note 61, at 30.
64 *Ibid.*, at 29.
65 *Ibid.*, at 59.
66 *Supra* note 60, at 62, 63.

Because the outcome desired by owners of private sector enterprises can be reduced, for the most part, to a simple profit calculus, a ready measure of the performance of an organization and individuals within it is available. To that extent, dependence on extensive formal rules can be reduced. In the absence of such a measure, rules must be substituted. A similar phenomenon can be observed in the regulation of markets for professional services, where clients or patients possess imperfect ability to judge the quality of service outcomes. Given further the highly particularized nature of professional services, which makes generalized regulation of outputs infeasible, public policies are often reduced to adopting input regulation, such as regulation of the quality of entrants to a profession on the assumption, often tenuous, that there is a high correlation between prescribed training inputs and desired service outcomes.[67]

However, there is a significant cost attaching to the substitution of detailed formal rules, primarily focussed on inputs, for measures of productivity focussed on outputs, such as profits. By constraining and prescribing the nature and mix of inputs, such rules also constrain the potential for innovation and dynamism in the system. These costs may not be high in many bureaucratic contexts, at least in cases of relatively routinized functions, but in an entrepreneurial setting they are likely to be substantial.

To the extent that Crown corporations are providers of goods or services in market settings, there are obvious advantages to emphasizing output measures of productivity rather than input measures; thus the case for removing such activities from the normal departmental setting. However, one must assume that to a greater or lesser extent every Crown corporation is intended to maximize some set of policy objectives in addition to, and indeed in opposition to, profits. If this were not so, it is difficult to conceive of any reason for a Crown corporation to exist. In relation to these non-market objectives, as in the case of bureaucratic objectives, output measures of effectiveness will be very difficult to specify. To the extent that a Crown corporation is expected to engage in any substantial balancing of market and non-market objectives, the intended joint output may be difficult to specify and measure. Thus, politically uneasy, and conceptually untidy, compromises between input and output measures of the value of a Crown corporation's activities seem unavoidable. How these compromises are struck is presumably in large part a matter of the relative weights of pecuniary wealth and political arguments in a corporation's objective function. These weights are likely to be reflected in institutional variations within the Crown corporation mode, *e.g.*, the presence or absence of both government and private sector shareholders maximizing competing objec-

---

[67] M. J. Trebilcock, C. J. Tuohy and A. D. Wolfson, *Professional Regulation: A Staff Study of Accountancy, Architecture and Law in Ontario Prepared for the Professional Organizations Committee* (Toronto: Ministry of the Attorney General, 1979) Chapter 4.

tives; the choice of accountability regimes—whether to schedule a Crown corporation under the *Financial Administration Act* or leave it unaccountable to government and Parliament in this respect.

b. Meeting the Competition

To the extent that a public enterprise is carrying on activities in competition with private sector enterprises, it is likely to be important that it be able to compete in both input and output markets on similar terms to those applying to its competitors. Thus, for example, if specialized expertise is required in the management of a public enterprise in order for it to be competitive in managerial skills with private sector enterprises in the industry, it will be necessary for the publicly owned enterprise to be able to offer executive remuneration arrangements and otherwise pursue personnel and hiring policies that are competitive with those prevailing in the industry, rather than being constrained in these respects by public service pay scales or personnel policies. Similarly, in the case of procurement or advertising policies freedom from government-wide practices and policies may be necessary to obtain the required flexibility.

c. "Fair" Competition

Somewhat related to the previous point is the notion that if publicly owned enterprises are carrying on market type activities in competition with private sector enterprises, on the one hand they should be sufficiently removed from the political process to be free to compete without excessive political intrusions that may compromise unduly this objective; on the other hand they should not be so heavily dependent on preferential treatment by the government that the other firms in the industry perceive themselves to be unfairly prejudiced in the terms on which they are able to compete, and perhaps leave the industry. The "distancing" of a public enterprise from the executive arm of government may promote these considerations.

d. Selective Responsibility

In particular cases, politicians will find it advantageous to be able to claim credit for activities of government or government agencies where these are positive, but at the same time be able to establish some distance from these activities where there are zero or negative political returns. The Crown corporation structure facilitates this "distancing" strategy to a greater extent than a departmental bureaucracy where the principle of Ministerial responsibility severely circumscribes its utilization.

e. Symbolism; Ideology

To the exent that a government wishes to espouse, or at least to seem to be espousing, a political philosophy of "keeping government out of business", or "reducing the size of government," the Crown corporation mode of organization may offer some advantages over direct departmental responsibility for the same activities.

f. Competing Considerations

The one major cost to adopting the Crown corporation mode over a departmental bureaucracy for organizing economic activity is that to the extent that non-market objectives are assigned to Crown corporations involving outputs that cannot be readily specified or measured, the greater distance between political decision-makers and a Crown corporation, contrasted with a bureaucracy, may increase the monitoring costs faced by government in effectuating its policies. Moreover, to the extent that competitive conditions in the industry in which a Crown corporation is operating compel remuneration arrangements for executives which are tied to market measures of effectiveness and productivity, and to the extent that executives perceive their future value elsewhere in the industry to be likely to be judged largely in these terms, to that extent incentive effects are set in motion to maximize market objectives over non-market objectives in much the same way as may have led politicians to reject private sector regulation in the first instance. The presence of non-government shareholders in a Crown corporation may exacerbate these effects.

We now turn, in the next section, to an examination of Canadian experience with Crown corporations to identify which of the above characteristics appear to be robust explanators of the utilization of this instrument in various classes of contexts.

IV. EXAMPLES OF THE CHOICE OF PUBLIC OWNERSHIP AS AN INSTRUMENT OF ECONOMIC REGULATION

(a) Introduction

Throughout this essay we have characterized public ownership as an instrument of economic regulation. As such, it is normally one of a number of different instruments including taxes, subsidies, loans, grants, direct regulation, procurement policies and the like, which may be used to achieve a given public purpose. In most situations, two or more of these instruments may be viewed as substitutes as each of them could be employed to achieve the same objective. A difficult question facing observers of government intervention in the market place is determining the factors which influence the choice of regulatory instrument in different situations. A central thesis of this essay is that the political choice among the substitute instruments including Crown corporations will be influenced by, and at the margin determined by, the characteristics, both legal and institutional, of the various instruments, which make them relatively more or less attractive to the decision-maker in achieving the stated objective. Having identified the critical legal and institutional characteristics of Crown corporations in the previous section we now turn to an examination of various settings in which Crown corporations have been chosen as the instrument of intervention with a view to determining the relative influence of these characteristics. While our discussion of examples does not generate an empirically testable hypothesis concerning instrument choice, it does, in our opinion, illustrate the usefulness of our approach as an analytical framework.

In order to place this approach to the study of Crown corporations in context, it is useful to examine briefly the traditional reasons cited for the establishment and operation of public enterprises. The reasons offered reflect an often rich mixture of political, economic, cultural, historical and ideological factors. Shepherd has suggested that the following potential gains can be derived from public ownerships:[68]

1. Improved efficiency and ability to innovate and take major risks.
2. Softening of the social impacts of the enterprise decisions, and improvement in regional and urban balance.
3. Improved social relations within the enterprise.
4. Improvements in equity, by reducing prices for needy citizens.

In similar vein, Pryor has identified the following principal influences which may lead to the establishment of public enterprise:[69]

1. Economies of scale leading to "natural monopoly".
2. Externalities, either positive (for example, multi-purpose river projects), or negative (for example, nuclear enrichment).
3. Public purchases where the government is a major or sole buyer.
4. Large "unearned" income—*i.e.*, mineral deposits.
5. Power and sovereignty, *i.e.*, weapons and in smaller export dependent countries, mineral production.

In a wide ranging study of alternative regulatory instruments undertaken by the United States Senate Committee on Governmental Affairs, the possible rationales for public ownership were surveyed. The conclusions can be summarized as follows:[70]

---

[68] W. G. Shepherd, ed., *Public Enterprise: An Economic Analysis of Theory and Practice* (Lexington: Lexington Books, 1976) at xii.

[69] Pryor, "Public Ownership: Some Quantitative Dimensions" in Shepherd, *ibid.*, at 9.

[70] United States. Congress. Senate. Committee on Governmental Affairs. *Study on Federal*

1. To regulate natural monopoly.
2. To serve as a yardstick competitor.
3. To ensure proper use of natural resources.
4. To assist in the rationalization and revitalization of sick industries.
5. To control the external benefits and costs of activities.
6. To achieve economic and social equity.

In the Canadian context, similar summaries of the rationales for public enterprise have been stated.[71] Particularly in Canada, these summaries must be sufficiently broad to describe the extensive and wide ranging activities of publicly owned firms in Canada. At the federal level, the Lambert Report has described this phenomenon as follows:

> That the corporate form is extremely versatile in its capacity to manage a great variety of undertakings is amply demonstrated by the range and importance of the tasks assigned to the organizations we have categorized as Crown Corporations. We observe that half of the total group are involved in transportation, the provision of facilities and services for transporting people and goods by rail and air, or the provision of port and harbour facilities designed to service the needs of water transportation. The twenty-three bodies associated with these services are all within the single portfolio of the Minister of Transport to whom, or through whom, each reports. The proposed addition of the Post Office Department to the ranks of Crown corporations would extend the reach of these agencies in the area of communications. Government financial institutions in corporate form range from a central bank to lending and guaranteeing activities for farmers, small businesses, housing, and export development. In manufacturing, Crown Corporations produce coins, airplanes, films, petroleum products, hydro-electric power, nuclear reactors, and nuclear materials. A government corporation operates the largest scientific research establishment in the country. An arts centre and several museums, as well as federally-owned real property in the national capital region are managed by Crown Corporations.[72]

To capture the full range of public ownership, one must add to this description of federal activity, a catalogue of the provincially[73] and municipally owned Crown corporations' activities. As a result, in order to encompass fully these diverse activities, any summary of the rationales for intervention becomes extremely expansive, reflecting the ubiquitous character of public enterprise and government intervention in Canada.

The striking common feature of all traditional summaries of the rationales for public ownership is their lack of explanatory power. That is, for

---

Regulation Prepared Pursuant to S. Res. 71 to authorize a Study of the Purpose and Effectiveness of Certain Federal Agencies: Volume 6—Framework for Regulation (Washington: U.S. Government Printing Office, Committee Print, 95th Congress, 2nd Session, 1978).

[71] Sexty, *supra* note 17.

[72] Lambert Report, *supra* note 1, at 327-28; see also Chapter 4, in this volume.

[73] See Vining and Botterell, Chapter 5, in this volume.

each rationale offered it is true that this rationale sometimes leads to public ownership but it virtually never leads exclusively to public ownership as the instrument of response. For example, while it is widely accepted that public ownership is one way to regulate natural monopoly, it is equally clearly accepted that it is not the only way. It is possible (and indeed commonly observed) to have a private firm regulated by a public regulatory board which is charged with regulating the private enterprise's behaviour so as to overcome the economic distortions induced by the economics of natural monopoly. Thus, in Canada, in the telephone industry which is often viewed as a natural monopoly, one observes both publicly owned firms (in the prairie provinces) and regulated private firms (in B.C., Ontario, Quebec and the Maritimes). As the introduction to this essay noted, similar substitutes and patterns can be observed in the other areas in which public ownership is sometimes utilized. As a result, it is not sufficient to invoke the banner of a field of activity requiring government intervention, such as natural monopoly, as a satisfactory explanation of the existence of public ownership, since such an approach fails to capture the diversity of alternative modes of government intervention. Rather, since the objectives of the intervention can normally be achieved in more than one way, one must go further to identify those characteristics of public ownership which will be influential in a particular context in determining the policy-maker's choice of instrument.

Just as it is insufficient to identify the rationales for intervention as a comprehensive explanation of the utilization of public ownership, it is equally inadequate simply to state that public ownership will be chosen in those situations in which it will maximize the self-interested goal of a politician's maximizing votes and then to conclude that a politician will choose public ownership in those situations where it will maximize his political support. While this may be true (indeed, it is virtually a tautology), it again offers very little in the way of predictive power as it does not explain why public ownership in a particular context is likely to be seen as the instrument which is most likely to maximize political support. Rather the analysis must again focus on the characteristics of public ownership which are likely to lead to the decision-maker's perception that his self-interest will be maximized through utilizing a Crown corporation as opposed to some other instrument of intervention in a particular context.

As a part of a search for an explanation for the utilization of public ownership with greater predictive strength than those above, the remainder of this section is devoted to an attempt to illustrate the utilization of public enterprise in terms of its critical legal and institutional characteristics developed in the preceding section. We have selected a number of examples of Crown corporations, drawn from fields of activity where public ownership is sometimes used as the regulatory instrument, and have used these examples to examine the influence of the characteristics of Crown corporations in determining the choice. The analytical approach is summarized in Table II, in which we have arrayed the characteristics of Crown corporations against the fields of activity in which they are observed, and then located within the matrix examples drawn from actual case histories of Crown corporations. These examples are by no means a comprehensive survey of the uses of Crown corporations; rather they are designed to be illustrative of the general thesis that the characteristics of the instrument will be influential in determining the choice among the range of substitutes.

Three limitations on this analysis must be acknowledged at the outset. First, we have made no attempt to make normative judgments about the desirability of the fact that there has been some form of intervention by the government in the particular setting. Our analysis is concerned exclusively with the question of the form of intervention that is adopted, not whether or not there should be intervention at all. Second, our examples focus on those situations in which public ownership has in fact been resorted to rather than those situations in which public ownership was considered but rejected in favour of some alternative instrument. This focus is determined both by the availability of public information and our desire to highlight the use of public ownership. However, it must be acknowledged that those situations in which public ownership was *not* selected as the instrument of intervention should also illuminate the characteristics of public ownership in the instrument choice process. Third, the examples in this section focus largely on the choice between public ownership and the other instruments of intervention and not on the choice of the particular form of public ownership. Although we deal briefly with the choice between departments and Crown corporations, the remainder of the final section utilizes examples wherein the Crown corporation is the particular form of public enterprise adopted.

Given the very large number of Crown corporations in Canada, including approximately 400 Crown corporations and their subsidiaries at the federal level, approximately 200 Crown corporations at the provincial level and uncounted public enterprises at the municipal and regional levels, to some cynical observers it may appear difficult to find areas of economic activity where there is *no* public enterprise. However, there are a number of fields of economic activity in which public ownership has been a dominant, although not exclusive, instrument of intervention and it is from these that we draw our examples, based on case studies prepared by others.[74] In par-

---

[74] The leading collection of case studies is Allan Tupper, "The Nation's Business: Canadian Concepts of Public Enterprise" (Kingston: unpublished Ph.D. Thesis, Queen's University, November 1977) from which the majority of our examples are drawn. See also C. A. Ashley and R. G. H. Smails, *Canadian Crown Corporations: Some Aspects of their Administration and Control* (Toronto: MacMillan, 1965); Kenneth McCarter, "The Legal Environment of Ontario Crown Corporations" (Toronto: unpublished manuscript on file with the Ontario Economic Council, 1979).

TABLE II
Legal and Institutional Characteristics

FIELDS OF ACTIVITY	Legal	Monitoring and Information Costs	Policy Co-ordination	Industry Structure	Legal Limitations on Substitute Instruments	Functional Limitations on Substitute Instruments	Low Visibility Taxation	Symbolism; Ideology	National Security; International Relations
Natural Monopoly Regulation	Hydros Prairie telephone		Hydros		Hydros Prairie telephone Auto insurance	Hydros Telesat Prairie telephone	Prairie telephone	Auto insurance Quebec Hydro	Telesat
Nation Building and Community Development	CN B.C. Hydro		P.W.A. Hydros	AECL TCA/Air Canada DeHavilland Canadair	P.W.A.	Telesat Air Canada		CBC Air Canada	Telesat Air Canada

FIELDS OF ACTIVITY						
Moderating Economic Transitions and Stabilizing Income	Cape Breton D.C. DeHavilland Saltfish	Cape Breton D.C. Saltfish	Saltfish	Saltfish	Saltfish	Cape Breton D.C. Canadair DeHavilland
Provision of Capital	CDC	IDC/FBDB	ODC IDC/FBDB			IDC
National Security and Security of Supply	Petro-Canada Polymer	Petro-Canada	Petro-Canada	Petro-Canada	Petro-Canada	Polymer Telesat Eldorado
Yardstick Competition	Petro-Canada			Petro-Canada	Petro-Canada	Petro-Canada
Control of Externalities	CN	CN	AECL Telesat	LCBO Lotteries	LCBO Lotteries	Telesat AECL LCBO Lotteries

ticular, we examine seven fields of activity in which Crown corporations are observed.[75] They are:

1. Natural Monopoly Regulation
2. Nation Building and Community Development
3. Moderating the Effects of Economic Transitions and Stabilizing Income
4. The Provision of Capital Funds
5. The Promotion of National Security and Security of Supply
6. The Creation of a Yardstick Competitor
7. Control of Externalities

Within each field of activity from which we have drawn examples, we state briefly the perceived rationale for intervention and then identify the range of possible instruments which might be adopted. We then analyze one or more examples in the Canadian context in which Crown corporations are observed and indicate the extent to which this selection might be explained in terms of one or more of the legal or institutional characteristics of Crown corporations.

(b) Fields of Activity

(i) Natural Monopoly Regulation

The existence of natural monopoly has been and continues to be the most widely accepted rationale for economic regulation.[76] A natural monopoly is defined as an industry where economies of scale are such that only one firm will emerge even if a large number of firms enter the industry; the inevitable conclusion of free competition will be a monopoly. The costs of production are minimized by having only one firm. In the theoretical textbook case, natural monopoly is characterized by falling average and marginal costs for a single firm in the region of total industry demand. In such a case, competitive entry is inefficient as the total market can be served at lowest cost by a single firm.

An unregulated natural monopoly, as with any unregulated monopoly, will lead to higher prices and lower output than the social optimum. As a

---

[75] Only point three of these fields of activity has an explicitly distributive element to it. However, income redistribution may be one of the government's objectives in any of the seven fields of activity. Indeed, as Borcherding in his companion essay makes clear, such redistribution is likely to be endemic to public ownership in many fields of activity.

[76] See Trebilcock, Waverman and Prichard, "Markets for Regulation: Implications for Performance Standards and Institutional Design" in *Government Regulation: Issues and Alternatives—1978,* Ontario Economic Council. ed. (Toronto: Ontario Economic Council, 1978) at 16-17; *Study on Federal Regulation, supra* note 70, at 9-12.

result, the case is made for some form of regulation in order to restrict the natural monopolist to a fair rate of return while designing a rate structure that will ensure that all those willing to pay the incremental costs of service can obtain it. The most prevalent regulatory instruments utilized to align the natural monopolist's behaviour with the social optimum are direct rate regulation and public ownership.

Under rate regulation, a private firm is normally granted a statutory monopoly in order to prohibit entry by other firms and is then subjected to rate regulation by a regulatory tribunal such as a public utility commission. The commission is charged with ensuring that the private firm receives a fair rate of return for invested capital. Normally this is done by devising a rate structure for the services of the firm based on projections of demand and the need to meet the firm's revenue needs. This rate structure can be modified within limits so as to achieve desired social objectives through the pricing structure. That is, the firm can be required to sell its product at low cost to certain groups of consumers so long as it is able to charge relatively higher prices to other groups of consumers in order to meet its overall revenue needs.

This form of regulation is commonly observed in Canada. At the federal level, the regulation of Bell Canada and B.C. Telephone by the Canadian Radio-Television and Telecommunications Commission is a very visible example. Similarly, at the provincial level in Ontario, the natural gas distribution companies are regulated by the Ontario Energy Board with regard to price and services. In the United States, this form of regulation is even more wide-spread as most electrical utilities are privately owned and subjected to state rate regulation.

An alternative regulatory response is public ownership. Once a natural monopoly is publicly owned, the notion of "excess profit" becomes largely irrelevant as a distributive issue since the revenues of the firm are the revenues of the state. In principle, publicly owned enterprises can set rates so as to meet its costs while serving all customers who are prepared to meet the incremental costs of service. The actual setting of the rate structure can be done either by the firm's management, subject to ministerial direction, or can be done with the assistance of an outside review body such as a public utility commission. Patterns in Canada vary in this regard, as some publicly owned natural monopolies are in part supervised by regulatory commissions (*e.g.*, the Ontario Energy Board reviews Ontario Hydro's rate proposals) while others are subject only to direct ministerial control (Saskatchewan Telephone).

The essential similarity of the two instruments is that each relies on a single enterprise to service the market. In the one case, the enterprise is privately owned and subject to rate regulation, while in the other, the firm is publicly owned thus reducing the need for rate regulation to control profits. The difficult question then, is why in some cases does government choose to regulate a private firm while in others it chooses to operate its own? The Canadian electric utilities, telephone companies, automobile insurance industry and Telesat all provide examples where conflicting patterns can be observed.

The publicly owned electric power utilities include some of Canada's largest Crown corporation as 54 percent of all assets held by provincial Crown corporations are held in the electric utility industry.[77] The production and distribution of electric power in Canada is dominated by the publicly owned firms with the five largest—Ontario Hydro, Quebec Hydro, B.C. Hydro, Manitoba Hydro and Saskatchewan Power—holding over $32 billion of the approximately $34 billion invested in the industry. While not all firms in the industry are publicly owned, there is no private ownership of great significance remaining in Canada. However, this dominance of public firms is a relatively recent phenomenon.

Although there has been public ownership in the industry since the turn of the century, it was only in 1955 that the assets held by the public sector outweighed the total private investment in the power utilities and it was only in the early 1960s when both British Columbia and Quebec nationalized their electric utilities that the balance swung decisively in favour of public ownership.

Part of this reliance on Crown corporations can be understood in terms of their legal characteristics. In particular, the decisions to nationalize the companies in British Columbia and Quebec resulted from a desire to avoid the taxes paid by the private utilities to the federal government. Since a provincial Crown corporation is immune from federal income tax, the governments in British Columbia and Quebec recognized that they would be able to reduce the cost of service to their provinces' consumers by eliminating the income tax as a cost of doing business. Thus the differential tax treatment of public and private firms created a significant direct incentive for public ownership as the regulatory instrument.[78]

---

[77] See A. R. Vining, "The History, Nature, Role and Future of Provincial Hydro Utilities", [unpublished paper on file with the author, Faculty of Commerce and Business Administration, University of British Columbia] for a survey of the Canadian electric utility industry. This paper is the source of most of the facts stated below in the text concerning the industry.

[78] The Premier of British Columbia emphasized the importance of taxes on a number of occasions. See *Monetary Times*, November, 1961, cited in Vining, *supra* note 77, at 50: " '. . . the position of British Columbia on the corporation tax levied by the Federal Government on private power utilities was made amply clear to the Liberal administration, which was relieved of office in 1957. 'Our position was made amply clear again, to the present Conservative administration in 1959, in 1960 and again in this year of 1961 at conferences held in Ottawa to work out a new federal-provincial tax agreement . . . at the federal-provincial conference of October 15-16, 1959, I stated British Columbia's feeling that the income tax on privately-owned public utilities should either be abolished or the province should get 100% of such a tax. I pointed out that privately-owned utilities operated under regulations similar to those governing Crown-owned utilities in the sense that their rates were controlled by public utility boards. I stated further that unless the Federal Government abolished its tax

The second legal characteristic influencing the choice of instrument has been the source of funds for provincially owned electric companies. It has been a standard practice for provincial governments to guarantee the debt obligations of the companies as if they were the province's, thereby supplying relatively low cost capital as a subsidy to the electric industry. While the same subsidy could be made available to a private electric utility it may be considerably more difficult for the government to distinguish between this industry and other industries seeking such assistance if the one were not publicly owned. Thus, to the extent that government wishes to provide a subsidy at apparently low cost to provincial consumers, the ability to lend government guaranteed funds to a carefully defined industry creates an incentive to turn to public ownership.

The superior ability to co-ordinate multiple objectives by internalizing them and certain of the functional limitations of the substitute instruments can also be seen as powerful influences on the choice of instrument in the electric industry. The provision of electric power is central to the industrial and economic structure of the province. As such, the provision of electricity as an incentive for development must be co-ordinated with the full range of government programmes and plans for the economic industrial development of the province. The availability of electric power at differential rates can be used as an incentive or disincentive for industrial location, private investment decisions, population distribution and almost any other aspect of the development of a province. Given the centrality of these objectives to provincial planning schemes, it is understandable that considerable stress would be put on the need to integrate the structure of electric prices and system expansion with these other policies. To the extent this can be achieved more readily through the internalization of decision-making in the public sector, Crown corporations become relatively more attractive. Certainly the history of the establishment of Ontario Hydro between 1905 and 1925 and the similar development of Quebec Hydro in 1963 can be traced, in part, to a desire to use the availability of electric services as a major policy in guiding the development of the respective provinces.

---

on private utilities, British Columbia would have to take over the B.C. Electric Company in order to protect our own consumers, and that the responsibility for such action would have to rest on the Federal Government . . .' 'Again, at the conclusion of the conference held in Ottawa last February 23 and 24, I reported fully, and plainly, to this House on the subject of power corporation taxes. I pointed out that whereas it had been estimated that British Columbia should receive $1,700,000 in 1970 as its share of this tax, we actually received only $349,500. I pointed out further that the Federal Government had refused to allow British Columbia to see the federal accounts and find out how this figure was arrived at.' " Subsequent to the nationalization decision in British Columbia and Quebec, federal-provincial tax negotiations eliminated the incentive to nationalize as the federal government agreed to return to provincial treasuries all amounts paid in federal income tax by private electrical utilities. This may in part explain the continued existence of a small number of private electrical utilities in Canada. What is less clear is why the differential taxation effect has not appeared to have an impact beyond the electric utility industry.

The relative advantages of Crown corporations in providing flexibility and reversibility also played a role in causing the dominance of Crown corporations in the electric power industry. In particular, given the links between the electric power industry and the development of the provinces, there was a need not only for co-ordination but also for continual marginal adjustments in the policy instructions issued to the utilities. As conditions and objectives changed, as political movements waxed and waned, as governments changed, and as the business cycles varied, the electric power utilities were necessarily required to modify their behaviour. All this no doubt could be done through a legal orders regime but it is probably more readily achieved through more subtle changes in policy communicated through the internal structures of the public sector. In the case of changes in political objectives, the political decision-makers may often wish to implement their plans with some lack of visibility. For example, if there is a desire to increase the degree of cross-subsidization of rural users by urban users, this may be an issue which the government would not wish to highlight with a specific and explicit legal order of compliance. Rather, it may prefer to communicate its wishes in a more subtle way so as to minimize the likely resistance by urban consumers. This appears to be one of the explanatory factors in Saskatchewan's switch in the 1930s from private, municipally based corporations, to a single, publicly owned provincial utility.

The change in Saskatchewan from private to public can also be explained in part by reference to the failure of competition policy. Saskatchewan was faced, in the 1930s, with what was perceived to be a cartelized private electric utility industry and an absence of effective anticombines legislation to counteract this anticompetitive behaviour. This situation fuelled political opposition to private ownership *per se* and created a further incentive for public ownership.

Also, in the electric power industry, Quebec's nationalization of the private utilities in 1963 displayed the importance of a number of the characteristics discussed above. In addition to the taxation and source of funds considerations, Quebec's nationalization showed the importance of low visibility, marginal adjustments in policy. There was a desire to deliver senior jobs in the industry for French-speaking rather than English-speaking Quebecers, but at the time it would have been politically difficult for the government to make this an explicit regulatory policy. Similarly, the co-ordination of Quebec's economic development was intimately related to the development of the electric industry with particular emphasis on northern development plans and the development of a strong hydraulics industry in the province. Finally, the decision can be seen as being motivated by the symbolism inherent in the issue of foreign ownership of the Quebec electric industry which was, at the time, a political concern of some magnitude.

The electric utility example shows perhaps the most pervasive influence of legal and institutional characteristics on the decision to prefer Crown corporations to regulated private firms in the case of natural monopolies. However, a number of other Canadian examples illustrate similar trends. An intriguing example of public ownership in Canada is the publicly owned telephone companies in Alberta, Saskatchewan and Manitoba.[79] These contrast with the privately owned companies enjoying statutorily protected natural monopolies in the other provinces. One explanation lies in the desire to provide low cost funds to meet the substantial capital expenditures involved in extending the telephone network to the thinly spread populations in the prairie provinces. As with the electric utilities, the provisions of government guaranteed loans represented a form of subsidy to a specific industry with the industry's distinguishing characteristic being its public ownership. However, perhaps the strongest explanatory characteristics are the functional and legal limitations on the available substitute instruments. The provincial telephone companies were largely owned by The Bell Telephone which was a company based in the East and difficult for the provincial governments to regulate. At the same time, the private firms were alleged to be deriving excess profits through an abuse of their monopoly position and were not investing sufficient funds in further expanding the provincial systems to satisfy politicians. This conflicted with the government's desire to expand substantially the degree of cross-subsidization of telephone rates, a goal which would impose very substantial costs on urban consumers because of the vast distances involved in servicing rural customers. This objective of providing services to all at reasonable cost points to the limits of the ability of private firms to cross-subsidize, thus creating a further incentive for public ownership. Also, to the extent that cross-subsidization is understood as a form of taxation,[80] public ownership may offer the least visible form of this tax.

The inadequacy and inaccessibility of competition policy and the shortcomings of direct regulation are also explanatory factors in the decisions by British Columbia, Saskatchewan and Manitoba to create Crown corporations with statutory monopolies to provide compulsory automobile insurance.[81] Prior to public ownership, the automobile insurance companies were primarily from other provinces and were alleged to be acting anti-competitively through arrangements which were well beyond the reach of provincial regulatory authorities. Thus it was perceived that the province, through a single publicly owned firm could offer automobile insurance services more cheaply than private industry could, despite the fact that the automobile insurance industry is not one which would normally be thought

---

[79] R. Collins, *A Voice From Afar: The History of Telecommunications in Canada* (Toronto: McGraw-Hill Ryerson Ltd., 1977) at 171-219 for an anecdotal history of the nationalization of the private telephone companies.
[80] Posner, "Taxation by Regulation" (1971), 2 *Bell J. Econ. and Mgmt. Sci.* 22.
[81] A. Tupper, *supra* note 74, at 198-230.

of as enjoying natural monopoly characteristics. The need for such a solution was enhanced by the symbolic cost of private provision of automobile insurance since the decision to create a single firm accompanied the decision to make automobile insurance mandatory in these provinces. There was a political concern that private firms should not be seen to be making profits as a result of the government's mandating of a demand for automobile insurance.

A last example of public ownership in a natural monopoly sector is that of Telestat Canada, the communications satellite which was created in 1969.[82] Telestat is a mixed enterprise with the federal government holding a majority ownership position and the major telecommunications carrier, CN/CP, and the Canadian public holding minority interests through equity ownership.[83] The decision to use public ownership in this case derived from both the existing industry structure and the functional limitations of direct regulation. While there were two competing private interests which indicated a desire to build and operate the satellite, there was a concern at the time that one of the firms lacked the capacity to complete the task, leaving the other firm, CN/CP Telecommunications, in virtually a monopolistic position with regard to the proposal to build. At the same time, the regulation of the completed satellite presented novel and uncertain regulatory issues. In particular, the question of the regulation of access to the satellite by different potential users was one on which it was difficult to make advance rulings which could then be included in the private builder's calculus as to the financial viability of the proposal. These regulatory matters involved decisions which were necessarily likely to evolve over time and the government was reluctant to commit itself in advance to any specific arrangement with a private firm. But at the same time there was a strong desire to use the satellite as a mechanism for cross-subsidizing geographically distant citizens and this goal added further uncertainty to the regulatory environment. Furthermore, one of the primary objectives in building the satellite was to enhance the development of the Canadian communications industry and its technological capacity. It was thought that there could be substantial potential positive externalities from the development of this technology and thus there was a desire to maximize the Canadian content in the building of the satellite. This was an extremely imprecise regulatory objective as it was so dependent on the capacity of Canadian suppliers to bid on the constituent parts of the building project. Since the objective was necessarily stated as a general constraint rather than a specific formula, it further contributed to the difficulty of entering any binding arrangements with a private builder.

---

[82] *Ibid.*, at 78-99.
[83] In 1978, Telesat became a member of the Trans-Canada Telephone System which is an agreement among the carriers concerning the division of interprovincial toll revenues. However, the government has maintained its ownership position in Telesat.

(ii) Nation-Building and Community Development

Perhaps the most common rationale offered for public enterprise is the encouragement of economic activities directed to nation-building and community development. In the Canadian context the objective has two major components:

(i) Integrating the country by making infrastructure investments and providing essential services, which private business is unable or unwilling to provide; and

(ii) Promoting Canadian nationalism, *i.e.*, developing a national identity and preserving Canadian control over certain services and sectors of the economy.

On a smaller geographical scale, provincial use of public enterprise can be seen as developing the provincial economies and identities in the same way.

The characterization of Canada as a vast, underdeveloped, sparsley populated country, rich in resources and with an inadequate private source of capital, is seen in the literature as often demonstrating the need for intervention by the government.[84] Often cited is the following passage by Professor Innis from *The Problems of Staple Production in Canada*:

> Government ownership in Canada is, fundamentally, a phenomenon peculiar to a new country, and an effective weapon by which the government has been able to bring together the retarded development and the possession of vast national resources, matured technique, and a market favourable to the purchasing of raw materials. It was essentially a clumsy, awkward means of attaining the investment of tremendous sums of capital, but it was the only means of accomplishing the task and of retaining a substantial share of the returns from virgin natural resources.[85]

The notion of nation building is discussed throughout the literature on public enterprise. For example, Tupper, labelling this concept "community development", emphasizes the function of "integrating and building robust autonomous political communities in inhospitable environments".[86] The inhospitable environment refers to the difficulty of developing integrated communities, given the American presence to the south, significant regional identities and the characteristics of the Canadian economy noted by Innis.[87] Tupper notes that private enterprise may not be willing to extend transportation, message communication and power facilities to isolated areas with small populations, since the cost may exceed any reasonable revenue expec-

---

[84] Plumtree, "The Nature of Political and Economic Development in the British Dominions" (1937), 3 *Can. J. Econ. Pol. Sci.* 489.

[85] (Toronto: Ryerson Press, 1933) at 80-81; see also Gracey, "Public Enterprise in Canada" in *Public Enterprise and the Public Interest, supra* note 8.

[86] *Supra* note 74.

[87] Gracey, *supra* note 85.

tations. As a related concern, there is also the threat of economic and political domination by the United States if the Canadian government fails to act in those situations where domestic private investment is not forthcoming. If the only real alternative to public enterprise is a foreign owned private firm, the government in some sectors may perceive its options to be foreclosed.

The varied patterns of public ownership furthering the objective of nation-building have been described by Tupper as follows:

> Provincial public ownership in the fields of transportation, communication and power, is an important means of promoting economic growth. It has contributed to the development of natural resources and has facilitated intra and extra provincial commerce. State enterprise has also been used to bind together disparate provincial communities in sub-provincial economies. Provincial governments, like their federal counterparts, have also used public ownership to ensure provincial, rather than private control of particular firms or industries.
>
> The community development seeks to influence the output of goods and services in several ways. For example, Air Canada and the Canadian Broadcasting Corporation were created to provide national services, which private enterprise had been tardy in establishing. On the other hand, the case of the Canadian National Railways illustrates how public enterprise was dictated by the importance to the community at large of the continued provision of vital transportation services. The CBC, telephone companies in the Prairie Provinces and Saskatchewan Transport, were established to extend services to previously neglected regions. Ontario Hydro and Hydro Quebec were prompted by the state's desire to make electric power widely available at lower rates than charged by private enterprise. Nationalization in 1963 of the entire hydro electric industry in Quebec was also dictated by the state's desire to provide high quality service to all parts of the province.[88]

While the objective of nation building and the strengthening of the economic infrastructure of the country or its regions is no doubt an objective of central importance to Canadian policy-makers, it does not, standing alone, offer an explanation of why public enterprise is so often selected as the instrument of intervention by which the government will pursue this objective. As in the case of natural monopoly, it is not difficult to conceive of, and indeed observe, a range of situations in which alternative instruments might be adopted. In particular, private firms, supported by government subsidies, loans, grants, tax incentives, guarantees and other forms of financial assistance, could in most situations offer an alternative vehicle by which the government could pursue its national building objectives. The failure to rely on these alternatives in a range of situations offers further insight into the influence of the characteristics of Crown corporations in the choice of instrument. We use the transcontinental railways, the electric power utilities, Air Canada and Pacific Western Airlines, Telesat Canada,

---

[88] *Supra* note 74, at 77-78.

the Canadian Broadcasting Corporation, DeHavilland and Atomic Energy of Canada Limited as illustrative of this proposition.

The legal characteristics related to the provision of funds to public firms can be understood as major determinants of the decision to national-ize the Canadian Northern and Grand Trunk Railways and to create the Canadian National Railway. Because part of the government's desire was to see the strengthening of east and west transportation corridors in Canada, the government provided subsidies and construction assistance to both of these railways as they embarked on building Canada's second and third trans-continental lines, between 1919 and 1923. These construction projects faced very substantial cost over-runs with a resulting deterioration of the financial position of both the Canadian Northern and Grand Trunk Rail-ways. The federal government was the guarantor of a substantial portion of the debt held by each railway and thus the credit of the government was at stake. The situation became so serious that in order to preserve the credit worthiness of the government and to provide a continuing source of finan-cial assistance to the railways, it became necessary to assume public owner-ship of the two railways and to merge them into Canadian National. As such, the government was able to provide a continuing source of financial assistance in the form of government guarantees of the debt obligations of the railways. This is similar to the cases noted above with regard to British Columbia and Quebec Hydro, where the governments of the day wished to provide financial assistance in the form of government guaranteed loans, thus creating an incentive to nationalize the firms.

The importance of policy co-ordination can also be seen as influential in the choice of public ownership. To the extent that the industries involved are strengthening the economic infrastructure, there is a need to achieve co-ordination of the government's assistance to the industries with other pro-grammes related to economic development. Thus, in the case of Alberta, its purchase of Pacific Western Airlines can be explained in part as the desire to integrate the province's plans for the development of the northern part of the province with the expansion of the necessary transportation infrastruc-ture. Similarly, the experience of the electric power utilities across Canada and their desire to link the energy infrastructure with other development policies created an incentive to adopt public ownership so as to internalize the task of co-ordinating the various programs.

The structure of the industries in which public ownership can be observed in this field of activity also offers a partial explanation of the deci-sion to rely on a Crown corporation instead of a regulated private firm. In the cases of the desire to build a transcontinental airline and a nuclear reac-tor, there was not a group of firms willing to compete for the opportunity to provide the service, subject to government support. In the case of the airline, while there were potential bidders in the form of the major national railways, there was no firm with any substantial experience in operating, or with the desire to engage in building, a major airline. The novelty and uncertainty surrounding the project made it relatively unattractive to firms outside the industry. Only American firms that had participated in the building of the American transcontinental airlines had experience in this area. Thus, the government created the publicly-owned firm, Trans-Canada Airlines as a subsidiary of Canadian National. Subsequently, in 1963, Trans-Canada Airlines became a separate Crown corporation under the name of Air Canada.[89] In the case of Atomic Energy of Canada Ltd. (A.E.C.L.) there was again no competitive market structure from which a bidder was likely to emerge to undertake the task of building a nuclear reactor. Rather, the only firms were American firms already engaged in the development of domestic nuclear power plants in the United States and thus disinclined to embark on the construction of a competitive product, even with Canadian government support.

A similar problem was seen in the case of DeHavilland which had become the only significant domestic aircraft producer. In considering further extension of various support programs for DeHavilland, the government was faced with the informational difficulty created by the absence of competitive firms able to assist the government in monitoring the performance at DeHavilland. As a result of the market structure, the government was not in a position to solicit bids from a number of firms to carry on aircraft manufacturing, since there were no real alternatives. Thus, to the extent this created substantial monitoring and information problems, public ownership became an increasingly attractive alternative.

Another dimension of market structure relates to those cases where the government is the primary purchaser of the services of the industry. This is the case with DeHavilland and Canadair and was to some extent the case in the early days of Trans-Canada Airlines. In the case of the two aircraft manufacturers, the government, through its defence procurement policies, has become the dominant purchaser of the firm's products and thus, to the extent this creates the risk of strategic behaviour and offers the potential gains from vertical integration identified above, the decision to assume ownership of the firm can in part be understood. In the case of Trans-Canada Airlines, the major customer for the transcontinental services in the early days was the Post Office as it built its airmail delivery service. While it was possible for the Post Office and potential private firms to negotiate terms of trade, it may have been that by internalizing the cost in the public sector a more satisfactory arrangement was reached. Indeed, the terms of contract agreed to, and reflected in the legislation creating the airline, involved an arrangement that would have undermined the advantages of relying on the private sector, since in effect the Post Office agreed to underwrite the losses suffered by the airline.[90]

---

[89] Although it became a separate Crown corporation in 1963, it continued until 1978 to report to the government through CN.

[90] Ashley and Smails, *supra* note 74, at 26.

The nation-building context also offers a relatively stark example of a legal limitation on alternative instruments, making the use of a Crown corporation sometimes the only viable alternative for the government. The case in point is Alberta's purchase of Pacific Western Airlines in the mid 1970s. Given the constitutional allocation of the regulation of aeronautics to the federal government, Alberta found itself relegated to essentially observer status in the regulation of air transport services within the province. However, by purchasing Pacific Western Airlines, which was the major regional carrier in the western part of Canada, the Alberta government was able to involve itself substantially in the development of air transport services in northern Alberta. Since Alberta perceived these services as being integral to its plans for economic development of the north, it turned to public ownership of the airline as the only way it could assure itself of a substantial role in setting the objectives and developing the plans of the airline. While Pacific Western Airlines remains subject to the jurisdiction of the Canadian Transport Commission, the Alberta Government is no longer a mere observer of the Transport Commission's decisions, but rather is an important participant.

While the Pacific Western Airlines case demonstrates the importance of legal limitations on substitute instruments, the Telesat Canada example demonstrates the importance of functional limitations on substitute instruments. Telesat Canada was established in the late 1960s in an atmosphere fuelled by the fear that if a domestic satellite communications system was not developed quickly, the United States would use up much of the available air space with its own satellites, and that Quebec might participate in a French satellite system in order to ensure French language services for Quebec residents. At the same time, the Canadian government perceived the development of the satellite communications system as an opportunity to strengthen the national identity of Canada as it would allow the extension of live television in both languages throughout Canada. Additionally, the system offered the opportunity to aid the development of the Canadian north, providing links between northern communities, decreasing the isolation of remote areas and removing the disparities in life-style between those living in and outside the main centres. Also, there was the desire to promote the principle of uniformity of service at reasonable rates analogous to the principle which guides the setting of postal service rates. In the case of the communications satellite, this involved very substantial cross-subsidization of rates. Finally, an important objective, already identified in the discussion of natural monopoly, was the maximization of Canadian content in the building of the satellite. As is argued above, this evolving regulatory objective strains the limits of direct regulation and creates incentives for public ownership.

In this context, while the government may have been able to turn to a private firm to build the satellite system, (although, as we noted above, the factors related to industry structure militated against this), the achievement of these multiple objectives of an evolving and imprecise nature made the use of the Crown corporation particularly attractive. Thus, when the government introduced the statute creating Telesat with the government holding the majority but not exclusive equity interest in the firm, the choice of instrument can be understood as a response to the difficulties that would have been faced in attempting to achieve these varied objectives through alternative regulatory instruments.

The symbolic dimensions of public ownership have also played a role in the selection of Crown corporations as the technique of intervention in the nation building and community development area. The commitment to public enterprise in the case of both the Canadian Broadcasting Corporation and Air Canada can be seen in part as promoting Canada's national identity by symbolically demonstrating Canada's commitment to control of its own destiny in these areas. While it is arguable that the same degree of control could be obtained by virtue of strict regulation of foreign-owned enterprises providing broadcasting or airline services, the political risks of testing this reality appear too great. Thus, at a time when the Canadian private sector appeared to be unwilling or unable to invest the resources necessary to build these Canadian institutions, public ownership became the only viable alternative.

Finally, both Telesat and Air Canada are good examples of situations in which co-ordination of Canada's posture in the international arena created an incentive for public ownership. Particularly at a time when international agreements regulating the conduct of international air transportation services were of major significance, it was important from Canada's point of view to speak with one voice in these settings. This could be accomplished more readily by a public sector firm subject to both a formal and informal direction from the government than by a private regulated firm. Similarly, in the telecommunication satellite area, where international agreements are of critical significance, it was again important that Canada have a Crown corporation speaking on behalf of the Government of Canada and preserving Canada's position in such negotiations.

(iii) Moderating the Effects of Economic Transitions and Stabilizing Income

The third major field of activity in which substantial public ownership is observed is in moderating the effects of economic transitions and stabilizing income. This reflects the political unacceptability of the abruptness of certain social dislocations caused by rapidly changing economic circumstances. This occurs in a number of related circumstances. One such situation is that of a private firm announcing its closing when the implications for the local community in terms of loss of jobs and economic base may be so substantial that government intervention is called for. Similarly, in situations in which a private firm is the dominant local employer and is undergoing a period of difficult economic transition, government intervention may be required so as to reduce the magnitude of the social dislocations caused to the work force. The firm may be threatened with bankruptcy as a result of mismanagement, obsolete technology or other sources of inefficiency, or falling demand for its products. In a situation where the relevant regional characteristics include an unskilled labour force not readily employable elsewhere, the desire of citizens not to move regardless of the long-term economic prospects, and the dependence of the local economy on the activity, all combine to encourage some form of government intervention. The need for income stabilization occurs in industries where exogenous factors have a substantial impact on the economic welfare of the producers. For example, in the agricultural industry changes in weather and world patterns of demand for food create highly variable incomes for producers. When the extent of the variances are very substantial, government intervention is called for. Government intervention in this sector may also be demanded to attempt to increase the relevant returns to producers where it is perceived that, because of structural factors in the market place, the returns to the primary producers are inadequate.

The range of instruments available to respond to these policy concerns are legion. It is possible, through the provision of subsidies, grants and loans to private industry, to assist them in overcoming periods of financial distress or in providing the capital necessary to modernize and revitalize an industry. Similarly, if the problem is an uncertainty of demand for the product, government procurement and stockpiling policies can be designed to assure the firm of some minimum level of demand for its product. Similarly, in situations of highly variable income, government guarantees of minimum income or government price supports for the product can accomplish a degree of stabilization. While these substitutes are commonly employed, public ownership of certain industries is also utilized. Thus we observe public ownership of certain industries occurring in times of extreme difficulty and publicly owned enterprises participating as middlemen in industries plagued by highly variable income.

Two leading examples of public ownership in this sector in Canada are the Cape Breton Development Corporation and the Canadian Saltfish Corporation. These examples are dealt with below.

The Cape Breton coal industry has had a history of poor economic performance, accounted for by intrinsically low productivity, poor labour relations and distance from markets.[91] Additionally, the labour force lacked skills other than mining, as the lack of emphasis on education related to the

---

[91] The development of the Cape Breton Development Corporation is described in Tupper, *supra* note 74, at 29-60.

traditional view of mining as an hereditary occupation. Prior to the decision of the federal government to assume ownership of the corporation in 1966, there was a long history of government involvement in the industry by means of various regulatory instruments. These included freight subsidies to allow Cape Breton coal to compete with imported coal in central Canadian markets, low interest loans to assist in the increased mechanization and rehabilitation of the industrial plant, financial incentives to the steel industry to encourage the use of Canadian coal, financial payments to encourage the use of local coal in electric power production, and benefits under the *Maritime Freight Rates Act.*[92]

These various forms of assistance were relatively modest in cost through the 1930s; by 1939 the support amounted to approximately $100 per employee. However, in the 1950s and early 1960s the cost escalated dramatically, reaching approximately $3,000 per employee in 1965. Simultaneously the market situation facing the industry deteriorated and in the early 1960s the private owners, DOSCO, announced that the capital requirements for rehabilitating the industry could not be met without further public funds. After a period of study the government agreed to provide the $25 million in capital funds required. Despite this promise of support, DOSCO announced that it was withdrawing from the industry and closing the mines, perceiving no economic future in the industry. Thus, in 1966 the government took over ownership of the industry, creating the Cape Breton Development Corporation.

Although massive expenditures were made, and further expenditures planned, for rehabilitation and re-organization of the mines, the industry was not expected to become a viable commercial operation. Rather, public ownership was viewed as a means of maintaining the livelihood of the dependent labour force and protecting the community from the collapse of the local economy which would occur if the mines closed. The continuing operation of the mines was designed to provide a period of time during which there would be an opportunity to revitalize and diversify the local economy with substantial public assistance.

There was no question that the intervention was dictated by social, political and humanitarian concern about the welfare of the Cape Breton community. As was stated by the Minister of Energy, Mines and Resources, at the time:

> It is because of its concern for the welfare of individuals and collectivities and not for the welfare of companies that the government intends to subsidize the regional economy so that it can move from a state of subjection to a declining natural resource toward a more wholesome economic situation.[93]

[92] R.S.C. 1970, c. M-3.
[93] Canada. Parliament. House of Commons. *Debates,* Second Session of the Twenty-Seventh Parliament, June 15, 1967 at 1553. Cited in Tupper, *supra* note 74, at 51-52.

The creation of the Canadian Saltfish Corporation in 1970 also grew out of the combination of a depressed industry and substantial previous government support programs.[94] The saltfish industry is based in Newfoundland and is primarily an export industry facing substantial international competition. In the post-war period it was characterized by very low incomes for fishermen and inefficient and disaggregated marketing strategies. Furthermore, to the extent that reasonable economic returns were being earned from the industry, they were accruing to participants other than the fishermen. The government support for the industry, when it was privately owned, came in various forms. There were credits and subsidies available for improving fishing boats, financial incentives for using modern gear, public provision of the infrastructure of harbours, wharfs, community stages and navigational aids, federal government support for scientific research relevant to the industry, provincial regulation of the export of saltfish, and deficiency payments to the saltfisheries. A study in the early 1960s rejected public ownership as a solution to the inadequate and unstable incomes earned by fishermen but did call for central processing plants. From 1963 through 1967 there was a substantial boom in the industry and the economic problems faded. However, in 1968 there was a crash in the international market of saltfish leading to substantial surpluses. The government responded through both procurement policies of the Canadian International Development Agency and a program of deficiency payments which had the effect of guaranteeing the record high prices of 1966 and 1967 for high quality saltfish. However, these deficiency payments were labelled as mere "bandaid" solutions and prices remained low until 1969 when the government reconsidered its position with regard to public ownership. Finally, in late 1969 the Canadian Saltfish Corporation was created and instructed to "market saltfish in an orderly manner, increase returns to fishermen and promote international and interprovincial markets for Canadian salt cod".

Tupper has described the functions of the corporation:[95]

In pursuit of these objectives the corporation was granted a monopoly over the purchasing, processing and marketing of all saltfish in participating provinces. The corporation was also able to make loans to salt cod fishermen. The corporation was to establish annual base prices to producers of various grades of salt cod and the price to producers would not fall below these base prices. If actual prices were less than the base price, the CSC would bear the loss. Alternatively, if actual prices exceeded the initial price the corporation would return, after deduction of operating expenses, all profits to the producers. The

---

[94] The development of the Canadian Saltfish Corporation is described in Tupper, *supra* note 74, at 237-60.
[95] *Ibid.*, at 253.

corporation did not immediately acquire processing, storage or shipping facilities. Rather these functions were to be performed by the trade in accordance with the corporation's guidelines and fee structures.

The corporation was to operate without appropriation by Parliament. The government would lend or guarantee loans of up to $10 million for the corporation and the corporation would be administered by a Board of Directors chosen by Ottawa and the participating provinces.

The creation of both the Cape Breton Development Corporation and the Canadian Saltfish Corporation raises the question of which factors were influential in causing the government to switch from a series of public support programs for the industries to public ownership of them. Some insights can be gained by focusing on a number of the characteristics of Crown corporations and their relative influence in these two cases.

In the case of the Cape Breton Development Corporation, the continuing decline in the potential financial viability of the industry led to an increasingly diminished residual interest by the private owners in the efficient operation of the firm, thus reducing the gains normally associated with the monitoring incentives generated by this residual interest. Simultaneously, the information problems facing the government, in negotiating its public support programs of subsidies, grants, and loans were increasing as the public sector involvement spread to essentially all aspects of the industry's activities. The spread of public programs also created an incentive to internalize the decision-making structure in the public sector in order to achieve greater co-ordination of the varied prográms of support for the industrial revitalization of the Cape Breton area. As it became clear that the future of Cape Breton lay not in enhancing the mining activities, but rather in organizing an orderly transition from a mining based economy to alternative economic activities, the range of programs which needed to be co-ordinated expanded beyond simply the support programs for the industry itself. Thus, by creating a Crown corporation with a mandate not only to operate the mines but also to revitalize the local economy, the government was able to focus and co-ordinate the wide range of programs which were necessary to arrange the economic transition. Finally, the extent of government support for the industry put the government in the position of bearing the entire downside risks of the operation of the mines in Cape Breton. Therefore, the symbolic concern about not allowing private firms to seem to be profiting from public support programs also contributed to the desire to put the government in the position of being able to capture some of the future financial returns if the economic transition were successful.

The creation of the Canadian Saltfish Corporation posed similar information and co-ordination problems as the degree of public support for the industry increased. Various public support programs which preceded public ownership reduced the incentive for efficient production while generating significant monitoring problems for the government. At the same time the growth of multiple programs increased the need for a centralized decision making structure for co-ordination. Another factor, not noted in the Cape Breton case, also was influential in determining the choice of public ownership as the regulatory instrument. The choice derived in part from the existence of competing public policies applicable to the industry. On the one hand competition policy legislation encouraged competitive behaviour among firms. On the other hand, to the extent that the saltfish industry is an export-based industry, in which Canada enjoys some market power, Canadians can be made better off in this sector by permitting the creation of an export cartel. Thus there was a desire to permit some monopolistic behaviour on the part of the industry while directing some of the returns from this behaviour to the fishermen.

The creation of a Crown corporation to be the exclusive marketing agency for export purposes is perhaps the only instrument which is clearly responsive to this objective. It also permits indirectly a form of low visibility taxation.

Other examples of the role of Crown corporations in moderating economic transitions and stabilizing income with similar features to the two just discussed can be identified. The assumption of public ownership of DeHavilland can be in part traced to the diminished residual interest maintained by the British owners. As the viability of the firm was called into serious question and as the degree of public support continued to increase, the position of the private owners became more and more that of merely managing a public enterprise. When the government determined that to allow the industry to close would cause unacceptable economic dislocations in the form of loss of jobs in the aerospace industry, the creation of a Crown corporation became the only realistic alternative, particularly since there were no competing firms which might become alternative recipients of the government support programs. The DeHavilland decision can also be seen as another situation in which the need to co-ordinate a variety of support programs called for the internalization to the public sector of the decision-making function. Finally, in the case of DeHavilland there was concern that if the government had reached the point of bearing all the downside risk, it should, given at least the possibility of substantial future financial success, assume an equity position so as to reap for itself some of the returns.

The purchase of Canadair Ltd. can also be seen as a situation in which the concern about a private firm's receiving substantial public assistance and then after a period of transition achieving financial success, was influential.

Crown corporations such as the Canadian Wheat Board can be seen as analogues to the situation raised by the Canada Saltfish Corporation case as once again there is a desire to create a single marketing agency in order to face the export market with a single seller, so as to generate maximum returns for the primary producers. They also provide a means of accomplishing low visibility taxation.

(iv) The Provision of Capital Funds

The pervasive presence of government intervention in the financial markets is well known. As Tupper has stated:[96]

> Canadian governments utilize many different means to achieve their goals in the financial system. A plethora of statutes and regulations provide a framework within which private financial institutions operate. That framework includes among other things financial disclosure laws, provisions of the Criminal Code regarding standards of conduct, anti-fraud and the proper means of acquiring and disposing of securities. The state is intimately involved with the financial system through central banking operations and related fiscal and monetary policies. Canadian governments are also active in the direct provision, through public enterprise, of a variety of financial services including loans and other financial services to farmers, fishermen, small businessmen and exporters.

The usual rationale for government intervention in the provision of capital is that "imperfections" exist in Canadian capital markets. As Mintz has stated, "by imperfect capital markets we mean that (i) the government has a technological advantage such that the state can intermediate among consumers and firms at less cost in comparison to direct trading on stock markets or indirect trading through private owned financial intermediaries or (ii) as a result of various institutional restrictions, created or tolerated by governments, privately owned institutions may be prohibited from operating in specific areas of capital market."[97]

In addition to this efficiency rationale for government intervention in the capital markets, it is also argued that in some circumstances, in order to stimulate economic activity, the government should provide capital to particular interests on terms and conditions different from those obtaining in the private market. That is, government may wish to intervene to make capital available at a lower price than the private market would charge given the level of risk of the investment. This may occur in situations in which there is a desire to promote economic growth through the expansion of the productive capacity of the particular industry. It may also be done in order to provide employment opportunities by making expansion plans more attractive to private firms than the market would dictate. Similarly, capital may be made available on below-market terms in order to encourage economic diversification, technologically innovative industries and regional development.

As the present patchwork of forms of intervention in the financial markets indicates, government has available to it a wide range of instruments for influencing the terms on which capital is made available.

---

[96] *Ibid.*, at 160-61.
[97] J. M. Mintz, *supra* note 56, at 12.

Among these instruments Crown corporations are an important sour
capital for the private sector as both the federal and provincial governme..
have created a number of Crown corporations for the purpose of
facilitating the provision of capital. Thus, at the national level the Federal
Business Development Bank (formerly the Industrial Development Corporation), the Farm Credit Corporation, the Canadian Development Corporation and the Export Development Corporation, create a substantital
federal presence in the financial market. Similarly, at the provincial level,
corporations such as the Ontario Development Corporation are involved in
the provision of both debt and equity funding for private enterprise.

The opportunities created for co-ordination of multiple forms of
assistance for private enterprise through the vehicle of the Crown corporation is one explanation as to the attractiveness of Crown corporations in this
area. Commonly development corporations such as the Ontario Development Corporation and the Federal Business Development Bank are
authorized to make loans, guarantee loans, take equity positions, provide
information and management consulting services, and otherwise generally
provide encouragement and support for private enterprises in need of
capital assistance. While each form of assistance might be offered through
different instruments, including government subsidization of private lending institutions, it would be difficult to achieve the same degree of co-
ordination and integration of assistance programs that is possible through
Crown corporations.

The dominant explanation for the existence of Crown corporations in
this area is the legal and structural limitations on the various substitute instruments already utilized in financial market regulations. As Mintz has
demonstrated, the net effect of the plethora of regulatory restrictions imposed by federal and provincial governments on lending institutions has
been the creation of gaps in the financial system.[98] In particular, these legal
restrictions have made it difficult for private lenders to provide medium and
long-term funds for small businesses. While it would certainly be possible to
modify the existing range of regulations governing the financial markets, so
as to eliminate these gaps, the costs associated with these changes in
regulatory patterns presumably outweigh the benefits to be obtained. That
is, the resulting increases in risk that might be incurred by various lending
institutions in order to fill these gaps indicate that these gaps are better filled
through the direct provision of capital by Crown corporations.

The fact that development corporations are normally permitted to take
equity positions in addition to providing loans to growing businesses allows
Crown corporations to participate more effectively in the potential suc-
cesses of firms receiving substantial public assistance in a way other than
that permitted by debt-oriented instruments. Therefore, by using a Crown

---

[98] *Ibid.*, at 12-18.

vernment can protect itself from the symbolic effect iden-
ing seen to bear only the downside risks in supporting

re making Crown corporations attractive in this field
pportunity for development corporations such as the
~~...~~ Development Corporation to create and acquire subsidiaries at
low cost and with low visibility in order to participate effectively in bidding
for equity positions in private firms. Thus, the Canadian Development Corporation has been in a position to take equity positions in firms without
having to first engage in substantial political and bureaucratic negotiation,
a process which might unduly constrain the corporation rather than furthering its role as an equity provider.

(v) The Promotion of National Security and Security of Supply

The national interest in the nation's security and the security of supply
of certain goods and services has at times dictated the use of Crown corporations. While we acknowledge that each of these examples must clearly
be understood in its historical context, the utilization of public ownership in
this area can also be interpreted in part as a recognition of the special
characteristics of Crown corporations. The leading examples relating to national security are perhaps the Polymer Corporation which was created in
1942 in order to produce synthetic rubber as part of the Allied war effort
and the Eldorado Mining and Refining Corporation (subsequently renamed
Eldorado Nuclear Limited) which was acquired by the federal government
in 1942 as part of the government's decision to participate as a supplier of
uranium in the Manhattan Project which was created to produce an atomic
bomb. In the security of supply area, the creation of Petro-Canada in 1975
is perhaps the clearest demonstration of the use of a Crown corporation as
an instrument of intervention.

The decision to operate Polymer as a Crown corporation was dictated
in part by the speed with which the plant had to be brought into operation in
light of the urgency of the war effort. Polymer's main plant at Sarnia was
completed in 1944 at a cost of $48.5 million and was North America's most
fully integrated synthetic rubber plant.[99] While the urgency of completing
the project was widely accepted, it is not clear from the historical record
why the government was confident that it could construct the plant more ex-
peditiously than the private sector, although it was widely publicized after
the fact that Polymer was constructed in half the time that such a project
would have required in peace time.[100] The explanation may lie in the reduc-

---

99 Tupper, *supra* note 74, at 301.
100 *Ibid.*, at 303.

tion of transactions costs achieved by internalizing in the public sector all decisions related to building the plant by using a Crown corporation. The use of a Crown corporation enabled funds to be made available, materials to be conscripted and priorities attached to the project without the monitoring costs which would be involved if a private firm were engaged in the project. That is, while a private firm may enjoy certain monitoring advantages in the actual production process, these advantages may be outweighed by the reduction in monitoring costs achieved by avoiding the need for the government to secure sufficient information in order to be able to negotiate the terms and conditions of the project on short notice with a private builder.

The expropriation of Eldorado Mining can be explained primarily in terms of the additional secrecy that could be achieved through incorporating the corporation into the public sector. In this case secrecy and confidentiality were at a premium as the Manhattan Project necessitated the greatest possible minimization of security risks. By vertically integrating in the uranium industry, the government was able to act as supplier of uranium for the Project without engaging in market transactions, transactions which by their very nature would have increased the risk of the release of confidential information.

Petro-Canada is a response to the government's perceived need for direct government intervention in the petroleum industry to assist in Canada's search for energy self-sufficiency by insuring the development of long-term Canadian oil resources through exploration and research which might otherwise be constrained by short-run profit considerations and capital scarcities. While Petro-Canada has been used as a vehicle for the government to assist in the undertaking of relatively high-risk exploration and research endeavours, as in all these fields of activities this is not the only way in which these goals might have been achieved. The complex array of tax incentive measures designed to encourage exploration expenditures is clear evidence of the simultaneous use of substitute instruments in the same industry. Similarly, to the extent that a scarcity of capital is a meaningful impediment to sufficiently aggressive exploration activities, existing Crown corporations in the business of providing capital could be relied upon. To the extent that these resources are inadequate the government could put further financial resources at the disposal of these firms.

While these substitute instruments exist, the choice of a Crown corporation as one of the instruments in this area is consistent with a number of the characteristics of Crown corporations. By seeking its objectives in part through a Crown corporation, the government may be able to reduce the costs associated with strategic behaviour by private firms in the industry seeking public assistance to supplement their exploration activities. To the extent that the bureaucracy is unable to monitor accurately the financial claims of the private sector and thus design support policy in light of this information, it may be necessary for the government to create a Crown corporation in order to generate its own source of information and provide a benchmark against which the claims of other firms can be judged. In addition, the structure of the petroleum industry in Canada may be a partial explanation of the choice of the Crown corporation. To the extent that the petroleum industry is perceived as lacking vigorous competition and to the extent that doubts are raised as to the degree of independent action of the major firms in the industry, the ability of the government to rely on providing incentives to the private sector to achieve its objectives is diminished. At the same time, certain functional limitations on the available substitute instruments limit the range of choice available to the government. The situations in which Petro-Canada is instructed to act are mainly areas of high-risk, great uncertainty and substantial novelty in that the exploration activities undertaken by Petro-Canada are highly speculative and at the frontiers of the petroleum industry's efforts. Each of these characteristics of the activity taxes the limits of policy makers' abilities to design adequately the alternative instruments. The use of a Crown corporation, while not eliminating this uncertainty, may be a superior vehicle for accommodating it as the financial implications of the anticipated projects need not be known in advance. Undoubtedly the symbolic characteristics of public ownership were also influential in the choice of Petro-Canada as one of the government's instruments in this sector. The public perception of the private firms in the petroleum industry as foreign owned, multi-nationals beyond the reach of national regulatory policies, makes it difficult for the government to rely exclusively on incentives designed to encourage exploratory activity by the private firms. Rather, a greater sense of public confidence may be achieved by devoting some public resources to a single, Canadian owned firm, free from incentives to align itself with the private firms in the industry. In addition, the potential upside gains from these exploratory activities are massive and the government may well be concerned to position itself so as to be able to participate in these potential gains as it is underwriting many of the potential losses from the exploration activities.

(vi) The Creation of a Yardstick Competitor

In a recent article on yardstick competition, Harrison identified three versions of this objective of public enterprise.[101] The first envisions the government entity not in direct competition with private firms but operating as a standard by which regulatory agencies may evaluate the prices and performance of private firms, serving as a source of information which can be

---

[101] Harrison, "Yardstick Competition: A Prematurely Discarded Form of Regulatory Relief" (1979), 53 *Tul. L. Rev.* 465.

used to monitor the private sector. The second version has the public enterprise competing directly with private firms, the objective being to keep prices competitive by making collusion and other anticompetitive behaviour more difficult. The third version of the yardstick firm is as a form of potential competition, discouraging private firms from taking full advantage of their market positions.

It is readily apparent from the statement of the rationale for the creation of a yardstick competitor that alternative instruments are available to achieve the same purposes. To the extent that information is required in order to evaluate the performance of private firms, this information can be obtained by disclosure requirements combined with comparative studies of private sector activity. To the extent that competitive market behaviour is desired, modification of competition policy legislation and enforcement strategies under it can be used to promote competitive practices. The desire for potential competitors in order to discourage the abuse of market position can be achieved by facilitating private entry into concentrated markets, through the provision of capital or other reductions in entry barriers.

While these instruments and others are possible alternative responses, the choice of a Crown corporation may in some circumstances appear to be the most attractive policy. In Canada, our review of the activities of existing Crown corporations does not indicate substantial reliance on Crown corporations in this area. It is difficult to find cases in which at least the articulated rationale for creating the Crown corporation was related to the concept of the yardstick competitor. Rather, the predominant rationales for the creation of Crown corporations in Canada have been the other objectives identified elsewhere in this section. However, one recent example of the creation of a yardstick competitor was the creation in 1975 of Petro-Canada as a major participant in the petroleum industry in Canada.

Section 3 of the statute incorporating Petro-Canada states:

> The purpose of this Act is to establish within the energy industries in Canada a Crown owned company with authority to explore for hydrocarbon deposits, to negotiate for and acquire petroleum and petroleum products from abroad, to ensure continuity of supply for the needs of Canada, to develop and exploit deposits of hydrocarbons within and without Canada in the interest of Canada, to carry out research and development projects in relation to hydrocarbons and other fuels and to engage in exploration for and the production, distribution, refining and marketing of, fuels.[102]

In pursuing this objective, Petro-Canada was given wide powers enabling it to act as a viable competitor in the petroleum industry, subject to any policy directions that the corporation might receive from the cabinet.[103]   ·

---

[102] *Petro-Canada Act,* S.C. 1974-75-76, c. 61.

[103] Section 7(2) of the *Petro-Canada Act* states: "In the exercise of its powers, the Corporation shall comply with such policy directions as may from time to time be given to it in writing by the governor in Council."

Petro-Canada can be seen as an example of a combination of the three versions of the yardstick concept identified by Harrison. Government policy-makers are able to obtain information and advice from the corporation about market conditions and industry performance without having to rely on the private firms to disclose this information. At the same time, Petro-Canada is free to compete vigorously in various sectors of the petroleum industry, making it more difficult for the major firms to collude successfully and discouraging anticompetitive practices. Furthermore, while to date Petro-Canada has not entered substantially into all sectors of the petroleum industry, its presence and access to capital through government assistance makes it a potential competitor in all aspects of the petroleum industry. As such, even in those aspects of the industry in which it is not yet involved, its very presence may discourage abuse of market position by private firms.

It would appear that the predominant characteristic of Crown corporations which influenced the choice to create Petro-Canada rather than relying on the alternative instruments related to questions of monitoring and information. The petroleum industry is one in which information is highly specialized and complex and is almost exclusively in the hands of the participants in the industry. Furthermore, to the extent that industry voluntarily or in response to regulatory demands releases information, it is information which is very difficult for non-industry sources to verify. A growing lack of confidence in the quality of information provided by the industry to the National Energy Board and other regulatory bodies involved in the industry through the 1960s and early 1970s led to increasing demands for the creation of a Crown corporation which would be able to independently generate information about the industry which could be used as a standard for evaluating the claims made by private firms. Only armed with this information would the other regulatory instruments already in place in the industry be made effective, since the other regulatory techniques, including tax incentives, export regulations, and price setting, all depend for their efficacy on the quality of the information on which they are based. Therefore the creation of Petro-Canada can be primarily understood as responding to the information deficiencies facing the government which plagued its ability to use any of the other instruments of regulation. Furthermore, by creating a Crown corporation the government is able to reduce the returns to strategic behaviour by private firms in the petroleum industry as the superior information the government could obtain through the Crown corporation would undermine their ability to succeed in influencing policy through the strategic release of information.

The informational dimension of Crown corporations can be seen in a broader context as adding a further reason for the creation of a Crown corporation. Long-range planning in the petroleum sector requires information about future availability of reserves and the costs associated with exploiting them. That is, decisions as to the rate of export of oil and gas must be based on assessment of the future resources available in the frontier areas for future Canadian consumers. Therefore, in order to reduce the uncertainty surrounding these policy decisions, the government faces incentives for the production of information about reserves somewhat different from those facing the private sector. The government may therefore wish to encourage exploration activity which may not be justified on purely financial grounds. Having settled on this objective, the government might contemplate creating financial incentives to encourage private firms to undertake this exploration activity but in doing so the government is still plagued by the informational problems identified above. Therefore, the Crown corporation, because of its superior informational and monitoring qualities, becomes an effective instrument for pursuing this goal as well.

(vii) The Control of Externalities

The final field of activity in which public ownership is sometimes observed is in the control of externalities, both positive and negative. With regard to the positive benefits, some forms of public enterprise generate external benefits not readily captured by the price system. Writing in the American context, the United States Senate Committee on Governmental Affairs has stated:[104]

> Many Government enterprises can or do provide services which confer external benefits. Some of these services could be or are now provided by regulated private enterprises. That is not true in every case. For example, Government insurance programs for banks and savings and loans, as well as the Federal Reserve System, can be viewed as assuring a well functioning monetary and credit system. Private providers would not be able to capture the full gains in terms of increased ease of commerce and improved allocation of credit, as these are widely diffused throughout the economy and so would provide too little service. Bank failures hurt many more people than just the bank stockholders, so Government insurance is much more credible for what is inherently an uninsurable risk. Another example would be urban commuter transportation, which is provided by a mix of generally regulated private firms and public enterprises, typically at the local level. In some areas such enterprises may be natural monopolies. Availability of high quality mass transit at low prices might reduce automobile traffic, and hence congestion and pollution. Today those enterprises usually are subsidized. Regulation could be used to moderate pricing, and take account of these externalities, while containing the size of the subsidy. Public enterprise could accomplish the same goals and could more directly improve service quality. At the Federal level, an analogy might be made with railroad vs. truck transport. Improving rail service might

---

[104] *Study on Federal Regulation, supra* note 70, at 116-17.

lessen highway congestion and truck use and reduce petroleum consumption and, hence dependence on foreign oil. Regulation by itself could have little impact on this problem; public enterprise or other subsidy could.

River basin development by the Department of the Interior's Bureau of Reclamation and the Army Corps of Engineers provides another example in which public enterprise may be justified by the importance of external costs and benefits. Dams on the Columbia River provide not only electricity but also flood control and irrigation. These benefits are widely diffused; it would be very difficult for a private enterprise to fully collect the value of the service. Thus, full private enterprise might underprovide such services. In addition, upstream dams assure a more stable flow and, therefore, more power out of the river downstream. There is a case for developing a river basin as a whole. Private enterprise may be unable or unwilling to organize such projects. Therefore, some form of Government intervention is justified. That, however, need not mean public enterprise is the best option. One alternative would be subsidies to private firms, perhaps administered under competitive bidding arrangements. Yet especially for projects of vast scale, such as the initial TVA, the Federal co-ordination and regulatory role would necessarily be so essentially a public enterprise.

In the Canadian context this notion can be seen as strongly related to nation building activity where the development of the economic infra-structure was discussed. Building the economic infra-structure including expansion of transportation and energy related facilities can be seen as part of nation building but can also be seen as a desire to use public ownership in order to generate the positive external benefits associated with these developments. Given the extensive discussion of nation building above, no further examples are developed here.

With regard to negative externalities, the most obvious examples in Canada are the Provincial Liquor Control Boards and the Provincial and Federal Lottery Corporations. In both the sale of liquor and the legalization of gambling, public ownership can be seen as a means of regulating the perceived negative externalities of the activities. To the extent that the excessive consumption of alcohol is seen to generate externalities in terms of health impairment, public rowdiness, moral degeneration and like effects, a case is made for regulating its distribution. Similarly, to the extent that concerns are raised about the terms on which gambling opportunities should be presented to the public and about the possible involvement of organized crime in the activity, a case can be made for public regulation of lotteries.

However, while the case for regulation of these externalities may be well accepted, it is less easily understood why Crown corporations such as the Liquor Control Board of Ontario and Lotto Canada are relied upon. An explanation may lie with the functional limitations on the alternative instruments, and in the symbolic effects of public ownership and the opportunities for low visibility taxation.

With regard to the functional limits of a legal orders scheme of regulation, a difficulty arises from the need for the regulations to be explicit and to specify the objectives of the regulatory scheme. That is, to the extent that there is a trade-off between permitting consumption of the product while controlling its external costs, it is necessary for the decision-makers to articulate the balance between these competing objectives if the private sector is going to undertake responsibility for providing the goods and services. This difficulty is magnified by the need for constant marginal adjustments in policy over time as the public assessment of the competing objectives varies. This requirement stretches the limits of a legal orders regime and creates an incentive for internalizing the decision-making in the public sector through a Crown corporation.

The second characteristic which explains the relative attractiveness of public ownership in this area is its symbolic effect. That is, by maintaining public ownership the government is able to make a symbolic statement that it is denying the forces of the market place and is determined to maintain control over the price, supply and channels of distribution of the product in order to encourage moderation in its consumption. Even where it may be possible to achieve the same substantial objectives through regulation of private producers and distributors, the assertion of public ownership may be reassuring to those interests most concerned about the external effects.

Finally, the use of Crown corporations in this area provides a form of low visibility taxation as the price of the product can incorporate a tax rather than having a tax more explicitly added to the private costs of production. As liquor control boards and lotteries have become important sources of government revenues, the significance of this ability to disguise the full extent of the revenue producing nature of the activity may create a substantial incentive favouring public ownership.

(viii) Conclusion

This extended review of examples of the utilization of public ownership as an instrument of intervention in various fields of activity reveals certain patterns regarding the relative importance of the legal and institutional characteristics of Crown corporations. With respect to the legal characteristics, the modes of creation and Crown immunity factors appear to be of little importance. The tax treatment of Crown corporations can be an important influence on the choice of instrument in specific situations but at the same time this factor can be neutralized relatively easily by federal-provincial tax agreements. The labour relations characteristic is unimportant at the public/private boundary since there is no significant change in the applicable legislation in a shift from Crown corporation to private sector status. However, as is developed below, the labour relations effect is most important at the Crown corporation/department boundary where the applicable legislation does change. The two important legal characteristics are sources of funds and mechanisms for accountability, the former as a result of the subsidization effects that can be achieved through public financial support and the latter as a result of the need to establish a balance between the co-ordination of policy and independence of action.

By comparison, certain of the institutional characteristics are much more important with the monitoring and information costs, policy co-ordination, functional limitations on substitute instruments and symbolic effects each being influential in a large number of cases. The monitoring and information costs associated with substitute instruments often make public ownership an attractive alternative particularly in those cases in which the extent of public involvement in the industry is so substantial that the residual monitoring incentives inherent in private ownership have been seriously weakened. The possibility of improving policy co-ordination by internalizing all decision-making to the public sector also favours the utilization of Crown corporations in situations in which either multiple support programs are being used or the development of the industry in question is integrally linked to other government programs or plans. The inherent functional limitations of substitute instruments which depend on the issuing of legal orders, broadly defined, also support the utilization of public ownership in numerous cases as the limits of direct regulation become apparent in situations involving novelty, uncertainty, evolving policies and continual marginal adjustments in policy and thus requiring flexibility and reversibility. Finally, in a substantial number of the examples studied, the symbolic characteristics of Crown corporations and the opportunities they provide for low visibility taxation played an important role in the calculus of choice. While important in some specific cases, the other institutional characteristics, like the majority of the legal characteristics, would appear to play a more modest role in the choice of instrument.

(c) Crown Corporations vs. Departmental Bureaucracies

While this section has concentrated on the substitutability of public ownership for alternative instruments of intervention, the same style of analysis can be utilized to study the choice between different forms of public enterprise. In particular, the choice between Crown corporations and departmental bureaucracies can be understood in terms of the legal and institutional characteristics which distinguish the two forms of public enterprise.

A current prominent example which illustrates the form of the analysis of this dimension of substitutability relates to the controversy over the appropriate form of organization for the Post Office. Previously organized as a department, after an analysis of the alternative organizational structures[105] it was converted to a Crown corporation.[106] Simultaneously in the United States, various legislative proposals call for converting the U.S. Postal Service, a public corporation, into a Post Office Department.[107] The impetus for the Canadian change can be traced to both the legal and institutional characteristics of Crown corporations. With respect to legal aspects, the dominant consideration is that the shift from departmental to corporate status would result in the application of the *Canada Labour Code* to postal service labour relations in place of the existing *Public Service Staff Relations Act*.[108] This would change the processes for the resolution of disputes, the determination of terms and conditions of employment and numerous other aspects of the labour relations. In light of the almost constant state of controversy concerning labour relations in the Post Office, it is not surprising that an organizational substitute which holds out the promise of a better era is seen as an attractive instrument. This legal consideration is complemented by numerous institutional characteristics. The Post Office produces a service which is substantially susceptible to output measurement; it operates in an increasingly competitive market; it is a source of constant political embarrassment which might be reduced through the "distance" inherent in the corporate form; and it is not so integrated with other government policies and programs that the monitoring and co-ordination costs are likely to become oppressive in the corporate form.

V. REFORM PROPOSALS

Two reform thrusts have won wide currency in Canada with respect to Crown corporations. First, it has been widely asserted that Crown corporations should be made more closely accountable to the executive and legislative arms of government. Second, it has been asserted in some quarters that a number of existing Crown corporations should be "privatized" by selling off their shares or assets to the private sector. In this section we evaluate some of the implications for the calculus of instrument choice that these reform thrusts seem likely to carry.

As we argued at some length in Section III, Crown corporations as a policy instrument possess characteristics that mark them off from private sector enterprises, including private sector enterprises that are subject to

---

[105] Canada. Canada Post. *Considerations Which Affect the Choice of Organization Structure for the Canada Post Office: Report of a Study Group to the Postmaster General* (Hull: Ministry of Supply and Services, 1978).

[106] *Canada Post Corporation Act*, S.C. 1981, c. 54.

[107] See generally, American Enterprise Institute for Public Policy Research, *Postal Service Legislative Proposals* (Washington, D.C.: American Enterprise Institute for Public Policy Research, 1977).

[108] See the discussion in the text at notes 44-47, *supra*.

government regulation, subsidy, or other forms of government influence. In addition, they possess characteristics which mark them off from departmental bureaucracies. Reform thrusts now current appear to imply a partial substitution of policy instruments falling outside both the boundaries which have hitherto delineated the realm of government activity where Crown corporations have often been viewed as possessing a comparative advantage over alternative policy instruments. In proposing these changes, policymakers appear to be proceeding from either of two possible premises. The first is that the values or interests that underlay the creation of Crown corporations as presently constituted are no longer regarded as worth promoting, and new values or interests require new policy instruments. If that is the case, we are probably entitled to insist that our political decision-makers make explicit these changes in purposes so as to facilitate an open and informed political debate about the wisdom of the changes. Second, the reform thrusts in particular cases may reflect a judgment on the part of the political decision-makers that while the purposes underlying the creation of a Crown corporation remain unchanged, a misjudgment was made in the choice of a policy instrument to effectuate those purposes; alternatively, if a misjudgment was not involved in the first instance, circumstances have changed over time so as to render some alternative policy instrument now more appropriate. In either case, again open and informed political debate requires that our political decision makers articulate precisely why a change in the choice of policy instrument is called for.

We now examine from this perspective each of the two major reform thrusts.

(a) Accountability

(i) The Proposals

At the federal level, the Privy Council Office's Blue Paper on Crown Corporations (1977), the Lambert Commission on Financial Management and Accountability (1979), and a Crown Corporations Bill (Bill C-27), tabled in Parliament by the Tory Government in 1979,[109] provide important reference points on current thinking amongst policymakers in this area.

First, as to modes of creation, it has been suggested by the Lambert Commission that the creation of a Crown corporation or a subsidiary or the acquisition of a company by a Crown corporation or a subsidiary should require express Parliamentary sanction in the relevant departmental or Crown corporation constituent Act and prior Governor in Council approval.[110]

---

[109] Bill C-27, First Reading, November 26, 1979.
[110] *Supra* note 1, Recommendation 19.2, at 335.

Similar proposals have been advanced by the Privy Council Office[111] and are contained in Bill C-27.[112]

As to *ex ante* approval by government of the activities of Crown corporations, the Lambert Commission recommends that capital budgets requiring appropriations be approved by the designated minister, by central agencies of government (*i.e.*, Treasury and Finance), by the Governor in Council and be tabled in Parliament with estimates. In the case of operating budgets requiring appropriations, approval of the designated Minister, Treasury Board and the Governor in Council is required. In the case of capital budgets not requiring appropriations, the approvals of the directors, designated minister, Finance, and Governor in Council, but not Treasury, are required. Operating budgets not requiring appropriations need only be presented to the designated minister for information.[113] The Privy Council Office proposed that all Crown corporations be required to submit capital budgets for Governor in Council approval and that agency corporations listed in Schedule C of the *Financial Administration Act*[114] should be required to submit operating budgets for the approval of the designated minister and the Treasury Board. Capital budgets, so approved, would be required to be laid before Parliament. Operating budgets, so approved, would be required to be laid before Parliament where, in the opinion of the government, continuing appropriations are likely to be needed.[115] Bill C-27 contemplated a basic distinction between Crown corporations ordinarily dependent on Parliamentary appropriations (Schedule I) and those that are not (Schedule II).[116] Amongst the latter, a further distinction was implicitly drawn between those operating in a monopolistic marketplace (Schedule II, Part I) and those that are operating in a competitive environment (Schedule II, Part II). Operating budgets of Schedule I corporations would have required Ministerial and Treasury Board approval. Capital budgets of Schedule I and Schedule II, Part I, corporations would have required similar approval. Operating and capital budgets so approved must be tabled in Parliament.[117]

The Lambert Commission also recommends that the chief executive officer of every Crown corporation be responsible for preparing a corporate strategic plan for the approval of the Board of Directors and for the information of the designated minister in evaluating proposed budgets on a year-to-year basis.[118] This corporate strategic plan would cover a period of three

---

[111] Blue Paper, *supra* note 14, at 29, 50.
[112] Section 11.
[113] *Supra* note 1, Recommendations 19.10-19.14, at 346.
[114] *Supra* note 9.
[115] *Supra* note 14, at 31-34, 63 *et seq.*
[116] *Supra* note 109, s. 3(1).
[117] *Supra* note 109, ss. 52-58.
[118] *Supra* note 1, Recommendation 19.3 at 336.

years or longer and would contain several basic components: (1) a situation review: the past year's performance, the environment ahead and the corporate outlook; (2) a statement of corporate objectives both general and specific; (3) corporate strategies for leading the enterprise toward its objectives and for achieving its goals; (4) corporate policies for implementation of strategies under certain prescribed circumstances; (5) a strategic financial plan, outlining the cost, timing, and financing of proposed capital commitments required to implement strategies.[119] The Privy Council Office proposes a similar requirement, except that corporate plans would require Governor in Council approval.[120] Bill C-27 would also have required such approval.[121]

In addition, the Lambert Committee recommends the introduction of a generalized directive procedure, whereby a designated Minister may issue policy directives to a Crown corporation, subject to Governor in Council approval and subject to tabling forthwith in Parliament.[122] The Privy Council Office proposes a similar directive power[123] as did Bill C-27.[124] The Lambert Commission,[125] the Privy Council Office,[126] and Bill C-27[127] have proposed that directives issued to a Crown corporation be binding on the corporation but that where these result in additional costs to the corporation, compensation on an agreed or independently arbitrated basis be awarded by the government.

As to *ex post* review of the activities of Crown corporations by the government and/or Parliament, the Lambert Commission proposes that, as at present, annual reports be furnished to the designated minister for tabling in Parliament,[128] and that the designated minister should in future be required to undertake a review of the mandate and operations of Crown corporations under his jurisdiction not less than once every ten years and that the results of such reviews be tabled in Parliament and referred automatically for study and appropriate action by the relevant Standing Committee.[129] Under separate proposals of the Commission, Parliamentary Committees would be given substantially enhanced powers and resources.[130] Under Bill C-27, every annual report of a Crown corporation would be

---

119 *Supra* note 1, at 335.
120 *Supra* note 14, at 34, 63.
121 *Supra* note 109, s. 49.
122 *Supra* note 1, Recommendation 19.4, at 338.
123 *Supra* note 14, at 22, 51.
124 *Supra* note 109, s. 9.
125 *Supra* note 1, Recommendation 19.5, at 338, 339.
126 *Supra* note 14, at 25, 51.
127 *Supra* note 109, s. 10.
128 *Supra* note 1, at 351; see also the Blue Paper, *supra* note 14, at 35, 67; Bill C-27, *supra* note 109, s. 60.
129 *Supra* note 1, Recommendation 19.21, at 353.
130 *Supra* note 1, chapter 22.

tabled in Parliament and automatically referred to the Parliamentary Committee charged with oversight responsibilities.[131] The auditor of a Crown corporation must also make periodic value for money examinations (at least every five years) and his report thereon may be tabled in Parliament if he considers this is warranted.[132] A scheme of review recently set up under the British Columbia *Crown Corporations Reporting Act*,[133] provides that a legislative committee must review the activities of every Crown corporation in the province at least once every three years. The Committee is given power to appoint expert advisors and to compel the attendance of witnesses and the production of documents. In Saskatchewan, the Select Standing Committee of the Legislature exercises, on an ongoing basis, the functions of a Public Accounts Committee with respect to all provincial Crown corporations.[134]

As to the duties of directors, the Privy Council Office, in a provision in the draft model bill attached to the Blue Paper, proposed that the legal duty of every director and officer of a Crown corporation be to:

> act honestly and in good faith with a view *to the best interests of Canada* and, insofar as is not incompatible with the best interests of Canada, the best interests of the Crown corporation.[135]

The Privy Council Office suggests that in the case of Crown corporations, "the government's interests are wider and more complex than those of maximizing return on investment and as a result the role of directors is broader and more complex".[136] Adopting the views expressed in the Lambert report,[137] Bill C-27 required directors of a Crown corporation only to act in the best interests of the corporation,[138] although early in the Bill it was declared that "every Crown corporation is constituted an instrument for advancing the national interests of Canada and that such interests are the primary of the best interests of every Crown corporation" (*sic*).[139] The Privy Council Office proposal also is at variance with at least the spirit of recommendations of the Ontario Committee on Government Productivity that government commercial services or products be priced at their true costs[140] and that the government clearly establish and publicize policies for govern-

---

[131] *Supra* note 109, s. 60.

[132] *Supra* note 109, s. 63.

[133] S.B.C. 1977, c. 49.

[134] See Gracey, *supra* note 85, at 39, 40.

[135] *Supra* note 14, at 56 (our emphasis).

[136] *Supra* note 14, at 27.

[137] *Supra* note 1, at 337.

[138] *Supra* note 109, s. 44.

[139] *Supra* note 109, s. 8.

[140] Ontario. *Committee on Government Productivity: Report to the Executive Council of the Government of Ontario: A Summary* (Toronto: Committee on Government Productivity, 1973) Recommendation 12.23, at 103.

ment enterprises to follow; within such policies boards of directors should be given as much freedom as possible to concentrate on economic performance.[141]

As to the borrowing powers of Crown corporations, Bill C-27 substantially expanded the access of Crown corporations (within the definition assumed in this paper) to private capital markets. The only governmental approval required was that of the Minister of Finance, and then only with respect to the timing of long-term borrowings. On the other hand, borrowings by such Crown corporations would not bind the Crown generally, unless an express guarantee was provided by the Minister of Finance.[142]

Finally, with respect to the definition of Crown corporations, as we indicated in Section II the Lambert Commission proposed a relatively restricted definition, but in addition suggested a new category of government-related corporations, to be called "shared enterprises". In the case of shared enterprises, which would principally be distinguished from Crown corporations by virtue of the fact that the government does not *wholly* own such enterprises, the accountability regime would be sharply different from that proposed for Crown corporations. In general, accountability would rest on the rights that the designated minister would possess as shareholder under the relevant federal or provincial corporations law. Thus, apart from his voting rights, he would be entitled to annual reports, which would be tabled in Parliament. The designated minister would be the accountability link between a shared enterprise and Parliament.[143] In particular, there would be no requirement for budget approval, no requirement of a strategic plan, no provision for ministerial directives, and no provision for periodic review either by the designated minister or by any Parliamentary Committee. Both the Privy Council Office[144] and Bill C-27[145] accepted the same distinction between wholly owned and mixed or shared corporations.

(ii) An Evaluation

Most of the following reactions to the foregoing proposals derive from a view that in the settings in which Crown corporations have been invoked in Canada in the past, the characteristics of this policy instrument which have influenced such a choice are extremely varied and subtle; a generalized accountability regime possessing the features of the kind proposed by the Lambert Commission is so indiscriminate in its application to Crown cor-

---

141 *Ibid.*, Recommendation 12.24, at 103.

142 *Supra* note 109, s. 23.

143 *Supra* note 1, Recommendations 20.1-20.4, at 359-363.

144 *Supra* note 14, at 37.

145 *Supra* note 109, s. 2.

porations as a class that substantial costs are likely to be incurred in particular cases in terms of reduced instrumental effectiveness, particularly where there is no close substitute instrument available. These proposals appear to flow from the premise that the large range of legal and constitutional variations that have hitherto been accommodated within the Crown corporation mode are accidental and/or undesirable. We question this premise. It seems more plausible to assume that these variations reflect the wide range of purposes and settings in which governments have found it useful to deploy Crown corporations in the past. The flexibility of the instrument has permitted a wide latitude for institutional custom-design, a central quality that is unlikely to be all negative. Conversely, homogenizing reforms are unlikely to be costless.

Taking first the case of the proposed rules restricting the creation of Crown corporations or subsidiaries, in cases such as Petro-Can and the Canadian Development Corporation which are charged with making investments in often highly competitive markets, the proposed restriction on the creation of subsidiaries may, in particular contexts, involve significant costs. For example, in the recent past, Petro-Can has been involved in a takeover battle for Pacific Petroleum and the Canadian Development Corporation for Texas Gulf Sulphur. Conceivably, in takeover settings such as these, the formation of subsidiaries to purchase shares anonomously through the market may be an important part of an effective takeover strategy. To require the formation of a subsidiary to be approved by the Governor in Council may involve highly damaging delays and publicity.

With respect to *ex ante* budget approval requirements, and the production of corporate strategic plans, Crown corporations facing competitors either in their output markets or their input markets, or both, are likely to find it costly, in many contexts, to have to telegraph strategically important information either to competitors or to parties with whom they are likely to be negotiating within the relevant timeframe. This is likely to be an especially acute problem in the case of yardstick enterprises (*e.g.*, Petro-Can) but even in the case of natural monopolies which face competition in input markets, bargaining strategies might be impaired (*e.g.*, negotiation of uranium supply contracts by Ontario Hydro). In addition, in the case of some Crown corporations, such as Atomic Energy of Canada, security reasons may make these requirements inappropriate.

In addition to these considerations, the requirement of the production and approval of a strategic plan against which ministers and their staffs will review budgets seems substantially to elevate the role of bureaucratic input in the decision-making processes of Crown corporations. Given that the only comparative advantage that bureaucrats have in this context is with respect to the non-market objectives of Crown corporations, one would expect that this proposal would lead to some shift in emphasis towards the maximization of these objectives. This tendency is likely to be accentuated by the dominant role played by central agencies of government, *i.e.*, Treasury Board and the Department of Finance, in the budget review process. With so centralized a bureaucratic perspective on the review process, the *sui generis* considerations that led to the creation of many Crown corporations are likely to be systematically depreciated.

A greater emphasis on non-market outputs, which cannot be readily valued is likely also to lead to a greater emphasis on bureaucratically-oriented input rules and regulations, with consequent costs in terms of reduced ability of the managements of Crown corporations to engage in innovative or dynamic behaviour. This suggests, in turn, a lower valuation on private sector skills in Crown corporation managements and greater difficulty in attracting persons possessing such skills to an environment of highly constraining political and bureaucratic oversight.

Differences should be noted between the Lambert Report, on the one hand, and the P.C.O. Blue Paper and Bill C-27, on the other, with respect to the above issues. The Lambert Report would require only that a corporate strategic plan be prepared for the information of the designated minister. Bill C-27 would have required the approval of the designated minister, the Minister of Finance, the President of the Treasury Board and the Governor in Council. On the other hand, Bill C-27 contemplated that Schedule II, Part II, corporations should not be required to obtain any governmental budget approval at all. Approval of corporate plans, in this context, was substituted for approval of budgets. In terms of relative political and bureaucratic inputs, it is not clear whether the Lambert Commission, with less emphasis on review of corporate plans and more emphasis on review of budgets, assumes more or less weight for such inputs than Bill C-27.

A further variant in mechanisms of centralized executive oversight is exemplified by the Saskatchewan Government Finance Office, which acts as a holding corporation of most provincial Crown corporations and reviews capital allocations. Traditionally, the majority of the Government Finance Office board of directors have been Cabinet Ministers, usually those who were chairmen of the boards of the individual Crown corporations.[146] Such an oversight mechanism would seem more sensitive to the policy considerations that led to the creation of individual Crown corporations than the Federal proposals, while providing a measure of centralized oversight.

A final concern with proposed requirements for budget approval is that to the extent that different approval mechanisms apply depending on whether appropriations are required or not, distortions are introduced into the approval process, and probably into the behaviour of affected parties, insofar as incentives are created to cross-subsidize unprofitable activities internally out of retained earnings rather than seek a politically debatable appropriation. Moreover, the distinctions drawn in Bill C-27 between Crown

---

146 Gracey, *supra* note 85, at 39.

corporations "ordinarily" dependent on government appropriations and those that are not, and between Crown corporations operating in monopolistic markets and those operating in competitive markets, even if relevant factors in designing accountability regimes, are extraordinarily difficult distinctions to operationalize.[147]

As to the proposed directive power to be given to ministers with respect to Crown corporations falling within their aegis, a similar point might be made to that already made with respect to proposed restrictions on modes of creation. If the government were to decide to direct Petro-Can or the Canadian Development Corporation to attempt to take over particular private sector enterprises, it would not seem conducive to the effectuation of this objective for the government to be required to table the directive "forthwith in Parliament".[148] Similarly, in the case of policy directives bearing on matters of national security, as may be the case, for example, with certain activities of Atomic Energy of Canada Limited.

As to the proposal that where directives impose costs on a Crown corporation, the Crown corporation should be compensated for these costs, a number of difficulties might be anticipated. First, such a proposal, if implemented, creates strong incentives for strategic behaviour on the part of management within Crown corporations to maximize subsidies paid under such a rule. For example, the management of a Crown corporation might decide to make no effort to maximize non-market objectives until positively directed to do so in order to trigger compensation payments for doing what the Crown corporation was intended to do from the outset. Crown corporations may also find it advantageous to present the government, in budgetary or strategic plan proposals, with a quite unrealistic menu of proposed projects, in the hope that directives will be received ordering abandonment of these projects, thus again arguably triggering the compensation requirement. A compensation requirement might also reduce incentives for management of Crown corporations to seek out the least cost methods for achieving a corporation's assigned objectives, if these costs can be externalized through invocation of the compensation mechanism. Finally, difficult problems of measurement seem likely to be raised by the proposal. For example, if a Crown corporation is directed not to build a nuclear plant in one location but instead to build it somewhere else, additional costs of building it in the second location might be difficult to measure, given the lack of serious cost data for the plant that was proposed in the first location.

One of the principal effects of a compensation rule may well be to induce corporations to behave very much like private sector corporations sub-

---

[147] For a detailed and damaging critique of recent Federal definition and classification proposals, see Langford, *supra* note 17.

[148] Lambert Report, *supra* note 1, Recommendation 19.4, at 338; Bill C-27 *supra* note 109, s. 9, requires a directive, and an estimate of any costs that it is likely to generate, to be laid before Parliament within the first 15 sitting days after the directive is given.

ject to regulation or subsidy. That is to say, management will maximize profits (because it may be in its interests to do so), and to the extent that the government wants management to maximize other objectives the latter will wait for directives to that effect and then demand subsidies, which may or may not bear a close relation to the costs actually imposed on the corporation by the directive. At this point, in terms of comparative monitoring costs, it is not clear that the Crown corporation is a more effective instrument of government policy than subsidization of private sector enterprises. In short, to what extent is it contemplated that the policy objectives of the government, both market and non-market, should be internalized into the behaviour of the management of Crown corporations, and to what extent is it assumed that maximizing non-market objectives will be a matter requiring continuous direction by political and bureaucratic overseers of the kind more usually associated with the administration of department bureaucracies?

The same ambivalence in terms of the behavioural expectations of the management of Crown corporations is reflected, on the one hand, in the Privy Council Office's proposal that the directors and officers of Crown corporations be required "to act . . . with a view to the best interests of Canada", compared, on the other hand, to the suggestion of the Ontario Committee on Government Productivity that the management of Crown corporations maximize economic returns subject only to such constraints as government might choose explicitly to impose on them. What this ambivalence may imply is that the balance between market and non-market objectives will vary significantly from Crown corporation to Crown corporation and that the duties of directives may have to be interpreted so as to recognize this fact.

As to proposals to provide freer access by Crown corporations to private capital markets on condition that the government's credit generally is not engaged, certain motivations seem to prompt these proposals: to expose Crown corporations more to market forces and market discipline in order to achieve greater efficiency in the use of capital; to curtail the cash drain on the Consolidated Revenue Fund; to provide greater flexibility to Crown corporations in their financing; to ensure that government expenditure commitments (even contingent) do not automatically flow from borrowings of Crown corporations (as agents of the Crown), without being subject to appropriate Parliamentary and other oversight mechanisms.

On the other hand, one can argue that the proposals, in implying a greater reliance on market constraints on Crown corporation behaviour, countervail other proposals which would increase political and bureaucratic constraints. The net effect of these countervailing proposals is not clear. In any event, the proposals on borrowing may seem more significant than they really are if formal guarantees by the Minister of Finance and informal governmental undertakings of support can be easily substituted for automatic commitment of the Consolidated Revenue Fund.

As to the distinction between "Crown corporation" and "shared enterprise" proposed by the Lambert Commission (and implicitly endorsed by the P.C.O. and Bill C-27), along with the sharply different accountability regimes applied to corporations falling within each category, it is clear that this will create substantial incentives (and associated distortions in institutional behaviour) to manipulate the application of accountability regimes by manipulating the applicability of definitional criteria. For example, a government and/or a Crown corporation wishing to avoid the accountability regime proposed for Crown corporations can simply ensure that its shareholding is less than 100 percent, and the corporation is then a shared enterprise.[149]

The general implications of this evaluation of current accountability proposals would seem to involve a much more case-specific application of accountability rules to Crown corporations. An alternative approach might be to identify discrete components in an accountability regime and make judgments as to the appropriateness of these accountability characteristics on a characteristic and corporation specific basis. Ideally, a legislative judgment might be made as to how to schedule particular Crown corporations with respect to each of the specified accountability characteristics. This is obviously a substantially more discriminating and exacting exercise than that contemplated by the broad sweep of the Lambert proposals. However, only such an exercise may fully recognize the importance of institutional variables in the promotion of the values or interests in whose service Crown corporations have hitherto been harnessed. Failure to undertake such an exercise will lead, we predict, to the substitution, over time, of other instruments of intervention designed to replicate, necessarily imperfectly, the set of characteristics formerly possessed by Crown corporations. Whether in the light of possible reductions in the instrumental effectiveness of Crown corporations and the substitution effects that proposed reforms are likely to engender, a net increase in social welfare, however measured, will be accomplished may be open to question.

(b) Privatization

(i) Introduction

The second major thrust of reforms regarding Crown corporations is privatization.[150] Privatization refers to the transfer to the private sector of

---

[149] Bill C-27, *supra* 109, s. 12 contemplates Governor-General-in-Council approval to an disposition of shares in a Crown corporation.

[150] Little has been written to date in Canada on privatization. See, however, Sexty, "The Profit Role in Crown Corporations" (1978), 5(3) *Can. Bus. Rev.* 9; T. M. Ohashi et al., *Privatization Theory and Practice: Distributing Shares in Private and Public Enterprises* (Vancouver: The Fraser Institute, 1980).

functions formerly undertaken by the public sector. In the case of Crown corporations, this normally refers to the transfer by sale or gift of the corporation's shares or assets to investors in the private sector. In this section we view proposals for privatization from the perspective of instrument choice, arguing that the decision to privatize a Crown corporation must be evaluated in terms of the relevant substitute instruments and their critical characteristics.

Privatization has recently become somewhat of a Canadian political *cause célèbre*. At the federal level, the election of the Progressive Conservative government in 1979 was accompanied by a pledge to reduce the size of the public sector in part by privatizing a number of Crown corporations. While the Conservatives had only begun action on this pledge by the time they were defeated in February, 1980, and while the new Liberal government divorced themselves from any such course of action[151], the issue remains politically sensitive. The Conservatives' campaign promise concerning privatization followed the widely acclaimed decision by the provincial government of British Columbia to create the British Columbia Resources Investment Corporation and then give its shares to all residents of the province. Advocates of privatization have claimed that substantial gains will be achieved through privatization, suggesting it may make a major contribution to both the reduction in size of the public sector and the restoration of the private sector to its rightful place of dominance in the production of goods and services. These claims for the role of privatization as a means of limiting the growth of government are reminiscent to a degree of the exaggerated boasts which accompanied the early discussions of sunset laws as their advocates saw them as a panacea for controlling the growth of regulation. Just as sunset proposals deserved (and received)[152] close scrutiny, so do the alleged benefits of privatization. In the remainder of this section we summarize the major recent privatization proposals and then comment on them from the perspective of instrument choice.

(ii) The Proposals

a. The British Columbia Resources Investment Corporation

The British Columbia Resources Investment Corporation (BCRIC) was created by statute in 1977 and began operation in 1979.[153] The rationale for its creation has been stated by its President:

---

151 "Liberals Shelve Plans to Sell Crown Firms", *Globe and Mail*, May 1, 1980, at 8: "Treasury Board President, Donald Johnston, indicated yesterday that the Liberals have shelved plans launched by the former Conservative Government to sell off more than $800 million worth of Crown corporations . . . 'It's not a priority with us', he said".

152 Behn, "The False Dawn of the Sunset Laws" (1977), 49 *The Public Interest* 103.

153 For a description of BCRIC, see David L. Helliwell, "Remarks for the Toronto Society of

B.C. Resources was initially conceived to be a vehicle to return to the private sector certain investments which were owned by the Province of British Columbia. The government wanted to avoid the conflicts which can arise where it had regulatory authority over the forest industry, for example, and yet had a direct holding in some forestry companies. In short, to separate exploitation from regulation.

In addition, the government felt the process could provide a mechanism to raise some badly needed equity capital that would at the same time enable its citizens, who were watching their bank deposit savings erode by inflation, participate directly, but individually, in resource ownership.

The architects of our concept patterned both the underlying principles and the resultant legislation very much after the Canada Development Corporation and the Alberta Energy Company.[154]

Consistent with this plan, the provincial government transferred to BCRIC its interest in four Crown corporations and oil and gas exploration rights in Northeastern British Columbia. The interests in the four Crown corporations included 81 percent of Canadian Cellulose, a public company and a major pulp and lumber producer in the province, 100 percent of two medium-sized lumber producers, Kootenay Forest Products and Plateau Mills, and 10 percent of the shares of Westcoast Transmission, a natural gas pipeline firm. In return for these assets BCRIC issued a promissory note to the government for 151½ million dollars.

After these initial transactions, the Corporation felt it would be unable to encourage individual equity investment in the corporation as a result of the substantial debt facing it. Accordingly, it was agreed that the government would accept 15 million shares in BCRIC as full settlement of its promissory note with the understanding that these shares would be distributed free to all eligible residents of British Columbia. Pursuant to that agreement, the government gave five free shares to each of 2.4 million eligible residents, giving birth to the new expression known as "bricing", *i.e.*, the giving away of shares in a publicly owned corporation. At the same time residents were entitled to purchase from the corporation further shares to a maximum of 5,000 per person.[155]

The final result of the share distribution and sale left BCRIC with 96½ million shares outstanding, 487½ million dollars in its treasury and the

Financial Analysts", September 27, 1979 and BCRIC Prospectus dated March 1, 1979. The statute creating BCRIC is the *British Columbia Resources Investment Corporation Act,* S.B.C. 1977, c. 47. For an account of the history of the creation of BCRIC, see Ohashi, "Privatization in Practice: The Story of the British Columbia Resources Investment Corporation" in T. M. Ohashi et al., *supra* note 150.

[154] Helliwell, *supra* note 153, at 4.

[155] A recent report (*Globe and Mail*, August 9, 1982, at B5) indicates that the provincial government has introduced legislation that would remove share ownership restrictions preventing individuals from purchasing more than 1 percent interest in the company and institutions more than 3 percent. Restrictions concerning Canadian ownership will remain in place. This legislation, if adopted, would appear to be responding to similar concerns to those expressed below in the text.

assets described above.[156] This represented the largest single equity distribution to date in Canadian history.

As a result of the share distribution the provincial government's interest in the corporation is less than 5 percent. All the investors are forbidden from holding more than 1 percent of BCRIC's shares except for mutual funds which are permitted to hold up to 3 percent.[157] All shareholders holding 100 or more shares are qualified to be registered and then to vote at company meetings and as a result BCRIC has about 130,000 shareholders entitled to participate in its affairs. All directors are elected by the shareholders and the government enjoys no privilege of appointment.[158]

Control of the BCRIC is further diffused by the "associated member" rule. Section 9 of the enabling statute provides that persons in various non-arms length relationships including "an agreement or arrangement a purpose of which, in the opinion of the Board (of Directors) is to require members to act in concert with respect to their interests in the company" are deemed to be associated members. Such members collectively may not hold more than 1 percent of BCRIC's shares.[159] Depending on the meaning given to the words "arrangement" and "concert" by the Board, almost any collective action by shareholders challenging a decision of the Board of Directors could be characterized as falling afoul of s. 9. One knowledgeable commentator has gone so far as to suggest that shareholders voting against the re-election of the Board of Directors could be classified as associated members.[160]

The President of BCRIC has made clear the corporation's objective: profit maximization. He has stated:

> First, BCRIC is not run by the government of British Columbia. . . . We have no function nor responsibility to carry out any aspect of government policy or direction other than that expected of any good corporate citizen. Second, B.C. Resources has as its principle objective the making of profits for its shareholders and the protection of their investment.[161]

The BCRIC has indicated that it is contemplating investing its cash assets by assuming equity interests in a number of private firms operating primarily,

---

[156] Helliwell, *supra* note 153, at 9-10.

[157] *British Columbia Resources Investment Corporation Act,* S.B.C. 1977, c. 47, s. 7, now the *Resource Investment Corporation Act,* R.S.B.C. 1979, c. 366, s. 6.

[158] Under s. 16 of the incorporating Act, the government was entitled to appoint a number of directors so long as it maintained 10 percent or more of the outstanding shares. However, as a result of the share distribution, the government's interest has fallen below this threshold thus, at least nominally relegating the government to equal status with all other shareholders.

[159] *Supra* note 157, s. 7(1)(b) [now s. 6(1)(b)]. Section 10 [now s. 9] modifies the impact of the associated member definition.

[160] Ohashi, *supra* note 153, at 15.

[161] Helliwell, *supra* note 153, at 13-14.

although not exclusively, in the West and has made some preliminary investments consistent with this indication.

In sum, the "bricing" process transferred ownership of four Crown corporations to the private sector without any financial return to the government for the assets. The corporations are now widely held, free from government control and directed toward profit maximization.

b. Privatization of Federal Crown Corporations

Although the federal Conservatives' proposals for privatization were shelved with the defeat of the government in February, 1980, they still present a useful contemporary case study. Upon its assumption of power in May, 1979, the new federal government made clear its intention to privatize a number of Crown corporations. Treasury Board President Sinclair Stevens stated:

> We are determined to get the federal government out of ordinary business and commercial operations and hand them over to private enterprise where they belong.[162]
>
> In a later news release, the government declared: Canada is distinctively different from other countries for reasons of history, geography and economics and it has been necessary at times to provide government services at uneconomic prices in the national interest. Nevertheless, the growth of the government sector in Canada and the high proportion of Crown corporations within the federal government has to be reversed. Some Crown corporations need the discipline of the marketplace and others are already mature enough to cope independently. Selling some Crown corporations will help us achieve a leaner and less expensive government.[163]

He also announced the creation of the Privatization Unit within the Treasury Board which was charged with the responsibility of identifying and preparing for sale Crown corporations suitable for privatization. By the time the government was defeated, eight corporations including Canadair, DeHavilland, Eldorado Nuclear and Northern Transportation Company Limited and their four subsidiaries were put up for sale.[164]

Two other developments related to the Conservatives' privatization efforts warrant special note. First, the government's most controversial decision regarding privatization was its determination to privatize Petro-Canada. Remaining true to its campaign promise, the government announced that it intended to proceed with privatization and appointed a task

---

[162] *Toronto Star*, June, 1979.
[163] "Crown Corporations for Sale", Treasury Board *News Release*, September 28, 1978, at 2.
[164] *Ibid.*

force to determine how the decision might best be implemented. By the time of their defeat, the Conservatives had not settled the details of the privatization mechanism.[165] However, the Task Force recommended that individual investors be limited to 1 percent and institutional investors to not more than 3 percent of the outstanding shares, and that while in the long-term total divestiture by the government of its interests in Petro-Canada was desirable, an interim stage wherein the government would retain an interest not in excess of 25 percent would be acceptable.[166]

The second development of note in the privatization debate was the government's plan to reduce its equity interest in the Canadian Development Corporation from the existing 66 percent to less than 50 percent.[167] This was consistent with the legislative scheme creating the Canadian Development Corporation (CDC) which envisions an eventual reduction in the public's holdings in the firm to a minimum of 10 percent of the equity. Initially, the Conservatives planned to reduce its holding to less than 50 percent of the equity. One effect of this would be to exclude the Corporation's 10,000 employees from the calculation of the number of federal employees since Statistics Canada treats the employees of companies in which the government holds less than 50 percent as being in the private sector.[168] In the result, the reduction of the government's equity by 17 percent would have reduced by 10,000 the total number of federal public employees.

The Conservatives' privatization plans were further complicated by an announcement by the CDC that it was interested in purchasing some of the Crown corporations the Conservatives were putting up for sale. Since the government had also indicated that it would be willing to take CDC shares in payment for such Crown corporations, there was the possibility that there would be an interim increase in the government's holdings before the stated objective of going below a 50 percent interest could be achieved.

(iii) Commentary

The growing political interest in privatization appears to have arisen from increasing concern about the growth and size of the public sector, a concern that was recognized in the Speech from the Throne in October, 1976 which said in part:

> In a further effort to reduce the size of government as well as expand the range of opportunities for private enterprise, all federal programs will be reviewed to

---

[165] Canada. Department of Energy, Mines and Resources. Petro Canada Task Force. *Report of the Task Force on Petro-Canada* [Ottawa: Department of Energy, Mines and Resources, 1979]. The Task Force was chaired by Donald J. McDougall.

[166] *Ibid.*

[167] *Globe and Mail,* November 20, 1979, at 1, 2, B1.

[168] *Ibid.,* at 1.

identify those government activities which could be transferred to the private sector without reducing the quality of service to the public.[169]

Similarly, in its paper entitled *The Way Ahead: A Framework for Discussion* which outlined a strategy for the post-wage and price control period, the government committed itself to considering "the possibility of the private sector providing goods and services that are now provided through government enterprises and programs."[170] These plans gained momentum with the creation of BCRIC and the federal Conservative government's attempt to reduce the size of the federal public sector in part through privatization.

From the perspective of instrument choice, these developments pose a puzzling question: what has changed that has led to the conclusion that certain Crown corporations are no longer the appropriate instruments of intervention? That is, given that the public decision-makers perceived the Crown corporations to be the most attractive instrument of intervention at the time they were created, what has changed that has altered that calculus of choice? Furthermore, can one derive from an identification of the cause of the change in choice calculus any implications for the way in which the privatization exercise might be undertaken?

An answer to these questions must begin by distinguishing two possible types of explanations for the change in the choice calculus. First, the change may be attributed to a shift in the government's substantive objectives for intervention. That is, the decision to privatize a Crown corporation may signal the abandoning of the public purpose for which it was first created or acquired or, similarly, it may signal a shift in the purpose such that the Crown corporation is no longer the most effective instrument to achieve the newly defined objective. Secondly, and alternatively, the change may be attributed to some change in the legal or institutional characteristics within the range of substitute instruments or some shift in the political perception of these characteristics such that the relative effectiveness of Crown corporations as the instrument of intervention has been diminished.

These two sources of change—a change in objective and a change in instrument effectiveness—have different implications for the process of privatization as they raise different issues regarding the appropriate procedures for, and the likely effects of, privatization.

a. Changes in Objectives

It is far from startling to acknowledge the likelihood that the rationale

---

[169] Canada. Parliament. House of Commons. *Debates,* "Speech from the Throne", Second Session of the Thirtieth Parliament, October 12, 1976, at 2. Cited in Sexty, *supra* note 150.

[170] Canada. [Privy Council Office.] *The Way Ahead: A Framework for Discussion: Working Paper* [Ottawa: Department of Finance, 1976] at 28.

supporting the creation or acquisition of certain Crown corporations has been eliminated or at least changed substantially as a result of changed political, economic and social circumstances. For example at the federal level, to the extent that the acquisitions of Polymer and Eldorado were dictated by the particular exigencies of the war effort, it is difficult to argue that their retention as Crown corporations can be based on the same rationale. Thus, the sale of Polymer (now named Polysar) to the CDC in 1974 and the Conservatives' decision to sell Eldorado Nuclear are clear examples of a shift in objectives being a primary explanation for the decision to privatize.

Similarly, the Conservatives' decision to sell Canadair and DeHavilland could also be argued as being consistent with a shift in objectives. To the extent that the original decision to assume ownership of these firms can be attributed to the need to provide a period of transition to allow them to establish their commercial viability and to the extent that this goal has been accomplished, their sale could be understood as signalling the completion of the period of transition. On the other hand, given the long history of government support for the aircraft manufacturing industry, in large part through its role as the major purchaser of the domestic products, it is not at all clear that the Conservatives intended to abandon the principal objective of maintaining the industry in Canada. Rather, to the extent that public assistance to the industry was to be continued through various substitute instruments, the decision to sell DeHavilland and Canadair may be more accurately understood as having been influenced primarily by a change in the government's perception of the relative effectiveness of the various instruments.

At the provincial level, the creation of BCRIC might also be explained in terms of a change in objective. At the time the constituent companies were turned over to BCRIC, they were all profitable, independent firms. However, except in the case of the interest in Westcoast Transmission, each of the companies had been acquired by the government in the early 1970s in order to moderate the potential economic dislocations caused by the threatened closing of the companies due to economic difficulties. By 1978 each of the companies had, with considerable government assistance and an absence of tax liability, been nurtured back to economic health and the transition periods were completed. Thus, the decision to privatize them through BCRIC can be seen as signalling the successful attainment of the stated objective of intervention.

The privatization of firms in situations in which there has been a change of objective is not a matter of great consequence. It reflects a presumption that for firms whose sole objective is profit-maximization, the incentive structures inherent to the private sector are more likely to lead to efficient business conduct. The tradeoff of competing monitoring costs favours private sector ownership and the absence of competing objectives makes it difficult to maintain a case for continued public ownership.

While at first blush this conclusion may appear non-controversial, its shortcoming is the difficulty in determining its applicability. That is, while there may be general agreement that the private sector is best suited to the pursuit of profit maximization, there is likely to be considerably less agreement on which cases qualify for classification as lacking any objective other than profit-maximization. This lack of agreement arises from the ambiguity concerning the objectives sought at the outset and the differing perspectives brought to bear on the question. The normative implication of this lack of agreement is the need for clarity on the part of any governmt as it embarks on its mission of privatization. Only if it is prepared to articulate the reasons for the change in objectives warranting the return of the firms to the private sector and to subject these reasons to debate in the appropriate political forums, can these privatization decisions be made politically accountable.

Once the decision to privatize a Crown corporation has been taken, the particular means to implement the decision must be selected. Various techniques are possible. They include:

1. *Complete Privatization*
This may include selling 100 percent of the equity through a public distribution, selling the entire equity to a private purchaser by tender, giving away the equity in a free public share distribution, selling the control block by tender with public distribution of the balance of the equity, and sale of viable subsidiaries or divisions and the subsidization or contracting out to the private sector of the non-profitable activities.

2. *Partial Privatization*
This may include the partial sale of the equity with the government retaining a percentage, thus creating a mixed enterprise, or the sale or transfer of the equity to an existing mixed enterprise in return for shares in that enterprise.

The choice of techniques will in large part be determined by the reason for privatization itself. That is, if the decision to privatize is a desire to return the activity to the private sector with no residual public control or responsibility, the complete privatization by sale is an attractive technique. However, so long as any non-profit objectives are retained, the straight sale option becomes less attractive. For example, if the government wishes to maintain Canadian ownership of the company, it may severely restrict the number of potential bidders and, in the case of large Crown corporations, may make it virtually impossible to find a Canadian owner with sufficient capital strength. In such cases, either partial privatization or a free share distribution may have to be considered. However, each of these solutions presents its own problems.

In the case of partial privatization resulting in a mixed enterprise, the problems of accountability and control raised by wholly owned Crown corporations are again raised although in a modified form. To the extent that an equity interest is maintained by the government to further its policy objectives (*e.g.*, Telesat), it is not difficult to argue that the gains thought to be associated with a dedication to profit by private owners may not be achieved. If the government's interest is maintained simply because of the absence of suitable investors, one wonders whether it would not be preferable to conceive of ways in which better access to capital by private investors might be achieved.

The proposal described above under which it was contemplated that the government would sell one or more Crown corporations to the CDC in return for equity in CDC is an example of the ambiguity created by the partial privatization solution. Under a plan such as this, the extent to which private ownership incentives would have been brought to bear on the privatized Crown corporation would turn on the extent to which these same incentives govern CDC. It is somewhat difficult to reconcile on the one hand the claim that ownership by the CDC would subject the Crown corporations to the discipline of the private profit incentive while on the other hand the government planned to remain the dominant shareholder in CDC.

The alternative solution—a distribution of free shares—presents a different problem, one underlined by the BCRIC experience in British Columbia. If on grounds of equity and democracy the government insists on the widest possible distribution of the free shares and, as in the case of BCRIC and the Petro-Canada proposal, prohibits the accumulation of a control bloc by any private investor by limiting individual owners to 1 percent and institutional investors to 3 percent of the equity, the distribution scheme runs the risk of freeing the management of the corporation from *any* meaningful controls. That is, by being privatized, the Crown corporation is freed from accountability to the government as it is no longer subject to the normal reporting, clearance and directive mechanisms which attach to Crown corporation status. At the same time, while management is nominally responsible to the shareholders of the company, the extremely wide shareholdings mean that no individual or group of individual shareholders has an adequate incentive to monitor the performance of the firm's management. Thus, while nominally these firms would be subjected to the discipline of the market, in fact they may well become paradigmatic examples of corporations in which the management is accountable to no one but itself.[171] One can predict that to the extent that this occurs there may well be calls for political intervention to increase accountability, thus beginning the process of a return to some form of political control over the corporation.

In sum, it can be seen that the decision to return Crown corporations to the private sector in situations in which the original rationale for the creation of the corporations has evaporated is not free from difficulty. As soon as a constraint such as insisting on Canadian ownership is imposed on the

---

171 Professor Spindler, in "'Bricking-Up' Government Bureaus and Crown Corporations" in *Privatization Theory and Practice, supra* note 153, at 170, while generally favouring privatization is highly critical of this aspect of the BCRIC initiative.

privatization process, the government may need to look beyond a simple sale of the equity and to consider mixed enterprise and free share distribution schemes. Each of these possibilities raises some doubts as to whether the full potential advantages of privatization will be attained since each may diminish the strength of the investors' monitoring incentives.

b. Perceived Changes in Instrument Effectiveness

The alternative rationale for privatization is that circumstances in a given context have changed such that some instrument or combination of instruments other than public ownership have become relatively more effective. In these cases the privatization decision represents not an indication of a change in objective but rather a desire to achieve the objective in a different way. Presumably, it is thought that the efficiency gains associated with a return to monitoring by private owners outweigh the costs which may be incurred in relying on alternative support instruments which, by definition, were second-best choices when the original decision to create the Crown corporation was taken.

As in the case of a change in objectives, there is no compelling reason to believe that the relative effectiveness of alternative instruments does not change over time. Indeed, the opposite is more plausible; changing circumstances are likely to alter the relative importance of the critical legal and institutional characteristics of Crown corporations with the result that in some cases alternative instruments will represent better choices. In these situations, the decision to privatize the corporation offers potential net gains as a result of the greater effectiveness of the substitute instruments put in place.

While gains are possible, their magnitude may not be great. It must be remembered that to the extent that the objective of intervention remains unchanged, the costs associated with the substitute instruments which must be put in place to accomplish the objective may diminish or even largely eliminate the gains to be derived from subjecting the corporations to private sector profit incentives. For example, if a Crown corporation is replaced by a private firm supported by a subsidy program, the monitoring costs associated with the subsidy program must be subtracted from the gains in efficiency attained by returning the firm to the private sector in order to calculate the net benefits from privatization.

Plans to privatize Petro-Canada are a good example of a perceived change in instrument effectiveness as the Conservative government announced that the objectives sought by Petro-Canada would not be abandoned. Rather, the government's presumption appears to have been that these same objectives could be achieved more efficiently by dividing the existing operations between a private, Canadian-owned petroleum company and a government agency charged with carrying on the activities which a corporation motivated by profit alone would not undertake. The conclusion that this combination of a private firm and a government agency could more effectively meet the government's objective of security of supply of oil and gas is not one we are competent to evaluate. However, two notes of caution should be sounded. First, the characteristics of Crown corporations which led to the creation of Petro-Canada would not appear to have changed a great deal between 1975 and 1979. Therefore, any claim that clear improvements in effectiveness were likely to occur after privatization might be viewed skeptically in the absence of some empirical evidence suggesting the initial evaluation of instrument choice was misinformed. Second, to the extent that the government would have been forced to rely on either a mixed enterprise or free share distribution solution to facilitate the privatization of Petro-Canada consistent with a desire to maintain Canadian ownership, the potential shortcomings of these solutions identified in the preceding section must be taken into account in any overall analysis of the benefits of privatization.

This discussion of changes in instrument effectiveness justifying privatization in some circumstances suggests that there may well be some legitimate cases in which privatization could lead to the attainment of certain public objectives at lower costs. As such, privatization plans should be welcomed to the extent that they apply to these cases. However, it is important not to overestimate the benefits that will accrue since much of the gain achieved by returning to the private sector will be offset by the costs of the inevitable substitute instruments.

The disturbing elements of much of the privatization movement arise from the lack of articulation and disclosure of either the anticipated substitute instruments or of the change in characteristics of the relevant instruments. Thus, when Crown corporations are put up for sale the terms of the sale must include not only the price of the equity or the assets but also the commitments, made openly or privately, with regard to future government support or regulatory programs bearing on the industry. There can be no doubt that the potential purchasers will require such information regarding future support or regulatory programs; the price they will be willing to pay for the corporations will be directly related to their evaluation of the programs. It is too easy for the government to inflate the apparent gains from privatization if it is permitted to proceed without disclosure of this same information to the public.

Similarly, a failure to be explicit with regard to the change in the characteristics of the alternative instruments could permit the government to make privatization decisions on the basis of symbolic but largely illusory changes in instrument effectiveness. A transparent contemporary case in this regard was the Conservative government's plan to meet its commitment to reduce the number of federal employees by 60,000 in part by privatization.[172] Since, for statistical purposes, employees of wholly owned Crown corporations and corporations in which the government holds 50 percent or more of the equity count as federal employees, privatization offered the prospect of substantially reducing the formal count of the number of public employees. However, to the extent that the privatization decisions were accompanied by the introduction of substitute instruments and unaccompanied by any net gain in instrument effectiveness (indeed, there may well have been a net loss in effectiveness), it is difficult to see any meaningful improvement in public policy. The extreme example of this phenomenon was the Conservatives' announcement regarding the reduction in equity in the CDC to below 50 percent to effect a statistical reduction of 10,000 federal employees and no other apparent objective. In such cases, the privatization decisions are, at best, an empty gesture and, at worst, a deliberate attempt to mislead the Canadian public.

---

[172] Statement by the Hon. Sinclair Stevens, President of the Treasury Board on Plans for More Efficient Government (August 15, 1979), at 1-3.

CHAPTER 2

TOWARD A POSITIVE THEORY OF
PUBLIC SECTOR SUPPLY ARRANGEMENTS

THOMAS E. BORCHERDING*

Nationalize B.C. Tel.
—Popular button and bumper sticker seen in British Columbia during the
B.C. Telephone Co.—Telecommunications Workers' Union dispute of
winter 1980-81.

The desire to avoid or suppress the effects of the profit making incentive is,
however, often the reason society resorts to public ownership . . . If public
ownership in some government activity were converted to private property, the
method of achieving the government objectives would be changed.
—Armen A. Alchian, "Some Economics of Property Rights,"
Il Politico (Fall 1965).

* Professor of Economics, Simon Fraser University.
    The idea for this essay was long in gestation, though in a formal sense the research of-
ficially commenced in the late fall of 1978. Many persons were very helpful to me, both well
before and since that time, but several deserve particular mention. These carefully read,
made thoughtful comments and sometimes offered sharp criticisms of earlier drafts: David
G. Davies (Duke University), John McManus, Keith Acheson and Stephen Ferris (Carleton
University), James Buchanan and Gordon Tullock (Virginia Polytechnic Institute), Stanley
Lebowitz (Western Ontario) and Michael Parkin (Western Ontario and the Hoover Institu-
tion), John Dales and Frank Mathewson (University of Toronto), Jack Knetsch, Stephen
Easton, Kelly Busche, Angus Oliver, and Zane Spindler (Simon Fraser University), C. M.
Lindsay (Emory University), Benjamin Klein, Harold Demsetz, George Priest and Earl
Thompson (U.C.L.A.), Robert O. Keohane (Stanford University), Douglass Morgan, H. E.
Frech, Walter Mead, Jon Sonstelie and Robert Deacon (U.C., Santa Barbara), Stephen C.
Littlechild (University of Birmingham) and my co-investigators in this volume Michael
Trebilcock and Robert Prichard (University of Toronto, Law), John Quinn (Western On-
tario, Law) and John Palmer (Western Ontario). John Todd (Research Director, Ontario
Economic Council) organized in a coherent fashion comments and criticisms of his review
committee. None of these scholars are responsible for any error I have added to the subject
at hand, nor should their assistance imply agreement with my thesis.
    The Law and Economics Programme (University of Toronto) and the Ontario
Economic Council (Toronto) made financially possible residence at the University of Toronto where research was undertaken during academic 1978-79. The Canada Council's and
Simon Fraser University's sabbatical year have contributed stipends to my support during
1979-80. The Earhart Foundation of Ann Arbor generously aided with research monies during 1980. My thanks also must go to the Faculty of Law, University of Toronto and the
Hoover Institution, Stanford University, for their kind hospitality and for provision of efficient typing services. Typing services at Simon Fraser University were provided through the
University's Programmes of Distinction. I am obliged to all those mentioned for their financial and "in-kind" assistance.

It does not appear that the existing range of regulatory institutions can be explained solely as a response to failures in private markets. Instead, much of the regulation we observe tends to redistribute income to specific groups. . . .
—M. J. Trebilcock et al., ''Markets for Regulation'' in *Government Regulation: Issues and Alternatives* (Toronto: Ontario Economic Council, 1978).

I. INTRODUCTION AND OUTLINE

We are determined to get the [Canadian] federal government out of ordinary business and commercial operations and hand them over to private business where they belong.
—Sinclair Stevens, *Toronto Star* (September 30, 1978)

Canada is distinctly different from other countries for reasons of history, geography and economics and it has been necessary at times to provide government services at uneconomic prices in the national interests.
—Sinclair Stevens, Chairman, Treasury Board, *News Release* (September 30, 1979)

Every exercise in positive economics should offer a solution to an interesting puzzle or, if a theoretical solution seems already well at hand, add more evidence to the explanation already offered. This is an essay largely in the style of explanatory economics. It concentrates more on presenting a plausible argument for why a ubiquitous institution—production by state owned and managed organizations—is observed than it does testing whether evidence conforms to the vision of conjectures presented. Put differently, the theory contained herein has not (yet) been refined to the point where an abundance of sharp implications emerges providing precise conditions to test the general hypothesis.

This may seem incomplete to those who assert that theory without operational implication is an empty set of assertions. My (polite) response to the latter group is to point out that a certain division of labour in scientific discourse is permitted whereby points of view may be offered prior to their formalizations in precise positivistic models. Thus, the title of my paper advertises what I believe I have, in fact, produced, a prologue to a useful theory of government enterprise. Given that my researches have uncovered no such theory to date, my approach stands favorably to its competitors.

(a) What is the Question?

I propose here to offer an explanation of why such a large fraction of the government budget (at least 50 percent) and national product (perhaps

25 percent) is supplied out of public bureaucracies of various sorts: government bureaus, Crown (or "independent") public corporations and so-called "mixed enterprises". Put differently, I want to explore why these functions are not undertaken by contracts let to private firms, by vouchers, or by the modern equivalent of the corvée, regulation. This question has long been part of the oral-puzzle traditions of the economists of the Chicago—UCLA—Virginia tradition and has, I can personally attest, appeared on exams or has been assigned as a term essay in universities associated with that tradition for, at least, two decades.[1] Nonetheless, I have never encountered this question in the formal literature save in an article where Pashigian opens his paper on public transit with this forthright statement:

> Public production of goods and services is somewhat of an embarrassment to most economists. It exists, and will in all likelihood increase in importance, but it is difficult to explain. An acceptable theory of public production has not yet appeared.[2]

Unfortunately, the study that follows does not satisfactorily resolve the puzzle. What Pashigian actually shows are the economic and political circumstances under which the state might intervene in the market which provides urban transit. He neglects to ask why the ends of urban transit policy could not as well be satisfied by any one (or combination) of the following two alternatives:

(A) *Public contracts.* Riders could receive subsidized coupons (vouchers) from a municipal agency charged with their distribution, but the ownership of the system would remain in private hands. Alternatively, this agency could pay these private owners a per-unit subsidy (not necessarily at the same rate on all lines or for all times of day). Finally, the municipality might offer private transit system owners complex pecuniary incentives for a stipulated set of services (contracting-out).

(B) *Regulations.* Using its constitutional "police powers", the municipality could create a regulatory agency. This agency could, in turn, promulgate various rules for allowable private pricing and specify the quantity and quality of services to be rendered as well as terms of entry or egress by the private firm(s).

Socialization by public enterprise or state bureaus (C) clearly is a substitute arrangement to (A) and (B). Still no one option is mutually ex-

---

[1] M. Olson and C. Clague, "Dissent in Economics: The Convergence of Extremes" (1971), 38 *Social Research* 751. Olson and Clague have an excellent discussion of the Virginia and Chicago School as well as the differences between them and the rest of the profession. Unfortunately, the article concentrates more on welfare economics rather than positivistic issues. The UCLA school which is methodologically akin to Chicago and Virginia is not mentioned at all.

[2] P. Pashigian, "Consequences and Causes of Public Ownership of Urban Transit Facilities" (1976), 84 *J. of Pol. Econ.* 239.

clusive. Combinations of (A), (B) and (C) can be, and in the real world are, employed.

The reader should note that in all the cases above the unique advantage that civilized states have, a monopoly over coercion, is employed, though as a matter of first-order approximation their incidence differs. In (A) and (C) monies to cover deficits between receipts and expenditures are made up by taxes, which may or may not be tied to specific assets that benefit from the scheme. (Some revenues may, in fact, also be generated by restricting the behaviour of competitors.) As for (B), at least in its purest forms, fiats simultaneously "tax" some activities while they "finance" others.

Pashigian, unfortunately, chooses to collapse the nonsocialization alternatives (A) and (B) into one instrumentality, an acceptable aggregation, *if* the relative prices of these alternative supply mechanisms remain constant over the jurisdictions analyzed. These other prices may well have remained constant or his choice of independent variables may have served as acceptable proxies for variations in these prices. Nonetheless, in his otherwise enlightening article, he does not address the issue why public enterprise has a comparative advantage over vouchers, contracting-out or government regulation.

This broader supply choice faces all levels of governments in every facet of their operations. Here is another very familiar example. Why for instance, are the so-called "Private Express" statutes not repealed in most countries permitting private individuals and firms to compete under regulatory constraints with the nationalized postal service? Or alternatively, while retaining the "Private Express" prohibitions why does the Canadian Post Office or the U.S. Postal Service not divest itself of its sorting and delivering functions and contract with private suppliers for these activities, as it does in transportation of mail between major population centers? One can ask similar questions about every activity carried out by government—prisons, libraries, schools, universities, courts, the military, fire, police, welfare, liquor control, etc. The interested reader can make up an indefinitely long list limited only by his or her patience and familiarity with state interventions.

(b) The Plan for the Study

It is my task to outline the choice among the three public supply alternatives—contracts, public bureaus and enterprises, and fiat rules—in a way that is consistent with our current understanding of economic theory. I shall do this rather leisurely, however, only explaining the phenomena in Section V. The impatient and/or well informed reader may simply skip to this section.

In Section II, I will endeavor to show the reader the degree that public production, *i.e.*, public supply by bureaus and independent state agencies, dominates public sector supply decisions and its size relative to the economy in general. No effort is made to quantify the regulatory alternative, unfortunately, since little systematic work yet exists. The reader may find useful the accompanying papers in this volume by Vining and Botterell[3] and Langford and Huffman[4] on provincial and federal Crown corporations, respectively.

In Section III, I take a highly selective, but I think not idiosyncratic, look at the discussion of the public supply decision in the development of classical and neo-classical economics, roughly from Smith's *Wealth of Nations*[5] to Friedman's *Capitalism and Freedom*.[6] I concentrate therein on but two activities: lower level education and so-called public utilities. I summarize the dominant theme of past writings on public sector supply alternatives which is twofold. First, the masters of the past were aware of the alternative supply instrument problem, but approached it from largely a normative or "what should be" point of view. Second, they were acutely aware that institutions mattered, since they predicted differential incentive effects under various regimes they proposed.

This leads directly to Section IV where this theme of incentives is considered in terms of the current literature with government bureaus and corporations, contracting-out and regulatory agencies, but where these institutions are taken as social givens. Writers here are divided, artificially in some cases, into two groups. In the first part, IV(a), the theory, predictions and findings of the "property rights" school associated with Armen Alchian (and others who focus on differential managerial incentives) are examined. In the next part, IV(b), the "public choice" analysis of bureaucracy, linked with the names of William Niskanen and the "Virginia School", is then reviewed. In the final part, IV(c) the problem of "waste" or "inefficiency" is considered, since the general finding of much of the research presented in the first two parts of this section is that the public firm or regulatory agency are inferior supply instruments when compared to contracts made with private suppliers, which includes, of course, vouchers and direct subsidies. I then point out that the term "waste" is a word that confuses and/or disguises what the real goals of the public sector are. When these are examined it it not surprising that relatively "costly" mechanisms receive public support, *i.e.*, the politicians' assent. The interested reader will find Chapter 6 by Palmer, Quinn and Resendes on an Ontario provincial Crown corporation, Gray Coach Lines, Ltd., a helpful complement to Section IV.[7]

In the final and, I believe, most original section of the paper, the question of alternative supply mechanisms is directly confronted. In Section V(a) the Coasian theory of the firm and market contract is delineated and in

---

[3] Vining and Botterell, in this volume, Chapter 5.
[4] Langford and Huffman, in this volume, Chapter 4.
[5] A. Smith, *The Wealth of Nations*, Cannan, ed. (1776; rpt. New York: Modern Library, 1937).
[6] M. Friedman, *Capitalism and Freedom* (Chicago: University of Chicago Press, 1962).
[7] Palmer, Quinn and Resendes, in this volume, Chapter 6.

V(b) its scope in the government supply decision for "productive" public goods is examined. The issue of who monitors contracts and how it is accomplished in a world where "shirking", "opportunism" and "chiseling" are endemic is pursued. In V(c) the possibilities for effecting forced transfers by each of the three means, what people generally mean by the opprobrious term "politics", are analyzed and, again, the comparative advantage of each of the three public supply instruments is apprised. Part V(d) studies the choice between the government bureau, the Crown corporation, and so-called mixed enterprises, an impure type of contracting-out. It also considers regulation as a complementary rather than substitute instrument to the two others. In the last part of the paper, V(e), I offer a few positive predictions and some empirical evidence that are helpful to my theory. I also suggest research that ought be pursued. Again, some detailed and confirming evidence based on the Gray Coach study is offered elsewhere in this volume by Palmer, Quinn and Resendes for those who wish to pursue my arguments in greater empirical depth.[8]

The reader is spared any welfare or policy judgments in my essay, but he will find the issue of institutional choice as a means of effecting efficient exchange developed by Trebilcock and Prichard in this volume.[9] These authors take up the theory of Section V and apply it with abundant illustrations, but from the point of view of scholar-as-helpful-social-engineer, informing the polity of superior options or institutional alterations.

One final comment needs to be made before I move on to the tasks outlined above. The discussions to follow, though subtle, are not couched in the vernacular of modern analytic (mathematical) economics, nor are the econometricians techniques or usual summary statistics employed. The nature of our understanding of the problem dictated the former to a large extent, but the desire to make the paper accessible to a wide range of non-economists was equally controlling for both decisions.

II. SOME BRIEF OBSERVATIONS ON THE MAGNITUDES

Let Pharaoh proceed to appoint overseers over the land, and take the fifth part of the produce of the land of Egypt during the seven plenteous years. And let them gather all the food of these good years that are coming and lay up grain under the authority of Pharaoh for food in the cities, and let them keep it. That food shall be a reserve for the land against the seven years of famine which are to befall the land of Egypt, so the land may not perish through the famine.

— *The Bible* (Revised Standard Version).

All governments, overtly or covertly, direct or at arm's length, are in business. . . . Often (but not always) these [state] objectives could be met by

---

[8] *Ibid.*
[9] Trebilcock and Prichard, in this volume, Chapter 1.

subjecting private enterprise to a mixture of taxation, subsidy, licensing and regulation (and opening the door to foreign investment). The reasons why the industries concerned do or do not pass into hands vary, more or less haphazardly, from case to case: (1) Accident . . . (2) Ideological [*reasons*] . . . (3) Revenue . . .(4) Private sector inadequacies . . . (5) Short-term vote catching . . . (6) Paymaster's control. . . .
— *The Economist*, "The State in the Market" (December 30, 1978).

Genesis 41:1-57 details how Joseph accurately forecast a 14-year agricultural cycle. The Bible is unclear whether Joseph acted for the Pharaoh in a private or public capacity for there was little difference in ancient authoritarian, but still proprietary states.[10] Nonetheless I would find it most interesting to see an account of private, non-Pharaonic accumulation during the "seven plenteous years" and their dispersals in the "seven years of dearth".[11] Since that time history has given us untold numbers of other examples, sometimes better documented, often not, of state firms supplying every conceivable kind of good and service. Table I, taken from *The Economist*, details for our own times the enterprise activities of several major relatively affluent societies, Canada and the United States among them.

Attempting to find patterns in Table I to explain why the state chooses to carry on economic activity under its own management is not very fruitful, though in the accompanying article *The Economist* showed much insight. Some theory is required to organize any general explanation and to subject such an explanation to the vicissitudes of empirical testing. Pure empiricism, measurement and hypothesizing without an organizing paradigm or theory, is extremely dangerous, if not a downright empty enterprise, since, often as not, the test of the theory is performed on the data from which the hypothesis is drawn. With this caveat in mind, let us pass on a few empirical tidbits anyway, largely confining ourselves to the U.S. and Canada.

One observes from colonial days in both countries strong interventionism, conventional wisdom about the U.S. notwithstanding. The post office in Britain from Elizabethan times[12], and the early colonial times in North America was supplied by state enterprise,[13] though the use of private

---

[10] J. H. Breasted, *A History of Egypt*, 2nd ed. (New York: Scribners, 1937); K. A. Wittfogel, *Oriental Despotism: A Comparative Study of Total Power* (New Haven: Yale University Press, 1957).

[11] Unfortunately, the Bible does not give us enough empirical evidence about the behaviour of private speculators to test whether the "inside information" that Joseph passed on to his king was efficiently filtered back into the market and, if so, why it was ignored—at least in the hinterlands east of the Sinai. Whether rational, but not God-informed, expectations were being formed seems important here, since if this was the case, private accumulation in those first seven good years should have fallen by the amount of Joseph's storage.

[12] R. H. Coase, "The Postal Monopoly in Great Britain: An Historical Survey" in *Economic Essays in Commemoration of the Dundee School of Economics, 1931-1955*, J. K. Easton, ed. (Pertshire: Coupas Angus, 1955); Coase, "The British Post Office and the Messenger Companies" (1961), 4 *J. of Law and Econ.* 12.

[13] G. Priest, "The History of the Postal Monopoly in the United States" (1975), 18 *J. of Law*

TABLE I
The Extent of Public Enterprise in Eighteen Countries

WHO OWNS HOW MUCH?

Privately owned: ○ all or nearly all

Publicly owned: ◔ 25%   ◑ 50%   ◕ 75%   ● all or nearly all

	Posts	Telecommunications	Electricity	Gas	Oil production	Coal	Railways	Airlines	Motor industry	Steel	Shipbuilding	
Australia	●	●	●	●	○	○	●	◕	○	○	na	Australia
Austria	●	●	●	●	●	○	●	●	●	●	na	Austria
Belgium	●	●	◑	◕	na	○	●	●	○	◕	○	Belgium
Brazil	●	●	●	●	●	●	●	◔	○	◕	○	Brazil
Britain	●	●	●	●	◕	●	●	◑	◑	●	●	Britain
Canada	●	◔	●	●	na	●	●	◑	○	◑	○	Canada
France	●	●	●	●	na	●	●	◑	◑	◑	○	France
West Germany	●	●	●	◑	◕	●	●	●	◕	○	◕	West Germany
Holland	●	●	◕	na	na	●	●	◑	○	◕	○	Holland
India	●	●	●	●	●	●	●	●	◕	●	●	India
Italy	●	●	◕	●	na	na	●	●	◕	●	●	Italy
Japan	●	●	○	○	na	○	◑	○	○	○	○	Japan
Mexico	●	●	●	●	●	●	●	◑	◕	◑	○	Mexico
South Korea	●	●	◕	○	na	◑	●	◑	◑	◕	○	South Korea
Spain	●	◑	●	◕	na	◑	●	◑	○	◕	○	Spain
Sweden	●	●	●	●	na	na	●	◑	○	◕	◕	Sweden
Switzerland	●	●	●	●	na	na	●	◑	○	○	na	Switzerland
United States	●	○	◔	○	○	○	◔*	○	○	○	○	United States

Source: *The Economist* (Dec. 30, 1978), p. 39.

na—not applicable or negligible production
* including Conrail

and Econ. 33; J. Haldi with J. F. Johnston, Jr., *Postal Monopoly: An Assessment of the Private Express Statutes* (Washington, D.C.: American Enterprise Institute, 1974); J. Kennedy, "Development of U.S. Postal Rates: 1845-1955" (1957), 33 *Land Economics* 93; Kennedy, "Structure and Policy in Postal Rates" (1957), 65 *J. of Pol. Econ.* 185.

contractors below the postmaster level was common.[14] Soon after the turn of the eighteenth century canals in both North American countries received state aid and often direction of the sort we associate with modern state development corporations or mixed-enterprises.[15] Publicly owned harbours actually preceded these, but the early railways were developed by capital subscribed by governments or by subsidized means where the state negotiated exchanges of land grants for extensions of road beyond the populous areas.[16] Schools were not uniformly free and public until the end of the nineteenth century, and then only after almost nine-tenths of the school-age population already was privately purchasing basic common school education.[17] Fire companies, usually contracting with insurance firms, were private,[18] but the police following Britain's Pealian example were publicly organized early on.[19] National defense, the collection of custom duties and excise taxes, even parts of the diplomatic service, were no longer following seventeenth and eighteenth centuries' practice of "putting-out" these services via government contracts.[20] In the post-U.S. civil war period some classes of military "hardware" were produced "in-house". Orphans were cared for, if that is not too generous a word for the Dickensonian attention lavished upon them, by a combination of state, private eleemosynary and for-profit firms. Roads were often private tollways, but publicly owned and maintained highways and post roads were becoming more common.[21] Libraries were operated both by private and eleemosynary institutions.[22]

As is well known, the government did not do all that much in the last century. It absorbed probably no more than 5 to 7 percent of income by tax-

---

[14] Priest, *supra*, note 13.

[15] C. Goodrich, ed. *The Government and the Economy, 1783-1861* (Indianapolis: Bobbs-Merrill, 1967); J. R. T. Hughes, *The Government Habit* (New York: Basic Books, 1977).

[16] Goodrich, *supra* note 15.

[17] M. B. Katz, *The Irony of Early School Reform* (Cambridge: Harvard Univ. Press, 1968); West, "The Political Economy of American Public School Legislation" (1967), 10 *J. of Law and Econ.* 101; E. G. West, *Education and the State*, 2nd ed. (London: Institute of Economic Affairs, 1970).

[18] M. Getz, *The Economics of the Urban Fire Department* (Baltimore: Johns Hopkins Press, 1979).

[19] Hughes, *supra* note 15.

[20] G. Tullock, *Politics of Bureaucracy* (Washington, D.C.: Public Affairs Press, 1965).

[21] Hughes, *supra* note 15; Innis, "Government Ownership in Canada" in *Problems of Stable Production in Canada*, H. A. Innis, ed. (Toronto: University of Toronto Press, 1933). No single source for Canada is definitive but the writings of the Innis School are instructive. See Tupper, "The State in Business" (1979), 22 *Can. Pub. Admin.* 124; H. V. Nelles, *The Politics of Development: Forests, Mines and Hydro Electric Power in Ontario, 1849-1941* (Toronto: Archon, 1974); Nelles, "Public Ownership of Electrical Utilities in Manitoba and Ontario, 1906-30" (1976), 57 *Can. Hist. Rev.* 461; T. Naylor, "The Rise and Fall of the Third Commercial Empire of the St. Lawrence" in *Capitalism and the National Question in Canada*, Temple, ed. (Toronto: Univ. of Toronto Press, 1972); V. Fowke, "The National Policy—Old and New" (1952), 17 *Can. J. Econ. Pol. Sci.* 271.

[22] M. Getz, *Public Libraries: An Economic View* (Baltimore: Johns Hopkins Press, 1979).

ation and borrowings, and direct public production, which then accounted for almost half of exhaustive spendings, a ratio only slightly less than that today.[23] This suggests that aggregate vertical integration in the traditional public sector changed very little over this century. "Off budget" public spendings, however, certainly did grow and independent public agencies and Crown corporations have definitely grown in both the numbers of firms and in total dollar assets.[24] Not only has growth been in absolute size, but it has increased relative to both the private economy and traditional government budgets.[25]

For the twentieth century, government's involvement in the economies of both Canada and the U.S. has been massive and its use of self-supply methods common. Added to the nineteenth century list of publicly supplied services are gas, electric and water utility companies, retail packaged liquor stores (almost 100 percent in Canada and one-third of the U.S. states), dams and reservoirs, city transit and even some railroads.[26] Furthermore, in Canada mixed corporations with government participating as an equity holder have, according to Mintz,[27] become a commonly used device to further government policy. In the U.S. such enterprises are less common, but the recent Lockheed, Penn Central and Chrysler "bailouts" suggest a possible upward trend. If President Carter's proposal to create an Energy Security Corporation had come to pass, it would have been in absolute size to mixed enterprises such as Canada's Syncrude what Safeway is to the corner convenience store.[28]

It also should be recalled that to a large extent timber and mineral resources in the West and a large area of land are owned by the state in both countries, but usually these are privately managed by contractual means.

---

[23] Borcherding, "One Hundred Years of Public Spending, 1870-1970" in *Budgets and Bureaucrats: The Sources of Government Growth*, T. E. Borcherding, ed. (Durham, North Carolina: Duke Univ. Press, 1977).

[24] F. L. Pryor, *Public Expenditures in Communist and Capitalist Nations* (Homewood, Illinois: Richard Irwin, 1968); Pryor, "Public Ownership: Some Quantitative Dimensions" in *Public Enterprise: Economic Analysis of Theory and Practice*, W. G. Shepherd, ed. (Lexington, Mass.: Lexington Books, 1976); R. A. Freeman, *The Growth of American Government: A Morphology of the Welfare State* (Stanford, California: Hoover Institution Press, 1975); and W. G. Shepherd, ed. *Public Enterprise: Economic Analysis of Theory and Practice ibid.*

[25] Pryor, *supra* note 24; Shepherd, *supra* note 24.

[26] Shepherd, *supra* note 24.

[27] J. M. Mintz, "Public-Private Mixed Enterprises: The Canadian Example" [Kingston: unpublished Discussion Paper #325, Institute for Economic Research, Queen's University, 1979].

[28] Hughes, *supra* note 15, notes the widespread partnership of states and private capital in the construction and operation of the canal companies. He suggests that three-fourths of the capital was governmentally supplied. The canals did badly, however, and this led to constitutional restrictions against this sort of partnership activity. See also Goodrich, *supra* note 15. This may explain why mixed enterprise at the state level in the U.S. is less prevalent than in Canada.

Canada has involved itself, however, in resource exploitation well beyond the role of mere owner of the natural resource stocks, *e.g.*, Petro-Canada and the National Energy Policy.

The Canadian Broadcasting Company and the much smaller Corporation for Public Broadcasting are publicly owned in both countries. Canada's public sector is (currently) more involved with "developmental" government corporations than is the U.S., while both countries have central banks whose independence from political control is the subject of continual scholarly attention and journalistic scrutiny.

Universities in Canada are almost all public while in the U.S. private institutions still make up the majority of "Top Ten" lists. That these latter universities really are mixed enterprises, receiving anywhere from one-third to one-half their funds from the public sector, ought to be interjected here, lest their private aspect be overemphasized. At the college level Canada has virtually nationalized all such institutions and it would appear the ratio of public to total college education (*i.e.*, nonresearch oriented, but higher level studies) in the U.S. is rising quickly. Canada has National Health Insurance, a sort of socialized Blue Cross, and though it is clearly not in the "fiscal cards" now, some scheme of this sort may well appear in the U.S. in the future, as it already has a base in Veterans' Administration programs and those for the poor and the aged in Medicaid and Medicare. Some hospitals in Canada are still nominally non-profit private, but moving toward public ownership. Most are state firms and few are for-profit. One sees, however, all three varieties of hospital firms in the U.S.: private for-profit, government and private-but nonprofit. Refuse collection, about which economists, ironically, know a great deal, lies in both sectors in the two countries. The courts, prisons and most police services are publicly operated as government firms in both countries, though the adversary role in Anglo-American justice allows wide scope for private suppliers. Fire services are generally socialized in both countries. Regulation of product safety by public fiat, rather than public provision of quality control in product production, is the rule for both countries, save for potable water systems.

But the list is too long to consider further, since the sectoral and qualitative aspects of public supply mechanism are well understood by the reader. Some detailed quantitative comparisons of Canadian and U.S. public enterprise (including public administration and supply of "traditional" government services) can be usefully offered, however.

Pryor, in a paper on international comparisons of public enterprise, has some crude indices of its economy-wide magnitude for the U.S. and Canada.[29] Excluding land, natural resources and housing, he found that in 1955 U.S. governments owned 15 percent of what he calls reproducible

---

[29] Pryor, *supra* note 24.

assets. For Canada the 1952 estimate was 23 percent. His figures exclude all mixed enterprise holdings, since the government here is either a bondholder or minority stockholder, so the 8 percent difference between Canada and the U.S. is probably not an understatement. (The casual impressions one gets suggests that this subtle form of corporate subsidy is much more common in Canada than in the U.S.)[30] In addition, given the relatively large ratio of land and natural resources to all assets in Canada compared to the U.S., it would seem likely that the differential is even still larger. In fact, given the recognized growth of both governments and a general agreement that the Canadian government has generally been more interventionist in the last two decades,[31] it would be safe to guess that the overall Canadian government reproducible asset ownership figures for 1980 would in percentage terms be somewhat higher than Pryor's estimates for the 1950s and still some 5 (or more) percentage points above that of the U.S., which Pryor elsewhere[32] claims to be 20 percent (again excluding mixed enterprise) for 1960. Vining and Boterell's[33] figures suggest, however, that the growth of provincially owned corporate-type assets has slowed up in the last decade and Langford and Huffman[34] show a similar, though not as pronounced, deceleration during this period at the federal level.[35] Thus, it seems reasonable to assert, all things considered, that governments now own and control at least one-quarter of the reproducible capital stock of the Canadian economy.

Assuming these crude estimates hold on closer inspection, what emerges is (a) the perception of a growing Canadian public sector influence on the overall structure of production, (b) rising at an exponential rate as to numbers of entities, but (c) at a much slower rate in asset value terms

---

30 L. D. Musolf, *Public Ownership and Accountability: The Canadian Experience* (Cambridge: Harv. Univ. Press, 1959); S. Ostry, "Government Intervention and Democratic Market Economics: A Comparison of Canada and the United States" [Washington, D.C.: unpublished paper presented to Brookings Institution Conference, May 18, 1978].

31 See Langford and Huffman, *supra* note 4; Shepherd, *supra* note 24; Vining and Botterell, *supra* note 3; Vining, A. R., "The History, Nature, Role and Future of Provincial Hydro Utilities" [Unpublished ms., University of British Columbia, 1979]; Ostry, *supra* note 30; S. P. Smith, *Equal Pay in the Public Sector: Fact or Fantasy* (Princeton, N.J.: Industrial Relations Section Series, Department of Economics, Princeton University, 1977).

32 F. L. Pryor, *Property and Industrial Organization in Communist and Capitalist Nations* (Bloomington, Illinois: Indiana Univ. Press, 1974).

33 Vining and Botterell, *supra* note 3.

34 Langford and Huffman, *supra* note 4.

35 Small, "Should Our Government Be in Business" (1979), *The Reader's Digest*, Canadian ed., January issue, claims that over 700 public corporations exist in Canada. A little perspective must be placed on this, however. Vining and Botterell *supra* note 3, demonstrate that while 70 percent of provincial Crown corporations were created since 1960, these accounted for only 20 percent of the currently held (1978) provincial assets. The five major provincial "hydros", all created before the early 1960s, account for over 60 percent of the total assets at the provincial level. At the federal level, Langford and Huffman, *supra* note 4, claim that almost 60 percent of Crown corporations have appeared since 1960 and these accounted for 30 percent of federal corporate assets. The result is, they say, that the size of federal and provincial controlling corporate holdings are roughly equal today.

relative to the private sector. Furthermore, if Table I is to be believed, this is a worldwide phenomenon in the developed world, both representative democracies and more authoritarian polities included.

This slowdown has, in fact, yielded a few experiments in "denationalizations" or "privatizations", but as the recent experience in Canada suggests[36] no real trend can yet be clearly seen.[37] For instance, if the role of public firm production grows as slowly as does public spending, state assets will decline relative to the private economy's.[38] However, if public firm growth emulates the rise of transfer payments and/or is influenced by the same factors affecting regulatory activity, it will continue to expand as a share of the overall economy.[39]

Finally and most unfortunately, as stated before, little is known of the absolute and relative magnitudes of the regulatory option in the U.S. over time, and nothing is written concerning Canada.[40] Weidenbaum argues it is a significant activity in the U.S. when compliance costs (more than 20 times the budgetary figures) are considered, perhaps 5 to 10 percent of GNP. Fur-

---

[36] Ohasi, T. M. et al., *Privatization: Theory and Practice-Distributing Shares in Private and Public Enterprises, BCRIC, PETROCAN, ESOPS, GSOPS.* (Vancouver: The Fraser Institute, 1980).

[37] The best known Canadian privatization scheme is the British Columbia Resource Investment Corp. ("Brick") whose stock was distributed—some free, most by market sale—to B.C. residents in 1979. Severe restrictions on share accumulation, however, mean that the usual capital market discipline on traded firms is diminished. As a result, the largest single shareholder, the B.C. government, was the dominant voice. (Recently the government donated the stock to a cancer research institute, but it did not change the accumulation constraints.) A similar proposed plan for the federal Crown corporation PetroCan failed when the Clark government was defeated in February, 1980. The Liberal government now in power does not favour "bricking" PetroCan, nor any other form of its denationalization. (The socialist NDP definitely opposed such a move and the Tories no longer do either.) See also Trebilcock and Prichard, Chapter 1, at pp. 83-97.

Currently in Manitoba (Progressive-Conservative government) four natural resource-based Crown corporations are being considered as candidates for privatization, while Quebec (Parti Quebecois government) is expropriating the Asbestos Corporation from General Dynamics.

Lest one think ideology is important in such matters, the reader should peruse both the Vining-Botterell, *supra* note 3, and the Langford-Huffman, *supra* note 4, studies which show no such factor existed in past provincial or federal decisions. Tory or Liberal, Socred or NDP, all exhibit the same propensities, more or less, to create public corporations. However, see Chandler, Chapter 3 in this volume.

[38] Recent studies of U.S. and Canadian spending, *e.g.,* R. M. Bird with M. W. Bucovetsky and D. K. Foot, *The Growth of Public Employment in Canada* (Montreal: Butterworth Institute for Research of Public Policy, 1979) indicate the trend of expansions of public budgets relative to the national economies is about over, though the relative growth of transfers may continue. Freeman, *supra* note 24, suggests, however, that expansion of "off-budget" items for the U.S. may, in fact, be rising. Since much public enterprise is "off-budget", this evidence bears further examination for Canada too.

[39] Borcherding, *supra* note 23, shows that for the U.S. the ratio of transfers to total government budgets continues to rise in this century to 1970. Bird, *supra* note 38, shows the same trend through the decade of the 1970s.

[40] M. L. Weidenbaum, *The Costs of Government Regulation* (St. Louis, Mo.: Center for the Study of American Business, Washington University, 1977).

ther, he indicates that this share has risen over the recent past and continues to do so.[41] For example, he shows that direct regulatory spendings by the U.S. federal government rose 600 percent from 1970 through 1976 and full-time positions have almost trebled. Given that regulation is a potential substitute for public production and/or contracting-out, the prediction of its future trends would seem upward. The few U.S. cases of deregulation (various aspects of the Interstate Commerce Commission, the Federal Communication Commission and the Civilian Aviation Board) hardly overwhelm the growth in the newer "social regulations" (*e.g.*, of the Occupational Health and Safety Administration and the Environmental Protection Agency). The promise of the new Reagan administration to dismantle both the Department of Energy and the Department of Education may not, in fact, be significantly realized. As for Canada, the surge of interventionism implicit in the creation and expansion of Petro-Can as well as in the recent National Energy Policy (plus the strengthening of the Foreign Investment Review Board's mandate and the new nationalistic tie-ins proposed by the Canadian Radio and Television Commission) indicate no diminution in regulatory efforts in absolute or relative terms. Whether in the U.S. an anti-regulatory trend similar to that of Proposition 13 builds with the Reagan victory is unclear. Even if such was the case, its effects on Canada would be unclear.

It seems nonetheless safe to say a few things about the history of the three intervention instruments in this century in the U.S. and Canada. First, with regard to "traditional" public spendings, the relative amount of public production has not markedly increased. Second, market interventions via public corporate or mixed enterprise has definitely risen relative to national products, but less dramatically compared to budgeted public spendings. Third, but with less certainty, employment of the regulatory mode appears to be rising both relative to the respective economies as a whole and to the aggregate of government interventions using all modes.

Still, it seems premature to predict on the basis of these trends exactly what the 1980s and the 1990s will bring in terms of the change in the employment of each sort of public supply mechanism. More to the point, without a theory such guesses are merely crude projections of past and current tendencies. What is required to understand past and future growth is some theory of the determinants of public sector supply decisions, not only as to magnitudes but to types of arrangements as well.

In the next section the second half of this task will begin by observing how distinguished economists of the distant and more recent past have at-

---

[41] Lilley and Miller, "The New 'Social Regulation'" (1977), 47 *Public Interest* 49, corroborate all this. Their quantitative measures and citations of other gross indicators in M. Friedman and R. Friedman, *Free to Choose: A Personal Statement* (New York: Harcourt Brace Jovanovich, 1979) show a growing (and centralizing) regulatory component of state action *vis-à-vis* the private sector.

tempted to structure the public sector supply problem, *i.e.*, what type of supply instrument will (or should) the state employ.

III. TWO EXAMPLES FROM PAST ECONOMIC THOUGHT

> . . . [G]ood management . . . can never be universally established but in con-sequence of that free and universal competition which forces everybody to have recourse to it for the sake of self-defence.
> —Adam Smith, *The Wealth of Nations* (1776; Cannan Ed.: New York: Modern Library, 1937)

> The real question is: what level of complexity did the law have to reach before significant degrees of supervision and discretion appeared in its administra-tion, the level at which we begin to approach 'intervention' in the strong sense? When does Smith's sovereign change from being a 'stage manager' to become a 'leading actor'?
> —E. G. West, "Adam Smith's public economics: a re-evaluation" (1977), 10 *Canadian Journal of Economics* 1.

From Smith and Mill through Pigou and Simons to Milton Friedman economists have not been reluctant to commend their views to their col-leagues and fellow citizens concerning the "ideal" role of the state. This op-timal agenda was unfortunately often a-politically and a-institutionally con-ceived and important positive aspects of the public supply decision were somewhat overlooked.[42]

On two activities, however, past economists were generally more forth-coming concerning alternative supply instruments, common level (primary) education and public utilities. These are worth considering to get a (limited) flavor of past professional thinking and to contrast it with modern and, I think, somewhat less romantic doctrine.

(a) Who Should Educate the Children?

Smith, whom Viner[43] and Stigler[44] both note gives a wide mandate for state intervention, was a proponent of publicly financed education, but

---

[42] See, *e.g.*, R. Turvey, ed. *Public Enterprises: Selected Readings* (Middlesex, England: Penguin, 1968) at 7. Turvey recognizes this in the foreword to his book. He states, ". . . what interests us . . . about public enterprise is how it ought to behave . . . (W)e are not so much concerned with understanding its behaviour and making predictions as with criticizing and making recommendations." How one can make policy suggestions without understand-ing the consequences of the choices is a mystery left unanswered.

[43] J. Viner, "Adam Smith and Laissez Faire" in *Adam Smith 1776-1926*, J. Hollander, ed. (Chicago: Univ. of Chicago Press, 1928).

[44] G. J. Stigler, "The Economist and the State" (1965), 55 *Am. Econ. Rev.* 1; Stigler, "Smith's Travels on the Ship of State" (1971), 3 *Hist. of Pol. Econ.* 265.

generally only for the poor. He was also an eclectic on organizational form. He worried that left to private choice the poor would not be educated at all, though he does not tell us whether this is because of a capital market imperfection or because of parental ignorance.

Another reason for publicly financing the activity is that

[t]he state . . . derives no inconsiderable advantage from their [the poor's] instruction. The more they are instructed, the less liable they are to delusions of enthusiasm and superstition, which, among ignorant nations, frequently occasion the most dreadful disorders [Smith, 1776/1937].[45]

Smith goes on to say how educated people add to the tranquility and good order of society. This was all the more important in a world where the increasing "division of labour" in the manufacturing sector would have, according to Smith's prediction, unfortunate psychological effects on the working class.

Smith then makes a plea for *partial* public financing of the activity. He suggests, in fact, that some level of fees should be paid directly to each teacher to insure that instruction is competent. He is a bit vague here, but I interpret him as suggesting that an endowment or annual grant should be given by the state directly to parochial, parish and county schools to keep up their capital structures and to offer a basic instructural stipend. Masters would, however, receive a non-negligible portion of their remuneration from their students' fees. (He thought, by the way, that system could be run at a small public expense.)

This is, of course, a contracting-out scheme using a two-part tariff. The first and greater part would be paid by the state, and the other, smaller share by the pupil's family (if they were not poor). It is also clear that Smith believed the wealthier orders would not generally use such schools. This is obviously no social loss, he suggests, since society would receive no positive *marginal* spillover from a subsidy of the rich who educate their children well beyond the basic level, a clear case of what we would now call an inframarginal or non-Pareto relevant externality.

John Stuart Mill also found for "market failure" in the basic education of poor children. "*Laissez-faire* should be the general practice," he says, "unless" in typical Millian equivocation, intervention "is required by some greater good."[46] Therefore, since he felt that parental ignorance dominated choice-making on common level education, and the poor were not capable of assessing the commodity's more subtle dimensions, he comes out in favor of intervention.

What is interesting about Mill is that he urged a policy of compulsory

45 Smith, *supra* note 5, at 740.
46 J. S. Mill, *Principles of Political Economy*, Ashley ed. (1848; rpt. London: Longman, 1915; rpt. New York: Sentry Press, 1965) at 950.

education (a) up to some age, (b) only at private schools, and (c) generally at the parent's expense. A proficiency examination would be given in the final year and financially able parents of a failed pupil would be dunned for the rest of the tuition necessary to bring the child's performance up to the minimum standard. Mill thought the incentives created by his regulatory scheme were just about right for all involved.

He reckoned, however, that private lower education was dreadfully undersupplied and that some financial aid ought to be given the needy. To mitigate the burdens on the poor Mill would have had the state institute some sort of scholarships and grants for poor children. Public schools might have to have been erected in the hinterlands, but even here some fraction of the fees would be paid by the financially able, so these schools would take on some aspects of private as well as contract supply. He wanted *no* public schooling unless it was absolutely clear no private, perhaps subsidized, supplying firm would be forthcoming.

His dislike of state schools was twofold. First, he thought, as did Smith, that a public, bureaucraticized teaching staff and its administration would have a smaller incentive to teach well. (How private teaching was to be efficiently monitored by the "uncultivated" parents of ignorant children is left unclear, but presumably some parental "learning" was assumed.) Second, he was dead set against any academic organization receiving an exclusive, *i.e.*, monopoly, charter. The control of information implicit in monopoly state schooling was particularly disturbing to Mill's nineteenth century liberal sensibilities.

By the end of the last century, and at the beginning of the neoclassical era, Mill's suggestions were forgotten, at least by Alfred Marshall, England's then most eminent economist. In his *Principles of Economics* Marshall refers with great approval to the "excellence of the common schools of the Americans"[47] and from there goes on to plead for increased British state finance in a long passage where he implicitly argues that human capital markets are imperfect and combine with ignorance and spillovers to make state subsidy of the activity desirable. Unlike Mill, it is clear that Marshall was not much concerned about the dangers of illiberal or incompetent common schooling provided by state firms. In fact, he restrained his criticism of the latter to but one of its characteristics; to wit: he believed that the children of the working classes were taught too much spelling and, implicitly, not enough writing and reckoning.

> The time spent on learning to spell is wasted; if spelling and pronunciation are brought into harmony in the English language as in most others, about a year will be added to the effective school education without any additional cost.[48]

---

[47] A. Marshall, *Principles of Economies,* 8th ed. (London: Macmillan, 1920) at 175.
[48] *Ibid.*, at 208.

Marshall would have been elated with at least one aspect of modern American and Canadian common school curriculum, the de-emphasis on standard spelling. He might not approve, however, of how this time saving is employed.

Veblen aside, hardly anything radically different was written about education by a well known economist until Friedman's famous chapter "The Role of Government in Education" in *Capitalism and Freedom.*[49] In this book Friedman departs from both Smith and Mill and, of course, Marshall by advocating that state financed schooling be provided competitively by a variety of private, nonprofit and even, if not differentially subsidized, by governmental firms. Under his scheme parents would receive state vouchers to purchase education for their children. Friedman's supply mechanism is determined by that which survives and would be forthcoming on the parentally directed, but voucher subsidized, competitive market. He dismisses (Mill's) concern with the natural monopoly argument of educational supply as appropriate more to the rural life of the nineteenth century than to our own time where innovations in transportation have reduced the difficulty of exhausting scale economies. His recent book departs not at all from this analysis.[50]

(b) Public Utilities and the Control of Natural Monopoly

The question of natural monopoly and its treatment by the state—*laissez-faire*, public ownership or regulation—drew the close attention of both the classicists and neoclassicists. Everyone, no doubt, is aware of the "utilities" problem, but at the risk of boring the technically informed reader, let me quickly outline the argument that natural monopoly leads to insufficient output.

If a good is produced under conditions of decreasing average costs over the relevant range of demand, competition will give way to at least some economic ruin and much consolidation. In the final result production will tend to the hands of only one producer. At best, competition "for the market"[51] will exist, *i.e.*, firms will compete to serve the whole of a market, but price must still exceed marginal cost. Second best consideration aside, since price, the value placed on consuming another (small) unit of production, exceeds incremental cost (less than average cost as the latter is declining), it necessarily follows that another unit of production would create more real income than it would displace elsewhere.

---

[49] Friedman, *supra* note 6, at 85.

[50] Friedman and Friedman, *supra* note 41.

[51] Chadwick, "Results of Different Principles of Legislation and Administration in Europe; of Competition for the Field, as Compared with Competition within the Field of Service" (1859), *Royal Statistical Society Journal.*

In recognition of this difficulty of maintaining competitive conditions in the face of large scale economies, Smith states that

> [t]he third and final duty of the sovereign or commonwealth is that of erecting and maintaining those public institutions and those public works, which, though they may be in the highest degree advantageous to a great society, are, however, of such a nature, that the profit could never repay the expense of any individual or small number of individuals.[52]

Public works were candidates for state subsidies and public ownership according to his policy. Smith gives four examples of "desirable" publicly owned and operated enterprises: canals, the post office, bridges and highways. He does not suggest a regulatory solution in *The Wealth* for this problem, perhaps because he correlated such a fiat instrument more closely with abuses of privilege, corruption and monopoly—all aspects of what today we call "rent-seeking" politics.[53] Smith later goes on to say, however, that he believes that charges and tolls would defray all of their expense. If this is so, why they could not be operated privately is unclear.

One possibility is that he sensed the privileged position the natural monopolist would be in and feared that given the lack of effective substitutes and the natural limitation on entry (any entrant would fear touching off a possibly no-win price war) private supply would be relatively inefficient. He might also have believed that public firms might have been more likely to produce larger outputs, though I should not put words in Smith's mouth that are not his.

Actually there is no firm evidence that he thought the shortfall in supply by monopolized agents to be an important social issue. In fact, he refers only to the latter evil once in *The Wealth* (and I loosely quote him) as a "derangement of stock". As Kochin[54] and West[55] both document, it was

---

[52] Smith, *supra* note 5, at 681.

[53] Rather than monopoly profit being a pure redistributional phenomenon with only a marginal misallocation (see A. Harberger, *Taxation and Welfare* (Chicago: Univ. of Chicago Press, 1974) of the magnitude $1/2 \triangle \times \cdot \triangle P$ where $\triangle X$ is the reduction of output due to the monopoly price increase $\triangle P$. Tullock, in "The Welfare Costs of Tariffs, Monopolies and Theft" (1967), 5 *W. Econ. J.* 224, argues that the anticipated profit ($\triangle P \cdot X$ when supply is inelastic) will cause resources to be devoted to its appropriation.

Crain and Zardkoohi, in "X-Inefficiency and Nonpecuniary Reward in a Recent-Seeking Society: A Neglected Issue in the Property Rights Theory of the Firm" (1980), 70 *Am. Econ. Rev.* 784, argue that the potential for misallocation of resources due to this quest for monopoly profit—rent-or transfer-seeking—may be greater under a regulated private utility than if the same activity was collectivized. Their empirics are not that persuasive, but their hypothesis bears closer scrutiny. Crain and Zardkoohi do not explictly recognize it, but they have rediscovered Simons' argument against regulated utilities and in favour of government ownership. See H. C. Simons, *Economic Policy for a Free Society* (Chicago: Univ. of Chicago Press, 1948).

[54] L. Kochin, "Monopoly Profits and Social Losses" (1980), 2 *Research in Law and Econ.* 201.

[55] West, "The Burden of Monopoly: Classical versus Neoclassical" (1978), 44 *S. Econ. J.* 829.

rent- or transfer-seeking behaviour that Smith thought socially costly.
Smith clearly recognized that such monopoly rent-seeking behaviour was
extremely resource using, the worse so the more competitive the means of
acquiring the privileges. It involved, he realized, investment choices on the
part of firms and individuals that from their private standpoint was no different in motivation than those involving the choice of products, market
areas or production capital. It was unlike the latter set of choices, however,
since it produced no net social utility, but, to the contrary, imposed a net
social loss. Smith discovered such appropriative maneuvers[56] in quest for
Crown franchises and regulated monopoly status to be both common and
costly under mercantilism and feudalism.

He essentially asks one question about public utilities' policy: what is
the "least worst" solution—government ownership, private unregulated
ownership or private, but stated regulated operations? A clear answer never
emerges in Smith, save in his general animus toward the regulatory mode. A
central government, parish, county or district utility commission was, in his
view, nothing more than a device to steal wealth from consumers in the
guise of the public interest.

Smith is fairly clear, however, on the appropriate jurisdictional level
for the financing and production of publicly owned works. Anticipating
modern day Tiebovians[57] he states

> [w]ere the streets of London to be lighted and paved at the expense of the
> [Central government's] treasury, is there any probability that they would be so
> well lighted and paved as they are at present, or even at so small an expense?[58]

This Smithian ambivalence toward his preference for collective ownership of natural monopolies, his choice among a bad set of alternatives, was
also reflected in the writings of Mill (who invented the term "natural
monopoly" and espoused as well a regulatory "capture theory") and most
classical economists, excepting Marx who felt public ownership of almost
every asset was historically inevitable, at some later and undated stage of
economic development. (Romantics like Proudhon, Fourier and assorted
millenialists seem hardly worth mentioning.)

One optimistic and brilliant *dirigiste*, Edwin Chadwick,[59] however, requires especial consideration here, since his arguments are the forerunners

---

[56] Hirshleifer's term. See J. Hirshleifer, "Towards a More General Theory of Regulation:
Comment" (1976), 19 *J. of Law and Econ.* 241.
[57] Tiebout's classic paper (Tiebout, "A Pure Theory of Local Expenditures" (1956), 64 *J. of
Pol. Econ.* 416) stresses the competition that exists between communities for citizens as a
check on inefficient public spending. To the extent that competition is muted or various activities subsidized by higher levels of government, this check is diminished. See Benjamin
and Kochin, "A Proposition on Windfalls and Taxes When Some But Not All Resources
Are Mobile" forthcoming *Econ. Inquiry.*
[58] Smith, *supra* note 5, at 689.
[59] See Chadwick, *supra* note 51.

to Demsetz's famous paper "Why Regulate Utilities?"[60] I will, in fact, now discuss both men's thoughts together, since in the main they are parallel, though Demsetz clearly belongs in Section IV.

The distinction Chadwick and Demsetz make between "competition for the field" and "competition within the field" is crucial.[61] Demsetz uses the example of license plates as a Chadwickian illustration. He asks: If average costs fall such that efficiency dictates but one firm, why should that firm be in the public sector? The state need merely call for competitors to bid and take the lowest price. As long as there is neither collusion in bidding among potential rivals, nor monopolization over any crucial input used, the price arrived at in this bidding would be "competitive", *i.e.*, yield a normal return.[62] With respect to utilities Demsetz, following Chadwick (whom he carefully acknowledges), opines that more complex franchising arrangements *could* be drawn up where presumably bids even of the negative sort *could* be solicited so that the government *could* "push" output beyond the point where price equaled average cost.[63] Demsetz however, does not answer the question why such bidding arrangements are not the socially dominant mechanism in the natural monopoly areas.

As Crain and Ekelund remind us, however, the original Chadwickian principle of "contract management" was applied by its coiner to justify government control of almost every economic activity where there was a shred of evidence of "market failure", including, in particular, the Chamberlinian area of monopolistic competition.[64] Chadwick was, in fact, a socialist, but quite a unique one. He advocated the government as regulator of many things, but as direct owner/manager of almost nothing.[65]

Even the undertaking and funeral service business, though in all likelihood highly though imperfectly competitive, would not have escaped Chadwick's socialist "rationalizations". Chadwick claimed that information and search cost economies lost to bereaved consumers could and would be internalized efficiently by the state via regulated franchises. He is interesting,

---

[60] H. Demsetz, "Why Regulate Utilities?" (1968), 11 *J. of Law and Econ.* 55.

[61] See M. Crain and R. Ekelund, "Chadwick and Demsetz on Competition and Regulation" (1976), 19 *J. of Law and Econ.* 149.

[62] Telser quite correctly points out this is still likely to lead to a short-fall in output from the price equals marginal cost desideratum, since competition for the field cannot push output beyond the point where the average revenue equals unit costs. See Telser, "On the Regulation of Industry: A Note" (1969), 77 *J. of Pol. Econ.* 937. Of course, the reply centers around the complex contracting possibilities, *i.e.*, the efficacy of price discriminations. See Demsetz, "On the Regulation of Industry: A Reply" (1971), 79 *J. of Pol. Econ.* 356.

[63] Demsetz, *supra* note 60.

[64] Crain and Ekelund, *supra* note 61.

[65] For those familiar with Demsetz's writings, I do not have to indicate his divergence from Chadwick on such interventions. The uninitiated reader should be informed, however, that Demsetz holds to a very market-oriented view of ideal organizations given their real world infirmities. See Demsetz, "The Exchange and Enforcement of Property Rights" (1964), 7 *J. of Law and Econ.* 11; Demsetz, *supra* note 62.

and virtually unique, for his time, as he attempts an empirical comparison of funeral and interment costs in London and Paris. He found, in fact, that the latter city, had the cheaper services and used a contract management scheme.[66]

It is clear, again according to Crain and Ekelund,[67] that Chadwick really had continuous regulation of private management in mind, since output characteristics (their quantity and qualities) and the price of the "bundle", required both policing by the government as agent for consumers and continual adjustments to account for unforeseen circumstances. In point of fact, the preferred regulatory commission Chadwick describes, as the negotiator, policer and enforcer of contract management, is very much like the present day U.S. Interstate Commerce Commission or the Canadian Transport Commission. The rent-seeking potential of public contract management is not discussed by Chadwick (or Demsetz for that matter).

Throughout the somewhat later, neoclassical treatment of the natural monopoly problem is a recognition that a collective enterprise solution has limitations. Stigler points out in his 1964 presidential address to the American Economic Association that Jevons seriously argued that government enterprise was, however, an acceptable solution to the natural monopoly problem under the following four conditions:

> (1) The work must be of an invariable and routine-line nature, so as to be performed according to fixed rules. (2) It must be performed under the public eye, or for the service of individuals, who will immediately detect and expose any failure or laxity. (3) There must be little capital expenditure, so that each year's revenue and expense account shall represent, with approximate accuracy the real commercial success of the undertaking. (4) The operations must be of a kind that their union under one all-extensive Government monopoly will lead to great advantage and economy.[68]

Stigler goes on to note, rather caustically, that all of the above was based on casual empiricism and *ad hoc* theoretical introspection, both with respect to municipal water companies. Given the investigatory tools, at hand, however, I find Jevons' statement to be not unsound [except for the gratuitous (4)].

"Gas-and-water socialism" pushed by Joseph Chamberlin, the Tory mayor of Birmingham at the century's turn,[69] does not seem to have much interested Marshall. He opined, however, that "there is . . . strong *prima facie* cause for fearing that . . . collective ownership . . . would deaden the

---

[66] B. W. Richardson, *The Health of Nations: A Review of the Works of Edwin Chadwick* (London: Dawsons of Pall Mall, 1965) I, at 148-149.

[67] Crain and Ekelund, *supra* note 61.

[68] Stigler, *supra* note 44, at 8-9.

[69] R. Nelson, "Public Enterprise and Investment Criteria" in *Public Enterprise: Economic Analysis of Theory and Practice,* Shepherd, ed. (Lexington, Mass: Lexington Books, 1976) at 50.

energies of mankind, and arrest progress,[70] though here he was speaking of total socialism, not a bit of piecemeal nationalization. He also questions (for the post office, not utilities) why, if the public activity is a truly natural monopoly, legislative entry barriers to private production are required. He obviously was not impressed with "cream skimming" arguments, which, perhaps he felt were just special pleadings in defense of preferential transfers.[71] Still, he never really questions the comparative advantage of the state in these endeavours.

Pigou, on the other hand, states in his *Economics of Welfare* that "[b]etween public operation and private operation, on the other hand, there is always and necessarily a fundamental difference of substance"[72] though what this is he does not speculate upon, other than to state that

> [t]here seems no general *a priori* grounds for holding, without reference to the special nature of controlling organizations evolved under them, that either public or private management is likely to prove technically the more efficient.[73]

Pigou, however, may have been making this non-judgment on feasibility grounds for he notes in the earlier version of the *Economics of Welfare, Wealth and Welfare* that "at the outset it must be clear that attempts to conduct such a comparison [of private vs. public production costs] by reference to statistics are fore-doomed to failure",[74] since both regimes operate under such differing circumstances. Stigler wryly notes (again) that all economic research would be ruled out by Pigou's exacting *ceteris paribus* standards.[75]

Pigou was prescient in his recognition of the public enterprise "control problem", however. This differential inability to monitor production efficiently by government firms is liable to be a cost-raising factor. Having shown that he has no illusions about the consequences of a policy of public ownership, Pigou argues, however, that legislative regulation of natural monopoly is worse than unfettered monopoly which he puts in an intermediate position. No Chadwickian, Pigou recognized, well before "capture" theories of regulation were in currency, that special interests influence regulatory authorities (and here he means legislative bodies, not independent agencies) more than the scholarly community at the time would admit.

> Government interference with relative prices is in the nature of arbitration of conflicts of interests between minority producer groups and consumers (the

---

[70] Marshall, *supra* note 47.
[71] R. H. Coase, "The Problem of Social Cost" (1960), 3 *J. of Law and Econ.* 1.
[72] A. C. Pigou, *The Economics of Welfare,* 4th ed. (London: Macmillan, 1932) at 382.
[73] *Ibid.,* at 387.
[74] A. C. Pigou, *Wealth and Welfare* (London: Macmillan, 1912).
[75] Stigler, *supra* note 44.

whole commnity); and such interference inevitably involves decisions which have regard primarily for the interest of the minorities.[76]

He explains the political inarticulateness of consumers in almost a Downsian fashion, *i.e.*, they are politically mute because the cost of organizing such a large, diverse, hence non-cohesive, group, exceeds the joint gains to its members and their organizing agents.[77] On the other hand, producer interests are overrepresented because the high stakes per individual or firm and their relatively smaller numbers make for greater cohesiveness.

In referring to a J. R. Commons' study on municipal electric companies, Pigou points out that claims over the wealth generated by managers charged with monitoring public managed activities are highly attenuated. He expects that higher unit costs would result. The issue to him was whether this loss of production efficiency was made up by the tendency to extend output beyond the wealth-maximizing, private monopoly level. He never answers this as he senses, like Stigler, that this is an empirical issue, not one for armchair econometrics.[78]

Without once mentioning Chadwick, Pigou also brings up the possibility of franchising public utilities, but dismisses this scheme as too complex and cumbersome, because, he says, of the constant need to adjust to new circumstances. Efficient contract management between private firms and governments to share this risk seemed, to Pigou, beyond the power of the market to negotiate, monitor and enforce, a point Williamson makes in criticism of Demsetz and with which we will deal in the next section.[79]

Pigou, unlike Chadwick, had faith that the private natural monopolies would soon "in these modern times" be operated subject to ". . . the recently developed invention of 'Commissioners', that is to say, bodies of men appointed by government for the express purpose of industrial operations or control".[80] This social innovation, he claimed, freed the legislature of the task of directly controlling this monopoly and got around the control problem of public ownership. Why such commissions would be more immune to capture than legislatures that created them is left unsaid. In fairness to Pigou, however, it was a "hope" generally shared by the bulk of

---

[76] Pigou, *supra* note 72.

[77] A. Downs, *An Economic Theory of Democracy* (New York: Harper and Row, 1957).

[78] Since first discovering the views of Pigou (by actually reading them), I have examined Goldberg's paper which convinces me Pigou has been distorted both by his Pigovian followers and his critics. His sense of subtlety and understandings of the multiplicity of margins is nowhere stressed by either group. See Goldberg, "Toward an Expanded Theory of Contract" (1976), 10 *J. of Econ. Issues* 45 and Goldberg, "Pigou on Complex Contracts and Welfare Economics" [Unpublished ms., University of California, Davis, July 1979].

[79] O. Williamson, "Franchise Bidding for Natural Monopolies in General with Respect to CATV" (1976), 7 *Bell J. of Econ. and Mgmt. Sci.* 73.

[80] Pigou, *supra* note 72.

Progressive Era welfare economists, given my casual sampling of their texts and writings.[81]

Nearer our own time that maverick Chicago economist, and man of uncommon directness, Henry Simons boldly states:

> In general, however, the state should face the necessity of actually taking over, owning, and managing directly, both the railroads and the utilities, and all other industries in which it is impossible to maintain effective competitive conditions.[82]

He unequivocally argues, further, that even unfettered private ownership of these resources is to be preferred to their state regulation.[83] Simons also offers no evidence for this ordering, save that gleaned from his own experiences.

Milton Friedman, another well-known Chicago economist, views the problem much differently. Monopoly for "technical" reasons, he believes, is a limited reality—"the telephone system, water system and the like . . .".[84] He goes on to say, echoing Marshall, Simons and Pigou, that the solution is "a choice among three evils: private unregulated monopoly, private monopoly regulated by the state, and government operation".[85] Further, he subscribes to the Simons' belief that the likelihood of "capture" by powerful, but special, *i.e.*, narrow, but politically cohesive, interests under regulation is high. He feels, however, that "dynamic" factors work through entry to undermine unregulated technical monopoly in the long run. Thus, unregulated natural monopoly poses no great threat, especially given their small size relative to the economy. The time length of that monopoly advantage and the misallocation costs incurred during it are acceptable to Friedman, compared with damages associated with the traditional solutions of regulation or government ownership both of which reduce to zero competitive entry potential. As to his choice between public firms and regulated private ones, Friedman is silent, though given his view of the irreversibilities of state ownership, we can safely guess he would put the public firm on the bottom of his welfare-generating list.

(c) The Message from the Far and Near Past

In this section I have attempted to give the reader a highly selective sample of "orthodox" utterings by eminent and learned economists work-

---

[81] H. Gray, "The Passing of the Public Utility Concept" (1940), 16 *Land Economics* 8.

[82] H. Simons, *supra* note 53, at 51.

[83] *Ibid.*, at 140, 184.

[84] Friedman, *supra* note 6.

[85] *Ibid.*

ing in the mainstream traditions of theory from classical times up to a couple decades ago. Two activities were surveyed: education, which without doubt could be privately supplied under competitive, if imperfectly so, circumstances, and natural monopoly, which by definition (except for the more sanguine Chadwickians) presents difficulties for competition.

The reader should note two things. First, little rigorous empirical evidence for social preferences among alternative supply regimens was given by any of these authors as such research along technical empirical lines was evidently not considered fruitful until the early 1960s. Even then Stigler thought the flow wholly inadequate, since his AEA presidential address is, among other things, a plea for some serious research along these lines.[86] Second, the discussion was largely normative, based on a tacit understanding of politics and of the nature of regulation and public enterprise. Further, the policy analysis is naively drawn in terms of admonitions to the "public interest", an end, Smith reminds us for the private sector, no man intends.

But this Stiglerian reading of these doctrines is, perhaps, too harsh. In my opinion, and Stigler agrees elsewhere,[87] today we stand intellectually on the shoulders of those classical and neoclassical mainstream economists. These past writers were convinced of two things. First, institutions mattered. The choice between substitute supply instruments involved wholly different distributions of costs and benefits among the various actors, even though the same nominal goals of policy were being pursued. Second, these differences altered incentives. If a policy goal did not have a proper set of private rewards to motivate its necessary actors, it would not be realized, regardless of how commendable its end. Alternatively, if the policy goal was realizable under several regimens, the side costs associated with each would systematically differ. Such an understanding is far from trivial.

We are now more blessed with research on the topic of alternative public supply means than when Friedman delivered his Wabash College lectures from which *Capitalism and Freedom* emerged. A great deal of empirical investigation of the various public supply mechanisms has been undertaken since and the theory of economic organization and exchange, though still crude, has developed to include politics, regulation and government bureaucracy.[88] In the next section I shall summarize this literature, though I will confine the discussion to those models which take the political choice of a supply instrument as exogenously given, waiting until Section V to relax this constraint.

---

[86] Stigler, *supra* note 44.

[87] See Stigler, "Does Economics Have a Useful Past" (1969), 1 *Hist. of Pol. Econ.* 217.

[88] Friedman, in his latest book with his wife, Rose, *supra* note 41, while still cheerfully admonishing the citizenry to decollectivize, deregulate and reduce public spending, is fully aware of the collective choice literature. He views his writings as socially useful input from an informational point of view, not as empty preaching. On this *see infra* note 225.

IV. THE EFFECTS OF PROPERTY RIGHTS AND PUBLIC CHOICE GIVEN THE COLLECTIVE SUPPLY DECISION

Without exception, the empirical findings indicate that the same level of output could be produced at substantially lower costs if outputs were produced by the private rather than the public sector.
— J. T. Bennett and M. H. Johnson, "Tax Reduction without Sacrifice: Private-Sector Production of Public Services," *Public Finance Quarterly* (October, 1980).

In the previous section almost two centuries of thinking about the public supply arrangements were selectively and discursively sketched. As indicated, these pronouncements, though fascinating, suggestive and insightful, lack important foundations, a positive theory of behaviour for the public bureau, firm or regulatory body. For at least the last century, however, economists have employed a robust "neoclassical" methodology to explore wealth pursuits by firms and individuals operating in private property contexts (under both competitive and monopolistic conditions). Intellectual bridges between this successful market model and the behaviour of the polity are currently being built, however, as I hope to demonstrate below.

One economist, Armen A. Alchian, is particularly important here. Beginning in the mid-1950s he and his many students and followers began to explore the question of how publicly operated and private-but-regulated firms differed from private-unregulated ones. In the first part of this section I shall review this literature, liberally adding my own thoughts and those of others who parallel this "property rights" approach.

In the second part of this section the "public choice" school's researches on input usage in bureaucratic and regulatory contexts will be explored. Here the names of James M. Buchanan, Gordon Tullock and William A. Niskanen, among others, are closely featured. Of course, some contributions straddle both the property rights and public choice approaches, hence my placement of such contributions under one or the other heading is necessarily arbitrary.

Finally, in the last part of this section, I will address the question of "waste" and the difficulties its recognition presents to economists of a neoclassical persuasion. Except for this last part, the question of why one sort of public supply mechanism is used rather than another will be more-or-less avoided. This follows since, in general, both the property rights and public choice groups take the organizational form on the supply side of government as a given.[89] The question of where the locus of public supply lies, private or public sector, or how control is shared, will be addressed in detail

---

[89] Lest this be interpreted as a criticism, let me point out that most price theory ignores the organizational unit of private exchange, but much useful explanation and prediction still follows from such a-institutional analysis.

in the section of the paper, where the chosen arrangement is made endogenous.

(a) The Property Rights Approach: Monitoring and Ownership Claims

Alchian, his followers and intellectual allies all point out that *the crucial difference between private and public firms is the practical difficulties in transferring ownership rights among individuals to public sector units and the relative ease with which these rights are passed around for private entities.* Likewise, they describe the government regulation of private behaviour as the equivalent to a partial attenuation of the rights to exchange private property. Since the road from private property to public ownership passes directly by the regulation milepost, the concept of a spectrum of rights naturally emerges.[90]

Exchange of ownership rights, the claims to the yield of an asset or the right to change its use or form, permits an assignment of authority over how a resource will be employed and permits various sorts of specializations in managerial inputs as well as in risk bearing.[91] Publicly owned firms lack this advantage, since democratic pressures on public management from what Hirschman calls "exit" and "voice" set more generous limits on a clientele's "brand loyalty".[92] Given the difficulties in exercising control over public officials charged with monitoring public entities, Alchian suggests that government managers will not organize inputs in a way that maximizes the wealth of the putative owners, *i.e.*, the general citizenry. He maintains that production efficiency constraints are far more effective in private firms. He predicts, therefore, that public firms will be found to be less efficient, *i.e.*, produce output at higher costs, their managers will enjoy "quieter" lives, and they will enjoy greater levels of discretion than their private counterparts.

Regulation of a private firm by state fiat, on the other hand, say Alchian and other property rights theorists, is the equivalent of partially nationalizing it. As such the connection between managerial choice and pecuniary profit is still "taxed" in an implicit sense, while non-pecuniary returns are "subsidized". In one of the earlier studies of this hypothesis, Alchian and (the late Reuben) Kessel[93] predicted and found evidence that

---

[90] A. A. Alchian and R. A. Kessel, "Competition, Monopoly and the Pursuit of Money" in *Aspects of Labor Economics*, National Bureau of Economic Research, ed. (Princeton: Princeton Univ. Press, 1962).

[91] A. A. Alchian, *Some Economics of Property* (Santa Monica: Rand Corporation Study P-2316, 1961); Alchian, "Some Economics of Property Rights" (1965), 30 *Il Politico* 816.

[92] A. O. Hirschman, *Exit, Voice and Loyalty* (Cambridge: Harvard Univ. Press, 1970).

[93] Alchian and Kessel, *supra* note 90.

the realization of non-pecuniary incomes in regulated firms was more nounced than in the unregulated ones. Since a regulated firm's owner rights are less attenuated than its totally government-owned equivalent, they advanced their hypothesis for public enterprises and agencies, too, but did not offer empirical substantiation. Recently, beginning with David G. Davies' study, this omission has been corrected.[94]

Those recalling the famous contribution of Adolf A. Berle and Gardner C. Means[95] may dispute the efficacy of this "discipline of differential transferability", recognizing that modern corporations have huge numbers of often ill-informed stockholders. This latter is obviously true, nonetheless, it remains that private firm asset transferability is demonstrably cheaper than a public firm's takeover. Those who have looked closely at private firms[96] have discovered an abundance of instruments employed which bring management's personal goals which rival a firm's profit into congruence with owners' desires for wealth. Takeovers, mergers, profit sharing, stock options and appreciation rights are some of these devices, to say nothing of the desire to maintain a good managerial reputation.[97] These carrot-stick disciplining instruments act then, albeit with imperfections when compared to more "heavenly" public interest constraints,[98] as incentives in the private pursuit of wealth. In effect, they impose shadow "taxes" on various margins for ignoring the "subsidies" on others. Empirical work by Hinley,[99] De Alessi,[100] McEachern and by Stano and Shelton (each re-

---

Aguirre

[94] Davies, "The Efficiency of Public versus Private Firms, The Case of Australia's Two Airlines" (1971), 14 *J. of Law and Econ.* 149.

[95] A. A. Berle and G. C. Means, *The Modern Corporation and Private Property*, Rev. ed. (New York: Harcourt, Brace, 1968).

[96] See H. Manne, "Mergers and the Market for Corporate Control" (1965), 73 *J. of Pol. Econ.* 110; R. K. Winter, *Government and the Corporation* (Washington, D.C.: American Enterprise Institute, 1978); R.A. Posner, *Economic Analysis of Law*, 2nd ed. (Boston: Little, Brown, 1977).

[97] E. Fama, "Agency Problems and the Theory of the Firm" (1980), 88 *J. of Pol. Econ.* 288.

[98] J. Palmer, in "Interaction Effects and the Separation of Ownership from Control" (1974), 21 *Rivisista Internazionale di Scienze Economiche e Commerciale* and in "The Profit-Performance Effect of the Separation of Ownership from Control in Large U.S. Industrial Corporations" (1973), 4 *Bell J. of Econ. and Mgmt. Sci.* 293; and R. Smiley in "Tender Offers, Transactions Costs and the Theory of the Firm" (1976), 58 *Rev. of Econ. and Statistics* 22, show, however, that such control means are not without "frictional" costs. By "frictions" is meant those transactions costs which limit the ability of owners to discipline and motivate management perfectly. Some slack will always emerge (unusefully referred to as X-inefficiency by Liebenstein in "Allocative vs. X-Efficiency" (1966), 56 *Am. Econ. Rev.* 392) as L. De Alessi in "An Economic Analysis of Government Ownership and Regulation: Theory and Evidence from the Electrical Power Industry" (1974), 19 *Public Choice* 1, and H. E. Frech in "The Property Rights Theory of the Firm and Competitive Markets for Top Decision Makers" [Unpublished ms., Harvard University, April 1977] show.

[99] B. Hindley, "Separation of Ownership and Control in the Modern Corporation" (1970), 13 *J. of Law and Econ.* 185.

[100] De Alessi, "Private Property and Dispersion of Ownership in Large Corporations" (1973), 28 *J. of Fin.* 839.

spectively cited by De Alessi)[101] are impressively in favor of this hypothesis.[102]

Since the public manager has no transferable equity in the public firm, and those who might otherwise discipline him, elected officials, do not either, the decision to choose a non-wealth maximizing course of action is relatively cheaper for him than for his private sector colleagues. Further, and more importantly, since public ownership is very diffuse, the constraints on his behaviour are likely to be less binding. This means that indulgence in personal, idiosyncratic inclinations will be less costly in terms of expected loss of income, jeopardy of tenure and possible promotion denials than in an equivalent private firm. This does not mean, however, that life is "sweeter" for public managers. Competition among this group plus the price "paid" to gain admittance to these ranks will roughly insure only normal (risk adjusted) returns.[103]

Another crucially important aspect of Alchian's approach is the recognition that limitations on ownership specialization in public firms means that future consequences of current management policy, which otherwise translate into immediately capitalized values in efficient markets for private ownership claims, will not impose the same kinds and degrees of discipline as they do on private management.[104] In addition, managers of publicly owned utilities have less incentive to adopt wealth maximizing pricing schedules and, instead, impose managerially simpler and convenient "rules of thumb". Thus, as Peltzman has so energetically argued, when a cost for one group is altered, it is likely that public enterprise-set prices will change for all groups, absorbing and buffering the former and with longer

---

101 De Alessi, "The Economics of Property Rights: A Review of the Evidence" (1980), 2 *Research in Law and Economics* 1.

102 M. Jensen and W. Meckling, "Theory of the Firm: Managerial Behaviour, Agency Costs and Ownership Structure" (1976), 3 *J. of Fin. Econ.* 305, have rigorously stated the conditions required for efficient discipline of managerial agents of stockholders by capital markets and cite much relevant literature from the finance discipline. They, also, take a great deal of pain discussing the "frictions" which diminish capital market discipline over inefficient managers.

103 De Alessi, *supra* note 98; De Alessi, "Managerial Tenure under Private and Government Ownership in the Electric Power Industry" (1974), 82 *J. of Pol. Econ.* 645; Frech, *supra* note 98; A. Breton and R. S. Wintrobe "The Logic of Bureaucratic Conduct" [Unpublished ms., Dec. 1980]. The notion that competition equalizes the real as opposed to nominal money incomes of managers is exceedingly convenient for theoretical purposes, since income effects, at least to a first order of approximation, are ruled out. Looking at relative prices then is all that matters. Alchian's work implicitly assumes this, but Frech is one of the first to state explicitly that real wages must equilibrate between private and public sectors for similar factors, entry barriers aside. When wages do not equalize because of entry barriers, resources will be devoted to "qualifying" for the higher remuneration such that the present value of the wage differential overtime equals the cost of overcoming these obstacles by whatever means the marginal chooser has at his or her disposal. See Alchian and Kessel, *supra* note 90.

104 De Alessi, "Implications of Property Rights for Government Investment Choices" (1969), 59 *Am. Econ. Rev.* 13; Shepherd, *supra* note 69.

lag than wealth maximizing firms would allow.[105] De Alessi[106] concurs v
this finding in his impressive summary based on many empirical studies and
his own elsewhere.[107] He finds that individual costs and marginal revenues
are less closely correlated for public than private firms, because the error
cost to a manager of not bringing separate costs and marginal returns in line
is smaller as the firm moves from private, but relatively unregulated, property through the collective path of regulation to fully nationalized ownership.

Another aspect of interest to the Alchian group is the question of adjustment to risk under various ownership regimens. Given that a few gross
errors of commission are more easily recognized than many small errors of
omission when specialized monitors are less active, riskier investments and
particularly innovative activities will be relatively shunned by publicly
employed managers. Arndt in comparing Australia's private and Crown
banks puts it this way: ". . . the private banks operate for profit and public
ones must at least avoid losses".[108] Davies' lengthy study[109] establishes
Arndt's speculation. He offers extensive evidence that the portfolios of
Crown banks exhibit a preference for lower risk, lower yield activities than
do the private banks where incentives to bear risk are less attenuated. He
also discovered that the Crown banks experienced both lower average
returns on capital and a reduced variance in these returns as compared to
their private counterparts.[110] In another study, Tilton found that private,
but regulated, firms were more likely to adopt cost-reducing innovations
than public firms.[111]

The reader may by now be wondering why general taxpayers are so
docile in such situations, frought with cross-subsidized inefficiences and
relative indifference to their interests. The answer, according to the property rights scholars, lies in the "gain-splitting" nature of public monitoring
activities. For any taxpayer (or small group of citizens) the gains from
monitoring public management must necessarily be shared with the larger

---

[105] S. Peltzman, "Pricing in Public and Private Enterprises: Electrical Utilities in the United
States" (1971), 14 *J. of Law and Econ.* 109; Peltzman, "Towards a More General Theory
of Regulation" (1976), 19 *J. of Law and Econ.* 211.

[106] De Alessi, *supra* note 101.

[107] De Alessi, *supra* note 98 and note 103; De Alessi, "Some Effects of Ownership on the
Wholesale prices of Electric Power" (1975), 13 *Econ. Inquiry* 526.

[108] Quoted by Davies, "Property Rights and Economic Behaviour in Private and Government
Enterprises, The Case of Australia's Banking System" (1981), 3 *Research in Law and Econ.*
111.

[109] *Ibid.*

[110] Davies also shows that the public bankers pursue the Hicksian "quiet life" and pursue
policies leading to larger staffs and faster growth of "sales". This latter Parkinsonian
prediction is pursued in depth in the next part of this section.

[111] J. E. Tilton, "The Nature of Firm Ownership and the Adoption of Innovations in the Electric Power Industry" [Unpublished paper presented at Public Choice Society Meetings,
Washington, D.C., March 1973].

group, yet he (or they) bear all the costs. Thus there is a bias against cost-saving reforms.

Of course, some monitoring is predicted lest public managers squander the assets of the firm. Such potential losses are large enough to get round even the heavy gain-splitting costs. Clarkson found in his study of non-proprietary hospitals, in fact, that managers of these firms were faced with much stricter guidelines than their proprietary counterparts acting where internal and external competitive checks act as disciplinary agents.[112] Presumably, these "bureaucratic rules" and "red tape" are attempts to reduce the discretion of non-proprietary managers. Nonetheless, Clarkson found a greater variance in factor combinations in public and nonprofit hospital care than in those of the private for-profit hospitals.[113] Presumably, other things being equal, this suggests greater variance in efficiency, too.

Ahlbrant's writings on private contracting vs. public supply of fire services found that the private firm turned out the same effective fire fighting services for almost half the cost.[114] Although Hirsch[115] and Collins and Downes[116] failed to find significantly lower unit costs for private as opposed to municipal trash collection, Savas,[117] Stevens[118] and Stevens and Savas[119] claim about 20 to 40 percent savings of private over public arrangements in this activity. Their explanation for the Hirsch and Collins and Downes findings is worth mentioning, especially since many other studies, cited in a survey by Savas, have found much lower cost differentials.[120] Savas *et al.*

---

[112] K. Clarkson, "Some Implications of Property Rights in Hospital Management" (1972), 15 *J. of Law and Econ.* 363.

[113] *Ibid.*

[114] R. Ahlbrandt, "Efficiency in the Provision of Fire Services" (1973), 16 *Public Choice* 1; Ahlbrandt, "Implications of Contracting for a Public Service" (1974), 9 *Urban Affairs Q.* 337.

[115] H. Hirsch, "Cost Functions of Government Services: Refuse Collection" (1965), 47 *Rev. of Econ. and Statistics* 87.

[116] J. Collins and B. Downes, "The Effect of Size on the Provision of Public Services: The Case of Solid Waste Collection in Smaller Cities" (1977), 12 *Urban Affairs Q.* 333.

[117] E. S. Savas, *Evaluating the Organization and Efficiency of Solid Waste Collection* (Lexington, Mass.: D.C. Heath, 1977); Savas, "Municipal Monopolies vs. Competition in Delivering Urban Services" in *Improving the Quality of Urban Management,* 8 Urban Affairs Annual Review, Hawley and Rogers eds. (Beverly Hills, Ca.: Sage Publications, 1974); Savas, "Policy Analysis for Local Government: Public vs. Private Refuse Collection" (1977), 3 *Policy Analysis* 49.

[118] B. Stevens, "Sale, Market Structure, and the Cost of Refuse Collection" (1978), 60 *Rev. of Econ. and Statistics* 438.

[119] Stevens and Savas, "The Cost of Residential Refuse Collection and the Effect of Service Arrangements" in *1977 Municipal Year Book* (Washington, D.C.: International City Management, 1978).

[120] See Savas, "Comparative Costs of Public and Private Enterprise in Municipal Services" in *Public and Private Enterprise in a Mixed Economy,* W. J. Baumol, ed. (New York: St. Martin's Press, 1980). Interestingly enough Pommerehne and Frey have found a great cost differential for Switzerland, but they do not distinguish private from contract variants. See Pommerehne and Frey, "Public vs. Private Production Efficiency in Switzerland: A

claim that there really are three alternatives in waste collection: public firms, unfettered competition among private firms and public sector contracting-out private firms. They find that municipal collection costs are 30 percent greater than private collection, but 60 percent higher than the contracting-out option. Evidently scale economies in co-ordination are quite important. Kemper and Quigley's study confirms this.[121] Only one study of Montana cities found in favor of municipal over private arrangement[122] and this is severely criticized by Pommerehne and Frey[123] and Savas[124] for "obvious" data and specification biases. Davies' two studies on domestic air service in Australia found that the private regulated firm enjoyed a higher productivity for its inputs than did the Crown airline though by law their routes and travel time are equal and equipment identical.[125]

All of the above have been criticized by Baldwin for not holding crucial variables constant though like Pigou, he does not specify for which differences to control.[126] However, in what Frech called a "natural experiment" where output characteristics were held constant, cost data for for-profit and nonprofit insurance companies contracted to process Medicare and Medicaid forms for the U.S. Social Security Administration were compared.[127] Alchian's theory predicts that for-profit firms should have lower costs, since the greater transferability of wealth claims and increased flexibility permitted to an efficient, market disciplined management occasion less non-pecuniary wealth-taking on their part. That prediction is confirmed on processing cost data, and two other productivity indices reinforced this conclusion. Frech also found that not only was the speed of processing the data and returning the results to the SSA faster by the for-profit firms, but

Theoretical and Empirical Comparison" in *Comparing Urban Service Delivery Systems,* 12 Urban Affairs Annual Review, Ostrom and Bish, eds. (Beverly Hills, Ca.: Sage Publications, 1977). Kitchen's study of Canadian cities is similar, though public costs are not so much higher. See H. Kitchen, "A Statistical Estimation of an Operating Cost Function for Municipal Refuse Collection" (1976), 4 *Pub. Fin. Q.* 56. Young's research also deserves mentioning. See D. Young, *How Shall We Collect the Garbage?* (Washington, D.C.: Urban Institute, 1972).

[121] P. Kemper and J. M. Quigley, *The Economics of Refuse Collection* (Cambridge, Mass.: Ballinger, 1976).

[122] W. Pier, R. Vernon, and J. Wicks, "An Empirical Comparison of Government and Private Production Efficiency" (1974), 27 *National Tax Journal* 653.

[123] Pommerehne and Frey, *supra* note 120.

[124] Savas, *supra* note 120.

[125] Davies, *supra* note 94; Davies, "Property Rights and Economic Efficiency: The Australian Airlines Revisited" (1977), 20 *J. of Law and Econ.* 223.

[126] J. R. Baldwin, *The Regulatory Agency and the Public Corporation: The Canadian Air Transport Industry* (Cambridge, Mass.: Ballinger Publishing, 1975). Baldwin argues, I believe correctly, that unit costs are not higher when the purposes of activity are properly considered. This theme will be adumbrated in the last part of Section IV and will be advanced in detail in Section V.

[127] Frech, "The Property Rights Theory of the Firm: Empirical Results from a Natural Experiment" (1976), 84 *J. of Pol. Econ.* 143.

the rate of error was lower.[128] He also found in a later study that even with-out the nonprofit category the degree of attenuation of wealth matters a great deal.[129] The tighter the nexus between an economic action and the receipt of profit or loss, Frech argues, the more it will pay management to oversee the operation closely and, as important, the more assiduously will owners monitor their agents, the firm's management. Frech's health insurance cost data tend to confirm this Alchianesque, spectral view of incentives.[130]

Bennett and Johnson also offer some interesting comparisons.[131] They discovered that the U.S. General Accounting Office has gauged the comparative efficiency of the private and public sectors in three services: debt collection, ship repair, and weather forecasting. No simple index emerges from any one of these, but Bennett and Johnson reckon that costs are often double, triple, or more in the public as opposed to the private sector. In their opinion, this order of magnitude difference swamps any differential that would emerge because output characteristics are not precisely identical between the two.[132]

One apparent piece of negative evidence is Meyer's comparative cost analysis of public and privately owned U.S. electric companies.[133] He found that over several sorts of operating costs public firms had significantly

---

128 Vincent Ostrom and his former students take this "mark-up" cost as almost an article of social scientific law, though they also find that the level of inefficiency is inversely proportional to the nearness of the level of government to its clientele and the degree of competition among the government units. Ostrom's views and those of his prominent students, R. Bish, R. Warren, and E. Ostrom are summarized in his survey paper. See Ostrom, "The Design of Public Organizational Arrangements" in *Perspectives on Property*, G. Wunderlich and W. Gibson, eds. (Institution for Research on Land and Water Resources, Penn. State Univ., 1972).

129 Frech, "Health Insurance: Private, Mutual or Government" in *Research in Law and Economics Supplement 1, The Economics of Nonproprietary Organizations,* K. Clarkson and Martin, eds. (Greenwich, Conn.: Jai Press, 1980).

130 Actually, some years before Frech's study, Nichols found stock-controlled California "Savings and Loans" to have 60 percent lower costs in processing new loans than the mutually-owned variety. See A. Nichols, "Stock versus Mutual Savings and Loan Associations: Some Evidence of Differences in Behaviour" (1967), 57 *Am. Econ. R.* 337.

131 J. T. Bennett and M. H. Johnson, *Federal Government Growth, 1959-78: Theory and Empirical Evidence* (College Station, Texas: Centre for Education and Research in Free Enterprise, 1980); Bennett and Johnson, "Tax Reduction Without Sacrifice: Private Sector Production of Public Services" (1980), 8 *Public Fin. Q.* 363.

132 U.S. taxpayers evidently believe what I have elsewhere referred to as this "Law of Two", see Borcherding, *supra* note 23. Opinion experts E. C. Ladd and S. M. Lipset and S. Raab cite survey findings to the effect that almost four-fifths of voters think that public budgets can be dramatically cut without affecting service levels in the public sector. See Ladd et al., "Polls: Taxing and Spending" (1979), 43 *Public Opinion Q.* 126; Lipset and Raab, "The Message of Proposition 13" (1978), 66(3) *Commentary* 42. This theme has recently been pressed by Bennett and Johnson, *supra* note 131. This is supply side public economics with a vengeance.

133 R. Meyer, "Publicly Owned versus Privately Owned Utilities: A Policy Choice" (1975), 57 *Rev. of Econ. and Statistics* 391.

lower costs. Mann and Mikesell, however, recognizing that control of input prices in multivariate analysis makes good theoretical and empirical sense, criticized Meyer for failure to take these into account. They chose to do their work on water systems, however, because of difficulties in obtaining input pricing data for Meyer's electricity study. They found that the Meyer hypothesis was inconclusive.[134] Morgan also attempted to analyze this difference using a multicharacteristic function and found a statistically significant higher unit cost for water from public systems.[135] He is modest in his claims and fails to offer an exact percentage difference, but I would gauge it to be some 15 percent. Crain and Zardkoohi, using simultaneous equations models of demand and cost (with data on input prices and indices of input use) incorporated in the familiar Cobb-Douglas production function, a highly specific attempt to use indirect cost functions, offered strong evidence that operating costs of publicly owned water companies exceed the private ones.[136] This was observed, they said, despite the well-known Averch-Johnson incentives which through rate-of-return constraints induce private regulated firms to over-capitalize their operations.[137]

One of the other few negative pieces of evidence for Alchian's hypothesis that public firms are more costly to operate than their private counterparts is an impressive study by Caves and Christensen.[138] They discovered no significant difference in operations costs between the Canadian National Railroad (CNR), a Crown corporation, and the Canadian Pacific Railroad (CPR), a private corporation. They wondered, perhaps, if this has to do with competitive pressures introduced in the mid-1960s when Canadian rail rate regulations were relaxed. Unfortunately, they take no direct account of regulations on line abandonment, except to argue that such constraints impinge more-or-less equally on both companies.

They argued that what made their examples differ from (almost) all the rest of the known studies comparing private and public firms was the per-

---

[134] P. Mann and J. Mikesell, "Ownership and Water Systems Operations" (1976), 12 *Water Resources Bulletin* 995.

[135] W. D. Morgan, "Investor Owned vs. Publicly Owned Water Agencies: An Evaluation of the Property Rights Theory of the Firm" (1977), 13 *Water Resources Bulletin* 775.

[136] Crain and Zardkoohi, "A Test of the Property-Rights Theory of the Firm: Water Utilities in the United States" (1978), 21 *J. of Law and Econ.* 395.

[137] H. Averch and L. Johnson, "Behaviour of the Firm under a Regulatory Constraint" (1962), 52 *Am. Econ. Rev.* 1052. Averch and Johnson hold that rate-of-return regulation acquisition of capital is more profitable than under unregulated circumstances. They argue that as long as the allowable rate exceeds the competitive market rate on capital, it pays a firm with higher than allowable profits to add to its capital stocks even if the resulting capital intensity is excessive in terms of unit costs. If \$1 implicit rental of competitive capital services permits the recapture of $\$1 + \epsilon$ (where $\epsilon > 0$) of profit nor otherwise realizable, it is in the firm's interest to invest, even if the capital is underutilized. Naturally, this raises production costs, but capturable profits increase by a larger magnitude.

[138] D. Caves and L. Christensen, "The Relative Efficiency of Public and Private Firms in a Competitive Environment: The Case of Canadian Railroads" (1980), 88 *J. of Pol. Econ.* 958.

vasiveness of competition in the product market. "Survival" of the CNR in the face of aggressive CPR marketing and rate deregulation since the mid-1960s forced the CNR management to look diligently for least-cost solutions. Before that period, competition from lightly regulated trucking acted as only a partial constraint, Caves and Christensen argued, and their data are consistent with this interpretation. In the late-1950s the CNR was only 80 percent as efficient as the CPR; for today Caves and Christensen can detect no (statistically) noticeable difference.

This Smithian notion that regulation causes a serious attenuation in the incentive to minimize social cost is also pursued in another paper by Christensen and Swanson.[139] Using a technique that Christensen (among others) developed to measure total productivity in the presence of both multiple inputs and outputs, Christensen and Swanson compared the large private, but regulated U.S. railroads with the CPR, the major private, but relatively unregulated Canadian railroad. They found that regulatory constraints add an immense burden on U.S. railroads, despite the fact that Canadian railroads operate with the same regulatory constraints on line abandonment and in a harsher physical climate. They concluded that regulation adds 15 to 20 percent to a firm's cost structure.

Spann provides the other serious piece of evidence which questions the strong form of Alchian's prediction that private firms necessarily operate more efficiently than public ones.[140] He discovered, like Christensen and Swanson, that regulation is a cost-raising factor, but he also found, for electric transmissions, when competitive alternatives for the public service exist, that costs are roughly comparable.[141]

---

139 L. R. Christensen and J. A. Swanson, "Economic Performance in Regulated and Unregulated Environments: A Comparison of U.S. and Canadian Railroads" [Unpublished ms., Univ. of Wisconsin, 1980].

140 S. Spann, "Public versus Private Provision of Governmental Services" in Borcherding, ed., *supra* note 23.

141 Spann's study, *ibid.*, of the electrical transmissions industry found that "'competition for the field'' is supplemented by "competition for the market" under certain circumstances in many communities. He argues that as competitive pressures on the product market increase efficiency in public firms approaches their private counterparts. Niskanen notes in a study of U.S. federal government productivity that the more competition facing an area, the closer was the productivity rate to its private counterpart. See W. Niskanen, "Bureaucrats and Politicians" (1975), 18 *J. of Law and Econ.* 617. Distressing as this sounds to economists trained to distrust "shock" theories of efficiency, the position can readily be explained within the neoclassical paradigm. This follows since the objective function being maximized in public agencies includes nonpecuniary sources of utility. "Taxes" on these items will induce their contraction, so that costs of the putative objective of the firm will appear to decline. As should be clear, there is an output composition effect confuting the efficiency estimations. For instance, Primeaux finds that the internal constraint placed on the public firm is important. Where utilities are subject to "break-even" rules, he finds costs are higher than where a minimum profit constraint is in place. See W. Primeaux, "An Assessment of X-Efficiency Gained through Competition" (1977), 59 *Rev. of Econ. and Statistics* 105.

Palmer and Smiley both find that the realization of profit in putatively unregulated but private firms is diminished as competition gives way to more non-competitive structures.

Given this demonstrated importance of regulation in attenuating profits and in limiting entry by competitive firms, it is well to mention the other general findings of private firm efficiencies under various regulatory regimes. (This will complete the comparison of the three broad institutional alternatives: private vs. public firms, public vs. private-but-regulated firms, and now, private vs. private-but-regulated firms.)

Because of De Alessi's survey of the U.S. electric utilities industry[142] and, in particular, Peltzman's imaginative research,[143] we know rather more about these matters than in times past. Their models and supporting data are fairly consistent with the previously mentioned findings that regulation *per se* is a cost-raising factor.[144] Unfortunately, Peltzman and De Alessi do not look directly at competition as a cost-limiting device, except by focusing

---

They argue that this reflects the high transactions costs of using the capital market as the managerial disciplining agent, relative to competition. See Palmer, *supra* note 98; Smiley, *supra* note 98. This is, of course, pure Adam Smith though Smith's dictum that monopoly is the parent of inefficiency is based more on his belief that in the long run no monopoly could exist without implicit state aid, *i.e.*, regulation. See Kochin, *supra* note 54. Smith argues, for tradeable goods, for instance, that oligopolistic structures would topple in the face of free-trade, a classic deregulation policy.

[142] De Alessi, *supra* note 98.

[143] Peltzman, *supra* note 105.

[144] Crain and Zardkoohi, *supra* note 53, argue, however, in the Henry Simons' tradition, that properly measured, it is possible that public firms with monopoly power are more efficient than a private regulated firm. They hypothesize the Averch-Johnson type incentives and various sorts of costly rent-seeking are absent in public firms. Thus, though the latter's unit costs may be higher than their private, regulated counterparts', they waste less on other margins protecting and enhancing their rights to earn monopoly returns. I do not find this argument persuasive, since the potential rents generated by the monopoly position in a public context may well be transferred to others besides consumers, *e.g.*, its employees via successful union demands or various sub-groups of consumers. De Alessi, *supra* note 98, and Peltzman, *supra* note 105, do find widespread evidence for the Averch-Johnson effect comparing regulated with unregulated firms, but they do not compare regulated private with public firms on this score. Both found, however, that municipally-owned electric firms did charge customers less than do private, regulated firms which usually are controlled by state level commissions. They discovered, in addition, that municipal firms price discriminated less between business and residential electricity uses, offered diminished variety of services, altered their prices less often, delayed innovations longer and exhibited a greater variation around a lower mean of returns than their private, unregulated equivalents. A study by R. Pryke, *Public Enterprise in Practice* (London: MacGibbon and Kee, 1971), of nationalized industry in the U.S. comes to the conclusion, however, that these government-owned firms are not demonstrably more inefficient than many private, but highly protected, firms, nor even than those private enterprises in the same industries with the socialized firms. G. Polanyi and P. Polanyi in "The Efficiency of Nationalized Industries" (1972), *Moorgate and Wall Street*, called Pryke's data into serious question and offer evidence to the contrary, as does I. Papps in *Government and Enterprise* (London: Institute for Economic Affairs, 1975). Unfortunately, the level of aggregation plus lack of econometric rigour make it impossible to pass on the merits of any of these findings without further investigation. Casual commentary by M. Deaglio in *Private Enterprise and Public Emulation: A Study of Italian Experience with IRI and the Lessons for Britain's IRC* (London: Institute for Economic Affairs, 1966) as to the alleged inefficiency of Italian public enterprise is similarly hard to assess as are the many discussions in W. J. Baumol's *Public and Private Enterprise in a Mixed Economy* (New York: St. Martin's Press, 1980), save that of Savas. See Savas, *supra* note 120.

on pricing decisions. To the extent competition can and does exist, the regulatory constraints ought not favor cost-raising strategies. If real prices are held down, by competition or other means, the firms cannot "afford" to substitute non-pecuniary sources of utility for productive efforts.

In the main, these last two mentioned studies find that private, regulated firms do appear to have slightly lower tariff structures (*i.e.*, lower prices) than unregulated (but presumably monopolistic) ones. However, in a recent study Jarrell disputes this interpretation.[145] He shows that in the era of "competitive" municipal franchising of electric utilities—after 1875 but before 1903—electric utilities were permitted to overlap geographically. Their services in this pre-regulation, competitive era were priced lower than after state commissions came into existence, which, by the way, is consistent with Spann's forementioned study.[146]

Jarrell, however, makes rather too much of this, since his data also show that merger and consolidation were the rule during this period and the pricing observed may have been of the temporarily competitive variety that precedes the movement toward natural monopoly. In fact, he demonstrates that from the 1880s when the Chicago area had over 15 franchised utilities —some with the same geographic markets and most with great border area overlaps—the members had diminished to two before the state government intervened with its commission. Jarrell's "unregulated" price structure would probably evolve into that of a single seller or at least not more than two. A Scotch verdict on competitive pricing in the private natural monopoly case seems the prudent judgment, at least for now.

In summary, this long and varied literature does appear to indicate that private and competitive suppliers provide cheaper contracted-for public services than do public firms not subject to competitive pressures. Further, it also appears that regulation can raise production costs of private firms, but probably not higher than their public, monopoly privileged equivalents. Finally, subject to sufficient competitive pressures and absent subsidies, public and private supplying firms need not differ markedly in their efficiencies. Thus, not only does the Alchian ownership transfer mechanism influence costs, but so also does the older, Smithian concern with market structure and entry regulation.

(b) Input Usage and Social Choice Theory

There is another approach to the comparison of public and private firms, again, both institutions taken as social givens. This literature considers the presence of bureaucracy more carefully than does that of

---

[145] G. Jarrell, "The Demand for State Regulation of the Electric Industry" (1978), 21 *J. of Law and Econ.* 269.

[146] Spann, *supra* note 140.

Alchian's group though there are notable exceptions, namely De Alessi. (Regulation has not been much studied using the models that follow save for Eckert.)[147]

Essentially this literature tries to develop a more political approach to the Alchian-Kessel notion that public firms' managers strive for a higher ratio of wealth-diversions to wealth-creations than do their private sector colleagues. This is done by speculating what particular arguments actually enter utility functions of public bureaucrats, the appointed agents of elected officials, and what political constraints limit their actions. This public choice approach recognizes that government employees have preferences concerning the behaviour of their own agencies that, in turn, direct or influence elected officials in predictable ways. Because civil servants have various avenues of expressing these preferences politically, the level of output chosen and the input combinations employed in public firms are said to be affected.

Perhaps the best known of this group is William A. Niskanen whose classic, *Bureaucracy and Representative Government*, is considered the (modern) beginning of this approach.[148] His hypothesis can be simply put: bureaucrats, like everyone in society, are interested in more pay, power and prestige. These "3 Ps" are closely correlated with budgets of public enterprises, a statement he bases on empirical observation, not on any *a priori* reasoning.[149] If this is the case, bureaucrats will "push" their programs, en-

---

[147] R. Eckert, "On the Incentives of Regulators: The Case of Taxicabs" (1973), 14 *Public Choice* 83; Eckert, "What do Regulators Maximize?" [Unpublished ms., Hoover Institution Conference on Regulation, July 1969].

[148] W. A. Niskanen, *Bureaucracy and Representative Government* (Chicago: Aldine, 1971).

[149] O. E. Williamson in *Corporate Control and Business Behaviour* (Englewood Cliffs, N.J.: Prentice-Hall, 1970), and R. Staaf in "The Growth of the Education Bureaucracy: Do Teachers Make a Difference?" in Borcherding, ed., *supra* note 23, offer supporting evidence for concentrating on budgets. T. Mayer in "The Distribution of Ability and Earnings" (1960), 42 *Rev. of Econ. and Statistics* 189, does as well, but his reasoning does not support Niskanen's argument. Mayer claims that higher salaries are paid to managers of large firms because they are more productive. Management, he claims, as do Alchian and H. Demsetz, "Production, Information Costs and Economic Organization" (1972), 62 *Am. Econ. Rev.* 777, J. McManus, "The Costs of Alternative Economic Organization" (1975), 8 *Can. J. Econ.* 334, and L. Cohen, "The Firm: A Revised Doctrine" (1979), 46 *S. Econ. J.* 580, involves the monitoring of productive inputs. The bigger the budget (or firm size), the more that can be gained or lost from poor monitoring. Given these stakes, owners of larger enterprises seek out superior managers. D. Roberts in "A General Theory of Executive Compensation Based on Statistically Tested Propositions" (1956), 34(3) *Harv. Bus. Rev.* 94, also observes the positive correlation of scale and salary. He explains the latter on the same grounds as does Mayer—responsibility requires competence and talent. Niskanen offers a "bootstraps" theory wherein public sector rules of thumb lead to more pay to bureaucratic managers of larger enterprises, holding managerial quality constant. Given mobility across governmental units and that some wage flexibility exists, this assumption is extremely questionable. See A. Breton and R. S. Wintrobe, "The Theory of Public Bureaus" [Unpublished ms., September, 1978], Breton and Wintrobe, "An Economic Analysis of Bureaucratic Efficiency" [Unpublished ms., 1979]; Breton and Wintrobe, *supra* note 103.

listing those Niskanen calls "high demand" representatives who control key positions in the legislature. The latter "capture" these positions because of the diffuse organizational nature of the low demanders. This reflects Stigler's view that high per capita stakes when coupled with small numbers yield differentially higher marginal returns in the political process because of the high transactions costs of forming countervailing coalitions.[15u]

Niskanen argues that since larger budgets are preferred by bureaucratic managers than smaller ones, bureaucrats will push their programs by offering the decision makers programs on a "take-it-or-leave-it" basis. The bureaucrat enlists the "high demand" group in the legislature to assist in the process, so it is possible, then, to offer a budget and program so large that the median demand group is only slightly better off than if there was none of the activity.

The absence of competition is, of course, absolutely crucial here, since bureaucrats can only coerce the median voters' representatives if bureaus are cartelized in such a way as to offer severely disadvantageous terms of trade, *i.e.*, without fear of retaliation or competition. Should alternative supply be privately forthcoming and/or non-collusive bargaining among various departments confront the legislature, these "all-or-none" prices will disappear. The legislature will then learn from competitors the true set of opportunities available at various budgetary costs.

Niskanen concludes that if the median group's demand, which approach all-or-none schedules at the limit of bureaucratic monopoly power, are (average value) elastic in the relevant range, the output of monopoly bureaus will be up to twice that forthcoming under competitive conditions.[151] Just as interesting as this prediction is the strong implication that this output will be produced at minimal budgetary cost or, at least, at the lowest cost considered relevant by the political reviewers. If, on the other hand, this intersection takes place on the inelastic portion of the all-or-none demand curve, more budget could be realized by reducing the output and "wasting" resources in ways that bureaucrats find congenial. To accomplish this, costs are artificially raised until the point of unitary price elasticity is reached.

Empirical tests of this model have not been directly put forward, since test conditions are extreme. Studies by Borcherding and Deacon,[152] Pom-

---

[150] Stigler, "The Theory of Regulation" (1971), 2 *Bell J. of Econ. and Mgmt. Sci.* 3; Stigler, "Free Riders and Collective Action: An Appendix to Theories" (1974), 5 *Bell J. of Econ. and Mgmt. Sci.* 359.

[151] If the marginal evaluation of the median voting group and the marginal cost schedule of bureaucratic supply are linear, the all-or-none and the average cost schedule have half the absolute slope of their marginals, respectively. It follows that the competitive rate is always half of the monopoly bureaucracy's given Niskanen's assumption about how monopoly rents are extracted, *i.e.*, through budget maximization.

[152] T. Borcherding and R. Deacon, "The Demand for the Services of Non-Federal Government" (1972), 62 *Am. Econ. Rev.* 891.

merehne and Frey,[153] Bergstrom and Goodman,[154] Deacon[155] and a number
of others surveyed by Deacon,[156] have established, however, that the observed demand price elasticities of public services are less than one in ab-   *clark*
solute value. Ott's study, finding a unitary price elasticity for 81 U.S. cities,
is the sole exception.[157] Thus, the evidence is not congenial to Niskanen's
prediction that they *must* be equal to or greater than unity.

Deacon's study of the Lakewood Plan in California—an institution
where smaller governments purchase services such as, but not limited to,
refuse collection, fire protection and policing from larger nearby communities under conditions that appear to be competitive—did find budgets
systematically higher by 20 percent in non-Lakewood communities.[158]
(Wagner and Weber using indices of competition among local jurisdictions
find similar results.)[159] Whether this is because demand curves are "pushed
out" or because, as Alchian believes, unit costs in public firms rise when
competition is lessened, cannot, at this time, be distinguished.

Using some evidence from Frech,[160] Davies[161] and the other forementioned studies in (a) The Property Rights Approach: Monitoring and
Ownership Claims, about differentially higher costs of nonmarket production, it is easy to show, however, a residual that might be consistent with
budget-push.[162] Residual explanations are not persuasive, however, since all
other factors have not been eliminated.

Niskanen has been criticized rather severely for what many consider to
be a caricature of budgetary politics. Because of this, milder versions of
Niskanen's model have been offered which, while claiming less about
bureaucracy, predict as much or more and, more importantly, are opera-
tionally testable.[163]

---

[153] W. Pommerehne and B. Frey, "Two Approaches to Estimating Public Expenditures" (1976), 4 *Public Fin. Q.* 395.

[154] T. Bergstrom and R. Goodman, "Private Demands for Public Goods" (1973), 63 *Am. Econ. Rev.* 280.

[155] Deacon, "A Demand Model for the Local Public Sector" (1978), 60 *Rev. of Econ. and Statistics* 184.

[156] Deacon, "Private Choice and Collective Outcomes: Evidence from Public Sector Demand Analysis" (1977), 30 *Nat. Tax. J.* 371.

[157] M. Ott, "Bureaucracy, Monopoly, and the Demand for Municipal Services" (1980), 18 *J. of Urban Econ.* 362.

[158] Deacon, "The Expenditure Effects of Alternate Public Supply Institutions" (1979), 34 *Public Choice* 381.

[159] R. Wagner and W. Weber, "Competition, Monopoly, and the Organization of Govern-ment in Metropolitan Areas" (1975), 18 *J. of Law and Econ.* 661.

[160] Frech, *supra* note 127.

[161] Davies, *supra* notes 94 and 125.

[162] Given that the observed demand price elasticity is around -0.5, the observation that unit costs are roughly 10 to 30 percent higher in slightly competitive (*e.g.*, local governmental) bureaucratic contexts suggests *total* expenditures ought to be only 5 to 15 percent greater. The residual 5 to 15 percent *could* reflect a budget-push element, which would support the Niskanen hypothesis.

[163] A later paper by Niskanen, *supra* note 141, indicates he realizes his original model has rather extreme noncompetitive assumptions.

One of the first of these more modest versions was De Alessi's.[164] Following the Parkinson hypothesis, he claims that public managers, among other things, want budgetary growth. A larger staff, more subordinates and more capital will (over some range at least) foster their own productivity, since budget may be viewed as complementary inputs to managerial efforts. Public managers will, therefore, employ relatively lower discount rates in evaluating their organization's projects than will those in privately operated firms. The latter must take the cost of acquiring capital and of committing themselves to future spending streams more seriously, because of the monitoring elements I have mentioned above. The results of this bias are larger public budgets and higher capital-labour ratios. The latter implication can be tested and De Alessi found some casual evidence consistent with this hypothesis.

Borcherding, Bush and Spann took a slightly more "populist" position on this issue.[165] They argued that public employees through their organizations over time "capture" civil service commissions, altering their rules in such ways that the effective supply of competing labor to public firms is more wage inelastic than a free market buyer would face. This public employee market power is enhanced, they claim, by the fact that public service employees contribute to the election of their ultimate "bosses", definitely not an option for a private sector union. In some sense then, public employees can alter the position of the derived demand schedule for their services by (a) "nudging" the final demand schedule for public services to the right and (b) specifying rules which lower both the elasticity of substitution between themselves and rival co-operant factors and the elasticity of supply of these other inputs. Both (a) and (b) will raise wages. They may raise employment, too, since, in effect, the budget and tie-in effects offset the usual substitution effects one might derive out of neoclassical models of labour demand in the presence of a labour monopoly.

Borcherding, Bush and Spann successfully tested this conception on non-federal U.S. government spending data using as crucial independent variables the presence or absence of civil service or the number of years that an activity had been controlled by civil service.[166] The position of public unions in the United States opposing constitutional spending limitations (*e.g.*, California's Proposition 13) is also evidence that public employees feel their (producer) interests are positively correlated with budgets.

Borcherding, *et al.* also suggests that given this labour oriented collective demand, capital-labour ratios ought to be lower than in private con-

---

[164] De Alessi, *supra* note 104.
[165] T. Borcherding, W. Bush and R. Spann, "The Effects on Public Spending of the Divisibility of Public Outputs in Consumption, Bureaucratic Powers, and the Size of the Tax-Sharing Group", in Borcherding, ed. *supra* note 23.
[166] *Ibid.*

texts.[167] Orzechowski tested this against De Alessi's obviously conflicting hypothesis by comparing state colleges and universities in the U.S. against their private institutional equivalents.[168] Orzechowski found that capital-labour ratios were, indeed, lower in the state systems. Of course, this could be true yet absolute capital intensities per unit of output might be higher in the public than in the private institutions. Unfortunately, output data or even good proxies for it were unavailable. Orzechowski did find elsewhere, however, on the basis of very aggregate data, that the public sector is significantly more capital-intensive than the private service sector and, in fact, it is more capital-intensive than for the economy as a whole.[169] If true, De Alessi's hypothesis[170] would have to be accepted and Orzechowski's first hypothesis discarded.[171] The data are not persuasive, however. First, as is well known among trade theorists, aggregates mask industry and firm factor combinations. Though Orzechowski's theory[172] applies to the latter alone, his data[173] are based on aggregations. Secondly, the data are exceedingly unreliable.[174]

But let us suppose Orzechowski's and De Alessi's respective, but different, empirical studies are both correct. Can they be reconciled? Perhaps. Government managers might well be pursuing De Alessi-type goals, while their employees pursue their own. Where the firm is "naturally" labour-intensive the political weight of the labour force works in the direction Orzechowski suggests. Below some level, however, this is cancelled out by the capital acquiring nature of bureaucratic managers. Needless to say, the theoretics of this *ad hoc*ery have not been fully worked out, nor, more importantly, has any "threshold" or "switch ratio" test been suggested.

De Alessi, in yet another paper, has argued that given the relative loose monitoring of bureaucratic managers by the political review authorities, a

---

167 *Ibid.*
168 W. Orzechowski, "Economic Models of Bureaucracy: Survey, Extension and Evidence" in Borcherding, ed., *supra* note 23.
169 Orzechowski, "Labour Intensity, Productivity, and the Growth of the Federal Sector" (1974), 19 *Public Choice* 124.
170 De Alessi, *supra* note 104.
171 Orzechowski, *supra* note 168.
172 *Ibid.*
173 *Ibid.*
174 In another context Orzechowski, *supra* note 169, claims that capital is used more intensively in the public sector, than under private auspices. L. Willmore and K. Acheson, in "Capital Utilization in Economic Development: An Interchange" (1974), 84 *Econ. J.* 159, point out that in certain cases the substitution of capital for labour is called for because labour's input is hard to monitor. This still does not solve the conflict between Orzechowski's studies and De Alessi's.
  For what it is worth, I offered weak evidence in my dissertation that non-federal U.S. government was slightly less capital-intensive than the private services sector. Again, the data were unreliable aggregates. Borcherding, "The Growth of Non-Federal Public Employment in the United States, 1900 to 1963" [Unpublished Ph.D. thesis, Duke University, 1965].

rational position for the latter given the gain-splitting results of assiduous monitoring, mangers will indulge their taste for security rather more than in private firms.[175] He finds evidence consistent with this risk-avoiding hypothesis. Public managers' tenures are more secure, of a longer duration and their fluctuations in real wages lower than private managers. Even limited competitiveness would suggest, however, that they "pay" for this in slightly lower salaries or in pre-employment queuing or qualification costs. Hendricks, in fact, found the more profit-regulated electric utilities firms to be no more generous with their wages paid their workers of a given quality than the unregulated ones.[176] Hendricks found, however, that tightly regulated firms tended to pay more than lightly regulated ones which is consistent with Alchian and Kessel.[177] The opportunity cost of a wage increase is lower in the former, since price can be raised nearer to the monopoly optimum as a result. A lightly regulated industry, on the one hand, is already so near that optimum that a wage increase is very costly to it. We should, as well, see the incidence of militant unionism more prevalent in the lightly regulated utilities than in the more profit-constrained ones. I have no evidence for this last implication, however.

This may have implications for public employee compensation, since public corporations or government bureaus can be thought of as firms operating under very severe profit constraints. I have discovered few sound empirical studies on this as yet, though both Orr[178] and Adie[179] have done rather interesting studies on wages in the U.S. public sector. They claim there is massive over-payment. Staats found evidence for the same,[180] though Borcherding in reviewing the evidence for the 1940s and 1950s in the U.S. did not.[181] All of these findings, drawn from fairly aggregative data, suffer from not holding crucial variables such as skill levels, education and age constant.

Luckily, Gunderson has carefully made such comparisons holding these variables constant for Canada.[182] He finds that the public sector in

[175] De Alessi, *supra* note 98.
[176] Hendricks, "Regulation and Labor Earnings" (1977), 8 *Bell J. of Econ. and Mgmt. Sci.* 483.
[177] Alchian and Kessel, *supra* note 90.
[178] D. Orr, "Public Employee Compensation Levels" in *Public Employee Unions: A Study of the Crisis In Public Sector Labor Relations*, Chickering, ed. (San Francisco: Institute for Contemporary Studies, 1976).
[179] D. K. Adie, *An Evaluation of Postal Service Wage Rates* (Washington: The American Enterprise Institute, 1977).
[180] Staats, "Weighing Comparability in Federal Pay" (1973), 34 *Tax Review* 1.
[181] Borcherding, *supra* note 174.
[182] M. Gunderson, "Decomposition of Public-Private Sector Earnings Differentials" in *Studies in Public Employment and Composition in Canada*, M. W. Bucovetsky, ed. (Montreal: Butterworth Institute for Research on Public Policy, 1979), Gunderson, "Earnings Differentials between the Public and Private Sectors" (1979), 12 *Can. J. of Econ.* 228, Gunderson, "Professionalization of the Canadian Public Sector" in *Studies in Public Employment in Canada, infra.*

Canada is currently paying labour no more than 10 percent more than does the private manufacturing sector for comparable jobs. Of that only 6 percent can be viewed as a rent. The remaining 4 percentage points is explicable by other characteristics which have alternative market values.[183]

The final study to cite is Pommerehne and Frey.[184] They found that bureaucracy does influence spending decisions, but what mattered more was the degree of representativeness of the government. Four types of government are represented among Swiss municipalities ranging from those where every citizen may participate, town meeting style, in formulating policy and these, in turn, are subject to referendum, to the least representative form where elected representatives make decisions that are not subject to referenda. Pommerehne and Frey discovered that spending rises, other things being equal, as the control "distance" increases between citizen and his government. The role of public managers and their employees in pushing budgets up by shifting demands appears, however, to be much less than the U.S. studies have so far suggested, even in the least democratic Swiss local government. The bureaucracy, Pommerehne and Frey argue, is but one of a number of competing special interests.

In conclusion, according to the public choice scholars, public firms have distinct biases favoring not only higher production costs, just as the Alchian literature suggests, but excessive outputs as well. The latter obtains because the bureaucracy can affect demand more readily under monopoly public ownership by the strength of its members votes. The absence of a civil service and the constraint on strong unions under more competitive types of supply, public or private, is thought to reduce the ability of members of such bureaucracies to offer their service on disadvantageous terms.

Only one study, with which I am familiar, has approached the regulatory decision within the Niskanen-type bureaucratic framework. Eckert claims that where regulatory authorities are organized as bureaus (complete with staffs and tiers of civil service employees) the pressure from the bureaucracy to expand their duties overcomes or offsets the regulated industry's desire to restrict the latter's output by limiting entry and other rivalrous practices.[185] When the agency is a small commission, no such countervailing incentives exist. Eckert finds evidence for his view looking at agencies which oversee taxicabs in large U.S. cities. Where agencies are charged with regulating an aspect of production among a broad range of industries, such as the U.S. Office of Occupational Health and Safety or

---

[183] Gunderson also found that the surplus wage to women in the Canadian public sector was 9 percent, adjusting for quality. This should lead to longer queues or to the imposition of higher qualification barriers for women than for men. He does not, however, address this interesting implication.

[184] Pommerehne and Frey, *supra* note 120.

[185] Eckert *supra*, note 147.

Canada's Product Safety Commission, Eckert's model is not as helpful (predictive), except that one would expect bureau interest would be relatively stronger, since the regulatees are more diffuse. Certainly casual impressions do not contradict this view. Recent work by Fiorina and Noll,[186] Owen and Braeutigam,[187] and Aranson[188] attempt to model the "Iron Triangle" between legislature, bureaucracy and interest group(s), but this richer context[189] is longer in descriptive reality and/or theoretical curiosities than it is in testable implications which conform to a wide range of situations. In any case, almost none of this latter political science oriented regulatory literature lends itself to summary statistics which address themselves to simple efficiency measurements.

(c) "Waste" as an Economic Puzzle

The theme of the first two parts of this section has been generally contrary to the view of efficient public supply, either through state owned firms or by regulatory means. This puts an economist in a rather awkward corner. Why would either supply device be used so often if they are both so inefficient? Economists use as their organizing principle the notion that waste will be minimized, given the transactions costs of engaging in exchange. This means that waste *per se* is a magnitude that rational economic actors will, mistakes and ignorance aside, attempt to reduce, at least as far as it pays to do so.[190]

This means that most of the forementioned analyses in the last two parts of this section need critical re-examination and amendment. "Red tape", rules against nepotism, encouragement of bureaucratic "professionalism", sealed bids and open negotiations, line item budgets, zero based budgets, sunset legislation, overlapping jurisdiction, legislative reductions of managerial discretion between current and capital budgets, must be reconsidered, too. Far from being (silly) impediments, generally absent in

---

[186] M. Fiorina and R. Noll, "Voters, Bureaucrats and Legislators: A Rational Choice Perspective on the Growth of Bureaucracy" (1978), 9 *J. of Pub. Econ.* 239.

[187] B. M. Owen and R. Braeutigam, *The Regulation Game: Strategic Use of the Administrative Process* (Cambridge, Mass.: Ballinger, 1978).

[188] P. H. Aranson, "The Uncertain Search for Regulatory Reform: A Critique of the American Bar Commission on Law and the Economy's Exposure Draft 'Federal Regulation: Roads to Reform' " [Unpublished ms., Univ. of Miami School of Law, March 1979].

[189] T. L. Lowi, *The End of Liberalism*, 2nd ed. (New York: W. W. Norton, 1979); J. Q. Wilson, *The Politics of Regulation* (New York: Basic Books, 1980).

[190] Two recent papers address this question in a straightforward way that is virtually unique. See C. Wolf, "A Theory of Nonmarket Failure: Framework for Implementation" (1979), 22 *J. of Law and Econ.* 107; C. Dahlman, "The Problem of Externality" (1979), 22 *J. of Law and Econ.* 141. Nothing said within either is new to economists familiar with the UCLA-Chicago-Virginia approach, yet what is lacking here in originality is made up by sharp reminders.

private organizations, they may well be defenses against even greater wastes. Perhaps civil service rules reducing favoritism and encouraging long tenures which elongate the views of bureaucratic managers have efficiency inducing aspects. The use of political appointees in top directorships of Crown corporations and independent agencies should, as James Q. Wilson long ago suggested, reduce monitoring costs.[191] They may well be receiving inefficient (resource dissipating) transfers, as tariffs are said to be,[192] but then again they may not. Even egregious corruption may have desirable side effects.[193] It would be useful to assume that transactions costs are such that some of these institutions represent least cost means of accomplishing productive as opposed to purely redistributive ends.[194]

Victor Goldberg[195] and Oliver Williamson[196] have great insight on this with respect to Demsetz's suggestion, mentioned in Section III, that private utilities be controlled by contract management, instead of by regulation or public ownership. Each focuses on a significant cost of operating under a Demsetz-style contract. Williamson stresses the likelihood of the incidence of "opportunism", on the part of the private supplier, together with the difficulties of post-contractual risk-sharing and day-to-day adjustments to non-anticipated shocks. All of these difficulties clearly raise the cost of Demsetz's preferred régime. Williamson attempts to document this in a case study of Oakland, California's operational difficulties associated with monitoring a contracting-out scheme for cable television to that area. Goldberg puts forth the argument, and offers evidence by citing a large number of legal cases, that pre-contractual problems are important as well. He argues that bureaucrats, who must at the very least act as a monitoring agent for the state under a contract management scheme, have little incentive to collect the right information. Since Goldberg claims that active mistakes are more easily monitored than inactions, bureaucratic behaviour will be excessively conservative and of a self-protective sort. Public agents, according to Goldberg, would manifest their concern by demanding excessive information and require "highly safe" contractual terms. In short, he argues that negotiating costs are generally high as a result of bureaucratic

---

[191] J. Wilson, "The Economy of Patronage" (1961), 69 *J. of Pol. Econ.* 369.

[192] T. L. Anderson and P. J. Hill, "The Social Cost of Transfers: A Reconsideration" [Unpublished ms., Public Choice Society Meeting, Washington, D.C., March 1980].

[193] E. Banfield, "Corruption as a Feature of Government Organization" (1975), 18 *J. of Law and Econ.* 587.

[194] P. Munch puts it well in "From Bismark to Woodstock: The 'Irrational' Pursuit of National Health Insurance, Comment" (1976), 19 *J. of Law and Econ.* at 368. ". . . if we adhere to the assumption that political markets function perfectly, this cannot explain a political decision in which the redistributive effects sum to a negative net outcome. . . ." Of course, as transaction costs rise this statement becomes less certain, a point Coase was the first to formally observe in "The Problem of Social Cost" (1960), 3 *J. of Law and Econ.* 1.

[195] Goldberg, "Regulation and Administered Contracts" (1976), 7 *Bell J. of Econ. and Mgmt. Sci.* 426; Goldberg, *supra* note 78.

[196] Williamson, *supra* note 79.

purchasing agents' excessive desire for security, while Williamson claims that policing costs will be high too.

In a recent critique of the public choice group's verdict on the inefficiency of bureaucracy, Breton and Wintrobe state their case counter to Niskanen *et al.* (including that made by myself and my colleagues in *Budgets and Bureaucrats*).[197]

> . . . although each bureau has, to a greater or lesser degree, a monopoly on the services it provides to citizens, bureaus are accountable to their political masters and there is certainly competition among political parties for office. Moreover, bureaus compete against each other for funds from the ruling government. Consequently, one would expect that inefficient bureaucrats would find themselves displaced by more efficient ones, either by transfers of personnel or by territorial encroachment. And a political party which tolerated inefficiency would find itself displaced from office. In short, if one is disposed to, one can in the competition among bureaucrats for funds or amenities, and in the competition among political parties for office, glimpse the operation of that same ghostly invisible hand which is said to insure efficiency in the private sector.[198]

Again, as in Caves and Christensen's model,[199] competition is said to act as an efficient substitute for the absence of ownership transferability present in private sector exchanges. The differences in efficiency, must be explained by differing "frictions", *i.e.*, the differential transactions costs associated with modes of behaviour under one institutional regime rather than another. Waste in a practical sense, then, cannot exist, unless there is persistent and remedial error in the choice of societal institutions. The latter possibility cannot readily be accepted, however, without seriously compromising the economists' commitment to the rational choice paradigm. If the latter is to be retained, the answer to the hypothesis that waste is present is to suggest the accuser look instead for other explanations.

For instance, what one (especially the uninformed outsider) might term waste might, in fact, be the best means of accomplishing an otherwise non-realizable end or it might be a transfer payment, accomplished at the least cost given the desire to discriminate among potential recipients. If it is neither, it should seem odd if it continues year after year.

This point of view should then give us some insights as to why governments behave as they do. Theory tells us that the deadweight effects of any institution employed will be minimized, subject to the transactions costs attendant to making the necessary marginal (and sometimes total) changes. It seems, therefore, implausible (to me, at least) that unit costs could be anywhere from 30 to 200 percent higher in the public sector for delivery of

---

197 Borcherding, *supra* note 23.
198 Breton and Wintrobe, *supra* note 149, at 6-7.
199 Caves and Christensen, *supra* note 138.

policies via public firms or regulatory agencies than they are under contracting-out systems. Baldwin in his excellent study of the Canadian Crown corporation Air Canada and its relationship to the Canadian Transport Commission declares as much,[200] as do Albert Breton,[201] Ronald Wintrobe,[202] John McManus,[203] Keith Acheson,[204] Acheson and John Chant,[205] Chant and Acheson[206] and Breton and Wintrobe[207] in various other contexts. All of these scholars, and I am tempted to lump them into something called the Canadian School, have shown in their studies of Canadian institutions that waste is an ill-considered term. As they clearly state the case, the very foundation of our theoretical methodology abhors the notion of systematic waste and remedial stupidity. Their position is that much of these excess costs are, in fact *transfers* taken in the form of higher wages, reduced intensity of effort, corruption, bribery, boondoggling and deliberate means of realizing some other redistribution.[208] But they also argue that some of these costs represent the price of delivering desirable, but unique outputs whose characteristics would be provided in different ratios using other supply instruments.

The error in the early property rights and public choice approaches (and orthodox welfare economics, in general) is in not recognizing that outputs have many and very subtle dimensions, whose intensity ratios are themselves a function of the institutions chosen. Later members of the Alchian group, *all* directed intellectually by Coase's two basic papers, "The Nature of the Firm"[209] and "The Problem of Social Cost",[210] have recognized this for choices among private sector arrangements.[211] Alchian himself

---

[200] Baldwin, *supra* note 126.

[201] A. Breton, "The Crown Corporation as an Alternative to Industrial Incentive Grants" in *The Challenge* (Winnipeg: Conference on Economic Development in Manitoba, 1971).

[202] R. Wintrobe, "The Economics of Bureaucracy" [Unpublished ms., Univ. of Western Ontario, Nov. 1977].

[203] McManus, *supra* note 149.

[204] K. Acheson, " 'Power Steering' and the Automotive Industry" [Unpublished ms., Carleton Univ., Jan. 1979].

[205] Acheson and Chant, "Bureaucratic Theory and the Choice of Central Bank Goals" (1973), 5 *J. of Money, Credit and Banking* 637.

[206] Chant and Acheson, "The Choice of Monetary Instruments and the Theory of Bureaucracy" (1972), 12 *Public Choice* 13.

[207] Breton and Wintrobe, *supra* note 103.

[208] My study on the B.C. Egg Marketing Board and McManus's on the Ontario Broiler Market reinforce this feeling. See, T. E. Borcherding, *The Egg Marketing Board: A Case Study of Monopoly and Its Costs* (Vancouver: The Fraser Institute, 1981); McManus, "On the Efficient Design of an Agricultural Marketing Board" in *Issues in Canadian Policy* (II), Wirick and Purvis, eds. (Kingston, Ont.: Institute for Econ. Research, Queen's Univ., 1979).

[209] Coase, "The Nature of the Firm" (1937), N.S. 4 *Economica* 386.

[210] Coase, *supra* note 194.

[211] Demsetz, "The Cost of Transacting" (1968), 82 *Q.J. of Econ.* 33; Cheung, "The Structure of a Contract and the Theory of a Non-Exclusive Resource" (1970), 13 *J. of Law and Econ.* 39; Williamson, "Hierarchial Control and Optimal Firm Size" (1967), 75 *J. of Pol. Econ.* 123; Williamson, "The Vertical Integration of Production: Market Failure Considerations"

hints at the application of this approach to the public/private firm choice,[212] as does Acheson.[213] Lindsay has applied the notion that characteristics of commodities supplied by public firms will differ from privately provided goods of the same class because of monitoring economies.[214] (Unfortunately, he leaves unsaid exactly why the goals of the government favor these different kinds of services.)

It is this interaction of goals (ends) and institutional choice (means) that will direct our attention in the next section. Here I shall pursue this newer line of argument at some length. What I offer, however, I do so only somewhat apologetically for its lack of technical rigor. I raise in my defense, Paul Baran's words from his famous Marxian *tour de force, The Political Economy of Growth*:

> . . . it is better to deal imperfectly with what is important than to attain virtuoso skill in the treatment of that which does not matter.[215]

V. THE NATURE OF THE PUBLIC SUPPLY DECISION

> . . . [W]e would like to make sure that the C.D.C. has a chairman who will understand and reflect, to a certain degree, the government priorities.
>   —Pierre Elliott Trudeau, remarks to Parliament on the Canadian Development Corporation. Canada. Parliament. House of Commons. *Debates,* 1st session of the 32nd Parliament, May 14, 1981 at 9574.

(1971), 61 *Am. Econ. Rev.: Papers and Proceedings* 112; O. E. Williamson, *Markets and Hierarchies: Analysis and Antitrust Implications* (New York: The Free Press, 1975), Williamson, "Transaction Cost Economics: The Governance of Contractual Relations" (1979), 22 *J. of Law and Econ.* 233; Alchian and Demsetz, *supra* note 149; Richardson, "The Organization of Industry" (1972) 82 *Econ. J.* 883; J. McManus, "The Organization of Production" [Unpublished Ph.D. thesis, Univ. of Toronto, 1971]; McManus, "The Costs of Alternative Economic Organization", *supra* note 149; Barzel, "An Alternative Approach to the Analysis of Taxation" (1976), 84 *J. of Pol. Econ.* 1177; Y. Barzel, "Measurement Cost and the Organization of Markets" (1979), 25 *J. of Law and Econ.* 27; B. Klein, R. Crawford and A. Alchian, "Vertical Integration, Appropriable Rents and the Competitive Contracting Process" (1978), 21 *J. of Law and Econ.* 297; Klein and Leffler, "The Role of Market Forces in Assuring Contractual Performance" (1981), 89 *J. of Pol. Econ.* 615; Cohen, *supra* note 149, J. McManus and K. Acheson, "The Cost of Transacting in Futures Markets" [Unpublished ms., Law and Econ. Workshop, Univ. of Toronto, Feb. 1979].

212 Alchian, *supra* note 91.

213 K. Acheson, "The Nature of a Bureau" [Unpublished ms., Carleton Univ., undated c. 1973].

214 C. M. Lindsay, *Veterans Administration Hospitals: An Economic Analysis of Government Enterprise* (Washington D.C.: American Enterprise Institute, 1975); Lindsay, "A Theory of Government Enterprise" (1976), 84 *J. of Pol. Econ.* 1061; Lindsay, "Is There a Theory of Public Organizations?" *Research in Law and Econ. Supplement 2, The Economics of Nonproprietary Organizations*, Clarkson and Martin, eds. (Greenwich, Conn.: Jai Press, 1980).

215 P. A. Baran, *The Political Economy of Growth* (New York: Monthly Review Press, 1957).

. . .[T]he schools belong to the public, not to the parents in favor of the [voucher] systems . . . [F]rom time to time you must go against parents' wishes.

> —Milo Gwosden, candidate for school board, Palo Alto [California] Unified School District. *The Peninsula Times Tribune* (October 5, 1979).

Instead of promising to give more multi-million dollar grants to the big auto companies to get new plants in Canada, Industry Minister Jack Horner should use the money to acquire one of them—Chrysler—outright and move its head office from Detroit to Windsor.

> —"Canada Should Buy Chrysler," editorial, *Toronto Star* (March 16, 1979).

Kirsch and Yale in their survey of Canadian Crown corporations (drawn heavily on Tupper)[216] list seven proximate reasons for the direct production of goods and services by government firms. Theirs is a typical analysis and leans heavily on alleged "market failures" of private supply. The list is offered here with Canadian examples:

(1) Attempts to realize cultural and political cohesion, *e.g.*, Canadian Broadcasting Company, Canadian National Film Board.
(2) Protection of "jobs", *e.g.*, Ocean Falls, Sydney Steel.
(3) Development by key "underdeveloped" sectors, *e.g.*, Industrial Development Bank, B.C. Resources Investment Co., SynCrude.
(4) Realization of scale economies and the control of natural monopoly, *e.g.*, Ontario Hydro. (This includes, as well, attempts to restrict the market power of "oligopolists", *e.g.*, the Insurance Corporation of British Columbia.)
(5) The stabilization or enhancement of particular prices or incomes, *e.g.*, Canadian Egg Marketing Agency, Canadian Wheat Board.
(6) Security in the supply of crucial activities, *e.g.*, PetroCan.
(7) Regulation and distribution of commodities with serious "social costs", *e.g.*, provincial liquor control boards, Lotto Canada.[217]

What is immediately obvious is that all of these activities could be carried out by the private sector and subjected to political control via subsidy/contracting-out procedures or by regulatory fiat. Such typologies though informationally useful and, in fact, the standard method of analysis are of little explanatory value, since they do not tell us why a particular supply arrangement was chosen.[218] They are useful, nonetheless, because of

---

[216] A. Tupper, "The Nation's Businesses: Canadian Concepts of Public Enterprise" [Unpublished Ph.D. thesis, Dept. of Pol. Stud., Queen's Univ., Nov. 1977].

[217] E. Kirsch and J. Yale, "Crown Corporations" [Unpublished paper, Univ. of Tor. Faculty of Law, Sept. 1979].

[218] See, Musolf, *supra* note 30; W. A. Robson, *Nationalized Industries and Public Ownership*

their authors' insistence that the goals of policy (the demand side of the public choice equations) are intimately linked with means of their execution (the supply side). If output characteristics were not idiosyncratically related to organizational form, such political attention would be frivolous.

The reader will recall, however, the general message of parts (a) and (b) of Section IV which "established" the proposition that the costs of government enterprise or regulatory mechanisms systematically exceed those of private firm provision of a public service desired by the policy makers. Yet as I said in part (c) of that section, economists are uncomfortable with such essentially Demsetzian/Chadwickian views. Our paradigm suggests, as I reminded the reader, that given the institutional constraints on public choice-making which bind market and government decisions, gains from trade must be exhausted. To put it differently, the inefficiencies remaining on any margin of choice must, save for ignorance, be smaller than the transactions costs of their removal.[219]

Now ignorance where public decisions are being made may be of a whole order of magnitude greater than for private decisions for reasons Downs,[220] Buchanan and Tullock,[221] Olson,[222] and others have discussed. Gaining information and disseminating it in order to effect superior decisions involves public goods' productions, hence, it will be subject to the familiar free-ridership strategy that guarantees its under-production. Political entrepreneurs and their firms, political parties, will, however, have great incentives to organize this activity. Nevertheless, their self-interest also leads them to dissemble, especially about future consequences, since their ownership claims on the government are incomplete, *i.e.*, their ability to capitalize future consequences is very limited.[223]

(London: Allen and Unwin, 1960); C. A. Ashley and R. G. H. Smails, *Canadian Crown Corporations* (Toronto: Macmillan of Canada, 1965); E. E. Barry, *Nationalization in British Politics* (Stanford: Stanford Univ. Press, 1965); D. Perry, "Government Enterprise" (1969), 17 *Can. Tax J.* 273; W. Willms, "Crown Agencies" in *Public Administration in Canada: Selected Readings*, 3rd ed., Willms and Kernaghan, eds. (Toronto: Methuen Press, 1977); Tupper, *supra* notes 21 and 216; D. Gracey, "Public Enterprise in Canada" in *Public Enterprise and the Public Interest*, A. Gélinas, ed. (Toronto: Institute of Public Administration, 1978).

[219] See Dahlman, *supra* note 190; C. J. Dahlman, "On the Nature and Function of Economic Institutions" [Unpublished ms., Sept. 1979]; Wolf, *supra* note 190.

[220] A. Downs, *Inside Bureaucracy* (Boston: Little, Brown, 1967).

[221] J. M. Buchanan and G. Tullock, *The Calculus of Consent* (Ann Arbor, Mich.: Univ. of Mich. Press, 1962).

[222] M. Olson, Jr., *The Logic of Collective Action* (Cambridge: Harvard Univ. Press, 1971).

[223] Parties can be thought of as having political lives longer than any of their members. Membership in parties is not, however, a divisible, privately transferable asset like a stock in a corporation. Thus, elements of common property are part of the claims associated with party membership. This means its "owners" will not exercise the kind of discipline over the elected from its ranks to the extent that stockholders constrain a firm's management. To the degree that "bossism" exists, parties do take on proprietary-like monitoring, but changes in membership requirements in the U.S. and Canada in recent years have all but extinguished those elements as "anti-democratic". Unfortunately, economists have not spent any time looking at the role of parties and the cost of joining them though some political scientists,

In this concluding section I am going to assume that ignorance in public choice-making is not affected by the supply arrangements chosen, except where I explicitly relax this assumption. Putting it differently, I will assume, following Becker,[224] that *rational expectations* characterize the market for political influence as much as they do the private sector market for bonds, money or labor. Thus, day-to-day issues get muddled, but people in political contexts act *as if* they understand the consequence of collective decisions among the three public service supply alternatives: subsidies and contracting-out methods, public firm production and regulation modes. Such an analytic defense against the presence of differential ignorance should not necessarily be taken as representing the way the world is at every moment in time, but as an attempt to make an already difficult problem more manageable for long-run analysis.[225]

Saying that long-run ignorance is absent, however, does not imply that "deadweights" are not part of the equilibrium.[226] The incidence of a tax on

Key, Wilson and Dahl in particular, are keenly aware of this appropriability issue. See V. O. Key, *Politics, Parties and Pressure Groups*, 4th ed. (New York: Thomas Y. Crowell, 1958); Wilson, *supra* note 191.

[224] Becker, "Toward a More General Theory of Regulation: Comment" (1976), 19 *J. of Law and Econ.* 245.

[225] The rational expectations methodology is just now becoming part of the theoretical tool kit of public choice economists and in no way has it yet swept the field. Essentially, the position of rational expectations scholars is that one cannot fool people forever. See B. McCallum, "The Political Business Cycle: An Empirical Test" (1978), 44 *S. Econ. J.* 504. Thus socially costly policies that persist do so not from ignorance, but because there is a political payoff that exceeds the cost of undoing it. Tariffs exist and persist for reasons well-known for 200 years. They are not mistaken policies.

On the other hand, the market also pays for the dispassionate (well, at least, scholarly) discussion of policy, implying that this additional information is valuable to participants. Analyses of policy, therefore, imply that otherwise unaided political equilibria are not efficient, and perforce, innovations in modelling and understanding of institutions are as valuable—on the margin—as intra-institutional innovations of technology or organization. Thus, when the theorist says that the aggregate of gains from exchange must be realized, he necessarily means this only in a static or provisional sense given existing information.

[226] In the short-run unanticipated events or consequences will lead individuals to wish they had acted differently. If the original decision "locks in" the chooser contractually—say by constitutional or dictatorial constraint—adjustments to the new equilibrium will be slower and perhaps even predictable. In this sense, politics can be thought to exhibit stable Phillips-curve like behaviour in the shorter-run. There is, however, some debate over this. See, *e.g.*, McCallum, *supra* note 225, who denies that political cycles are empirically relevant even in the short run and W. Nordhaus in "The Political Business Cycle" (1975), 42 *Rev. of Economic Studies* 169, who uses adaptive expectations testings, suggesting people do not learn, hence finds these cycles exist. I suspect that the "final" position that will emerge will be a weak version of rational expectations where people are "fooled" only because (a) they have locked themselves into "contracts" because greater flexibility is *ex ante* costly, and (b) they cannot reasonably be expected to have anticipated the action. Foreign policy adjustments may be of this latter variety, but highway expenditures strategies where incumbent parties attempt to win last minute votes by judicious spendings in certain key districts will have less effect because they are so predictable. Still, given the optimal nature of ignorance that characterizes politics, it would seem that "fooling" people ought to be easier for longer periods of time than in private markets, since the expected costs of learning will for free-rider reasons be very high, provided the deception involves non-repetitive policies.

corporate profits may be understood for what it is by everyone, but it will still place a wedge between price of products and incremental costs and (second best consideration aside) this will impose social costs. It does mean the institutions serve the purposes of those who have the power to create, maintain, change and destroy them. Thus the ends are realized, *ignorance aside*, at minimum excess burdens. It is in this spirit that I will proceed.

In part V(a) of this section, I shall outline the theory of the private firm as interpreted by Ronald Coase[227] and expanded upon by Alchian and Demsetz,[228] McManus,[229] and Williamson[230] and apply it in part V(b) to the notion of the public supply choice. There I will emphasize the difficulties of monitoring contracts, but with the strong assumption that the goods produced are, in fact, "public" in consumption and that redistribution is neither an intended nor foreseeable consequence of public decisions, except where it is a form of Pareto-optimal charity. This assumption allows me to hold constant with respect to distributional considerations the demand schedules for public services as supply instruments are changed.

In part V(c) the possibility of "politics" enters, by which I mean the social act of one group coercively appropriating to itself the wealth of another under the protection of the state's constitution. The transactions costs notion from part V(b) will be carried along on the supply side, but the assumption that demand functions are unaffected by the supply mechanism chosen is relaxed, *i.e.*, the supply instrument chosen is a function of the demand for redistribution. In part V(d) the choice of type of public firm is analyzed and the possibility of using other instruments as complements to the public firm is briefly discussed. Finally, in part V(e) some implications of my theory are offered and a few (more) suggestions made.

(a) Coasian Analysis of Contracts and Private Organizations

In 1937 Coase wrote the classic paper, "The Nature of the Firm", which attempted to explain why firms vertically integrate productive relationships to the extent they do rather than employ market contracts. He argued that the private firm is a social mechanism to reduce transactions costs. Its function is to replace market directives (prices) with authoritative commands (orders) or as he puts it, "[to] supercede the price mechanism".

This theme has been pursued by Lindsay and Zycher under the rubic of the "fog factor". See C. M. Lindsay and B. Zycher, "Porkbarrel Politics and the Fog Factor" [Unpublished ms., Univ. of Calif. Los Angeles, 1978].

227 Coase, *supra* note 209.
228 Alchian and Demsetz, *supra* note 149.
229 McManus, *supra* note 149.
230 Williamson, *supra* note 211, *Markets and Hierarchies* and "Transaction Cost Economics: The Governance of Contractual Relations".

Contracts are part of both methods of co-ordination, but are of wholly different sorts in each. In a pure market relationship an individual promises a set of very specific things for a consideration, a price. Under a firm, the individual gives wide command over his resources to another for a given price subject to a (possibly implicit) set of limitations. In practice firm and market co-ordinations blend into one another, but the polar cases are still worth examining.

The great saving from the use of firms, offers Coase, is not having continuously to employ the price system. Of course, he recognizes that the latter is an excellent mechanism for giving information about scarcities, but it is not without its costs. For one, as Coase intuited and Williamson directly notes,[231] prices are not "sufficient statistics", contrary to what Hayek[232] tells us. That is, market prices as exchange ratios do not convey *all* the information needed about the characteristic of the resources purchased or sold. In fact, Coase recognizes that scarce resources will be used to gain information to corroborate or supplement that given by market prices alone. This is referred to as the transactions costs of using the market as the means of co-ordinating behaviour.

Coase suggests, therefore, that the supercession of prices by hierarchial fiat is the way to economize on private co-ordination costs. It is an alternative, a substitute managerial input, if you will, to searching out better market price information. But not using the price mechanism, Coase reminds his readers, has its costs too. He is not at all clear exactly what these are, but I am confident he meant the cost of information distortion that necessarily accompanies private bureaucratic organizational structures, a point Herbert Simon makes in his classic study, *Administrative Behavior*[233] and Simon's student Oliver Williamson[234] at one time built up on to explain the level of a firm's vertical integration caused by defects in market information and "organizational slack".[235]

Recognizing these two distinct costs, Coase goes on and predicts that firms will vertically integrate until the marginal benefit from not using the price system equals the incremental costs suffered because of internal organizational diseconomies. Unfortunately, in this form the model is empty, *i.e.*, does not admit directly of testable implications, since the factors that in particular circumstances favor one form of organization over

---

231 Williamson, *supra* note 211, "Transaction Cost Economics: The Governance of Contractual Relations".

232 F. Hayek, "The Use of Knowledge in Society" (1945), 35 *Am. Econ. Rev.* 519.

233 H. A. Simon, *Administrative Behavior*, 2nd ed. (New York: Macmillan, 1961).

234 Williamson, *supra* note 211, "Hierarchial Control and Optimal Firm Size".

235 R. M. Cyert and J. G. March, *A Behavioral Theory of the Firm* (Englewood Cliffs, N.J.: Prentice-Hall, 1963). Cyert and March's discussion of "organizational slack" and Simon's concept of "satisficing", *supra* note 233, are attempts to recognize these kinds of distortions as part of "real world" organizational costs.

another are left unstated. It provides, however, an important point of view, since it directs attention to those factors that enhanced private decision-making inside and outside of firms.

For 35 more years the Coase paper gained minor fame and was assigned on the reading lists of most introductory graduate price theory courses in the English-speaking world. Teachers passed over the paper in their lectures, however, going to the a-institutional "theory of the firm" and the "theory of markets" they understood. Coase's speculations on the degree of vertical integration was not a "good" problem to bring up in lecture, since there were few if any theoretical implications for the instructor to comment upon.

In 1972, however, Alchian and Demsetz published a paper that gave more substance to Coase's notions.[236] They claim that the essence of production is "team effort", because output is produced in most important instances by non-separable production functions. Because of problems in measuring individual efforts, the tendency for "shirking" will be larger than is desirable for the joint wealth of the "team". The firm is the solution since the "team's" leader is the owner, who claims the residual rent or profit, hence has an incentive to monitor behaviour. Let me give their "lifting" example as illustration.

A very heavy trunk is to be carried up a long, steep grade by four strong men. Ascertaining what each will add to the product is a very difficult task. Detailed contracts could be drawn by the owner of the trunk or moving firm specifying individual obligations, but they would not self-enforce. Some of the team might still "go light". A monitor could be employed, but who will monitor the monitor? A solution, say Alchian and Demsetz, is a profit-seeking firm. The entrepreneur, the residual claimant, becomes the monitor. (If a finer division of labour is desired, a hired monitor is placed in a set of circumstances by the actual residual claimant where he acts *as if* he was owner.) The monitor's unique job inside the firm is to police shirking while combining input services in a wealth maximizing way.

McManus looks at it only slightly differently.[237] The problem with each sort of contractual schema, market or firm, he believes, is that people breach contracts in both capacities. Team production is not the problem; it is enforcement of contracts. He offers an interesting example, which I quote at length:

> . . . suppose the owner of a dump truck and the driver of a truck choose a price system to co-ordinate their action, and suppose that it is prohibitively expensive (i.e., measurement costs are higher than gains from trade) to measure

236 Alchian and Demsetz, *supra* note 149.
237 McManus, *supra* note 211, "The Organization of Production" and "The Costs of Alternative Economic Organization", *supra* note 149.

changes in the mechanical condition of the truck resulting from the care with which it is operated by the driver. If the driver's income directly depends on his rate of output, he has a pecuniary incentive to drive the truck in a manner that will inefficiently (by a perfect standard) depreciate its value.

The establishment of a centralized organization weakens the relationship between an individual's income and his actions. If the owner of the dump truck and the driver choose to co-ordinate their actions within a firm, one of them, say the owner, will direct the behavior of the other within limits that are mutually agreed upon. The driver's income will become less sensitive to his rate of output and he will therefore have less pecuniary incentive to depreciate the value of the truck in his use of it.[238]

What McManus is talking about is "chiseling", to put it quite bluntly. It is the well documented *tendency of economic men to ignore the damages inflicted in an exchange unless held accountable or bribed to act otherwise.* It is present in every two or more party contract, because contractual terms are not totally enforceable at zero cost, and for the usual economic reasons, it never pays to draw up "iron clad", all-contingency contracts.[239] Williamson has written on this extensively too and has called this the problem of "opportunism".[240] The choice of means for co-ordination, according to Alchian and Demsetz, McManus and Williamson, will depend on the relative damage done by the one sort of chiseling along the pecuniary dimensions in markets (short weights, intentional delays, quality cutting, etc.) as opposed to that suffered on the non-pecuniary dimensions in the firm (indifference to workmanship, laziness, insubordination, etc.).

As said before, McManus points out that team production is not the issue (though it no doubt adds to the enforcement problem) and Williamson amplifies this.[241] To see his point, the reader is urged (by Williamson) to recall Adam Smith's classic discussion of the pin factory.[242] Each step is quite separate, but time/space co-ordination is crucially important so that large (costly) buffer stocks of pins-in-process need not be kept near each worker's bench. All this could have been accomplished by "putting out" to specialists, but deliveries on strict schedule, the "sequencing" problem, to keep the flow of pins-in-process smooth and steady, will be difficult to assure. At the very least, under market co-ordination a tallyman is required to count things, a quality control specialist must be employed, and the services of a flow control specialist purchased. But these specialists have to be monitored, too. One can quickly see how monitoring costs to protect the integrity of market contracts necessarily build. Some of this transaction cost

---

[238] McManus, *supra* note 149, at 344.

[239] S. Macaulay, "Non-Contractual Relations in Business: A Preliminary Study" (1963), 28 *Am. Soc. Rev.* 55.

[240] Williamson, *supra* note 211, *Markets and Hierarchies*.

[241] Williamson, *supra* note 211, "Transactions Cost Economics: The Governance of Contractual Relations".

[242] Smith, *supra* note 5.

can be avoided by substituting authoritative contracts within firms, but only by willingness to bear another kind of cost, shirking, opportunism or chiseling within the firm.

Recently, using this chiseling methodology, Klein, Alchian and Crawford analyzed vertical integration when individuals are subject to "hold-up" tactics.[243] They give an example of where an individual is engaging in an activity where sizeable quasi-rents are at stake. Efforts can be directed at their expropriation by opportunistic owners of crucially co-operative factors. "A distortion arises", they say, echoing McManus though not citing him, "because each [party] sees a distorted marginal revenue or marginal cost." Such hold-ups can make vertical integration attractive when the alternative market costs of enforcement and chiseling are considered.[244]

(b) Monitoring Efforts and Efficient Public Goods Provision

Let us after this long, but I hope not uninstructive discussion of the private firm, ask if production of public goods by government firms might not be desirable under certain conditions, too, though ineffective internal monitoring efforts raise their production costs.

Would the choice of contracts with private firms (which includes, as a special case, direct subsidies to private citizens to expend these funds in particular ways) or a regulatory procedure which would direct citizens by fiat to produce public goods be superior? I think not always. The ability of a private contractor to chisel or act opportunistically on contractual terms rises with the complexity of a contract.[245] Would citizens be better off put-

---

[243] Klein, Crawford and Alchian, *supra* note 211.

[244] Klein and Leffler, *supra* note 211, and L. Telser, "A Theory of Self-enforcing Agreements" (1980), 53 *J. of Bus.* 27, spend some time on what Tullock calls the "discipline of continuous" dealings as a restriction on or warranties against breach of market contracts. See G. Tullock *Explorations in the Theory of Anarchy* (Blacksburg: Centre for Study of Public Choice, 1972).

[245] L. Bezeau, in "Complexity as a Characteristic of Policies in Albert Breton's 'Economic Theory of Representative Government' " (1979), 34 *Public Choice* 494, makes much of complexity in the public sector as does Simon in "Rationality as Process and as a Product of Thought" (1978), 68 *Am. Econ. Rev.: Papers and Proceedings* 1, and in *Administrative Behaviour, supra* note 233. Particularly interesting is Bezeau's brief survey of the political science and organization behaviour literature. The civil service, according to this literature, is viewed as an indispensable "bridge" between politicians and their clientele. The politician and voters willingly share their power with the bureaucracy via the delegation of broad authority in order "to work out the bugs". The sensitive nature of politics, say Bezeau (explicitly) and Simon (implicitly), clearly limits the scope for the dull tool of contracting-out. Barzel, *supra* note 211, though confining himself to private exchanges, claims the issue really is difficulty in measureability, but surely this is the essence of complexity. On the issue of complexity and measurement difficulty over a whole range of physical and social scientific issues see M. Polanyi, *The Tacit Dimension* (Garden City, N.J.: Doubleday, 1966).

ting Canada's Department of External Affairs or the U.S. Department of State in the hands of ITT, "Ma Bell" or General Motors? Consider the Pentagon's problems if instead of just contracting out for its hardware and many "soft" services, it also made contracts with private mercenary firms to supply manpower, tactical information, strategy, etc. The CIA and the RCMP are yet two others that many, if not most, citizens might not want constrained by price-contractual means alone. The "discipline of continuous dealings"[246] in all of these pursuits is not sufficient to rule out a one time opportunistic sell-out and continuous and unrelieved chiseling in minor ways would require a monitoring effort that might itself rival in size and cost the public bureaucracy displaced.[247]

How would some of these security functions be efficiently carried out by regulation? Requiring every able bodied person to own a rifle or handgun and heed the "hue-and-cry" is fraught with enforcement difficulties and presents an insuperable challenge with respect to heavy national armaments. Would consumer subsidies for the latter really get around the dangers implicit in neighbors or private firms who possess parts of complex missile systems? Posses can be summoned by fiat, but what insures they search in an efficient manner?

Less far fetched are the Becker and Stigler suggestions to privatize certain aspects of the courts and the police via private regulatory incentives.[248] Awards to private parties for the ferreting out of malfeasance indeed has historical precedent. That such "bounty hunting" involves predictable distortions must be admitted as well.[249]

Klein, Crawford and Alchian[250] and Klein[251] argue that while permitting the private supply of *fiat* money has attractive features (its competitive quantity), the enormous gains from a one-shot sell-out (by massive devaluation) makes opportunism likely unless huge sums are paid in bonding

---

[246] Tullock, *supra* note 244.

[247] Savas, *supra* note 117, gives an instructive history of waste collection and disposal from ancient through modern times. Regulation was the first mode and everyone was his own "waste disposal engineer". This was not satisfactory to authorities, for enforcement reasons, and in late classical and medieval times, scavengers were hired via contracts tied to the license regulation of draymen, a common medieval cross-financing mechanism. See D. C. North and R. P. Thomas, *The Rise of the Western World: A New Economic History* (New York: Cambridge Univ. Press, 1973). Contracting out continued in a formal, market constrained setting in the nineteenth century, but scandal in the form of corruption and nonfulfillments caused the practice to be abandoned in favour of public sanitation departments in the Progressive Era. Today Savas reckons that about two-thirds of cities use some form of waste disposal contracting or require private pick-ups of refuse.

[248] G. Becker and G. Stigler, "Law Enforcement, Malfeasance and Compensation of Enforcers" (1974), 3 *J. of Legal Studies* 1.

[249] W. Landes and R. Posner, "Adjudication as a Private Good" (1979), 8 *J. of Legal Studies* 235.

[250] Klein, Crawford and Alchian, *supra* note 211.

[251] Klein, "The Competitive Supply of Money" (1974), 6 *J. of Money, Credit and Banking* 423, Klein, "Competing Monies: A Comment" (1976), 8 *J. of Money, Credit and Banking* 513.

premia. In some sense, the absence of private monies competing with "local" U.S. and Canadian money is proof of this, even given the current inflation rates.

Consider now the question of the private provision of goods whose stability in supply is highly valued by the general citizenry such as the courts or police services. Private firms will have strong incentive to quantity adjust along various dimensions of output as the relative cost of their production alters even though their contracts provide otherwise.[252] How, for example, would one expect a mercenary army or police force to operate in the presence of an invasion of a superior force or a serious civil insurrection? Historical discussions of the behaviour in the era of private armies, *e.g.*, the *condottieri*, suggests grave difficulties along crucial margins because of enforcement problems.[253] Contracts to insure that citizens are properly "insured" against such fluctuations in service quality may be difficult to draw up and exceedingly hard to enforce.

But even if chiseling could be constrained on specific margins as input prices change, there still remains the problem of "reading" the demands for complex public goods. Individuals under each institution, though identical in their abilities and tastes, will "survive" by taking different factors into account. A very subtle set of policy goals will require a continuous sampling of demand. Since these are in a public sector context revealed politically, they may require individuals to carry them out who are politically "attuned" or connected,[254] *i.e.*, those who constantly receive and are disciplined by political signals.

As I earlier pointed out in Section II, the best evidence for U.S. public sector budget suggests that even in the politically less expensive, and, no doubt, less redistributive era of 1902, the degree of bureaucratization, "non-contracting outs", was not significantly smaller than in 1970.[255] This strongly suggests that utility from public firms exists that cannot be realized in many activities by contracting-out or regulatory procedures.[256]

It may be for this reason, paradoxically, why the Lakewood Plan, a highly studied example of contracting-out, is successful. The latter is a system used in the Los Angeles area where small governments purchase their services from larger governments. The purchasing cities involved are

---

252 Chiselling is an equilibrium concept which involves, among other things the costs of inputs used to produce the contracted-for output. Given their prices, a certain level of private opportunistic substitution is to be expected. *A fortiori*, when the price of certain inputs rises, a still further substitution is to be expected.

253 B. W. Tuchman, *A Distant Mirror: The Calamitous 14th Century* (New York: Alfred A. Knopf, 1978).

254 W. W. Wilms, *Public and Proprietary Vocational Training* (Lexington, Mass.: Lexington Books, 1974); Bezeau, *supra* note 245.

255 Borcherding, *supra* note 23.

256 For instance, R. Schmalensee in *The Control of Natural Monopolies* (Lexington, Mass.: Lexington Books, 1979), claims that by 1875 one-half of all water companies in the U.S. were publicly owned and operated. Today he finds that the ratio has risen to three-fourths.

neither large nor heavily urbanized.[257] They are often surrounded by larger jurisdictions that can come to their aid, if the situation warrants. These contracting firms are not for profit, however, but "professionally" oriented public bureaucracies unlikely to count the cost as input prices change in the short period.

Governmental dealings with wealth maximizing, opportunistic private firms and factor owners are not the sole difficulty with the contracting problem. Hettich points out that if education was provided only by private firms competing for the custom of parents of students supplied with state subsidized vouchers, less civics and other broad forms of social propaganda would be supplied and more of the 3Rs.[258] Since the latter is more likely a private good, and the former a public one, the characteristics of the output privately chosen are apt to diverge from those collectively desired. Further, vouchers will also encourage sectarianism which may have negative external consequences.[259]

Here is another example of complexity problems from education.[260] If what is desired by taxpayers is a certain number of effective units of education per child and children's rates of transforming schooling into effective units of education differ, a system that gives each child the same voucher will not equate the relevant margins taxpayers are willing to pay for. Bright (or socially advantaged) children will require less of a subsidy than do dull (or deprived) ones to raise them to the levels of education where they will be honest, independent citizens. Providing the bright (advantaged) children with the same resources as the dull (deprived) youngsters will reduce the total effectiveness of any given outlay. A public school is ideal for this, says Acheson, since the professional caste running it will more likely make the necessary transfers than would a private school which will be consumer directed.[261] Pauly,[262] however, argues that such differential transfers to ac-

---

[257] R. Bish and R. Warren, "Scale and Monopoly Problems in Urban Government Service" (1972), 8 *Urban Affairs Q.* 97.

[258] W. Hettich, "Mixed Public and Private Financing of Education: Comment" (1969), 59 *Am. Econ. Rev.* 210.

[259] This may well be offset by the ethical norms instilled by such education. Smith in his other famous, but less well-known book, *The Theory of Moral Sentiments,* West ed. (1759: rpt. Indianapolis, Ind.: Library Classics, 1975), makes much out of the power of sectarian relations to reduce people's proclivity to chisel on one another. Casual empiricism, based on observation of Mormon communities, suggest this is definitely so, though most of these are small towns. Smith notes in *Sentiments* that his "impartial Spectator", a conscience-like agent acting to remind individuals of their ethical duties to one another, worked better where communities were smaller. He reckoned in the *Wealth of Nations* that as communities became larger the "brother's keeper" function of social norms grew less effective.

[260] Acheson, *supra* note 213.

[261] Unfortunately, the evidence also shows that teachers have personal preferences for bright over dull children. This leads to the notorious tracking systems much discussed in the courts in the 1960s. This evidence is surveyed by Borcherding in "The Economics of School Integration: Public Choice with Tie-Ins" (1977), 31 *Public Choice* 53.

[262] M. Pauly, "Mixed Public and Private Financing of Education: Efficiency and Feasibility" (1967), 57 *Am. Econ. Rev.* 120.

complish social ends could be accomplished by vouchers that were inversely distributed according to family income.[263]

Of course, an alternative to educational vouchers and public schooling is some sort of Chadwickian/Demsetzian contracting out. This would necessarily involve the evaluation of teacher/school performance. As has been demonstrated in other contexts, this leads to the "prepping" of children to pass specific tests.[264] Such specific coaching is not necessarily correlated with quality education. This is, of course, the same sort of prediction that Williamson[265] and Goldberg[266] made with respect to contract management of public utilities. Wilms[267] offers evidence, in fact, that such difficulties plague the U.S. job-training programs as do Farag-Ott[268] and Marvel.[269]

Thus, a system of direct subsidies or contracting-out of public services to avoid chiseling clearly requires (a) a contract specifying monitorable dimensions, and (b) a motivated monitor. Disagreements over contractual intentions and actual results require continual adjudications. This is perhaps why refuse collection and garbage disposal are so widely provided by contracting-out procedures.[270] Obviously, these services pose no great measurement problem as citizens easily observe their provision and provide massive monitoring. Becker and Stigler's suggestion to contract out the police, on the other hand, engenders little enthusiasm, even among those who otherwise are sympathetic to market provisions of public services.[271] Tax farming, an ancient contracting out device whereby kings sold to private persons or groups the right to extract certain kinds of taxes of cer-

---

[263] James Buchanan in private correspondence has suggested that introduction of vouchers would also be objected to by proponents of equalitarianism. Under the current set of institutions, a child receives an in-kind subsidy for state-provided education. Little leeway is available for private supplementation. (I have been told that it is even illegal in the State of Washington for a private tutor to come to a child's school and use the latter's facilities in any way to provide the child extra tutorial assistance.)

Under vouchers this cost discontinuity discouraging supplementation would no longer obtain. The prediction would be that the variance among individuals in dollar spendings on education would increase and such differences would be income-related. Of course, this is probably true. Whether the relative disadvantage a poor child suffers would grow is another thing, however, as Friedman and Friedman, *supra* note 41, address. If the real value of the basic subsidy rises, the predicted differential would decline in effective terms.

[264] Wilms, *supra* note 254.

[265] Williamson, *supra* note 79.

[266] Goldberg, "Regulation and Administered Contracts", *supra* note 195.

[267] Wilms, *supra* note 254.

[268] A. Farag-Ott, "Should Public Employment be Viewed as a Public Good or a Case of a Wage Subsidy" [Unpublished ms., Intl. Institute of Public Finance Congress, Jerusalem, August 1980].

[269] M. Marvel, "The Social and Political Consequences of Manpower Training Programs" in *Labor and Employment Policy*, Bulmer and Carmichael, eds. (Lexington, Mass.: Heath-Lexington, 1981).

[270] Savas, *supra* note 117.

[271] Becker and Stigler, *supra* note 248; Landes and Posner, *supra* note 249.

tain rates from certain classes of factors, generates zero voting interest nowadays, though Tullock notes,[272] it was well received in the Spanish port of Cadiz in the seventeenth century when it was employed to collect customs duties.[273]

Requiring that private individuals supply their own units of the public service has obvious faults as well, as I have earlier discussed, and these would have to be recognized if we employed a "regulatory public finance" scheme to paraphrase both Posner[274] and McManus.[275] Mills' rule for education requiring parents to educate their children to a certain standard would require a great army of state inspectors, if it were to insure that parents actually were *exceeding* the level of schooling purchase where they would otherwise stop. After all, if the externality is infra-marginal or non-existent, one needs no such rules. Only if private provision is suboptimal, must one force a larger purchase.

Furthermore, it should be clear that unless regulation involves an enforceable *quid pro quo* to the regulatees, it will be resisted by the individuals on whom it is imposed. Coercion does not come free, nor is it ever totally

---

[272] Tullock, *supra* note 20.

[273] Thomas Mayer has pointed out in a letter that "the problem with tax farming is probably that the tax farmer, unlike the sovereign, does not bear the cost of treating the taxpayer brutally." My discursive reading on the subject suggests that sovereigns did attempt to limit the more egregious deadweights of this system. Tullock's example is one where the monitoring to accomplish this end was probably fairly easy. Earl Thompson in conversations argues that if the relationship between the government and private supplier is characterized by bilateral monopoly there is a double or reciprocal holdout problem. This well-known phenomenon is liable to be very costly in terms of rent dissipation due to negotiation costs. Integrating the activity by government enterprise, he claims, may be resource saving on net, especially if the demand for the public good is fairly inelastic.

I have also treated chiseling and holdups as something a firm does to the government purchasers, but the reverse is clearly possible. Since political agents have less of a stake in the future value of their organization, it follows then that extreme opportunism on the part of a purchasing agent might, in some cases, require the government to supply services that an effective bonding mechanism would cause to be privately produced. Governments in unstable parts of the world may have great difficulty finding willing suppliers for as mundane a reason as fear of nonpayment and/or confiscation of firms' assets, an extreme case of post-contractual holdup.

Consumer chiseling is another problem worth mentioning. Young claims that one difficulty of the private franchising-regulatory mode of garbage collection is simply non-payment of bills by customers. *Supra*, note 120. This is one reason Savas feels that a contracting out scheme municipally financed has some advantages. *Supra* note 117.

[274] Posner, "Taxation by Regulation" (1971), 2 *Bell J. of Econ. and Mgmt. Sciences* 22; McManus, "On the New Transportation Policy After Ten Years" in *Studies on Regulation in Canada*, W. T. Stansbury, ed. (Montreal: Institute for Research on Public Policy, 1978).

[275] One large city, Texarkana, Arkansas, was prominently featured in the television news and national magazine media some years ago. It had no city-provided refuse removal service, publicly owned or privately contracted out, though its sister city of the same name in Texas did. Of course, it did have a municipal regulation requiring that residents and businesses dispose of their trash by hygenic and public health-considerate ways. Many residents did, in fact, comply and purchased private refuse collection services. Many did not, however, and this Arkansas town came to be known as the "rat capital" of the U.S. The city now has a municipally contracted, but privately supplied, refuse collection system.

effective.[276] Thus, regulation, if it is not a trivial economic exercise, requires that people behave in ways that are different than they would otherwise choose. The greater the number or margins that must be controlled and the larger the elasticity of substitution over the items in the regulated bundle, the more likely the regulatee will attempt to substitute around the intention of the authority. Coercion, by employing the use of penalties, is, of course, one means of deterrence. But positive "shadow prices" can be substituted on some margins for implicit taxes on others to better effect, B. F. Skinner notwithstanding.

To the extent, however, that the regulatory authority possesses the political and economic power to "purchase" alterations in behaviour by offering in-kind subsidies, this mechanism begins to resemble the subsidy/contracting-out option. Acheson's study of the North American Auto Pact is instructive here, since he shows that the legislation is employed in ways to "purchase" quantum differences in behaviour by permitting various trade flows that otherwise would have or have not been subject to quotas or tariffs.[277]

This point brings us to the conclusion of this part of Section V. The discussion has concentrated entirely on monitoring efforts and the comparative advantage each of the three institutional types have in delivering that vector of real outputs (beyond that otherwise forthcoming in private markets) considered desirable. Another issue, financing, needs to be discussed before closing, however, since the choice between regulation and more orthodox public goods supply methods (in-house production or contracting-out/subsidy schemes) involve very different taxation requirements. This difference, noted originally by Posner,[278] could have fairly profound effects on the supply decision. The marginal social cost of $1 in U.S. federal revenues has a deadweight taxation cost range of from 15 to 30 cents according to Browning.[279] Non-federal jurisdiction taxation marginal deadweight costs surely exceed this, since the supply and demand functions for most outputs and inputs are more elastic than at the national level. Now most estimates of the social regulatory costs attendant to the necessary cross-subsidization are around or within this range—rent- or transfer-seeking aside.[280] Browning, however, does indicate in his work on redistribution that in-kind redistributions do add another 6 percent more than price subsidies require.[281] Thus, employing regulation as a public finance alter-

---

[276] As mentioned earlier Weidenbaum, *supra* note 40, and Lilley and Miller, *supra* note 41, estimate that private compliance with regulations costs at least $20 for every $1 in public administrative outlays. The returns to "avoison", that murky area between legal avoidance and illegal evasion, are not negligible.

[277] Acheson, *supra* note 204.

[278] Posner, *supra* note 274.

[279] E. Browning, "The Marginal Cost of Public Funds" (1976), 84 *J. of Pol. Econ.* 283.

[280] See Borcherding, *supra* note 208.

[281] Browning, "The Externality Argument for In-Kind Transfers: Some Critical Remarks" (1975), 28 *Kyklos* 526.

native may make economic sense, if extra monitoring costs from non-compliance, *i.e.*, regulatee chiseling, are not significantly higher than taxation inefficiencies.[282] The well-known literature on effluent charges and bribes versus standards involves, in a rather primitive way, exactly these sorts of considerations.

For the nonce, therefore, it seems prudent to dismiss the deadweight "tax" effects on the choice of supply instruments, fiscal or regulatory. Further, even if these could be brought into the analysis they could not explain the supply choice between contracts to private entities and bureaucratic vertical integrations.

(c) The Politics of Discrimination

A few years ago I published a paper on why U.S. blacks wanted integrated schools in the period 1920 through the mid-1960s.[283] The evidence indicated, however, that they have been less interested in integration in recent years just as they were uninterested in the immediate post-Civil War period up until the 1890s. The answer I gave for this curious pattern is that public education was discriminatorily supplied from the late 1890s to the early 1960s, but not nearly so much in either the earlier or later decades. After the Civil War lower school education in the South was largely segregated, but effective black political power and Reconstruction monitoring by federal troops, carpetbaggers and assorted scalliwags assured blacks (in a given county) roughly the same amount of education in dollar terms per child as whites. After the federal troops left in the 1870s, "Jim Crow" politics ascended and the result was a dramatic fall in the ratio of black to white per pupil spending. Only then did blacks decry segregation, and some black leaders like Booker T. Washington and his famous protege, W. E. B. DuBois, suggested that vouchers might be a desirable alternative to public schools. Only later when this goal became unobtainable, because of white control over fiscal decisions, did the black leadership press for integrated public schooling.

The conventional wisdom still has it, however, that in the 1954 land-

---

[282] R. Zerbe and N. Urban argue in "Towards a Public Interest Theory of Regulation" (1979), *Research in Law and Econ.*, based on survey data, that certain regulatory activities at the state level in Washington are highly popular, indicating the coercive redistributional component attendant to them is not great. Following Tiebout, *supra* note 57, it would seem possible that purely local government regulation may be even more likely to be public good, rather than redistribution, intensive. This follows since the ability of local governments to exploit consumer and factor owners is limited, at least in relation to the opportunities available to higher level jurisdictions.

Even at the federal level the average U.S. citizen finds much regulation desirable though he or she favors adjustments to reduce the powers of special interests (including bureaucrats who have gone rather farther imposing social or environmental rules than those in this group think useful). See Lipset and Schneider, "The Public View of Regulation" (1979), 2 *Public Opinion*.

[283] Borcherding, *supra* note 261.

mark decision, *Brown v. Topeka Board of Education*,[284] the Supreme Court was swayed by the social psychological evidence presented by Kenneth Clark's famous *amicus* brief. This is not clear. In the other three cases jointly decided along with *Brown*, evidence of fiscal discrimination was presented by the other plaintiffs and noted by the court. It is my hypothesis that the federal courts had always in the past adhered to the view that equal expenditures per child (within a given jurisdiction) was the required rule. They found it exceedingly difficult to enforce this dictum, however, and went along instead with an institutional alteration to alleviate fiscal discrimination implied in *Brown* that, I am sure, several on the Supreme Court, despite its unanimous agreement, felt was premature.

The point of this long story is that political favoritism is at the heart of much that the state does, a point Breton has effectively made in his many writings[285] and Migué has recently concluded,[286] all studies for Canada. No one, in fact, currently writing denies this.

Studies of demands for public services carried out by Deacon and Borcherding[287] and later replicated elsewhere[288] have determined that on the margins, at least, collective economies in consumption or externalities are not strong, with the exception of the local level where for obvious reasons redistribution is severely constrained.[289] Looser studies uncovering the real beneficiaries of state spending on public activities also suggest that redistribution is common. Stigler argued this rather vigorously in his enunciation of Director's Law of Public Expenditure[290] and in his writings since then as does Becker,[291] Peltzman,[292] and Lindsay.[293]

Some economists may be distressed by this, since such transfer-seeking uses scarce resources,[294] but they are not surprised.[295] The state, positive col-

---

284 *Brown v. Board of Education of Topeka County, Kansas* (1954), 75 S. Ct. 753.

285 Breton, "The Economics of Nationalism" (1964), 72 *J. of Pol. Econ.* 376; Breton, *Discriminating Government Policies in Federal Countries* (Montreal: Private Planning Association of Canada, 1967); Breton, "The Crown Corporation as an Alternative to Industrial Incentive Grants", *supra* note 201.

286 J. L. Migué, *Nationalistic Policies in Canada: An Economic Approach* (Montreal: C. D. Howe Research Institute, 1979).

287 Borcherding and Deacon, *supra* note 152.

288 Deacon, *supra* note 156.

289 Deacon, *supra* note 155.

290 Stigler, "Director's Law of Public Income Redistribution" (1970), 13 *J. of Law and Econ.* 1.

291 G. S. Becker, "Competition Among Pressure Groups and the Political Redistribution of Income," forthcoming *Quart. J. of Econ.*

292 Peltzman, "The Growth of Government" (1980), 23 *J. of Law and Econ.* 209.

293 C. M. Lindsay and B. Zycher, "Pork Barrel Politics and the Fog Factor", *supra* note 226.

294 Tullock, *supra* note 53; Posner, "The Social Costs of Monopoly and Regulation" (1975), 83 *J. of Pol. Econ.* 807; Borcherding, *supra* note 208.

295 G. Kolko, *Railroads and Regulations, 1877-1916* (Princeton: Princeton Univ. Press, 1965); E. W. Hawley, *The New Deal and the Monopoly Problem: A Study in Economic Ambivalence* (Princeton: Princeton Univ. Press, 1966); Stigler, *supra* note 150; W. Jordan, "Producer Protection, Prior Market Structure and the Effects of Governmental Regulation" (1972), 15 *J. of Law and Econ.* 151.

lective choice theorists tell us, besides producing public good, is the only legitimate device for coercing individuals to transfer income to others without compensation.[296] The representation method used to accomplish this in modern Western jurisdictions is not via full Greco-political democracy, but the election of agents who represent geographic sub-units of a jurisdiction. Periodic and open elections decide who has usufructory rights over the state, bounded only by written and unwritten constitutions (and they are not on stone either).[297] People organize around political entrepreneurs who compete for office by offering legislation in exchange for support. Some of this legislation will, no doubt, take the form of financing of productive or public goods, but not all. Redistribution by discriminatory taxes and expenditures and by regulatory interventions will be another predictable outcome as political entrepreneurs and parties attempt to bring the political marginal product of each instrument they command into line with one another so as to maximize political income (which in a competitive system means survival with little long-run rents).

In this current (but also Smithian)[298] view of the state, one expects political representatives to examine the redistributive possibilities of each public supply instrument and to impute benefits to them depending upon their distributional effects on individuals as political actors.[299] That given these goals and constraints they will choose the lowest "cost" method has not until quite recently been well understood by economists.[300] The essence of this emerging awareness has been captured by the political scientist Robert Wood. He puts it well and with a touch of humor:

> It is not so much inefficiency of bureaucracy we complain about as its efficiency for purposes other than those we feel appropriate.[301]

With this redistributional goal of government in mind, it is obvious that private contracting out of public services has at least two *political* liabilities. First, it is necessarily more open than policy carried out within

---

[296] Goldberg, "Institutional Change and the Quasi-Invisible Hand" (1974), 18 *J. of Law and Econ.* 461.

[297] Recall Mr. Dooley's comment that the "courts follow the 'lection returns". Even less cynically put, it should be realized that resources can and will be used to alter the interpretation of the constitution in favour of those making these investments. The difference between legislative as opposed to a constitutional shift is the former is more costly to accomplish. Moynihan's recent discussion is useful here. D. P. Moynihan, "What do you do when the Supreme Court is Wrong?" (1979), 51 *The Public Interest* 3.

[298] West, "Adam Smith's Public Economics: A Re-Evaluation" (1977), 10 *Can. J. of Econ.* 1.

[299] Explaining the supply mode on tax deadweights has other liabilities too; to wit, it does not conform to the casual evidence. Take the Private Express Statutes which give the U.S. and Canadian government postal systems a monopoly on first-class mail delivery. No doubt this does provide a means of cross-subsidizing rural and remote patrons, but it is not clear that the attendant excess burdens are smaller than if direct taxes and subsidies were employed.

[300] For a prominent early exception, see A. Breton, *The Economic Theory of Representative Government* (Chicago: Aldine, 1974).

[301] Cited in R. Bartlett, *Economic Foundations of Political Power* (New York: Free Press, 1973).

c bureaus and independent government agencies in their roles as sup-
s or regulators. This openness makes monitoring by non-coalition
members much easier and interferences by courts on constitutional grounds
more likely. David Tuerck in a much neglected, but important, paper has
carefully focused on how the U.S. courts have vigorously attempted to
police the tax system to prevent discrimination.[302] No similar attempt to enforce "due process" or what Canadians and English legal scholars call
"natural justice" has accompanied the expenditure or regulatory side when
the supplies are made in-kind and beneficiaries are not named in legislation.
This is an important limitation that has not been fully recognized, but
should. *If goods are private, the recipients must be openly specified in the
contracting-out process; not so for either the bureaucratic or regulatory
modes of supply.* Lindsay and Zycher refer to this preference of public officials for secrecy as the "fog factor"[303] and "fog" is certainly not enhanced
by open, contractual methods.[304]

But a second, and far more important, reason can be given why regulation and supply by public firms are preferred to contracting-out methods:
the former two are necessarily more selective. A private firm will not have
the same incentive to tailor benefits to the politically "worthy", since its objective function contains pecuniary wealth arguments, not political ones. It
will, to the eyes of politicians, act irresponsibly, since it has, in fact, no incentive to dole out the transfers "optimally," but rather as cheaply as possible. Further, since legislators' time is scarce, they could not possibly
monitor closely these private agents who contract manage discriminatorily
without incurring a very high control cost. Creation of competitive-like but
politically sensitive suppliers reduces this loss, though, of course, at the expense of raising unit costs. Regulation, bureaucracy or public enterprise are
efficient responses to political necessity in this light.

Given the problem of selectivity, the reader can also see why redistributions are not made directly in terms of money, but rather as in-kind
transfers. Given that the demand by potential recipients for monetary
grants is highly elastic, means must be found to choke off excess demand.
Stigler,[305] Becker and Stigler[306] and Landes and Posner[307] explain the in-kind
transfer as an efficient rationing device. The reason is that U.S. due process
and English-Canadian natural justice considerations restrict the selectivity
capacity of the legislature to write discriminatory law involving taxes and
monetary transfers. The courts, using the "classification doctrine", will

---

302 D. Tuerck, "Constitutional Asymmetry", *Papers on Non-Market Decision Making II*,
   1967.
303 Lindsay and Zycher, *supra* note 226.
304 See also Lowi, *supra*, note 189, and D. G. Hartle, *A Public Policy Decision Model: The
   Case of Government Regulation in Canada* (Ottawa: Economic Council of Canada, 1979),
   for a complete expansion on this theme, replete with much evidence, albeit of a casual sort.
305 Stigler, "The Theory of Regulation", *supra* note 150.
306 Becker and Stigler, *supra* note 248.
307 Landes and Posner, *supra* note 249.

find it relatively difficult, however, to establish that a bureaucratically administered program which the legislature puts forth as a "public good" really is no more than a discriminatory transfer.[308] At least since the late nineteenth century the courts in the U.S. have given up scrutinizing the regulatory purposes with much thought to classification for discrimination, save in race and sex discrimination cases.[309] Almost no extension of public enterprise or regulation has been disallowed either, the courts holding, instead, that they cannot fathom the real intentions of the legislature, but must accept the implied and explicit "police powers" as giving wide latitude to legislative choice.

Studies by Breton, Nelles, Migué and Acheson[310] suggest that for Canada discrimination as a part of regulation and public enterprise is a non-trivial part of the activities undertaken. Tupper's dissertation[311] and recent writings[312] on Canadian public enterprise makes this a key consideration, too, as do Kennedy and Tullock[313] for the U.S.

One must recognize the wide scope of this principle. For instance, E. G. West documents the rise of "free" public schooling in Britain and the U.S., long after the vast numbers of children (90 percent) had voluntarily been educated and county and parish vouchers had been employed to extend parental purchase.[314] Who were those agents behind the movement? Teachers, say West and Katz,[315] who wanted a vehicle to restrict competition. The public school system, with its take-it-or-leave-it style subsidy, pro-

---

[308] K. Leffler in "Government Output and National Income Estimates" in *Public Policy in Open Economies: Journal of Monetary Economics,* Supplement, Brunner and A. H. Meltzer, eds. (1978), (citing private conversations with C. M. Lindsay) agrees with this position. He believes a great deal of public activity is transfer, not public good oriented. He offers an intriguing econometric test suggesting that government output is not productive on the margins and argues that the comparative advantage of government in coercion is guaranteed to cause such misallocations. He agrees, however, that this is in some sense unavoidable, though costs can be reduced somewhat by sensible changes in institutions and policies.

[309] Terry Anderson and Peter Hill in *The Birth of a Transfer Society* (Stanford, Calif.: Hoover Institution Press, forthcoming 1980) point to the Granger cases of the 1870s, particularly *Munn v. Illinois* (1876), 94 U.S. 113 (Sup. Ct.), as pivotal historically, since at that point the police powers of government were extended dramatically. Canadian doctrinal history, according to conversations with Univ. of Toronto law professor, Hudson Janisch, parallels the U.S. though interventionism has always been easier given the theoretical supremacy of Canadian Parliament checked only by the *British North America Act*, now the *Constitution Acts, 1867-1982* and unwritten custom.

[310] Breton, *supra* note 285; Nelles, "The Politics of Development", *supra* note 21; Nelles, "Public Ownership of Electrical Utilities", *supra* note 21; Migué, *supra* note 286; Acheson, *supra* note 204.

[311] Tupper, *supra* note 216.

[312] Tupper, *supra* note 21.

[313] Kennedy, *supra* note 13 (both articles); Tullock, *supra* note 53.

[314] West, "The Role of Education in Nineteenth Century Doctrines of Political Economy" (1964), 12 *British J. of Educ. Studies* 161; West, *supra* note 17; West, "A Measure of the Effect of Government Intervention upon the Growth of the 19th Century British Education" (1980), *Annals of Econ. Hist.* (forthcoming).

[315] Katz, *supra* note 17.

vided one important element in creating a more favourable market for teachers' services. Control of this system by educators (never total, of course) insured that substitute outputs faced severe purchase barriers. Standards for entry into the profession itself provided the second condition for monopolistic control. The third condition, that general taxpayers would acquiesce, is readily explained by both the small losses they incur on per household bases and the diffuseness of their numbers as opposed to the large benefits to the teachers and their compactness as a group.[316]

The works of Niskanen[317] and that found in *Budgets and Bureaucrats*[318] are useful here too. This research suggests, and finds evidence for, the hypothesis that the public sector is a useful way for *specialized* factor owners selling services that produce public activities to gain rents, since it can be thought of as a device for civil servants not only to restrict entry, but to increase their demand. Thus, if factor owners fail to achieve some monopoly advantage under say a subsidization or contracting-out program, they may press for collectivization, since entry can then be constrained via public service commission directions.

The political supply decision between regulation and the public firm as "efficient" means for accomplishing redistributions must now be considered.[319] One obvious explanation is the degree and scope of control. Regulatory commissioners have very small staffs and are observed to adjudicate differences between small numbers of private interests that organize themselves to plead for cross-subsidies.[320] The scarcity of information available to commissioners and the limitations on time imposed by this mode severely limit their abilities to choose with political finesse when the number of competing groups is large, however.[321] This is reinforced by com-

---

316 It should also be noted that when per capita stakes rise or technical or constitutional means lower the cost of diffuse interests, the original redistribution may be offset to a certain extent. The "taxpayers" revolution sweeping the U.S., and possibly being imported into Canada is a case in point. With respect to education the attempt to place a voucher scheme on the ballot in California for referendum consideration is, according to Friedman and Friedman, *supra* note 41, a reaction to a continuing depreciation of the quality of public education.

317 Niskanen, *supra* notes 148 and 141.

318 Borcherding, ed., *supra* note 23.

319 Jarrell, *supra* note 145; Owen and Braeutigam *supra* note 187; Posner, *supra* note 274; Stigler, *supra* note 150; and Peltzman, *supra* note 105; using U.S. data, consider regulation to be a substitute for public enterprise directed transfers. The Canadian choice has been put similarly by Nelles, *supra* note 21 (both articles), Breton, *supra* note 285 (all three articles), Migué, "Controls versus Subsidies in the Economic Theory of Regulation" (1977), 20 *J. of Law and Econ.* 213; Migué, *supra* note 286; McManus, *supra* notes 211 and 274; Stegeman and Acheson, "Canadian Government Purchasing Policy" (1972), 6 *J. of World Trade Law* 442; Acheson and Chant *supra* note 205; Chant and Acheson, *supra* note 206; Acheson, "The Allocation of Government Deposits Among Private Banks: The Canadian Case" (1977), 9 *J. of Money, Credit and Banking* 447; Acheson, *supra* note 204; and Borcherding, *supra* note 208, explain why redistribution is to be expected by one or the other means.

320 Eckert, *supra* note 147 (both articles); Lowi, *supra* note 189.

321 G. Hilton, "The Basic Behaviour of Regulatory Commissions" (1972), 62 *Am. Econ. Rev.: Papers and Proceedings* 47.

missioners' relatively short tenures which reduce their interest in the future consequences of a decision.[322]

Government bureaus on the other hand have larger staffs, are composed of career civil servants and are more politically sensitive to groups whose "voice" may require a higher level of organizational effort. Eckert's comparison of commissions and agencies indicates the more parochial nature of commissions and concludes that the former are more likely to support producer monopolies while the latter are concerned with many interests.[323] Thus, it would seem that regulatory bureaus are more useful when the number of politically relevant competitive interests is small *and* the enforcement problems are not severe.

To conclude this part, I would argue holding aside the technical monitoring issue mentioned in part V(b), and concentrating on distributional considerations alone, that the preference ordering of decision-makers among instruments to effect redistributions among large numbers of interest ought to rank the government bureau or public enterprise highest followed on by regulatory commissions and, finally, by private contracting-out. However, where coercive redistribution is the dominant goal but the number of effective contending groups is small, I would predict, absent monitoring considerations, that the regulatory option would receive a higher ranking than public production. Further, in cases where great redistributional selectivity is openly and administratively feasible, the subsidy/contracting-out procedures will be preferred to public production.[324] Thus, only in those activities where monitoring complexities are minimal *and* redistribution unlikely, will private contracting become the commonly observed arrangement. The only noticeable opponents to non-municipal garbage collection, for example, have been the public employee unions and only in certain jurisdictions have they been successful.

(d) Variations Among Public Firm Types and Hybrid Solutions

Until now I have not attempted to draw distinctions between bureaus, Crown corporations (or independent agencies), and mixed enterprises, though the descriptive literature's comparisons are extensive.[325] They are,

---

[322] Eckert, *supra* note 147, "On the Incentives of Regulators: The Case of Taxicabs".

[323] Eckert, *supra* note 147 (both articles).

[324] Farmers in the United States and Canada have been chiefly aided by quotas (regulation), parity and price supports (subsidies), though basic agricultural research, possibly a public good to some extent, has been accomplished through more-or-less a contracting-out procedure to agriculture scholars in public universities and to private for-profit consultants. In-house production within the U.S. or Canadian federal farm bureaucracies has certainly not been the dominant mechanism for effecting redistribution to farmers. See Borcherding *supra* note 208.

[325] A. Abel, "The Public Corporation in the United States" in *Government Enterprise: A Comparative Study*, Friedman and Gurner, eds. (London: Stevens, 1971); H. J. Abraham,

however, organizationally distinct and ought, therefore, to cause their managements to respond rather differently to their various incentive structures. As such, each has unique advantages and disadvantages as to both monitoring costs and ability to engage in discriminatory supply effort.

Bureaus, part of the traditional or "line" operations of government administration, are headed by a chief officer who is of cabinet rank or directly reports to one of such rank. As such the officials are "sensitive" to political articulations of demand to a degree that is a quantum level beyond that of firms whose relationship to the government are drawn in terms of contracts. Crown corporations or independent agencies, on the other hand, are usually headed by officers who are appointed by cabinet officials and only in rare cases are managed by those of cabinet rank. Because a major fraction of their outputs are financed by market sales revenues, their managements are more market directed than those of bureaus whose revenues are generally realized by legislative authorization and appropriations.[326] As such, Crown corporations are necessarily more sensitive to market signals generated by their clientele than are bureaus. Nonetheless, they are ever aware of their public status and receive either publicly or, more often secretly, instructions from cabinet or the minister in charge.[327]

Government as Entrepreneur and Social Servant (Washington, D.C.: Institute for Public Affairs, 1956); Ashely and Smails, *supra* note 218; Canada, Privy Council. *Crown Corporations: Direction, Control, Accountability: Government of Canada's Proposal* (Ottawa: Queen's Printer, 1977); Barry, *supra* note 218; Gracey, *supra* note 218; Canada. Lambert Commission. *Royal Commission on Financial Management and Accountability* (Ottawa: Ministry of Supply and Services, March 1979); Key, *supra* note 223; Musolf, *supra* note 30; Perry, "Crown Corporations and Government Enterprises" in *Proceedings of the Institute of Public Administration of Canada,* 1956; Perry, *supra* note 218; Robson, *supra* note 218; H. Seidman, "The Government Corporation in the U.S." (1959), 37 *Pub. Admin. Rev.* 103; R. W. Sexty, "Government Owned Corporations in Canada: Review of Recent Developments" [Unpublished ms., Memorial Univ. of Nfld. Nov. 1978]; Sexty, "Autonomy Strategies of Government and Business Corporations in Canada" [Unpublished paper, Conference on State-Owned Enterprises in Industrialized Market Economies, March 1979]; Sexty, "Canadian Cellulose Company Limited: A Case Study of Government Rescue and Turnabout" [Class discussion paper, School of Business and Commerce, Memorial Univ. of Nfld., 1979]; Tupper, *supra* note 216; A. H. Walsh, *The Public's Business: The Politics and Practices of Government Corporations* (Cambridge: MIT Press, 1978); Willms, *supra* note 218.

326 The post offices of the U.S. and Canada have historically been the prominent exceptions, though since 1971 the U.S. Postal Service has been an independent agency and the Canadian Postal Service became a Crown corporation under Bill C-42, *Canada Post Corporation Act,* S.C. 1980-81, c. 54. Explaining this puzzle is an important task, but at a superficial level I would argue that in the past when substitutes for the services were poor and the number of affected interests large, that efficient redistribution required a political administration of the service. (See Kennedy, *supra* note 13, in *Land Economics* for a discussion of the political pricing of the U.S. Post Office over its history.) As mentioned earlier, it has only been in the delivery and sorting that in-house production has been important, *i.e.,* the marketing segments.

327 Bill C-42, *ibid.,* in s. 20(1) through (3), explicitly gives the government the powers to issue secret directives to the Crown corporation. This appears not to be exceptional *de facto,* but it is so *de jure.*

Mixed-enterprises, private firms with sizeable numbers of shares—not necessarily a majority—owned by government, are perhaps a step closer to the contracting-out or Demsetzian/Chadwickian solution. Government's executive arm appoints an official (or officials) to oversee its interests and to exercise voting rights on the corporation's board of directors if it has sufficient shares. If it has enough shares, the government may actually have officials or its appointees, often with congenial political views, on the firm's board of directors. A very subtle variation of this mode is the purchase of bonds or other debt instruments of a private firm in exchange for certain output and input decisions by government. The current U.S. and Canadian governments' Chrysler bailouts are of exactly this sort.

These three organizational variants of public firms can be viewed as lying along a spectrum where signals received are, in the case of bureaus, largely those given by the legislature while for mixed-enterprises the firm is more market sensitive. Attenuation of ownership claims via non-transferability of asset ownership together with more limited product competition reduce the more obvious indices of productive efficiency of the bureau, but they combine to enhance the political readings of public demands. For mixed enterprises productive efficiency is very high, but willingness to read political valuations is diminished, but not nearly so much as in the extreme case of contracting-out.[328] Crown corporations represent a highly politicized, but also market directed, institution somewhere between government bureaus and mixed-enterprises. As such they are about as attuned to the market as they are to politics and, given competitive pressures, often differ little from counterpart private firms in their behaviour.[329]

So far I have taken the position that supply instruments were mutually exclusive or, to use the economist's jargon, perfect substitute inputs. This means that the *one* with the least transactions costs ought always be chosen, a corner solution. This may roughly be the case, though I doubt it, for it is easy to point to cases where two, possibly three, instruments are combined.

Consider, for a moment, an independent agency, the United States Postal Service.[330] The Private Express Statutes act as a regulatory device giving the post office some monopoly power on the handling of first class mail. It is instructed by law to cover costs, but in the past it did not always do so nor does it now. To the extent it did not, it received subsidies with "strings attached" so that it resembled a bureau which, of course, it was before 1971. Its rate structure is still subject to regulatory review. Although it sorts and delivers using its own employees, it contracts out much of the intercity transportation of mail to air, truck and railroad freight specialists, who, in

---

[328] The agreement between Chrysler and the two national governments is quite detailed, but it is obvious the continuous nature of the relationship insures that Chrysler's management is politically attuned.

[329] Caves and Christensen, *supra* note 138.

[330] Adie, *supra* note 179; Priest, *supra* note 13; Haldi and Johnson, *supra* note 13.

turn, compete for contracts on the basis of complex, closed and sometimes negotiated bidding. In this case, one can see the combination of several instruments though the independent agency is the dominant form to which the others attach.

Take another example, Air Canada. Baldwin clearly shows that this Crown corporation pursues wealth, but it attends to political interests as well.[331] Regulation of entry, routes, service and prices prevent other private airlines from "cream skimming", *i.e.*, from competitors providing customers in low service cost locations with low priced air services, since net revenues from non-competitive runs finance extensions of services (cross-subsidize) to loss generating routes elsewhere.

Still another case of the employment of mixed instruments is lower education. State and provincial boards regulate public school curriculum and specify broad requirements for private schools. The schools do not produce their own blackboards and chalk, but purchase these and many other inputs in the market. Parents by "voting with their feet" as well as pressuring school boards influence policy as do teachers' associations and administrative groups. There is much vertical integration here, but not so deep as to require the creation of state nurseries and the public production of pencils and papers. Instead, regulation of parental choice is substituted for the former and tender bids for the latter.

Were the theory more tightly formed, one would be able to determine whether the employment of regulation and contracting/subsidy modes as sub-organization forms are complement or substitute inputs to public enterprise. As of this juncture, I am willing only to conjecture that they are useful, co-operative structures that enhance the public goods monitoring and redistributive aspects of government supply decision-making.

(e) Implications, Conjectures and Concluding Notes

So far I have argued that a range of government enterprise—and I use this term generically over the full organizational spectrum from bureaus through mixed enterprises—(a) is a response to dealing with the contractual difficulties that attend private contracting (including vouchers and subsidies) or regulation and/or (b) is a means to effect more precise redistributions than could be obtained by direct transfers or by regulation. Given what are generally called public services, therefore, the incidence of public enterprise ought to be higher as their complexity in terms of number of relevant characteristics grows and/or as the political possibilities for redistribution increase.

The Lakewood Plan in Los Angeles is helpful to consider here for

---

[331] Baldwin, *supra* note 126.

distinguishing between these hypotheses. Police and fire protection and a host of other services are provided small communities on contractual bases, but mostly by other large governments, all under an exchange system most economists would term as workably competitive. Because of factor and citizen mobility, however, the possibility of local redistribution is severely limited, so competition for citizens and factor owners by the political managers of these jurisdictions is brisk as Bish and Warren,[332] following Tiebout,[333] have demonstrated. A perusal of Lakewood Plan cities suggests that the fire service is a prime candidate for private supply, while police is a bit trickier to supply efficiently. Garbage collection appears clearly to be one of those that is efficiently supplied privately by government franchise and contract and this is becoming more prevalent all over North America.

Sonenblum, Kirlin and Ries's study of the Lakewood Plan is instructive here.[334] They take as given that redistribution is highly limited at the city and county level. The choice of public supply instrument, bureaucratic vs. contract supply, will, in their view, be determined by comparing what they call "contract control" costs against "bureaucracy control" savings. They find that political sensitivity is enhanced by public production, but internalization of scale economies, lowering of start-up costs, and mitigation of "personnel problems" are better realized under contracting-out schemes. (They, unfortunately, do not explore the pure regulatory option.) They go on to say that simpler technologies are more likely to be found in the contracting out scheme, while those items where "sensitivity" matters are more likely to be served by bureaucratic techniques. Where citizens are homeowners, more wealthy and, where invisible qualitative aspects might necessarily loom large, again own-supply dominates public supply choice. On the other hand, in communities where businesses and industries are a more important part of the tax base, contracting-out is more common. This is also true where younger, more mobile, house renting and poorer individuals are found. None of this contradicts the hypothesis I have offered, but is quite consistent.

Pryor has studied the existence of independent public agencies across national boundaries where the outputs are not the traditional public services, but akin to what in ordinary usage we think of as commerce and manufacturing.[335] He limited his data set to what I would call "western democracies" and found public enterprise more prevalent at levels above the local jurisdiction. At the municipal level government ownership is common only in the utilities' field—gas, water, sewage, and electricity. Further, he discovered that the incidence of public firms increases from state/provin-

---

[332] Bish and Warren, *supra* note 257.

[333] Tiebout, *supra* note 57.

[334] S. Sonenblum, J. J. Kirlin and J. C. Ries, *How Cities Provide Services: An Evaluation of Alternative Delivery Structures* (Cambridge: Bollinger, 1977).

[335] Pryor, *supra* note 24 (both articles).

cial jurisdictions to the central government,[336] mirroring his findings of transfer activities on the budgetary side of public expenditures.[337]

Education and welfare, on the other hand, two traditional state/ provincial level responsibilities since before the 1890s (though also locally administered), clearly involve a great deal more redistributional possibilities as well as severe political complexity problems. The unwillingness of governments to turn them over to private agencies is, therefore, understandable given the control loss. The reaction of California citizens to current and forthcoming attempts to put a voucher scheme on referenda ballots will be instructive. So too is the study of the future of the guaranteed income as a substitute for traditional, bureauctratic welfare schemes.

One implication of all this immediately comes to mind. As mobility and ability to escape "taxation" by regulation or nationalized industry administration increase, the elasticities of the associated productive factors rise. It follows, therefore, that nationalization ought to be more a central than a subnational phenomenon, except where government enterprise is a response to complexity. Therefore, one reason that Canada may have a greater incidence of public ownership and government enterprise, especially at the provincial level, than the U.S. is the more limited ability of disadvantaged resources to flee.[338] Note also that at the provincial level the productive factors nationalized are often in the natural resource oriented or natural monopoly sort. Both are geographic specific. That all the provinces maintain public retail distribution of packaged liquor (with Quebec the one partial exception) has much to do with the inability to smuggle, a border effect that in the U.S. according to studies by Smith, Wales, and Whalen,[339] severely constrains a U.S. state's behaviour.[340] A Canadian Confederation of 30 provinces with triple the current population and, hence, with many and much denser markets continuously blending into one another would reduce the provincial possibilities of redistribution and damp the demand

---

336 Pryor, *supra* note 24, "Public Ownership: Some Quantitative Dimensions".

337 Pryor, *supra* note 24, *Public Expenditures in Communist and Capitalist Nations*.

338 Nelles appears to subscribe to this hypothesis, *supra* note 21, "The Politics of Development. . .".

339 J. Smith, "The Legal and Illegal Markets for Taxed Goods: Pure Theory and Application to State Government Taxation of Distilled Spirits" (1976), 19 *J. of Law and Econ.* 393; Wales, "Distilled Spirits and Interstate Consumption Effects" (1968), 58 *Am. Econ. Rev.* 853; T. Whalen, "State Monopoly of Packaged Liquor Retailing" (1967), 75 *J. of Pol. Econ.* 197.

340 Only 13 states monopolize the sale of spirits and not one monopolizes beer and wine, though Washington State limited the sale of wine to state liquor stores until 1968. It is interesting to note that two-thirds of its population lived almost 200 miles from the closest open border area, Portland, Oregon. The change in Washington's policy came about, I believe, because legislative reapportionment changed the distribution of political assets in favour of the "wetter" residents of the Puget Sound area and against the sterner drys east of the Cascades. Something like this appears to be taking place in British Columbia where the current (Social Credit) government is exploring via sample surveys, the desirability of selling wine and beer at grocery stores.

for transfer-seeking via provincial public enterprise or regulation. As important, the larger the number of political units the less likely any one region would have the political power to supply the marginal contribution necessary for a party's national survival reducing the incidence of federal intervention. That the call for the creation of "jobs" in the Maritimes is answered by various public development agencies in Canada, but Maine, other poor parts of New England and Appalachia receive less particularized assistance is not so inexplicable.

This observation also can be made of the Swiss system.[341] Here continuous national referenda and strong constitutional guarantees of cantonal rights severely limit redistribution. Little public enterprise exists outside of railroads, the post office, certain communications, and hydropower, all of which are highly Ricardian specific for both the cantons' or the federal government's purposes. The low cost to capital from relocating from one canton to another would, according to my hypothesis, leave largely "productive" rather than transfer activities in non-federal government hands, but probably the constitution is really the limiting factor.

Hong Kong, a British Crown Colony, is another interesting example of these constraints.[342] Low taxes and a free-trade policy imposed on Hong Kong by London severely restricts its ability to engage in redistribution by taxation, public enterprise, or regulatory means. The one factor whose income is vulnerable to transfer is land and Hong Kong has had rent control and land use regulation for almost a half century. This is not surprising in an area where current densities are over 10,000 persons per square mile. The incidence of other government intervention is, on the whole very low, but not absent from schools, universities, hospitals and utilities. Crown corporations in the general market sector are rare, however, and for good reason. The products sold would compete with those of a world market. Regulation for purposes of coercive redistribution in tradeable goods would lead capital to flee.

Hong Kong's neighbor state to the west, Singapore, free of British oversight since 1959, still operates under a regime of free trade with the rest of the world, but on "nontradeables" intervention is much more common than Hong Kong. Regulation and public enterprise interventions are, therefore, less uncommon schemes, as are mixed-enterprises.[343] Like Hong Kong, land is highly regulated by the government. The politics of fiscal

---

[341] K. Katzarov, *The Theory of Nationalization* (The Hague: Martinus Nijhoff, 1964).

[342] A. Rabuska, *Hong Kong: A Study in Economic Freedom* (Chicago: Univ. of Chicago Press, 1979).

[343] According to "Survey: Singapore, the Sovereign Municipality" in *The Economist*, December 29, 1979, bureaucracy is organized very competitively in Singapore. For example, no less than four or five bureaus are involved in commercial and private housing and mixed enterprises and contracting out also supplement this market reducing "concentration" of any agency or bureau.

redistribution exists in Singapore to an extent well beyond Hong Kong, *e.g.*, income taxes are much higher and progressive, reflecting the absence of the external check of London.

Historian N. V. Nelles,[344] following in the tradition set by Harold Innis,[345] points out that the history of Canada has been a continual struggle of economic interests waged through the public sector.[346] One weapon, Nelles points out, is the tariff; the other, he notes, is the government firm. I invite other scholars to join me in the future in examining this thesis more closely and eventually generalizing and testing this proposition with the end in mind of understanding what particular activities of the state are conducive to the generation of net wealth and what merely transfer it about. Only when this is well understood will policy discussions about the proper role for Crown corporations, as well as calls for "privitizations", contracting-out and de-regulation, be informed by more than ideologically intense speculations. Furthermore, only by realizing the difference between the efficient policing and enforcement of exchange of truly public goods and the efficient, but coercive, transfer of rents between citizens can politically feasible "reorganizations" be made, reducing both the resistance from producers of public services and self-interested seekers of costly transfers.

This paper has much in common with the early work of Coase[347] and Stigler[348] and of the recent contributions of McManus.[349] First, I have spelled out, in detail, a vision of a model, but like the similar models of Coase and McManus upon which it closely draws, mine is not overly rich in implications. Operationalizing the theory will require ways of measuring the notion of complexity, *i.e.*, bargaining, monitoring and enforcement difficulties, and those factors that enhance and make more selective redistributions. Rather too many possibilities are being explained to be of great theoretical use so far. Saying what cannot happen is more important than

---

[344] See Nelles, *supra* note 21 (both articles).

[345] Innis, *supra* note 21.

[346] A large and long literature in Canadian economic history, with its intellectual roots in Innis' methodology ought to be mentioned here, since it stresses the redistribution aspects of state intervention, but also recognizes the complexity monitoring issue as well. Authors to peruse are H. Aitken, "Defensive Expansion: The State and Economic Growth in Canada" in *The State and Economic Growth*, Aitken, ed. (New York: Social Science Research Council, 1959); C. A. Ashley, *The First Twenty-Five Years—A Study of Trans-Canada Airlines* (Toronto: MacMillan, 1963); G. E. Britnell, "Public Ownership of Telephones in Prairie Provinces" [Unpublished Master's thesis, Univ. of Toronto, 1934]; Gracey, *supra* note 218; Fowke, *supra* note 21; F. W. Peers, *The Politics of Canadian Broadcasting 1920-1950* (Toronto: Univ. of Toronto Press, 1969); D. W. Smythe, "A Study of Saskatchewan Tele-communications" [Unpublished paper, Dept. of Communications, Gvt. of Canada, July 1974].

[347] Coase, *supra* note 209.

[348] Stigler, *supra* note 150.

[349] McManus, *supra* note 211; *supra* note 274; and *supra* note 208.

what is possible.[350] Concentrating on selected cases rather than broad aggregates is clearly called for here, if the maze of constraints and myriad of interests are to be sorted out.

This paper, except for the brief, descriptive part V(d), also makes rather too much of a distinction between the various means of affecting public supplies. Just as Stigler and others recognize the limitation of the capture theory of regulation (one interest owns the authority), so I do not believe supply choices are mutually exclusive. My corner solution analytics need to be relaxed more than my small discussion in part V(d) permitted. It should be realized that any policy will be carried out by "bits" of each supply institution in the real world.[351] More work on the possibility of complementarities as well as substitutions between alternative supply mechanisms is clearly called for.[352]

The major task for economists studying politics is the modeling of the articulation of political demands and supplies where transactions costs must necessarily be the main set of predictive variables. Though far away from a satisfactory solution, intelligent forays are currently being made. I trust this essay will aid those formulating specific economic models of politics and their application to highly specific sets of public supply decisions.

---

[350] This criticism is John McManus' based on conversations. Cheung, "A Theory of Price Control" (1974), 17 *J. of Law and Econ.* 53 at 55, puts it more precisely in the context of price floors and ceilings: "To interpret the effects of price control, as to interpret any economic behaviour, the specified constraint must be rigid enough to yield implications refutable by facts. . . . If certain outcomes are to be attributed to the control, and that one control usually differs from another, it is highly unlikely that the actual constraints can be guessed correctly."

[351] This admonition was reinforced in a communication to me by Keith Acheson.

[352] Enrichment of a theory seldom comes without cost. If readers endeavour to explain the institutional mix on the basis of the various indicators of contractual difficulties and precise redistributive desires, they will at once run into one significant problem—assigning effects *a priori*. When the relative price between the two items changes, all other things being equal, the First Law of Demand can be invoked. When two prices change between three closely related goods, no such statement can be made since cross-effects confound predictions. The only way the latter can be ignored is to assume they sum to zero. This has a rather strong implication, however, namely that the choice among instruments is all-or-none, the corner solution case. See Borcherding and Silberburg, "Shipping the Good Apples Out: The Alchian and Allen Theorem Reconsidered" (1978), 86 *J. of Pol. Econ.* 131.

Supplemental Bibliography

Acheson, K.   "Revenue vs. Protection: The Pricing of Wine by the Liquor Control Board of Ontario" (1977), 10 *Can. J. Econ.* 246.

Akerlof, G. A.   "The Market for 'Lemons': Quality Uncertainty and the Market Mechanism" (1970), 84 *Q.J. Econ.* 488.

Ames, E.   *Soviet Economic Processes* (Homewood, Illinois: Irwin, 1965).

Arrow, K. J.   *Limits of Organization* (New York: W. W. Norton, 1974).

Baratz, M. S.   *The Economics of the Postal Service* (Washington: Public Affairs Press, 1962).

Barzel, Y.   "Some Fallacies in the Interpretation of Information Costs" (1977), 20 *J. Law and Econ.* 291.

Bator, F. M.   *The Question of Government Spending: Public Needs and Private Wants* (New York: Harper and Row, 1960).

Bendix, R.   *Work and Authority* (New York: Wiley, 1956).

Bennett, J. T. & Johnson, M. H.   "Paperwork and Bureaucracy" (1979), 17 *Economic Inquiry* 435.

_____.   "Public Versus Private Provisions of Collective Goods and Services: Garbage Collection Revisited" (1979), 34 *Public Choice* 55.

Bergson, A.   *The Economics of Socialist Planning* (New Haven: Yale University Press, 1964).

_____.   "Optimal Pricing for a Public Enterprise" (1972), 86 *Q.J. Econ.* 519.

Blakeney, A. W.   "Saskatchewan Crown Corporations" in *The Public Corporation: A Comparative Symposium*, W. Friedmann, ed. (Toronto: Carswell, 1954).

Blankart, Beat   "Zur ökonomischen Theorie der Bürokratie" (1975), 30 *Public Finance* 166.

Bös, D.   *Economic Theory of Public Enterprise* (New York: Springer-Verlag, forthcoming 1982).

Breton, A.   "Modelling the Behavior of Exchequers" in *Issues in Canadian Economics*, L. H. Officer and L. B. Smith, eds. (Toronto: McGraw-Hill Ryerson, 1974).

Breton, A. & Wintrobe, R. S.   "The Equilibrium Size of a Budget-Maximizing Bureau: A Note on Niskanen's Theory of Bureaucracy" (1975), 83 *J. Pol. Econ.* 195.

Browning, E. K.   *Redistribution and the Welfare System* (Washington: American Enterprise Institute, 1975).

Cabney, C. W.   "Public Enterprise in Saskatchewan" in *Public Enter-*

prise: A Study of Its Organization and Management in Various Countries, A. H. Hanson, ed. (New York: International Institute of Administrative Science, 1955).

Campbell, J. I., Jr. "Politics and the Future of Postal Service" in *Perspectives on Postal Service Issues*, R. Sherman, ed. (Washington: American Enterprise Institute for Public Policy Research, 1980).

Canadian Tax Foundation "Crown Corporations" in *The National Finances: An Analysis of the Revenue and Expenditures of The Government of Canada, 1929-79* (Toronto: Canadian Tax Foundation, 1979).

Canes, M. *Telephones—Public or Private* (London: The Institute of Economic Affairs, 1966).

Coase, R. H. *British Broadcasting: A Study in Monopoly* (London: Longmans Green, 1950).

————. "The Lighthouse in Economics" (1974), 17 *J. Law and Econ.* 357.

Corbett, D. C. "Liquor Control Administration in British Columbia: A Study in Public Enterprise" (1959), 2 *Can. Pub. Admin.* 19.

————. *Politics and the Airlines* (London: George Allen and Unwin, 1965).

Courant, P., Gramlich E. & Rubinfeld, D. C. "Public Employee Market Power and the Level of Government Spending" (1979), 69 *Am. Econ. Rev.* 806.

Courchene, T. J. "The Theory of Bureaus and the Bank of Canada" [unpublished ms. presented to the Canadian Economics Association Meetings, June, 1974].

Crozier, M. *The Bureaucratic Phenomenon* (Chicago: University of Chicago Press, 1964).

Darby, M. R. & Karni, E. "Free Competition and the Optimal Amount of Fraud" (1973), 16 *J. Law and Econ.* 67.

Demsetz, H. "Information and Efficiency: Another Viewpoint" (1969), 12 *J. Law and Econ.* 1.

Drache, D. "Rediscovering Canadian Political Economy" (1976), 11(3) *J. Can. Studies* 3.

Dye, T. R. *Politics, Economics and the Public: Policy Outcomes in the American States* (Chicago: Rand McNally, 1966).

Edwards, F. R. "Managerial Objectives in Regulated Industries—Preference Behavior in Banking" (1977), 85 *J. Pol. Econ.* 147.

Feiwal, G. R. *The Economics of Socialist Enterprise* (New York: Praeger, 1965).

The Financial Post "Taxpayer's Guide to the Business of Government" January 1, 1978.

Fitch, L. C. "Increasing the Role of the Private Sector in Providing

Public Services" in *Improving the Quality of Urban Management, Vol. 8 Urban Affairs Review Annual,* W. D. Hawley and D. Rogers, eds. (Beverly Hills, California: Saga, 1974).

Foster, C. D.   *Politics, Finance and the Role of Economics: An Essay on the Control of Public Enterprise* (London: Allen and Unwin, 1971).

Friedman, M. "The Monetary Theory and Policy of Henry Simons" (1967), 10 *J. Law and Econ.* 1.

Friedman, W. G. & Garner, J. F.   *Government Enterprise: A Comparative Study* (New York: Columbia University, 1970).

Furubotn, E. & Pejovich, S.   "Property Rights and the Behavior of the Firm in a Socialist state: The Example of Yugoslavia" (1970), 30 *Zeitschrift for National Ökonomie* 431.

_____. "Property Rights and Economic Theory: A Survey of Recent Literature" (1972), 10 *J. Econ. Lit.* 1137.

Fuss, M. A.   "Cost Allocation: How Can the Costs of Postal Services Be Determined?" in *Perspectives on Postal Service Issues,* R. Sherman, ed. (Washington: American Enterprise Institute for Public Policy Research, 1980).

Goldberg, V.   "Peltzman on Regulations and Politics" [Unpublished ms., University of California at Davis, July 1979].

Hayek, F. A.   ed. *Collectivist Economic Planning* (London: Allen and Unwin, 1935).

Hazlewood, A.   "Telephone Service" in *Public Enterprises: Selected Readings,* R. Turvey, ed. (Middlesex, U.K.: Penguin, 1968).

Herzlinger, R. & Kane, N. M.   *A Managerial Analysis of Federal Income Redistribution Mechanisms: The Government as Factory, Insurance Company and Bank* (Cambridge, Mass.: Ballinger, 1979).

Hirsch, W. Z.   "The Economics of Shirking and Its Implications for the Public Sector" in *Secular Trends of the Public Sector,* 23rd Session, Congres d'Edinborough 1975, H. C. Recktenwald, ed. (Paris: Editions Cujas, 1978).

Holland, S.   *The State as Entrepreneur: New Dimension in Public Enterprise* (London: Weidenfeld, 1972).

Horsefield, J. K.   "British and American Postal Services" in *Public Enterprises: Selected Readings,* R. Turvey, ed. (Middlesex, U.K.: Penguin, 1968).

Hughes, J. R. T.   "Roots of Regulation" in *Regulatory Change in an Atmosphere of Crisis,* G. Walton, ed. (New York: Academic Press, 1979).

Jewkes, J.   *Public and Private Enterprise* (London: Routledge and Kegan Paul, 1965).

Joskow, P. L.   "Pricing Decisions of Regulated Firms: A Behavioural Approach" (1973), 4 *Bell J. Econ. and Mgmt. Sci.* 118.

Knight, F. H.   *Risk, Uncertainty and Profit* (New York: Harper and Row, 1965).

Kohlmeir, L. M., Jr. *The Regulators* (New York: Harper and Row, 1969).

Kristjanson, K. "Crown Corporations: Administrative Responsibility" (1968), 11 *Can. Pub. Admin.* 454.

Lange, O. & Taylor, F. M. *On the Economic Theory of Socialism* (Minneapolis: University of Minnesota Press, 1938).

Lerner, A. P. *The Economics of Control* (London: MacMillan 1944).

McCormick, R. E. & Tollison, R. D. "An Economic Theory of Legislation: Some First Principles" in *Towards a Theory of a Rent Seeking Society*, R. D. Tollison, G. Tullock, and J. M. Buchanan, eds. (College Station, Texas: A. & M. Press, 1980).

MacEachern, W. A. "Corporate Control and Risk" (1976), 14 *Econ. Inquiry* 270.

McKean, R. N. "Divergences between Individual and Total Costs Within Government" (1964), 54 *Am. Econ. Rev.: Papers and Proceedings* 243.

————. "Government and The Consumer" (1973), 39 *S. Econ. J.* 481.

————. "The Unseen Hand in Government" (1965), 55 *Am. Econ. Rev.* 496.

McManus, J. "The Theory of the International Firm" in *The Multinational Firm and the Nation State*, G. Pacquet, ed. (Toronto: Collier-McMillan, 1972).

MacNeil, I. R. "The Many Futures of Contracts" (1974), 47 *S. Cal. L. Rev.* 691.

Mallory, J. R. "Commentary: The Political Economy Tradition in Canada" (1976), 11(3) *J. Can. Studies* 18.

Malmgren, H. "Information, Expectations and the Theory of the Firm" (1961), 75 *Q.J. Econ.* 399.

Mann, P. C. " User Power and Electricity Rates" (1974), 17 *J. Law and Econ.* 433.

————. "Publicly-Owned Electric Utility Profits and Resource Allocation" (1970), 46 *Land Economics* 478.

Mann, P. C. & Mikesell, J. L. "Tax Payments and Electric Utility Prices" (1971), 38 *S. Econ. J.* 69.

March, J. C. & Simon, H. A. *Organizations* (New York: Wiley, 1958).

Marshall, J. M. "Private Information and Public Information" (1974), 64 *Am. Econ. Rev.* 373.

Meade, J. E. *Planning and the Price Mechanism* (London: George Allen and Unwin, 1948).

Migué, J. L. & Belanger, G. "Towards a General Theory of Managerial Discretion" (1974), 17 *Public Choice* 27.

Moore, T. G. "The Effectiveness of Regulation of Electric Utility Prices" (1970), 36 *S. Econ. J.* 365.

Moreland, R. Scott "Managerial Discretion, Property Rights and The Theory of Firms" (unpublished ms., March 1972).

Moses, R.   *Public Works: A Dangerous Trade* (New York: McGraw-Hill, 1970).

Nelson, P.   "Political Information" (1976), 19 *J. Law and Econ.* 215.

Newhouse, J. P.   "Toward a Theory of Nonprofit Institutions: An Economic Model of a Hospital" (1970), 60 *Am. Econ. Rev.* 64.

Nove, A.   "The Problem of 'Success Indicators' in Soviet Industry" (1958), N.S. 25 *Economica* 1.

_____.   *The Soviet Economy: An Introduction* Rev. Ed. (New York: Praeger, 1966).

Panzar, J. C. & Willig, R. D.   "Economies of Scale in Multi-Output Production" (1977), 91 *Q.J. Econ.* 481.

Parkinson, C. N.   *Parkinson's Law and Other Studies in Administration* (Boston: Houghton-Mifflin, 1957).

Pauly, M.   "The Economics of Moral Hazard" (1968), 58 *Am. Econ. Rev.* 531.

Pauly, M. & Radisch, M.   "The Not-for-Profit Hospital as a Physician's Co-operative" (1973), 63 *Am. Econ. Rev.* 87.

Peterson, G. M.   "Voter Demand for Public School Experience" in *Public Needs and Private Behavior in Metropolitan Areas*, J. E. Jackson, ed. (Cambridge: Ballinger, 1975).

Peterson, W. assisted by Heath, M.   "Crown Corporation Boards" in *Canadian Directorship Practices: A Self-Examination of Ottawa* (Ottawa: Conference Board of Canada, 1977).

Polyani, M.   "Towards a Theory of Conspicuous Production" (1960), 34 [*Soviet*] *Survey* 90.

Portes, R. D.   "The Enterprise under Central Planning" (1969), 36 *Rev. Econ. Stud.* 197.

Posner, R. A.   "Natural Monopoly and Its Regulation" (1969), 21 *Stan. L. Rev.* 548.

_____.   "Theories of Economic Regulation" (1974), 5 *Bell J. Econ. and Mgmt. Sci.* 335.

Rabuska, A. & Shepsle, K. A.   *Politics in Plural Societies: A Theory of Democratic Instability* (Columbus: Charles Merril, 1972).

Recktenwald, H. C.   ed., *Secular Trends of the Public Sector*, 23rd Session, Congres d'Edinborough 1975 (Paris: Editions Cujas, 1978).

Ripley, R. B. & Associates   *CETA Prime Sponsor Management Decisions and Program Goal Achievement*, Employment and Training Monograph No. 56 (Washington: Government Printing Office, 1978).

Robbins, L.   *The Theory of Economic Policy in English Classical Political Economy* (London: Macmillan, 1952).

Roberts, P. C.   "Drewnoski's Economic Theory of Socialism" (1968), 76 *J. Pol. Econ.* 645.

_____.   "The Polycentric Soviet Economy" (1969), 12 *J. Law and Econ.* 163.

Roberts, P. C. & Stephenson, M. A.   "Alienation and Central Planning in Marx" and "Reply: The Oneness of Socialism and Central Planning in Marx" (1968), 27 *Slavic Review* 470, 477.

Ruttan, V. W.   "Bureaucratic Productivity: The Case of Agricultural Research" (1980), 35 *Public Choice* 529.

Selznick, P.   *TVA and Grass Roots* (Berkeley: University of California Press, 1949).

Sexty, R. W.   "Direction, Control and Accountability of Crown Corporations: Review and Analysis of Government Proposals" (1979), 17 *Osgoode Hall L.J.* 193.

_____.   "Independent Strategies of Crown Corporation Management" (1978), 9(3) *Optimum—A Forum for Management* 5.

_____.   "Profit Role in Crown Corporations" (1978), 5 *Can. Bus. Rev.* 9.

Shapiro, D. L.   "The Nature of the Public Firm" in *Frontiers of Economics*, Vol. I, G. Tullock, ed. (Blacksburg, Virginia: University Publications, 1975).

Shenfield, A.   "The Public versus the Private Sector in Britain" (1961-62), 6(1) *Modern Age*, 43.

Shepherd, W. G.   *Economic Performance under Public Enterprise* (New Haven: Yale University Press, 1965).

_____.   "Cross-Subsidization in Coal" in *Public Enterprises: Selected Readings*, R. Turvey, ed. (Middlesex, U.K.: Penguin, 1968).

_____.   "Residential Telephone Service in Britain" in *Public Enterprises: Selected Readings*, R. Turvey, ed. (Middlesex, U.K.: Penguin, 1968).

Shonfield, A. *Modern Capitalism: The Changing Balance of Public and Private Power* (New York: Oxford University Press, 1969).

Simon, J. L.   "The Economic Effects of State Monopoly of Packaged-Liquor Retailing" (1966), 74 *J. Pol. Econ.* 188.

Simons, H. C.   "Hansen on Fiscal Policy" in *Economic Policy for a Free Society*, H. C. Simons, ed. (Chicago: University of Chicago Press, 1948).

_____.   "A Positive Program for Laissez-Faire: Some Proposals for a Liberal Economic Policy" in *Economic Policy for a Free Society*, H. C. Simons, ed. (Chicago: University of Chicago Press, 1948).

Smith, S. P.   *Equal Pay in the Public Sector: Fact or Fantasy* (Princeton, New Jersey: Industrial Relations Section Series, Department of Economics, Princeton University, 1977).

Sorkin, A.   *The Economics of the Postal System: Alternatives and Reform* (Lexington, Mass.: Lexington Books, 1980).

Stigler, G. J.   "The Division of Labor is Limited by the Extent of the Market" (1951), 59 *J. Pol. Econ.* 185.

_____.   "The Economics of Information" (1961), 69 *J. Pol. Econ.* 213.

_____.   "A Theory of Oligopoly" (1964), 72 *J. Pol. Econ.* 44.

Stigler, G. J., in collaboration with Friedland, Clare   "What can Regulators Regulate?: The Case of Electricity" (1962), 5 *J. Law and Econ.* 1.

Stockfish, J. A. "Analysis of Bureaucratic Behavior: The Ill-Defined Process" (Santa Monica: Rand Corporation, January, 1976).

_____. *The Political Economy of Bureaucracy* (New York: General Learning Press, 1972).

Trebilcock, M. H. "The De-Regulation Debate: Interests and Ideologies" [unpublished ms., Faculty of Law, University of Toronto, May, 1979].

Trebilcock, M. H., Waverman, L. & Prichard, J. R. S. "Markets for Regulation: Implications for Performance Standards and Institutional Design" in *Government Regulation—Issues and Alternatives 1978* (Toronto: Ontario Economic Council, 1978).

Tullock, G. "The Transitional Gains Trap" (1975), 6 *Bell J. Econ. Mgmt. Sci.* 671.

Vining, A. R. "The History, Nature, Role and Future of Provincial Hydro Utilities" [unpublished ms., University of British Columbia, 1979].

Wallace, R. L. & Junk, P. E. "Economic Inefficiency of Small Municipal Electrical Generating Systems" (1970), 46 *Land Economics* 98.

Waverman, L. "Pricing Principles: How to Price Post Office Services" in *Perspectives on Postal Service Issues*, R. Sherman, ed. (Washington: American Enterprise Institute for Public Policy Research, 1980).

Weisbrod, B. A. "Some Collective-Good Aspects of Non-Government Activities: Not For-Profit Organizations" in *Secular Trends of the Public Sector,* 23rd Session, Congres d'Edinborough 1975, H. C. Recktenwald, ed. (Paris: Editions Cujas, 1978).

Williamson, O. E. *The Economics of Discretionary Behavior: Managerial Objectives in a Theory of the Firm* (Englewood Cliffs, New Jersey: Prentice Hall, 1964).

Wilson, J. Q. "The Politics of Regulation" in *Social Responsibility and the Business Predicament,* J. K. McKie, ed. (Washington, The Brookings Institution, 1974).

CHAPTER 3

THE POLITICS OF PUBLIC ENTERPRISE*

MARSHA A. CHANDLER†

I. INTRODUCTION

Studies of public ownership in Canada have commonly had as their objectives the specification of the characteristics of government enterprise and the categorization of many structural forms and mechanisms for political control.[1] This has meant an emphasis on description and typology in which the central anlytical issues have been the problems of the extent and nature of the accountability of Crown corporations to government authority.

No one would question the importance of this kind of structural analysis, but at the same time it is essential to recognize that exclusive reliance on these concerns has led to a number of rather critical gaps in our understanding of public ownership as an instrument of policy. In particular such analysis has neglected questions concerning the establishment and impact of Crown corporations. Under what conditions and why are Crown corporations created? What are the economic and social functions performed by these entities? Who benefits and who is disadvantaged by their actions?

Essentially, the politics of public ownership has had a one-sided focus with the bulk of attention on the policies of control, that is, the process by which corporations are linked to the government. It is as if one were to ex-

* This study was funded by the Law & Economics Programme, the Faculty of Law at the University of Toronto. I would like to thank George Cadbury for his helpful comments.
† Associate Professor, Department of Political Science, University of Toronto.
[1] See, *e.g.,* Hodgetts, "The Public Corporation in Canada", in *The Public Corporation,* W. Friedman, ed. (Toronto: Carswell, 1954); C. A. Ashley and R. G. H. Smails, *Canadian Crown Corporations* (Toronto: Macmillan of Canada, 1965); Balls, "The Financial Control and Accountability of Canadian Crown Corporations" (1953), 31 *Public Administration* 127; Langford, "The identification and classification of federal public corporations: a preface to regime building" (1980), 23 *Can. Pub. Admin.* 76; Sexty, "Direction, Control and Accountability of Crown Corporations: Review and Analysis of Government Proposals" (1979), 17 *Osgoode Hall L.J.* 193; Hodgetts, "The Public Corporation in Canada" in *Government Enterprise,* W. Friedmann and J. F. Garner, eds. (New York: Columbia University Press, 1970); Kristjanson, "Crown Corporations: Administration Responsibility and Public Accountability" (1968), 11 *Can. Pub. Admin.* 454; Langford, "Crown Corporations as Instruments of Policy" in *Public Policy in Canada*, 2nd ed., G. B. Doern and P. Aucoin, eds. (Toronto: Macmillan of Canada, 1979).

amine public expenditures as instruments of policy focusing only on supply procedures, the Public Accounts Committee and the Auditor General. Clearly a great deal would be missing, and large parts of the political process would be ignored.

The purpose of the essays in this volume is to expand the systematic analysis of the policy processes in which the state plays a direct role in the economy. The object of this particular essay is to address the issue of the origins of public ownership by examining the relationship between public ownership and political parties. Because they recruit political elites through elections and bear responsibility for public policy as governments, political parties are inevitably at the centre of the political process.[2] No thorough treatment of political decision-making can succeed without some consideration and clarification of the role of political parties. The question before us is whether partisan political forces influence the use of public ownership, and if so, how.

The analysis is divided into four main sections. The first is a review and evaluation of prevailing explanations of state intervention in the economy. This is followed by a discussion of the theoretical basis for associating partisanship with public enterprise. In the third section we assess the empirical linkages between party politics and patterns of public ownership. By examining provincial public enterprise since 1920 we will trace the effect of party ideology by comparing the policies of provincial governments controlled by parties of the left with those controlled by nonleft parties. And in the final section we seek to explain the apparent anomaly of public ownership produced by the nonleft and to show that the nature of Crown corporations established by social democratic parties differs significantly from those created by other parties. Taken together the analysis will provide a framework to explain the effects of partisanship on the development of state enterprise.

II. EXPLANATIONS OF STATE INTERVENTION

(a) Environment, Culture and Pragmatism

Extensive direct intervention in the economy by both provincial and federal governments is a major characteristic of Canada's political economy. Whether the activity involves the provision of the transportation or other infra-structure, direct financing of industrial development or the ex-

---

2 Any Canadian political science text attests to the centrality of political parties. See, *e.g.*, R. J. Van Loon and M. S. Whittington, *The Canadian Political System*, 2nd ed. (Toronto: McGraw-Hill Ryerson, 1976); and P.W. Fox, *Politics: Canada*, 4th ed. (Toronto: McGraw-Hill Ryerson, 1977).

ploitation of natural resources, the state has continued to play a crucial role in shaping the economy. Indeed, a major point of comparison between the United States and Canada has been the far greater use of public enterprise in Canada. Although examples of collectivism antedate Confederation, there has been a recent expansion in the size and scope of public ownership. Some 70 percent of the existing Crown corporations have been created since 1960. What factors have contributed to the development of government enterprise? Although each instance of public ownership may be explained in part by its own unique circumstances, more general explanations have been put forward. Environmental factors, political culture and ideological pragmatism constitute the main factors that have been used to explain why Canadian governments have turned to public ownership.

The *environmental* explanation is based on a geographic, economic, and social functionalism. It argues that the pattern of public enterprise is due in large part to the effect of certain characteristics of the environment. Gracey states one version of the thesis:

> In the main, our significant reliance on public enterprise can be attributed to the Canadian situation: a vast country, rich in natural resources but small in population, bordering on the U.S., the most dominant economic power in the world.[3]

It is sometimes argued that whereas the opening of the American West spawned an agrarian-based, rugged individualism which pre-empted extensive state involvement, in Canada the "hard frontier" created barriers to economic development which demanded collective action beyond the scope of any individual. State support was further necessitated by the scarcity of capital, the need to facilitate production and marketing and the persistent threat of an aggressive American economy.[4]

The provision of railroads and hydro-electric power were two of the most important functions taken on by governments to facilitate economic development. As succeeding staples became the basis for economic growth, early patterns of public sector support for private economic development have been continued into the present.[5] Provincial (as well as federal) governments have sought to mitigate the effects of an inhospitable environment by taking on those tasks necessary for economic development which were often felt to be beyond the capacity of the private sector.[6] Crown cor-

---

[3] Gracey, "Public Enterprise in Canada" in *Public Enterprise and the Public Interest*, A. Gélinas, ed. (Toronto: The Institute of Public Administration of Canada, 1978) at 25.

[4] See, *e.g.*, S. D. Clark, *The Developing Canadian Community* (Toronto: University of Toronto Press, 1962).

[5] Aitken, "Defensive Expansion: The State and Economic Growth in Canada" in *Approaches to Canadian Economic History*, W. T. Easterbrook and M. H. Watkins, eds. (Toronto: McClelland and Stewart, 1967).

[6] Allan Tupper, "The Nation's Businesses: Canadian Concepts of Public Enterprise" [Kingston: unpublished Ph.D. Thesis, Queen's Unversity, 1977].

porations in British Columbia, Ontario, Alberta, Saskatchewan and Quebec which subsidize the development of each province's northern region are modern examples of the state's effort to overcome the limits of geography. A variant of the functional mode of explanation is found in the argument that widely differing western provincial governments have all increased their use of public ownership in a common response to the problem of regional dependency and hinterland status.[7]

Unlike the environmental explanation which focuses on objective external conditions, the concept of *political culture* suggests a dominant belief system within each polity which structures the definition and solution of social problems. It must be emphasized that political culture implies a more broadly held and a more diffuse set of shared attitudes and values than contained in the concept of ideology.

In Canada the "fragment theory" is the most prevalent form of the political culture argument. Formulated by Louis Hartz, the fragment theory contends that North American political cultures are derived from the European ideologies carried over by succeeding waves of immigrants.[8] Those who have applied Hartz' thesis to Canada argue that Canada is a dual fragment society, in which both Liberal and Conservative values took hold.[9] Gad Horowitz has further developed this interpretation by contending that the conservative concern for the organic unity of the community and the consequent willingness to use public power to preserve the organic unit constitutes a distinctive part of Canadian political culture.[10] This "Tory touch", Horowitz claims, is deeply woven into the fiber of Canadian beliefs and has generated a willingness among political and business elites to use the power of the state for purposes of economic growth. Thus there is some consensus running through socialists, liberals and conservatives in Canada which has provided the basis for a solid tradition of government enterprise.[11]

The cultural predisposition towards interventionism may in principle be found among any elites regardless of partisan affiliation and may therefore provide an explanation for the lack of fit between party and policy. In this additional sense it is quite distinct from manifest ideology which can be associated with particular political parties.

---

[7] Berkowitz, "Forms of State Economy and the Development of Western Canada" (1979), 4 *Can. J. Socio.* 287.

[8] L. Hartz, *The Founding of New Societies* (New York: Harcourt, Brace and World, 1964).

[9] See McRae, "The Structure of Canadian History" in *ibid.* For a comparison of various interpretations of Hartz' thesis see D. Bell and L. Tepperman, *The Roots of Disunity* (Toronto: McClelland and Stewart, 1979).

[10] Horowitz, "Conservatism, Liberalism, and Socialism in Canada" (1966), 32 *Can. J. Econ. Pol. Sci.* 143.

[11] For a disscussion of the cultural thesis see H. V. Nelles, *The Politics of Development* (Toronto: Macmillan of Canada, 1974) and H. Hardin, *A Nation Unaware* (Vancouver: J. J. Douglas, 1974).

Pragmatism, the third approach to public ownership is somewhat of a catchall explanation. Because it focuses on specific adaptations to unique events, pragmatism in fact encompasses a host of explanations; but because pragmatic adaptation has been used so often as an explanation in and of itself it is best seen as a distinctive approach.[12] Alexander Brady states the pragmatist perspective:

> This collectivism is throughout empirical shaped by the thinking of those who are concerned with practical problems of the moment and the exigency of given situation.[13]

The common thread in this view of public ownership is that when in power political leaders regardless of ideology respond similarly to stimuli. Although distinctive party ideology may be one of the factors to be included in the calculus, other forces and events vitiate its impact.[14] The pragmatic argument holds that the creation of public enterprise can be traced to particular situations rather than the workings of any political philosophy. Tupper describes the basis of this explanation:

> Public enterprise is pragmatic because it emanates neither from socialism nor from any clear consistent or principled preference for state provision of goods or services. . . . Public enterprise is also pragmatic because it is nonpartisan and not consistently related to the party struggle. Most Canadian political parties have established government business despite their espoused belief in private enterprise and individual initiation.[15]

(b) Problems of Explanation

Taken individually or in conjunction, the environmental, cultural and pragmatic explanations are of limited utility for the analysis of provincial state enterprise. Environment and cultural explanations have been used mainly at the national level and in most cases much of the argument is developed in the context of comparison with the United States or United Kingdom.[16] The focus of comparison tends to be gross policy distinctions among nation-states rather than more specific decisions within a single national setting.

As Richard Simeon argues, environmental approaches are best viewed

---

[12] The pragmatic approach is illustrated in L. D. Musolf, *Public Ownership and Accountability* (Cambridge: Harvard Unversity Press, 1959).

[13] Brady, "The State and Economic Life" in *Canada,* G. W. Brown, ed. (Berkeley: University of California Press, 1950) at 366.

[14] See D. Corbett, *Politics and the Airlines* (Toronto: Allen and Unwin, 1965).

[15] Tupper, *supra* note 6, at 8.

[16] See, *e.g.*, King, "Ideas, Institutions and the Policies of Governments: A Comparative Analysis: Parts I, II, III" (1973), 3 *Br. J. Pol. Sci.* 291 (Parts I, II) and 409 (Part III).

as starting points of analysis.[17] Although they constitute conditions that are the basis for political demands and also set constraints on decision-makers in terms of the availability of resources, there is no mechanism whereby environmental factors are automatically translated into public policy. Environmental circumstances should be seen as providing the potential for political cleavages and policy choice. For policy effects to occur, these conditions must be translated into politically significant factors. Explanations that are based solely on environmental factors tend to ignore the crucial conversion process.

Within Canada, there is little evidence of significant cultural variation that can be systematically related to the wide differences in patterns of public enterprise. Where there are findings of variation among regional or provincial cultures the differences are in terms of individual feelings of efficacy and trust of government, rates of participation and bases of electoral cleavage, none of which appear to be related to public intervention.[18] Moreover, where regional orientations toward state intervention or attitudes on economic issues have been studied, the findings support a convergence hypothesis. There is evidence of a cross-regional, general trend toward greater sympathy for an expanded role of government.[19]

As formulated by Horowitz, political culture describes a constant value in Canadian political life which cannot help us to explain the variations in government entrepreneurship. Clearly in many situations, governments have preferred other instruments such as subsidies, tax incentives or regulation which normally carry with them a more restricted role for state involvement. If the cultural hypothesis is to be useful, we must formulate it as a variable.

The pragmatic approach provides no general criteria for analysis. Each case is considered to be the result of a particular constellation of forces. The major generalization to be derived from this approach is the proposition that when conditions have been favourable, governments have created Crown corporations. Although the pragmatic approach, like case study analysis generally, can yield a rich volume of detail and information about a particular set of circumstances, its explanatory power is not based on a systematic framework and therefore it has little predictive value.

---

[17] Simeon, "Studying Public Policy" (1976), 9 *Can. J. Pol. Sci.* 548.

[18] For these findings on regional differences, see Simeon and Elkins, "Provincial Political Cultures in Canada" in *Small Worlds: Provinces and Parties in Canadian Political Life*, D. J. Elkins and R. Simeon, eds. (Toronto: Metheun, 1980); W. Mishler, *Political Participation in Canada: Prospects for Democratic Citizenship* (Toronto: Macmillan of Canada, 1979); Wilson, "The Canadian Political Cultures: Towards a Redefinition of the Nature of the Canadian Political System" (1974), 7 *Can. J. Pol. Sci.* 438; Jenson, "Party Systems" in *The Provincial Political Systems*, D. J. Bellamy et al., eds. (Toronto: Methuen, 1976).

[19] Simeon and Blake, "Regional Preferences: Citizens' Views of Public Policy" in *Small Worlds: Provinces and Parties in Canadian Political Life, supra* note 18.

III. PROVINCIAL POLITICS AND PARTY IDEOLOGY

(a) Party-Policy Linkages

Running through all three explanatory approaches is a striking disregard for political forces. Although each explanation is concerned with the outputs of the political process there is little attention to the ways in which parts of the political system regularly influence policy-making. The major assumption appears to be that political institutions have little independent effect, and variations in policy are due mainly to factors outside political structures. In the cases of the environmental and pragmatic approaches, public policy is pre-eminently the result of responses to exogenous forces. Even in the cultural case, the focus is on the common characteristics that determine the way all Canadian governments deal with social problems, rather than the variations among governments.

In its tendency to disregard political forces the study of public enterprise is quite distinct from the general analysis of public policy. Nowhere is this more apparent that in the consideration of the role of political parties. There is little evidence of the debate that has been a central point of controversy in the policy literature: the question of whether the characteristics of the party in power shape the nature of public policy.

The proposition that variations in policy outputs might be explained by the differences in the party in power is predicated on the ideological distinctiveness among parties and/or differences in each party's constituent groups. For even if the parties fail to articulate different policies, it is assumed that their actions in government will reflect the differences in their sources of support. Policy impact may also result from variation in the provincial party system in which parties compete. In other words, the structure of the situation may have a predictable effect on the policy-making of the party in power. For example, the nature of the opposition or the extent of one-party dominance over time may affect the kinds of policies promulgated by the party in power.

Despite the broad theoretical bases for expecting partisanship and other party-related variables to influence policy, the early empirical studies in the United States and Canada found little evidence of such relationships.[20] Subsequent research has pointed to a number of serious methodological and conceptual flaws in these studies but perhaps the most important

---

[20] For a summary of the U.S. material see T. R. Dye, *Politics, Economics, and the Public* (Chicago: Rand McNally, 1966). For the Canadian findings see D. J. Falcone and M. S. Whittington, "Output Change in Canada: A Preliminary Attempt to Open the 'Black Box' " [unpublished paper presented to Canadian Political Science Association, June 1972]. See also R. M. Bird, *The Growth of Government Spending in Canada* (Toronto: Canadian Tax Foundation, 1970).

criticism is the inadequate conceptualization and operationalization of the dependent variable—public policies.

By relying on expenditures as the sole indicator of policy these initial studies failed to consider other modes of policy-making, such as regulation and taxation, that are not well represented by expenditures. Also by focusing solely on expenditures, the analysis fails to consider the important distributive element of policy-making. Who bears the burdens and who receives the benefits?[21]

Although expenditure data can provide a consistent measure of a limited range of public activities, even here there are important difficulties. The amount spent does not necessarily equal the degree of service provided. As Sharkansky describes the spending-service fallacy, ". . . a number of factors not directly connected with the magnitude of government spending can affect the quantity and quality of public services."[22] Another problem with the use of expenditures is the large proportion of uncontrollables or relatively fixed costs within government budgets. This bears directly on comparisons within a single political unit. The presence of uncontrollables limits the extent to which political factors can influence expenditure levels. Any significant political impact must likely be viewed in terms of marginal expenditure changes rather than gross budgetary figures.

Finally, there is the additional problem of the ambiguous interpretation of variations in expenditures. For example, it is often assumed that spending on social policies such as education is associated with left-wing governments, however, the impact of spending on university and post-secondary education is in fact regressive: due to class-related rates of usage, public expenditures on education are of greater benefit to the well-off.[23] The same problem occurs in the case of funding for public dental insurance.

When the conceptualization and measurement of the dependent variables have been refined to better reflect not only the scope, but also the various instruments and redistributive effects of policy, partisanship has been found to be of considerable utility in explaining policy choice. There is evidence that, when in power, parties of the left have implemented policies in keeping with their ideology. In contrast to more conservative governments, social democratic ones are more likely to pursue macroeconomic policies that counter unemployment rather than inflation, to increase taxation and to reduce social inequality. They also are in general more likely to be innovative.[24]

Even though some research appears to have reinstated party variables

---

21 On redistributive issues see Simeon, *supra* note 17.

22 I. Sharkansky, *The Politics of Taxing and Spending* (Indianapolis: Bobbs-Merrill, 1969) at 177.

23 See O. Mehmet, *Who Benefits from the Ontario University System?* (Toronto: Ontario Economic Council, 1978).

24 See Hibbs, "Political Parties and Macroeconomic Policy" (1977), 71 *Am. Pol. Sci. Rev.* 1467; E. R. Tufte, *Political Control of the Economy* (Princeton: Princeton University Press,

as significant factors in policy-making, there remains great skepticism concerning their importance for explaining decisions to establish Crown corporations. The object of this paper is to begin an assessment of the impact of partisanship on public ownership.

(b) Party Ideologies

Ideological distinctions among political parties are usually portrayed along a left-centre-right continuum. However, the translation of party positions into a spatial ordering, typified by Downs' depiction of an array of parties along a single dimension, has been subject to a number of criticisms.[25] Perhaps the most fundamental is that party positions are multidimensional and cannot be represented unidimensionally. As Sartori points out, one dimensional explanations have been sufficient for explaining party competition in Italy, Germany and Sweden but in France, the Netherlands, Israel and Switzerland a second dimension is required.[26] Federally, and in the case of some provinces, there is evidence that the analysis of Canadian parties also requires more than a single dimension.[27]

The Downsian spatial model has also been criticized because of the difficulty in assessing the distances between parties and the problem of estimating the extent of ideological overlapping. Moreover, estimates of the true nature of party system configurations may depend on the kind of evidence selected. Is party position to be judged by platform announcements, opinions of party leaders or popular support?[28] Even when a single basis, such as mass opinion is employed, the precise ranking of all parties along a left-right continuum may still not be a matter of unanimity.[29]

1978); Cameron, "The Expansion of the Public Economy: A Comparative Analysis" (1978), 72 *Am. Pol. Sci. Rev.* 1243; Hewitt, "The Effect of Political Democracy and Social Democracy on Equality in Industrial Societies: A Cross-National Comparison" (1977), 42 *Am. Socio. Rev.* 450; Poel, "The Diffusion of Legislation among the Canadian Provinces: A Statistical Analysis" (1976), 9 *Can. J. Pol. Sci.* 605.

[25] See, *e.g.*, G. Sartori, *Parties and Party Sytems* Vol. I (Cambridge U.K.: Cambridge University Press, 1976); and B. Parry, *Sociologists, Economists and Democracy* (London: Collier-MacMillan, 1970); Converse, "The Problem of Party Distances in Models of Voting Change" in *The Electoral Process*, M. K. Jennings and L. H. Zeigler, eds. (Englewood Cliffs: Prentice-Hall, 1966).

[26] Sartori, *supra* note 25, at 335, 336.

[27] See, *e.g.*, Elkins, "The Perceived Structure of the Canadian Party Systems" (1974), 7 *Can. J. Pol. Sci.* 502.

[28] See Ogmundson, "On the Measurement of Party Class Positions: The Case of Canadian Federal Political Parties" in *The Canadian Political Process*, 3rd ed., O. M. Kruhlak et al., eds. (Toronto: Holt, Rinehart and Winston, 1979); F. C. Engelmann and M. A. Schwartz, *Canadian Political Parties: Origin: Character, Impact* (Scarborough, Ont.: Prentice-Hall, 1975).

[29] See, *e.g.*, La Ponce, "Note on the Use of the Left-Right Dimension" (1970), 2 *Comp. Pol. Stud.* 481 and A. Kornberg et al., "Elite and Mass Perceptions of Canadian Party Location on Issue Space: Some Tests of Two Theories" [paper presented at the International Political Science Association Meetings, 1973].

In this study we use an ordering of provincial parties that avoids the problems of multidimensionality and inconsistent ordering. First, in order to cope with multidimensionality the analysis is focused on a single issue area and thus on only one aspect of party ideology. Although party positions may consist of economic, social, constitutional, international and other elements, our concern here is solely with the economic criterion. Certainly other beliefs may well relate to and reinforce the economic sphere, but the basic categorization of left-nonleft rests on party positions concerning the relationship between the state and the economic system. The left connotes state intervention in the economy; the right, on the other hand, is associated with the principle of free enterprise unfettered by public control. The left favours a positive role for the state while the right leaves the economy to be shaped by market forces. Social democratic parties are committed to goals of economic and political equality, and are therefore critical of the distributive consequences of the market. They are willing to intervene and use the power of the state to change those consequences. Linking economic and political resources, those on the left argue that the deconcentration of economic power is necessary for the decentralization of political power.

The Canadian left's attitude regarding public ownership has shifted somewhat. The resounding commitment in the Regina Manifesto of 1933 has been replaced by the more tempered position of the Winnipeg Declaration of 1956 which declared that public ownership is now considered to be one of several instruments that the left can use to further its economic and social goals. Although the New Democratic Party (NDP) no longer accords public ownership the pre-eminent position it once did, there can be no doubt that as an instrument of policy, state enterprise is still considered favourably. For example, Premier Blakeney of Saskatchewan expressed his government's view of public enterprise,

> At the outset let me make it clear that this Government will encourage the continued operation and expansion of Crown corporations. We will develop our resources for the benefit of Saskatchewan people. Where appropriate this will be done through Crown corporations.[30]

The second problem of inconsistent ordering along even a single dimension (in this case the economic criterion) is mitigated to a large extent by collapsing the parties into two categories: left and nonleft. The left is composed of the Cooperative Commonwealth Federation (CCF)/New Democratic Party (NDP) and Parti Québecois (PQ). Whatever ambiguities may exist in ordering provincial parties the CCF/NDP has been consistently ranked to the left of other parties.[31] Under highly competitive conditions it

---

[30] Saskatchewan Treasury Department. *Budget Speech of 10 March 1972,* [Regina: Lawrence Amon, Queen's Printer, 1972] at 12. The speech was delivered by the Hon. A. E. Blakeney.
[31] See McLeod, "Explanations of Our Party System" in P. W. Fox, *supra* note 2, and Fox, "Politics and Parties in Canada" in P. W. Fox, *supra* note 2; W. Christian and C. Camp-

has been shown that the NDP may cause its opponents to shift leftward, but there is no argument that the competition ever overtakes the NDP.[32]

The other provincial party that is placed in the left category is the Parti Québecois. Even though there is much debate over the nature of the Parti Québecois it is generally agreed that the PQ is a social democratic party that occupies the left of the spectrum in Quebec politics.[33] Besides their obvious differences on issues of federalism, the most important distinction between the PQ and the NDP is that, unlike most social democratic parties including the NDP, the PQ has no formal links with the trade union movement. Otherwise, the similarity of their positions on economic and social issues is well established.[34]

The category of nonleft is composed of the other parties that compete in provincial elections (Liberal, Progressive Conservative, Union Nationale and Social Credit).[35] Although there are significant differences among provincial parties with the same label, on economic issues they have shared a commitment to a market economy and have accepted as a goal in and of itself the perpetuation of an economic order based on private property. This public commitment to the private sector is a shared characteristic of the nonleft parties. For example, a former Liberal Premier of Saskatchewan states this shared position.

> May I reiterate that it is the philosophy of this government to encourage the industrial development of Saskatchewan by 'private enterprise'.[36]

The question then is whether the policy outputs of party governments reflect their ideological distinctiveness. If there is a causal relationship between partisanship and public ownership, we can expect social democratic governments to be more heavily associated with public ownership than other governments. It has been argued, however, that since all parties have been associated with public ownership initiatives, partisanship or party

---

bell, *Political Parties and Ideologies in Canada: liberals, conservatives, socialists, nationalists* (Toronto: McGraw-Hill Ryerson, 1974).

[32] On the impact of CCF/NDP as an opposition force see W. Chandler, "Canadian Socialism and Policy Impact: Contagion from the Left?" (1977), 10 *Can. J. Pol. Sci.* 755.

[33] See K. McRoberts and D. Posgate, *Quebec: Social Change and Political Crisis* (Toronto: McClelland and Stewart, 1980); Niosi, "The New French-Canadian Bourgeoisie" (1979), No. 1 *Studies in Political Economy* 113; Fournier, "The New Parameters of the Quebec Bourgeoisie" (1980), No. 3 *Studies in Political Economy* 67.

[34] For a comparison of the two parties, see J. Avakumovic, *Socialism in Canada* (Toronto: McClelland and Stewart, 1978), at 210-215. For an analysis of the programme of the P.Q., see V. Murray, *Le Parti québécois: de la fondation à la prise du pouvoir* (Montréal: Éditions Hurtubise HMH, 1976), chapters 2 and 3.

[35] Other parties such as the U.F.A., U.F.O. and Progressives have contested and won provincial elections. Also in Manitoba and B.C. governments have been formed by coalitions rather than a single party. Because none of these "other" parties or coalitions have created any Crown corporations we have not sought to include them in the analysis.

[36] Saskatchewan Treasury Department. *Budget Speech of 25 February, 1966*, [Regina: Lawrence Amon, Queen's Printer, 1966] at 9. The speech was delivered by the Hon. W. R. Thatcher.

ideology has little to do with such decisions.[37] Certainly the observation that all provincial parties have at times utilized public ownership raises doubts about the ideological hypothesis. In assessing the hypothesis one must ask whether parties of the left have used this particular instrument more than other parties, and why other parties have used it at all? Section IV of this essay looks at the first issue—the left and public ownership, Section V considers intervention through public ownership by other parties.

IV. THE LEFT AND PUBLIC OWNERSHIP

(a) The Meaning of Crown Corporations:
Defining the Dependent Variable

Prior to exploring the relationship between politics and state enterprise we must be precise about what is meant by public enterprise. The creation of Crown corporations has in reality involved the state in myriad activities. Without refinement and specification, generalizations about the impact of parties on public ownership are likely to be extremely risky and even misleading.

The concept of state or public enterprise is often quite loosely applied to a wide variety of seemingly disparate structures which range in size, organization and degree of autonomy. Moreover, since control rather than ownership *per se* is the more important definitional criterion, mixed enterprises (Syncrude, for example) which are owned by government and private interests are often included in the general category of state enterprise.[38] The problems of definition that exist at the federal level are multiplied at the provincial level since across the provinces there is not even a classificatory or organizing statute like the federal *Financial Administration Act*.[39]

Identification is obviously the first step in the analysis of public ownership and it is to this end that a number of definitions have been put forward. For example, Ashley and Smails define a Crown corporation as "an institution with corporate form brought into existence by action of the government . . . to serve a public function".[40] Tupper refines the definition to refer to organizations owned wholly or partially by the state, engaged in the production of goods, the marketing of natural products and the provision

---

[37] Gracey, *supra* note 3, at 25.
[38] On mixed enterprise in general see L. D. Musolf, *Mixed Enterprise: A Developmental Perspective* (Lexington: D.C. Heath, 1972). For Canada see Swedlove, "Business-government joint ventures in Canada" (1978), 1 *Foreign Investment Review* 13, and Langford, *supra* note 1, at 246.
[39] R.S.C. 1970, c. F-10.
[40] C. A. Ashley and R. G. H. Smails, *supra* note 1, at 3.

of services, sold at a price according to use.[41] Recently, John Langford has brought together a number of definitional approaches which were developed in various governmental reform proposals.[42] In all of these cases the object is to derive a conceptual definition that is wide enough to encompass the various forms that public ownership may take, yet narrow enough to isolate those basic characteristics of public ownership that distinguish it from other forms of public and private activity. In their discussion of provincial public enterprise in this volume, Vining and Botterell have singled out three defining characteristics of public enterprise: provincial ownership or control, organization outside the regular departments, and provision of goods and services. Using these components as their working definition they have developed an inventory of over 200 instances of provincial public enterprise. With some revisions these data will be used here to assess the role of state enterprise as an instrument of partisan policy.[43]

(b) Problems of Analysis

The conclusion that the use of public ownership as an instrument of policy cannot be associated with any single party or ideology is based primarily on the observation that although the ideology of left is more sympathetic to public ownership, empirical evidence indicates that parties of the nonleft have been responsible for creating more Crown corporations than the left. Of the 200 cases of public enterprise 75 percent (148) were established by nonleft governments (see Table I). Unfortunately this seemingly straightforward description of the partisan origin of Crown corporations across the ten provinces is misleading in three fundamental respects: (1) it fails to take into account differences in the party systems among the provinces; (2) it does not reflect differences in opportunity due to time in office; and (3) it focuses attention on political parties rather than provincial governments as the units of analysis. Aggregating the data in this way results in a loss of information and in obscuring the impact of partisanship rather than in the identification of nation-wide trends in public policy.

---

[41] A. Tupper, *supra* note 6, at 8.

[42] Langford, *supra* note 1.

[43] The general methodology for compiling the inventory can be found in Vining and Botterell, "An Overview of the Origins, Growth, Size and Functions of Provincial Crown Corporations", Chapter 5, in this volume. In some cases in which several Crown corporations were later consolidated into a single entity such as Saskatchewan Wool Products (1945) and Saskatchewan Leather Products (1945) becoming part of Saskatchewan Industries (1949), we include the original corporations in the data because although it may inflate the overall number, each represents an instance of decision-making. Vining and Botterell used only the consolidated units. The electoral data are based on the characteristics of the 119 provincial governments since 1920. The description of these data can be found in M. Chandler and W. Chandler, "Parliamentary Politics and Public Policy" [paper presented at the Mid-Western Political Science Association Meetings, 1974].

(i) Multiple Party Systems

The first problem with a combined analysis of provincial policy-making is that it fails to recognize that the provinces represent ten distinct political systems.[44] Nowhere is this variation more evident than in their party systems: the provinces differ in terms of which parties compete, how many parties there are and the degree of competition among them. For example, the Atlantic provinces all have fairly stable competitive two-party systems in which the Liberals and the Progressive Conservatives vie for office. In the West each province has had its unique party system, none of which is similar to those in the East. Manitoba has a three-party system in which one of the major competitors is the NDP, while Alberta politics have been characterized by long periods of one-party dominance, first by Social Credit and now by the Progressive Conservatives. In British Columbia the unstable party system has as its main contenders the NDP and Social Credit parties. Saskatchewan's party system is one in which there has been long-term dominance by the NDP. In the central provinces there is still more variation. Ontario's three-party system is marked by the dominance of the Progressive Conservatives, and the unstable two-party system in Quebec has undergone two important transformations: the long-dominant Union Nationale was replaced in the 1960s by the Liberals and in the 1970s the Parti Québécois has become a major contender.

Due in part to their individual party systems the provinces have presented rather dissimilar electoral opportunities. Since the left has never formed a government in six of the provinces (Alberta, Ontario, Newfoundland, Prince Edward Island, Nova Scotia and New Brunswick) it could not have been responsible for any public enterprise in those provinces. No matter how few Crown corporations were created in those provinces, the record of the left will always be less than the governing parties. On the other hand where the left has formed at least one government, the differences in party record may be submerged by aggregating across provinces.

The results in Table I indicate that is just what occurred in the aggregated observations. A provincial breakdown of the number of Crown corporations established by each partisan category yields a very different picture than the one drawn from the combined data.

In each of the three provinces in which there has been a CCF or NDP government, the left has created more Crown corporations than all other parties combined. This record of the CCF/NDP is even more striking when we consider that *regardless* of how long they were in power they *always* created more public enterprises than the rest of the parties.

---

44 On various aspects of provincial party systems see M. Robin, ed. *Canadian Provincial Politics*, 2nd ed. (Scarborough, Ont.: Prentice-Hall, 1978); M. A. Chandler and W. M. Chandler, *Public Policy and Provincial Politics* (Toronto: McGraw-Hill Ryerson, 1979), chapter 3; D. J. Elkins and R. Simeon, eds., *supra* note 18; D. J. Bellamy et al., eds., *supra* note 18.

TABLE I
Number of Crown Corporations by Partisanship of Government
(1920-1979)

	B.C.	Alta.	Sask.	Man.	Ont.	Que.	N.B.	N.S.	P.E.I.	Nfld.	Total**
Left	16	—	24	7	—	5	—	—	—	—	52
Nonleft	10	20	3	5	25	30	8	9	8	40*	148

* The large number in Newfoundland is due to the inclusion of some 17 different Crown corporations for school financing and hospital management.
** The Crown corporations established before 1920 are not included in these tables because there are no corresponding electoral data. Also not included are those for which no date of origin could be established.

The only province in which this impact of a social democratic government is not observable is Quebec. Although the Parti Québecois, which has formed only one government, was responsible for a number of Crown corporations, the Liberals and the Union Nationale were more active in creating public enterprise. We believe that the explanation for the Quebec findings is due to the fact that since 1960 every government in Quebec has used state intervention to foster nationalistic goals. The nationalistic pressures have been in addition to the partisan pressure described above. In the analysis below of types of public ownership it will be demonstrated that once the economic and nationalistic dimensions are separated, the evidence will show that the PQ has acted differently than other parties in Quebec and in keeping with other left governments.

(ii) Time in Office

An aggregated analysis of Crown corporations also fails to reflect differences in the opportunities the left has had to make policy. In this case it is not a question of interprovincial differences but rather less opportunity within the province. Since 1920, in those provinces in which the left has formed a government (except Saskatchewan) these parties have been in power for fewer years than the other parties. As Vining and Botterell have shown, in order to control for differences in opportunity to make policy, it is best to use a measure of the rate of creation of public enterprise. By calculating the number of corporations created compared to the party's years in office the parties' records are put on a comparable footing.[45]

Once the time factor is taken into account the nation-wide results reveal that the left parties have created Crown corporations at a rate that is almost triple that of the combined nonleft parties. But significantly when the

---

[45] See Vining and Botterell, *supra* note 43.

calculation is performed on a province by province basis the results are even more striking. In comparing the rates of the parties within each province we are comparing the actions of parties operating within a similar environment. It is easier to isolate the effects of partisanship when they are not confounded by pressures from the differing economic and social systems. The rates reported by Vining and Botterell and reproduced below illustrate the same situation as in the case of the absolute scores in Table I: the combined data obscure significant variations among provinces. In every province except Quebec in which the left have formed the government, the rate of creation for parties of the left is higher than the rate of the other parties.

TABLE II
Rate of Establishment of Crown Corporations for each Province
(Crown Corporations per year in office)
(1961-1979)

	B.C.	Alta.	Sask.	Man.	Ont.	Que.	N.B.	N.S.	P.E.I.	Nfld.	Total
Rate of Left Govts.	5.3	—	1.14	.63	—	1.33	—	—	—	—	1.5
Rate of Nonleft Govts.	.44	.63	.14	.18	.74	1.43	.26	.31	.50	.63	.52

An alternative possible explanation for the differences in rates within each province is that left governments have been in power during times that were more conducive to creating Crown corporations. In other words, similar environmental circumstances rather than party ideology might account for the left's higher scores. If we take the 1940s, the decade in which the first social democratic government came to power, it was a period of relatively little activity in the field of public enterprise in which only about ten percent of all state enterprises were established. However, even in that period, the two CCF governments in Saskatchewan established almost half of the total number of provincial Crown corporations.[46] While some like the Reconstruction Housing Corporation were related to the circumstances at the end of the war and were phased out in a few years, others like Saskatchewan Power Corporation and Saskatchewan Government Insurance Office were central to the general objectives of the government and continue today to be important parts of the public sector.

In the 1970s, a period in which there has been much greater use of state enterprise, social democratic governments account for a disproportionately

---

[46] Saskatchewan. Government Finance Office. "Public Enterprise in Saskatchewan", [paper for seminar, held in June 1977, at Institute for Public Administration, 897 Bay St., Toronto M5S 1Z7].

high fraction of the total number of enterprises created. In this period, left of centre parties formed the governments in four provinces. They held office for 23 percent of the time but accounted for almost half (43 percent) of the Crown corporations. Thus it would appear that regardless of the overall level of public enterprise, the actions of the left may be distinguished from the others.

(iii) Party vs. Government

The third way in which one may be misled into thinking that partisanship makes no difference for public entrepreneurship derives from the fact that a majority of Crown corporations are the product of nonleft parties. In this case the faulty inference results from collapsing all the years in which Liberals, Conservatives, etc., have formed provincial governments and comparing their policy records. Analysis based on blending all of the governments of each party into a single construct of years in power and combining all of the records of each of those governments into a total measure of Crown corporations does not address the basic issue because it conceals information about government policy-making. It simply relates years in power, disassociated from the structure of a term in office, unique environmental pressures, or other elements of the political process, to the total number of Crown corporations.

Inferring relationships from the general record of the party rather than individual governments is an example of ecological fallacy. The relationship identified by the summarized data is incorrectly assumed to be applicable to individual cases. It is as if we assumed, for example, that the establishment rate of 1.14 for the left in Saskatchewan told us something about the rate by which any government in Saskatchewan created Crown corporations. That of course is the problem: it does not reveal anything about the policy-making of any particular government. Perhaps even more importantly it obscures the variation among governments of the same party and thus detracts from the possibility of exploring the circumstances that may heighten or decrease the impact of ideology. The basic objective is to investigate whether the partisanship of a government affects its policy-making. Thus each government is a case in point. In order to generalize about the relationship that exists in each government between its ideology and its policy record, it is necessary to treat governments as discrete units.

(c) Establishing Public Enterprise

With this sharper focus on decision-making the first question is whether or not the partisanship of a government affects the overall likelihood of its using public ownership as an instrument of policy. In Table III the governments are grouped by whether they opted for public enterprise.

TABLE III
Establishment of Crown Corporations

	% Left Governments	% Nonleft Governments
Established no Crown Corporations	25	46
Established one or more Crown Corporations	75	54
	n = 12	N = 107

About one half of the nonleft governments established no public enterprises at all during their terms of office. Among left governments, on the other hand, only one in four used no public ownership. Arrayed in this manner, the data indicate that public enterprise is more likely under social democratic governments.

Among those governments that have established state enterprises there is a wide range in the extent of their use of Crown corporations. Does partisanship help to explain frequency? In order to answer this question each government has been categorized by its rate of Crown corporation creation. In Table IV the governments have been grouped into categories. Those governments that established no public ownership are in the zero group. In the low category are those governments that have created at least one Crown corporation but whose rate was *below* the average rate. Those governments whose rate was above the national average were placed in the high category.

Not only are governments of the left more likely to employ Crown corporations, they also do so with greater frequency. Two-thirds of the social democratic governments were above the average rate, while only 26 percent of the other governments were in the high category.

Taking government as the unit of analysis permits us to look more closely at those cases which do not fit the predicted pattern. Obviously there

TABLE IV
Rates of Crown Corporations Creation by Partisanship

		% Left Governments *(12)*	% Nonleft Governments *(107)*
	zero	25	46
Rate of creation of Crown corps.	low	8	28
	high	67	26

are any number of factors that can account for those instances in which a particular government did not appear to act in keeping with its ideological disposition. Are there any shared characteristics of the deviant cases that can explain why these governments differ from the predicted party-policy relationship that applied in most of the other cases? Is there some attribute of the government itself rather than a characteristic of its environment that might dampen the effect of ideology? One possibility is the age of the government. Do governments that succeed themselves act differently in their subsequent terms of office? Specifically in the case of the left do they lose their ideological edge? Does coming to office from the government side rather than from the opposition mitigate their critical stance and thus their impulse to act? Certainly once they have achieved power, even the most innovative governments must spend some time securing their accomplishments before they can take on new ones.

Is there a kind of political aging process or "life cycle" in which as parties remain in power over the course of several elections they become less innovative, more committed to their prior policy record and hence more defensive of the status quo?[47] If so, one could predict that all new governments would have a greater tendency to initiate new policy direction or opt for new policy instruments. We would naturally expect that this inclination would be strongest among radical, protest parties as they gain power but that the process of growing old would breed in all of them a certain sclerosis in their policy function.

To analyze these questions, the public ownership activity records of new and old governments of the left and nonleft are compared in Table V. Old governments are defined as ones formed by the same party as that of the preceding government.

TABLE V
Crown Corporations Created by Old and New Governments

		Left Governments		Nonleft Governments	
		New	*Old*	*New*	*Old*
Rate of Crown Corps.	zero		43% (3)	35% (9)	50% (40)
	low		14% (1)	30% (8)	27% (22)
	high	100% (5)	43% (3)	35% (9)	23% (19)

---

[47] For a discussion of the effects of longevity in office at the federal level, see J. Meisel, *Working Papers on Canadian Politics* (Montreal: McGill-Queen's University Press, 1973), chapter 5, "Howe, Hubris and '72: An Essay on Political Elitism".

For the left the results are quite dramatic. Not only did all new, left governments opt for public ownership, their rates were all high. In contrast all of the less active governments were old ones. The results for the nonleft indicate that this pattern of differentiation between old and new does not apply consistently for all parties; new governments of the nonleft were only marginally more likely to use Crown corporations than old ones. Thus time in office does not seem to alter the basic orientation toward public ownership of the nonleft. Why is it that only the impulses of left ideology appear to be dampened in old governments?

The governments in Saskatchewan in the 1950s are cases in point. By 1945, the first CCF government had created nine corporations. They were comprised of two reconstruction corporations, intended to last only a few years, a government printing corporation and six others, based primarily on the production and sale of various resources and natural products (e.g. Saskatchewan Clay Products and Saskatchewan Timber Board). By 1951, after some reorganization and consolidation as well as new efforts in transportation and power, the total number of public enterprises reached 14. The succeeding CCF governments of 1951 and 1955 created no new public enterprises. How can this slackening of the pace be explained without falling back to the idiosyncratic explanation of pragmatic politics? Should this decline in activity be attributed to a diminution of the impact of ideology? Looking at the Saskatchewan cases there seem to be three factors that have unique bearing on old governments: the need to build upon past policies, the limitations of provincial economies, and coping with instrument failure.[48] Together these elements help to explain why the policy records of succeeding governments may differ from those of new governments.

First, following a period of great activity there appears to be a time of consolidation and extension rather than a steady expansion of new projects. A party succeeding itself in power does not start with a clean slate. The incoming government is tied to the record of its predecessor. Some of its energy must be spent in defending its record and adapting its past policies, while new governments are more likely to focus on establishing a break with the past and the policies of the previous government. This means that old governments are more inclined toward taking stock and building on previous policies. Much policy-making is taken up with responses to past actions which, although no less significant than some totally new policies, may appear to be less innovative.

During the 1950s the Saskatchewan Power Corporation was expanded dramatically. Its electricity service capacity increased 500 percent in ten

---

[48] For excellent discussions of Saskatchewan under CCF government, see S. M. Lipset, *Agrarian Socialism* (Garden City, N.Y.: Doubleday, 1968), and J. Richards and L. Pratt, *Prairie Capitalism: Power and Influence in the New West* (Toronto: McClelland and Stewart, 1979).

years, and it was one of the few utilities in Canada given authority to also distribute natural gas (1950). By 1961, the power and telephone corporations had grown to the point where they represented well over 90 percent of the assets of Saskatchewan public enterprise. Also, instead of creating new corporations, governments in the 1950s continued to support social ownership in another way, by relaying heavily on co-operatives. For example, despite the government's decision not to move directly into oil exploration and production, the co-operatives were given first option in exploiting Crown lands. They also operated the major refinery in Regina. These represented another mode of public ownership, no less in keeping with the left's desire to deconcentrate economic and social power.

A time of taking stock and consolidation may be even more understandable in conjunction with a small provincial economy. After a period of vigorous activity by a new government, all the most likely candidates for public ownership had been taken over and the obvious Crown corporations had been created. In contrast to larger, more diversified economies, aside from utilities, transportation and insurance, there are few other significant provincial possibilities for government entrepreneurship. The exception, of course, is natural resources, for which the CCF governments did not feel they had adequate capital to take over oil or potash. The CCF did, however, move into small scale resource industries like Saskatchewan Wool Products and Leather Products.

The failure of these small retail Crown corporations is the basis of the third part in the explanation of the behaviour of the government in the 1950s. The CCF commitment to public enterprise must be viewed within the context of its overall social and economic objectives. Public ownership, as we have indicated, represents one means or instrument that can be used to achieve these goals. The small scale resource corporations were created to generate employment, develop provincial resources and lessen the dependence on imports from the East. Whatever symbolic value they might have had, they were not successful and did not result in import substitution or development of the provincial economy. Some, like the Leather Products Division of Saskatchewan Industries, were shut down, while others were reorganized. But there was little impetus to start up any new ones. Recognizing these failures, succeeding governments looked to other policy instruments to generate economic development and diversify the economy.[49]

Before proceeding to the next section which analyzes the objectives of public ownership, it is best to summarize the findings so far. The record of provincial governments since 1920 has revealed that governments of the left are more likely to turn to public ownership and use this instrument more frequently than are those of the nonleft. The differences in propensity to establish Crown corporations applied during periods in which public enter-

---

[49] Saskatchewan, *supra* note 46.

prise was a rarely used instrument of policy as well as in periods in which it was more popular.

Analysis of the conditions in which left governments did not use public ownership indicates the nature of the left's commitment to public ownership. It is after all a means of policy rather than an end in itself, and its continued use must be evaluated on those terms. As we have seen in the case of Saskatchewan in the 1950s, and in the early 1960s, public ownership was not always believed to be the most effective means of achieving government goals.

To this point in the essay, the focus has been on the positive influence of left ideology on the use of public enterprise and the reasons why this relationship is not always predictive of the actions of left governments. The other side must now be considered. As seen in Table IV, some 50 percent of nonleft governments have established Crown corporations. Indeed in this regard the records of a few nonleft governments rival those of the most vigorous social democratic governments.[50] Can the policy-making of the nonleft be interpreted in the context of ideology or is there a need to return to pragmatism to explain this?

V. IDEOLOGY AND THE OBJECTIVES OF PUBLIC ENTERPRISE

The effects of the ideological preferences of the party in power need not be confined to variations in the *extent* to which public enterprise is used as an instrument of policy. It is also possible that governments of the left use public ownership for different purposes than do other governments.

In studies of other policy instruments such as budgetary expenditures and taxation it is clear that total figures are often an unsatisfactory basis for analysis. Thus, for example, expenditures are divided into functional (*e.g.,* transfer payments, goods and services) and substantive (*e.g.,* health, education) categories. Similarly, taxation is often divided by target (*e.g.,* income, property) and incidence (*e.g.,* progressive, regressive). The point is, each of these instruments is used for more than one function and with varying impacts. Policy analysis must recognize that diversity and draw, where necessary, distinctions within the category of a single type of instrument.

The problem with analysis based on simple aggregations of Crown corporations is that it treats all instances of public ownership as identical. Even on the most intuitive level, this assumption is untenable. For example, if we are told that one province has ten Crown corporations and another has 37, what can we conclude? Very little, for in order to make any assessment of the role of public enterprise in policy-making more information is required.

---

50 See, *e.g.,* Neil Swainson, "The Crown Corporation in the Government of British Columbia" [paper presented to Canadian Political Science Association, May 1981] for a comparison of the Barrett and Bennett governments.

(a) Dimensions of State Enterprise

What then are the relevant criteria for distinguishing among Crown corporations? As we have noted, the traditional mode of analysis has focused on legalistic characteristics, especially those related to accountability. Vining and Botterell[51] differentiate public enterprises by such factors as the size of assets, functional sector of the economy and size relative to private sector. These characteristics are useful and important starting points for the analysis of policy choice, for they place each Crown corporation in the perspective of its operational environment and at the same time provide some means of comparison.

Other recent studies have gone further. They have sought to identify dimensions of public ownership that can be specifically related to its role as an instrument of policy.[52] In Chapter 1 of this volume Prichard and Trebilcock categorize Crown corporations in terms of the economic activities for which they may be employed. They then focus on the attributes of public ownership that bear on its substitutability with other policy instruments in performing specific economic and political functions.[53] In his discussion of public ownership, Allan Tupper uses seven concepts: job maintenance, community development, sector building, captive markets, income enhancement, supply security and regulation, to differentiate public enterprises in Canada. These concepts refer not only to the goal of the enterprise, but also the way it is achieved and who benefits from this activity by the state.[54] There can be no doubt that both Prichard and Trebilcock and Tupper's work do much to augment and clarify our understanding of the functions of social ownership and its place in the political process.

Do, however, refinements in the notion of public enterprise shed any further light on the impact of ideology? Do they uncover any link between partisanship and the use of Crown corporations in either certain fields of economic activity or specific concepts of public enterprise? The answer is no. All three studies conclude that public ownership decisions are not associated with party differences.[55]

These findings that party ideology does not seem to be related to the various dimensions of public ownership may, however, be more a reflection of the conceptualizations of public enterprise than of the weakness of ideological pressures. Based on the dimensions they pose are there any

---

[51] Vining and Botterel, *supra* note 43.

[52] See the articles in W. G. Shepherd et al., *Public Enterprise: Economic Analysis of Theory and Practice* (Lexington: D.C. Heath, 1976). See also Swainson, *supra* note 50.

[53] Trebilcock and Prichard, "Crown Corporations: The Calculus of Instrument Choice", Chapter 1 in this volume.

[54] Allan Tupper, *supra* note 6, chapter 1.

[55] *Ibid.*, and M. J. Trebilcock et al., *The Choice of Governing Instrument: A Study Prepared for the Economic Council of Canada* (Ottawa: Ministry of Supply and Services Canada, 1982).

reasons to hypothesize that such linkage might exist? Do the dimensions of public ownership they use as indicators of policy output tap differences in party ideologies? The problem with using fields of activity or concepts as the dependent variable when assessing the relationship between party and policy is that these categories do not correspond to differences in party ideology. For example, using Tupper's concepts there is little reason to think the nonleft would be less interested in security of supply that the left. Or that other parties, for example, the Progressive Conservatives, would be less concerned with community development than the NDP. In the same vein, in choosing among policy instruments to accomplish particular economic activities it is not readily apparent how much variation there can be in the perceptions of instrument attributes. And as Prichard and Trebilcock point out, it is the differences in attributes that are the primary basis for political choice.[56] For example, is there any reason to suspect that some political parties are willing to incur higher monitoring costs than others?

An additional reason why it may be inappropriate to use these and other similar dimensions of public enterprise for assessing the impact of partisanship is that policy-making is conceived too narrowly. Although the concepts and economic activities used by Tupper and Prichard and Trebilcock are quite general, the analyses tend to rest on the consideration of specific instances and often narrow choices. From other policy research, it is clear that when party ideology has been found to be an important factor in policy-making it has been in the context of such broad policy directions as economic policy and tax effort.[57] With some obvious exceptions,[58] the constraints operating on any government may limit its maneuverability on any single decision, and it is therefore much more likely to be in regard to the broad contours of policy that the impact of ideology may be observed.[59]

If partisan control does make a difference in the use of public enterprise, these differences are more likely to be observable within a framework of analysis that is based on broad, ideologically-relevant dimensions of public ownership, which allow for the critical connection between policy-making and provincial political forces. This underscores the fact that Crown corporations are means to various ends and it is in the pursuit of distinctive ends that ideologies and perhaps governments differ.

Conflicts over the role of the provincial state in the economy have continued to be at the centre of the provincial political process. it has been not so much a question of whether to use the state but rather how and for what

---

[56] Trebilcock and Prichard, *supra* note 53, and M. J. Trebilcock et al., *supra* note 55.

[57] See E. R. Tufte, *supra* note 24, and Cameron, *supra* note 24.

[58] *E.g.*, Poel, *supra* note 24, points out the clear impact of the CCF/NDP on the initiation of various policies.

[59] Simeon, *supra* note 17.

purpose(s). Provincial governments have intervened in the economy in order to foster economic development, redistribution and nationalism. These three objectives have constituted the enduring themes of provincial politics. It is within the context of the pursuit of these objectives that public enterprises may be viewed as policy instruments that reflect party ideology. Each objective refers to a particular relationship between the private and public sectors, and each may be further differentiated by its intended beneficiaries.

(b) Facilitating Economic Development

Provincial governments have had a long standing interest in promoting the development of their economies. Toward this end, many Crown corporations have been used to foster the growth of the private sector. As in the case of other instruments, there are a number of ways in which public ownership can be used to facilitate development. Although the methods vary, facilitative Crown corporations all boil down to what Pierre Fournier describes as a sophisticated subsidy system in which costs and risks are absorbed by the state, but control is left to private firms.[60]

Public enterprises designed to foster economic development are not challenges to the private sector. On the contrary, they involve the use of public resources to supplement and support the private sector. The view that business is always against public enterprise is based on a misperception that intervention always poses a threat to the private sector. The business community very much benefits from this particular form of state activity, and there appears to be little loss of autonomy or control in return. Whittaker describes this as profit at public expense.[61]

The facilitative type of Crown corporation is the most frequently used. It includes such traditional modes as the creation of transportation infrastructure, (Ontario Northland, B.C. Railway, Alberta Resources Railway) provision of cheap power (Saskatchewan Power Corporation, Ontario Hydro) access to low cost and/or last resort financing (Manitoba Development, N.S. Industrial Estates Ltd., Newfoundland Fisheries Loan Board) and marketing facilities (Ontario Food Terminal Board, Saskatchewan Fur Marketing Company). The more modern efforts include corporations to provide low cost computer services (Manitoba Data Services, B.C. Systems Corp.) and to develop and distribute new technology (Ontario Transporta-

---

[60] P. Fournier, *The Québec Establishment* (Montréal: Black Rose Books, 1976) at 193.

[61] Whitaker, "Images of the state in Canada" in *The Canadian state: political economy and political power,* L. Panitch, ed. (Toronto: University of Toronto Press, 1977). In the same vein see Lloyd, "State Capitalism and Socialism: The Problem of Government Handouts" in *Essays on the Left,* L. LaPierre et al., eds. (Toronto: McClelland and Stewart, 1971).

tion Development Corporation, Alberta Oil Sands Technology and Research Council).

Even when the state may appear to be taking on some function usually performed by private firms, such as mineral exploration, the facilitative nature becomes apparent. For example, through its involvement in joint ventures, SOQUEM (Quebec Mining Exploration Corporation) diminishes private costs and, moreover, it sells back to the private sector those ventures that are profitable.

A subset of the general category of facilitative corporation consists of the several provincial corporations devoted to northern development. In British Columbia, Saskatchewan, Ontario, Alberta and Quebec public corporations have been established to the development of the economy within a distinct area of the province.

Crown corporations created to take over closing plants are also a case of facilitation (*e.g.*, Harmon Corporation in Newfoundland, Ocean Falls, B.C.). Although the initial motivation is to save the jobs that would otherwise be lost, those public enterprises may properly be seen as policy designed to maintain the economic structure of a region or town. Public takeovers to save jobs do not occur every time a factory closes. They tend to occur when the jobs are important in the context of the existing development of the private sector in the region. In other words, loss of jobs is not a sufficient condition for public ownership. However, public takeovers have occurred when there are critical implications for the economic system. These Crown corporations are similar to unemployment insurance in that although there is a humanitarian element, it should not be forgotten that by dealing with dislocations the state is maintaining the basic economic system. As in the case with other facilitative corporations, provincial governments have not used these instances of public ownership to assert control or give new direction to the economy.

The supportive relationship between private and public sectors and the nature of the interests that derive the benefits influence the politics of facilitative corporations. There is little sign of conflict, because these Crown corporations are not seen as intrusive or as an extension of state control. Because the costs are not obvious, those who ultimately stand to lose from the policy are unlikely to oppose it. Moreover, although the direct recipients of the assistance are specific interests within the private sector, it is usually claimed that the increased development means more jobs and revenues and therefore entails benefits to the entire province.

In many ways the character of the political process is similar to the "distributive" arena described by Lowi.[62] Conflict is minimal since varying interests can be indulged with seemingly little cost to each other. Moreover,

---

[62] Lowi, "American Business, Public Policy, Case-Studies, and Political Theory" (1964), 16 *World Politics* 677.

those interests that stand to lose or at least bear the bulk of the costs are generally not represented in the policy-making process.

(c) Redistribution

Redistribution refers to public policies intended to change the distribution of economic and/or political benefits. In the case of public ownership it is direct use of intervention in the economy by the public sector to change some of the impacts of the private sector. This translates into action not only to bring about a more equitable distribution of economic benefits but also to disperse the political and social power that accompanies the concentration of economic benefits. Prime examples of redistributive public enterprise are public insurance corporations in British Columbia, Manitoba, Saskatchewan and Quebec which provide benefits to the public in two ways: they have lowered the rates of insurance for individuals and whatever profits accrue go to the public treasury. Similarly in the case of the Potash Corporation of Saskatchewan economic rents as well as all "normal" returns on investment go directly to the public treasury rather than being split between the public and private sectors through royalties, etc.

The redistributive Crown corporation represents a definite intrusion in the private sector and an extension of state control over the economy. The redistributive corporation alters the existing arrangement of benefits. In many instances, including insurance and natural resources, the benefits may go to the entire population, but this need not be the case. For example the Saskatchewan Trading Corporation was created because of the high prices the Hudson's Bay Company was charging to natives in the North. The purpose in setting up a competitor to Hudson's Bay was not to enter into a new line of commercial enterprise to raise revenues or to facilitate northern development, but to offset the power of the Hudson's Bay Company monopoly and to redistribute those profits to the natives through lower prices. In this case the beneficiaries were a small segment of the population.

Unlike the facilitative type, redistributive corporations are more threatening to the private sector because they are directed toward changing some aspect of the economy. Far more than the facilitative, they can be used as a power base by the provincial government for asserting control over the economy. Another difference between the two types is the greater visibility of the winners and losers in the case of redistributive enterprise. Most significantly, those who stand to lose tend to be aware of the potential threat and are more likely to pose some opposition.[63] This means that in the politics surrounding redistributive Crown corporation there is likely to be more

---

[63] Molot and Laux, "The Politics of Nationalization" (1979), 12 *Can. J. Pol. Sci.* 227.

conflict.[64] Moreover, such conflict will tend to correspond to the basic ideological cleavage which divides the right from the left, so that even those who do not stand to directly lose or gain, may, because of their ideology, be involved in the conflict over the adoption of redistributive policy instruments.

(d) Nationalism

Public enterprise directed toward nationalistic objectives represents the third category. In these cases state ownership is used to enhance provincial interests at the expense of those interests outside the province. Nationalistic Crown corporations combine elements of both the facilitative and redistributive, albeit in a distinctive manner that requires separate treatment.

Nationalistic state enterprises are facilitative because they are established to assist indigenous economic interests. Providing special assistance for local firms, rather than to the private sector in general, gives rise to a redistributive element. Benefits and some economic power are wrested from one part of the private sector (external interests) and distributed to intra-provincial interests. This may take the form of direct assistance to local firms as in the case of the Quebec General Investment Corporation whose role is to accelerate industrial development in Quebec by promoting and financing Quebec enterprises. Alternatively the promotion of provincial interests may be via the establishment of heavy industry like Sidbec in which a major consideration was to provide for Francophone participation in Canadian heavy industry.

The nationalistic objective is unique because, although it is certainly related to the promotion of economic growth, it is not growth at any cost. It is a more complex and restricted kind of incentive system and in this regard represents a greater interference by the state in the economy than does the purely facilitative enterprise.

The defining characteristic of the nationalistic Crown corporation is the importance of regional or territorial distinctions. In contrast the public-private sector boundary is not particularly significant. The power of the state is used to increase local control (which may be either private or state-directed) at the expense of external interests (which also may be private or public from other jurisdictions). In *Prairie Capitalism* the nationalistic motivation of Alberta's Conservative government is described.

Fear of new federal incursions and distrust of a market economy under outside control have manifested themselves in a series of related policy interventions,

---

64 This is demonstrated in the conflict that arose around Manitoba's Hydro Corporation. See Nelles, "Public Ownership of Electrical Utilities in Manitoba and Ontario, 1906-30" (1976), 57 *Can. Hist. Rev.* 461.

virtually all of which have been justified in the name of Alberta public enterprise.[65]

Although all provinces have established some nationalistic Crown corporation, this aspect of state enterprise is especially important in Quebec. Unlike other provinces where the facilitative is the most common form of public enterprise in Quebec there is a clear preponderance of the nationalistic type. Since 1960 a network of state enterprises have been created. Coming one after another, such enterprises as SGF, SOQUEM, SOQUIP, Rexfor and Sogefer have been initiated in accordance with one basic idea—the development of the Quebec economy by and for Québecois. Described as the economic liberation of Quebec, the object has been to create a specifically Francophone economic base.[66]

Nationalism has also been an important basis for public enterprise outside Quebec. In the West especially, provincial governments have a long history of acting to favour the growth of locally controlled economic development. Western alienation—the traditional feeling that the western economy has been exploited for the benefit of the East—has been an important motivation behind nationalistic enterprise. This surfaced clearly in the import substitution strategy that was a major element in the first CCF government's creation of Crown corporations and in later efforts in all western provinces to diversify their economies.

It has been shown that much of the public enterprise activity in Alberta has centred on replacing eastern dominance with control by Albertans.[67] Tupper's analysis of the acquisition of Pacific Western Airlines argues that the Alberta government bought the company after it was unable to persuade private interests in Alberta to purchase it. In any case the overriding objective was to have Albertans control this transportation link, believed to be crucial to the province's development, rather than allow it to be controlled by interests outside the province.[68]

More than the other two types, nationalistic corporations reflect some of the impact of the federal system on policy-making. Besides attempting to develop the provincial sector at the expense of outside private interests, nationalist Crown corporations are used by provincial governments in their conflicts with Ottawa. For example, the Société d'Habitation du Québec, was established to compete in the housing field with the federal government's Central Mortgage and Housing Corporation. Similarly B.C. Petroleum Corporation and Alberta Gas Trunk Link and the Société Québecois

---

[65] J. Richards and L. Pratt, *supra* note 48, at 237.

[66] P. Fournier, *Les Sociétés d'État de les objectifs économiques du Québec: une évaluation preliminaire* (Québec: Éditeur officiel du Québec, Ministère des Communications, La Documentation québécoise, 1977).

[67] J. Richards and L. Pratt, *supra* note 48, chapter 9.

[68] Allan Tupper, *supra* note 6, at 99-113.

D'Initiatives Petrolières (SOQUIP) were established to counter federal initiatives in the distribution of natural gas. Similarly, in Quebec's jurisdictional dispute with Ottawa over cable television the Office de Radio-Télé Diffusion du Québec (ORTQ) is an important factor.

The politics surrounding nationalistic corporations reflect their unique characteristics. As with other nationalistic policy-making, although everyone is said to gain, the benefits are in fact less widely distributed than they might appear to be.[69] Pratt describes the impact of Alberta's policies in the 1970s.

> Alberta's recent experiments in state enterprise should be understood as a form of public works undertaken for the benefit of the province's business community and urban middle class.[70]

The level of conflict will in part reflect the extent to which these policies are believed to benefit the entire province, rather than any one segment. The extent to which losers within the province are mobilized, will also be a function of the organization and representation of external interests. Much depends on the degree to which the province's actions are characterized as scaring off vitally needed venture capital rather than as strengthening the provincial economy.

(e) Partisanship and Instruments of Policy

Do differences in policy-making between governments of the left and non-left go beyond variations in the extent to which each is likely to turn to public ownership? Can analysis by objective bring to light, systematic differences in the use of public ownership? At issue here is whether the partisanship of the party in power is related to the kinds of state ownership it creates, and more specifically, whether analysis of the objectives of Crown corporations can help to explain the circumstances in which the nonleft employs state ownership?

At the provincial level there is clear evidence that non-socialist governments have used public ownership almost *exclusively* to facilitate economic development. Starting with the early cases in which hydro and other services were provided, nonleft governments have continued to promote private sector growth. Industrial development corporations, the largest single functional category of public enterprise, have, since 1960, been an important policy instrument. Out of the 30 provincial industrial development corpora-

---

69 See, *e.g.*, Guindon, "Social Unrest, Social Class and Quebec's Bureaucratic Revolution" (1964), 71 *Queen's Quarterly* 150.

70 Pratt, "The State and Province-Building: Alberta's Development Strategy" in Panitch *supra* note 61, at 155.

TABLE VI
Facilitative Corporations

Sector	Total Number	Number created by nonleft
Industrial Development	30	26
Research and Development	10	9
Power	8	7
Transportation	18	14

tions, only four have been created by a left government. In other areas in which the enterprises are usually facilitative such as power, research and development, and transportation facilities and systems—the nonleft have created the overwhelming majority of these corporations. Thus, despite the greater overall likelihood and higher rate of public ownership by the left, more facilitative corporations are established by the nonleft.

Although facilitative enterprises demonstrate a willingness by the nonleft to use the state, this mode of intervention has not been employed to assert public control over the economy. The distinction, which has been drawn in other national settings, between the state as lender and subsidizer as opposed to entrepreneur and manager, is relevant here.[71] It is quite possible for the state to provide much needed capital through loans, guarantees, etc., and yet permit the private sector and market forces to continue to determine the direction of the economy. It cannot be assumed that public enterprises are always used to intrude on the private sector or to force it into line with the objectives of the state. A good example of a provincial government acting as a promoter but eschewing any direct control is the Société du Development Industriel du Québec. Established by the Liberal government in 1971, the fund was prohibited from owning more than 30 percent of any venture while being specifically confined to providing capital and not external control.

Crown ownership to promote rather than control is a policy tool well within the ideological ken of nonsocialists. Based on the shared interest of the state and the private sector, it involves the use of the state to further those interests. Although, as with other instances of public enterprise, it does involve a blurring of the boundary between the private and public; it must be looked upon as "nonintrusive intervention".

Redistributive Crown corporations present a very different picture of the origins of public enterprise. With the insurance and some of the resource corporations as the main examples, the left has borne the sole

---

[71] See S. Holland, ed. *The State as Entrepreneur* (London: Weidenfeld and Nicolson, 1972); Bennett and Sharpe, "The State as Banker and Entrepreneur: The Last-Resort Character of the Mexican State's Economic Intervention, 1917-76" (1980), 12 *Comparative Politics* 165.

responsibility for this kind of state enterprise. However, some, like the insurance companies, have been retained by incoming Conservative or Liberal governments. As a tool of public policy, the redistributive Crown corporation is especially attractive to the left for a number of reasons. Not only is it a means for providing a more equitable distribution of economic benefits, it is also an instrument for deconcentrating economic power. In both British Columbia and Manitoba, for example, a major element in the government's entry into the resource arena was the high degree of corporate concentration in these areas.

In direct comparison with facilitative actions, redistribution represents a greater intrusion into the economy. For left governments, the use of Crown corporations as a channel of access for planning and focusing the economy is as important as whatever direct redistribution the enterprise generates. It is the redistributive, and to some extent the nationalistic, corporations that have been used by the left as instruments for asserting public control over the economic system. In British Columbia, for example, the NDP government was committed not only to redistribution of income but also to the notion of controlled growth—the regulation of unrestrained resource development.[72]

The nationalistic Crown corporations illustrate yet another pattern of partisan use. It appears that both socialist and nonsocialist governments have instituted nationalistic Crown corporatons. Since 1960, in Quebec, the Liberals, Union Nationale and Parti Québécois have all used public ownership to further provincial autonomy. In the pursuit of nationalistic objectives the post-1960 Quebec governments created a large number of Crown corporations. Unlike the others, the PQ, however, has instituted a tightening of government control over the state corporations.[73]

Nationalistic Crown corporations have tended to arise in the perephery provinces and in Quebec, which has its own unique set of grievances. In the West, for example, Richards and Pratt have illustrated the ways in which the NDP in Saskatchewan and the Progressive Conservatives in Alberta have tried to enhance provincial control over their economies.[74] It is perhaps indicative of the changes in Canadian federalism that Ontario, the province generally associated with dominance within the federal system, has seen fit in the 1970s to set up a nationalistic Crown corporation. The Ontario Energy Corporation whose main purpose is to enhance the availability of energy in Ontario may be viewed as one response to Ontario's vulnerability in the field of energy.

---

[72] Raymond Payne, "Corporate Power, Interest Group Activity and Mining Policy in B.C., 1972-77" [paper presented to the Canadian Political Science Association, 1980]. See also Government of Manitoba, *Guidelines for the Seventies, Vol. 1, Introduction and Economic Analysis* (Winnipeg: Office of the Queen's Printer, 1973).

[73] Fournier, *supra* note 33, at 75.

[74] J. Richards and L. Pratt, *supra* note 48.

Although partisanship appears at first not to have much utility in the analysis of nationalistic Crown corporations, it can, in fact, further our understanding of the actions of party governments. For nonleft governments it is the potential basis for their greatest control over the economic system. Under the rubric of nationalism, in Alberta, for example, it has meant abandonment of a passive rentier strategy and the development of a far more positive role for the provincial state.[75] As external forces are believed to have an impact on the provinces' well-being the justification for action grows.

The degree of openness of the economy, and hence its vulnerability, has been found in other national settings to be the most important factor in determining the size of the public economy.[76] Thus it may be expected that all governments, including the nonleft, will turn increasingly to public ownership as one way of coping with this vulnerability. Nationalistic state ownership may be a modern form of defensive expansion. Since 1960 both the left and nonleft have used public enterprise as an instrument of nationalism. The nationalistic Crown corporation reflects the provinces' response to problems of economic development in vastly different economic and political milieux. Advanced technology may require efforts beyond the private sector and the changed federal system has prompted governments to become more than passive actors in that economic development.

For the left, nationalistic public ownership can be a politically more acceptable instrument that performs some of the same functions as the redistributive corporation. It can permit some reallocation of benefits as well as government planning and the deconcentration of economic power. For example, in British Columbia under the Barrett government and in Quebec under the PQ, nationalistic Crown corporations have been used to assert provincial control over the economy. Given the degree of foreign ownership and extent of federal power over the economy, as well as the dominance of the central provinces, much of the left's concerns with the skewed distribution of wealth and the concentration of economic power can be directed toward external forces and hence nationalistic corporations rather than internal divisions and redistributive enterprise.

VI. CONCLUSION

An understanding of provincial public ownership cannot rest on any unicausal explanation. Undoubtedly many factors have had their impact on this form of public policy. This essay has been primarily devoted to an

---

[75] See Stevenson, ''Political Constraints and the Province-Building Objective'' (1980), 6 *Canadian Public Policy/Analyse de Politiques* 265.
[76] Cameron, *supra* note 24.

evaluation of the role of party politics in shaping the extent and form of governmental entrepreneurship. Contrary to many widely held impressions, the evidence presented here shows that partisan and ideological characteristics must be taken into account when analyzing this facet of public policy.

Parties of the left are likely to turn to state ownership more frequently than other governments. However, even more crucial than distinctive partisan propensities to establish Crown corporations is the difference in the purposes for which Crown corporations have been employed. Like other policy instruments, state enterprise can serve a number of functions. For the most part, Conservatives, Liberals and other parties of the nonleft have viewed public ownership not as an instrument for controlling or shaping the economy but rather as an alternative to incentives, subsidies and the like in support of the private sector. The left on the other hand have used Crown corporations as instruments of economic and social control in line with the goals of redistribution and deconcentration of power. While governments of diverse ideologies have used Crown corporations, they have used them for diverse objectives. The trend toward an expanded use of Crown corporations is a result of several factors that are related to the various functions of state ownership.

CHAPTER 4

THE UNCHARTED UNIVERSE OF FEDERAL PUBLIC CORPORATIONS*

JOHN W. LANGFORD†
AND
KENNETH J. HUFFMAN†

I. INTRODUCTION

It has been widely noted in recent literature that public corporations are key elements in government as suppliers of goods and services at the federal level.[1] In addition, the activities (and misadventures) of a few select federal public corporations, such as Petro-Canada, Air Canada, and VIA Rail, are occasionally brought to the attention of Canadian citizens by the media. However, there have been few attempts to provide detailed comprehensive data on the scope and significance of federal public corporations within the wider public sector. Various official lists of public corporations and data collections on public enterprise do exist;[2] but—as Bird and others

* This study was funded by the Ontario Economic Council. The authors wish to thank the Editor of *Canadian Public Administration* for permission to reprint in revised form parts of an article by John W. Langford in (1980), 23 *Can. Pub. Admin.* 76.
† School of Public Administration, University of Victoria.

[1] See Tupper, "The State in Business" (1979), 22 *Can. Pub. Admin.* 124; Langford, "The Identification and Classification of Federal Public Corporations: A Preface to Regime Building" (1980), 23 *Can. Pub. Admin.* 76.
[2] See Canada. Office of the Comptroller General. "Corporations in which the Government Has an Interest" Revised (Ottawa: May, 1980); Canada. Office of the Comptroller General. "Information Requested by Mr. Cossitt on Crown Corporations and Other Such Separate Entities" (Ottawa: August 29, 1980).
  To construct our data package for the 1978-79 fiscal year, we used a mailed questionnaire and the following sources in addition to the available Annual Reports of corporations: Canada. Treasury Board. *Estimates for the fiscal year ending March 31, 1979* (Ottawa: Ministry of Supply and Services, 1978); Canada. Department of Finance. Receiver General for Canada. *Public Accounts of Canada 1979: Volume III Financial Statements of Crown Corporations* (Ottawa: Ministry of Supply and Services, 1979); Canada. Auditor General of Canada. *Report of the Auditor General of Canada to the House of Commons for the fiscal year ended March 31, 1976* (Ottawa: Ministry of Supply and Services, 1976); Canada. Statistics Canada. Public Finance Division. *Federal Government Enterprise Finance: Income and expenditure, assets, liabilities and net worth: 1978* (Ottawa: Ministry of Supply and Services, Statistics Canada #61-203, 1980); Canada. Statistics Canada. Business Register Division. "Business Register Master File" (Ottawa: Statistics Canada unpublished computer printout, updated on request); Canada. Statistics Canada. Public Finance Division. *Federal*

have noted—none of these provide the interested observer with the necessary disaggregated data with which to analyze the boundaries of the federal public corporate universe, historical and functional patterns of usage of public corporations as instruments of policy, and the size and signficance of the corporate enterprise sector relative to the wider federal public sector, the corporate efforts of the provincial governments, and the comparable activities of the private sector.[3] Parallelling the efforts of Vining and Botterell with respect to provincial public corporations, this essay is designed to provide a "snapshot" of the federal public corporate universe as it was constituted in 1980, and more detailed data for 1978-79 on a narrower range of federal government enterprises within that corporate universe. While our data by no means provide a suitable basis for all of the analytical tasks outlined above, they hopefully establish a rough foundation for further work on this largely ignored component of the public sector.

The following section is directed towards the problems of identifying a public corporation. The discussion centres around the contemporary debate at the federal level on the need to distinguish this species from other forms of government organization (*e.g.*, departments, branches, commissions), on the one hand, and corporations which may have a variety of links with the government but which may not usefully be thought of as directly accountable corporate instruments of federal public policy, on the other. Those seeking an analytical tool for sharply delineating the federal public corporate sector from its private counterpart may not be in the best of spirits at the end of this discussion.

Overriding a number of the problems raised in the previous sections, Section III of the paper and, in particular, Table I, present a list of federal public corporations. Figures 1-3 examine the data in Table I in more detail and, specifically provide an analysis of the data on "year of incorporation or acquisition", "designated minister", and "corporate headquarters" location for all the corporations in which the federal government has a direct ownership or membership interest. This section concludes with the division of members of the above corporate universe in which the government has a *direct* involvement (*i.e.*, excluding subsidiaries, sub-subsidiaries and associated corporations) on the basis of functional groupings compatible with the product groupings used in the Statistics Canada Standard Industrial Classification series. The results are displayed in Table II.

---

government employment, 1978-80 (Ottawa: Ministry of Supply and Services, Statistics Canada #72-004 Quarterly, 1978-81); Canada. *Royal Commission on Financial Management and Accountability: Final Report, March 1979* (Ottawa: Minister of Supply and Services, 1979) Chapter 16 and Appendix A (Allen Thomas Lambert was Chairman of the Commission: hereinafter cited as the "Lambert Commission"); Canadian Tax Foundation. *The National Finances, 1978-79* (Toronto: Canadian Tax Foundation, 1979) Chapter 19 "Crown Corporations".

[3] See especially R. M. Bird, *Financing Canadian Government: A Quantitative Overview* (Toronto: Canadian Tax Foundation, 1979) at 1-7.

The fourth section, which attempts to make the leap from public corporation to corporate enterprise, may prove equally contentious to the compulsive boundary drawer. In this section and the accompanying Table III, "non-enterprise" federal public corporations are discarded and economic data are provided on those which remain. The problems associated with collecting and using this data are also outlined. The essay concludes with some comments on the growth and performance of this enterprise group, and, where possible, comparisons with the Vining and Botterell findings and comparable data on the private corporate sector.

II. WOULD YOU RECOGNIZE A FEDERAL PUBLIC CORPORATION IF YOU MET ONE?

While it would seem to be perfectly understandable that Vining and Botterell would have difficulty constructing a definition of a "public" or "Crown" corporation which would be adaptable to the usages of ten provincial governments, it might be anticipated that this would be an easy task at the federal level. Nothing could be further from the truth. No such definition exists and the federal government is still a long way from developing an identification and data integration package which would be of use to lawyers, economists, political scientists, parliamentarians and members of the general public interested in defining the boundaries of the federal public corporate universe as a basis upon which to analyze the accountability of the public corporate sector, its growth, or its performance. This is clearly a task for the federal government because, as this essay will adequately demonstrate, it is an extremely difficult assignment for an outside observer.

The need to identify federal public corporations is obviously part of the wider problem of fully understanding the extent of the entire spectrum of government's non-departmental growth at the periphery, a problem shared with many other jurisdictions and reflected in the use and abuse in recent years of concepts such as "Crown corporations", "mixed enterprises", "joint enterprises", "quasi-public corporations", "quagos", "quangos" and "fringe bodies".[4] What is patently clear in the federal context is that the legislatively endorsed approach to the identification of the public corporate sector has been inadequate from the outset. It is a widely repeated part of our administrative mythology that in 1951 the term "Crown corporations" and the newly minted schedules of the Financial Administration Act[5] (FAA) satisfactorily covered the waterfront of the federal govern-

---

[4] See C. Hood, "The World of Quasi-Government" (unpublished paper presented at the Annual Conference of the Public Administration Committee, York, England, September 3-5, 1979).

[5] *Financial Administration Act*, S.C. 1951 (2nd Session), c. 12, ss. 76-88 and Schedules B, C, and D.

ment's corporate involvement in the economy and the wider society. The fact is that while 33 corporations were listed under the three schedules of the new Act, as many as eight others (including the Canadian Wheat Board, the Bank of Canada and various joint enterprises with provincial governments) remained unscheduled from the beginning.[6] This situation has become progressively worse until, in1980, only 56 (just over 12 percent) of 464 corporations in which the government claims to have "an interest" are clearly designated as Crown corporations, scheduled under the Act, and, therefore, subject to its financial management and accountability provisions.

This rather unsatisfactory turn of events is, in part, due to the linguistic shortcomings of the FAA, specifically the ambiguous meaning attached to "Crown corporations"—a term invented for the legislation. For all intents and purposes, the federal government in 1951 equated the universe of public corporations with what it referred to in the FAA as Crown corporations. This term seemed to embrace only corporations the shares of which the federal government wholly owned, or corporations created by special act for which the government—by analogy—was the sole shareholder. However, no useful definition of a Crown corporation was given in the Act (or at any subsequent time in the next 28 years) other than it "means a corporation that is ultimately accountable, through a Minister, to Parliament for the conduct of its affairs, and includes the corporations named in Schedule B, Schedule C and Schedule D".[7] Amongst the other ambiguities of this definition, it was never clearly established whether it excludes corporations which have not been named in the schedules. Some of the corporations outside the schedules have been referred to as "unclassified" or "para" Crown corporations, although the continued stretching of the term "Crown corporation" to cover a much wider universe of corporations than those scheduled has contributed to the modern sense that it is a term without substantive meaning.

A number of significant conceptual and empirical problems stand in the way of the achievement of a comprehensive list and data set encompassing all federal public corporations. Christopher Hood has observed that "to count 'quangos' . . ., is rather like trying to count the stones on the seashore between the tidemarks".[8] Surely, as a subset of that problem, identifying and counting public corporations should not be quite so difficult.[9] Can one not say—as the "corporate" part of the test—that all public cor-

---

6 See Balls, "Financial Control and Accountability of Canadian Crown Corporations" (1953), 31 *Pub. Admin.* 127, at 132; and the Lambert Commission, *supra* note 2, at 292.

7 *Financial Administration Act*, R.S.C. 1970, c. F-10, s. 66 (am. Schedule B, SOR/78-285, 378; Schedule C, SOR/71-404; SIR/76-376; SOR/79-441; Schedule D, 1974-75-76, c. 14, s. 56, c. 61, s. 15, c. 77, s. 8; SOR/78-287).

8 Hood, *supra* note 4, at 10.

9 For a discussion of the problem in the British context, see Chester, "Public Corporations and the Classification of Administrative Bodies" (1952), 1 *Political Studies* 34.

porations, as corporations, except for a couple of anachronistic corporations "sole" (*e.g.*, Director of Soldier Settlement), have a common corporate organizational form distinguished by a board of directors, and a separate legal existence under a special constituent act or individual articles of incorporation by which powers and responsibilities are delegated to the board? Is this test for corporate status immediately rendered irrelevant because some public corporations appear to function managerially as departments, and perform tasks which resemble "departmental tasks" (*e.g.*, Canada Employment and Immigration Commission)? Or does the similarity of the tasks and management styles of two agency types merely raise questions about the logic of the government's choice on certain occasions of a specific agency type?[10] We would support the latter position. Surely a more critical conceptual problem in the confusion of the mixed economy is the clarification of the nature of "public"; some satisfactory way of drawing a line between those corporations for which the government and the corporation board are to be held accountable *to some degree* for their governance to Parliament and those for which they are not. For this do we not have to develop a widely accepted and testable group of indicators or criteria of "public"? Candidates might include: the source or form of the delegation of power to a corporation; evidence of government ownership or membership (regardless of how indirect or minor); evidence of government sponsorship;[11] the status of the corporation as an agent *vis-à-vis* the Crown; the provision by government of capital or operating funds; or the corporation's use of government grants. Ideally, the criteria should not be based on characteristics of the corporation which flow directly from the regime of government direction and management under which it presently operates as this would have the effect of short-circuiting the underlying issue of "publicness".

The empirical problems confronting the identification exercise are no less daunting. Until recently, there was virtually nowhere one could go for any reliable data on this far-flung universe. The FAA schedules are, as we have indicated, hopelessly inadequate. The Public Accounts are worse. Some interesting additions to these traditional sources of corporation names may occasionally be the reward for a close study of departmental expenditures in the Blue Book of Estimates. In the absence of any publicly available directory of appointments made by ministers, one wonders what could be gleaned from the list of available directorships drawn up by the dispensers of patronage within the Prime Minister's Office? As we shall see,

---

[10] See Hood, "Keeping the Centre Small: Explanations of Agency Type" (1978), 26 *Political Studies* 30.

[11] On sponsorship, see Chester, "Fringe Bodies, Quangos and All That" (1979), 57 *Pub. Admin.* 51, at 52; and B. L. R. Smith, ed., *The New Political Economy: The Public Use of the Private Sector* (New York: MacMillan Press, 1975).

the government's list of public corporations, first compiled in 1977, is inadequate for both conceptual and empirical reasons; nevertheless, it is light years ahead of any previous listing and remains, to date, the only comprehensive survey of public corporations available.

The government has trouble establishing the boundaries of its own corporate universe, in part, because the simple discovery of many subsidiaries, sub-subsidiaries, associated corporations, etc., and other more curious forms of corporations depends on the co-operation of parent public corporations, ministers, and senior government officials which in the past has not always been forthcoming. What chance does the outside researcher have of checking these results? In any case, what is the usefulness of playing the identification game if all one is left with is names? To check the accuracy of one's judgment and to make a list useful for economic, political or legal analysis requires more substantial information. The contemporary concern about this issue dates from the Auditor General's (A.G.) insistence in his 1976 Report that the government's dereliction with respect to the identification and grouping of all government-owned and controlled corporations was one of the root causes of the failure to develop adequate financial management and control practices for the corporations which his office audits.[12] How can you monitor the practices of corporations, the existence of which you are unaware? Specifically with respect to the identification of public corporations, the A.G. stated that he requested a complete listing of "government-owned or controlled" corporations from the Treasury Board, the Department of Finance and the Privy Council Office. "None could provide it."[13] But the A.G. did not stop at a general indictment. He went on in his 1976 Report to note that a preliminary survey by his staff had identified "more than 30 corporations not scheduled in the FAA". Consequently, he recommended that "all government-owned and controlled corporations should be scheduled in the FAA and subject to its provisions".[14] This is really the sum of the A.G.'s contribution. It is noteworthy, that while his proposal provoked significant reaction, it made only a minor addition to the methodological and empirical knowledge of the public corporate sector. The A.G. did not know how to approach the problem of identification himself, but he needed no tutoring in how to turn his "discovery" of the shortcomings of the FAA to political advantage.

The A.G.'s Report put the government on the spot. Despite the fact that the Treasury Board Secretariat (TBS) and the Privy Council Office (PCO) had been conscious for a decade of the inadequacies of the FAA as a boundary marker, only desultory efforts had been made to catalogue

---

12 Auditor General of Canada, *supra* note 2, at 231.
13 *Ibid.*
14 *Ibid.* For the Auditor General's list of "government-owned and controlled corporations", see 289-292.

Crown corporations and their subsidiaries. This had never been seen as a priority. Although the TBS lamented that it did not have the legislative authority under the FAA or any other statute to collect and collate this particular kind of data, an inventory of 366 "government-owned and controlled corporations" was rushed to completion by May, 1977, in response to the A.G.'s criticism. The accuracy of the A.G.'s charge that the government did not even know the names or number of the corporations which it owned and controlled is reflected in the fact that between the publication of the list and its first revision in January, 1978, the government "found" 17 more corporations. A still later version released by the Office of the Comptroller General (OCG) in August, 1979, contained 401 corporations. The most recent edition, revised in March, 1980, is entitled more vaguely "corporations in which the government has an interest" and lists 464 corporations.[15] Ranging well beyond the FAA's 56 Crown corporations, this most recent edition of the list enumerates a further 23 "other government corporations" "owned or controlled solely by the Government of Canada" which are not included in the three Crown corporation schedules. The next category is labelled "mixed enterprises", "corporations owned or controlled jointly with other governments and/or other organizations" and numbers 25. By far the largest groups in this catalogue are the 210 "subsidiary corporations and their subsidiaries" and 124 "associated corporations" of previously listed Crown corporations, other government corporations, and mixed enterprises. Finally, out of the farthest reaches of the corporate universe, according to the list, are a disparate group of 26 corporations arcanely labelled "other entities and associates" and defined with inexcusable imprecision, by an office devoted to exactitude as "bodies corporate, established by treaty, special act or by letters patent, and not operating as a branch of a department". Informally, the OCG refers to this as a "fuzzy catch-all group".

Although the list performs an extremely important service by alerting observers to the existence of a vast number of what would appear to be public corporations beyond the confines of the FAA schedules, it by no means provides a clear and unassailable photograph of the government's corporate entanglements. On the most practical level, as a data base it is incomplete. It is widely believed within the central agencies concerned— although not openly discussed for obvious political reasons—that there are still a large number of corporations unidentified, in part because of the lack of co-operation on the part of departmental officials and corporation managers in tracking them down. Another problem is the paucity of the data contained in the list. The only information provided for each corporation is the portfolio of which it is part and the name of its auditor; this

---

[15] See Office of the Comptroller General, *supra* note 2, "Corporations in which the Government has an interest".

hardly provides a well-rounded picture of the public corporate sector.[16] In addition, this lack of data contributes to the sense of suspicion that the distinctions made between groups within the list (*e.g.*, "other government corporations" and "other entities and associates") are artificial at best, although the government makes no pretence that these groupings (other than the three FAA schedules) should be considered relevant for classification purposes.

A far more significant consideration is the overarching conceptual imprecision of the list itself. The title of the list—"corporations in which the government has an interest"—is not defined, except in the sense that, like the title of the previous editions of the list "government-owned and controlled corporations", it is commonly used by interested senior public servants as a synonym for "public". The user of the list is given no definitive statement of what test or tests the drafters employed to draw the line between the public and private sectors in the course of scouring the countryside for federal public corporations. From this arises a number of conceptual questions. For instance, the list contains several non-shareholding corporations (*e.g.*, Vanier Institute of the Family, Forest Engineering Research Institute of Canada) which can not be properly termed as "owned" by the government because they are non-share capital corporations and could not be described in any of the common legal senses of the word as "controlled" because the government does not have the power to name a majority of the members of the board of directors.[17] In what sense specifically does the government have "an interest" in such corporations? Why are some of them listed as "other government corporations" and others as "other entities and associates"? Similarly, what kind of "interest" does the government have in international banking and aid operations such as the International Bank for Reconstruction and Development and the African Development Fund which would qualify them for this list? A related and potentially more interesting example of corporations which would not appear to qualify for status as public corporations—again, despite the presence on the list of examples—are those share capital and membership corporations (*e.g.*, Federal Insolvency Trustee Agency) which have been started up by individual Ministers or public servants acting—in their own minds at least—on behalf of government, but, in fact, without the blessing of either statutory

---

16 The Office of the Comptroller General—in answer to a question in the House of Commons—provided some additional information (date of incorporation or acquisition, location of corporate headquarters, statement of corporate function) for a number of corporations on the list. See Office of the Comptroller General, *supra* note 2, "Information requested by Mr. Cossitt". The O.C.G. is presently reviewing its whole approach to data collection in this area.

17 *Canada Corporations Act*, R.S.C. 1970, c.C-32, Part II, ss. 153-157, provides for the incorporation and administration of non-profit organizations.

authority or even the knowledge of the governor-in-council.[18] While individuals in government may have an "interest" in such corporations, it is not clear what the government's "interest" is. This casual and often covert approach to incorporation raises the question of what kind of legal connection—if any—the government has with these corporations, beyond the fact that such corporations are often funded, at least in part, by federal money. On at least one occasion (Dungarvon Forestry Project Inc.), the government has apparently been obliged to meet the financial obligations of such a corporation when it was declared insolvent. Finally, the list's title not only raises questions about what is included, but also about what is omitted. From the mixed enterprise grouping are those corporations in which the government holds some shares on a temporary basis to secure a loan. This approach is probably legitimate if the involvement is indeed temporary, and the government's "interest" in the firm's affairs does not extend beyond the prerogatives normally granted a short term creditor in the private sector. However, the government's actual mode of behaviour in these cases has never, to our knowledge, been adequately analyzed, and, therefore it would seem premature to exclude such corporations without further investigation. In general, then, these problems throw doubt on the validity of the list as an accurate boundary marker of government's corporate involvement, raise complicated and significant legal issues related both to the definition of "corporations in which the government has an interest" and to the question of the government's liability (as the "deepest pocket") for the operations of corporations formed by its Ministers and senior officials, and begs wider questions about what Ministers and public servants are and should be doing "on behalf of the government".

The only significant alternative to the government's half-hearted and disjointed efforts to establish a framework for the identification of the federal public sector was presented by the Royal Commission on Financial Management and Accountability (the Lambert Commission). The Commission's proposals were but part of a far more ambitious scheme for the identification and classification of the entire "motley" of federal non-departmental bodies.[19] The Commission recognized that both the FAA schedules and definitions and the TBS/OCG list were conceptually inadequate as tools for the identification of public corporations. The Commission's conceptual approach to identification was to set down three criteria based on characteristics against which all corporations could be measured. The

---

[18] Even in cases where corporations are created by Ministers or public servants under federal or provincial corporation law with cabinet approval or direction and thus have a strong aura of legality, it has been argued that without prior statutory authority, the legality of the incorporations is in doubt and the status of the corporations (*e.g.*, Loto Canada, Via Rail Canada, Hockey Canada), as "government" corporations, is questionable. See Lambert Commission, *supra* note 2, at 334 and at 364-365.

[19] *Ibid.*, at 279.

characteristics were *direct* delegation of authority (in contrast to indirect delegation through a minister as it is for departments), the presence of a board of directors, and the presence of managerial and decision-making processes characterized by collective board responsibility for the corporation's "care and management" in keeping with the private sector (*i.e.*, entrepreneurial) nature of the corporate task.[20] Operationalizing these criteria leads the Commission to identify three types of public corporations making up the federal corporate universe:

(1) "Crown corporations" which are wholly owned by government;
(2) "shared enterprises" in which government has taken a direct equity position in common with other participants;
(3) "Quasi-public corporations" which are non-profit or membership corporations, "encouraged" or "sponsored" by government, of which government is a member.

The application of the criteria also lead to some unexpected and curious results. The Commission recommended that a number of corporations (*e.g.*, Canadian Arsenals Ltd., Canadian Film Development Corp., Social Science and Humanities Research Council) be excluded from public corporate status and recast as departmental or "independent deciding and advisory" type agencies. It also raised questions about the validity of including ten marketing and commodity agencies in the public corporate universe. At the "edge of the public sector" a number of membership corporations (*e.g.*, Hockey Canada, Vanier Institute of the Family) are declared to be "quasi-public corporations", something less "public" in nature than their status in the government's eyes as "government-owned and controlled" corporations.[21] At least with this approach, the boundaries of the public corporate sector begin to appear. We are entitled to ask if the Commission's recommendations might have the makings of an ideal solution to the identification dilemma.

An immediate concern has to be that the Commission's proposals exclude from the public corporation field, organizations which would appear to be corporations by the test we outlined earlier. Why? The Lambert test for corporations is somewhat more ambitious than our own in that it employs a criterion dictating that a public corporation's board must have a certain kind and degree of collective managerial authority appropriate to the entrepreneurial nature of the corporate task. The use of this criterion is a reflection of the Commission's desire to accomplish more than the mere identification of public corporations. The criteria package is established with an eye to rooting out those corporations which in the Commission's

---

20 *Ibid.*, at 279-85. See also Auditor General of Canada, *supra* note 2, at 232.
21 Lambert Commission, *supra* note 2, in Appendix A.

view are really some other type of agency in corporate disguise. In short, it is designed to test for "corporateness" as well as "publicness" in order to demonstrate cases where the corporate organization form is being abused or is inappropriate. This "positive" approach to identification is a new and extremely interesting wrinkle. However, fixated by the desire to rid the schedules of non-corporate corporations, the Commission sidestepped the conceptual questions associated with basing a test for "corporateness" on a characteristic which at least in part is not inherent to the organization being tested but is dependent exclusively on the regime for direction and management which the government has chosen to apply to it.

The Lambert Commission also adds the criterion of "direct delegation" to its test for public corporation status. This is the criterion which appears to be most relevant to the Commission's inclination to exclude membership corporations from public corporate status. However, the Commission is clearly not convinced on the basis of its test that these corporations are not public. Its acceptance of a nether-world of "quasi-public corporations" is a reflection of the inadequacy of its criteria package for making knife-edge distinctions between public and private on the outer edge of the putative public corporation universe. The Commission does not go on to discuss whether or not the addition of other criteria such as government sponsorship or funding would make the test more viable. Nor does it clarify other conceptual problems which might arise from the widest application of the "direct delegation" criterion. For instance, would the "direct delegation" test threaten the public corporation status of subsidiary and associated corporations which have no *direct* relationship with government? In large part, the Commission was aware of the shortcomings of its analysis. It recognized the need to develop a comprehensive conceptual framework for the identification of public corporations and worked towards that end. However, short of resources (by comparison with the government) and pressed for time, it did not push the development of its approach to the limit and questions remain.

III. PERSPECTIVES ON FEDERAL PUBLIC CORPORATIONS

In the list of 454 federal public corporations contained in Table I we have tried to combine the best aspects of the Lambert Commission's conceptual approach to identification with the encyclopedic efforts of the OCG's list and supplementary data offerings. Conceptually, the primary intention is to identify and list all administratively active public corporations in which the government was continuously involved as an owner or member in May, 1980. Therefore, Table I is divided into three groups with different types and, in a sense, descending degrees of government involvement: 81 corporations which the government owns solely (Group I); 20 corporations which the government owns jointly with other governments, private organizations, or individuals (Group II); and 18 corporations in which the government has a sponsorship and continuing membership interest (Group III). All subsidiary, sub-subsidiary and associated corporations with which the government is *indirectly* involved are displayed immediately following the name of the corporation with which the government is directly involved as an owner or member. In addition, Table I contains data on the "designated minister", "function", and "year, headquarters, and mode of incorporation or acquisition" for each corporation with which the government is directly involved.[22]

Our list, therefore, discards the ponderous and misleading eight-part division featured in the OCG approach in favour of a "status relationship" approach based largely on the Lambert Commission recommendations. However, out of step with Lambert, our list accepts as *bona fide* public corporations all ostensibly corporate organizations with which (according to the OCG) the government is continuously involved, directly or indirectly, as an owner or member. No corporation is excluded, therefore, because it lacks "corporateness". In addition, we gather those membership corporations which the Commission labels "quasi-public" into our "public" net. Corporations on our list (and the subsidiary and associated corporations attached to them) are public to some degree *because* of the government's direct or indirect ownership or membership relationship with them and, therefore, some measure of accountability to Parliament for their activities should be expected. In short, as implied earlier, our tests for "corporateness" and "publicness" are simpler and less demanding than those proposed by the Lambert Commission.

The fact that our list contains virtually all of the corporations included in the OCG's May, 1980, list is a reflection of simple necessity. We had neither the resources nor the powers to duplicate across the board the government's less than satisfactory survey. Therefore, we would argue that while Table I is more effectively organized than the OCG list, it is only marginally more comprehensive or authoritative in terms of the size of the corporate universe "captured". We do add three corporations of long-

---

22 The "designated minister" data is drawn from the Office of the Comptroller General's May, 1980 list, *supra* note 2. The "function" and "year of incorporation" data comes primarily from the Office of the Comptroller General, "Information Requested by Mr. Cossitt . . .", *supra* note 2. Statements of function for a small number of subsidiary corporations are available in Statistics Canada. *Federal Government Enterprise Finance, supra* note 2, at 20-26. The "mode of incorporation or acquisition" data is drawn from a variety of sources including: Canada. Interdepartmental Committee on the Organization of the Government of Canada. *Organization of the Government of Canada 1976*, 11th ed. (Ottawa: Ministry of Supply and Services, 1976); Canada. Treasury Board. *Organization of the Government of Canada 1978/79*, 12th ed. (Ottawa: MacMillan Co. and Ministry of Supply and Services, 1979); Statistics Canada. *Federal Government Enterprise Finance, supra* note 2; and our own questionnaire.

standing (Agricultural Products Board, Army Benevolent Fund, and National Farm Products Marketing Council) which appear to have been omitted from the OCG list in error. In addition, we remove from the list 11 corporations which are presently inactive for various reasons (*e.g.*, bankruptcy or insolvency) and are being wound up or phased out. Those removed include five wholly owned corporations (Centennial Commission, CN West Indies Steamship Ltd., Custodian of Enemy Property, Federal Insolvency Trustee Agency, and Radio Engineering Products Ltd.), five joint ownership corporations (Abenaki Motel Ltd., Crane Cove Oyster Farm Ltd., Mainland Investments Ltd., Mohawk St. Regis Lacrosse Ltd. and Shong Way Shi Corporation Ltd.) and one membership corporation (Canadian Colour and Fashion Trend Service). Three other corporations are relocated within the list as subsidiaries.

This is the extent of the changes, however. We were unable to add anything to the sum of knowledge of those joint ownership corporations in which the government has taken an equity position as a "short-term" creditor. Similarly, our list follows the example of the OCG list in displaying the names of corporations with which the government claims to be involved, even though—due to the somewhat freewheeling approach to incorporation which has gripped Ministers and senior public servants in the past—the government's exact legal status with respect to the corporation may be open to question.[23] Nor do we add membership corporations (*e.g.*, the Institute for Research in Public Policy) which the OCG steadfastly ignores despite the fact that they meet the criteria for inclusion. Finally, corporations which the government or listed corporations have begun since May, 1980 (*e.g.*, Canertech Inc.—a new corporation to promote the development of renewable energy technology and energy conservation, to be located in Winnipeg) have also been ignored in Table I.

In the case of Group I, it should be made clear that government ownership is, on occasion, ownership by analogy as there are no shares to be owned (*e.g.*, CBC, Canada Employment and Immigration Commission, National Harbours Board). In the case of Group II, jointly-held corporations generally appear on this and the OCG list if the federal government has established a majority or substantial minority share ownership position. Only in one case, Nanisivik Mines Ltd., does the government appear to own less than 40 percent of the outstanding shares. In at least three cases (Newfoundland and Labrador Development Corporation, La Société Inter-port de Québec, and La Société du parc industriel et commercial aéroportuaire de Mirabel), corporations on the federal list also appear on the provincial list prepared by Vining and Botterell due to the presence of provincial governments as major participants. In addition to Newfoundland and

---

[23] The government has recently begun taking steps to rectify the ambiguity of its status with respect to these corporations. See Langford, *supra* note 1, at 93-94.

Quebec, other provinces participating with the federal government in the ownership of public corporations include New Brunswick (St. John Harbour Bridge Authority), Saskatchewan (POS Pilot Plant Corp.), and Ontario (Consolidated Computer Inc.). Other participants in joint ownership corporations with the federal government include national and state governments (*e.g.*, Hawaii), private and public utilities, native people's, organizations, private corporations and individual investors.

Obviously there are a large number of governments associated with the international development banks, the fund, and the development association included in the jointly-owned group. It is questionable whether Group III—membership corporations—would not be a more appropriate category for these latter organizations. The government appears to be a shareholder in these organizations in the sense that it subscribes funds on a share basis. The legal and practical differences between this practice on an international level and shareholding in a jointly held share corporation need to be examined more thoroughly.

Finally, a number of directly owned corporations in Groups I and II have subsidiary and associated corporations listed with them. For the purpose of this collection, a subsidiary corporation is almost always one in which the parent corporation owns more than 50 percent of the shares. The same principle applies to sub-subsidiaries. The accounts of subsidiaries are consolidated into the accounts of the holding corporation. Associated corporations, by contrast, are less than 50 percent held by the holding company, and their accounts are not generally consolidated into the holding company's accounts. We were not in a position to investigate the accuracy of the OCG's subsidiary and associated corporation listings.

TABLE I

Corporations in which the Government of Canada has a Continuing Ownership or Membership Involvement

Corporation—Headquarters	Designated Minister	Function	Year and Mode of Incorporation or Acquisition
GROUP I. Corporations Owned Directly and Solely by the Government of Canada and Their Subsidiary and Associated Corporations			
Agricultural Products Board—Ottawa, Ontario	Agriculture	To buy, sell or import agricultural products. It may purchase and hold commodities for later sale, emergency relief in Canada or assistance programs abroad.	1951 Special Act
Agricultural Stabilization Board—Ottawa, Ontario	Agriculture	To stabilize prices of agricultural products by either buying the products, granting a deficiency payment or by making a fixed payment to the producer.	1958 Special Act
Air Canada—Montreal, Quebec Air Transit Canada [S]* Airline Maintenance Buildings Ltd. [S] Nordair Ltd. [S]	Transport	To provide a publicly owned air transportation service, with powers to carry out business throughout Canada and outside of Canada.	1937 Special Act

* [S]designates a subsidiary corporation, [SS] a sub-subsidiary corporation, [SSS] a subsidiary of a sub-subsidiary corporation, [SSSS] a subsidiary of a subsidiary of a sub-subsidiary corporation, [SSSSS] a subsidiary of a subsidiary of a subsidiary of a sub-subsidiary corporation, [SSSSSS] a subsidiary of a subsidiary of a subsidiary of a subsidiary of a sub-subsidiary corporation, [A] an associated corporation, [AS] an associated corporation of a subsidiary corporation, [ASS] an associated corporation of a sub-subsidiary corporation, [SA] a subsidiary of an associated corporation, [SAS] a subsidiary of an associated corporation of a subsidiary corporation, [SASS] a subsidiary of an associate of a sub-subsidiary corporation, [SSAS] a sub-subsidiary of an associate of a subsidiary corporation, [SSAS] a subsidiary of a sub-subsidiary of an associate of a subsidiary corporation, and [SSSAS] a subsidiary of a sub-subsidiary of an associate of a subsidiary corporation.

TABLE 1—*Continued*

Corporation—Headquarters	Designated Minister	Function	Year and Mode of Incorporation or Acquisition
Air Canada—*Continued* Nordair (Haiti) S.A. [SS] Nordair (Ontario) Ltd. [SS] Sudair Ltd. [SS] Treasure Tours (Canada) Ltée [SS] Treasure Tours International Ltd. [SS] Venturex Ltd. [S] Touram Group Service, Inc. [SS] Air Jamaica (1968) Limited [A] Matac Cargo Ltd. [A]			
The Army Benevolent Fund Board—Ottawa, Ontario	Transport	To make grants of financial assistance to World War II army veterans or their dependents to relieve distress when such has arisen from unexpected contingencies.	1947 Special Act
Atlantic Pilotage Authority—Halifax, Nova Scotia	Energy, Mines and Resources	Section 12 of the Pilotage Act: "12. The objects of an Authority are to establish, operate, maintain and administer in the interests of safety an efficient pilotage service within the Region set out in respect of the Authority in Schedule."	1972 Special Act
Atomic Energy of Canada Limited—Ottawa, Ontario	Energy, Mines and Resources	To develop a competitive and safer nuclear fuel cycle.	1952 Companies Act**

Corporation	Objectives	Department	Year / Authority
	To engineer successfully operating nuclear reactor power systems. To design and construct support nuclear production facilities. To foster the sales of power reactors to other countries. To transfer nuclear technology to Canadian industry. To provide an adequate return on the investment made in the nuclear field.		
Atomic Energy Control Board—Ottawa, Ontario	To control the development, application, and use of atomic energy through the authority of the Act and through Regulations approved by the Governor-in-Council.	Energy Mines and Resources	1946 Special Act
Bank of Canada—Ottawa, Ontario	Formulation and implementation of monetary policy.	Finance	1934 Special Act
Canada Council-Ottawa, Ontario	To support the creation and production of all forms of art and to facilitate public access to the arts. To foster cultural exchanges. To co-ordinate UNESCO activities in Canada and Canadian participation in UNESCO activities abroad apart from political questions and assistance to developing countries.	Communications	1957 Special Act

---

** The Companies Act and the Canada Corporations Act [CCA], Part I are the vehicles for the federal incorporation of business companies which preceded the Canada Business Corporation Act [CBCA].

TABLE 1—*Continued*

Corporation—Headquarters	Designated Minister	Function	Year and Mode of Incorporation or Acquisition
Canada Deposit Insurance Corporation—Ottawa, Ontario	Finance	To insure Canadian currency deposits, up to $20,000 per person, in banks, incorporated trust and loan companies that accept deposits from the public. It is also empowered to act as a lender of last resort for member institutions.	1967 Special Act
Canada Employment and Immigration Commission—Hull, Quebec	Employment and Immigration	To further the attainment of national economic and social goals by realizing the full productive potential of Canada's human resources, while supporting the initiatives of individuals to pursue their economic needs, and, more generally, their self-fulfillment through work. To administer the admission of immigrants and non-immigrants in accordance with economic, social and cultural interests of Canada.	1977 Special Act
Canada Mortgage and Housing Corporation—Ottawa, Ontario	Public Works	To administer the National Housing Act. Under this Act, the Corporation is authorized to insure mortgage loans made by approved lenders and to make loans directly for new and existing homeowner housing, new rental housing and dwellings built by cooperative associations.	1945 Special Act

Corporation	Department	Objective	Year / Creation
Canadair Limited—Montreal, Quebec 　Canadair Flextrac Limited [S] 　　Canadair GmbH [S] 　Canadair Incorporated [S] 　Canadair International Ltd. [S] 　Canadair Services Limited [S] 　Canadian General Atomic Corporation Limited [S] 　Canarch Limited [S]	Industry, Trade and Commerce	Aircraft Manufacturing	1975 Share Acquisition
Canadian Arsenals Limited—Ville de la Gardeur, Quebec	Supply and Services	The primary objective of the Company is to maintain for Canada a centre of excellence together with a production capability of medium to large calibre ammunitions and complementary products for the purpose of National Defence and to provide the base for expansion in the event of a conflict.	1945 Companies Act
Canadian Broadcasting Corporation—Ottawa, Ontario 　CJBR Radio Limitée [S] 　CJBR Télévision Limitée [S] 　Master FM Limited [A] 　Télévision St-François Limitée [A] 　Visnews Limited [A]	Communications	To develop and provide a national broadcasting service for all Canadians in both official languages, in television and radio, and an international service, both of which should be primarily Canadian in content and character.	1936 Special Act
Canadian Chicken Marketing Agency—Brampton, Ontario	Agriculture	To operate a national supply management program for the orderly marketing of chicken in Canada, subject to federal/provincial agreements.	1978 Regulation***

*** Regulation refers to the creation of a corporation usually by order-in-council under the authority of an existing statute.

TABLE 1—Continued

Corporation—Headquarters	Designated Minister	Function	Year and Mode of Incorporation or Acquisition
Canadian Commercial Corporation—Ottawa, Ontario Hermes Electronics Limited [A]	Industry, Trade and Commerce	To assist in the development of trade between Canada and other nations. To assist persons in Canada in obtaining goods and commodities from outside Canada. To dispose of goods and commodities that are available for export from Canada.	1946 Special Act
Canadian Dairy Commission—Ottawa, Ontario	Agriculture	To maintain a national dairy policy and to achieve a sound, healthy and viable industry. It administers the price stabilization program for manufacturing milk and cream, that forms part of the mechanism for controlling the industry and enforcing policies.	1966 Special Act
The Canadian Egg Marketing Agency—Ottawa, Ontario	Agriculture	To ensure the orderly marketing of eggs.	1972 Regulation
The Canadian Film Development Corporation—Montreal, Quebec	Communications	To foster and promote the development of a feature film industry in Canada.	1967 Special Act
Canadian Livestock Feed Board—Montreal, Quebec	Agriculture	To ensure: the availability of feed grain to meet the needs of livestock feeders; the availability of adequate storage space in	1966 Special Act

Eastern Canada for feed grain to meet the needs of livestock feeders; reasonable stability in the price of feed grain in Eastern Canada and British Columbia; fair equalization of feed grain prices in Eastern Canada and British Columbia.

Canadian National Railways—Montreal, Quebec	Transport	To operate and manage a national system of railways.	1919 Special Act

Autoport Limited [S]
The Canada and Gulf Terminal Railway Company [S]
Canadian National Express Company [S]
The Canadian National Railways Securities Trust [S]
Canadian National Realties Limited [S]
Canac Consultants Limited [SS]
Canac Distribution Limited [SS]
Canadian National Hotels (Moncton) Ltd. [SS]
Canalog Logistics Limited [SS]
Canaven Limited [SS]
CN Tower Restaurants Limited [SS]
Canaprev Inc. [AS]
Metro Centre Developments Limited [AS]
Canadian National Steamship Company Limited [S]
Canadian National Telegraph Company [S]

TABLE 1—*Continued*

Corporation—Headquarters	Designated Minister	Function	Year and Mode of Incorporation or Acquisition
Canadian National Railways—*Continued*			
The Great North Western Telegraph Company of Canada [SS]			
Canadian National Transfer Company [S]			
Canadian National Transportation Limited [S]			
Chapman Transport Limited [SS]			
Eastern Transport Limited [SS]			
Hoar Transport Limited [SS]			
Husband Transport Limited [SS]			
Cronin Transport Limited [SSS]			
Husband International Transport (Ontario) Limited [SSS]			
Husband Transport (Quebec) Limited [SSS]			
Chalut Transport (1974) Inc. [SSSS]			
Midland Superior Express Limited [SSS]			
Empire Freightways Limited [SSSS]			
Provincial Tankers Limited [SSS]			
Royal Transportation Limited [SSS]			
Swan River—The Pas Transfer Ltd. [SSS]			

The Toronto—Peterborough Transport Company Limited [SSS]
The Canadian Northern Quebec Railway Company [S]
Canat Limited [S]
CN Exploration Ltd. [S]
CN (France) S.A. [S]
CN M Inc. [S]
CN Marine Inc. [S]
Coastal Transport Limited [SS]
Halifax Industries (Holdings) Limited [AS]
Halifax Industries Limited [SAS]
CN Tower Limited [S]
Grand Trunk Corporation [S]
Central Vermont Railway Inc. [SS]
Domestic Four Leasing Corporation [SSS]
Domestic Three Leasing Corporation [SS]
Domestic Two Leasing Corporation [SS]
Duluth, Winnipeg and Pacific Railway Company [SS]
Duluth, Rainy Lake & Winnipeg Railway Company [SSS]
Duluth, Winnipeg & Pacific Railroad Company [SSS]
Grand Trunk Land Development Corporation [SS]

TABLE 1—*Continued*

Corporation—Headquarters	Designated Minister	Function	Year and Mode of Incorporation or Acquisition
Canadian National Railways—*Continued*			
Grand Trunk Radio Communications, Inc. [SS]			
Grand Trunk Western Railroad Company [SS]			
Grand Trunk—Milwaukee Car Ferry Company [SSS]			
The Belt Railway Company of Chicago [ASS]			
Chicago & Western Indiana Railroad Company [ASS]			
The Detroit & Toledo Shore Line Railroad Company [ASS]			
Detroit Terminal Railroad Company [ASS]			
The Minnesota and Manitoba Railroad Company [S]			
The Minnesota and Ontario Bridge Commission [S]			
Mount Royal Tunnel and Terminal Company Limited [S]			
Newfoundland Dockyard and Engineering (CN) Ltd. [S]			
The Northern Consolidated Holding Company Limited [S]			

Northwest Telecommunications Inc. [S]
The Quebec and Lake St. John Railway
    Company [S]
Terra Nova Telecommunications Inc. [S]
Compagnie de Gestion de Matane
    Inc. [A]
Computer Sciences Canada Limited [A]
East Yard Development Limited [A]
Eurocanadian Shipholdings Limited [A]
Cast Containers Ltd. [SA]
Cast Shipping Ltd. [SA]
Eurocanadian Shipholding (UK)
    Ltd. [SA]
European Transportation Associates
    Ltd. [SA]
General Cargo Holding Associates
    Ltd. [SA]
North America Transportation
    Associates Ltd. [SA]
Task Terminals Ltd. [SA]
Halterm Limited [A]
Intercast S.A. [A]
    Cast Europe N.V. [SA]
    Cast North America Ltd. [SA]
    World Trade Chartering Ltd. [SA]
Northern Alberta Railways Company [A]
The Public Markets Limited [A]
The Shawinigan Falls Terminal Railway
    Company [A]

TABLE 1—*Continued*

Corporation—Headquarters	Designated Minister	Function	Year and Mode of Incorporation or Acquisition
Canadian National Railways—*Continued* Société du port ferroviaire de Baie Comeau-Hauterive [A] Telesat Canada [A] The Toronto Terminals Railway Company [A]			
Canadian Patents and Development Limited—Ottawa, Ontario	Industry, Trade and Commerce	To secure the optimum exploitation for the benefit of Canada of licenseable material accruing to the Crown and publicly funded institutions and agencies	1947 Companies Act
Canadian Saltfish Corporation—St. John's, Nfld.	Fisheries and Oceans	To regulate interprovincial and export trade in saltfish in order to improve the earnings of primary producers of cured cod fish.	1970 Special Act
The Canadian Turkey Marketing Agency—Brampton, Ontario	Agriculture	To ensure the orderly marketing of turkeys.	1974 Regulation
Canadian Wheat Board—Winnipeg, Manitoba	Designated Minister	To buy, take delivery of, store, transfer, sell, ship, or otherwise dispose of grain.	1935 Special Act
Cape Breton Development Corporation—Sydney, Nova Scotia Cabot Craft Industries Limited [S] Cape Breton Lamb Limited [S] Cape Breton Marine Farming Limited [S]	Regional Economic Expansion	To help resolve problems on Cape Breton Island occasioned by the planned closure of coal mines and a steel plant that was operated by the Dominion Steel and Coal Company.	1967 Special Act

Corporation	Department	Purpose	Year / Authority
Cape Breton Woolen Mills Limited [S] Darr (Cape Breton) Limited [S] Dundee Estates Limited [S] Whale Cove Summer Village Limited [S] Cape Breton Vegetable Company Limited [A] Cape Breton Welsh Black Limited [A]			
Crown Assets Disposal Corporation—Ottawa, Ontario	Supply and Services	To provide a specialized sales service to government departments and certain agencies and Crown companies in the disposal of their surplus goods and assets located in Canada and abroad.	1944 Special Act
Defence Construction (1951) Limited—Ottawa, Ontario	National Defence	To carry out the construction of major military projects and the maintenance projects required by the Department of National Defence. Also the company provides on request of government departments and agencies certain technical and administrative assistance relative to construction matters. Such services are recovered on a cost-recovery basis.	1951 Companies Act
The DeHavilland Aircraft of Canada, Limited—Downsview, Ontario DeHavilland Canada, Inc. [S]	Industry, Trade and Commerce	Aircraft manufacturer	1974 Share Acquisition
Director of Soldier Settlement—Ottawa, Ontario	Veterans Affairs	To assist in the postwar rehabilitation of Veterans of World War I through settlement on the land and the expansion of the agricultural industry in Canada.	1931 Special Act

TABLE 1—*Continued*

Corporation—Headquarters	Designated Minister	Function	Year and Mode of Incorporation or Acquisition
Director, The Veteran's Land Act—Ottawa, Ontario	Veterans Affairs	A post World War II rehabilitation measure to provide financial assistance on favourable terms to veterans wishing to settle on land as full or part-time farmers, or in conjunction with their occupation of commercial fishing.	1942 Special Act
Economic Council of Canada—Vanier, Ontario	Prime Minister	To advise and recommend how Canada can achieve the highest possible levels of employment and efficient production in order that the country may enjoy a high and consistent rate of economic growth and that all Canadians may share in rising living standards.	1963 Special Act
Eldorado Nuclear Limited—Ottawa, Ontario Eldorado Aviation Limited [S] Eldor Resources Limited [S]	Energy, Mines and Resources	Briefly stated, the company's objective as a proprietary corporation is to make a contribution to Canadian energy requirements while maximizing Canada's position in international markets for nuclear fuels, and to do that on a commercially viable basis without recourse to public funds.	1944 Companies Act
Export Development Corporation—Ottawa, Ontario	Industry, Trade and Commerce	Export Development Corporation is a commercially self-sustaining enterprise that	1969 Special Act

Corporation	Department	Objects	Year	
		provides financial facilities to assist Canadian export trade.		
Farm Credit Corporation—Ottawa, Ontario	Agriculture	To meet long-term mortgage credit needs of Canadian farmers.	1959	Special Act
Federal Business Development Bank—Montreal, Quebec	Industry, Trade and Commerce	The objects of the Corporation are to promote and assist in the establishment and development of business enterprises in Canada by providing, in the manner and to the extent authorized by its Act, financial assistance, management counselling, management training, information and advice and such other services as are ancillary or incidental to any of the foregoing.	1975	Special Act
Federal Mortgage Exchange Corporation—Ottawa, Ontario	Finance	To develop a secondary mortgage market.	1973	Special Act
Fisheries Prices Support Board—Ottawa, Ontario	Fisheries and Oceans	To recommend price support measures when severe price declines occur. The The Board has authority to buy fish products and to sell or otherwise dispose of the products, or to pay producers the difference between a price prescribed by the Board and the average price the product actually commands.	1944	Special Act
Fraser River Harbour Commission—New Westminster, British Columbia	Transport	Management and control of the harbour and the works and property therein under its jurisdiction.	1913	Special Act

TABLE 1—*Continued*

Corporation—Headquarters	Designated Minister	Function	Year and Mode of Incorporation or Acquisition
Freshwater Fish Marketing Corporation—Winnipeg, Manitoba	Fisheries and Oceans	To regulate interprovincial and export trade in freshwater fish.	1969 Special Act
Hamilton Harbour Commissioners—Hamilton, Ontario	Transport	To regulate and control navigation and all works and operations within the harbour.	1912 Special Act
Harbourfront Corporation—Toronto, Ontario	Public Works	To create at Harbourfront a mixed use, Urban Waterfront Area integrating a significant proportion of public places and activities with residential, commercial and institutional uses.	1973 Provincial Companies Legislation
International Boundary Commission (Canadian Section)—Ottawa, Ontario	External Affairs	To keep the boundary vista entirely free of obstruction and plainly marked for the proper enforcement of customs, immigration, fishing and other laws of Canada and the United States. The Commission is concerned with fixed things on the boundary line or near it, not with movement across it.	1908 Treaty
The International Development Research Centre—Ottawa, Ontario	External Affairs	To initiate, encourage, support and conduct research into the problems of the developing regions of the world and into the means	1970 Special Act

for applying and adapting scientific, technical and other knowledge to the economic and social advancement of those regions.

Name—Location	Department	Year / Authority	Description
International Fisheries Commissions Pension Society—Ottawa, Ontario	Environment	1957 CCA Part I	To arrange for and administer the provision of pensions and insurance for the employees of any international fisheries commission whose seat or headquarters is in Canada or the United States of America.
International Joint Commission—Ottawa, Ontario	External Affairs	1909 Treaty	To deal with the use, obstruction and diversion of boundary waters and rivers crossing the boundary between Canada and the United States; additional responsibilities conferred under Great Lakes Water Quality Agreement, November 22, 1978.
Lakehead Harbour Commission—Thunder Bay, Ontario	Transport	1958 Special Act	Management and control of the harbour and the works and property therein under its jurisdiction.
Last Post Fund—Montreal, Quebec	Veterans Affairs	1909 Federal Charter	To give honourable sepulchre to any ex-service member who has served on an active basis in a branch of Her Majesty's forces or the forces allied with Her Majesty during the South African War, World War I, World War II and the Korean Conflict, who might at death be in destitute circumstances, friendless, indigent or liable to become a public charge.

TABLE 1—*Continued*

Corporation—Headquarters	Designated Minister	Function	Year and Mode of Incorporation or Acquisition
Laurentian Pilotage Authority—Montreal, Quebec	Transport	Section 12 of the Pilotage Act: "The objects of an Authority are to establish, operate, maintain and administer in the interests of safety an efficient pilotage service within the region set out in respect of the Authority in Schedule."	1972 Special Act
Loto Canada Inc.—Ottawa, Ontario	Labour	To conduct and manage a national lottery according to approved regulations, and for which the net revenue to December 31, 1979 shall be distributed according to a specified formula.	1976 CBCA
Medical Research Council—Ottawa, Ontario	Health and Welfare	To promote and support research in the health sciences in Canada. To this end it maintains a balanced program of support to research investigators, to the costs of research programs in Canadian universities, hospitals and related institutes and to promotional activities designed to stimulate new research efforts in significant areas.	1969 Special Act
Municipal Development and Loan Board— Ottawa, Ontario	Finance	To administer the Municipal Development and Loan Act.	1963 Special Act

Corporation	Minister	Purpose	Year	
Nanaimo Harbour Commission—Nanaimo, B.C.	Transport	Management and control of the harbour and the works and property therein under its jurisdiction.	1960	Special Act
National Arts Centre Corporation—Ottawa, Ontario	Secretary of State	To operate and maintain the National Arts Centre, to develop the performing arts in the National Capital Region, and to assist the Canada Council in the development of the performing arts elsewhere in Canada.	1966	Special Act
The National Battlefields Commission—Quebec, Quebec	Environment	To acquire, restore and maintain the historic battlefields at Quebec to form a National Battlefields Park.	1908	Special Act
National Capital Commission—Ottawa, Ontario	Public Works	To prepare plans for and assist in the development, conservation and improvement of the National Capital Region in order that the nature and character of the seat of the Government of Canada may be in accordance with its national significance.	1958	Special Act
National Farm Products Marketing Council—Ottawa, Ontario	Agriculture	To assist Canadian agriculture to maintain and promote an efficient, competitive and expanding agriculture industry.	1970	Special Act
National Harbours Board—Ottawa, Ontario	Transport	The board has jurisdiction over the harbours of St. John's, Nfld., Halifax, N.S., Saint John and Belledune, N.B.; Chicoutimi, Baie des Ha! Ha!, Quebec, Sept-Iles, Trois-Rivières and Montreal, Quebec; Churchill, Man., Prince Rupert and Vancouver, B.C., and the grain elevators at Prescott and Port Colbourne, Ontario.	1936	Special Act

TABLE 1—*Continued*

Corporation—Headquarters	Designated Minister	Function	Year and Mode of Incorporation or Acquisition
National Museums of Canada—Ottawa, Ontario	Communications	To demonstrate the products of nature and the works of man, with special but not exclusive reference to Canada, so as to promote interest therein throughout Canada and to disseminate this knowledge.	1968 Special Act
National Research Council—Ottawa, Ontario	Science and Technology	To initiate and conduct research in the natural sciences and technology for the economic and social benefit of Canadians. To provide an independent, versatile, broadly based source of expertise, available to assist in the achievement of national objectives.	1916 Special Act
Natural Sciences and Engineering Research Council—Ottawa, Ontario	Science and Technology	(a) To promote and assist in the natural sciences and engineering other than the health sciences; and (b) to advise the Minister in respect of such matters relating to such research as the Minister may refer to the Council for its consideration.	1978 Special Act
North Fraser Harbour Commission—Vancouver, B.C.	Transport	Management and control of the harbour and the works and property therein under its jurisdiction.	1913 Special Act

Northern Canada Power Commission—Edmonton, Alberta	Indian and Northern Affairs	To construct and operate public utility plants in the Northwest Territories, the Yukon Territory, and subject to approval of the Governor-in-Council, elsewhere in Canada.	1948 Special Act
Northern Transportation Company Limited—Edmonton, Alberta Grimshaw Trucking and Distributing Ltd. [S] Yellowknife Transportation Company Limited [S]	Transport	To provide a general marine transportation service throughout Northern Canada and the Arctic, together with related intermodal services.	1947 Companies Act
Oshawa Harbour Commission—Oshawa, Ontario	Transport	Management and control of the harbour and the works and property therein under its jurisdiction.	1960 Special Act
Pacific Pilotage Authority—Vancouver, B.C.	Transport	Section 12 of the Pilotage Act: "The objects of an Authority are to establish, operate, maintain and administer in the interests of safety an efficient pilotage service within the region set out in respect of the Authority in the Schedule."	1972 Special Act
Petro-Canada—Calgary, Alberta Petro-Canada Consulting Corporation [S] Petro-Canada Exploration Inc. [S] Asher American, Inc. [SS] Bailey Selburn Oil & Gas Ltd. [SS] Big Eagle Oil & Gas Ltd. [SS] Aquilla Holdings Ltd. [SSS] Fifth Pacific Stations Ltd. [SS]	Energy, Mines and Resources	Article 6 of Petro-Canada Act: ". . . to explore for hydrocarbon deposits, to negotiate for and acquire petroleum and petroleum products from abroad to assure a continuity of supply for the needs of Canada, to develop and exploit deposits of hydrocarbons within and without Canada in the interests of Canada, to carry out	1975 Special Act

TABLE 1—Continued

Corporation—Headquarters	Designated Minister	Function	Year and Mode of Incorporation or Acquisition
Petro-Canada—*Continued*		research and development projects in relation to hydrocarbons and other fuels, and to engage in exploration for, and the production, distribution, refining and marketing of fuels."	
GMI Co. (Bahamas) Ltd. [SS]			
Opal Oils Limited [SS]			
Commodore Oils Limited [SSS]			
First Pacific Stations Ltd. [SSSS]			
Fourth Pacific Stations Ltd. [SSSS]			
Second Pacific Stations Ltd. [SSSS]			
Third Pacific Stations Ltd. [SSSS]			
Pacific Energy Resources Ltd. [SS]			
Pacific Petrochemicals Ltd. [SS]			
Pacific Petroleums Espanola, S.A. [SS]			
Pacific Petroleums, Inc. [SS]			
Pacific Pipelines, Inc. [SSS]			
Pacific Petroleums (Overseas) Limited [SS]			
Petro-Canada Industries Inc. [SS]			
Petro-Canada Inc. [SSS]			
Petro-Canada Norway A/S [SS]			
Petroleum Transmission Company [SS]			
Rocair Limited [SS]			
Tri-Mountain Petroleums Ltd. [SS]			
Value Serve Stations Ltd. [SS]			
Venezuelan Canadian Oils, C.A. [SS]			

Venezuelan Pacific Petroleums, C.A. [SS] Western Natural Gas Company Ltd. [SS] Panarctic Oils Ltd. [A] Syncrude Canada Ltd. [A] Westcoast Transmission Company Limited [A]			
Port Alberni Harbour Commission—Port Alberni, B.C.	Transport	Management and control of the harbour and the lands and property therein under its jurisdiction.	1947 Special Act
Public Works Lands Company Limited—Ottawa, Ontario	Public Works	Initial function was to acquire a leasehold interest on Crown lands in London, England to be the site of new Canadian offices, to overcome the problem of the Crown not being able to contract with itself; this leasehold is now managed by Dept. of External Affairs. In 1979, its mandate was extended to include management of Mirabel peripheral lands, but curtailed by the subsequent Cabinet. Present mandate of corporation is uncertain.	1956
Roosevelt Campobello, International Park Commission—Campobello Island, New Brunswick	External Affairs	The Commission was established to accept title to the former Roosevelt Estate on Campobello Island, N.B.; to restore the Roosevelt home to its condition when occupied by President Roosevelt; to administer as a memorial the Roosevelt-Campobello International Park.	1964 Special Act

TABLE 1—Continued

Corporation—Headquarters	Designated Minister	Function	Year and Mode of Incorporation or Acquisition
Royal Canadian Mint—Vanier, Ontario	Supply and Services	To produce and arrange for the production and supply of coins of the currency of Canada; produce coins of currency of countries other than Canada; melt, assay and refine gold, silver and other metals; buy and sell gold, silver and other metals etc. To mint coins and carry out other related activities in anticipation of profit.	1969 Government Orgaization Act
The St. Lawrence Seaway Authority—Ottawa, Ontario Great Lakes Pilotage Authority [S] Jacques Cartier and Champlain Bridges Incorporated [S] The Seaway International Bridge Corporation Ltd. [S]	Transport	To acquire lands for and construct, maintain and operate all such works as may be necessary to provide and maintain a deep waterway between the port of Montreal and Lake Erie; bridges connecting Canada with the United States as authorized by the St. Lawrence Seaway Authority Act; and lands necessarily incidental to works undertaken pursuant to the St. Lawrence Seaway Authority Act.	1954 Special Act
Science Council of Canada—Ottawa, Ontario	Science and Technology	To assess Canada's scientific and technological requirements, to increase public awareness of these requirements and of the	1966 Special Act

Social Sciences and Humanities Research Council—Ottawa, Ontario	Communications	interdependence of various groups in society in the development and use of science and technology and to advise the government on the best use of science and technology. To promote and assist research and scholarship in the social sciences and humanities.	1977	Special Act
Standards Council of Canada—Ottawa, Ontario	Industry, Trade and Commerce	To foster and promote voluntary standardization in fields relating to the construction, manufacture, production, quality, performance and safety of buildings, structures, manufactured articles and products and other goods, not necessarily provided for by law, as a means of advancing the national economy, benefiting the public and protecting consumers.	1970	Special Act
Teleglobe Canada—Montreal, Quebec Teleglobe Canada Limited [S]	Communications	To establish, maintain and operate in Canada and elsewhere external telecommunications services for the conduct of public communications; to carry on the business of public communications by cable, radio telegraph, or any other means of telecommunication between Canada and any other place; to co-ordinate Canada's external telecommunication services to other nations.	1950	Special Act

TABLE 1—*Continued*

Corporation—Headquarters	Designated Minister	Function	Year and Mode of Incorporation or Acquisition
Toronto Harbour Commissioners—Toronto, Ontario	Transport	To regulate and control navigation and all works operations within the harbour.	1911 Special Act
Uranium Canada Limited—Ottawa, Ontario	Energy, Mines and Resources	To act on behalf of the Minister of Energy, Mines and Resources in the performance of certain duties relative to the acquisition and disposal of uranium concentrate stockpiles.	1971 CCA Part I
VIA Rail Canada Inc.—Montreal, Quebec	Transport	Railway passenger service.	1977 CBCA
Windsor Harbour Commission—Windsor, Ontario	Transport	Management and control of the harbour and the works and property therein under its jurisdiction.	1957 Special Act
GROUP II: Corporations which the Government of Canada Owns Jointly with Other Governments, Private Organizations and Individuals			
African Development Fund—Abidjan, Côte d'Ivoire	External Affairs (CIDA)	To assist the African Development Bank in making an increasingly effective contribution to i) the economic and social development of the Bank's members and ii) to the promotion of co-operation and international trade.	1972 Regulation

Asian Development Bank—Manila, Philippines	External Affairs (CIDA)	To promote economic growth and co-operation in Asia and the Far-East, and help to accelerate the economic development process in developing countries of this part of the world, either in individual countries or in the whole region.	1965 Regulation
Blue Water Bridge Authority—Point Edward, Ontario	Transport	To hold, operate, maintain and repair the Canadian portions of the Blue Water Bridge which links Sarnia, Ontario and Port Huron, Michigan, U.S.A. across the St. Clair River.	1964 Special Act
Canada Development Corporation—Vancouver, B.C. CDC Data Systems Limted [S] AES Data Ltd. [SS] AES Nederland B.V. [SSS] AES A.G. [SSSS] AES Belgium S.A. [SSSS] AES GmbH [SSSS] AES Schweiz A.G. [SSSS] AES Wordplex Europe Ltd. [SSSS] AES Wordplex Ireland Ltd. [SSSS] AES Wordplex Ltd. [SSSS] AES Wordplex Leasing Ltd. [SSSSS] International AES N.V. [SSS] OMS Nederland B.V. [SSSS]	Finance	To develop and maintain strong Canadian controlled and managed corporations in the private sector, to widen the investment opportunities open to Canadians, and to operate profitably and in the best interests of all shareholders.	1971 Special Act

TABLE 1—*Continued*

Corporation—Headquarters	Designated Minister	Function	Year and Mode of Incorporation or Acquisition
Canada Development Corporation—*Continued*			
Wordplex Corporation [SSS]			
CDC Energy & Metals Limited [S]			
CDC Nederland B.V. [SS]			
Texasgulf Inc. [ASS]			
Cia. Exploradora del Istmo, S.A. [SASS]			
Sulphur Export Corporation [SASS]			
Texasgulf of Australia Ltd. [SASS]			
Texasgulf Canada Ltd. [SASS]			
Texasgulf Export Corporation [SASS]			
Texasgulf Panama Inc. [SASS]			
Texasgulf Potash Company [SASS]			
CDC Oil & Gas Limited [S]			
CDC Minerals Ltd. [SS]			
CDC Oil & Gas International B.V. [SS]			
CDC Producing Company [SSS]			
CDC Oil & Gas (U.K.) Limited [SS]			

CDC Life Sciences Inc. [S]
Bio-Research Laboratories Limited [SS]
    Steele Chemicals Limited [SSS]
Connaught Laboratories Limited [SS]
    Connaught Biologics Ltd. [SSS]
    Canada Serum Co. Ltd. [SSSS]
    Connaught Laboratories Inc. [SSS]
    Connaught Laboratories Export Inc. [SSSS]
    Connlab do Brasil Industries Commercio Lta. [SSS]
Comex Nederland B.V. [SS]
A/S Dumex [SSS]
    A/S Dumex, Norway [SSSS]
    Dumex Australia (Pty.) Limited [SSSS]
    Dumex B.V. [SSSS]
    Dumex GmbH [SSSS]
    Dumex (Pty.) Ltd. [SSSS]
    Dumex Lakemedel AB [SSSS]
    Dumex SPA [SSSS]
    OY Dumex AB [SSSS]
    Dumex of Mexico [ASSS]
Comprator AG (Switzerland) [SSS]
Omnimedic Inc. [SS]
    Canada Pharmacal (1975) Ltd. [SSS]
Nordic Laboratories Inc. [SSS]
Raylo Chemicals Limited [SS]
    R&L Molecular Research Limited [SSS]

TABLE 1—*Continued*

Corporation—Headquarters	Designated Minister	Function	Year and Mode of Incorporation or Acquisition
Canada Development Corporation—*Continued*			
Dominion Biologicals [AS]			
CDC Ventures Inc. [S]			
Canwest Capital Corporation [AS]			
Crown Trust Company [SAS]			
Global Ventures Western Limited [SAS]			
The Monarch Life Assurance Co. [SAS]			
Na Churs Plant Food Company [SAS]			
Universal Subscription & Television Inc. [SAS]			
Innocan Investments Ltd. [AS]			
Cancoat Papers Ltd. [SAS]			
Cremanco Systems Ltd. [SAS]			
Glen Falls International Corp. [SAS]			
Innotech Aviation [SAS]			
International Systems Ltd. [SAS]			
Lorcon Inc. [SAS]			
Sentrol Systems Ltd. [SAS]			
Ventures West Capital Ltd. [AS]			
Brown, Farris & Jefferson Ltd. [SAS]			

Canadian Shields Exploration Ltd. [SAS]
Castlemain Exploration Ltd. [SAS]
Controlled Environments Ltd. [SAS]
Freen Screen, Inc. [SAS]
A. Freen Ltd. [SAS]
Frio Oil Ltd. [SAS]
Highpoint Properties Ltd. [SAS]
Hypoint Resources Ltd. [SAS]
International Mobile Data Inc. [SAS]
Malabar Mines Ltd. [SAS]
MMN Holdings Ltd. [SAS]
Spectre Exploration Ltd. [SAS]
Ventures West Minerals Ltd. [SAS]
Ogilvy Mineral Corporation [SSAS]
Venturetek International Ltd. [AS]
Conat Industries Limited [SAS]
Hermes Electronics Limited [SAS]
McPhar Instrument Corporation [SAS]
Northway-Gestalt Corporation [SAS]
PoP Shoppes International Inc. [SAS]
PoP Shoppes of America [SSAS]
PoP Shoppes of Canada [SSAS]
Kist of Canada [SSSAS]
Stake Technology Ltd. [SAS]
Water Coaster International Ltd. [SAS]

TABLE 1—*Continued*

Corporation—Headquarters	Designated Minister	Function	Year and Mode of Incorporation or Acquisition
Petrosar Limited [S]			
Polysar Limited [S]			
Bellaplast Nederland B.V. [SS]			
Com-Share Limited [SS]			
Computer Sharing of Canada Ltd. [SSS]			
Kayson-Mammoth Limited [SS]			
Polysar United States, Inc. [SSS]			
Polcrete Properties Incorporated [SS]			
Polymer Corporation Canada Limted [SS]			
Polysar Australia Pty. Ltd. [SS]			
Polysar Handelmaatschappij B.V. [SS]			
Polysar Holdings Limited [SS]			
Polysar Nederland B.V. [SSS]			
Bellaplast A.G. Für Kunststoff- verpackungen [SSSS]			
Bellaplast Kunststoffverpackungen Gesellschaft mbH [SSSS]			
Bellaplast Maschinenverkaufs A.G. [SSSS]			
Bellaplast Inc. [SSSSS]			
Polysar Belgium N.V. [SSSS]			

Monoplast S.A. [SSSSS]
Polysar Cayman Ltd. [SSSSS]
Polysar GmbH [SSSSS]
Bellaplast GmbH [SSSSSS]
Komfortplast GmbH [SSSSSS]
Polysar (Deutschland) GmbH [SSSSSS]
Polysar Europa S.A. [SSSS]
Polysar France S.A. [SSSS]
Polysar Incorporated [SSSS]
Polymer Services Ltd. [SSSSS]
Polysar Latex Inc. [SSSSS]
Polysar International S.A. [SSSS]
Polysar do Brasil Produtos Quimicos Ltda. [SSSSS]
Polysar de Venezuela S.A. [SSSSS]
Polysar Insurance Services Ltd. [SSSSS]
Polysar Italiana S.P.A. [SSSS]
Polysar (UK) Limited [SSSS]
Bellaplast (UK) Limited [SSSSS]
Polysar Skandinaviska A.B. [SSSS]
Polysar Technical Services Centre N.V. [SSSS]
Société Française Polysar [SSSS]
Société de Latex S.A. [SSSS]

TABLE 1—*Continued*

Corporation—Headquarters	Designated Minister	Function	Year and Mode of Incorporation or Acquisition
Polysar Limited—*Continued* Synthetic Elastomers Development S.A. [SSSS]			
Ain-Ke-Jig Limited [AS]			
Bellaplast Maschinenbau GmbH [AS]			
Comshare Inc. [AS]			
Comshare A.G. [SAS]			
Comshare B.V. [SAS]			
Comshare International B.V. [SAS]			
Comshare Limited (U.K.) [SAS]			
Comshare S.A. (Belgium) [SAS]			
Hules Mexicanos, S.A. [AS]			
Nippon Polymers Company Ltd. [AS]			
Petrosar Limited [AS]			
Ventek Limited [S]			
Canada-France-Hawaii Telescope Corporation—Honolulu, Hawaii	Science and Technology	To design, construct and operate a major astronomical installation on Mauna Kea on the Island of Hawaii and other related activities.	1974 Foreign Companies Legislation
Canadian Arctic Producers Co-operative— Ottawa, Ontario Imanco Marketing Limited [S]	Indian and Northern Affairs	To carry on the business of a marketer and distributor of and to buy, sell, manufacture, import, export and generally deal in Eskimo goods, wares and merchandise of all kinds.	1965 Canada Co-operatives Association Act

Corporation	Department	Purpose	Date / Authority
Canarctic Shipping Company Limited—Ottawa, Ontario	Transport	Ship owning and operating.	1975 CCA Part I
Caribbean Development Bank—Wildex, St. Michael, Barbados	External Affairs (CIDA)	To contribute to the harmonious economic growth and development of the member countries, especially the less developed ones.	1969 Regulation
Consolidated Computer Inc.—Ottawa, Ontario	Industry, Trade and Commerce	Computer manufacturer.	1968 Share Acquisition
Inter-American Development Bank—Washington, D.C.	External Affairs (CIDA)	To contribute to the acceleration of the process of economic development of the member countries, individually and collectively.	1959 Regulation
International Bank for Reconstruction and Development—Washington, D.C.	Finance	To assist in the reconstruction and development of territories of member countries by facilitating the investment of capital for productive purposes and by guaranteeing or supplying capital.	1945 Treaty
International Development Association—Washington, D.C.	Finance	To make "soft" loans to the poorest of the under-developed countries.	1960
International Finance Corporation—Washington, D.C.	Finance	To promote private sector growth in the under-developed countries through equity investment in companies.	1956
Nanisivik Mines Limited—Calgary, Alberta	Indian and Northern Affairs	To test the feasibility of mining lead and zinc in the Canadian Arctic, providing jobs for the Inuit people, and increasing the Canadian presence in the Arctic.	1974 Provincial Companies Legislation

TABLE 1—*Continued*

Corporation—Headquarters	Designated Minister	Function	Year and Mode of Incorporation or Acquisition
Newfoundland and Labrador Development Corporation Limited—St. John's Nfld.	Regional Economic Expansion	To assist small and medium-sized businesses in Newfoundland and Labrador through loan and equity financing, management advisory services, and other related services and means of support.	1972 Provincial Companies Legislation
Baie Vista Inn Ltd. [A]			
Bernard W. Bartle Ltd. [A]			
East Coast Recyclers Ltd. [A]			
Fort Amherst Seafoods Ltd. [A]			
Glass Fibre Plastics Ltd. [A]			
Glenwood Forest Products Ltd. [A]			
P. Janes and Sons Ltd. [A]			
Loreb Steel Fabricators Ltd. [A]			
Maritime Service and Supply [A]			
Newfont Ltd. [A]			
Newfoundland Paper Converting Ltd. [A]			
A. Northcott Ltd. [A]			
Notre Dame Bay Fisheries Ltd. [A]			
Port Enterprises Ltd. [A]			
Rayo Forest Enterprises Ltd. [A]			
Terra Nova Envelopes Ltd. [A]			
Terra Nova Shoes Ltd. [A]			
Truck Bodies Ltd. [A]			
Vinland Export Company Ltd. [A]			
Walken Enterprises Ltd. [A]			

Watkins Enterprises Ltd. [A]
Western Farm Feeds Ltd. [A]

Saint John Harbour Bridge Authority—Saint John, N.B.	Finance	To investigate and make such surveys and studies as may be necessary for the erection of a bridge across the Harbour of Saint John and to purchase or otherwise acquire any lands necessary for the construction of such bridge and to construct or cause to be constructed a bridge and to raise money by borrowing and to enter into agreement with Federal, Provincial and Municipal and Private governments, persons or corporations respecting the financing and construction of such bridge.	1962 Provincial Companies Legislation
La Société Inter-Port de Québec—Québec	Regional Economic Expansion	To develop and implement plans and programs for an industrial complex using the infrastructure of the Quebec harbour and contributing to the development of that same infrastructure.	1974 Special Act Provincial
La Société du parc industriel et commercial aéroportuaire de Mirabel (SPICAM)—Montréal, Québec	Regional Economic Expansion	To plan, arrange and manage an industrial park at Mirabel and to plan joint services within the park.	1976 Special Act Provincial
Telesat Canada—Ottawa, Ontario	Communications	To establish a multi-purpose domestic satellite communications system.	1969 Special Act
Thousand Islands Bridge Authority—Landsdowne, Ontario	Transport	To administer the Thousand Islands Bridge and some other related properties.	1933 Special Act

TABLE 1—*Continued*

Corporation—Headquarters	Designated Minister	Function	Year and Mode of Incorporation or Acquisition
GROUP III: Corporations in which the Government has a Membership Interest			
Association for the Export of Canadian Books—Ottawa, Ontario	Secretary of State	Assisting in expanding the export of Canadian published books.	1972 CCA Part II*
Board of Trustees of the Queen Elizabeth II Canadian Fund to Aid in Research on the Diseases of Children—Ottawa, Ontario	Prime Minister	To provide salary support for investigators working or training in the field of children's diseases.	1959 Special Act
Canada Grains Council—Winnipeg, Manitoba	Industry, Trade and Commerce	To provide a forum in which council members representing all facets of the grain industry could discuss mutual problems, study particular issues and provide advice and recommendations to Government.	1969 CCA Part II
Canadian Centre for Occupational Health and Safety—Hamilton, Ontario	Labour	To promote the fundamental right of Canadians to a healthy and safe working environment through study, encouragement and co-operative advancement of occupational health and safety, with the participation of workers, trade unions, employers, federal, provincial and territorial authorities, professional and scientific communities, and the general public.	1978 CCA Part II
Canadian International Grains Institute—Winnipeg, Manitoba	Industry, Trade and Commerce	To offer to selected possible users outside Canada courses in grain technology and	1972 CCA Part II

	handling as a means of technical market development for Canadian grain.		
Canadian Law Information Council—Ottawa, Ontario	To promote the acquisition of knowledge of the law in Canada and its dissemination within Canada. To enhance the quality and increase the availability of information pertaining to the law in Canada for the benefit of the Canadian community.	Justice	1973 CCA Part II
Commonwealth War Graves Commission—Ottawa, Ontario	To maintain graves, memorials and records of the members of the Commonwealth and Empire who died in the two World Wars. The cost is shared by the Partner Governments in the proportion of the number of their graves.	Veterans Affairs	1917 Royal Charter
Costpro Inc.—Ottawa, Ontario	To simplify international trade procedures.	Industry, Trade and Commerce	1975 CCA Part II
Fashion Canada Incorporated—Ottawa, Ontario	To increase the international competitiveness of Canadian apparel and textiles.	Industry, Trade and Commerce	1973 CCA Part II
Footwear and Leather Institute of Canada—St. Laurent, Quebec	To assist the Canadian footwear manufacturing and tanning industries, especially the small and medium sized firms, through provision of the expertise required to assist them in achieving their growth potential and maintaining and improving their performance and viability through greater efficiency.	Industry, Trade and Commerce	1976 CCA Part II

---

* The Canada Corporations Act (CCA), Part II is the most common vehicle for the federal incorporation of non-profit membership corporations.

TABLE 1—*Continued*

Corporation—Headquarters	Designated Minister	Function	Year and Mode of Incorporation or Acquisition
The Forest Engineering Research Institute of Canada—Point Clair, Quebec	Environment	To carry out research and development projects to demonstrate pratical measures for increasing the efficiency of wood harvesting in Canada.	1974 CCA Part II
Forintek Canada Corp.—Vancouver, B.C.	Environment	To carry out research and development on the forest industry, develop new products and processes, and perform other functions to facilitate the expansion of markets for Canadian forest products.	1979 CCA Part II
Hockey Canada—Vanier, Ontario	Labour	To support a national hockey team to represent Canada in international competition and to support generally the playing of hockey in Canada.	1969 CCA Part II
National Sport and Recreation Centre, Inc.—Vanier, Ontario	Labour	To assist national organizations concerned with the development of Canadian sport by providing support services in the area of administration, technical development and promotion.	1974 CCA Part II
OPCAN—Montréal, Quebec	Employment and Immigration	A non-profit corporation to act in the area of training youth, administering a program called "KATIMAVIK".	1977 CCA Part II

POS Pilot Plant Corporation (*i.e.*, Protein, Oilseed & Starch) —Saskatoon, Saskatchewan	Industry, Trade and Commerce	Development of value-added technologies pertaining to Canadian cereal grains, oilseeds and vegetables.	1973	CCA Part II
Sport Participation Canada—Montréal, Québec	Labour	To promote the fitness of Canadians through their participation in sports and physical recreation.	1971	CCA Part II
Vanier Institute of the Family—Ottawa, Ontario	Health and Welfare	To promote the spiritual and material well-being of Canadian families and in furtherance thereof and without limiting the generality of the foregoing, to study their social, physical, mental, moral and financial environment and characteristics.	1965	CCA Part II

What can we learn from the data presented in Table I? The most obvious point is that the government, through its 454 corporations, is involved in producing an incredible number and variety of goods and services (from supporting a national hockey team and marketing Inuit art to constructing nuclear reactors and building aircraft). The available data only suggest the full richness of the activities carried on within the federal corporate sector as no precise information is provided on the tasks of corporations with which the government is indirectly involved. These latter activities are carried on at some remove from the government through the network of subsidiary, sub-subsidiary and associated corporations. For instance, Texasgulf Inc., a huge mining conglomerate is held as an associated corporation status by a foreign sub-subsidiary of the Canada Development Corporation which the government owns in concert with a large number of other shareholders. Overall, a full 335 corporations are indirectly held—most by three corporations, the Canada Development Corporation, the CNR and Petro-Canada.

Table I also gives us the basic data with which to make some tentative comments about the historical pattern of the use of public corporations as instruments of policy at the federal level. Figure 1 focuses on the "year of incorporation" data and demonstrates that while the public corporation has been used more frequently at the federal than the provincial level in the period before 1960, there was still a remarkable period of growth in the 20-year period between 1960-80.[24]

Since 1960, 58 percent of all federal public corporations were created. Between 1940-60, 27 percent of the extant corporations were created; the remaining 15 percent were begun in the 32-year period beginning in 1908. In the ten-year period 1970-79, over 36 percent of this universe was incorporated. While the birth rate for the wholly owned corporations within the universe is more constant over the 72-year period of our survey, Figure 1 demonstrates that 80 percent of the shared ownership and 89 percent of the membership corporations were created in the last 20 years. The use of these latter instruments was a rare event before 1960. But since that time, the government has clearly found both corporate forms to be convenient vehicles for co-operative profit and non-profit-making ventures with other governments and individuals and organizations in the private sector.

The correlation of the "year of incorporation or acquisition" data with the periods of Liberal and Conservative majority and minority governments suggests on the surface that "party in power" might be a useful tool for ex-

---

[24] Analysis based on the "year of incorporation or acquisition" excludes corporations which are no longer extant in 1980 (*e.g.*, most of the 32 companies created during WW II and dissolved shortly after the hostilities ended). The date chosen is that year during which the federal government became involved with the corporation (*i.e.*, the year the corporation entered the public sector). Where a corporation's name has been changed but the function has not altered at all, the date of original incorporation or acquisition has been chosen (*e.g.*, Crown Assets Disposal Corporation).

FIGURE 1

Year of Incorporation or Acquisition of Federal Public Corporations

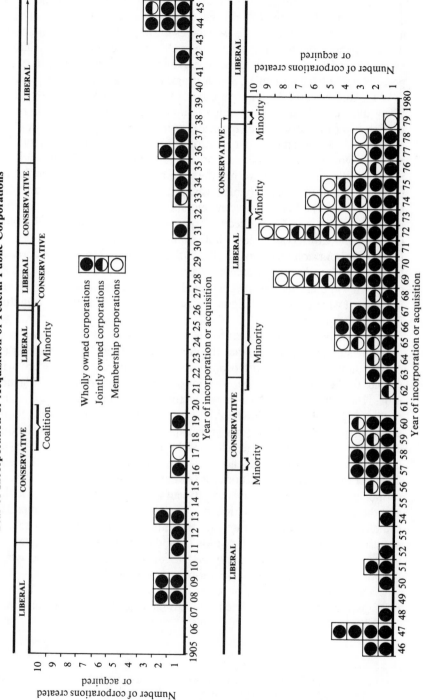

plaining why more corporations were created during one particular period than another. Clearly the Liberals have been involved in the creation of far more corporations than the Conservatives during the period of our survey. Roughly, the Liberals have been responsible for the creation of 100 corporations in 50 years of rule (2 per year), and the Conservatives for 19 corporations in 22 years of rule (.86 per year), including the coalition years of WW I. Moreover, the Liberals employed the public corporation form extensively during WW II—a fact which is not reflected in Table I due to the winding up of most of these corporations in the post-war period. Looking more closely at the extant incorporations or acquisitions of both parties it is also noteworthy that the Liberals are responsible for creating most of the major public corporations within the federal public sector. Except for the CNR, the Bank of Canada (which was, in fact, begun as a private corporation in 1934 by the Bennett government and later made a public corporation by the Liberals), the Farm Credit Corporation, and the National Research Council, the Conservative contributions to the public corporate stable are largely harbour commissions, bridge authorities and other minor corporations masking rather traditional government services or programs (*e.g.*, Director of Soldier Settlement, National Capital Commission, the International Fisheries Commissions Pension Society and the Agriculture Stabilization Board).

To qualify these findings, it is worth remembering (and we will raise the issue again in Section V) that the number of corporations created or acquired may not be the most persuasive measure of a party's record with respect to the use of public corporations as instruments of policy. Furthermore, the Liberals have been in power for long periods (*e.g.*, the time between 1963-79 when a majority of corporations were created) during which government activity of all types grew exponentially in all western nations. The Liberal record is further clouded by the fact that it has to varying degrees been under the influence of a form of "contagion from the left" during a recent period of minority government in which the NDP played a supporting role.[25] Due to the lags between policy initiation and legislation and the complexity of the relationship between the NDP and the Liberals it is difficult to comment accurately on the impact of the NDP on the Liberal pattern of public corporation creation. There is no doubt, however, that the whole question of "party in power" as an explanatory variable would benefit from more careful consideration at the federal level.

Three other interesting observations arise from the data in Table I. First, as Figure 2 illustrates, the provinces have not benefited equally from

---

25 On the general phenomenon of "left contagion", see Chandler, "Canadian Socialism and Policy Impact: Contagion from the Left?" (1977), 10 *Can. J. Pol. Sci.* 755.

FIGURE 2

Location of Corporate Headquarters for Federal Public Corporations

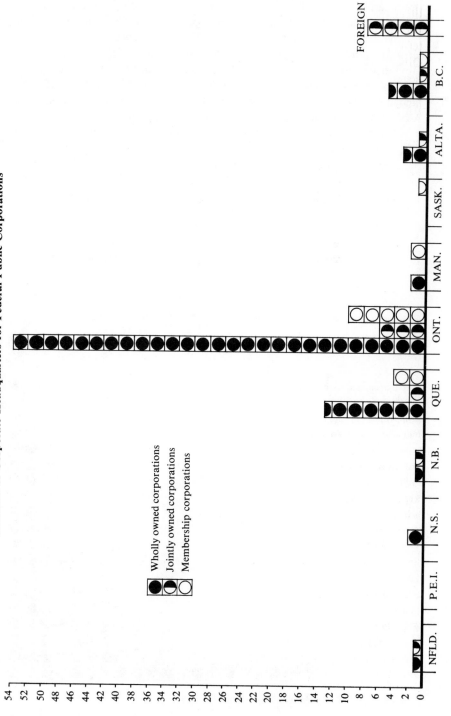

the location of the headquarters of federal public corporations. Ignoring the actual economic significance of the location of individual corporations for the moment, it is obvious that Ontario and Quebec are the winners in terms of numbers of corporate headquarters, with Ontario the clear victor. Obviously, Ottawa is the city of choice, with 52 of Ontario's 69 corporate headquarters located in the capital. Prince Edward Island has been by-passed entirely, Saskatchewan has one minor membership corporation, and Alberta has only four—but one of them is Petro-Canada.

Policy areas suffer from similar imbalances of representation. Public corporations have been used as instruments of policy far more frequently in the areas administerd by the Department of Industry, Trade and Commerce and Transport Canada, as Figure 3 (which displays the distribution of the 119 corporations in Table I according to the "designated minister" to

FIGURE 3
Designated Minister for Federal Public Corporations

Wholly owned corporation ●
Jointly owned corporation ◐
Membership corporation ○

MINISTERS

National Defence
Other*
Justice
Employment and Immigration
Health and Welfare
Prime Minister
Indian and Northern Affairs
Environment
Fisheries and Oceans
Public Works
Regional Economic Expansion
Science and Technology
Supply and Services
Veterans Affairs
Energy, Mines and Resources
Labour
External Affairs
Finance
Agriculture
Communications/Secretary of State
Industry, Trade and Commerce
Transport

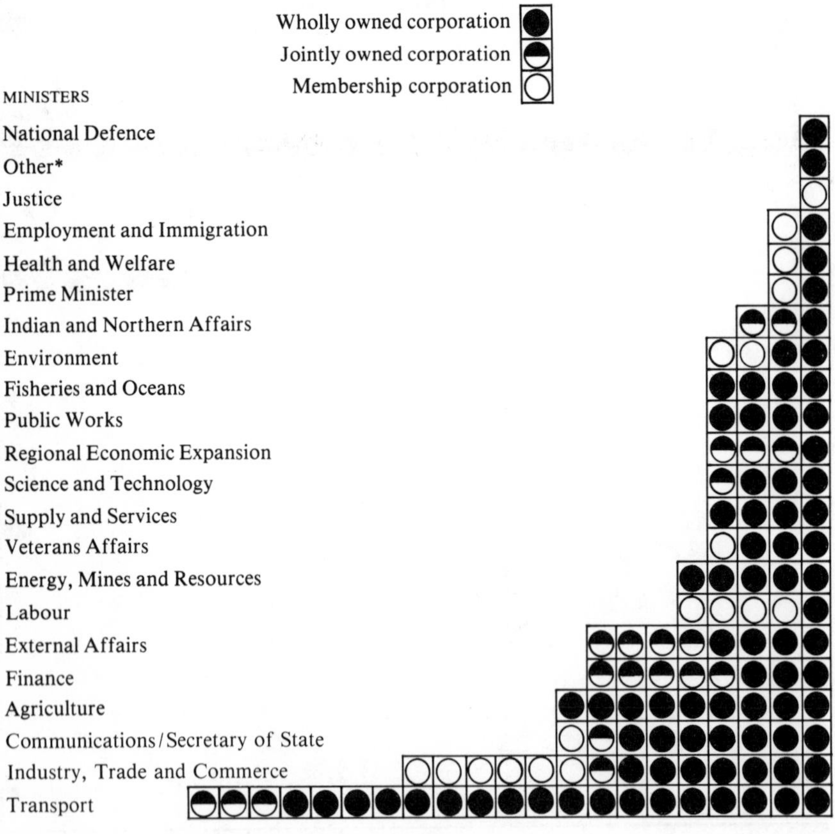

* Minister of State Responsible for the Canadian Wheat Board

whom they are responsible) demonstrates.[26] It would appear that Ministries such as Justice, Consumer and Corporate Affairs, Employment and Immigration, National Defence, and National Revenue have not found the corporate form compatible with their respective policy needs.[27]

Finally, Table I provides a statement of function for each of the 119 corporations in which the government is directly involved. These statements were used as the basis for a rough division of this universe into 15 functional groupings as set out in Table II. Then, where necessary, adjustments were made to the groupings to bring them as closely as possible in line with the groupings suggested by the Statistics Canada Standard Industrial Classification (SIC) system. The resulting 15 functional groupings, a SIC code number for each corporation, and a "comparable SIC grouping for each functional grouping" are displayed in Table II.[28] Undoubtedly, one could take issue with the functional categorizations upon which we have settled. The amalgam of SIC three digit categories required to create a comparable grouping to match our functional grouping in a couple of cases (*e.g.*, Financing, Insurance and Busines Services) suggests the underlying problems associated with the attempt to closely match "functional" and "product" oriented groupings. This problem is accented by the presence on our corporations list of a number of multi-division or multi-subsidiary public corporations (*e.g.*, Canada Development Corporations, CNR), each with multiple functions and each producing a wide variety of goods and services. Nevertheless both the functional grouping and SIC matching exercises are extremely useful. The latter provides a basis for rough comparisons between the public and private corporate sectors, while the former suggests a gross distinction between functions which tend to be "enterprise" and those which tend to be "governmental" in character. This distinction is implicit in Table II, and will be explored in detail in Section IV.[29]

---

[26] The Transport figures are somewhat distorted by the presence on the list of nine harbour commissions as separate corporate entities.

[27] Responsibility for several "cultural" corporations (*e.g.*, C.B.C., Canadian Film Development Corporation, Canada Council) has recently been transferred from the Secretary of State to the Minister of Communications.

[28] The SIC number for each corporation is drawn from Statistics Canada. "Business Register", *supra* note 2. Some corporations are not listed, and we have not arbitrarily chosen a grouping for these. The SIC product groupings have been revised twice since their original development in 1960. See Canada. Dominion Bureau of Statistics. *Standard Industrial Classification Manual: Revised 1970* (Ottawa: Information Canada, Statistics Canada #12-501, 1970); and Canada. Statistics Canada, *Corporation financial Statistics 1977* (Ottawa: Minister of Supply and Services, Statistics Canada #61-207, 1980). However, it does not appear that the "Business Register" coding has entirely kept pace with these revisions. Where the "Register" coding is clearly out of date, we have made the appropriate revision in the coding of individual corporations. For the purposes of comparison with the private sector, we have generally conformed to the product groupings used in the *Corporation Financial Statistics* series.

[29] For an earlier attempt at a similar division, see Irvine, "The delegation of authority to Crown Corporations" (1971), 14 *Can. Pub. Admin.* 556.

As a further preface to Table II we provide a brief sketch of each of the functional categories employed in this analysis.

1. *Communications*—There are three corporations in this grouping or 2.5 percent of the corporations with which the government is directly involved. Their functions include the operation of television and radio networks, telecommunications systems, and a domestic satellite communications system.

2. *Culture and Recreation*—This group is made up of two corporations (or 1.7 percent of the total) involved in operating a theatre and a national lottery respectively.

3. *Financing, Insurance and Business Services*—This category contains eight corporations (or 6.7 percent of the total) involved in banking, the provision of mortgages, loan and equity financing to facilitate domestic businesses and exports, and the provision of management advisory services.

4. *Industrial Development*—This grouping is made up of five corporations (or 4.2 percent of the total) involved in the creation or development of businesses, resources, properties and industries on a national or regional basis through the operation of diversified holding companies or industrial "parks" or the provision of funds and assistance to a specific industry.

5. *Manufacturing Industries*—This category contains eight corporations (6.7 percent of the total) producing a wide variety of manufactured products including computers, aircraft, petrochemicals, nuclear reactors and coins.

6. *Marketing, Wholesaling and Trading*—This is a rather diverse group of 11 corporations (9.2 percent of the total) providing orderly marketing arrangements for a wide variety of farm and fishing products, patents, international trading arrangements for importers and exporters, and wholesaling facilities for Inuit artisans.

7. *Resource Development*—This is a group of two corporations (1.7 percent of the total) involved in mining and hydro power development respectively.

8. *Transportation Sytems and Facilities*—This grouping contains 22 corporations (18.5 percent of the total) involved in moving passengers and freight by rail, air and water modes of transport, and providing way (bridges, waterways), terminal (harbours) and ancillary facilities (*e.g.*, pilotage) for transportation carriers.

9. *General Government Services*—This is a "catch-all" group of nine corporations (7.6 percent of the total) providing a wide variety of services that are traditionally viewed as being governmental in nature (*e.g.*, administering employment and immigration programs, parks, "greenbelt" areas, museums and government real estate holdings).

10. *Economic Support*—This is a 12-member group of corporations (10.1 percent of the total) operating domestic price or supply stabilization or subsidization programs, or acting on an international level as conduits for development funds for third world nations.

11. *Foreign Affairs and Defence*—This category contains four corporations (3.4 percent of the total), three of which administer discrete foreign relations programs (boundaries, environment and war graves) and the other provides construction services for the Department of National Defence.

12. *Promotion and Training*—This group consists of 12 corporations (10.1 percent of the total) involved in trade, health, sports, and social welfare promotion as well as technical and youth training.

13. *Regulation*—This is a one corporation category (0.8 percent of the total) involving the regulation of the nuclear energy industry.

14. *Research, Granting and Advising*—This category is made up of 16 corporations (13.4 percent of the total). Nine of these corporations primarily conduct research on their own, three are largely advisory in nature and four primarily provide grants for outside research.

15. *Social Welfare*—The last group contains four corporations (3.4 percent of the total) all of which operate programs designed to enhance the welfare of armed services veterans.

TABLE II

Federal Public Corporations by Functional Grouping

Functional Grouping	Corporations	SIC Code Number	Comparable SIC Product Grouping for each Functional Grouping[1]
1. Communications	Canadian Broadcasting Corporation	543	543-548 Total Communications
	Teleglobe Canada	545	
	Telesat Canada	543	
2. Culture and Recreation	Loto Canada[2]	700	
	National Arts Centre Corporation	845	859 Other Recreational Services
3. Financing, Insurance and Business Services	Bank of Canada	701	
	Canada Deposit Insurance Corporation	731	
	Canada Mortgage and Housing Corporation	703	
	Export Development Corporation	721	712, 713, 718 Banks
	Farm Credit Corporation	703	721, 727, 729 Other Credit Agencies
	Federal Business Development Bank	703	781 Insurance and Real Estate Agencies
	Federal Mortgage Exchange Corporation		
	Newfoundland and Labrador Development Corporation	703	
4. Industrial Development	Canada Development Corporation	756	
	Canadian Film Development Corporation	756	
	Cape Breton Development Corporation	756	752, 756 Other Investment Companies

Category	Code	Corporation	Industry Code
	931	La Société Inter-Port de Québec	791, 793 Real Estate Operators and Developers
	737	La Société du parc industrial et commercial aéroportuaire de Mirabel	931 Provincial Administration[3]
5. Manufacturing Industries	864	Atomic Energy of Canada Limited	295-298 Smelting and Refining
	321	Canadair Limited	304 Metal Stamping
	379	Canadian Arsenals Limited	315, 318 Other Machinery
	318	Consolidated Computer Inc.	321 Aircraft and Parts
		The DeHavilland Aircraft of Canada Limited	365 Petroleum Refineries
	321	Eldorado Nuclear Limited	371, 373, 379 Other Chemicals
	295	Petro-Canada	864 Engineering and Scientific Services
	365	Royal Canadian Mint	
	304		
6. Marketing, Wholesaling and Trading	629	Canadian Arctic Producers Co-operative	111 Fish Products
	869	Canadian Chicken Marketing Agency	604 Grain Wholesale Trade
	909	Canadian Commercial Corporation	614 Food Wholesale Trade
	602	Canadian Egg Marketing Agency	629 Other Wholesale Trade
	909	Canadian Patents and Development Limited	861, 866, 869 Other Business Services
	614	Canadian Salt Fish Corporation	909 Other Federal Administration[4]
	869	Canadian Turkey Marketing Agency	
	602	Canadian Wheat Board	
	629	Crown Assets Disposal Corporation	
	102	Freshwater Fish Marketing Corporation	
	629	Uranium Canada Limited	
7. Resource Development	059	Nanisivik Mines Limited	053-057, 059 Other Metal Mining
	572	Northern Canada Power Commission	572 Electric Power Utilities

TABLE II—Continued

Functional Grouping	Corporations	SIC Code Number	Comparable SIC Product Grouping for each Functional Grouping[1]
8. Transportation Systems and Facilities	Air Canada	501	501, 502 Air Transport
	Atlantic Pilotage Authority	505	504, 505 Water Transport
	Blue Water Bridge Authority	516	506 Railways
	Canadian National Railway	503	516, 517, 519 Other Transportation
	Canarctic Shipping Company Limited	504	
	Fraser River Harbour Commission	505	
	Hamilton Harbour Commissioners	505	
	Lakehead Harbour Commission	505	
	Laurentian Pilotage Authority	505	
	Nanaimo Harbour Commission	505	
	National Harbours Board	505	
	North Fraser Harbour Commission	505	
	Northern Transportation Company Limited	504	
	Oshawa Harbour Commission	505	
	Pacific Pilotage Authority	505	
	Port Alberni Harbour Commission	505	
	St. John Harbour Bridge Authority	516	
	St. Lawrence Seaway Authority	505	
	Thousand Islands Bridge Authority	516	
	Toronto Harbour Commissioners	505	
	VIA Rail Canada Inc.	503	
	Windsor Harbour Commission	505	

9. General Government Services	Canada Employment and Immigration Commission	909	
	Harbourfront Corporation[5]	—	
	International Fisheries Commissions Pension Society	909	
	Municipal Development and Loan Board	909	801-828 Community and Public Services
	National Battlefields Commission	909	909 Other Federal Administration
	National Capital Commission	909	
	National Museums of Canada	807	
	Public Works Lands Company Limited	909	
	Roosevelt Campobello International Park Commission	909	
10. Economic Support	African Development Fund	NA	
	Agricultural Products Board	909	
	Agricultural Stabilization Board	909	
	Asian Development Bank	NA	
	Canadian Dairy Commission	909	
	Canadian Livestock Feed Board	909	909 Other Federal Administration
	Caribbean Development Bank	NA	
	Fisheries Prices Support Bank	909	
	Inter-American Development Bank	NA	
	International Bank for Reconstruction and Development	NA	
	International Development Association	NA	
	International Finance Corporation	NA	
11. Foreign Affairs and Defence	Commonwealth War Graves Commission	NA	
	Defence Construction (1951) Limited	902	902 Defence Services
	International Boundary Commission	909	909 Other Federal Administration
	International Joint Commission	909	

TABLE II—*Continued*

Functional Grouping	Corporations	SIC Code Number	Comparable SIC Product Grouping for each Functional Grouping[1]
12. Promotion and Training	Association for the Export of Canadian Books	899	
	Canadian Centre for Occupational Health and Safety	909	
	Canadian International Grains Institute	869	801-828 Community and Public Services
	Costpro Inc.	867	
	Fashion Canada Incorporated	891	859 Other Recreational Services
	Footwear and Leather Institute of Canada	869	861, 866, 869 Other Business Services
	Hockey Canada	849	871, 872, 879-899 Other Services
	National Sport and Recreation Centre Inc.	849	909 Other Federal Administration
	Opcan	NA	
	Sport Participation Canada	849	
	Standards Council of Canada	909	
	Vanier Institute of the Family	828	
13. Regulation	Atomic Energy Control Board	909	909 Other Federal Administration
14. Research, Granting and Advising	Board of Trustees of the Queen Elizabeth II Canadian Fund to Aid in Research in the Diseases of Children	NA	

Canada Council	909	861, 866, 869 Other Business Services
Canada-France-Hawaii Telescope Corporation	NA	864 Engineering and Scientific Services
Canada Grains Council	891	871, 872, 879-899 Other Services
Canada Law Information Council	866	909 Other Federal Administration
Economic Council of Canada	909	
Forest Engineering Research Institute of Canada	864	
Forintek Canada Corporation	NA	
International Development Research Centre	864	
Medical Research Council	909	
National Farm Products Marketing Council	NA	
National Research Council	909	
Natural Sciences and Humanities Research Council	864	
POS Pilot Plant Corporation	864	
Science Council of Canada	909	
Social Sciences and Humanities Research Council	909	
15. Social Welfare Army Benevolent Fund	NA	
Director, Soldier Settlement	NA	
Director, Veteran's Land Act	NA	871, 872, 879-899 Other Services
Last Post Fund	899	

[1] With the exception of the Public Administration groupings (902, 909, 931), the comparable SIC product groupings are drawn from the *Corporation Financial Statistics* which, in most cases, reverts to the coding used in the original 1960 SIC Manual.
[2] Loto Canada's SIC number has no comparable grouping in the *Corporation Financial Statistics*.
[3] No comparable financial data is available for the federal administration groupings.
[4] No comparable financial data is available for the provincial administration group.
[5] Harbourfront Corporation has a Business Register designation which is no longer appropriate to the function of the Corporation.

While federal public corporations are undoubtedly involved in a diverse set of tasks, they are to a significant degree a different set of tasks than those for which the provincial governments have employed public corporations. In part this difference in emphasis is dictated by the separation of power under Canadian federalism. There are no federal corporations involved in automobile insurance, liquor sales, municipal financing, water supply or school and hospital financing. The two federal government corporations involved in fishing, forestry or mining (excluding the marketing corporations) are located in the territories, where the federal government exercises provincial resource development powers.[30]

IV. FROM PUBLIC CORPORATION TO CORPORATE ENTERPRISE

One of the most valuable spinoffs of the grouping of the federal public corporation universe on a functional basis is the distinction it suggests between the mass of public corporations and that subset of the universe which we will refer to as corporate enterprises. To our mind, the corporate enterprise group is made up of all of the corporations contained in the first eight categories of our functional division (communications; culture and recreation; financing, insurance and business services; industrial development; manufacturing industries; marketing, wholesaling and trading; resource development; transportation systems and facilities). Our corporate enterprise group contains all 61 corporations in these eight categories. In addition to identifying this corporate enterprise group, we also provide a data set made up of seven economic indices (total assets, total revenue, government derived revenue, net income, long term loans from federal government and other sources, and employment) for each enterprise for the year-end closest to March 31, 1979. We believe that this data set covers a far more comprehensive universe of public corporations on a more disaggregated basis than all the other available sources combined.

Before proceeding to present and consider this data, we should note that our definition of corporate "enterprise" is far more liberal than the traditional interpretations. The standard definition is that put forward by Statistics Canada as the basis for its *Federal Government Enterprise Finance* series:

> Government enterprises are agencies engaged primarily in operations of a commercial industrial nature, which either compete actively with similar operations in the private sector or monopolize activities that would otherwise be carried out in the private sector . . . . Enterprises reflect government activities which involve the production of economic goods and provision of services for sale to the consumer, at a price which is intended to compensate wholly or largely for their costs and, in some cases yield a profit.[31]

---

[30] See Vining and Botterell, Chapter 5 in this volume.
[31] Statistics Canada. *Federal Government Enterprise Finance, supra* note 2, at 5.

Such enterprises are distinguished from activities in the government sector:

> Services of a general nature such as protection of persons and property, health and social welfare, education and public works are common to all levels of government and are usually financed out of ordinary revenue. . . .[32]

Using this approach to the meaning of enterprise, Statistics Canada identifies only 29 corporations with which the government is directly involved as "government enterprises".[33] Our data set contains more than double that number. The major difference between the two approaches is that we place less emphasis on the issue of how the enterprise's activities are financed (*e.g.*, by sales, appropriations, or a combination of the two), and more emphasis on the type of task which the enterprise performs—its function. Following Vining and Botterell, we subscribe to Green's approach to enterprise which focuses on the production of "generally marketable goods and services".[34] If the mandate of our investigation extended beyond the corporate universe, there are even branches within federal government departments (*e.g.*, Air Administration, Transport Canada) which we would argue should be labelled as government enterprise. Many of our corporate enterprise universe already operate in a competitive environment. Several operate on a cost-recovery or profit-making basis. It would not be stretching a point to argue that almost all of the tasks performed by the corporations listed in Table III would be performed by private sector corporations if the government was not already active. In our view, the over-emphasis of the criteria "cost-recovery" or "profit-making" with respect to corporations which perform social functions hand in hand with commercial tasks is needlessly restrictive and leads to a significant understatement of the scope of the corporate enterprise universe.

Before presenting the financial data in Table III, some prefatory comments are in order on the problems encountered and practices established in our effort to retrieve comparative information from the myriad accounting styles employed by our corporate enterprise group. Financial results for the 61 corporations consolidate the operations of 213 subsidiaries but generally exclude the operations of associated corporations beyond the inclusion of "investments" in assets. The plethora of accounting formats combined with reporting omissions and obfuscations create a comparative environment which is confusing and open to wide discretionary interpretation. For example, some corporations (DeHavilland) are precise in detailing their

---

[32] Canada. Statistics Canada. *Federal Government Enterprise Finance, 1971* (Ottawa: Information Canada, Statistics Canada #61-203, 1973) at 17; as cited in Statistics Canada. *The input-output structure of the Canadian economy 1961-74* (Ottawa: Ministry of Industry, Trade and Commerce, Statistics Canada #15-508E, 1979), at 19.

[33] The Auditor General takes an even more restrictive approach employing the "financial viability" criterion. See Auditor General of Canada., *supra* note 2, at 239.

[34] See C. Green, *Canadian Industrial Organization and Policy* (Toronto: McGraw-Hill Ryerson, 1980) at 251; and Vining and Botterell, Chapter 5 in this volume.

financial relationships with the federal government to the extent that funds received under manpower training programs are included in the "government derived revenue" note to the financial statements. Conversely, other corporations secrete contributions from government in a variety of locations (*e.g.*, as a reduction of expenses, or as items of contributed capital, equity, or funds provided).

To develop a "total revenue" figure for each corporation we have aggregated all its income items at a gross level; that is, any reductions for expenses or commissions are transferred to the expense statement, while positive items from the non-operating statement (such as foreign exchange gains and interest earned) are included as revenue. Unfortunately some corporations (*e.g.*, CNR, Canadian Wheat Board) provide only net interest figures. Extraordinary items such as gains from the sale of fixed assets and tax reductions arising from previous losses, have been excluded from revenues but included in net income. Also included in "total revenue" is "government derived revenue", which includes such components as operating subsidies, parliamentary appropriations, and services provided without charge by government departments—where the latter accounting is presented (*e.g.*, Laurentian Pilotage Authority). The "government derived revenue" category is probably substantially understated by the failure, in many cases (*e.g.*, Canarctic Shipping, Uranium Canada) to include the full imputed income of services provided and personnel seconded (formally or informally) from government departments to perform corporate tasks. The importance of "government derived revenue" can be crudely gauged by noting the magnitude of this column in relation to "net income". The latter figure is overstated in some cases by the non-applicability of income taxation to some enterprises.

Turning to the "debt" section of Table III it should be noted that long term debt is net of current portions. In cases where no breakdown between "Government of Canada" and "other" long term debt was available current debt was apportioned relative to the overall shares of total long term debt. Long term debt also includes interest accrued and interest in arrears. The "Government of Canada" debt section includes loans made to the enterprise by other federal corporate enterprises, while loans from provincial governments to federal enterprises are classified as "Other".

The employment data in Table III are a compendium of the results of our questionnaire, annual reports and interviews. In some cases, *Estimates*[35] person-year figures have been utilized as a 'best' approximation of actual employment levels and, finally, a small number of missing values were filled with 1976 and 1977 figures gleaned from business directories.

---

[35] Treasury Board, *supra* note 2.

TABLE III
Financial Data on Corporate Enterprises
(For Year End Closest to March 31, 1979)

Corporate Enterprise	Total Assets (000's)	Revenue (000's)		Net Income (000's)	Long Term Debt (000's)		Employment
		Total	Government Derived		Government of Canada	Other	
Air Canada	1,333,494	1,367,836	0	47,485	305,978	256,626	20,964
Atlantic Pilotage Authority	1,883	3,776	874[a]	(97)	802	0	100
Atomic Energy of Canada Ltd.	1,859,182	397,746	119,120	5,197	1,372,682	94,374	6,563
Bank of Canada	15,105,642	989,493	0	925,031	0[b]	0	1,854
Blue Water Bridge Authority[c]	26,000	1,089	0	0	0	100	24
Canada Deposit Insurance Corporation	147,608	10,573	0	5,459	0[d]	0	5
Canada Development Corporation[e]	3,411,700	1,356,750	0	65,400	0	794,700	24,000
Canada Mortgage and Housing Corporation[f]	10,774,747	1,789,275	694,075	31,621	9,898,072	0	3,848

[a] Appropriations to purchase fixed assets have been excluded as has the liability due to Canada with respect to parliamentary appropriations. Similar practice has been followed when dealing with capital grants to other corporations (example: National Harbours Board, Cape Breton Development Corporation, Atlantic Pilotage Authority, C.B.C., Canadian Arsenals).

[b] The Bank holds more than $4.4 billion on deposit, largely to satisfy chartered bank reserve requirements and provide leverage in the formulation and conduct of monetary policy. Because they are a reflection of the current level of charter bank customer deposits, we have omitted these holdings.

[c] The bridge and ancillary buildings have an estimated asset value of $25 million, although recorded at a nominal value of $1. In addition to operating on a break-even basis, the Authority provides services to Customs and Immigration and Agriculture Canada without charge.

[d] The $145 million Deposit Insurance Fund can only be considered to be a liability in the sense of insurance contingencies. Under s. 35(a) of the incorporating legislation, funds must be invested in Government of Canada securities (1978—$140 million).

[e] Data include operations of unconsolidated associated corporations, C.D.C. *Annual Report*, 1978, p. 19.

[f] The operations of the Insurance, Guarantee and Contribution Funds are consolidated, with the exception of ministerial contributions which are assumed to be included in Schedule V, "Grants, Subsidies and Contributions on Behalf of the Minister," Canada, Department of Finance, Receiver General for Canada, *Public Accounts of Canada, 1979*, Vol. III (Ottawa: Ministry of Supply and Services, 1979), at 80, 84. It is important to note that all funds in excess of the $5 million statutory limitation are paid to the Receiver General. In 1978, this transfer amounted to $6.69 million.

TABLE III—*Continued*

Corporate Enterprise	Total Assets (000's)	Revenue (000's) Total	Revenue (000's) Government Derived	Net Income (000's)	Long Term Debt (000's) Government of Canada	Long Term Debt (000's) Other	Employment
Canadair	246,525	83,294	0	3,229	0	83,744	5,093
Canadian Arctic Producers Ltd.	1,804	2,398	0	5	339	0	24
Canadian Arsenals Ltd.[g]	47,282	15,438	883	1,064	4,383	0	341
Canadian Broadcasting Corporation	452,622	595,296	481,671	(53,868)	268,146	0	12,487
Canadian Chicken Marketing Agency (created Dec. 1978)	N/A	N/A	N/A	N/A	N/A	N/A	N/A
Canadian Commercial Corporation	131,130	193,309	8,271	(4,586)	3,300	0	108
Canadian Egg Marketing Agency	12,783	35,939	0	3,864	0	0	38
Canadian Film Development Corporation	2,948	5,378	4,412	813	0	0	22
Canadian National Railways[h]	4,531,148	3,156,064	352,684	136,105	264,615	1,057,650	78,247
Canadian Patents and Development Ltd.	943	1,419	317[i]	63	0	0	24
Canadian Saltfish Corporation	9,977	24,150	60	(32)	884	0	32[j]
Canadian Turkey Marketing Agency	575	1,263	0	225	0	0	N/A
Canadian Wheat Board[k]	1,914,177	2,403,323	0	391,320	0	974,788	662
Canarctic Shipping Co. Ltd.[l]	33,738	4,069	2,232	(546)	0	31,319	22
Cape Breton Development Corporation	166,265	146,053	18,038	(19,019)	10,250	35	4,534
Consolidated Computer	22,878	23,047	0	614	0	4,445[m]	296
Crown Assets Disposal Corporation	9,294	12,671	0	101[n]	4,945	29	69
DeHavilland Aircraft of Canada Ltd.	190,180	173,311	5,344	3,738	110,411[o]	70,000	4,564
Eldorado Nuclear Ltd.[p]	314,882	131,429	0	17,618	93,542	36,824	1,499
Export Development Corporation[q]	2,359,183	187,086	0	29,458	975,755	779,039	361
Farm Credit Corporation	2,869,719	212,492	394	2,287	2,756,818	0	626

Federal Business Development Bank	1,631,671	N/A	11,129	541	1,387,852	0	2,207
Federal Mortgage Exchange Corporation^r	N/A	N/A	N/A	N/A	N/A	N/A	N/A
Fraser River Harbour Commission	21,843	4,655	0	1,872	611	9,150	7
Freshwater Fish Marketing Corporation	17,152	35,275	1,171[s]	8	4,289	0	330
Hamilton Harbour Commissioners	21,844	4,219	0	126	2,049	0	248
Lakehead Harbour Commission	18,556	1,325	0	191	634	0	20
Laurentian Pilotage Authority	4,353	17,004	114	561	0	0	306

g Canadian Arsenals Ltd. considers fixed assets to be Crown owned and Company administered. The Auditor General attacks this practice and suggests that fixed assets should be included on the Balance Sheet and a corresponding amount should be included as parliamentary appropriations in the Statement of Deficit. We have included fixed assets in our asset total. Government revenue is an appropriation which was "Due to Canada"; however, we have classified it as government derived revenue and long term debt because it was not repaid in 1979. The other item of debt is a working capital loan, a category which is normally outside the ambit of long term but included because of the absence of repayment dates.

h Legislation in June, 1978 capitalized $808 million in debts payable to the Government and initiated the payment of annual dividends equal to at least 20 percent of net income. Subsidies to C.N.R. include $2.4 million from the Province of Quebec to support Montreal commuter services.

i Government derived revenue includes $67,000 which represents an indirect subsidy by the National Research Council which pays certain employee benefits for Canadian Patents and Development Ltd.

j Excludes up to 400-500 seasonally employed processing workers.

k Revenue figures for the Canadian Wheat Board include inventories of grain and sales made subsequent to the fiscal year-end. Bank loans are guaranteed by the Government of Canada and are almost entirely used to finance grain export sales.

l Through appropriations, the Government of Canada is providing funds for Canarctic to meet its obligations to other parties, with the proviso that future profits will first be used to repay these obligations. We have excluded the accumulated appropriations from long term debt.

m This item excludes inventory purchases made by the Ontario Development Corporation and held until shipments to customers are made.

n Subsequent to a 1970 Order-in-Council, any surplus in excess of $300,000 must be paid to the Receiver General.

o Training assistance has been omitted from our calculations since such grant programs are independent of federal corporate status. Government loans are repayments due on assistance to finance research and development of the DHC-7 which become due when aircraft production is yielding returns.

p The results of Eldorado Nuclear consolidate the operations of the Eldorado Aviation subsidiary. Government debt includes $45 million in uranium concentrates borrowed from Uranium Canada Ltd.

q Export Development Corporation data excludes accounts administered for the Government of Canada, where there is no direct financial involvement by the Corporation.

r Federal Mortgage Exchange Corporation is not yet operational.

s Government assistance is *not* disaggregated between federal and provincial contributions.

TABLE III—Continued

Corporate Enterprise	Total Assets (000's)	Revenue (000's) Total	Revenue (000's) Government Derived	Net Income (000's)	Long Term Debt (000's) Government of Canada	Long Term Debt (000's) Other	Employment
Loto Canada Inc.[t]	41,414	263,871	0	62,472	0	0	120
Nanaimo Harbour Commission	6,501	3,189	0	974	16	0	14
Nanisivik Mines Ltd.[u]	93,904	65,802	0	1,716	10,181	44,774	218
National Arts Centre Corporation	2,311	18,563	10,430[v]	(150)	0	0	624
National Harbours Board[w]	526,260	119,682	4,138	(16,625)	418,067	24,343	1,967
Newfoundland and Labrador Development Corporation[x]	19,346	2,770	1,346	0	17,500	1,700	24
North Fraser Harbour Commission	2,766	304	0[y]	117	0	0	16
Northern Canada Power Commission	205,070	45,180	0	(64)	189,879	0	334
Northern Transportation Co. Ltd.	58,743	27,386	397	(341)	38,577	121	792
Oshawa Harbour Commission	3,191	596	133	117	0	0	4
Pacific Pilotage Authority	2,595	9,450	0	448	201	0	144
Petro-Canada	3,348,913	205,095	0	13,740	0	300,277	850
Port Alberni Harbour Commission	5,981	2,081	0	495	1,391	0	146
Royal Canadian Mint[z]	48,326	83,856	0	4,572	24,393	0	674
St. John Harbour Bridge Authority	N/A	N/A	N/A	N/A	N/A	N/A	N/A
St. Lawrence Seaway Authority[aa]	702,187	61,060	1,832	(3,278)	315,131	8	1,473
La Société Inter-Port de Québec	278	303[bb]	0	214	0	0	N/A
La Société du parc industriel et commercial aéroportuaire de Mirabel[cc]	6,261	N/A	N/A	N/A	N/A	N/A	10
Teleglobe Canada[dd]	259,185	96,467	0	19,864	18,247	0	1,240
Telesat Canada	150,848	40,092	0	5,595	0	4,500	360

Thousand Islands Bridge Authority	N/A	N/A	N/A	N/A	N/A	N/A	N/A
Toronto Harbour Commissioners	123,525	7,341	0	(2,748)	0	0	368
Uranium Canada Ltd.	103,933	11,060	0	8,815	0	0	N/A[ee]
VIA Rail Canada[ff]	75,344	64,209	29,117	102	37,338	11,961	4,200
Windsor Harbour Commission	1,139	217	0	141	0	0	3
TOTAL	53,481,749	14,710,785	1,748,182	1,692,024	18,537,328	4,580,507	183,106

[t] The operations of Loto Canada are winding down to probable dissolution in 1981. At present there are three employees.

[u] With the exception of debt, these figures are for the majority shareholder (53.6 percent), Mineral Resources International Ltd. (The Government of Canada holds 18 percent of Nanisivik Mines.) Since the Nanisivik mine is the only *major* operating holding of MRI, the figures provide a rough indication of Nanisivik operations. Under a financing agreement, 35 percent of net profit goes to Texasgulf Inc. Employment data is for the Arctic mine and excludes management employees in Calgary and Toronto.

[v] Government derived revenue includes a municipal grant of $135,000.

[w] Statements include 11 months of operations of the Jacques Cartier and Champlain Bridges, which were transferred to the St. Lawrence Seaway Authority on December 1, 1978. Loans and interest in arrears totalling $252 million were cancelled in 1978 and added to contributed capital.

[x] Government derived revenue appears to be primarily reimbursements from "governments" for bad debts written off. The Corporation estimates that its loans and investments in 1978-9 provided 583 full-time and 226 part-time jobs.

[y] The harbour commissions receive dredging services from the federal government without charge. North Fraser Harbour Commission does make a reference to this service in its accounts.

[z] The Mint has a statutory limitation of $1 million with all excess funds going to the Receiver General.

[aa] Data for the St. Lawrence Seaway Authority consolidates the operations of subsidiaries. Employment totals exclude the operations of the Seaway International Bridge Corporation and financial results for the Jacques Cartier and Champlain Bridges Incorporated include only the four months following the transfer of the assets from the National Harbours Board and consequent incorporation in November, 1978.

[bb] Included in total revenue is a grant of $284,700 from the Ministry of Industry and Commerce, Government of Quebec.

[cc] The industrial park is at the development stage with no significant revenue flows and costs being assumed by the shareholder partners. The annual report provides no statement of operations.

[dd] Both Telesat and Teleglobe include an allowance for funds used during construction. This unusual accounting practice seems intended to portray some sense of the opportunity cost of capitalizing investments, as opposed to some alternative use of the funds or method of financing.

[ee] The Department of Energy, Mines and Resources provides all staff and administrative support.

[ff] The figures for VIA Rail Canada Ltd. are for the nine month period following the commencement of operations on April 1, 1978.

V. PERSPECTIVES ON FEDERAL CORPORATE ENTERPRISE

The 61 federal corporate enterprises examined in Table III represent a significant force within the government and the economy, accounting overall for almost $53.5 billion in assets and over 183,000 employees as of March 31, 1979. During the 1978-79 fiscal year (depending on the closest year-end for individual corporations), they generated $14.7 billion in revenues, of which almost $1.8 billion (12 percent) was paid by the federal government. The enterprise group had an overall net income of $1.7 billion and owed $18.5 billion in long term debt to the federal government and a further $4.6 billion to other long term lenders. Ignoring the effect of "government derived revenue" on the income statements of our corporate enterprises, only 14 corporations lost money during 1978-79. If "government derived revenue" is subtracted from net income, a further 11 corporate enterprises would have operated in the red. However, the latter calculation would be misleading in the case of those corporations (*e.g.*, CMHC, CNR) which receive revenue from government to cover the costs of servicing specific national interest objectives or programs (*e.g.*, lower freight rates for specific regions).

It is interesting to compare the size and significance of our corporate enterprise group with that of the Statistics Canada "government enterprise" group. Statistics Canada clearly understates the importance of federal enterprise despite the fact that its corporate universe contains most of the major corporations in our group. For the comparable time period, Statistics Canada records federal government enterprise total assets to be $35.1 billion (66 percent of our figure), employment to be 148,918 (81 percent of our figure), total revenue to be $10.5 billion (71 percent of our figure), and government derived revenue to be $660 million (38 percent of our figure).[36]

Figure 4 relates 1978-79 asset and employment data for the corporate enterprise group to the "year of incorporation or acquisition" data presented in Table I and Figure 1. An examination of the relative growth rate of these three indicators on this basis provides some interesting insights. For most of the period up to the end of WW II, assets and employment grew at a much faster rate than the number of corporate enterprises. *In terms of present day significance*, therefore, the relatively small number of incorporation and acquisition decisions made in the first quarter-century of our survey were more important than those made in the following 35 years—despite the fact that over 3/4 of the corporate enterprise group were

---

[36] See Statistics Canada. *Federal Government Enterprise Finance*, and *Federal Government Employment, supra* note 2. The difference in the "government derived revenue" figures clearly reflects the differences in our respective approaches to the criterion for inclusion in the enterprise group.

created or acquired in the latter period. By 1945, only 23 percent of the corporate enterprise group had been created; however, in present terms, that group accounts for over 2/3 of all corporate enterprise assets and employment. These figures also increase the significance of the role of the Progressive Conservatives as initiators of public enterprise. Again, in present day terms, the Conservatives or Conservative-led governments are responsible for the creation or acquisition of roughly 44 percent of the assets and employment of the corporate enterprise group. Obviously, such calculations are extremely superficial, as they depend on present day data and ignore the political complexity of individual incorporations or acquisitions (*e.g.,* as previously noted, the Conservatives began the Bank of Canada in 1934 as a private rather than a public corporation). If it is concerned about its place in the history books, the present Liberal government can assure its long-term domination of the corporate enterprise employment and asset statistics by turning the Post Office into a public corporation (thereby adding 70,000 postal employees to the ranks of enterprise employees) and allowing Petro-Canada to continue to amass assets at the same astounding rate it has established over the last three years.

Table III leads us, finally, to what is the most problematic task undertaken in this essay—financial comparisons between our corporate enterprise group and, the wider federal public sector, provincial corporate enterprise, and appropriate private sector groupings. Establishing the relative importance of federal corporate enterprise in the context of the overall federal public sector is reasonably straightforward although there are some problems of comparability. In 1978-79, federal corporate enterprise assets ($53.5b) represented roughly 68 percent of the total assets ($78.3b) of the federal government.[37] Enterprise employment (183,106) represented almost 32 percent of total federal government employment (578,378 *including* the armed services and all "federal government enterprise" employment).[38] Finally the total revenue of the corporate enterprise group for 1978-79 ($14.7b) was approximately 37 percent of the total federal government revenue of $39.3b.[39] These rough comparisons clearly suggest that our corporate enterprise group is a significant component within the federal public sector.

Comparisons of federal corporate enterprise with provincial public enterprise are more difficult. Vining and Botterell calculate the 1977 total

---

[37] See Canada. Department of Finance. Receiver General for Canada. *Public Accounts of Canada 1979: Volume I Summary Report and Financial Statements* (Ottawa: Ministry of Supply and Services, 1979) at 2.8; and *Federal Government Enterprise Finance, supra* note 2. The federal government total asset figures are apparently understated. See Canadian Tax Foundation. *The National Finances: An analysis of the revenues and expenditures of the Government of Canada 1979-1980* (Toronto: Canadian Tax Foundation, 1980) at 276-280.

[38] *Federal Government Employment, supra* note 2, January-March 1979.

[39] See *Public Accounts, supra* note 37, at 1.13.

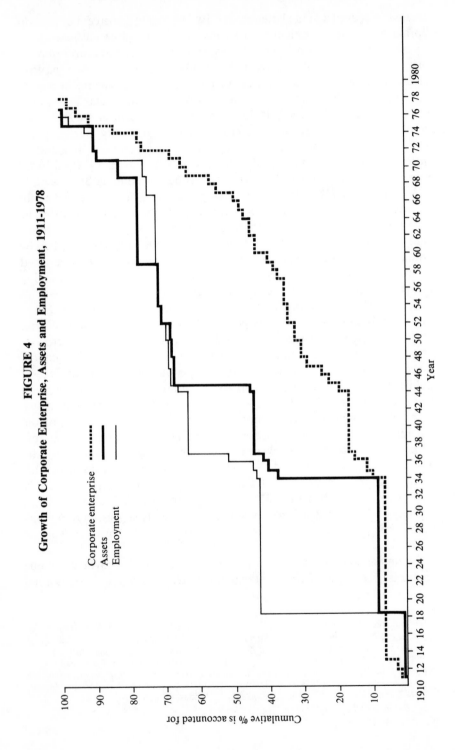

FIGURE 4

Growth of Corporate Enterprise, Assets and Employment, 1911-1978

Corporate enterprise
Assets
Employment

assets of what they define as "provincial Crown corporations" to be $62.3 billion, approximately $8.8b more than the 1978-79 total for our federal enterprise group.[40] The bases of calculation are not strictly comparable either in this instance or in the case of the available employment date. Statistics Canada—using a more narrow corporation base than either we or Vining and Botterell would be inclined to adopt—calculates provincial enterprise employment for January-March, 1979 to be 146,262.[41] If these figures were comparable, federal corporate enterprise employment would exceed its provincial counterpart by 36,844.

The final measure of the relative importance of federal corporate enterprise is based on loose comparisons between the number of corporations, assets and revenues in our eight functional groupings and the analogous eight SIC product groupings representing the private sector. These comparisons, contained in Table IV, reflect the fact that on average—both in terms of assets and revenues—federal corporate enterprise represents roughly 12-13 percent of the total public and private sector activity across the eight groupings—despite the fact that the federal corporate enterprises for which we display data (57 for assets, 56 for revenue of the universe of 61) are obviously, in terms of "numbers of corporations," insignificant relative to the total population of private corporations.[42] From the perspective of "total assets," four corporate enterprise functional groupings (financing, insurance, and business services; manufacturing industries; marketing, wholesaling and trading; and transportation systems and facilities) represent prominent components relative to their respective private sector groupings.[43] On the basis of "total revenue", five corporate enterprise groupings (communications; culture and recreation; financing, insurance and business services; industrial development; and transportation systems, and facilities) are significant relative to their analogous private sec-

---

[40] See Vining and Botterell, Chapter 5 in this volume. They appear to take an even more liberal approach to the identification of an "enterprise" than we do.

[41] See Canada. Statistics Canada. *Provincial Government Employment: January-March 1979* (Ottawa: Ministry of Supply and Services, Statistics Canada #72-007, 1979).

[42] SIC product grouping data is not available for 1978. While comparing 1978-79 corporate enterprise data and 1977 SIC product grouping data tends to overstate the importance of the former, Table IV provides a rough approximation of the magnitude of federal participation *vis-à-vis* comparable SIC groupings. We would add a further cautionary note, however, on the tenuous nature of the comparisons, *viz*, the problem of the presence of one relatively small federal enterprise in a functional grouping "dragging in", for purposes of analogy, a major SIC product grouping. For example, the classification of Canadian Saltfish Corporation in the "wholesale food trade" category, necessitates the inclusion of a SIC product grouping with 1977 revenues of $11.2b.

[43] Although the November, 1978 takeover of Pacific Petroleums Ltd. by Petro-Canada (helping to boost Petro-Canada assets 280 percent over 1977) tends to skew any comparisons of the manufacturing groups, it is illustrative of the magnitude and significance of some individual public corporate enterprises. It is interesting to note that, while some functional groups are minor relative to their SIC analogues, they display greater importance within the corporate enterprise group (*e.g.*, industrial development assets represent 6.7 percent of the total corporate enterprise assets ($53.5b)).

TABLE IV
Financial Comparisons of Public Corporate Enterprise Functional Groupings and Private SIC Product Groupings

Functions	No. of Corporations		Total Assets (000's)		Total Revenue (000's)	
	Per Corporate Enterprise Grouping 1978-9	Per SIC Product Grouping 1977	Corporate Enterprise Grouping 1978-9	SIC Product Grouping 1977	Corporate Enterprise Grouping 1978-9	SIC Product Grouping 1977
1. Communications	3	812	862,655	13,629,500	731,855	5,537,000
2. Culture & Recreation	2	3,974	43,725	2,370,300	282,434	1,723,200
3. Financing, Insurance & Business Services	7	11,358	32,907,916	153,042,700	3,387,455	14,645,700
4. Industrial Development	5	73,894	3,587,452	87,380,800	1,508,484	3,817,200
5. Manufacturing Industries	8	7,685	6,078,168	25,819,500	1,113,216	28,444,000
6. Marketing, Wholesaling & Trading	10	30,073	2,201,768	13,123,800	2,720,807	28,103,300
7. Resource Development	2	562	298,974	49,114,100	110,982	12,482,900
8. Transportation Systems & Facilities	20	4,242	7,501,091	15,760,100	4,855,552	10,311,900
TOTAL	57	132,600	53,481,749	360,240,800	14,710,785	105,065,200

tor groupings.[44] By both measures, the transportation systems and facilities corporate enterprise grouping is almost half the size of its analogous private sector grouping.

Overall, these rather tenuous comparisons suggest that the corporate enterprise set which we have segregated from the wider universe of federal public corporations is a key component of the federal public sector, roughly comparable in size to its provincial public enterprise counterpart, and a significant if not overwhelming component of the total economy, relative to the presence and activity of analogous private sector corporations.

---

[44] The absence of revenue data on one corporation in the industrial development group necessitates the excision of the comparable SIC product group, thus removing 10,663 corporations from the 73,894 in the overall analogous SIC grouping. This significantly alters the relationship between the two revenue figures.

CHAPTER 5

AN OVERVIEW OF THE ORIGINS, GROWTH, SIZE AND FUNCTIONS OF PROVINCIAL CROWN CORPORATIONS*

AIDAN R. VINING†
AND
ROBERT BOTTERELL†

I. INTRODUCTION

The recent activities of the British Columbia Resources Investment Corporation (BCRIC) in British Columbia and la Société Nationale de l'Amiante in Quebec highlight both the diversity and the dynamism of the "Crown corporation" format at the provincial level. Thus while BCRIC has been partially "privatized" by the Bennett government in Victoria, la Société Nationale de l'Amiante is the spearhead of asbestos expropriation of the Levesque government of Quebec City.

While such corporations, along with the perennial favourites, the major hydros, may be the "glamor stocks" of the provincial Crown corporations (PCCs hereafter) portfolio they are only the tip of the iceberg. There are, in fact, a vast array of PCCs—over 200 depending on the definition utilized—ranging from Ontario Hydro, with assets of $12,682 billion, to Crown Development Corp. of B.C., with assets of $9,723. While we can say with certainty that there is "a vast array" of PCCs it is not clear, however, how vast. The problem is partially one of definition; each province has developed its own terminology, procedures and taxonomy. It is also a problem of continual evolution and change: PCCs are continuously created, altered and terminated.

The objective of this paper is to place the PCCs in perspective—historically, politically, economically and comparatively. The paper first provides a brief overview of taxonomies as utilized by various provinces. Second, we develop a simple taxonomy of PCCs based on "functional category". The development of such a taxonomy is a necessary prerequisite of the following attempt to anlyze the historical development, growth, size

* This study was funded by the Institute for Research on Public Policy, Montreal.
† Policy Analysis Division, Faculty of Commerce and Business Administration, University of British Columbia.

and importance of PCCs. It is also of central importance in comparing the role of PCCs among the provinces.

II. WHAT IS A PROVINCIAL CROWN CORPORATION?

(a) Government Perspective

Ideally, the appropriate definition of PCCs would be that utilized by provincial governments. Unfortunately a perusal of provincial practices shows that there is often no clear distinction between provincial entities which appear to be obviously corporate in both content and form and other provincial entities which are obviously departmental in nature. Rather the provinces have developed a variegated array of agencies, commissions, authorities, and corporations. Even the "corporate" label itself can be deceptive. It is often not a good indicator of the functional separateness of an entity; that is, that an entity is not, in fact, a government department. On the other hand, the absence of the corporate label does not guarantee that the entity is not, for all practical purposes, a functionally autonomous Crown corporation: a simple example is the British Columbia Hydro and Power *Authority*. To fully appreciate this lack of consistency it is valuable to consider the classification system used by several provinces.

In Ontario agencies are divided up into four categories:[1]

(1) Those agencies which have the status of a board, agency or commission but which are subject to most, if not all, of the normal administrative controls, practices and procedures of government. In nearly all cases, support services such as accommodation and staff resources are provided by the parent Ministry. In addition, the personnel and administrative costs of many of these bodies are limited to per diem fees and out-of-pocket expenses paid to members for meetings or hearings. Examples of agencies in this category include the Eastern Ontario Development Corporation, the Construction Industry Review Panel and the Board of Censors.

(2) Those which are wholly, or largely, self-financing and which are commercial in nature. Each of these boards, agencies and commissions prepares and makes public, an annual report. Examples of agencies in this category include Ontario Hydro, the Workmen's Compensation Board and the Ontario Lottery Corporation.

(3) Those agencies which, although supported by the Consolidated Revenue Fund, enjoy a degree of operating independence from the

---

[1] Ontario Management Board of Cabinet. *Boards, agencies and commissions to which the Government of Ontario appoints all or some of the members, listed by Ministry* (Toronto: Government of Ontario, 1978).

Government. In the majority of cases the Province of Ontario provides only part of the fundings of these boards, agencies and commissions. Examples of agencies in this category include the Essex County District Health Council, the Wilfred Laurier University Board of Governors, and the Alcoholism and Drug Addiction Research Foundation.

(4) Those agencies which do not directly receive funds from the Province. The majority have been given legislative authority to regulate professional activities and operate with minimal government involvement, other than the involvement of some of the members. Examples of agencies in this category include the Durham Regional Board of Commissioners of Police, the Ontario Cream Producers' Marketing Board, and the Land Surveyors Board of Examiners.

Newfoundland, on the other hand, divides non-departmental entities into two major categories:[2] (1) Provincial government enterprises (19 enterprises), and (2) Special funds (38 funds). These funds include the Newfoundland and Labrador Development Corporation and the Newfoundland Farms Product Corporation—candidates for inclusion in any definition of Crown corporations. However, in addition the funds include the Public Libraries Board and the Workmen's Compensation Board—candidates for exclusion.

New Brunswick considers 22 entities to be Crown corporations, including the Workmen's Compensation Board and the New Brunswick Dairy Products Commission. These Crown corporations are divided into five functional categories.[3] The first grouping consists of Operational-Commercial corporations. For example, King's Landing Corporation's responsibility is "to collect, preserve and exhibit buildings and artifacts which are part of the province's historical resources".[4] Operational-Financial corporations make up the second category, including the Farm Adjustment Board. The third category is Operational-Program and includes the New Brunswick Museum which has the responsibility "to manage, control and administer the affairs of the Museum".[5] The final two categories are Regulatory-Economic and Regulatory-Judicial. The Natural Products Control Board and Workmen's Compensation Board are examples of corporations which fall in these categories.

The picture is clearer in Saskatchewan where 20 Crown corporations are organized for reporting purposes into four major categories:[6] (1) financial and insurance corporations; (2) resource corporations; (3) utility cor-

[2] Personal contact, Government of Newfoundland.
[3] New Brunswick. *New Brunswick Crown Corporations* [Fredericton: Queen's Printer, 1978].
[4] *Ibid.*, at 2.
[5] *Ibid.*, at 2.
[6] Saskatchewan. Crown Corporations. *Annual Reports of Crown Corporations of the Province of Saskatchewan, 1977* [Regina: Queen's Printer, 1978].

porations; and (4) service corporations. Even here, however, it is not clear what exactly a Crown corporation is—only nine of the 20 corporations are covered by the province's *Crown Corporations Act, 1978*.[7] The Act itself does not specify either whether a Board of Directors is needed or the role of the Chairman of the Board. Additionally, the Saskatchewan Liquor Board—the largest liquor supply and distribution agency in terms of assets among the provinces—is not organized as a Crown corporation.

British Columbia simply lists 30 entities which it describes as "Crown Corporations and other Government Agencies". Again the agencies include the Worker's Compensation Board of British Columbia and the Legal Services Commission.[8] All 30 produce an annual balance sheet.

(b) The Classification Problem

The preliminary evidence, then, suggests that the term Crown corporation is one of art, rather than science. As Green points out ". . . it is probably impossible to provide a single unambiguous and generally accepted definition for the term 'public enterprise' which can clearly differentiate among the numerous activities governments undertake."[9] In order to produce a working definition which successfully differentiates Crown corporations from both private sector enterprises and from other public sector entities, several assumptions have been made. The rationale in making these assumptions has been to provide a wide net of public organizations which will assist both political scientists interested in the accountability of extra-departmental organizations and economists interested in the efficiency implications of government enterprise, especially where it is monopolistic.

The first requirement of any classification is that it exclude private sector corporations. However, the distinction between private and public enterprise is not always clearcut. A minority, but substantial, shareholding in many corporations can ensure effective control. A provincial government may, therefore, effectively "nationalize" a private corporation via share ownership. Here we arbitrarily assumed that if a province has a 50 percent or greater interest in a corporation it is under the control of the province. Thus, for our purposes the Alberta Energy Corporation is treated as a PCC as the Province of Alberta holds 50 percent of the outstanding shares. There are a number of corporations where, due to the wide dispersion of share ownership, ownership of a small segment of the shares gives a province ef-

---

[7] R.S.S. 1978, c. C-50.1.

[8] British Columbia. Ministry of Finance. *Public Accounts 1976-77* [Victoria: The Queen's Printer, 1977] in Section F, "Financial Statements of Crown Corporations and other Government Agencies."

[9] C. Green, *Canadian Industrial Organization and Policy* (Toronto: McGraw-Hill Ryerson, 1980) at 249.

fective control. These corporations have been treated on a case-by-case, judgmental basis.

The second requirement of the classification scheme is that it screen out those agencies, corporations, etc. which are not, in fact, provincially-controlled. This task is complicated by linkages between federal and provincial programs which suggest that while some corporations are provincially-sponsored their programs are heavily influenced by Federal priorities. As there is no obvious method of gauging this type of control, this study treats as PCCs those which are outwardly controlled by provinces. As a result, the regional lotteries and the corporations in the NorthWest Territories and Yukon are considered to be of provincial nature and origin.

The final, and most problematic, requirement of a classification scheme is that it differentiates PCCs from other government organizations. Two questions were utilized to assist in a classification of Crown corporations: (1) Is the entity organized and run as a government department? (2) Is the entity involved in large-scale government enterprise? We utilize the term government enterprise in the same manner as the *Dictionary of Social Sciences* which defines public enterprises as vehicles for "public services which are economic enterprises, i.e. ones which may be expected to [but often do not] pay for themselves".[10] Our definition is also generally consistent with Green's definition: "publicly owned enterprises producing generally marketable goods and services".[11]

If we posit that both questions can be answered with a yes or no, it is possible to develop a simple four-cell matrix of candidates for inclusion. Figure 1 presents such a matrix:

FIGURE 1
Classification Framework for Crown Corporations
Large-Scale Public Enterprise?

		Yes	No
DEPARTMENTAL ORGANIZATION?	Yes	*Example* – Alberta Liquor Control Board 1	Excluded 4
	No	*Examples* – Cansteel – Ontario Hydro 2	*Example* – Nova Scotia Research Foundation 3

---

[10] J. Gould and W.L. Kolb, ed., *A Dictionary of the Social Sciences* (New York: The Free Press, for UNESCO, 1964) at 560; as cited in Green, *supra* note 9, at 249.
[11] Green, *supra* note 9, at 251.

Cell 2 entities are the most obvious candidates for inclusion as PCCs. These entities—such as Ontario Hydro and Cansteel—engage in large-scale enterprise and are autonomously organized. Cell 4 entities are obvious candidates for exclusion. Cells 1 and 3 are problematic. With some exceptions, entities in these two cells were included in the analysis. Therefore, the study focuses on provincially-controlled entities in cells 1, 2, and 3 of the matrix. In practice the only PCCs in cell 1 are the provincial liquor agencies. Cell 2 covers most obvious examples of Crown corporations—companies producing steel, hydro electric power, ships, etc. Cell 3 conceptually is the most problematic and is where some arbitrary exclusions have been made. Here we find entities engaged in activities that cannot readily be called enterprise, such as the Saskatchewan Educational Communication Corporation and the Nova Scotia Research Foundation Corporation. We have excluded from this category entities which are primarily involved in judicial, quasi-judicial, regulatory or government sanctioned self-regulation functions. Thus, worker's compensation boards and provincial marketing boards have been excluded from this analysis. This classification applied to Canadian public and private sector entities yields 233 PCCs for analysis (see Appendix I for a listing).

(c) Functional Perspective

For the purpose of this analysis, PCCs are grouped into "functional" categories. As we have seen, some provinces do not utilize functional classifications while the classifications of other provinces are idiosyncratic, making them unhelpful for a interprovincial comparison.

The approach adopted in this study is to cluster corporations in narrow generic groupings. While this results in 24 categories, some with only two corporations, it provides maximum flexibility. Here, we provide a brief description of the functional categories and give an indication of both the relative and absolute size of each category. Additionally, examples of the stated aims and objectives of PCCs are included. (For a list of the PCCs included under each functional heading see Appendix II.)

1. *Agricultural Development*—There are 13 corporations which fall in this category, or approximately 5.6 percent of total PCCs. They serve a variety of functions including the provision or guaranteeing of loans, agricultural insurance, and the leasing of land. Several also consolidate and manage farm land. Two examples of corporations that fall into this category are the Prince Edward Island Land Development Corporation and the Alberta Agricultural Development Corporation. Their respective objectives are as follows:

> To conserve, develop and assist in improving the use of land in Prince Edward Island in relation to its capability and in accordance with the public interest,

but with a primary objective of consolidating good agricultural lands for the purpose of increasing farmer and agricultural sector income.[12]

The Agricultural Development Corporation is an agency of the Crown established within Alberta Agriculture, which provides financial assistance to primary producers of agricultural products, the owners of associated businesses and agricultural industries. . . . The function of the Corporation is not to replace other lenders, but to meet the legitimate credit needs of Albertans involved in the agricultural industry, who are unable to borrow from other sources at reasonable terms and conditions. All other sources of credit should be investigated before applying to the Agricultural Development Corporation.[13]

2. *Banking, Saving,* and *Investment*—There are five corporations which fall into this category and they make up roughly 2 percent of PCCs. They provide a wide range of banking functions. Two such corporations are the Saskatchewan Development Fund Corporation and the Caisse de dépôt et placement de Québec. Their respective objectives are:

It [the Saskatchewan Development Fund Corporation] administers the Saskatchewan Development Fund, an investment vehicle for the savings of Saskatchewan residents which is used for minimum risk investments and to provide a source of capital to assist in the retention of control of the Saskatchewan economy by residents of the province.[14]

The general investment policy adopted by the Caisse at its founding in 1966 always has remained consistent with four primary objectives: protection of capital, attainment of a return compatible with the risks taken, sound diversity in investments, and promotion of the economic growth of Quebec.[15]

3. *Forest Development* and *Manufacturing*—There are 13 corporations within this category and they make up about 5.6 percent of total PCCs. Many different aspects of forestry are represented, ranging from linerboard facilities to sawmills. For example, the operations of Kootenay Forest Products Ltd. were described as follows in the British Columbia Resources Investment Corporation Prospectus:

Kootenay carries on logging operations primarily through independent contractors and operates a sawmill, a plywood plant and related facilities in Nelson on approximately 30 acres of land and nine acres of lease foreshore lots served by two railway lines. Kootenay also sells wood chips to CanCel's pulp

---

[12] Prince Edward Island. Land Development Corporation. *Annual Report of the Prince Edward Island Land Development Corporation 1976* [Charlottetown: Queen's Printer, 1976].

[13] Alberta. Alberta Agricultural Development Corporation. *Loan Programs* [Edmonton: Alberta Government Services, 1978].

[14] Saskatchewan. Government Finance Office. *Public Enterprise in Saskatchewan* [unpublished paper prepared for a seminar held June, 1977, at the Institute for Public Administration, 897 Bay St., Toronto] at 12-13.

[15] Québec. Caisse de Dépôt et placement. *Onzième Rapport annuel de gestion: Caisse de dépôt et placement* [Québec: Éditeur Officiel du Québec, 1977] at 9.

mill at Castlegar and to Georgia-Pacific Corporation in Bellingham, Washington.[16]

Other PCCs within this category are primarily vehicles for forest management; one example is the New Brunswick Forest Authority:

> The New Brunswick Forest Authority was organized to supervise the harvest and direction of Crown Land wood to its best end use. A prime purpose is to find use for all the merchantable wood obtained by harvesting all trees from areas not larger than three hundred acres.[17]

4. *General* and *Auto Insurance*—There are five corporations in this category, comprising approximately 2 percent of total PCCs. These corporations often provide both auto and general insurance coverage. An indication of the rationale behind such corporations is contained in the following quote from the first annual report of the Régie de l'assurance automobile du Québec:

> Une autre source de satisfaction réside dans le fait que la Régie a pu contribuer à réaliser les objectifs fondamentaux de la réforme maintes fois énoncés, à savior une indemnisation meilleur, plus rapide et au meilleur coût possible.[18]

5. *Government Buildings*—There are three corporations in this category making up just under 1.3 percent of the total. These corporations own, manage, and construct buildings for provincial government departments and agencies. The B.C. Buildings Corporation has the following mandate:

> . . . to identify the short and long-term accommodation and related accommodation service requirements of the British Columbia Government, and to satisfy those needs in a responsive and cost-effective manner.[19]

6. *Government Computer Services*—There are four corporations in this category (2 percent of total PCCs), often providing services to both the public and private sectors. Apparently the rationale is that the centralization of these services will generate economies of scale. The two main tasks assigned to Manitoba Data Services are indicative:

1. Offer a wide range of data processing services at competitive rates to Manitoba businesses.

---

16 British Columbia Resources Investment Corporation Prospectus dated March 1, 1979, at 10-11.
17 New Brunswick. Ministry of Natural Resources. *New Brunswick Forest Authority Annual Report 1974-75* [Fredericton: Queen's Printer, 1975] at 6.
18 Québec. Ministre des Consommateurs, Coopératives et Institutions financières. Régie de l'assurance automobile du Québec. *Rapport annuel 1978/79* [Québec: Éditeur Officiel du Québec, 1979] at 5.
19 British Columbia. Ministry of Highways and Public Works. British Columbia Buildings Corporation. *British Columbia Buildings Corporation Annual Report 1977* [Victoria: The Queen's Printer, 1978] at 4.

2. Absorb the provincial government computer centre and centralize government and Crown corporation computing for maximum efficiency.[20]

7. *Housing*—There are 18 housing corporations which form almost 8 percent of total PCCs. These corporations are involved in the construction of homes, leasing of lands, and subsidization of mortgages. The targets of such programs can include senior citizens, whole communities, rural areas, low to middle income groups, etc. This broad set of functions is reflected in the objectives of the Alberta Housing Corporation:

> The prime objectives of the Alberta Housing Corporation are twofold: to provide rental accommodation at a reasonable cost for families of low and middle income and to encourage home ownership where possible. As well, through long-range planning, the Corporation endeavors to promote increased housing supply, reduced housing costs and the repair and renovation of existing homes.[21]

8. *Industrial Development*—There are 31 Crown corporations in this category and they constitute just over 13 percent of total PCCs. The range of functions performed by industrial development corporations and their rationale is reflected in the mandate of the Newfoundland and Labrador Development Corporation:

> The Government of the Province of Newfoundland and the Government of Canada recognizing that small and medium size businesses play a major role in realizing the objectives of expanded employment and effective use of resources, capital and skills in the Province, signed an agreement in 1972 establishing the Newfoundland and Labrador Development Corporation Limited. The Corporation's mandate was to assist in the establishment, modernization and expansion of small and medium size business by the provision of:
>
> > Business/technical information
> > Management advisory services
> > Project information
> > Loan financing
> > Equity financing
> > Related services and assistance.[22]

9. *Liquor*—There are 12 entities or 5 percent of total PCCs in this category. Liquor agencies are involved in the distribution of liquor products and may also be involved in licencing activities. An example of a province where the two functions are separated is New Brunswick:

---

[20] Manitoba Data Services, "The Computer Utility", [information brochure, n.d.].

[21] Alberta. Alberta Housing Corporation. *Alberta Housing Corporation Annual Report: April 1, 1976/March 31, 1977* [Edmonton: Alberta Government Services, 1977] at 4.

[22] Newfoundland. Newfoundland and Labrador Development Corporation. *Newfoundland and Labrador Development Corporation Annual Report 1976-77* [St. John's: Queen's Printer, 1977] at 4.

As a Crown Corporation, NB Liquor has the sole responsibility to handle the products, distribution and retail sales of liquor in the Province. Liquor Licensing and related areas are no longer a part of its function.[23]

10. *Lotteries*—There are four lottery corporations which make up just under 2 percent of total corporations. An example of the rationale and objectives for such corporations are contained in this statement on the Ontario Lottery Corporation:

> The Ontario Lottery Corporation is a Crown Corporation established on February 7, 1975, by an Act of the Ontario Legislature to develop and manage lotteries within the Province.
> Through the Ministry of Culture and Recreation, funds from Wintario are used to promote physical fitness, sports and cultural activities and through the Ministries of Health, Environment and Labour, funds from the Provincial are used for health research and health-related environmental projects, thereby contributing to the overall quality of life in Ontario.[24]

11. *Miscellaneous Marketing* and *Brokerage Facilities*—Eighteen (or roughly 8 percent of the total) PCCs provide marketing services to companies within their respective provinces that cannot generate the economies of scale to effectively market their goods. One example is the Prince Edward Island Market Development Corporation (formerly Centre) which has the following objectives:

> The Market Development Centre provides a marketing consulting service which is available to all Prince Edward Island primary producers, processors and manufacturers. This service is provided freely, or, in cases of a major project, at shared cost.
> The objectives are as follows:
> —to strengthen domestic markets for Agriculture, Fisheries and Manufactured Products originating on Prince Edward Island;
> —to explore, determine and develop international markets for Prince Edward Island products;
> —to determine market potential and encourage businessmen to take advantage of identified opportunities;
> —to improve the image of Prince Edward Island primary, processed and manufactured products in all major markets;
> —to provide assistance in package design, labelling, sales promotion, to primary producers, processors and manufacturers;
> —to develop new products, reformulate existing products and provide quality control services;
> —to provide a market information service to Island producers and processors

---

23 New Brunswick. Ministry of Finance. New Brunswick Liquor Corporation. *New Brunswick Liquor Corporation Annual Report 1977* [Fredericton: Queen's Printer, 1977] at 2.
24 Ontario. Ministry of Culture and Recreation. Ontario Lottery Corporation. *Ontario Lottery Corporation Annual Report 1977/78* [Toronto: Government of Ontario, 1978] at 24.

including pricing data, tariffs, patents, franchises, technical innovations, market reports, etc.[25]

12. *Mineral, Mining* and *Development*—The ten corporations, or just over 4 percent of total corporations, in this classification include all mineral extraction activities except for those related to oil and gas exploration and production. The Charter of the Société Québecois d'Éxploration Miniére (SOQUEM) has a representative set of objectives:

a) to carry out mining exploration by all methods;
b) to participate in the development of discoveries, including those made by others, with power to purchase and to sell properties at various stages of development and to associate itself with others for such purposes;
c) to participate in the bringing into production of mineral deposits, either by selling them outright or by transferring them in return for a participation.[26]

13. *Miscellaneous Manufacturing*—Ten of the corporations, or about 4 percent, are engaged in diverse manufacturing activities that cannot be readily segmented by function unless each were given its own category. This classification contains such companies as United Cotton Mills and the Quebec Sugar Refinery.

14. *Municipal Finance Corporations*—These five corporations make up just over 2 percent of the total. They generally obtain funds on capital markets and provide these funds to municipalities in exchange for debentures. The rationale behind such corporations is stated succinctly in the 1977 annual report of the Alberta Municipal Financing Corporation:

The Alberta Municipal Financing Corporation is a non-profit corporation established to assist municipal jurisdictions within the Province to obtain capital funds at the lowest possible cost through access to a wider range of the capital markets which would not be available to the various municipal governments on an independent basis.[27]

15. *Oil* and *Gas Production*—There are five PCCs in this category and their principal activities include the development and/or marketing of oil and gas resources. Two examples are the Ontario Energy Corporation and B.C. Petroleum. Their respective aims are as follows:

The Province of Ontario is dependent on other provinces and foreign sources for over 80% of its energy needs. In order to support the efforts of the Government of Ontario in implementing its policy of improving the security of energy supply to the Province, legislation was introduced in November 1974 to

[25] Prince Edward Island. Department of Industry and Commerce. Market Development Centre. *Market Development Centre Annual Report 1977* [Charlottetown: Prince Edward Island Market Development Centre, 1978] at 2.
[26] *Loi sur la Société québécoise d'exploration minière*, L.R.Q. 1977 c. S-19, s. 3.
[27] Alberta Municipal Financing Corporation. *Alberta Municipal Financing Corporation Annual Report 1977* [Edmonton: Alberta Municipal Financing Corporation, 1978] at 3.

establish the Ontario Energy Corporation which would have the object of investing or otherwise participating in energy projects in Canada or elsewhere.[28]

The British Columbia Petroleum Corporation was established in November 1973. The Corporation acts as the marketing agent for all of the natural gas produced in the Province of British Columbia. It purchases gas from the producers at the wellhead and sells it, through Westcoast Transmission Co. Limited, to B.C. Utility companies and to its American purchaser, Northwest Pipeline Corporation.[29]

16. *Power Utilities*—There are 11 companies in this category forming 4.7 percent of the total number. The principal activities of these companies involve the production and distribution of electrical power. However, the mandate for such corporations can be much wider as the mandate for Manitoba Hydro demonstrates:

Manitoba Hydro is a Crown corporation owned by the Province of Manitoba. Its purpose is to provide for the continuance of a supply of power adequate for the needs of the Province and to promote economy and efficiency in the generation, distribution, supply and use of power.[30]

Another example is Saskatchewan Power:

1. To bring the advantages of power and gas to the people of Saskatchewan efficiently, safely and economically.

    This includes attempting to bring power and gas to as many of the people of the province as possible, even in distances where this cannot be done with a profit on the new investment. It will be done responsibly and in such a way that the government of the day realizes the financial and economic effects.

    In achieving the first objective, it will be the intent of the Corporation to earn a reasonable surplus or profit. This, at a minimum, will be aimed at enabling the financing of necessary system expansion to be accomplished in a manner which does not adversely affect the credit of the Province. It will also be aimed at maintaining an annual dividend payment to the people of Saskatchewan acceptable to the government of the day.

2. To charge all customers fair and reasonable rates.

    Rates should not be discriminatory, and may, when the Corporation considers it advisable in the public or Corporation interest, favour lower income customers or be promotional to industry.

3. To serve the changing needs and desires of customers as well as they can be reasonably accomplished.

---

28 Ontario. Ministry of Energy. Ontario Energy Corporation. *Ontario Energy Corporation Annual Report: Period ended March 31, 1975* [Toronto: Government of Ontario, 1975] at 1.
29 British Columbia. Organization of the B.C. Public Service [Victoria: The Queen's Printer, 1981], at 22.
30 Manitoba Hydro-Electric Board. *The Manitoba Hydro-Electric Board 26th Annual Report for the year ended March 31, 1977* [Winnipeg: Office of the Queen's Printer, 1977] at 5.

4. To develop an able management and staff, adequate not only to maintain existing standards of service, but to improve the contribution the Corporation can make to the Province.

It follows that the Corporation must be a good employer, paying salaries and wages competitive with those in the private sector, and should aim at providing a high standard of security for all its employees.

The Corporation must also expect and demand a high standard of contribution from all its employees, management and staff.

5. To operate according to the laws of Saskatchewan and always respecting the rights of customers, landowners and employees.

The Corporation must go further and try at all times not to take unreasonable advantage of the wide powers granted to it by the Legislature.[31]

17. *Research* and *Development*—These 13 corporations conduct, or finance, research in areas ranging from agricultural machinery to hydroelectric technology. An example is the Manitoba Research Council whose stated aims are as follows:

a) promote and carry on, or cause to be promoted or carried on, research and scientific enquiries respecting agriculture, natural resources, industry, or other segments of the economy of the Province; and

b) help to secure for Manitoba the benefits of research and scientific enquiries carried on elsewhere.[32]

18. *School* and *Hospital Financing*—There are 17 PCCs operating in this area, 12 in Newfoundland alone. They provide much the same services as municipal finance corporations, albeit to schools and hospitals. An example in point is the B.C. School Districts Capital Financing Authority:

The Authority is the marketing agent for school district capital fund requirements and as such supplied $88,368,000 in investment funds in the fiscal year ended March 31, 1975.[33]

19. *Shipyards*—There are two companies in this category and their functions are exmplified by Georgetown Shipyard:

Georgetown Shipyard specializes in the construction of all types of steel and aluminum vessels up to 180′ length overall. It has facilities to undertake major refits, conversions, and overhauls to vessels. Services include a 100-ton and a

---

[31] *Power Corporation Act,* R.S.S. 1978, c. P-19, s. 8 as am. 1979, c. 53.

[32] Manitoba. Department of Industry and Commerce. *The Manitoba Department of Industry and Commerce; Manitoba Trading Corporation; Manitoba Research Council; Manitoba Design Institute Annual Report 1975-1976* [Winnipeg: Office of the Queen's Printer, 1977] at 50.

[33] British Columbia, *supra* note 29, at 21.

600-ton marine railway. There are also complete facilities for sandblasting and painting, steel work, marine outfitting and heavy industrial fabrication.[34]

20. *Steel*—There are three PCCs in this category and they act to develop and/or operate steel production facilities. The mandate for Cansteel Corporation is indicative of the former objective:

A Nova Scotia Crown corporation established to provide the organization and the vehicle to bring a new steel complex to Cape Breton.[35]

21. *Telephones* and *Communications*—The eight corporations in this category provide telephone service to residents and businesses, several also provide more specialized communication services. An example is the Alberta Educational Communications Corporation:

Its purpose is to provide a framework within which educational broadcasting and the development, production and distribution of educational programs and materials can take place. Aside from self-generated revenues, ACCESS is funded by provincial government grants.[36]

22. *Transport Facilities*—There are seven corporations or just over 3 percent of total PCCs in this category. They manage, and develop transportation facilities. This excerpt from an annual report of the Waterfront Development Corporation gives an indication of the range of activities this can include:

The Corporation is provided with funds of $35,154,000 for the purpose of land acquisition, planning, operation and for installation of infrastructure including landfill, dredging, seawalls, wharf construction and repairs, buried utility services, such as water, storm and sanitary sewers, power and telephone distribution conduit and for renovation of specific historic buildings.[37]

23. *Transport Systems*—The 14 corporations in this classification control rapid transit, airline, and rail transport systems. The following is an example of the rationale for having a corporation in this area:

With the increased emphasis being placed on public transportation in many urban areas in Canada, and the increase in work trips across Municipal boundaries, it is evident that the needs of the commuter cannot be met without the

---

34 Prince Edward Island. *Government Services Directory 1977-78* [Charlottetown: Queen's Printer, 1978] at 37.
35 Nova Scotia. Cansteel Corporation. *Cansteel Corporation Second Annual Report for the Fiscal Year Ended March 31, 1977* [Halifax: Nova Scotia Government Bookstore, 1977] on the title page.
36 Alberta. Alberta Educational Communications Corporation. *Access Alberta Fourth Annual Report: The Fourth Annual Report of the Alberta Educational Communications Corporation: October 17, 1976—October 16, 1977* [Edmonton: Alberta Government Services, 1978] at 2.
37 Nova Scotia. Waterfront Development Corporation Ltd. *Waterfront Development Corporation Annual Report 1977* [Halifax: Nova Scotia Government Bookstore, 1977] at 4.

co-operation and co-ordination of all transit properties in an urban area. The formation of a Transit Operating Authority for the Toronto Area is the first attempt by the Province of Ontario to establish an appropriate Agency to carry out the functions necessary to achieve an integrated network of transit operations.[38]

24. *Water Supply*—The two corporations in this category provide centralized administration and development of water supply systems. The specific objectives of one of these corporations, The Manitoba Water Services Board, are as follows:

a) The obtaining of supplies of potable water for domestic and other uses within the province; and the selling of water to municipalities and water districts.

b) The acquisition or construction and the operation and maintenance of all plants and works necessary for obtaining, collecting, storing, treating, purifying and transmitting water.

c) The transmission of water from a source of supply or a point of storage to a point of acceptance by a municipality or water district either within or without the municipality or water district.

d) The acquisition or construction and the operating and maintenance of works for the distribution of water.

e) The acquisition or construction and the operating and maintenance of works for the collection of sewage.

f) The acquisition or construction and the operating and maintenance of works for the treatment and disposal of sewage.[39]

III. PROVINCIAL CROWN CORPORATIONS IN PERSPECTIVE

(a) Size

The 233 Provincial Crown Corporations analyzed here control approximately $62.26 billion in assets. This total is made up of $45.54 billion in fixed assets, $12.77 billion in current assets and $3.94 billion in other assets. The mean level of assets per corporation is $305 million. However, as Figure 2 demonstrates, a few power corporations control a high percentage of total assets. (For a detailed discussion of the Tables and Figures utilized in the text see Appendix III.)

These asset figures can be compared to: (1) assets controlled by private

---

[38] Ontario. Ministry of Transportation and Communications. Toronto Area Transit Operating Authority. *Aims and Objectives* [Toronto: Government of Ontario].

[39] Manitoba. Minister of Agriculture. Manitoba Water Services board. *The Fifth Annual Report of the Manitoba Water Services Board—year ending March 31, 1977* [Winnipeg: Office of the Queen's Printer, 1978] at 5.

TABLE I

PCC Assets Compared to: (1) Private Sector Assets; (2) Federal Government Assets; (3) Provincial Financial Assets directly held ($000,000's)

	A Provincial Crown Corps.	B Corporate Assets	Ratio A/B	C Federal Assets	Ratio A/C	D Provincial Financial Assets	Ratio A/D
Current Assets	$12,772.51	$297,988.3	4.3%				
Fixed Assets	45,542.55	173,673.9	26.2%				
Other Assets	3,941.71	148,053.4	2.7%				
Total Assets	62,256.77	619,715.6	10.1%	50,672,9	123%	32,666.7	191%

sector Canadian corporations; (2) assets of the federal government; and (3) assets of the provincial governments directly held. As Table I demonstrates, PCCs have assets equal to 10.1 percent of corporate assets. However, PCCs have fixed assets equal to 26.2 percent of corporate fixed assets. Moving to a comparison of PCC assets with other government assets, we find that the assets of PCCs exceed the total assets of the Federal and Provincial Governments, the former by 23 percent and the latter by 91 percent (this is somewhat misleading as government fixed assets are not depreciated but expensed immediately). An alternate comparison is current and other assets of PCCs as a percentage of total Provincial and Federal assets. When these ratios are calculated, PCC assets represent 33 percent of Federal assets and 51 percent of Provincial assets. In sum, PCCs control significant assets and as such their decisions have an important impact on the economy.

FIGURE 2
Distribution of Total Assets Among PCCs

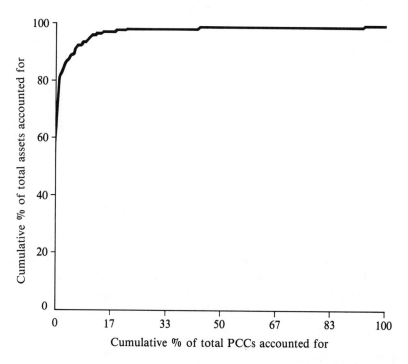

(b) Growth

Figure 3 demonstrates that there has been an almost exponential increase in the number of PCCs. In fact since 1960, 76 percent of all Crown corporations have been created. This compares with 2 percent for the period 1900-1920, 7 percent for 1920-1940, and 15 percent for 1940-1960. Since 1970, 48 percent of all PCCs were brought into existence.

While the recent growth in numbers has been rapid, the increase in assets has been modest. Figure 4 shows that since 1970 only 13 percent of present total assets were created. The percentage is even lower for fixed assets (7 percent), while higher for current assets (27 percent). The major growth thus took place in the periods 1900-1920 and 1940-1960 when 20 percent and 34 percent, respectively, of present total assets were created.

FIGURE 3
Growth of PCCs, 1900-1980

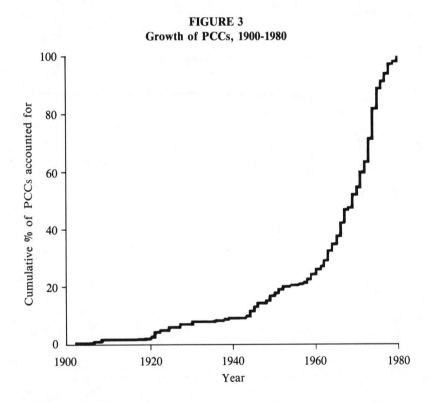

(c) Political Origins

Overall "Right of Centre" parties (Conservatives, Social Credit, Union Nationale) were responsible for the creation of 38.6 percent of all PCCs, while the Liberals were responsible for 35.1 percent and "Left of

FIGURE 4
Growth of PCC Assets, 1900-1980

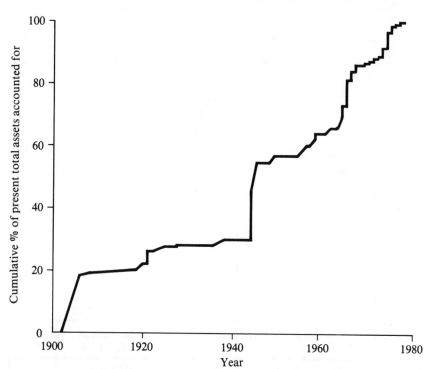

Centre'' parties (the Co-operative Commonwealth Federation (CCF), New Democratic Party (NDP), and Parti Québecois (PQ)), 21.2 percent (see Figure 5).[40] The official opposition during the creation period of PCCs was Liberal for 38.5 percent of the Crown corporations, Right of Centre for 47 percent and Left of Centre for 10 percent (see Figure 6). Thus, Right of Centre parties created the largest percentage of PCCs.

A related point of interest is the historical trend of party involvement in PCC creation. As Figure 7 shows, between 1900 and 1920 the Conservatives were responsible for the highest creation rate. However, in the period 1920 to 1940 the percentage created by both the Liberals and Conservatives stabilized or dropped. From 1940 to 1960 the Liberals' share remained close to 40 percent, while the Conservatives and Social Credit boosted the Right of Centre total to 31 percent. The CCF also gained power in the priod and were responsible for 20 percent of PCCs created. In the most recent period, 1960 to 1980 (the greatest growth period) the Right of Centre share has in-

---

[40] Such labelling involves a certain degree of arbitrariness. Social Credit presents the greatest problem; obviously Social Credits philosophical orientation has changed over time.

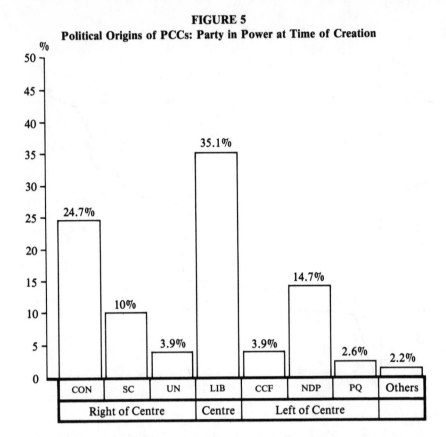

FIGURE 5

Political Origins of PCCs: Party in Power at Time of Creation

creased to 40 percent and the Left of Centre share (the NDP and the PQ) has risen to 24 percent while the Liberal share has dropped to 33 percent.

Thus, in absolute terms, Right of Centre parties are the most frequent utilizers of the PCC instrument. However, the above statistics are somewhat misleading as each party has not had the same temporal opportunity to introduce PCCs. An alternate measure is the ratio of PCCs created to years in office. As Table II shows, utilizing this measure, Left of Centre parties assume a greater responsibility for the recent growth in PCCs. While the Liberals and Right of Centre parties have introduced an average of between .91 and .59 PCCs for each year in office between 1960 and 1980, Left of Centre parties created PCCs at a 1.5 rate, or an average of three corporations for every two years in office.

In sum, PCCs are an important component of the public and private sector in terms of total and fixed assets. Their temporal growth in numbers has been almost exponential, although growth in assets has been more even over time. Their creation has been the result of actions by all parties with Right of Centre parties responsible for the largest share and Left of Centre parties creating them the most rapidly when in office.

FIGURE 6
Political Origins—Party in Opposition at Time of Creation

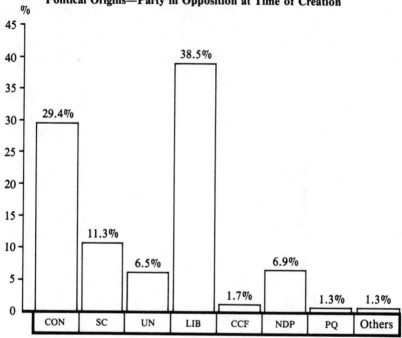

FIGURE 7
Political Party Creation of PCCs, 1900-1980

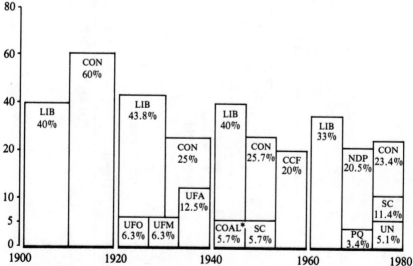

* Coalition

TABLE II
PCCs Created per Year in Office by Political Parties (1960-80)

		A Yrs. in Office 1960-80 10 Provinces	B Corps. Created	B/A	A' Years in Office	B' Corps. Created	B'/A
Right of Centre	Conservative	84	46	.55	118	70	.59
	Union Nationale	4	9	2.25			
	Social Credit	30	15	.50			
Left of Centre	NDP	22	35	1.59	28	42	1.5
	CCF	2	1	.50			
	Parti Quebecois	4	6	1.33			
Centre	Liberal	64	58	.91	64	58	.91
TOTAL		210					

IV. PROVINCIAL UTILIZATION OF THE PROVINCIAL CROWN CORPORATION

(a) Size

All provincial governments have used the PCC form of organization as can be seen from Table III. Newfoundland and Quebec have used this organizational form most frequently, while the other three Atlantic provinces and the Northwest Territories and Yukon have utilized PCCs least. When PCC data is broken down regionally we find that the four Western provinces have the largest number of PCCs with 95 in total (40 percent), followed by the Atlantic provinces with 71 and Ontario and Quebec combined with 62.

TABLE III
Provincial Utilization of PCCs by (1) Total Number; (2) Percentage; (3) Regional

	Total No.	Percentage of Total
1. Newfoundland (NFLD)	42	18.0%
2. British Columbia (BC)	36	15.5%
3. Quebec (QUE)	35	15.0%
4. Ontario (ONT)	27	11.6%
5. Saskatchewan (SASK)	25	10.7%
6. Alberta (ALTA)	20	8.6%
7. Manitoba (MAN)	13	5.6%
8. Nova Scotia (NS)	10	4.3%
9. Prince Edward Island (PEI)	10	4.3%
10. New Brunswick (NB)	9	3.9%
11. Northwest Territories (NWT)	2	0.9%
12. Yukon	2	0.9%
13. REGIONAL	2	0.9%
1. Western Provinces	95	40.8%
2. Atlantic Provinces	71	30.9%
3. Ontario and Quebec	62	26.6%
4. Yukon and Northwest Territories	4	1.7%

Another size measure is the assets controlled by PCCs within each province (see Table IV). Here Quebec ranks first with $20,020 billion in assets, followed by Ontario with $17,372 billion. The next group of provinces have asset levels between $7.9 billion and $2.6 billion and include, in declining order of size, British Columbia, Alberta, Manitoba, Newfoundland and Saskatchewan. The group of provinces with the lowest total assets are New

TABLE IV
PCC Asset Comparison between Provinces

Rank	Total Assets ($'000,000)		Total Assets			
			Per Capita		Prov. Gov. Fin. Assets	Provincial[1] GDP
1.	Que.	20,020.6	Nfld.	$5,645	Nfld. 3.18	Nfld. 123 %
2.	Ont.	17,372.2	Man.	3,419	B.C 2.93	Man. 47.4%
3.	B.C.	7,927.0	B.C.	3,214	N.B. 2.31	Que. 46.7%
4.	Alta.	5,377.8	Que.	3,211	Que. 2.40	Sask. 32.9%
5.	Man.	3,492.8	Alta.	2,926	Ont. 1.96	N.B. 32.8%
6.	Nfld.	3,148.2	Sask.	2,858	Man. 1.78	B.C. 32.0%
7.	Sask.	2,632.7	Ont.	2,102	Sask. 1.15	Alta. 24.8%
8.	N.B.	1,302.1	N.B.	1,923	Alta. .98	Ont. 23.3%
9.	N.S.	848.9	N.W.T.	1,178	N.W.T. .83	N.S. 18.8%
10.	P.E.I.	57.9	N.S.	1,025	N.S. .67	P.E.I. 12.9%
11.	N.W.T.	50.2	Yukon	590	P.E.I. .44	
12.	Yukon	12.9	P.E.I.	490	Yukon .39	

[1] Figures n.a. for N.W.T. and Yukon

Brunswick, Nova Scotia, Prince Edward Island, the Northwest Territories and the Yukon.

While absolute total assets are of interest, provincial commitment to PCCs can also be measured by assets per capita. Referring to Table IV we find that although Newfoundland ranks in sixth place in total assets it ranks first in PCC assets per capita, at $5,645, Manitoba is second with $3,419 assets per capita and B.C. third spot with $3,214. The most notable change in rank is the drop of Ontario from second in terms of total assets to seventh in assets per capita.

Two other measures of interest are the size of the PCC sector relative to provincial government financial assets and to the economic activity within a province. Table IV shows that while New Brunswick and Ontario have relatively low assets per capita, they rank higher when their investment in PCCs relative to other governmental assets, is gauged. Conversely, Manitoba and Alberta rank higher in terms of assets per capita and lower in terms of their relative investment in PCCs.

The other relationship summarized in Table IV—size of the PCC sector compared to size of the economy—has been approximated by the ratio of total PCC assets to Provincial Gross Domestic Product. As Table IV also shows, Newfoundland dominates in this area, while the rest of the provinces range from a low of 12.9 percent for Prince Edward Island to a high of 47.4 percent for Manitoba.

A question of some interest is the liquidity of PCC asset portfolios. This can be estimated by breaking down the total assets of each province into fixed and current assets. In Table V, we find that Prince Edward

TABLE V
Distribution of Asset Types by Province

	Fixed	Current	Other
Alta.	32.1%	56.0%	11.9%
B.C.	68.2	17.3	14.5
Man.	86.6	8.3	5.1
N.B.	79.2	16.9	3.9
Nfld.	80.8	10.5	8.7
N.S.	87.9	10.2	1.9
N.W.T.	82.2	17.8	—
Ont.	70.0	28.0	2.0
P.E.I.	36.1	61.7	2.2
Que.	85.6	9.8	4.6
Sask.	67.3	21.5	11.1
Yukon	82.1	17.1	.8
TOTAL	73.2%	20.5%	6.3%

Island, Alberta, Ontario and Saskatchewan have the greatest percentages of current assets with 61.7 percent, 56 percent, 28 percent and 21.5 percent respectively. Manitoba, Newfoundland, Nova Scotia, Northwest Territories, Quebec and the Yukon all have over 80 percent fixed assets.

It is also valuable to consider the particular functional areas that provinces have entered with PCCs and the relative size of their investments in the various functional areas. For this purpose the provinces are compared by the number of PCCs in each functional area and the size of investment in each functional area. In addition, the importance of each function within a province has been gauged by calculating the percentage of total PCC assets that function controls.

Drawing information from summary Tables VI and VII provincial involvement in each functional area can be summarized:

1. *Agricultural Development*—Alberta, Manitoba, Prince Edward Island, Quebec, Saskatchewan, and Ontario have PCCs in this area. Not surprisingly, prairie provinces are responsible for seven of the 13. The prairie provinces also control a significant share of assets with Alberta controlling 18.6 percent of total agricultural assets and Saskatchewan controlling 14.0 percent. However the largest share of assets is controlled by Quebec with 46 percent. In terms of importance to the individual province we find that in Prince Edward Island agricultural development is in third place making up 13.7 percent of that province's assets.

2. *Banking, Saving*, and *Investment*—Alberta, Ontario, Quebec and Saskatchewan have PCCs in this area. The largest share of assets is held by Quebec's Caisse de Dépôt et Placement du Québec with 84.5 percent, followed by Alberta and Saskatchewan with 15.3 percent and .2 percent. When intra-provincial comparisons are made, la Caisse de Dépôt et Placement du Québec occupies second position behind power utilities in Quebec with 24.7 percent of the province's PCC assets. In Alberta banking ranks third after telephones and communications and municipal finance with 16.6 percent of that province's PCC assets.

3. *Forest Development* and *Manufacturing*—British Columbia, Manitoba, Ontario, New Brunswick, Newfoundland, Quebec and Saskatchewan all have PCCs in this area. Newfoundland has a large percentage of the assets with 39.3 percent of the total while the next two ranking provinces are British Columbia and Manitoba with 23.8 percent and 16.8 percent of total assets. Forestry is relatively unimportant in all provinces except Newfoundland where it is responsible for 7.8 percent of assets and ranks only behind power utilities in importance.

4. *General* and *Auto Insurance*—Alberta, British Columbia, Manitoba, Quebec and Saskatchewan have PCCs in this area. British Columbia has the highest percentage of assets (69.6 percent) and Saskatchewan and Manitoba follow with 16 percent and 10 percent respectively. In all three provinces these PCCs rank fourth in terms of provincial assets: British Columbia 8.5 percent, Saskatchewan 5.9 percent and Manitoba 3.0 percent.

5. *Government Buildings*—Only British Columbia, Prince Edward Island and Newfoundland have government buildings PCCs. The B.C. Building Corporation controls 96.1 percent of the assets in this category and is the only important PCC of this type, ranking fifth within British Columbia, with 4.6 percent of total British Columbia assets.

6. *Government Computer Services*—British Columbia, Manitoba, Newfoundland and Saskatchewan have computer PCCs. We find that British Columbia controls 51.9 percent of total assets, followed by Manitoba with 25.7 percent and Newfoundland with 13 percent. Intraprovincially, none of the corporations rank in the top five in terms of assets.

7. *Housing*—All provinces except Nova Scotia have housing corporations. In terms of total assets the leaders are Ontario, Quebec and Alberta, controlling 54.1 percent, 15.8 percent and 13.0 percent of total housing assets respectively. There are nine provinces where the housing PCC is one of the top five corporations in terms of provincial total assets. In general the percentage of assets these corporations control ranges from 3 percent to 13 percent. However in Prince Edward Island, the Yukon and the Northwest Territories, the percentage is much higher, (*e.g.,* 21.9 percent in Prince Edward Island).

8. *Industrial Development*—Only the Northwest Territories and the Yukon do not have industrial development corporations. The largest percentage of assets are held by Quebec, Ontario and Saskatchewan with 39.1 percent, 28.4 percent and 9.9 percent. Industrial development PCCs are relatively important within several provinces ranking first in Prince Edward Island (41.7 percent), second in Nova Scotia (15.6 percent) and third in Newfoundland (6.1 percent).

9. *Liquor*—Not surprisingly all provinces and territories have liquor corporations. Ranked by assets we find that liquor PCCs in Saskatchewan, Quebec and Ontario control 23.9 percent, 22.7 percent and 22.5 percent of total PCC assets respectively. On an intraprovincial basis, liquor corporations rank in the top five in Prince Edward Island, New Brunswick and Nova Scotia, controlling 7.5 percent, .7 percent and 1.9 percent of provincial assets. And in the Yukon and The Northwest Territories they rank second with 11 percent and 6.2 percent of assets respectively.

10. *Lotteries*—There are two regional lotteries and a Quebec and Ontario lottery corporation. Ontario controls 42.8 percent of the assets in this area followed by Quebec and the regional lotteries with 32.1 percent and 25 percent. The lottery corporations are not of any importance intraprovincially.

11. *Miscellaneous Marketing* and *Brokerage Facilities*—Alberta, British Columbia, Newfoundland, Ontario, Prince Edward Island, Quebec and Saskatchewan have PCCs. We find that Quebec has the most assets with 97.8 percent (due to the Régie des Installations Olympiques), followed by Ontario with 1.8 percent and Saskatchewan with .3 percent. None of these PCCs are of significant importance intraprovincially.

TABLE VI

Provincial Utilization of the Various Functional Areas by (1) Number of PCCs; (2) Total Assets (% of Total PCC Assets in Functional Area*)

Area	Rank	Province		Area	Rank	Province	
Agricultural Development (AGRI)**	1	Que.	46.0	Miscellaneous Manufacturing (MMAN)	1	Nfld.	69.3
	2	Alta.	18.6		2	Que.	19.0
	3	Sask.	14.0		3	B.C.	11.6
Banking, Savings and Investment (BANK)	1	Que.	84.5	Municipal Finance (MUNI)	1	Alta.	92.0
	2	Alta.	15.3		2	Nfld.	4.0
	3	Sask.	0.2		3	Ont.	2.2
Forest Development and Manufacturing (FORE)	1	Nfld.	39.3	Oil and Gas Production (OILG)	1	Alta.	39.9
	2	B.C.	23.8		2	Ont.	18.5
	3	Man.	16.8		3	B.C.	16.2
General and Auto Insurance (GAUT)	1	B.C.	69.6	Power Utilities (POWE)	1	Ont.	33.0
	2	Sask.	16.0		2	Que.	31.0
	3	Man.	10.0		3	B.C.	14.0
Government Buildings (GBUI)	1	B.C.	96.1	Research and Development (RESE)	1	Que.	85.6
	2	Man.	2.3		2	N.S.	4.8
	3	P.E.I.	1.6		3	Sask.	3.9
Government Computer Services	1	B.C.	51.9	School & Hospital Financing	1	Ont.	71.9
	2	Man.	25.7		2	B.C.	25.8

Functional Area	Rank	Province	%		Functional Area	Rank	Province	%
(GCOM)	3	Nfld.	13.0		(SCHO)	3	Nfld.	2.2
Housing (HOUS)	1	Ont.	54.1		Shipyards (SHIP)	1	Nfld.	88.0
	2	Que.	15.8			2	P.E.I.	12.0
	3	Alta.	13.0					
Industrial Development (INDU)	1	Que.	39.1		Steel Production (STEE)	1	Que.	99.9
	2	Ont.	28.4			2	N.S.	0.1
	3	Sask.	9.9					
Liquor (LIQU)	1	Sask.	23.9		Telephones and Communications (TELE)	1	Alta.	56.7
	2	Que.	22.7			2	Man.	22.0
	3	Ont.	22.5			3	Sask.	20.3
Lotteries (LOTT)	1	Ont.	42.8		Transport Facilities (TFAC)	1	Que.	79.1
	2	Que.	32.1			2	N.S.	10.0
	3	Regional	25.0			3	B.C.	6.0
Misc. Marketing & Brokerage Facilities (MARK)	1	Que.	97.8		Transport Systems (TSYS)	1	B.C.	59.0
	2	Ont.	1.8			2	Ont.	23.7
	3	Sask.	.3			3	Alta.	15.3
Mineral Mining and Development (MINE)	1	Sask.	76.8		Water Supply (WSUP)	1	Man.	54.6
	2	Que.	20.2			2	Sask.	45.4
	3	Nfld.	2.1					

* Percentage of total provincial PCC assets in a functional area accounted for by particular province's functional assets.

** These abbreviations are used in Tables VII, XII—XVI.

12. *Mineral Mining* and *Development*—Manitoba, New Brunswick, Newfoundland, Nova Scotia, Quebec and Saskatchewan have PCCs. Excluding New Brunswick and Nova Scotia from the analysis, Saskatchewan controls the largest share of total assets with 76.8 percent, followed by Quebec with 20.2 percent and Newfoundland with 2.1 percent. Mining is the third most important Crown corporation in Saskatchewan with 12.7 percent of that province's total assets.

13. *Miscellaneous Manufacturing*—British Columbia, Newfoundland, Nova Scotia and Quebec have PCCs of this type. We find that Newfoundland has 69.3 percent of total assets, Quebec has 19 percent, and British Columbia has 11.6 percent. Miscellaneous manufacturing is not of significant importance in any province.

14. *Municipal Finance Corporations*—Alberta, Newfoundland, Ontario, Quebec and Saskatchewan have PCCs. The dominant province, is Alberta with 92 percent of the total municipal finance assets. Municipal finance is the most important area in Alberta controlling 37.6 percent of total provincial PCC assets.

15. *Oil* and *Gas Production*—Alberta, British Columbia, Ontario, Quebec and Saskatchewan have corporations in this area. We find that Alberta controls 39.9 percent of total assets, Ontario controls 18.5 percent, and British Columbia controls 16.2 percent.

16. *Power Utility*—Only Alberta, Prince Edward Island, the Northwest Territories and the Yukon do not have power PCCs. The largest three power PCCs are Ontario, Quebec and British Columbia with 33 percent, 31 percent and 14 percent of total assets respectively. In all provinces with power PCCs power ranks first in importance with between 40 percent to 89 percent of total provincial assets.

17. *Research* and *Development*—Alberta, Manitoba, British Columbia, New Brunswick, Newfoundland, Nova Scotia, Quebec and Saskatchewan have PCCs. Quebec corporations control 85.6 percent of all R & D assets followed by Nova Scotia with 4.8 percent and Saskatchewan with 3.9 percent. Within Nova Scotia R & D ranks fifth with .5 percent of assets.

18. *School* and *Hospitals Financing*—British Columbia, Newfoundland and Ontario are involved in this area. Ontario controls 71.9 percent of total assets, British Columbia 25.8 percent and Newfoundland 2.2 percent. In both British Columbia and Ontario, school and hospital financing ranks second to power PCCs, controlling 11.3 percent and 14.4 percent of total provincial PCC assets respectively.

19. *Shipyards*—Only Newfoundland and Prince Edward Island have PCCs in this category with Newfoundland holding 88 percent of total assets and Prince Edward Island the remainder. In Prince Edward Island shipyards rank fourth, after industrial development, housing and agriculture PCCs, with 10.5 percent of total assets.

20. *Steel Production*—Nova Scotia and Quebec have corporations in

TABLE VII

Intra-Provincial Importance of Functional Areas by Assets

Prov.	B.C.		Alta.		Sask.		Ont.		Que.		N.B.	
Rank	Area	% of Assets	Area	% of Assets	Area	% of Assets	Area	% of Assets	Area	% of Assets	Area	% of Assets
1	POWE	60.7*	MUNI	37.6	POWE	40.9	POWE	65.5	POWE	53.2	POWE	88.6
2	SCHO	11.3	TELE	23.4	TELE	17.1	SCHO	14.4	BANK	24.7	HOUS	7.2
3	TSYS	9.3	BANK	16.6	MINE	12.7	HOUS	13.3	STEE	4.7	TFAC	2.0
4	GAUT	8.5	HOUS	10.3	GAUT	5.9	INDU	3.2	INDU	3.8	INDU	0.8
5	GBUI	4.6	AGRI	4.0	INDU	4.6	TSYS	1.7	HOUS	3.5	LIQU	0.7

Prov.	Man.		P.E.I.		N.S.		Nfld.		Yukon		N.W.T.	
Rank	Area	% of Assets	Area	% of Assets	Area	% of Assets	Area	% of Assets	Area	% of Assets	Area	% of Assets
1	POWE	68.8	INDU	41.7	POWE	75.5	POWE	74.3	HOUS	89.0	HOUS	93.8
2	TELE	14.1	HOUS	21.9	INDU	15.6	FORE	7.8	LIQO	11.0	LIQO	6.2
3	HOUS	7.0	AGRI	13.7	TFAC	6.5	INDU	6.1				
4	GAUT	3.0	SHIP	10.5	LIQU	1.9	HOUS	3.5				
5	AGRI	2.8	LIQU	7.5	RESE	0.5	SCHO	2.8				

* All percentage figures are the percentage of province's total PCC assets invested in particular functional area.

this area. Within Quebec, Sidbec ranks third (after the power utilities and banking) with 4.7 percent of total provincial PCC assets.

21. *Telephones* and *Communications*—Alberta, British Columbia, Manitoba, Quebec and Saskatchewan have PCCs of this type. Alberta controls 56.7 percent of the assets followed by Manitoba and Saskatchewan with 22.0 percent and 20.3 percent. In Alberta, Saskatchewan and Manitoba, telephone corporations rank second in importance holding between 14.1 percent and 23.4 percent of total provincial assets.

22. *Transport Facilities*—British Columbia, New Brunswick, Nova Scotia, Ontario and Quebec have corporations in this area. Excluding Ontario we find that Quebec controls 79.1 percent of assets followed by Nova Scotia with 10 percent and British Columbia with 6 percent.

23. *Transport Systems*—Alberta, British Columbia, Ontario, Quebec and Saskatchewan have PCCs of this type. British Columbia leads the other provinces controlling 59 percent of total assets. It is followed by Ontario and Alberta which control 23.7 percent and 15.3 percent. In British Columbia transport systems corporations rank third controlling 9.3 percent of provincial assets and in Ontario rank fifth controlling 1.7 percent of total provincial assets.

24. *Water Supply*—Manitoba and Saskatchewan have PCCs. Manitoba controls 55 percent of the assets and Saskatchewan the remainder. Neither corporation is of significant importance intraprovincially.

(b) Growth

The growth of PCCs in each of the provinces generally reflects the overall pattern of growth: high recent growth in numbers and early major growth in assets. The data is summarized in Tables VIII and IX. For example 55 percent of Alberta's PCCs have been founded since 1970. The equivalent percentages for British Columbia are 77 percent, for Saskatchewan 60 percent, Manitoba 54 percent and Ontario 48 percent. Thus the 1970s was a period of major growth in most provinces. Only Quebec, among the larger provinces, created few PCCs during this period. Major growth in Quebec occurred in the periods 1940-1950 and 1960-1970.

(c) Political Origins

The nationwide description of the party origins of PCCs hides significant variations in the party origins of a particular province's PCCs. Using the information summarized in Tables X and XI the following is a brief description of party origins in each province:

British Columbia—Both the NDP and Social Credit are responsible for

TABLE VIII
Percentage Growth of PCCs (Number) in Each Province, 1910-1980

Prov./Yr.	Alta.	B.C.	Man.	N.B.	Nfld.	N.S.	N.W.T.	Ont.	P.E.I.	Que.	Sask.	Yukon
1910	—	3%	8%	—	—	—	—	7%	—	—	—	—
1920	—	3	8	—	—	10%	—	7	—	—	—	—
1930	5*%	9	23	25%	—	10	—	15	—	.4%	4%	—
1940	15	9	23	25	—	20	50	15	—	.4	4	—
1950	20	14	23	25	7%	20	50	22	10%	57	32	50%
1960	30	14	31	38	29	40	50	30	10	59	32	50
1970	45	23	46	75	86	50	50	52	70	95	40	50
1980	100	100	100	100	100	100	100	100	100	100	100	100

* All percentage figures are cumulative percentage of PCCs in a given province created by a given date.

TABLE IX

Percentage Growth of PCC Assets in Each Province, 1910-1980

Prov. Yr.	Alta.	B.C.	Man.	N.B.	Nfld.	N.S.	N.W.T.	Ont.	P.E.I.	Que.	Sask.	Yukon
1910	—	—	14%	—	—	—	—	66%	—	—	—	—
1920	—	—	14	89%	—	75%	—	66	—	—	—	—
1930	.7%*	9%	83	89	—	75	—	67	—	.4%	3%	—
1940	17	9	83	89	1%	77	6%	67	—	.2	3	—
1950	17	70	83	89	31	77	6	67	7%	55	51	—
1960	78	70	85	89	48	99	6	68	7	55	51	—
1970	81	81	92	97		99	6	92	73	94	57	—
1980	100	100	100	100	100	100	100	100	100	100	100	100

* All percentage figures are cumulative percentage of total present PCC assets in given province created by a given date.

42.9 percent of PCCs. Indicative of the NDP's commitment to PCCs is the fact that they were responsible for the formation of five PCCs per year in office compared to a rate of .83 for the Social Credit between 1960 and 1980. The British Columbia NDP creation rate is the highest among provincial parties.

Alberta—Right of Centre parties (Conservatives and Social Credit) are responsible for the creation of 88 percent of PCCs. The United Farmers of Alberta (UFA) were responsible for 10 percent. In the last 21 years this translates into a creation rate of .67 PCCs per year in office for Right of Centre parties.

Saskatchewan—The NDP and its predecessor, the CCF, are responsible for the formation of 88 percent of the PCCs, at a creation rate of 1.15 corporations per year in office. The Liberals have only created 12 percent of the PCCs.

Manitoba—The NDP are responsible for 46.2 percent of the PCCs, followed by the Conservatives with 38.5 percent. The Liberals and the United Farmworkers of Manitoba (UFM) are each responsible for 7.7 percent of the province's PCCs. In the last 21 years the NDP has created .75 corporations per year in office and the Conservatives only .23 per year.

Ontario—The Conservatives are responsible for the creation of 92.6 percent of the PCCs, while the Liberals and the United Farmers of Ontario are each responsible for 3.7 percent. The Conservatives have held office over the last 21 years creating an average of .9 corporations each year.

Quebec—Three parties have created PCCs: the Liberals with 57.1 percent, the Union Nationale with 25.7 percent and the Parti Québécois with 17.1 percent. All the parties have created PCCs at a rate exceeding one a year with the Union Nationale leading with a rate of 2.25 per year in office.

New Brunswick—The Conservatives and the Liberals have each created half the PCCs. In the last 21 years the Liberals have edged the Conservatives with a creation rate of .30 compared to .18 for the Conservatives.

Nova Scotia—The Liberals have created 70 percent and the Conservatives 30 percent of the PCCs. In the last 21 years the Liberals have created an average of .63 corporations per year in office while the Conservatives have the lowest rate of all provincial parties at .08.

Prince Edward Island—The Liberals are responsible for the creation of all the PCCs, many of which were created between 1960 and 1980 at a rate of .69 per year.

Newfoundland—The Liberals and the Conservatives are responsible for 78.6 percent and 19.0 percent respectively of the PCCs. The creation rate for the Liberals over the last 19 years has been 1.92, and for the Conservatives .78.

TABLE X
Ranking of Party Responsibility for the Creation of PCCs by Province

Rank Province	1	2	3	4	Total Corps. With Data	Total Corps.
B.C.	NDP 42.9%	SOCR 42.9%	LIBE 5.7%	COAL 5.7%	34	35
Alta.	CONS 55.0%	SOCR 33.0%	UFA 10.0%	UFA —	19	19
Sask.	NDP 52.0%	CCF 36.0%	LIBE 12.0%	—	25	25
Man.	NDP 46.2%	CONS 38.5%	LIBE 7.7%	UFM 7.7%	13	13
Ont.	CONS 92.6%	LIBE 3.7%	UFO 3.7%	—	27	27
Que.	LIBE 57.1%	UN 25.7%	PQ 17.1%	—	35	35
N.B.	CONS 50.0%	LIBE 50.0%			8	8
N.S.	LIBE 70.0%	CONS 30.0%			10	10
P.E.I.	LIBE 100%				10	10
Nfld.	LIBE 78.6%	CONS 19.0%			42	42

TABLE XI
Party Creation of PCCs per Year in Office, 1960-1980

	Alta.	B.C.	Man.	N.B.	Nfld.	N.S.	Ont.	P.E.I.	Que.	Sask.
Liberal Years				10	12	8		13	13	8
Corps. Created				3	23	5		9	16	2
Corps/Year				0.30	1.92	0.63		0.69	1.23	
Left of Centre Years		3	8						4	13
Corps. Created		15	6						6	15
Corps/Year		5.0	0.75						1.50	1.15
Right of Centre Years	21	18	13	11	9	13	21	8	4	
Corps. Created	14	15	3	2	7	1	19	—	9	
Corps/Year	0.67	0.83	0.23	0.18	0.78	0.08	0.90	—	2.25	

V. FUNCTIONAL AREA ANALYSIS

(a) Size

The size of the functional areas vary a great deal when measured by assets. Table XII demonstrates that power utility PCCs control by far the highest dollar value of assets ($34,458 million) while shipyards control the lowest amount with $21.8 million dollars. Figure 8 illustrates the asymetrical distribution of assets among PCCs. This graph plots the cumulative percentage of PCCs on the horizontal axis and cumulative percentage of assets on the vertical axis. If all PCCs have the same amount of assets the graph would be a straight line. However, as Figure 8 demonstrates, a few PCCs control most of the assets. More specifically, two of the functional areas, Power and Banking, account for 65 percent of all assets. Housing, schooling, telephone and communications PCCs add another 16 percent, thus fully 81 percent of total PCC assets are accounted for by just three functional categories. When municipal finance, industrial development and transport systems are added, percentage of assets accounted for rises to 90 percent.

Another comparison of interest is the size of PCCs within the particular functional areas. Using mean assets in each functional category, (see Table XII) we find that schools and hospitals financing corporations drop from fourth position in terms of absolute assets to seventh position in terms of mean assets with $204 million per corporation. Housing corporations drop from third position to sixth position with an average of $250 million per corporation. Industrial development corporations drop from seventh position to thirteenth position with $75 million per corporation.

The importance of the various functional categories can also be gauged by comparing their assets with total assets in that functional area held by both the private sector and public sector (directly). As a first approximation to this relationship the ratio of PCC assets to private sector and public sector corporate assets has been calculated for 23 of the 24 functional categories. In Table XII this ratio is presented as a percentage. Obviously the ratio is affected by the definition of private sector assets deemed to fall into each of the functional categories (the assumptions which underlie this calculation are contained in Appendix III). For the purpose of this analysis the ratio results are grouped into three percentage categories; those cases where: (1) PCCs assets are greater than 30 percent of private and public assets; (2) PPC assets are between 10 percent and 30 percent of private and public assets, and (3) PCC assets are between 0 percent and 10 percent.

30% plus—There are three functional areas where PCCs fall into this percentage range: power utilities with 81.51 percent, school and hospital financing with 43.52 percent, and general and auto insurance with 38.28 percent. Clearly PCCs play a significant to dominant role in these sectors of the Canadian economy.

TABLE XII

Size of Functional Areas by: (1) Numbers; (2) Total Assets; (3) Percentage of Private Sector Total Assets; (4) Mean Assets

Function	No. of Corps*	% of Total No.	Total Assets ($000,000's)	% of Total Assets	% of Private Sector Total Assets**	Rank	Mean Assets/ Corp.	Rank
POWE	11	5%	$34,458.3	55.35%	81.51%	1	3,132.57	1
BANK	4	2	5,847.3	9.39	3.88	13	1,461.83	2
HOUS	17	8	4,256.5	6.84	5.37	11	250.38	6
SCHO	17	8	3,478.3	5.59	43.52	2	204.60	7
TELE	7	3	2,223.3	3.57	16.31	8	317.61	5
MUNI	5	2	2,198.5	3.53	27.51	4	439.71	4
INDU	26	12	1,948.3	3.13	8.73	9	74.94	13
TSYS	11	5	1,242.3	2.00	5.04	12	112.93	10
GAUT	5	2	967.6	1.55	38.28	3	193.52	8
STEE	2	1	940.4	1.51	16.36	7	470.20	3
MARK	12	6	784.6	1.26	—	—	65.38	14
AGRI	13	6	716.7	1.15	6.81	10	55.13	16
FORE	13	6	620.4	1.00	3.64	14	47.72	17
TFAC	6	3	548.6	0.88	2.23	18	91.44	12
OILG	5	2	542.1	0.87	2.82	16	108.42	11
MINE	7	3	435.3	0.70	2.28	17	62.18	15
GBUI	3	1	382.9	0.61	0.86	21	127.63	9
LIQU	12	6	367.1	0.59	16.39	6	30.59	18
RESE	8	4	92.1	0.15	2.95	15	11.52	21
MMAN	9	4	62.5	0.10	0.24	23	6.95	24
LOTT	4	2	53.5	0.09	1.84	19	13.37	20
GCOM	4	2	37.8	0.06	0.52	22	9.46	23
WSUP	2	1	30.4	0.05	16.74	5	15.21	19
SHIP	2	1	21.8	0.04	1.49	20	10.41	22

* Number of corporations included in analysis.
** See Appendix III for definition of private sector total assets.

FIGURE 8
Distribution of Assets Across Functions

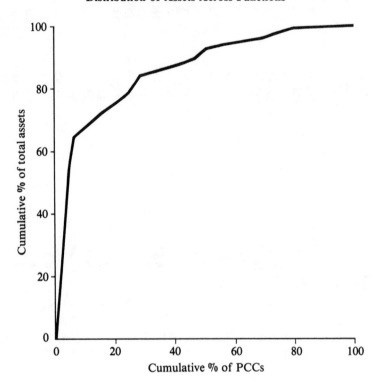

10%-30%—There are five functional categories where PCCs make up from 10 percent to 30 percent of total sector assets. PCCs in these classifications either form a major subsegment of the total sector or represent viable alternatives to existing public and private sector organizations. They include municipal finance at 27.5 percent, water supply at 16.7 percent, liquor with 16.4 percent, steel production with 16.4 percent, and telephones and communications with 16.3 percent.

0-10%—There are 15 functional classifications in this category. While obviously not a major threat to the private sector these corporations could be of considerable importance in a specialized segment of the market. An example in point is lotteries, although they do not rank of any importance when compared with total assets in the entertainment sector, they are in a monopoly position in their specialized segment of the market. The percentages in this category range from .2 percent for miscellaneous manufacturing to 8.7 percent for industrial development with four functions, housing, agriculture, and transport systems in the 4-7 percent range.

(b) Growth

The functional categories are grouped according to the decade in which the first PCC was created. For the purposes of discussion this is further aggregated into four periods: prior to 1940, the 1940s, the 1950s, and the 1960s (see Tables XIII and XIV for summarized data).

Prior to 1940—Eight functional categories originated prior to WW II: marketing, liquor, power, telephones, transport systems, banking, research and agriculture. While banking, research, agriculture and liquor distribution PCCs were first created in the 1920s and 1930s the other functional categories had members by 1910. For three of these functional areas a major portion of their growth in assets, if not numbers, was experienced prior to WW II. In particular, by 1940, 75 percent of liquor PCCs (representing 96 percent of liquor assets) had been formed, 36 percent of power PCCs had been formed (representing 45 percent of assets), 14 percent of transport system corporations had been formed representing 69 percent of transport assets, and finally 7.7 percent of agricultural PCCs had been formed (representing 46 percent of assets). The exceptions were: research, where only 8 percent of the corporations and a insignificant percentage of assets had been created; telephones, where 13 percent of PCCs and 22 percent of assets had been created, and banking where 40 percent of corporations and only 15 percent of assets had been formed.

1940s—The 1940s saw the addition of six functional areas: forestry, housing, mining, general and auto insurance, industrial development, and miscellaneous manufacturing. These areas experienced modest initial growth. By 1950 8 percent of forestry PCCs with 6 percent of the functions assets had been formed. The percentages for housing and mining were 6 percent and .3 percent and 11 percent and 2 percent respectively. A major part of the growth in these areas was experienced in the 1970s. Until 1970 only 8 percent of forestry assets, 64 percent of housing assets, and 8 percent of mining assets had been formed.

1950s—In this period the provinces entered several new areas with PCCs: government buildings, municipal finance, transport facilities, and school and hospital financing. The 1950s represented the major asset growth period for municipal finance with 94 percent of total assets added by 1960.

The other functional areas did not grow rapidly until the 1960s and 1970s. In this period 67 percent of the corporations and 98 percent of the assets in government buildings were added, 85.7 percent of PCCs and 91 percent of assets in transport facilities were created; 95.7 percent of the PCCs and 99.7 percent of the assets in school and hospital financing were formed.

TABLE XIII
Growth of PCCs by Functional Areas, 1910-1980

Year Function	1910	1920	1930	1940	1950	1960	1970	1980
MARK	5.6%	5.6%	5.6%	5.6%	28%	28%	50%	100%
LIQU		—	5.8	75	92	92	92	100
POWE	9	18	36	36	64	73	82	100
TELE	13	13	13	13	25	28	38	100
TSYS	7	7	14	14	21	21	28	100
BANK	—	—	20	40	40	40	60	100
RESE	—	—	—	8	16	16	46	100
AGRI	—	—	—	7.7	7.7	23.1	53.9	100
FORE	—	—	—	—	8	22	22	100
HOUS	—	—	—	—	6	6	40	100
MINE	—	—	—	—	11	22	33	100
GAUT	—	—	—	—	40	40	40	100
INDU	—	—	—	—	3.3	10	50	100
MMAN	—	—	—	—	10	40	80	100
TFAC	—	—	—	—	—	14.3	43	100
GBUI	—	—	—	—	—	33	66	100
MUNI	—	—	—	—	—	40	60	100
SCHO	—	—	—	—	—	4.3	43	100
GCOM	—	—	—	—	—	—	25	100
OILG	—	—	—	—	—	—	20	100
SHIP	—	—	—	—	—	—	50	100
STEE	—	—	—	—	—	—	67	100
WSUP	—	—	—	—	—	—	50	100
LOTT	—	—	—	—	—	—	—	100

TABLE XIV

Growth of PCC Assets in Functional Areas, 1910-1980

Year / Function	1910	1920	1930	1940	1950	1960	1970	1980
MARK	—	—	—	—	2%	2%	2%	100%
LIQU	—	—	91%	96%	100	100	100	100
POWE	33%*	35%	45	45	93	96	96	100
TELE	22	22	22	22	22	79	79	100
TSYS	11	11	69	69	69	69	78	100
BANK	—	—	—	15	15	15	100	100
RESE	—	—	—	—	—	—	89	100
AGRI	—	—	—	46	46	66	70	100
FORE	—	—	—	—	6	8	8	100
HOUS	—	—	—	—	.3	.3	64	100
MINE	—	—	—	—	2	4	8	100
GAUT	—	—	—	—	16	16	16	100
INDU	—	—	—	—	.6	7	62	100
MMAN	—	—	—	—	19	34	88	100
TFAC	—	—	—	—	—	9	94	100
GBUI	—	—	—	—	—	2	4	100
MUNI	—	—	—	—	—	94	98	100
SCHO	—	—	—	—	—	.3	99	100
GCOM	—	—	—	—	—	—	13	100
OILG	—	—	—	—	—	—	15	100
SHIP	—	—	—	—	—	—	88	100
STEE	—	—	—	—	—	—	100	100
WSUP	—	—	—	—	—	—	45	100
LOTT	—	—	—	—	—	—	—	100

* All percentage figures are cumulative percentage of total present PCC assets in a given functional area created by a given date.

1960s—This was the period of initiation for PCCs in steel, shipyards, oil and gas, and government computer services and water supply. By 1970 two of the areas, shipyards and water supply, had experienced half their growth in numbers and between 45 percent and 88 percent of their growth in assets. On the other hand, government computer services and oil and gas corporations grew mainly in the 1970s. In particular, 87 percent of government computer services assets and 85 percent of oil and gas assets were formed.

(c) Political Origins

The political responsibility for PCCs in each functional area is diffuse. There is only one area in which one political party has been responsible for all the PCCs, shipyards. However, particular parties have been responsible for a larger percentage of growth in some areas. This can be gauged by outlining the functional categories in which a party has created the largest percentage of PCCs and the largest percentage of assets (see Tables XV and XVI).

Right of Centre parties have led in the creation of several types of PCCs. These areas include: agriculture (38.5 percent of the total number); housing (46.7 percent); industrial development (50 percent); marketing (55.6 percent); research (61.5 percent); telephone and communications (62.5 percent); transport facilities (57.1 percent); and transport systems (57.1 percent) of numbers. When measured on an asset basis Right of Centre parties no longer lead in the areas of agriculture, industrial development, marketing, and transport systems. However they have created the most assets in: government buildings 96 percent, government computers 64.9 percent, lotteries 42.8 percent, municipal finance 99.3 percent, oil and gas 73.6 percent, and schools and hospital financing 97.1 percent. The Liberals have matched or closely followed the Conservatives in terms of the number of PCCs created. In eight areas: government buildings, liquor, miscellaneous manufacturing, municipal finance, school and hospital financing, shipping, steel, and most importantly power, they have led the way by creating 66.6 percent, 40 percent, 90 percent, 60 percent, 70.6 percent, 100 percent, 67 percent and 55 percent of the PCCs respectively. On an asset basis they have led the way in five of the eight above functional categories.

Left of Centre parties have taken a leading role in the creation of banking, forestry, general and auto insurance, and mineral development PCCs. The percentage of PCCs created in these areas by the Left of Centre parties ranges from 40 percent in banking to 80 percent in auto insurance. Forestry and mining are in-between at 53.9 percent and 55.6 percent respectively. When the Left of Centre party responsibility is measured in terms of assets, the picture is somewhat different. In banking, responsibility (or credit) can

TABLE XV

Party Responsibility for Growth by Functional Area

Function	Left of Centre %	#	Centre %	#	Right of Centre %	#	Other %	#	PCCs Included	Total PCCs
AGRI	30.8	4	30.8	4	38.5	5	—	—	13	13
BANK	40.0	2	20.0	1	20.0	1	20	1	5	5
FORE	53.9	7	23.1	3	23.1	3	—	—	13	13
GAUT	80.0	4	—	—	20.0	1	—	—	5	5
GBUI	—	—	66.6	2	33.3	1	—	—	3	3
GCOM	50.0	2	—	—	50.0	2	—	—	4	4
HOUS	26.7	4	26.7	4	46.7	7	—	—	15	18
INDU	13.3	4	36.7	11	50.0	15	—	—	30	31
LIQU	40.0	4	40.0	4	—	—	20	2	10	12
LOTT	50.0	1	—	—	50.0	1	—	—	2	4
MARK	22.2	4	22.2	4	55.6	10	—	—	18	18
MINE	55.6	5	44.4	4	—	—	—	—	9	10
MMAN	10.0	1	90.0	9	—	—	—	—	10	10
MUNI	—	—	60.0	3	40.0	2	—	—	5	5
OILG	40.0	2	—	—	40.0	2	20	1	5	5
POWE	9.1	1	54.5	6	27.3	3	9.1	1	11	11
RESE	7.7	1	15.4	2	61.5	8	15.4	2	13	13
SCHO	5.9	1	70.6	12	23.5	4	—	—	17	17
SHIP	—	—	100.0	2	—	—	—	—	2	2
STEE	—	—	66.7	2	33.3	1	—	—	3	3
TELE	25.5	2	12.5	1	62.5	5	—	—	8	8
TFAC	—	—	42.9	3	57.1	4	—	—	7	7
TSYS	21.4	3	21.4	3	57.1	8	—	—	14	14
WSUP	—	—	50.0	1	50.0	1	—	—	2	2

be taken for only .2 percent of the assets assembled, while in forestry the percentage is 46.1 percent. However, Left of Centre parties do lead in the creation of assets in auto insurance, government computers, mining and water supply. In sum, the "productivity" of Left of Centre parties in terms of absolute numbers has not been fully matched by a similar productivity in assets.

TABLE XVI

Party Responsibility for Creation of Assets by Functional Area

Function	Left or Centre % of Assets	Centre % of Assets	Right of Centre % of Assets	Other % of Assets	PCCs Incl.	TOT PCC
AGRI	14.1	47.1	38.8	—	13	13
BANK	.2	84.5	15.3	—	4	5
FORE	46.1	5.6	38.3	—	13	13
GAUT	99.8	—	0.2	—	5	5
GBUI	—	3.9	96.1	—	3	3
GCOM	35.1	—	64.9	—	4	4
HOUS	4.6	4.8	90.6	—	16	18
INDU	8.7	46.5	44.6	—	26	31
LIQU	—	54.8	32.1	13.1	12	12
LOTT	32.2	—	42.8	25.0	4	4
MARK	0.6	97.1	2.3	—	12	18
MINE	77.6	22.3	—	—	7	10
MMAN	11.6	88.4	—	—	9	10
MUNI	—	5.7	99.3	—	5	5
OILG	26.4	—	73.6	—	5	5
POWE	3.1	45.7	37.2	14.0	11	11
RESE	3.9	7.1	89.0	—	8	13
SCHO	0.7	2.2	97.1	—	17	17
SHIP	—	100.0	—	—	2	2
STEE	—	100.0	—	—	2	3
TELE	20.3	0.5	79.3	—	7	8
TFAC	—	10.1	89.9	—	6	7
TSYS	1.1	70.0	28.9	—	11	14
WSUP	54.6	45.4	—	—	2	2

VI. SUMMARY

Provincial Crown corporations, as a sector of the Canadian economy, are of considerable size and importance and recently have experienced rapid growth in numbers. In particular, it was found that total assets of PCCs represent 180 percent of provincial financial assets, and that fixed assets of PCCs amount to 36 percent of Canadian corporate fixed assets. In the period since 1960, 72 percent of all provincial Crown corporations were created, representing only 37 percent of total assets.

The examination of PCCs by province of creation and by functional role reveals several further insights. While Quebec and Ontario rank first and second in terms of total assets, Newfoundland has the largest per capita investment in PCCs with $5,456 assets per capita, while Ontario occupies eighth position with assets of $1,888 per capita.

Moving to the functional level of analysis, it was found that several functional categories have experienced major growth in assets since 1970, contrary to the general pattern of early growth in assets and recent growth in numbers. Namely: forestry (93 percent), mining (77 percent), industrial development (79 percent) and agricultural development (77 percent). In terms of political responsibility for functional growth, it was found that Right of Centre parties lead in many functional categories including housing and school and hospital financing, while Left of Centre parties lead in a few areas including auto insurance and mining. In sum, PCCs are an important sector of the Canadian economy and yet are diverse in size, growth and political origins, when viewed either by province of creation or functional specialization.

APPENDIX I
Provincial Crown Corporations
(alphabetically)

Agricultural Development Corp. of Saskatchewan
Alberta Agricultural Development Corp.
Alberta Agricultural Research Trust
Alberta Art Foundation
Alberta Educational Communications Corp.
Alberta Energy Corp.
Alberta Environmental Research Trust
Alberta General Insurance Company
Alberta Government Telephone Comm.
Alberta Hail and Crop Insurance Corp.
Alberta Home Mortgage Corp.
Alberta Housing Corp.
Alberta Investment Fund (Inactive Sept. 1, 1977)
Alberta Liquor Control Board
Alberta Municipal Financing Corp.
Alberta Oil Sands Technology and Research Authority
Alberta Opportunity Company

Alberta Resources Railway Corp.
Algonquin Forestry Authority
Atlantic Gypsum Ltd.
Atlantic Lottery
Bell Island Hospital Building Corp.
Burgeo Fish Industries Ltd.
Burgeo Seafoods Ltd.
B.C. Buildings Corp.
B.C. Cellulose Company
B.C. Development Corp.
B.C. Educ. Institutions Capital Financing Authority
B.C. Ferry Corp.
B.C. Harbours Board
B.C. Housing Management Comm.
B.C. Hydro and Power Authority
B.C. Liquor Distribution Branch
B.C. Petroleum Corp.
B.C. Place Corp.
B.C. Railway Company
B.C. Regional Hospital Districts Financing Authority
B.C. Research Council
B.C. School Districts Capital Financing Authority
B.C. Steamship (1975) Ltd.
B.C. Systems Corp.
CANSTEEL
Caisse de Dépot et Placement du Québec
Canadian Cellulose Company
Centrale d'Artisant du Québec (CAQ) Private Ownership
Centre de recherché Industrielle du Québec (CRIQ)
Churchill Falls (Labrador) Corp. Ltd.
Community Improvement Corp.
Corner Brook Hospital Building Corp.
Crop Insurance Commission of Ontario
Crown Development Corp. (Inactive)
The Discovery Foundation, Discovery Parks, Inc.
Dunhill Development Corp. (Inactive 1978)
E. Ontario Development Corp.
Elizabeth Towers (Inactive March 31, 1976)
Exhibition Stadium Corp.
Fish Building Ltd. (Inactive March 31, 1976)
Fisheries Loan Board of Newfoundland
Freshwater Fish Marketing Corp.
Gander Hospitals Corp.

Georgetown Shipyards
Grace Hospital Extension Corp.
Grand Falls Hospital Building Corp.
Halifax-Dartmouth Bridge
Halifax International Containers
Harmon Corp.
Hotel Building Ltd.
Housing Corporation of B.C.
l'Hydro-Québec
Industrial Enterprises Incorporated
Industrial Estates Ltd.
Institut de Recherché de l'Hydro-Québec
Insurance Corp. of B.C.
Knowledge Network of the West Communications Authority
Kootenay Forest Products Ltd.
Labrador Linerboard (Inactive Dec. 1978)
Liquor Control Board of Ontario
Liquor Control Commission of Manitoba
Lower Churchill Development Corp. Ltd.
Manitoba Agricultural Credit Corp.
Manitoba Data Services
Manitoba Development Corp. (Inactive—Legal Entity only)
Manitoba Forestry Res.
Manitoba Housing and Renewal Corp.
Manitoba Hydro
Manitoba Mineral Resources Ltd.
Manitoba Public Insurance Company
Manitoba Research Council
Manitoba Telephone System
Manitoba Trading Corp.
Manitoba Water Services Board
Market Development Corp.
Marystown Shipyard Ltd.
Memorial University of Newfoundland Building Corp.
Metro Transit Operating Company
Mooring Cove Building Company Ltd.
Municipal Financing Corp.
Municipalité de la Baie James (Affiliated to SDBJ)
NORDCO Ltd.
NOVACO
Newfoundland Farm Products Corp.
Newfoundland Fiberply
Newfoundland Government Building Corp.

Newfoundland Hardwoods
Newfoundland Industrial Development Corp.
Newfoundland and Lab. Computer Services Ltd.
Newfoundland and Lab. Development Corp.
Newfoundland and Lab. Housing Corp.
Newfoundland and Lab. Power Corp.
Newfoundland Liquor Corp.
New Brunswick Coal
New Brunswick Development Corp.
New Brunswick Electric Power Commission
New Brunswick Forest Authority
New Brunswick Housing
New Brunswick Liquor Control
New Brunswick Research and Productivity Council
New Brunswick Transportation Authority
North Start Cement Corp.
Northern Hospitals Building Corp.
N. Ontario Development Corp.
N. Pickering Development Corp.
Northwest Territories Housing Corp.
Northwest Territories Liquor System
Nova Scotia Liquor
Nova Scotia Power Corp.
Nova Scotia Research Foundation Corp.
Nurses Training School Building Corp.
Ocean Falls Corp.
Office des Autoroutes du Québec
Office du Crédit Agricole
l'Office de Radio-Télé Diffusion du Québec (ORTQ)
Ontario Development Corp.
Ontario Education Capital Aid Corp.
Ontario Energy Corp.
Ontario Food Terminal Board
Ontario Housing Corp.
Ontario Hydro
Ontario Junior Farmer Establishment Loan Corp.
Ontario Land Corp.
Ontario Lottery Corp.
Ontario Mortgage Corp.
Ontario Municipal Improvement Corp.
Ontario Northland Transportation Commission
Ontario Place Corp.
Ontario Stock Yards Board

Ontario Transportation Development Corp. (Inactive)
Ontario Universities Capital Aid Corp.
Pacific Coach Lines Ltd.
Pacific National Exhibition
Pacific Western Airlines
Pepperell Hospital Reconstruction Corp.
Plateau Mills Ltd.
Potash Corp. of Saskatchewan
Power Distribution District of Newfoundland and Labrador
Prairie Agricultural Machinery Institute
P.E.I. Crop Insurance Agency
P.E.I. Crown Building Corp.
P.E.I. Economic Improvement Corp. (Inactive)
P.E.I. Housing Corp.
P.E.I. Land Development Corp.
P.E.I. Lending Authority
P.E.I. Liquor Control
Province of Ontario Savings Office
Province of Saskatchewan Liquor Board
Provincial Rental Housing Corp.
Raffinerie de Sucré du Québec
Régie des Installations Olympiques (RIO)
Régie de l'Assurance Automobile du Québec
Research Council of Alberta
SIDBEC
SOTEL INC. (Affiliated to SDBJ)
SYSCO
St. John's Housing Corp.
St. John's Infirmary Building Corp.
Saskatchewan Computer Utility Corp.
Saskatchewan Crop Insurance Corp.
Saskatchewan Development Fund
Saskatchewan Development Fund Corp.
Saskatchewan Econ. Development Corp.
Saskatchewan Educational Communications Corp.
Saskatchewan Farmstart
Saskatchewan Forest Products Corp.
Saskatchewan Fur Marketing Service
Saskatchewan Government Insurance
Saskatchewan Government Printing Co.
Saskatchewan Housing Corp.
Saskatchewan Minerals
Saskatchewan Mining Development Corp.

Saskatchewan Oil and Gas Corp.
Saskatchewan Power Corp.
Saskatchewan Telecommunications
Saskatchewan Trading Corp. (Changed to Agri. Dev. Corp. of Sask.)
Saskatchewan Transportation Company
Saskatchewan Water Supply Board
Science Council of B.C.
Société des Alcohols du Québec (SAQ)
Société d'Aménagement de l'Outaouais (SAO)
Société de Cartographie du Québec
Société de Développement de la Baie James (SDBJ)
Société de Développement Coopératif (SDC)
Société de Développement Immobillier du Québec (SODEVIQ)
Société de Développement Industriel (SDI)
Société Générale de Financement du Québec (SGF)
Société d'Habitation du Québec (SHQ)
Société Inter-Port de Québec
Société des Loteries et Courses de Québec (LOTO-QUÉBEC)
Société Nationale de l'Amiante (SNA)
Société du Parc Industriel du Centre du Québec (SPICQ)
Société du Parc Industriel et Comm. Aéro de Mirabel (SPICAM)
Société Québecois de Développement des Industries Culturelles
Société Québecois d'Exploration Miniére (SOQUEM)
Société Québecois d'Initiatives Agro-Alimentaires (SOQUIA)
Société Québecois d'Initiatives Pétroliéres (SOQUIP)
Société de Récupération d'Exploitation et de Dévelop. Forestiers du Québec
    (REXFOR)
Société des Traversiers du Québec (STQ)
Société de Tourisme de la Baie James (Affiliated to SDBJ)
Surrey Farm Products Investments Ltd.
T.S. Holdings Ltd.
Technical College Building Corp.
Toronto Area Transit Operating Authority
Transportation 86 Corp.
Treasury Branches Dep. Fund
Twin Falls Power Corp. Ltd.
United Cotton Mills Ltd.
Urban Transit Authority of B.C.
Urban Transportation Development Corp.
Vocational Schools (Western) Building Corp.
Waterfront Development Corp.
Western Canada Lottery
Yukon Housing Corp.
Yukon Liquor Corp.

APPENDIX II
Provincial Crown Corporations by
Functional Category

	Creation Year	Prov.
Agricultural Development (AGRI)		
Agricultural Development Corp. of Saskatchewan	1978	Sask.
Alberta Agricultural Development Corp.	1972	Alta.
Alberta Hail and Crop Insurance Corp.	1969	Alta.
Crop Insurance Commission of Ontario	1966	Ont.
Manitoba Agricultural Credit Corp.	1959	Man.
Office du Crédit Agricole	1936	Que.
Ontario Junior Farmer Establishment Loan Corp.	1952	Ont.
P.E.I. Crop Insurance Agency	1967	P.E.I.
P.E.I. Land Development Corp.	1969	P.E.I.
Saskatchewan Crop Insurance Corp.	1974	Sask.
Saskatchewan Farmstart	1973	Sask.
Saskatchewan Trading Corp. (Changed to Agri. Dev. Corp. of Sask.)	1974	Sask.
Soc. Québecois d'Initiatives Agro-Alimentaires (SOQUIA)	1975	Que.
Banking, Saving and Investment (BANK)		
Caisse de Dépot et Placement du Québec	1965	Que.
Province of Ontario Savings Office	1921	Ont.
Saskatchewan Development Fund	1974	Sask.
Saskatchewan Development Fund Corp.	1974	Sask.
Treasury Branches Dep. Fund	1938	Alta.
Forest Development and Manufacturing (FORE)		
Algonquin Forestry Authority	1975	Ont.
B.C. Cellulose Company	1973	B.C.
Canadian Cellulose Company	1973	B.C.
Kootenay Forest Products Ltd.	1974	B.C.
Labrador Linerboard (Inactive Dec. 1978)	1972	Nfld.
Manitoba Forestry Res.	1971	Man.
New Brunswick Forest Authority	1973	N.B.
Newfoundland Fiberply	1959	Nfld.
Newfoundland Hardwoods	1950	Nfld.
Ocean Falls Corp.	1973	B.C.
Plateau Mills Ltd.	1973	B.C.
Saskatchewan Forest Products Corp.	1949	Sask.
Société de Récupération d'Exploitation et de Dévelop.		

	Creation Year	Prov.

Forest Development and Manufacturing (FORE)—Continued

Forestiers du Québec (REXFOR)	1971	Que.

General Auto and Insurance (GAUT)

Alberta General Insurance Company	1948	Alta.
Insurance Corp. of B.C.	1973	B.C.
Manitoba Public Insurance Company	1970	Man.
Régie de l'Assurance Automobile du Québec	1977	Que.
Saskatchewan Government Insurance	1945	Sask.

Government Buildings (GBUI)

B.C. Buildings Corp.	1977	B.C.
Newfoundland Government Building Corp.	1958	Nfld.
P.E.I. Crown Building Corp.	1962	P.E.I.

Government Computer Services (GCOM)

B.C. Systems Corp.	1977	B.C.
Manitoba Data Services	1975	Man.
Newfoundland and Lab. Computer Services Ltd.	1969	Nfld.
Saskatchewan Computer Utility Corp.	1973	Sask.

Housing (HOUS)

Alberta Home Mortgage Corp.	1976	Alta.
Alberta Housing Corp.	1970	Alta.
B.C. Housing Management Comm.	1975	B.C.
Dunhill Development Corp. (Inactive 1978)	1974	B.C.
Elizabeth Towers (Inactive March 31, 1976)	1966	Nfld.
Housing Corporation of B.C.	1976	B.C.
Manitoba Housing and Renewal Corp.	1967	Man.
New Brunswick Housing	1967	N.B.
Newfoundland and Lab. Housing Corp.	1967	Nfld.
Northwest Territories Housing Corp.	1975	N.W.T.
Ontario Housing Corp.	1964	Ont.
Ontario Mortgage Corp.	1974	Ont.
P.E.I. Housing Corp.	1975	P.E.I.
Provincial Rental Housing Corp.	1973	B.C.
St. John's Housing Corp.	1944	Nfld.
Saskatchewan Housing Corp.	1973	Sask.
Société d'Habitation du Québec (SHQ)	1967	Que.
Yukon Housing Corp.	1972	Yukon

	Creation Year	Prov.

Industrial Development (INDU)

Alberta Investment Fund (Inactive Sept. 1, 1977)	1965	Alta.
Alberta Opportunity Company	1972	Alta.
B.C. Development Corp.	1974	B.C.
Community Improvement Corp.	1965	N.B.
Crown Development Corp. (Inactive)	N/A	B.C.
The Discovery Foundation, Discovery Parks Inc.	1979	B.C.
E. Ontario Development Corp.	1973	Ont.
Fisheries Loan Board of Newfoundland	1949	Nfld.
Harmon Corp.	1967	Nfld.
Industrial Enterprises Incorporated	1965	P.E.I.
Industrial Estates Ltd.	1957	N.S.
Lower Churchill Development Corp. Ltd.	1978	Nfld.
Manitoba Development Corp. (Inactive—Legal Entity only)	1971	Man.
Manitoba Trading Corp.	1974	Man.
New Brunswick Development Corp.	1959	N.B.
Newfoundland Industrial Development Corp.	1967	Nfld.
Newfoundland and Lab. Development Corp.	1973	Nfld.
N. Ontario Development Corp.	1972	Ont.
N. Pickering Development Corp.	1975	Ont.
Ontario Development Corp.	1966	Ont.
Ontario Land Corp.	1974	Ont.
P.E.I. Economic Improvement Corp. (Inactive)	1966	P.E.I.
P.E.I. Lending Authority	1969	P.E.I.
Saskatchewan Econ. Development Corp.	1963	Sask.
Société d'Aménagement de l'Outaouais (SAO)	1969	Que.
Société de Developpement Immobillier du Québec (SODEVIQ)	1971	Que.
Société de Développement Industriel (SDI)	1971	Que.
Société Générale de Financement du Québec (SGF)	1962	Que.
Société du Parc Industriel du Centre du Québec (SPICQ)	1968	Que.
Société du Parc Industriel et Comm. Aéro de Mirabel (SPIC-AM)	1976	Que.
Société de Tourisme de la Baie James (Affiliated to SDBJ)	1971	Que.

Liquor (LIQU)

Alberta Liquor Control Board	1924	Alta.
B.C. Liquor Distribution Branch	1921	B.C.

	Creation Year	Prov.

Liquor (LIQU)—Continued

Liquor Control Board of Ontario	1927	Ont.
Liquor Control Commission of Manitoba	1922	Man.
New Brunswick Liquor Control	1927	N.B.
Newfoundland Liquor Corp.	1949	Nfld.
Northwest Territories Liquor System	1939	N.W.T.
Nova Scotia Liquor	1930	N.S.
P.E.I. Liquor Control	1948	P.E.I.
Province of Saskatchewan Liquor Board	1925	Sask.
Société des Alcohols du Québec (SAQ)	1921	Que.
Yukon Liquor Corp.	1970	Yukon

Lotteries (LOTT)

Atlantic Lottery	1976	Reg.
Ontario Lottery Corp.	1975	Ont.
Société des Loteries et Courses du Québec (LOTO-QUÉBEC)	1978	Que.
Western Canada Lottery	1974	Reg.

Misc. Marketing and Brokerage Facilities (MARK)

Alberta Art Foundation	1972	Alta.
B.C. Place Corp.	1980	B.C.
Centrale d'Artisant du Québec (CAQ) Private Ownership	1963	Que.
Exhibition Stadium Corp.	1975	Ont.
Fish Building Ltd. (Inactive March 31, 1976)	1966	Nfld.
Freshwater Fish Marketing Corp.	1969	Ont.
Market Development Corp.	1972	P.E.I.
Ontario Food Terminal Board	1946	Ont.
Ontario Place Corp.	1972	Ont.
Ontario Stock Yards Board	1944	Ont.
Pacific National Exhibition	1908	B.C.
Régie des Installations Olympiques (RIO)	1975	Que.
Saskatchewan Fur Marketing Service	1945	Sask.
Saskatchewan Government Printing Co.	1945	Sask.
Société de Cartographie du Québec	1969	Que.
Société de Développement Coopératif (SDC)	1977	Que.
Société Québecoise de Développement des Industries Culturelles	1978	Que.
Transportation 86 Corp.	1980	B.C.

	Creation Year	Prov.

Mineral, Mining and Development (MINE)

Manitoba Mineral Resources Ltd.	1970	Man.
NOVACO	1978	N.S.
New Brunswick Coal	N/A	N.B.
North Star Cement Corp.	1951	Nfld.
Potash Corp. of Saskatchewan	1975	Sask.
Saskatchewan Minerals	1946	Sask.
Saskatchewan Mining Development Corp.	1974	Sask.
Société de Developpement de la Baie James (SDBJ)	1971	Que.
Société Nationale de l'Amiante (SNA)	1978	Que.
Société Québecoise d'Exploration Miniére (SOQUEM)	1965	Que.

Misc. Manufacturing (MMAN)

Atlantic Gypsum Ltd.	1952	Nfld.
Burgeo Fish Industries Ltd.	1954	Nfld.
Burgeo Seafoods Ltd.	1969	Nfld.
Halifax International Containers	1977	N.S.
Hotel Building Ltd.	1966	Nfld.
Mooring Cove Building Company Ltd.	1966	Nfld.
Newfoundland Farm Products Corp.	1963	Nfld.
Raffinerie de Sucré du Québec	1943	Que.
Surrey Farm Products Investments Ltd.	1974	B.C.
United Cotton Mills Ltd.	1951	Nfld.

Municipal Financing (MUNI)

Alberta Municipal Financing Corp.	1956	Alta.
Municipal Financing Corp.	1970	Sask.
Municipalité de la Baie James (Affiliated to SDBJ)	1971	Que.
Newfoundland Municipal Finance Corp.	1964	Nfld.
Ontario Municipal Improvement Corp.	1950	Ont.

Oil and Gas Production (OILG)

Alberta Energy Corp.	1973	Alta.
B.C. Petroleum Corp.	1973	B.C.
Ontario Energy Corp.	1975	Ont.
Saskatchewan Oil and Gas Corp.	1973	Sask.
Société Québecoise d'Initiatives Pétroliéres (SOQUIP)	1969	Que.

	Creation Year	Prov.
Power Utility (POWE)		
B.C. Hydro and Power Authority	1945	B.C.
Churchill Falls (Labrador) Corp. Ltd.	1958	Nfld.
l'Hydro-Québec	1944	Que.
Manitoba Hydro	1921	Man.
New Brunswick Electric Power Commission	1920	N.B.
Newfoundland and Lab. Power Corp.	1974	Nfld.
Nova Scotia Power Corp.	1919	N.S.
Ontario Hydro	1906	Ont.
Power Distribution District of Newfoundland and Labrador	1971	Nfld.
Saskatchewan Power Corp.	1949	Sask.
Twin Falls Power Corp. Ltd.	1960	Nfld.
Research and Development (RESE)		
Alberta Agricultural Research Trust	1970	Alta.
Alberta Environmental Research Trust	1971	Alta.
Alberta Oil Sands Technology and Research Authority	1974	Alta.
B.C. Research Council	1944	B.C.
Centre de recherché Industrielle du Québec (CRIQ)	1969	Que.
Institut de Recherché de l'Hydro-Québec	1967	Que.
Manitoba Research Council	1963	Man.
NORDCO Ltd.	1975	Nfld.
New Brunswick Research and Productivity Council	1962	N.B.
Nova Scotia Research Foundation Corp.	1977	N.S.
Prairie Agricultural Machinery Institute	1974	Sask.
Research Council of Alberta	1930	Alta.
Science Council of B.C.	1978	B.C.
Schools and Hospital Financing (SCHO)		
Bell Island Hospital Building Corp.	1963	Nfld.
B.C. Educ. Institutions Capital Financing Authority	1975	B.C.
B.C. Regional Hospital Districts Financing Authority	1967	B.C.
B.C. School Districts Capital Financing Authority	1963	B.C.
Corner Brook Hospital Building Corp.	1965	Nfld.
Gander Hospitals Corp.	1961	Nfld.
Grace Hospital Extension Corp.	1962	Nfld.
Grand Falls Hospital Building Corp.	1960	Nfld.
Memorial University of Newfoundland Building Corp.	1959	Nfld.

| | *Creation* | |
	Year	*Prov.*
Northern Hospitals Building Corp.	1963	Nfld.
Nurses Training School Building Corp.	1960	Nfld.
Ontario Education Capital Aid Corp.	1966	Ont.
Ontario Universities Capital Aid Corp.	1964	Ont.
Pepperell Hospital Reconstruction Corp.	1964	Nfld.
St. John's Infirmary Building Corp.	1963	Nfld.
Technical College Building Corp.	1960	Nfld.
Vocational Schools (Western) Building Corp.	1962	Nfld.

Shipyards (SHIP)

Georgetown Shipyards	1974	P.E.I.
Marystown Shipyard Ltd.	1966	Nfld.

Steel Production (STEE)

CANSTEEL	1974	N.S.
SIDBEC	1964	Que.
SYSCO	1967	N.S.

Telephones and Communications (TELE)

Alberta Educational Communications Corp.	1973	Alta.
Alberta Government Telephone Comm.	1958	Alta.
Knowledge Network of the West Communications Authority	1980	B.C.
Manitoba Telephone System	1908	Man.
l'Office de Radio-Télé Diffusion du Québec (ORTQ)	1969	Que.
SOTEL INC. (Affiliated to SDBJ)	1971	Que.
Saskatchewan Educational Communications Corp.	1974	Sask.
Saskatchewan Telecommunications	1974	Sask.

Transportation Facilities (TFAC)

B.C. Harbours Board	1968	B.C.
Halifax-Dartmouth Bridge	1951	N.S.
New Brunswick Transportation Authority	1973	N.B.
Office des Autoroutes du Québec	1961	Que.
Ontario Transportation Development Corp. (Inactive)	1973	Ont.
Société Inter-Port de Québec		
Waterfront Development Corp.	1976	N.S.

Transportation Systems (TSYS)

Alberta Resources Railway Corp.	1965	Alta.

	Creation Year	Prov.
Transportation Systems (TSYS)—Continued		
B.C. Ferry Corp.	1976	B.C.
B.C. Railway Company	1924	B.C.
B.C. Steamship (1975) Ltd.	1975	B.C.
Metro Transit Operating Company	1980	B.C.
Ontario Northland Transportation Commission	1902	Ont.
Pacific Coach Lines Ltd.	1978	B.C.
Pacific Western Airlines	1974	Alta.
Saskatchewan Transportation Company	1946	Sask.
Société des Traversiers du Québec (STQ)	1971	Que.
T.S. Holdings Ltd.	1975	B.C.
Toronto Area Transit Operating Authority	1974	Ont.
Urban Transit Authority of B.C.	1979	B.C.
Urban Transportation Development Corp.	1974	Ont.
Water Supply (WSUP)		
Manitoba Water Services Board	1972	Man.
Saskatchewan Water Supply Board	1966	Sask.

APPENDIX III

The tables and figures in this paper are based on a common set of dimensions. These are: year of creation, party in power or opposition, total, fixed, current and other assets, population, and gross domestic product. The first section of this appendix will outline the sources of this data and the second section will provide an outline of the coverage of data used in the paper.

SOURCES

The following sources were used:

A. *Asset Data*

(1) *PCC Asset Data*—This data was developed from Annual Reports for 1976 and 1977 where possible. In some cases the PCCs do not produce annual reports or release the information publicly, or are of such recent creation that they have not yet released their first annual report. Where possible a variety of other sources were used to overcome this problem.

(2) *Corporate Asset Data*—The total corporate asset figures and the figures

for the individual corporations were obtained for the year 1977. Both figures were drawn from Statistics Canada catalogue 61-207.

(3) *Federal Government Asset Data*—This data was obtained for March 31, 1978 from Statistics Canada catalogue 68-211.

(4) *Provincial Government Asset Data*—This data was obtained for March 31, 1977 from Statistics Canada catalogue 68-209.

B. *Party in Power*

(1) *Provincial Party in Power*—This information was obtained from the Canadian Parliamentary Guide.

(2) *Provincial Party in Opposition*—Same as above.

C. *Year of Creation*

PCC Year of Creation—This was obtained from annual reports, accompanying literature, news clippings, etc.

D. *GDP*

Provincial Gross Domestic Product—This was obtained from Wood Gundy and Co., *Financial Statistics: Canada's Provinces and Representative municipalities,* Toronto, 1978.

E. *Population*

Provincial Population—This data was obtained from Canada Year Book Special Edition 1976-1977.

COVERAGE

There are two aspects of coverage that deserve discussion, discrepancies in year of data sources, and limitations on the coverage of particular data sources. The year of data sources varies in part because Crown corporations, like private corporations, have differing year ends. As a result, the PCC asset data used in this study is drawn from the period 1975 to 1979 with 80 percent of the asset data from the years 1976 and 1977.

The coverage of particular data sources can best be described as it relates to the sections of the paper. In the first most general section, "Provincial Crown Corporations in Perspective", the findings are based on the following:

233—total PCCs
231—year of creation available
231—party in power available
205—asset data available

In the second section "Provincial Utilization of The Provincial Crown Corporation" the findings are based on the following:

	Total Corps	Year of Creation Avail.	Assets of PCCs Avail.	Party in Power Avail.
Alta.	20	20	16	20
B.C.	36	35	25	35
Man.	13	13	13	13
N.B.	9	8	7	8
Nfld.	42	42	41	42
N.S.	10	10	7	10
N.W.T.	2	2	2	N.A.
Ont.	27	27	24	27
P.E.I.	10	10	9	10
Que.	35	35	32	35
Sask.	25	25	25	25
Yukon	2	2	2	N.A.
Regional	2	2	2	N.A.
	233	231	205	231

In the third section, "Functional Category Analysis" the findings are based on data opposite.

In order to compare the size of Crown corporations in a functional area as measured by total assets with the size of the economic sector in that area, corporation statistics published by Statistics Canada were used. The coverage of the Statistics Canada data is described as follows in the report,

> This report contains data on some 346,640 corporations. Included are joint ventures and partnerships of participating corporations, unincorporated branches of foreign incorporated companies, limited dividend housing corporations, other public and private corporations, federal proprietary Crown corporations and their subsidiaries, provincial Crown corporations, federal agency Crown corporations, co-operatives and municipally owned corporations. Credit unions, caisse populaires, insurance carriers, non-profit organizations and foreign business corporations are not included, nor are corporations which, for all practical purposes, can be considered inactive as they declared less than $500 in sales, assets, equity, profits and taxable income. In addition no data derived from personal income tax returns is included.

For the purposes of this study the categories into which the Statistics Canada data was classified were matched with the functional categories developed in this analysis.

	Total	Year of Creation	Asset Data	Party in Power
AGRI	13	13	13	13
BANK	5	5	4	5
FORE	13	13	13	13
GAUT	5	5	5	5
GBUI	3	3	3	3
GCOM	4	4	4	4
HOUS	18	18	17	18
INDU	31	30	26	30
LIQU	12	12	12	12
LOTT	4	4	4	4
MARK	18	18	12	18
MINE	10	9	7	9
MMAN	10	10	9	10
MUNI	5	5	5	5
OILG	5	5	5	5
POWE	11	11	11	11
RESE	13	13	8	13
SCHO	17	17	17	17
SHIP	2	2	2	2
STEE	3	3	2	3
TELE	8	8	7	8
TFAC	7	7	6	7
TSYS	14	14	11	14
WSUP	2	2	2	2
	233	231	205	231

As can be seen from the results in Table A-I, it was not possible to obtain a close match in all categories because the Statistics Canada data is more aggregated. However, with the exception of Miscellaneous Manufacturing a match has been made and forms the basis for the comparison summarized in Table XII in the main text.

TABLE A—I

Categories of Corporations Used for Asset Comparison

Functional Area	Sic Code	Stats. Can. Corporate Categories
Agriculture 721,727	729	Other credit agencies
	781	Insurance and real estate agencies
Banking	712	Chartered banks
	713	Quebec Savings Banks
	718	Savings Banks
721,727	729	Other credit agencies
Forest Development	251-259	Wood industries
& Manufacturing	261-268	Furniture and fixture industries
	271-274	Total paper and allied industries
General & Auto Insurance	781	Insurance and real estate agencies
Government Buildings	791,793	Real estate operators and developers
Govt. Computer Services	861-869	To total services to business management
Housing	404	Building construction
	715	Mortgage loan companies
	791,793	Real estate operators and developers
Industrial Development	721-729	Total Credit Agencies
Liquor	696	Liquor, wine and beer stores
	699	Retail stores, n.e.s.
Lotteries	851	Motion picture theatres and film exchanges
	853	Bowling alleys and billiard parlours
	859	Other recreational services
Minerals, Mining &	051-059	Metal mines
Development	061	Coal mines
	071-099	Non-metal mines, quarries and sand putts, services incidental to mining
Miscellaneous	101-139	Food industries
Manufacturing	161-169	Rubber industries
	183,193,197	Cotton yarn, cloth and woolen mills
	271-274	Paper and allied industries
Municipal Finance 721,727	729	Other credit agencies
Oil and Gas Production	064	Oil and gas wells
	092-099	Mining Services
Power Utilities	572-579	Electric power, gas and water utilities

Functional Area	Sic Code	Stats. Can. Corporate Categories
Research & Development	864	Engineering and scientific service
School & Hospital Financing	721	Export finance
	727	Business financing corporations
	729	Other credit agencies
Shipyards	326	Railroad rolling stock industry
	327	Shipbuilding and repair
	328	Boatbuilding and repair
	329	Miscellaneous vehicle manufacturers
Steel	291	Iron and steel mills
	292	Steel pipe and tube mills
Telephones & Comm.	543-548	Communication industry
Transport Facilities	501-519	Transportation industry
Water Supply Transport Systems	576	Water systems
	501-519	Transportation industry
	579	Other utilities

CHAPTER 6

A CASE STUDY OF PUBLIC ENTERPRISE: GRAY COACH LINES LTD.

JOHN PALMER*
JOHN QUINN
RAY RESENDES

I. INTRODUCTION

In Chapter 2 of this volume, Borcherding provided an up-to-date summary of the literature concerning the behaviour of public enterprises and some extensions of the theoretical models that have been offered by scholars in the field. We adapt these models, and some logical extensions, to a specific case—that of Gray Coach, Ltd., which is owned entirely by the Toronto Transit Commission (TTC), an independent subdivision of the Metropolitan Toronto political structure. The major purpose of this study is to provide some empirical confirmation for a positive theory of managerial behaviour in public enterprise. Section II contains a description of Gray Coach, Ltd.; it outlines the chain of political authority, and relates it to the management of the TTC and Gray Coach. It also describes the southwestern Ontario market for inter-city bus passenger service, including the supply and demand conditions, as well as a description of some of the competition in the market. In Section III we develop our theory and relate it to the political, institutional, and economic forces shaping the decisions of the TTC-Gray Coach management. The theory assumes that the managers of public enterprises sell their products and/or services in a market which often offers reasonably close substitutes, and that they are accountable (albeit weakly) to a legislative authority.

The general model developed in Section III relies on foundations provided by three different areas of economic analysis: property rights, mana-

* The authors are, respectively, Associate Professor of Economics and Director of the Centre for Economic Analysis of Property Rights, University of Western Ontario, Associate Professor of Law, Osgoode Hall Law School, York University and member of the firm of Osler, Hoskin & Harcourt. Research assistance was provided by Heather Crisp. Helpful comments were received from Bruce Feldthusen, Stan Liebowitz, Steven Margolis, Geoffrey Carliner, John Nordin, and from numerous members of the industry.

gerialism, and political economy. The results of previous work in these areas are blended together with the specific institutional facts presented in Section I to generate empirically testable hypotheses concerning the behaviour of public firms. In Section IV we present the results of our tests of these hypotheses. Although we have sufficient concerns about the reliability of some of the data employed in these tests that we would not place much confidence in any one of them alone, the preponderance of evidence is so strong that the results of all the tests, taken as a whole, cannot be dismissed. We find that Gray Coach has been operated in such a fashion as to create substantial allocative distortions and sizeable redistributions of wealth.

Several features of Gray Coach's institutional environment make it an especially attractive subject for a detailed case study. First, the firm sells its services to customers who, for the most part, are not members of the political constituency to which the firm is ultimately responsible. This divergence between the scope of the firm's market and the determinants of the political controls to which it is subject give rise to some interesting potential for conflict in managerial incentives; Sections III and IV explore the behavioural implications of conflicts between political and market incentives. Moreover, the case study was initiated about one year after Gray Coach was informed forcefully, though perhaps not explicitly, that the provincial regulatory body, the Ontario Highway Transport Board (OHTB), would no longer guarantee it freedom from entry competition on lucrative routes to enable its cross-subsidization of unprofitable routes. While the firm may previously have been operating under what it believed to be regulatory pressure to engage in cross-subsidization, it could no longer be under that impression, and we were curious as to how it would respond to the removal of this perceived constraint.

One final point that we wish to emphasize is that although our theory and results are fairly cynical in their attribution of complex and apparently nefarious designs to the management of Gray Coach and the TTC, such is probably not the case. Each of the authors has done enough research concerning industries experiencing considerable political involvement to be able to say that generally the managers involved are sincere in their belief that they are promoting social welfare. We suspect, however, that as rational humans with utility functions similar to those of most people, these managers are merely responding in a predictable manner to the incentives offered them and only behave *as if* they are not concerned about the societal good. This observation points out the necessity for careful consideration of the incentives offered to managers in such firms. We hope that our part of the study, and the study as a whole, will help advance the behavioural knowledge that economists, lawyers and politicians require for the design of institutions which can accommodate private motives while creating incentives more closely linked to the promotion of social objectives.

II. GRAY COACH LINES LTD.—INTERNAL STRUCTURE, MARKET AND POLITICAL ENVIRONMENT

(a) Gray Coach Lines Ltd.

Gray Coach Lines Ltd. is a wholly owned subsidiary of the Toronto Transit Commission (TTC), an independent municipal authority, which provides most forms of public transportation within the Toronto metropolitan area.[1] Gray Coach was incorporated in 1927 by the TTC's predecessor, the Toronto Transportation Commission. When motor bus transport was first introduced in the early 1920s, private operators established bus lines in competition with the interurban electric railways then operating in Toronto. The private bus operators were also carrying local passengers into the city centre and diverting patronage from the publicly owned municipal transit system. In order to eliminate this source of competition, the city secured amendments to the *Toronto Radial Railway Act, 1921*[2] which authorized the Commission to purchase the assets of the private bus lines. The Commission subsequently organized a separate corporation, Gray Coach Lines Ltd., to assume the assets and functions of the private carriers which had operated inter-city routes radiating from Toronto.[3] The Commission justified its acquisition of a monopoly over inter-city carriage on the ground that the bus service would attract profitable tourist trade to Toronto.[4] The Commission also asserted that Gray Coach's operations would complement its municipal services by facilitating the realization of economies of scale and specialization in maintenance and repair functions.[5]

The capital structure of Gray Coach consists solely of common shares —there is no debt capital. In terms of relative firm size, Gray Coach is dwarfed by the TTC. In 1977, the TCC held assets with a book value of $118,508,000 and had total expenditures of $179,981,000;[6] Gray Coach held assets with a book value of $15,883,000 and had total expenditures of $26,928,000.[7] Gray Coach is, however, one of the largest firms in its in-

---

[1] *Municipality of Metropolitan Toronto Act*, R.S.O. 1980, c. 314, ss. 98-115.

[2] S.O. 1921, c. 24 as amended by S.O. 1927, cc. 58 and 134, ss. 4-5.

[3] Toronto Transit Commission. *Transit in Toronto: The story of the development of public transportation in Toronto, from horse cars to a modern, high speed subway system* (Toronto: Toronto Transit Commission, 1976) at 11-12.

[4] Toronto Transit Commission. *Wheels of Progress: a story of the development of Toronto and its public transportation services* [Toronto: Toronto Transit Commission, 1940] at 69. Gray Coach Lines, Ltd. was incorporated June 28th 1927 as a subsidiary of the TTC.

[5] *Ibid.*, at 71.

[6] Toronto Transit Commission: *1977 Annual Report* (Toronto: Toronto Transit Commission, 1978) at 7-9.

[7] Gray Coach Lines, Ltd. *Annual Report 1977* (Toronto: Gray Coach Lines, 1978) at 5-6. Since 1978 it has been the company's policy not to release their Annual Reports to the general public.

dustry. With gross revenues of $26,483,000 in 1977 from its interurban and suburban services, the firm ranked as the third largest bus carrier in Canada.[8]

Gray Coach provides interurban passenger and freight service along a broad route system radiating out in a spoke-like manner from Toronto. The system's terminal points include London, Buffalo, North Bay, Sudbury and Owen Sound. Some intermediate points with fairly heavy traffic include Barrie, Orillia, Guelph, Kitchener and St. Catharines. In 1977, Gray Coach's interurban passenger and freight services accounted for 43 percent of its total revenue.[9] In addition to its regularly scheduled interurban service, Gray Coach derives a significant proportion of its total revenue (15 percent in 1977) from the operation of charter trips and sightseeing tours.[10]

About 32 percent of Gray Coach's revenues are attributable to its suburban commuter runs.[11] These services are provided on a cost-plus basis under a contract with the Toronto Area Transit Operating Authority (TATOA), a provincial Crown corporation. TATOA was established by the provincial legislature in 1974 to provide integrated rail-bus commuter service in the area adjacent to the municipal limits of Metropolitan Toronto.[12] Gray Coach was awarded the contract because it held the original operating licenses (issued in 1926) for the routes which TATOA now serves. TATOA is wholly funded by the provincial government. The Authority performs its own maintenance and repair functions and supplies a substantial proportion of the buses employed in its commuter system.

Gray Coach's suburban commuter operations, performed under contract with TATOA, are generally excluded from direct consideration in this study. The privately owned bus carriers operating in Ontario do not provide services comparable to Gray Coach's commuter services. Because of significant disparities in the revenue and cost characteristics of suburban and interurban route systems, direct performance comparisons with the private interurban carriers would be very difficult. Moreover, Gray Coach performs its commuter services for the province on a cost-plus basis under the direct supervision of TATOA. These unique institutional factors would render any comparative analysis inherently suspect.

Gray Coach owns its main terminal facility, located on Bay Street in Toronto. In addition to its main terminal, the firm owns other terminals at major points in its route system, such as Barrie, North Bay and Guelph. At other points, Gray Coach rents terminal space; the company, in turn, leases a substantial amount of owned terminal space to other bus lines.

---

[8] *Ibid.*, at 5.

[9] *Ibid.*, at 5-6.

[10] *Ibid.*

[11] *Ibid.*

[12] *Toronto Area Transit Operating Authority Act, 1974,* S.O. 1974, c. 69, proclaimed in force June 28, 1974; now R.S.O. 1980, c. 505.

Buses constitute, by far, the firm's largest asset category, accounting for 64 percent of total invested capital in 1977. The Gray Coach bus fleet, excluding the vehicles used to operate the TATOA commuter system, numbered 184 in 1977. The company's vehicle stock had an average age of 5.9 years.[13]

The internal structure of Gray Coach has been primarily shaped by the firm's subordinate relationship to the TTC. During the period covered by our study, the Gray Coach board was composed of all five TTC commissioners and five of Gray Coach's senior managers. The TTC commissioners, all Metro Council appointees who pursued full-time careers in addition to their Commission responsibilities, were either prominent citizens with a background in municipal politics or career civil servants. The five senior Gray Coach managers were also officers and employees of the TTC, dividing their managerial efforts between the Commission and Gray Coach. The only full-time senior manager of Gray Coach, Mr. Musgrove, did not sit on the Board of Directors. Since our study began, the Board's membership has been altered with the objective of increasing its regional representation, and to increase the firm's responsiveness to communities outside Toronto. The reorganized Board is now composed of two TTC commissioners: the Chairman, Mr. Porter (a Toronto lawyer and political figure), and Mr. Warren (the general manager of the TTC); Mr. Kearns (the first full-time president of Gray Coach), Mr. Hicks (a Toronto lawyer), and two regional representatives appointed by the TTC.

It should be emphasized that there is a substantial identity of senior management between Gray Coach and the TTC. Examples of this overlap in senior positions are the offices of General Counsel, Secretary and Treasurer, which were at the time of our study, filled by the same people in both organizations. The working time of the TTC-Gray Coach management is generally allocated between the two firms as the need arises, with the result that most of their time is devoted to Commission matters. Management expenses are prorated between the firms on a loose "percentage-of-time-worked" basis.[14]

The TTC supplies approximately 75 percent of Gray Coach's financial and administrative services. The TTC personnel department hires, transfers and fires Gray Coach employees. All Gray Coach employees receive TTC paycheques. Most of Gray Coach's accounting and legal services are performed by TTC personnel. Moreover, all maintenance and repair services for Gray Coach vehicles are supplied by the TTC in the Commission's garage facilities. The TTC's transfer prices for these services are determined by a "time-worked" allocation formula. Although the practise may vary

---

[13] Gray Coach, *supra* note 7, at 5-6.
[14] Interview with Mr. Terence Hancock, Chief Accountant, Treasury Department, Toronto Transit Commission.

slightly between departments, TTC accountants estimate the actual time spent in performing Gray Coach-related services on a departmental basis and calculate an appropriate transfer price on the basis of each department's wage, supplies and overhead expenses.[15] In 1977, administrative costs transferred from the TTC to Gray Coach totalled about $3,500,000. These transferred services constituted about 12 percent of Gray Coach's total operating expenses in 1977.[16] It should be noted that shortly after the commencement of the study, some administrative services, such as budgeting and purchasing were being increasingly performed in-house by Gray Coach personnel. All Gray Coach's maintenance and repair requirements are still supplied by the TTC. In 1977, transfer charges to Gray Coach for maintenance and repair services constituted 7 percent of Gray Coach's total operating expenses.

Gray Coach's own personnel are primarily responsible for route scheduling, planning and direct operations. Bus drivers constitute the most numerous employee category at Gray Coach; in 1977, this group accounted for 62 percent of Gray Coach's total employees. All drivers are, in fact, hired, trained and paid by the TTC. The drivers' union, the Amalgamated Transit Workers Union, also represents all of the TTC's unionized employees. The TTC bargains with the union on behalf of Gray Coach. Since the conditions of interurban driving render some of the provisions in the TTC agreement inappropriate for Gray Coach drivers, the firm's drivers are covered in a special appendix to the collective agreement. Wage rates are roughly the same for unionized staff in both firms.

Gray Coach also employs ticket agents at many of its regularly scheduled stops on a commission basis.

(b) The Market for Inter-City Bus Transportation in Ontario

Most interurban bus routes in Ontario are assigned on an exclusive basis to either Gray Coach or a private carrier by the Ontario Highway Transport Board. The regulatory scheme and its effect on intra-modal competition will be discussed later. First, however, the general contours of the market must be described. This section identifies the major inter-city bus firms operating within, or in a close proximity to, the Gray Coach route system; it also provides a brief description of the key sources of inter-modal competition in Gray Coach's market area.

Gray Coach's principal rival is Eastern Canadian Greyhound Lines, a wholly owned subsidiary of Greyhound Lines of Canada Ltd. Greyhound Lines of Canada Ltd. is a privately owned inter-city carrier, headquartered

---

15 *Ibid.*
16 Gray Coach, *supra* note 7, at 8.

in Calgary. With combined revenues from its passenger, freight and charter operations of $75 million in 1978, Greyhound ranks as the largest bus carrier in Canada.[17] The firm's Canadian operations are carried on through several wholly owned regional subsidiaries. For example, passenger and freight services in Alberta and British Columbia are provided by Coachways System Ltd., a regional subsidiary of Greyhound Lines. Eastern Canadian Greyhound Lines provides passenger, freight and charter service throughout Ontario. Eastern Canadian Greyhound's route system is largely restricted to major centres on the main highway corridors radiating from Toronto, such as Windsor, London, Chatham, Brantford and Hamilton. In late 1977, Eastern Canadian Greyhound was granted operating licenses to provide express passenger service between Sudbury and Toronto and Buffalo and Toronto in direct competition with Gray Coach. Since these routes are the most profitable part of the Gray Coach system, Eastern Greyhound is now Gray Coach's primary competitor.

Voyageur Ltd., is a privately owned inter-city bus carrier, headquartered in Montreal. The firm is a wholly owned subsidiary of Canada Steamship Lines, which in turn is controlled by Power Corporation. Voyageur Ltd. has one wholly owned subsidiary, Voyageur Colonial. Together these two inter-city bus carriers rank as the second largest bus line in Canada.[18] Voyageur Ltd. is a major interurban carrier in Quebec; Voyageur Colonial operates regularly scheduled inter-city services between major centres in eastern Ontario. Voyageur Colonial serves Ottawa, Peterborough, Oshawa, Toronto, and smaller cities in eastern Ontario. It does not provide any notable direct competition to Gray Coach.

Travelways Ltd. is a privately owned inter-city bus carrier, headquartered in Toronto. It is a relatively small bus line, and its route system is mainly restricted to points in the resort areas north and west of Toronto. Some of the firm's major regularly scheduled stops are Peterborough, Haliburton, Huntsville, and Orillia. Travelways does provide some direct competition for Gray Coach, especially on the Orillia and Barrie to Toronto portions of its route system.

Charterways Ltd. is a small privately owned inter-city carrier, operating from London, Ontario. Charterways provides regularly scheduled service to Sarnia, Windsor, Kitchener and Owen Sound, on a route system which radiates from its London headquarters. The firm's route system is characterized by numerous intermediate stops in small towns and villages. Charterways does not provide any direct competition to Gray Coach.

---

[17] Rea, J.C. et al., "Inter-city Passenger Transportation in Canada: A Quantitative Comparison of Strategies" (an unpublished paper prepared for the Economic and Regional Analysis Directorate, Strategic Planning Group, Transport Canada, Ottawa, 1975) at 20.
[18] *Ibid.*, at 22.

Gray Coach faces inter-modal competition throughout its route system from railroads, commercial air carriers, and the private auto. Canadian National Railways and Canadian Pacific Railways provide extensive rail passenger and freight service throughout Gray Coach's market area. Their combined transcontinental passenger service, called VIA RAIL, serves about 78 percent of the regularly scheduled stops in Gray Coach's route system.[19] The intensity of the competition offered by VIA RAIL differs from route to route throughout the Gray Coach system, depending on the relative frequency of train service to various centres. For example, Gray Coach faces fairly stiff competition on its London route because VIA RAIL provides frequent regular service to major cities and towns along that route. In other portions of its system where train service is relatively infrequent (*e.g.*, the Sudbury route), Gray Coach faces very little rail competition.

All inter-city bus lines face strong competition from the private auto. The intensity of this competition varies depending on such factors as trip length, traffic congestion, parking costs and convenience, or door-to-door travel time. It should also be noted that bus transportation is generally regarded as an inferior good; in an era of steadily rising personal incomes, inter-city bus transit has suffered from a steady decline in demand as former bus passengers switched to the private auto. For relatively short trips, despite the very competitive position of the bus mode in terms of seat/mile costs, the greater convenience and flexibility of the auto make bus transit a much less attractive substitute. There is some evidence that consumers regard the bus as a somewhat more attractive alternative to the auto as trip length and travel time increase.[20]

Over longer trip lengths, the unit costs of air travel decline to a level roughly comparable to those of rail and bus travel.[21] Given the relatively short trip lengths throughout most of the Gray Coach route system, commercial airlines would seem to offer little competition to the bus carriers. Air transport may, however, offer some limited competition on a few of Gray Coach's longest runs—London to Toronto or Sudbury to Toronto. Even on these routes, the relatively high cost and lengthy door-to-door travel time for regularly scheduled commercial air services will often make it only marginally more attractive than the bus. It should also be noted that many smaller Ontario communities are fairly remote from airports which receive regularly scheduled commercial air service.

(c) The Toronto Transit Commission

The TTC was first established in 1921 as a politically independent and

---

[19] See Section IV of this chapter, "Performance Aspects of Gray Coach", *infra* at 401.
[20] Rea, *supra* note 17, at 63-68.
[21] *Ibid.*, at 64.

financially autonomous corporation with statutory authority to create and manage a public transit system in Toronto. Although the Commission acquired some additional responsibilities when the provincial legislature adopted a regional form of municipal government for the Toronto metropolitan area in 1954, its formal structure is still the same as it was in 1921. The Commission has five members; each member's appointment must be ratified by a "special bylaw" of the Metro Toronto Council. The enactment of a "special bylaw" requires an affirmative vote of two-thirds of the councillors present and voting. A commission appointment carries a rather small salary, which is fixed by Metro Council.[22] Service on the Commission has always been regarded as a strictly part-time affair, a prestigious "civic duty". All of the recent Commissioners have been prominent lawyers, businessmen or municipal civil servants who have continued to carry on their normal occupations during their tenure in office. The Commissioner's three-year terms are staggered and renewable, subject to the required two-thirds vote of Council. During the 1950s and early 1960s, the TTC was the focus of a hot political battle between the largely urban supporters of the Commission's ambitious subway projects and the suburban interests who favoured more expressways and commuter buses. Now that the subways have been completed, the Commission's visibility as a political forum has declined. One prominent student of the Commission has characterized its orientation a basically "administrative" and rather apolitical.[23]

The Commission operates a huge urban transportation complex which includes bus, trolley and subway services for the entire Metro area. The TTC's chief concern in recent years has been its growing operating deficit, attributable to both declining patronage and rapid cost increases.[24] Thus, the politics of municipal transit at the TTC are now largely the politics of subsidization—who will pay the subsidy and how much?

The provincial government provides some funding for every municipal transit system in Ontario under a rather complex scheme established by the *Highway Improvement Amendment Act, 1971*.[25] The municipal transit subsidy fund, administered by the Ministry of Transportation and Communications, is allocated among the province's municipalities under a revenue-expense ratio formula which varies according to the size of the city's population. Under the existing formula established by the Ministry, a city of 100,000-150,000 is assigned a revenue-cost ratio "target" of 55 percent, and the province funds one-half of the "targeted deficit". This means that the province will pay 22.5 percent of the city's total transit operating costs. Generally, the provincial subsidy decreases as the size of the city increases;

---

[22] *Municipality of Metropolitan Toronto Act*, R.S.O. 1980, c. 314, s. 100(11).

[23] Kaplan, "The Toronto Transit Commission: A Case Study of the Structural-Functional Approach to Administrative Organizations" (1967), 33 *Can. J. of Econ. and Pol. Sc.* 171.

[24] Toronto Transit Commission, *supra* note 6, at 21-22.

[25] S.O. 1971, c. 67, s. 14 [am. 1973 c. 67, s. 21(1)]; now *Public Transportation and Highway Improvement Act*, R.S.O. 1980, c. 421, ss. 94-95.

for example, the maximum subsidy for a city of 201,000-1,000,000 is 17.5 percent of total transit costs (*i.e.*, the city's cost-revenue target is set at 65 percent). Moreover the provincial subsidy remains the same regardless of whether the municipality falls short of or exceeds its targeted deficit ratio. Thus, if a system manages to cut its deficit below the targeted ratio, the city's share of the subsidy burden is reduced by an equal amount.

Since Toronto is so much larger than other Ontario municipalities, its deficit target has been the subject of direct negotiation between Metro and the province. Metro's revenue-cost ratio target has been fixed at 72.5 percent for the last several years. In 1977, the province also agreed to pay a special three-year subsidy to help Metro meet the costs of the new Spadina subway line. This subsidy, which expired in December, 1980, brought the total current provincial subsidy up to approximately 15 percent of total system costs, and reduced the effective cost-revenue target to about 70 percent.[26] In the last two years, however, the TTC's ridership has been decreasing, and relatively sharp fare increases have been used to keep the TTC's revenues near the 70 percent target. In 1977, when the TTC's revenue-cost target was 70 percent, the province provided about $27 million, which was approximately 14 percent of TTC operating expenses. In the same year, Metro paid a subsidy of about $32 million, which was about 16.3 percent of total operating expenses.[27] It should be noted that the provincial subsidy is specifically earmarked for the support of municipal transit services and cannot be diverted to fund operating deficits incurred in the provision of other transportation services. Provincial auditors check the accounts of municipal systems to insure that the conditions of eligibility for the subsidy are satisfied.

The architects of the TTC were progressive reformers who believed that a financially and politically independent public transit authority would best achieve a high degree of responsiveness to public needs and the efficiency of a private business. With chronic annual operating deficits, it is clear that the TTC's fiscal independence is a thing of the past. Moreover, fiscal independence and political autonomy are strongly interrelated. In recent years, as the TTC subsidy burden has steadily increased, Metro Toronto has subjected the TTC's financial affairs to increasingly strict scrutiny and has used other strategies to secure a greater degree of control over TTC management.

Metropolitan Toronto, a regional municipal corporation, is governed by a Council which is composed of representatives from the City of Toronto, and the six surrounding area municipalities. Metro councillors are elected from the councils of each of the constituent municipalities; representation in the Metro Council is apportioned on the basis of the populations

---

[26] Toronto Transit Commission, *supra* note 6, at 10.
[27] *Ibid.*

of the constituent municipalities. Metro Council's most important control over the TTC is its power to appoint the Commission's members. Since appointment to the Commission requires an affirmative vote by two-thirds of Metro Council, a successful candidate must secure the support of both the urban and suburban blocs of the Council. It is also important to note that one of the five TTC Commissioners, Paul Godfrey, has been for several years the Chairman of Metro Council, the chief executive officer and de facto political leader of Metro.

Metro Council also engages in a detailed review of TTC operations as a part of its annual budgetary process. The Commission is required by statute to submit an annual report to Metro Council, accompanied by audited financial statements. Metro Council employs two full-time auditors to monitor the TTC accounts. A standing Committee of Council, the joint Metro-TTC Planning Committee, reviews the Commission's report and financial statements annually. The TTC report and financial statements are included as agenda items for Council's budget debates. Municipal officials, in interviews with the authors, indicated that the political saliency of TTC's finances is largely attributable to the Commission's large operating deficits. These deficits, as indicated earlier in our discussion of the provincial subsidy scheme, are financed in roughly equal proportions by provincial and municipal revenues. Since the TTC possesses neither taxing nor borrowing powers, it is wholly dependent on the Metro and provincial governments to meet its current account deficits. The especially large TTC deficits in recent years have aroused some sharp criticism of TTC management in Metro Council, especially from suburban councillors whose constituents generally benefit least from TTC services.

Curiously, Gray Coach's financial affairs seem to receive no attention in Metro Council debates on the TTC's annual subsidies. Several officials interviewed by the authors stated that they could not recall a single occasion upon which Gray Coach's financial performance was discussed in Council proceedings.[28] Audited financial statements for Gray Coach, as a wholly separate accounting entity, are included with the TTC's annual report to Metro Council; the TTC also prepares a separate annual report for Gray Coach, with full audited financial statements, for limited public distribution. In the past few years, Gray Coach has paid only negligible dividends to its sole shareholder, the TTC. Since Gray Coach accounting profits, which have also been negligible in recent years, would have the consequence of reducing the Metro subsidy to the Commission without affecting the size of the provincial grant, it is somewhat surprising that Gray Coach's poor profit record has not received more critical attention in Council budget debates. Perhaps Gray Coach's small size in relation to the huge TTC

---

[28] Interview with Mr. R. Biggart, Administrative Assistant to Metro Chairman, Toronto City Hall.

system, and the fact that very few Metro taxpayers regularly use its services, account for its lack of political visibility.

(d) The Ontario Highway Transit Board and the Regulatory System

(i) Entry Regulation

Entry and fare regulation by the provincial government has shaped both the structure and conduct of the interurban bus industry in Ontario. Responsibility for the administration of the provincial regulatory scheme is divided between the Ontario Highway Transit Board (OHTB) and the Ministry of Transportation and Communications (MTC). Under the *Public Vehicles Act*,[29] the OHTB controls entry into the interurban bus industry through a system of route licensing applicable to all bus carriers operating in Ontario. The Minister of Transportation and Communications exercises statutory authority over rates charged by all interurban carriers for passenger, freight and charter services, although the OHTB assists the Ministry by conducting hearings on fare change applications and providing the MTC with factual findings and recommendations in rate cases. It should be noted that Gray Coach, although it is wholly owned by the TTC, is subject to precisely the same entry and rate controls as the private firms in the industry.

The OHTB is a quasi-judicial body which exercises regulatory jurisdiction over the intra- and extra-provincial "for hire" trucking industry in addition to its duties relating to intercity bus carriers.[30] Only about 10 percent of the Board's caseload involves matters relating to bus carriers.[31] The Board's members are appointed by the Lieutenant-Governor in Council; at the time of this study the Board was composed of a chairman, two vice-chairmen, and seven other members. The OHTB's enabling statute permits any single member to hear and dispose of any application or reference to the Board.[32] OHTB hearings are rather formal trial-type proceedings; they inevitably follow an adversary pattern with bus carriers holding existing operating licenses opposing the license applications of potential competitors. There are generally two avenues of appeal from a final decision of the Board. Upon the petition of an "interested party," the provincial Cabinet may confirm, rescind or vary any Board decision, or require the

[29] R.S.O. 1980, c. 425.
[30] *Ontario Highway Transport Board Act*, R.S.O. 1980, c. 338.
[31] Bonsor, "The Development of Regulation in the Highway Trucking Industry in Ontario" in Ontario Economic Council. *Government Regulation: Issues and Alternatives* (Toronto: Ontario Economic Council, 1978).
[32] *Supra* note 30, s. 6.

Board to rehear the case. In addition, an appeal lies from a Board decision to the Ontario Court of Appeal, but only on a "question of law".[33]

Regulatory control over entry into the Ontario inter-city bus industry is effected through a comprehensive system of route licensing. Licenses, which are usually referred to as "operating authorities" in the industry, are required not only for regularly scheduled passenger and freight operations, but also for ancillary activities such as the provision of charter and tour services.[34] The operating authorities issued by the OHTB are always limited to specific routes. Some licenses may allow the carrier to serve all points along the approved route, while other operating authorities may restrict the points at which regularly scheduled stops may be made, or the number of daily trips provided along the route. Since the composition of the inter-city bus industry in Ontario is very stable, most of the Board's caseload involves applications for extensions or modifications of existing licenses, which generally pose only negligible threats of potential competition to other established carriers. The legal standard which governs the Board's disposition of all license applications is whether ". . . public necessity and convenience . . ." would be served by the grant of an operating authority.[35] The legal effect of the public necessity and convenience standard is that the Board possesses very broad discretion in the formation of regulatory policy. Since Board orders only rarely contain any coherent articulation of its decisional criteria, the best evidence of its regulatory objectives can be obtained from its public pronouncements and from published accounts of interviews with Board members. Generally, the Board views its goal in entry regulation as ensuring ". . . a competitive balance . . ." while avoiding ". . . a destructive over-supply of carriers . . .".[36] This concern with the dangers of "destructive competition" in the transportation industry is, of course, the traditional rationale for entry control in the bus industry, and is consistent with the legislative history of the Ontario regulatory scheme. Prior to its seminal decision in the Greyhound-Gray Coach entry dispute of 1976-77, the OHTB had generally followed a policy of exclusivity with respect to routes for regularly scheduled inter-city passenger and freight services.[37] With its decision in the Greyhound-Gray Coach case, the Board signaled a departure from this long-standing policy.

---

[33] *Supra* note 30, s. 23.

[34] The OHTB also exercises control over inter-city charter bus service. Unless prohibited by the terms of his operating license, a licensee may operate a public vehicle on any chartered trip originating from a point on the highway designated in his license or from any other point on a competitor's route so long as that other licensee does not maintain a public vehicle at that point or within ten miles thereof. Although there is no legal requirement that a carrier run regularly scheduled service over routes that he wishes to obtain charter rights for, there does appear to be a *de facto* requirement that charter rights are to be conditional upon the provision of regularly scheduled service to the area for which charter rights are sought.

[35] *Public Vehicles Act, supra* note 29, s. 6.

[36] Bonsor, *supra* note 30.

[37] *Ibid.*

Prior to the filing of Greyhound's license applications, Gray Coach held exclusive operating rights to the two most heavily traveled routes in the Ontario market—the Toronto-Buffalo and Toronto-Sudbury routes. At that time, Greyhound had a pooling agreement with Gray Coach, designed to eliminate the inconvenience to passengers of having to change buses in Sudbury and Buffalo, which are also terminal points on Greyhound's inter-continental route system. A passenger traveling from, for example, Van-couver to Toronto would ride a Greyhound bus along Greyhound's Trans-Canada route to Sudbury. At Sudbury, a Gray Coach driver would take charge of the Greyhound bus and continue the trip to Toronto. The same arrangement was employed by the firms at their ''inter-line'' connection in Buffalo. The fares for these ''inter-line'' trips were set by agreement be-tween the two carriers, and passenger and freight revenues were shared ac-cording to a formula in the inter-line agreement. In the summer of 1976, Greyhound, apparently recognizing the opportunities for large profits on these heavily traveled routes, or perhaps unhappy with the driver-exchange system as a link in its transcontinental route, applied for licenses to provide regularly scheduled service on these routes in direct competition with Gray Coach. A hearing on Greyhound's license applications was held by the Board in the fall of 1976; Gray Coach intervened in the proceeding and vigorously opposed the Greyhound applications.

Greyhound's arguments in support of its application focused on its ability to improve the quality of passenger and freight service on the Sud-bury—Toronto and Buffalo-Toronto routes.[38] Greyhound asserted that its inter-line arrangements with Gray Coach were not functioning in a satisfac-tory manner and adduced evidence of passenger complaints of delays and scheduling problems. Greyhound also argued that passengers who traveled these routes were not being offered a sufficient number of non-stop or ex-press trips. The petitioner offered only fragmentary and rather weak con-sumer survey evidence on this latter point. Moreover, it offered no convinc-ing explanation for Gray Coach's failure to provide additional express ser-vice, if in fact a sufficient demand for increased express service existed. It should be noted that Greyhound did *not* argue that it could provide the same or better service than Gray Coach at lower fares. Members of the in-dustry, and at least one academic commentator, have observed that the Board is generally unreceptive to arguments for entry based on the potential for price competition.[39] Perhaps, this is the reason why Greyhound avoided any discussion of lower fares in its arguments to the Board.

Gray Coach denied Greyhound's allegations concerning deficiencies in the service offered on its Buffalo-Toronto and Sudbury-Toronto routes and argued that there was insufficient demand to justify additional express

---

[38] Greyhound brief to the OHTB, 1976.
[39] Bonsor, *supra* note 30.

trips.[40] Its main rebuttal argument, however, focused on the claim that Greyhound was attempting to "skim the cream" from its route system. Gray Coach asserted that many of its routes, essentially those serving sparsely populated rural areas, were unremunerative and that the firm required the profits from its more heavily traveled routes to subsidize its rural services.[41] It should be recognized that arguments against allowing the entry of potential competitors on "cream-skimming" grounds are notoriously difficult to verify empirically.[42] For example, in this case, Gray Coach never really distinguished between its short-run average total costs of providing service along the rural routes and its long-run marginal costs of providing those services. But assuming that the rural routes were generating revenues below their marginal costs of operation, there was implicit in the Gray Coach argument an assertion that the OHTB had endorsed, at least tacitly, a policy of cross-subsidization—a policy which required Gray Coach to use its profits from the main Toronto runs to subsidize rural riders.[43] Counsel for Gray Coach characterized the Board's tacit policy of cross-subsidization as "long-standing" and argued that a reversal of such an important policy should be a matter for legislative resolution.[44] The only substantive gap in Gray Coach's argument was its inability to identify any Board regulation or order which required the firm to continue to provide service on its rural routes as a condition to maintaining its licenses for the more profitable routes.

Greyhound countered Gray Coach's "cream-skimming" argument with the assertion that many of Gray Coach's rural routes could be operated profitably by a more efficient carrier. While Greyhound admitted that some of the rural routes generated revenues that were below the industry "break-even" averages, it argued that the average firm in the industry could realize a normal rate of return on most of Gray Coach's rural routes. Greyhound adduced a great quantity of economic evidence which depicted Gray Coach as a "high-cost operator" in the industry. Most of the evidence employed standard productivity ratios to compare the operating performance of Gray Coach and Greyhound with average performance data for the industry in North America.[45] The evidence generally portrayed Greyhound as one of the industry's most efficient firms, while Gray Coach was shown to have costs well above the industry's average cost levels. The basic thrust of Greyhound's counter-argument was that Gray Coach could meet the potential competition on its more profitable runs by improving the efficiency of its

---

[40] Gray Coach petition to the Cabinet, 1977.
[41] *Ibid.*
[42] A. E. Kahn, *The Economics of Regulation: Principles and Institutions, Volume 2: Institutional Issues* (New York: John Wiley and Sons, 1971) at 220-250.
[43] Interview with the OHTB chairman, July, 1972.
[44] Gray Coach petition, *supra* note 40.
[45] Greyhound brief, *supra* note 38.

entire system and that if Gray Coach could reduce its operating costs down to the average level for the industry, it would not be necessary for the firm to reduce or terminate service on the rural routes. Greyhound also suggested that the OHTB consider offering Gray Coach's rural routes to other Ontario bus carriers if Gray Coach petitioned the Board for discontinuance of its rural service.

Gray Coach denied that it was an inefficient carrier. While it failed to offer evidence to contradict Greyhound's productivity comparisons, Gray Coach argued that any direct comparison between its operating performance and that of Greyhound was unreliable and misleading because of the dissimilarities in their route systems.[46] Gray Coach pointed out that Greyhound operates a huge transcontinental route system characterized by relatively long-distance trips and high bus speeds. It noted that its own system is regional in scope, with shorter trips and slower speeds, mainly because of the relatively large number of intermediate stops along its routes. Gray Coach argued that many of the productivity measures employed in Greyhound's evidence, such as maintenance costs per mile, driver productivity measures based on miles traveled, etc., are highly sensitive to the basic structural characteristics of particular route systems.[47] Gray Coach did not, however, present any evidence or substantive argument, apart from summary denials, to rebut Greyhound's contention that its costs were substantially higher than the industry's average levels. Gray Coach did argue that it was unfair to compare its performance with industry averages derived solely from privately owned firms; it asserted that, as a public enterprise, it pursued other goals in addition to profit.[48]

In November, 1976, the Board decided to grant Greyhound's license applications, and by December the firm was operating four express trips a day on the Sudbury-Toronto and Buffalo-Toronto routes.[49] Gray Coach appealed the Board's decision to the provincial Cabinet, and in April, 1977, the Minister of Transportation and Communications directed the Board to rehear the case and, more specifically, to review the effect of its decision on the rural communities served by Gray Coach. The Board held a new hearing for the original parties and several new intervenors. Virtually all the intervenors, such as several rural municipalities, the Consumers Association of Canada, the Canadian Motor Bus Association, among others, opposed the decision to allow Greyhound to operate the disputed routes. Greyhound and Gray Coach put on more evidence and argument; actually, many of the

---

[46] Gray Coach petition, *supra* note 40.

[47] *Ibid.*

[48] *Ibid.*

[49] *Re Greyhound Lines of Canada Ltd. and Eastern Canadian Greyhound Lines Ltd.,* unreported decision of the Ontario Highway Transport Board (Hearing date: April 21-29, 1976, decision dated Nov. 22, 1976). Decisions are available in the OHTB library and are filed by hearing date.

arguments and much of the evidence recounted above were heard at this later stage of the proceedings. In July, 1977, the Board forwarded a lengthy report to Cabinet, which recommended that its original decision be affirmed.[50] The Board's report embraced virtually all of Greyhound's economic analysis and gave special emphasis to the evidence of Gray Coach's inefficiency. The Board also leveled sharp criticism at Gray Coach's internal structure and the performance of TTC management. The Report asserted that Gray Coach's practise of purchasing most of its administrative, maintenance, and repair services from the TTC was the major cause of the firm's higher than average operating costs.[51] Moreover, the Report argued that Gray Coach urgently required its own full-time managers, and that its time-sharing arrangement with the TTC was a primary source of the firm's inefficiency. In regard to Gray Coach's rural routes, the Board endorsed Greyhound's argument that many of the routes could be operated remuneratively by carriers of average efficiency. The Board suggested that there would be no lack of applicants eager to serve these routes if Gray Coach should decide to discontinue serving them.[52] One aspect of the Board's Report was rather curious. In spite of all the attention given at the hearing to the Board's alleged tacit policy of cross-subsidization, there is no mention of such a policy in the Report. The Report never actually acknowledged that the Board had either required or ratified Gray Coach's decision to use the profits from its "mainline routes" to subsidize rural bus riders.

In the fall of 1977, the provincial Cabinet affirmed the Board's decision, but imposed a condition on Greyhound's continued operation on the disputed routes. Greyhound was required to negotiate an explicit market division agreement with Gray Coach in order to minimize the competitive impact of its entry on the public firm. The result of the negotiations was an equal sharing of the most profitable and least profitable trips on the routes, with depature times spaced to avoid direct competition. When this study was initiated in the fall of 1978, there was no evidence of any price competition between the two carriers on the bitterly contested routes. More than two years after the Cabinet decision, Gray Coach has discontinued only one of its smaller rural routes, the Alliston route, which is now served by a small local carrier. Gray Coach has not announced any future plans to discontinue any other rural routes. Also, since our study was initiated, Gray Coach has moved to perform more of its administrative functions in-house, such as budgeting, some accounting and purchasing. Most administrative and all maintenance and repair services are still provided for Gray Coach by

---

[50] Ontario. Ministry of Transportation and Communications. *Ontario Highway Transport Board Report to Minister of Transportation and Communications 1977*, (Toronto: Ontario Highway Transport Board, 21 June 1977).

[51] *Ibid.*, at 66.

[52] *Ibid.*, at 74.

the TTC. As noted earlier, the TTC has increased the number of non-TTC directors on the firm's Board, but the TTC-related directors still constitute a majority. Most important, the same unity of upper management continues between Gray Coach and the TTC; since the Cabinet decision, there does not appear to have been any substantial alteration in Gray Coach's internal structure or its basic mode of operation.

(ii) Fare Regulation

As mentioned before, the Ministry of Transportation and Communications administers a system of maximum and minimum fare regulation which is applicable to all interurban bus carriers in Ontario. There are neither statutory standards nor formal regulations governing the rate regulation process; the *Public Vehicles Act* simply authorizes the Minister to regulate all fares charged by licensed carriers. From interviews with Ministry personnel, the authors learned that the Minister uses a guideline formula, usually referred to as an "operating ratio", which tracks the relationship between a carrier's operating expenses and revenues. Although the rate formula is not published and serves only as a rough guideline, we were told that, in most cases, when a carrier's operating expenses exceed approximately 85 percent of its total revenues, a fare increase sufficient to bring the ratio back down to the targeted 85 percent level would be allowed.[53] The Ministry's procedure for the disposition of rate change applications can be briefly summarized. The carrier submits its application to the Ministry, along with the financial information necessary to evaluate the merits of the proposed fare change. Since the Ministry refused to allow the authors to inspect its rate case files, we have no first-hand knowledge of the nature and detail of the financial data generally submitted by applicants. We were informed by Ministry personnel that expense and revenue data are carefully scrutinized to ensure that a rate change is justified. After the financial documentation is submitted and scrutinized by the Ministry's staff, the application is usually forwarded to the OHTB for further study. The Board's practise is to publish notices of rate applications in the *Ontario Gazette* and in newspapers in the applicant's market area; these notices generally provide a brief description of the proposed fare changes and invite submissions from the public. If objections are filed, the Board convenes a public hearing to allow interested parties to express their views. Whether or not a public hearing is held, the Board's staff examines the application's supporting documentation and makes a recommendation to the Minister on the appropriate disposition of the case. Since the Board's role in the fare setting process is merely advisory, the Minister need not accept the Board's recommendation

---

[53] Interview with Mrs. M. Grant, Director of Tariffs, Ministry of Transportation and Communications.

in resolving the case. From our inspection of rate cases over the last six years, it would seem that the Minister always adopts the Board's recommendations. When the application is approved by the Minister, the revised fares must be published in the carrier's official schedule of tariffs and made available for public inspection prior to their effective date.

It is difficult to assess the precise impact of the rate regulation process on the behaviour of the Ontario bus carriers. Our study of the most recent six years of fare changes showed that the Minister grants virtually all applications in full. In the handful of cases in which the Minister declined to grant a proposed fare increase in full, the applicant nevertheless received a substantial increase. For example, in late 1975, Gray Coach applied for a 15 percent across-the-board increase of its inter-city passenger rates. The Minister declined to provide the full increase, citing the recent imposition of wage and price controls by the federal government. Gray Coach was, however, granted a 10 percent across-the-board fare increase. It should be noted that in virtually all rate cases the Minister's final order does not provide any reasons or justification for the action taken in the case. The general pattern observed by the authors, with only negligible variations, was that all carriers in the industry applied for and received the equivalent of 10 percent increases on an annual basis during the last six years. The uniformity of the treatment accorded to all carriers may be partially explained by the fact that the time period covered by our rate case study was coincident with a period of continuous and severe inflation in Canada. Thus, it should be recognized that our findings may not be indicative of the Ministry's fare regulation policies prior to the early 1970s. Since we were not permitted to inspect the Ministry's rate files, it is difficult to draw any firm conclusion concerning the incentive effects of the regulatory process. Our findings strongly suggest that the Ministry fails to monitor the carrier's costs and revenues with any real rigor. Our general impression is that the profit constraint imposed on the industry by the Ministry's method of fare regulation has a negligible impact on firm behaviour. It should be emphasized, however, that to the extent that the regulatory system does constrain the profit-seeking behaviour of industry managers, it affects the behaviour of the private firms and Gray Coach in precisely the same ways. With these background facts in mind we now turn to the general question of how the behaviour of a public enterprise might be expected to differ from that of private firms.

III. A POSITIVE THEORY OF GOVERNMENT ENTERPRISE BEHAVIOUR

(a) Introduction

This case study provides some empirical confirmation for a general positive theory of public enterprise. This theory attempts to explain and predict the behaviour of government owned or controlled firms, which sell their products in a market and are directed by managers who are ultimately accountable to a legislative authority. The development of general theories which facilitate the assessment of the allocative and distributive consequences of public enterprise should illuminate some of the issues in the current political debate on the strengths and limits of government ownership as a policy instrument. We also hope that this case study will advance the behavioural knowledge that economists and lawyers require for the design of institutions which accommodate private motives with social objectives.

The general model of the public firm employed in this paper is constructed from three related strands of economic theory: the "property rights" theory of the firm; the managerial theory of the firm and public bureau; and the economic theory of representative democracy. Each of these components is animated by the behavioural assumption that all actors, both public and private, are strongly motivated to pursue their perceived self-interest. Moreover, each of the theories builds on the fundamental insight that certain alterations in the institutional features of the firm, bureau or political system change the cost-reward structures of utility maximizing decision-makers in ways which systematically affect their behaviour. Thus, these theories provide the basic building blocks for more general theories which provide testable predictions about the welfare consequences of alternative institutional arrangements, such as the public firm, the regulatory commission, and the private firm (among others) as mechanisms for the pursuit of collective goals. In this section, we attempt to construct a general model of public firm behaviour, which is primarily derived from the three somewhat distinct bodies of theoretical work mentioned above, and to relate the basic components of our model to the specific institutional facts of our case study.

(b) The Property Rights Theory

The modern property rights theory of the firm formulated by such theorists as Alchian and Demsetz attempts to explain how alternative ownership forms affect firm performance.[54] These theorists argue that the crucial difference between public and private enterprise is the specialization of the ownership or entrepreneurial function which is attainable in the latter form. The relatively low cost of transferring property rights in private firms has two key consequences. First, it strengthens incentives for owner control

---

54 Alchian, "Some Economics of Property Rights" (1965), 30 *Il Politico* 816; Alchian and Demsetz, "Production, Information Costs, and Economic Organization" (1972), 62 *Am. Econ. Rev.* 777; Alchian and Demsetz, "The Property Rights Paradigm" (1973), 33 *J. Econ. Hist.* 16; Demsetz, "The Exchange and Enforcement of Property Rights" (1964), 7 *J. Law and Econ.* 11.

by encouraging specialization in ownership. The concentration of owner-ship in the hands of an individual or control group creates a large personal stake in promoting efficient wealth maximizing behaviour by the firm's managers. Peltzman argues that ownership or entrepreneurship is a produc-tive input which organizes and combines managerial inputs, much like the manager organizes labour and capital.[55] Thus, low-cost transferability of ownership rights permits specific control groups to specialize in those in-dustries where the return to their particular entrepreneurial talents is highest. The second important consequence of a property rights system which permits the relatively inexpensive transfer of ownership interests is that it reduces the owner's cost of monitoring and his costs of supervising the firm's managers. The owner's monitoring costs are reduced because a reasonably efficient market for ownership shares provides an objective per-formance standard, a market price, which facilitates a comparative evalua-tion of managerial performance. In other words, the existence of a market mechanism which operates to capitalize the future consequences of current production decisions into the present value of a firm's shares reduces the owner's cost of obtaining information concerning his manger's relative per-formance.[56] Moreover, the private property rights system reduces an owner's direct costs of exercising control over management. First, the trans-ferability of equity shares permits the concentration of ownership in the hands of an individual or a group who can directly hire and fire top management through their control over the firm's board of directors.[57] Sec-ond, the existence of a market for equity shares permits owners to lower their control costs by simply linking their managers' pecuniary compensa-tion with the market value of the firm's shares. Stock options and other profit sharing devices bring the interests of owner and manager into closer alignment by permitting the manager to capture a portion of the net monetary gains from profit-seeking behaviour.[58]

---

[55] Peltzman, "Pricing in Public and Private Enterprises: Electric Utilities in the United States" (1971), 14 *J. Law and Econ.* 109, at 111.

[56] W. Crain and A. Zardkoohi argue that "since the direct benefits can only be internalized by a public manager during his tenure in office and the costs of his decisions beyond his career horizon do not affect his net worth, we would expect managers of a political firm to have a higher rate of time preference than private enterpreneurs". The results of their comparative study of public and private water utilities confirmed their prediction that the input choices of public managers tend to be biased away from long-term capital investment and towards utilization of labour and other variable factors. Crain and Zardkoohi, "A Test of the Prop-erty Rights Theory of the Firm: Water Utilities in the United States" (1978), 21 *J. Law and Econ.* 395, at 398.

[57] See, *e.g.*, Manne, "Mergers and the Market for Corporate Control" (1965), 73 *J. Pol. Econ.* 110.

[58] Several empirical studies support the basic behavioural proposition that individuals work more productively if they can appropriate the marginal gains resulting from their efforts. See, *e.g.*, Stano, "Executive Ownership Interests and Corporate Performance" (1975), 42 *So. Econ. J.* 272; De Alessi, "Private Property and Dispersion of Ownership in Large Cor-porations" (1973), 28 *J. Fin.* 839.

Contrast the incentives and relative costs of control which confront the owner of a public enterprise. Individual citizen-taxpayers own shares in government firms, just as they do in private firms. Like private shareholders, shareholders in public firms are interested in improving the value of their shares, or more specifically, they have an interest in lowering their tax burdens. In attaining this objective, however, the incentives of government shareholders are limited by the fact that their shares of the firm's profits or losses are tied by the tax laws to either their taxable incomes or other taxable wealth. There is no organized market for shares in government firms; transfers of shares in public enterprises can occur only through a citizen-taxpayer's change of residence or through a legislated change in the tax structure. The very high costs of transferring shares in government firms preclude the concentration of ownership which generates strong incentives for owner control. It does not generally pay a citizen-taxpayer to monitor the activities of public enterprise managers because, even if he detected inefficiencies and had them rectified, he would be able to, at best, capture an amount roughly equal to the gain divided by the number of taxpayers.[59]

Moreover, the control mechanisms available to the public firm shareholder are more costly than those available to his private counterpart. First, the owner's cost of obtaining information about the performance of public firms is higher because their shares are not traded in organized capital markets; the market values of private firm shares are one very useful index (unavailable for public firms) of management's relative success in maximizing owner wealth. Second, the public manager's inability to hold equity shares or some similar stake in the government enterprise precludes one very effective method of reducing the owner's costs of control. Third, and perhaps most important, is the point that the citizen-taxpayer, or rather a group of citizen-taxpayers, possess no direct supervisory power over the managers of a government firm. The owners of public firms can only influence the decisions of management through political intermediaries, elected representatives who monitor and supervise the operations of government firms. Thus, the costs of control which confront the owners of public firms are generally coterminous with the costs of using the political system. The costs of using a political system to achieve any specific objective, such as greater efficiency in a particular public enterprise, depend on that system's institutional characteristics, such as voting rules, information costs, or the frequency of elections. These features of the Metro Toronto political system and their implications for the behaviour of Gray Coach's management will be discussed below.

Many students of public enterprise have asserted that the attentuation of ownership rights in public firms is causally linked to observed differences

---

[59] This argument does, of course, assume that the tax burden is apportioned equally within the political community; citizens with higher tax burdens would have relatively stronger incentives to influence the policies of government firms.

between the behaviour of public managers and their private counterparts. Davies provides some evidence on the comparative efficiency of public versus private airlines using data on Australia's two airlines, one of which is privately owned and the other publicly owned.[60] His findings for three types of efficiency indexes support the hypothesis that property rights in the public enterprise are less conducive to efficient operation. Albrandt tested for the relative efficiency of public and private fire companies.[61] His findings indicated that many municipal fire departments generated operating costs that were almost twice as high as the costs of private firms providing comparable fire protection services. Spann's study of the relative efficiency of private versus public garbage collection services found that communities using private contractors have significantly lower costs.[62] Clarkson examined the impact of alternative ownership forms on managerial behaviour in profit-seeking and non-profit hospitals.[63] He found a higher degree of variance in the input combinations employed by the non-profit managers and inferred that this was an indication of the superior efficiency of the profit-seeking hospitals. It should be noted, however, that Clarkson's findings were impaired by his inability to control for other variables, such as factor prices or flexible production methods, which might also influence the observed differences in input variability. Crain and Zardkoohi investigated the comparative efficiency of public and private water utilities.[64] They found that operating costs were significantly higher in the publicly owned utilities. They attributed the observed cost differential between the two types of firms to differences in labour productivity.

(c) The Political Market

All of the studies mentioned above attempt to explain observed differences between public and private firm behaviour (*i.e.*, greater variability in input combinations, lower labour productivity, or a bias toward capital intensive production methods) by reference to the public manager's relative autonomy from owner control. Because of the structural differences in ownership forms, the public manager is less likely to bear the costs or internalize the rewards from profit-seeking behaviour. Thus, the public manager's opportunity cost of economic inefficiency is reduced. As De Alessi

---

[60] Davies, "The Efficiency of Public versus Private Firms, the Case of Australia's Two Airlines" (1971), 14 *J. Law and Econ.* 149; Davies, "Property Rights and Economic Efficiency—The Australian Airlines Revisited" (1977), 20 *J. Law and Econ.* 223.

[61] Ahlbrandt, "Efficiency in the Provision of Fire Services" (1973), 16 *Public Choice* 1.

[62] Spann, "Rates of Productivity Change and Growth of Local Government Expenditures" in *Budgets and Bureaucrats: The Sources of Government Growth*, T. E. Borcherding, ed. (Durham, North Carolina: Duke University Press, 1977).

[63] Clarkson, "Some Implications of Property Rights in Hospital Management" (1972), 15 *J. Law and Econ.* 363.

[64] Crain and Zardkoohi, *supra* note 56.

says, "managers of political firms have greater opportunities to increase their own welfare at the expense of the employer's [citizen-taxpayer's] wealth."[65] This then leads to the general hypothesis tested in these studies: that managerial efforts aimed at organizing, co-ordinating and monitoring productive activity to maximize owner wealth will be reduced in the public enterprise. Specific predictions about public firm behaviour are then derived from attempts to identify the pecuniary and non-pecuniary objectives of autonomous, utility-maximizing public managers. But this essentially managerial theory of the public firm is incomplete because it ignores the role of the political intermediary in shaping public firm behaviour. In other words, many of the observed differences in public and private firm behaviour may be attributable, in whole or in part, to the deliberate choices of political entrepreneurs, responding to the incentives generated by the political system in which they compete for voter support. A few studies attempt to dissolve the analytic problem created by the potential for goal conflict between public managers and politicians by assuming either that politicians are perfect brokers for their own objectives, or that politicians and public managers share a substantial identity of interest in shaping public firm policies. Thus, for example, Peltzman assumes that "an important object of utility to the management of government enterprises, one for which they are willing to trade owner wealth, is the maintenance of political support for the enterprise."[66] Baldwin achieves the same result by assuming that public managers trade profits for political support because they are constrained to do so by their politican-supervisors.[67] One of the primary objectives of this study is to separate the effects of political constraints from the effects of managerial discretion on public firm behaviour. In order to pursue that objective, we require a general model of the political process within which both politicians and public managers pursue their respective goals.

Economic theorists have developed a general model for political systems organized around the principle of representative democracy.[68] This model views the political process as a type of market in which citizens bid votes, or other resources which may be used to influence votes, in order to receive benefits from the state.[69] Politicians, or groups of politicians called

[65] De Alessi, "Management Tenure under Private and Government Ownership in the Electric Power Industry" (1974), 82 *J. Pol. Econ.* 645, at 646.

[66] *Supra* note 55, at 112.

[67] J. R. Baldwin, *The Regulatory Agency and the Public Corporation: The Canadian Air Transport Industry* (Cambridge, Mass.: Ballinger Pub. Co., 1975).

[68] See, *e.g.*, A. Downs, *An Economic Theory of Democracy* (New York: Harper and Row, 1957); R. Bartlett, *Economic Foundations of Political Power* (New York: Free Press, 1973); A. Breton, *The Economic Theory of Representative Government* (Chicago: Aldine; 1974); Peltzman, "Toward a More General Theory of Regulation" (1976), 19 *J. Law and Econ.* 211; Stigler, "The Theory of Economic Regulation" (1971), 2 *Bell J. Econ. and Mgmt. Sci.* 3.

[69] See Trebilcock, Waverman, and Prichard, "Markets for Regulation: Implications For Performance Standards and Institutional Design" in Ontario Economic Council., *supra* note 31, at 11 for a very useful formulation of the "political market" paradigm.

"parties", attempt to maximize their political support through promises to supply benefits. Thus benefits, or simply transfers of wealth, are exchanged in political markets, with voters on the demand side and their elected representatives on the supply side. As with any market, the political market distributes more benefits to those constituents whose effective demand is highest, *i.e.*, voters or coalitions of voters who can bid the greatest political support for the policies they favour. The model also incorporates the specific institutional features of representative democracies which shape the incentives of voters and politicians and the costs they confront in using the political process to pursue their goals.

The economic theory of representative democracy focuses on two types of costs which must be borne by voters or politicians in their efforts to organize a successful political coalition. First, political markets are characterized by relatively high information costs.[70] Voting occurs infrequently (*i.e.*, municipal councillors are elected for two-year terms) and pertains to an entire package of issues. As to any particular policy issue, it will be costly for a voter to obtain information concerning the issue's implications for his own wealth. Moreover, since the election is for candidates and not specific policies, the voter must also expend time and money ascertaining the positions of the various candidates on particular issues. Thus, the prediction emerges that a voter with a small per capita stake in a particular issue is unlikely to cast an informed vote for a candidate solely on the basis of that issue because his expected costs will generally more than offset his prospective gains.[71] The second major type of costs incurred in using the political system is the direct cost of organizing political coalitions. It is not enough for the successful coalition to merely secure the information it requires to correctly perceive its interests; the groups must also organize its members to provide effective support for the candidate or party that will implement the policies it favours. Thus, the coalition must effectively mobilize the votes of its members and also contribute time and money to persuade other voters to support, or at least not oppose, its candidate or party. The strength of the incentives to organize for political action is, of course, a function of the group's per capita stake in the policies it supports or opposes. The group's costs of organizing an effective coalition are, however, a function of the group's numerical size. The costs of the organization generally rise faster than group size for two reasons.[72] First, as the numerical size of the group that seeks the benefit or transfer increases, the size of the opposing coalition contracts. As the numerical size of the opposing coalition decreases, the per capita stakes of its members increase and this has the effect of increasing the

---

[70] See Bartlett, *supra* note 68, at 27-58, for an insightful discussion of information costs in political markets.

[71] See Borcherding, Chapter 2, this volume.

[72] M. Olson, *The Logic of Collective Action: Public Goods and the Theory of Groups* (Cambridge, Mass.: Harvard University Press, 1965). The relation between coalition size and organization cost is derived from Olson's theories of group action.

intensity of their efforts to block the transfer. Second, the costs of neutralizing the ubiquitous "free rider" problem also increase as the numerical size of the potential coalition increases.

This summary of an economic model of representative democracy predicts that the success of any specific political coalition will be a function of the intensity of its members' interest (*i.e.*, their per capita stakes) in a particular policy and the numerical size of the voter group. The group's costs of obtaining information and organizing for political action may also be affected by the decisions of politicians or other third parties. For example, a candidate or the media may decide to provide information about particular issues, or there may be electoral laws which limit the size of campaign contributions. The model, however, abstracts from system-specific strategic and institutional details to focus on the strength of pecuniary incentives and the costs of organizing winning coalitions. This rather simple model can be employed to generate some predictions about the kinds of operating policies which Metro politicians might wish Gray Coach managers to adopt.

Metro Toronto councillors will promote the adoption of Gray Coach policies which have the effect of maximizing their political support. Consider the Metro electorate as being divided into two groups—users and non-users of Gray Coach services. Since non-users will receive a reduction in their tax liabilities as a result of profits earned by Gray Coach, they will favour operating policies aimed at profit maximization. The political impact of the preferences of the non-user group is, however, likely to be relatively small. Since the non-user group constitutes a very large majority of the Metro population, the per capita benefit to the group's members will be very small relative to the participation costs they would have to incur in order to influence the firm's policies. Moreover, the costs of obtaining information regarding the degree to which Gray Coach's managers fail to maximize potential profits must be relatively high; Gray Coach's management has a strong interest in concealing this sort of information. There is also the related point that operating losses are more visible to non-users and are much more likely to be publicly deplored, especially when private firms exist that claim they could perform the same service without costs to the municipal treasury.[73]

Metro voters who use Gray Coach services may favour policies which subsidize the services they consume rather than policies directed toward profit maximization. The user's cost-benefit calculus would entail balancing the benefits he might receive from lower fares or greater frequency of service against the increased tax liability he must bear as a result of lower profits. Since users are a very small proportion of the taxpaying population and since an increase in tax liabilities must be shared by users and non-users

---

[73] See Baldwin, *supra* note 67, at 92-105, for a discussion of the political saliency of Air Canada's operating deficits during the firm's early years.

alike, the benefits to users from lower fares or higher quality services are likely to be larger than their share of increased tax liabilities. Moreover, the information cost argument mentioned above suggests that the user group is likely to appreciate the benefits they receive from a policy of subsidization more readily than they perceive the costs it imposes on them as taxpayers. The one crucial factor that may influence a user's preferences on firm policy is the frequency of his consumption of Gray Coach services. [74] If the average Metro user rides Gray Coach buses only infrequently, his anticipated benefit from a policy of subsidizing users would be relatively small. Because of the nature of Gray Coach's route system, we would expect that only Metro residents commuting to jobs located a substantial distance from the Metro area would be frequent riders.

There is, however, a third group of Metro voter-taxpayers who might favour a policy of subsidizing Gray Coach riders. The owners of Metro businesses, and to a lesser extent the individuals and firms that supply labour and other inputs to Metro businesses, might wish Gray Coach to adopt a policy of subsidizing bus travel to Toronto. Lower fares on bus trips to and from Toronto might induce a larger number of Ontario residents to shop or spend their leisure time in Toronto. The pecuniary benefits from increased patronage would be concentrated on a relatively small and cohesive group, the owners of Metro's shops, hotels, theaters, etc., while the increased tax liabilities that would result from subsidizing travel to Toronto would be shared by all Metro residents. It should be noted, however, that business owners also bear a disproportionate share of the municipal property tax burden. The ultimate incidence of municipal property taxes is a subject of much recent controversy. [75] If we assume that a substantial proportion of the business owners' tax burden is shifted to consumers or landlords, Metro business owners are likely to favour a policy of subsidization in spite of its effect on their nominal tax bills. Moreover, the group's relatively small size confers a comparative advantage in organizing an effective political lobby. [76]

Based on this analysis of the Metro electorate, one would expect Metro

---

[74] When a consumer of a public firm's services is also a taxpayer, any departure from profit maximizing policies will have two separate effects on his welfare. These two effects are (1) the subsidized price change times the quantity of the firm's services consumed, and (2) the change in the consumer's tax liability attributable to the firm's policy of granting subsidies to all consumers. See Peltzman, *supra* note 55, at 113-21 for a similar analysis in which all consumers are assumed to be taxpayers.

[75] See, *e.g.*, H. J. Aaron, *Who Pays the Property Tax? A New View* (Washington, D.C.: The Brookings Institution, 1975) at 18-56; R. W. Lindholm, ed., *Property Taxation and the Finance of Education* (Madison: University of Wisconsin Press for the Committee on Taxation, Resources and Economic Development, 1974).

[76] If a substantial proportion of the costs of using the political process are fixed, groups with stable organizational structures (*i.e.*, chambers of commerce, labour unions, etc.) would enjoy comparative advantages in political competition.

councillors to promote Gray Coach policies aimed at: (1) subsidizing bus trips to and from Toronto; and (2) avoiding operating losses. The subsidization of fares for trips, either beginning or ending in Toronto, would benefit Metro business owners and frequent Metro users. Metro councillors should favour profit-maximizing fares for all other Gray Coach trips; they would have no incentive to subsidize non-residents on trips neither beginning nor ending in Toronto. It should be noted that bus fare schedules do not impede this sort of price discrimination.

There are two additional factors which may influence the positions adopted by Metro councillors in regard to Gray Coach. First, the political independence of the TTC may weaken the councillors' incentives to take an active role in shaping Gray Coach policies.[77] Although the Commission is legally responsible to Metro Council, many Metro voters may have difficulty perceiving the connection between Gray Coach policies, which they favour or oppose, and the initiatives of Metro councillors. The members of Metro Council would, of course, wish to publicize the benefits conferred on their constituents, but their ability to do so without also calling attention to the increased tax burden on all voters must be impaired by the formal separateness of the Commission. Second, the costs of monitoring and supervising Gray Coach-TTC management will impose limits on the councillors' ability to achieve their political objectives. As Lindsay and others have noted, certain attributes of public enterprise performance can be monitored relatively cheaply by politicians, while other aspects of firm behaviour may be difficult to evaluate.[78] For example, operating losses are highly visible and their welfare implications are readily perceived by politicians and their taxpayer-constituents. On the other hand, in order to monitor effectively a policy of cross-subsidization, Metro politicians would require detailed information about route profits that is usually either unavailable or unreliable because of the vagaries of allocating costs and revenues among routes. Faced with these high information costs, politicians are likely to focus on those aspects of public enterprise output which are most visible to their constituents. Instead of concentrating on the absolute level of fares or the difference between the profit-maximizing fare and the fare currently being charged, the Metro politician anxious to promote a policy of cross-subsidization is more likely to focus on the fare per mile differential between Toronto and non-Toronto trips. Without route-specific

---

77 Walsh criticizes the design of public corporations in the United States on the ground that they are too remote and insulated from the constraints generated by pluralist legislative politics. A. Walsh, *The Public's Business: The Politics and Practices of Government Corporations* (Cambridge, Mass.: MIT Press, 1978). For a similar critique of independent authorities in American municipal government, see R. Caro, *The Power Broker: Robert Moses and the Fall of New York* (New York: A. A. Knopf, 1974).
78 Lindsay, "A Theory of Government Enterprise" (1976), 84 *J. Pol. Econ.* 1061; see also C. Lindsay, *Veterans Administration Hospitals: An economic analysis of government enterprise* (Washington, D.C.: American Enterprise Institute for Public Policy Research, 1975).

data on costs and revenues, this sort of crude monitoring is about the best the politician can do for his constituents. We explore the implications of monitoring costs for firm behaviour in Section IV.

(d) Managerial Discretion and the Public Firm

While public enterprise managers will be subject to political constraints of varying intensity, a positive theory of the public firm must also incorporate some conception of managerial objectives. As discussed above, public managers are less likely than their counterparts in private firms to bear costs or internalize rewards from profitable performance. Thus, they possess an expanded set of opportunities to pursue goals which increase their own welfare. If we assume that public firm managers seek to maximize their utility, a theory of managerial behaviour can be derived by attempting to specify both the sources of utility in public manager's utility functions and the constraints they confront in pursuing their goals. There is a vast theoretical and empirical literature on managerial behaviour, both private and public, which we will not attempt to summarize here.[79] Following Niskanen and others, we assume that a public manager's utility function will, at a minimum, contain the following arguments: (1) pay, power and prestige; (2) ease of management; and (3) security of tenure.[80] Subject to the political and market constraints which limit his choices, a manager may pursue certain objectives more aggressively than others, but at the margin all sources of utility are substitutable. Our analysis proceeds by attempting to identify plausible management policies for Gray Coach that might be consistent with these managerial objectives.

Parkinson, Niskanen and others argue that a public manager's pay, power and prestige are closely correlated with the size of his firm, or in the case of a public bureau, the size of the bureau's budget.[81] Gray Coach is, of course, unlike a public bureau in that its operations are not funded by legislative appropriations. But measures like asset size and number of employees are generally correlated with a civil servant's rank and salary level.

---

[79] See, *e.g.*, W. J. Baumol, *Business Behavior, Value and Growth: Revised Edition* (New York: Harcourt, Brace and World, 1967); R. Cyert and J. March, *A Behavioral Theory of the Firm* (Englewood Cliffs, N.J.: Prentice Hall, Inc., 1963); R. Marris, *The Economic Theory of 'Managerial' Capitalism* (New York: The Free Press of Glencoe, 1964); O. E. Williamson, *The Economics of Discretionary Behavior: Managerial Objectives in a Theory of the Firm* (Chicago: Markham Pub. Co., 1967). For a comprehensive review of the literature, see Orzechowski, "Economic Models of Bureaucracy: Survey, Extension and Evidence" in Borcherding, ed., *supra* note 62, at 229.

[80] W. A. Niskanen, *Bureaucracy and Representative Government* (Chicago: Aldine-Atherton, 1971); Williamson, *supra* note 79.

[81] C. N. Parkinson, *Parkinson's Law and Other Studies in Administration* (Boston: Houghton Mifflin Co., 1957); Niskanen, *supra* note 80.

This suggests that the managers of Gray Coach and the TTC will trade potential profits for more staff and a larger bus fleet. The expansionary policies chosen, however, are likely to be shaped by Gray Coach's subordinate relationship to the TTC. Our theory of managerial behaviour would predict that the TTC-Gray Coach management will wish to adopt operating strategies that would have the effect of maximizing the combined size of the TTC and Gray Coach.

As discussed in Section II, the TTC receives subsidies from both the provincial government and Metro to finance the deficits from its municipal transit services. Only the TTC's municipal operations are subsidized; Gray Coach's costs and revenues are excluded from the calculations on which the joint subsidy is based. Because of obvious political constraints, any accounting profits realized by Gray Coach will be applied to reduce Metro's share of the annual TTC subsidy. While the TTC management will probably be indifferent as to expanding Gray Coach or its municipal activities, it will clearly not wish to adopt operating strategies for Gray Coach which have the effect of reducing the size of its subsidy from Metro. This suggests that TTC managers will desire inter-firm arrangements which allow the transfer of profits from Gray Coach to the TTC in order to expand its municipal operations. This objective can be attained by preserving the firms' separate legal status while integrating many of their functions. In short, the TTC's transfer prices for administrative and maintenance services may be employed to shift Gray Coach profits to the TTC without the realization of accounting profits which would reduce its Metro subsidy.

In pursuit of their objective of maximizing the joint size of Gray Coach and the TTC, the TTC managers confront both political and market constraints which will shape the expansion paths of both firms. One might predict that the TTC managers would promote profit maximization by Gray Coach in order to increase the disguised profit transfer between the two firms. Profit-maximization by Gray Coach, however, would entail a substantial reduction in its route system. A bus company which operates fewer routes will have fewer buses and less staff. Thus, contractions in the size of Gray Coach's assets and staff will reduce the scope for profit transfer because the profit-shifting mechanism is, in large part, based on the relative size of Gray Coach's assets and employees. The scope for increases in nominal inter-firm transfer prices will be generally limited by the relative size of Gray Coach's assets and staff because Metro politicians, and their auditors, will have incentives to monitor just this sort of disguised profit-shifting between the two firms.

The probable expansion paths of the two firms can be illuminated by a concrete example. Assume that Gray Coach-TTC management have the opportunity to add a bus route to Gray Coach's existing operations. Management expects its annual revenue from the route to be $90,000, and its expenses to be $100,000. Assume also that the new route will enable the TTC to charge Gray Coach for $30,000 of expenses, that $20,000 of these transfer charges are actually attributable to Gray Coach operations, and $10,000 of the charges are in fact a disguised transfer of Gray Coach profits from other routes. So long as the $10,000 of losses attributable to the new route can be offset by profits earned on other routes, management may increase the combined size of the firms by operating the new route. In other words, management's expansionary activities will be subject to the political constraint that Gray Coach not show accounting losses. This argument can be demonstrated algebraically. Let R_o be the initial TTC revenues, X_o the initial TTC expenses. Assume initially the provincial subsidy constraint is binding so that $R_o/X_o = .725$. Now let the TTC bill Gray Coach for $10,000 of TTC-specific expenses. The ratio then changes to $R_o/X_o - 10,000) > .725$. The TTC can expand its own activities, increasing R by $\triangle R$ and X by $\triangle X$ such that:

(i) $$\frac{R_o + \triangle R}{X_o - 10,000 + \triangle X} = .725$$

This equation can be rewritten as:

(ii) $R_o + \triangle R = .725X_o - 7250 + .725 \triangle X$

Recalling that $R_o = .725X_o$ by assumption, (ii) can be rewritten as:

(iii) $\triangle R + 7250 = .725 \triangle X$, or

(iv) $$\frac{\triangle R + 7250}{\triangle X} = .725$$

Equation (iv) tells us that expansion in TTC-specific operations need not generate sufficient additional revenues to cover the additional expenses attributable to them; they need not cover even 72.5 percent of the additional expenses. In fact, even if these activities generate no additional revenues, $\triangle X$ can be $10,000 and the political constraint will be satisfied. It is more likely, though, that an additional TTC-specific activity would generate some additional revenue, allowing the managers to expand the TTC by more than $10,000. For example, a new municipal bus route may have expenses of $200,000 per year and revenues of only $140,000 per year. It should be recalled that costs will not be fully subsidized (directly) by the province and Metro. If the TTC now spends the $10,000 transferred from Gray Coach on this new bus route (or more precisely has the $10,000 available to cover some of the losses on the route), it can operate the route within the constraints of the provincial subsidy scheme and increase the size of its system. In summary, overbilling Gray Coach for expenses and/or billing Gray Coach for the TTC expenses, allows disguised transfers of Gray Coach profits to the TTC. The transfer price scheme thus provides

Gray Coach-TTC management the flexibility to adopt operating policies aimed at expanding the joint size of the firms. At a minimum, our analysis suggests that Gray Coach's decision to operate routes which generate deficits can be explained by their desire to promote expansionary policies which enhance their pay power and prestige.

A second assumed argument in managers' utility functions is ease of management or, more simply, an easy life.[82] Our theory of the public firm suggests that government managers have expanded opportunities to pursue operating policies which will provide them with easier, more convenient and pleasant work than their counterparts in the private sector. What sort of operating policies might inter-city bus managers adopt in pursuit of an easy life? Since a good deal of managerial work time in the inter-city bus industry is devoted to planning bus trips, we might anticipate that public managers would adopt operating policies designed to ease their planning and scheduling problems. A larger bus fleet would provide reserve capacity to alleviate scheduling difficulties. In addition, of course, a larger number of subordinates would also ease planning burdens. A larger driving staff may also alleviate managerial headaches arising from driver absenteeism. Moreover, an inter-city bus firm manager might also desire a relatively new fleet of buses in order to minimize consumer complaints and scheduling problems arising from breakdowns.

Finally, one might expect that public managers in a regulated industry would adopt price policies or other strategies which would minimize the burdens of dealing with regulatory officials. Thus, public managers may request fare increases less frequently than the private managers of other regulated firms. One might also anticipate that public mangers would tend to favour more "blunt" or across-the-board fare increases because they are less constrained than private managers to formulate a fare structure more sensitive to marginal revenue-cost conditions on specific routes. All these potential strategies for pursuing an easy life are discussed in Section IV.

A third assumed argument in public managers' utility functions— security of tenure—is closely related to the survival of the government firm.[83] It might be equally plausible to regard the public manager's survival motive as a constraint on the pursuit of other goals. In other words, public managers may adopt policies aimed at maximizing firm size and an easy life subject to the constraint that the firm's probability of survival not fall below some tolerable level. As Baldwin has noted, the question of whether tolerable limits to public enterprise survival can be achieved without actually pursuing survival as an independent goal primarily depends upon the nature of the political system in which the firm operates. In regard to Air Canada, Baldwin notes:

---

[82] Hicks, "Annual Survey of Economic Theory: The Theory of Monopoly" (1935), 3 *Econometrica* 1.

[83] See, *e.g.*, De Alessi, *supra* note 65.

It is not inconceivable that a Crown Airline may have some "organizational slack" to play with under certain regimes—for instance, a socialist government—whereas, on other occasions it may be hard pressed to defend itself.[84]

To a large extent, the survival of a public enterprise, like other government departments, will depend upon its demonstrating to political monitors that the firm's services have elicited significant support from a politically important sector of the electorate. Following our analysis of the Metro political system, we would expect Gray Coach managers to adopt policies aimed at subsidizing Toronto bus trips and, perhaps more important, reducing the risk of accounting losses. Because of the high costs of monitoring faced by Metro politicians, it is likely that Gray Coach managers will regard the survival motive as a constraint on the pursuit of their other goals. One might, however, predict that survival-oriented managers would adopt accounting methods which reduce the risk of recognizing operating losses because of the relative visibility of these losses to Metro taxpayers. Finally, it should be noted that Gray Coach managers who desire enhanced security of tenure would have no incentive to maximize firm profits. Accounting profits provide an inducement for private bus lines to attempt to obtain operating licenses for Gray Coach routes. Moreover, political entrepreneurs may interpret high accounting profits as an indication that the firm should be sold to the private sector. We explore the behavioural implications of the survival motive in Section IV.

IV. PERFORMANCE ASPECTS OF GRAY COACH

(a) Introduction

In Section III we presented a general behavioural model which can be used to explain and predict the performance of public enterprises. The theoretical content of our model led to the expectation that firms which are publicly owned will generally be operated so as to maximize the utility of their managers subject to constraints in the market for control, constraints in the product market, and constraints in the political arena. Because of the diffuse ownership by political constituencies, the market for control typically presents only a weak constraint on the behaviour of publicly owned firms, primarily as a result of the extremely high information, transactions and negotiations costs involved in any attempt to transfer the ownership and control of the firm. The product market, does, however, constrain public firms like Gray Coach in several ways. First, the managers must take cognizance of, and maximize their utility subject to, the demand conditions in the market. Second, the managers need not in most cases fear the threat

---

[84] Baldwin, *supra* note 67, at 71.

of potential entry, but recent events discussed in Section II suggest that it is a mistake to assume that the threat of potential entry is completly non-existent.

The third constraint is the political constraint, which can manifest itself in many different forms for different firms or even for one firm. Because the politicians nominally in control of a public firm usually represent a broad constituency which forms a loose coalition of varied vested interests, they will often desire the firm to pursue several different and sometimes apparently inconsistent goals. The politicians' articulation of multiple and seemingly inconsistent performance goals merely represents an attempt to satisfy the wishes of competing vested interests within his constituency; this voter-support-maximizing strategy is the consequence of the variablility in the intensity of diverse voter preferences and forms the basis of log-rolling in representative democracies.

More specifically for Gray Coach, the intersection of the theories of managerial utility maximization with the theory of political voter-support maximization gives rise to behavioural predictions which are shaped by the specific institutional environment which has evolved. We assume that the joint managers of Gray Coach and the Toronto Transit Commission increase their utility by increasing their pay, power, prestige and job security; and following related arguments, we assume that an important determinant of pay, power, prestige, and job security is the combined size of Gray Coach and the TTC. An important implication of these assumptions is that we should expect to find that Gray Coach operates at a scale which is greater than the profit-maximizing scale.

How the size of Gray Coach has been increased, though, has been strongly affected by the constraints impinging upon managerial behaviour. One important constraint is that Gray Coach must not *appear* to be drawing a subsidy from the Metropolitan Toronto taxpayers. This constraint operates for several reasons. First, Gray Coach losses cannot, by law, be subsidized by provincial grants to the TTC. So long as Gray Coach can avoid reporting accounting losses, increased scrutiny and time-consuming bother, at least in this regard, can be avoided. Second, there may reasonably be some fear on the part of the joint managers of Gray Coach and the TTC that Metro Council would balk at specifically using Metro funds to subsidize Gray Coach accounting losses. With these thoughts and fears in mind, the managers are constrained in their utility-seeking behaviour to report at least non-negative accounting profits. In fact, Gray Coach has reported negative accounting profits only *three* times in its 50-year history, and these have been very small.[85]

A second influence on the managers stems from the political power of some vested interests in Metro who would like the firm to give people riding to and/or from Toronto a discount. These vested interests might be Metro

---

[85] Gray Coach Lines, Ltd. Annual Reports for various years.

residents and taxpayers who frequently travel via Gray Coach, they might be business groups who benefit from increased tourism and commerce, or they might be some broader coalition incorporating each of these groups.

A third constraint on the managers is provided by the formula for provincial subsidization of municipal transit in Ontario. Essentially the province is concerned that it not subsidize non-municipal transit services, and hence requires that Gray Coach and TTC books be kept separate. Since Metro makes a substantial contribution to the TTC subsidy, any dividends paid by Gray Coach to the TTC have the effect of doing nothing more than reducing the size of the Metro subsidy (recall that they will not reduce the net provincial subsidy). A result of the subsidy scheme is that we should expect Gray Coach rarely to report much profit and rarer still to declare a dividend. We should also expect that the TTC would like to acquire indirectly some of the Gray Coach potential economic profits in order to expand its TTC operations and hence expand the basis on which provincial and Metro subsidies are calculated. The implication, of course, is that although Gray Coach and the TTC have been organized as separate economic entities, we might expect to observe a considerable amount of managerial discretion to allocate expenses between the two firms (*e.g.*, the TTC provides many services to Gray Coach). In this fashion, some of the Gray Coach profits could be paid to the TTC in a very non-visible form and be employed to increase the joint size of both firms.

Other forces are also at work influencing the behaviour of public enterprise managers and hence shaping the performance of the firm. For one, the managerial utility functions probably include as an argument the minimization of hassles in addition to pay, power, prestige, and job security. This treatment of managerial utility underlies or animates theories of organizational slack and X-inefficiency.[86] In a public enterprise, and in Gray Coach in particular, these theories suggest that we should observe organizational structures which are changed only infrequently. We should also observe the use of additional inputs to provide a smoother functioning of the bureaucracy. And we should rarely, if ever, find behaviour likely to irritate or alienate an important interest group.

Finally, because Gray Coach, like many public firms, is exempt from the federal corporation profits tax, it has an incentive to use a higher capital/labour ratio than would private firms. Because the profits tax is primarily a tax on the return to capital, removal of the tax in effect reduces the user cost of capital to the firm. Consequently, despite the existence of incentives for Gray Coach to report low profits, to the extent that they do report positive profits and retain them for future investment, their expansion path should have a slight capital bias relative to the expansion paths of private firms. Furthermore, unless capital is an inferior or regressive input

---

[86] See Cyert and March, *supra* note 79; and Leibenstein, "Allocative Efficiency vs. 'X-efficiency' " (1966), 56 *Am. Econ. Rev.* 392.

into the production process, the tax-related decreased cost of capital will induce the firm to increase its rate of output.

In this section we examine available evidence on Gray Coach performance to test these implications of our behavioural theories. We look first at some balance sheet and income statement data to get an overview of the profitability of the firm. Next we examine several aspects of technical efficiency. And, finally, we develop and estimate a pricing model of the firm to examine the firm's pricing decisions and the extent of cross-subsidization in its fare structure.

Before beginning our analysis, however, we must point out that while there are many similarities between the bus firms operating in Ontario, there are also many differences. For example, some of the smaller firms appear to be running their regularly scheduled trips at a loss, but are willing to do so in order to maintain some exclusive charter rights.[87] For the larger firms, especially Greyhound, there are numerous subsidiary and ancillary operations which cloud the statistical picture, since often the data for various operations are difficult to disentangle. Also, the firms have quite different route structures; some (*e.g.,* Greyhound) typically have longer but fewer routes, while others have shorter routes along highways which may necessitate slower travel time.[88] These differences in route structure could seriously affect maintenance and operating expenses. To some extent the potential problems for our analysis which might be created by such differences can be obviated by a judicious use of appropriate ratios of data and by the use of appropriate variables in our regression model. Nevertheless, the cloud of non-comparability still hangs over the study, to some degree, and deserves recognition, especially since there are so few firms involved in the study. It must be recognized, however, that the route structure is not, in the long run, completely exogenous to the firm. Gray Coach may be operating many unprofitable routes because doing so increases its size and complexity, generating additional pay, power, and prestige for the managers.

(b) Profit Performance

Tables I and II present some very basic profit and net worth data for Gray Coach and Greyhound, respectively.[89] For the years 1969 to 1977,

---

[87] It is not completely clear to us whether firms must maintain regularly-scheduled service at a loss in order to maintain charter rights; the regulations of the province are somewhat vague on this point. More importantly, however, the managers of several different firms indicated to us that they believed that the OHTB enforced such regulations. See note 34, *supra.*

[88] Average distances for each of the five major firms operating in southwestern Ontario are given later in Table III.

[89] The other three firms did not respond to our requests for balance sheet data. At least two of them are wholly-owned subsidiaries of other corporations and hence were unlikely to be able to respond with any data useful for this study.

Gray Coach had an average rate of return on net worth of only 6.3 percent. This figure is well below a "normal" rate of return for most firms in competitive industries over that period, and it is even below the Gray Coach unofficial target rate of return of 8 percent. It is compatible, however, with their implicit profit constraint of "break-even plus a bit".[90] For the period of 1974-1978, Greyhound had an average rate of return of 20.4 percent on its net worth, a figure well above a normal rate of return, but perhaps affected by Greyhound's bus manufacturing subsidiary and its other ancillary operations.

TABLE I
Selected Balance Sheet and Income Statement
Data for Gray Coach (in $000's)

	I	II	III	IV	V	VI
			Profits from Disposal of	*Total Payments to the*	*Annual Increase in Payments to the*	*Payments to the TTC*
Year	*Profits*	*Net Worth*	*Assets*	*TTC*	*TTC*	*for admin.*
1977	207	11,510	275	5211	130	N/A
1976	271	11,303	211	5081	194	1316
1975	574	11,032	120	4887	1007	1167
1974	268	10,458	113	3880	333	1005
1973	1068	10,189	140	3547	598	825
1972	1037	9,321	105	2949		725
1971	558	8,385				
1970	718	8,186				
1969	644	7,790				
1968	-39	7,146				

TABLE II
Profits and Net Worth for Greyhound
(in $000's)

Year	*Profits*	*Net Worth*
1978	11,051	59,717
1977	10,357	53,152
1976	9,551	47,085
1975	9,538	41,513
1974	7,355	35,708

---

[90] Interviews with Gray Coach and Toronto Transit Commission managers.

Of course, a finding that Greyhound is much more profitable than Gray Coach is not conclusive evidence of Gray Coach's relative inefficiency. Gray Coach, because of geographic, historical, political, and regulatory circumstances, may simply be operating on a less-profitable route structure. Gray Coach may well be very efficient at operating along its routes. Or, however, it may be operating "efficiently" on unprofitable routes in order to increase the size of the firm. If such routes involve Toronto as an origin or destination, increasing the size of the firm could be consistent with politicians' desires to encourage travel to Toronto from surrounding communities.

Using the data from these same tables, the standard deviations of the rates of return were calculated over the same time periods. For Greyhound, the sample standard deviation was .015 and for Gray Coach it was .035. In terms of coefficients of variation (sample standard deviations divided by sample means), Gray Coach had even more variable rates of return than Greyhound. This fact is not surprising for a number of reasons, though the size of the difference is, perhaps, a bit greater than might be expected.

Generally, economists have observed that larger firms tend to have less variable rates of return.[91] This empirical observation may be due in part to greater diversification of larger firms. Certainly Greyhound is larger and somewhat more diversified than Gray Coach, and for these reasons alone can be expected to report more stable rates of return over time.[92] Although the profits of both firms were affected by employee strikes, train strikes, and postal strikes, these exogenous shocks appear to have had a smaller impact on the overall performance of the larger, more diversified firm.

Yet these results are also consistent with managerial theories of the firm and some of the results of testing these theories. For example, it has been found that management-controlled firms, under some conditions, report both lower and more variable profits than owner-controlled firms.[93] If, as is argued in the property rights literature, the managers of public enterprises are subject to less monitoring than the managers of private enterprises, an extension of the managerial hypotheses would predict precisely what we have observed: Gray Coach, the public enterprise, has lower and more variable profit rates than Greyhound, the private enterprise. The managers of the less closely monitored firm, according to these theories, would have less incentive to report high and stable profits.

---

91 Hall and Weiss, "Firm Size and Profitability" (1967), 49 *Rev. Econ. Stat.* 319; and Palmer, "The Profit Variability Effects of the Managerial Enterprise" (1973), 11 *Western Econ. J.* 228.

92 Greyhound is more diversified than Gray Coach in several ways. First, it has a bus manufacturing subsidiary; second, it operates along a greater geographical diversity of routes; and third, it provides a broader range of sightseeing and charter services.

93 See Palmer, *supra* note 91. Also see Boudreaux, "The Profit Variability Effects of the Managerial Enterprise: Comment" (1975), 13 *Econ. Inquiry* 124; and Palmer's reply, "A Further Analysis of Profit Variability and Managerialism", *ibid.* at 127.

A more careful examination of Table I reveals some evidence that the managers of Gray Coach and the Toronto Transit Commission have, to some extent, attempted to reduce the variablility over time in the reported rates of return for Gray Coach. For example, a comparison of columns I and III indicates that Gray Coach profits were bolstered in low-profit years, especially 1976 and 1977, by the disposal of fully depreciated assets.[94] Clearly one way to smooth out reported profit rates over time is to depreciate assets fully and more quickly than the actual depreciation takes place and then to sell these assets in times of lower-than-normal profits. This is not to say that Gray Coach pursued such a policy, for there may have been legitimate reasons for its accounting practices, but their behaviour is nevertheless consistent with this notion.[95]

Another example of this type of practice appears in a comparison of columns I and V of Table I. Here we see that there is a strongly similar movement over time in the firm's profits and in the increase in payments to the Toronto Transit Commission. When profits were high, payments to the TTC increased by more than when profits were low (see Figure 1).[96] On one hand this observation is explicable by the fact that when profits were high, Gray Coach had more extensive and/or intensive operations involving greater costs, including costs for which they were billed by the TTC. On the other hand, it can be argued that payments to the TTC mask the true profits of Gray Coach and that these payments are adjusted annually in an attempt to avoid politically visible and perhaps unpopular losses or profits which might seem excessive to voter-riders; or they may be adjusted to appropriate Gray Coach profits for the TTC in ways that are not obvious to politicians and auditors.[97]

One implication of these data is that if payments to the TTC are based more on potentially reportable profits than on incurred expenses, then using data on TTC costs which are allocated to Gray Coach for services provided by the TTC may yield very misleading impressions about the operating efficiency of Gray Coach. Conceivably Gray Coach could report certain ex-

---

[94] Gray Coach depreciates its buses quite rapidly relative to other firms in the industry, a practice criticized by Greyhound as highly anomalous in its presentation to the OHTB entitled "1977 Pro Forma Statement for a Competitive Gray Coach Lines, Ltd., Case V," at Schedule 506.

[95] Greyhound emphasized in the Prom Forma Statement, *supra* note 94, that this practice was unique to Gray Coach in the bus passenger service industry.

[96] Although payments to the TTC for administrative services do not follow this pattern so neatly, it is interesting that Gray Coach has ceased making a separate reporting of this portion of its payments to the TTC. As is clear in Figure 1, first-differences of payments to the TTC move in lock-step with both profits and the first-differences of profits.

[97] In fact, although the theories of managerial behaviour suggest that we should observe *more* variable profits in Gray Coach, these apparent attempts to reduce the variability of Gray Coach profits are quite consistent with our earlier prediction that the TTC-GC managers have an incentive to reduce the reported profits of Gray Coach (in good years) by appropriating them indirectly through TTC billing of expenses.

penses which are over-billed to them by the TTC and which would yield performance ratios for Gray Coach which cast the firm in a very unfavourable
light relative to other bus companies. Gray Coach might appear to be
operating very inefficienty when in fact they are merely passing on some of
their profits to the TTC in a less visible form. It is with this caveat in mind
that we turn next to a discussion of operating efficiency and some traditional ways of analyzing efficiency.

FIGURE 1

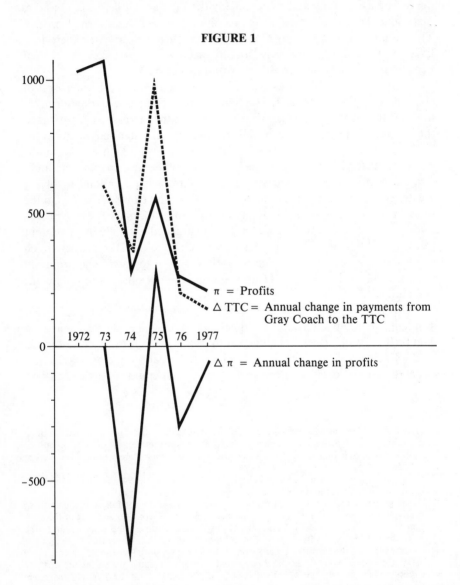

(c) Technical Efficiency

An examination of the technical efficiency of a firm generally involves a comparison of its performance with the performance of other firms (usually designated as "competitive" or something similar) or with some absolute or arbitrary standard. The former technique assumes that the market is the relevant standard and is often used by economists, while the latter is sometimes used in specific cases by management consultants. Studies of the technical efficiency of public enterprises have typically been of the former type, generally comparing them with private enterprises producing similar products or services.[98]

Complete and detailed reviews of these studies have been provided by Borcherding (Chapter 2, Section I) and in Section III of this Chapter. What stands out in these reviews of the literature is that only rarely have economists been able to approximate an assumption of *ceteris paribus* either by finding firms producing a nearly homogeneous output with nearly homogeneous inputs or by including enough important variables in their regressions to allow for the more important noncomparabilities.

We have already discussed the nature of the noncomparabilities between Gray Coach and the other firms operating in Ontario, especially Greyhound, for which we have the most data. We have also pointed out that because of the unique relationship between Gray Coach and the TTC, the data for Gray Coach may not be particularly helpful in discussing comparative technical efficiency. Consequently, the material presented in this section, while it may yield some useful insights into the relative performance of Gray Coach and Greyhound, must be viewed and interpreted with some caution. Not only were we concerned about the quality of data that were available, we also found it impossible to acquire other data and were unable to engage in comparative cost funciton analysis similar to that done in Caves and Christensen.[99] Most of the data used in this section were taken from evidence presented in the Greyhound-Gray Coach entry case, and the OHTB's report to the Provincial Cabinet.[100]

---

[98] References to the more important examples of these studies are provided by Borcherding, Chapter 2 in this volume. See also Section III, "A Positive Theory of Government Enterprise Behaviour", in this chapter.

[99] Caves and Christensen, "The Relative Efficiency of Public and Private Firms in a Competitive Environment: The Case of Canadian Railroads" (1980), 88 *J. Pol. Econ.* 958.

We were also reluctant to employ the Caves-Christensen methodology (which relies on duality theorems) because we had strong reasons to believe that revenues are not entirely cost-determined among our sample of firms.

[100] *Supra* note 50. The details of the case are presented in Section II, "Gray Coach Lines Ltd.— Internal Structure, Market and Political Environment", in this chapter.

(i) Mechanics

According to its own analysis,[101] Greyhound has fewer mechanics per bus than Gray Coach: 85/388 = .251 vs. 99/322 = .307, respectively. This analysis involved the allocation of TTC employees by occupational category to Gray Coach in accordance with TTC-Gray Coach arrangements. However, the use of buses as the base on which the ratios were calculated may be inappropriate due to noncomparabilities in the route structures. It might be more meaningful to examine mechanics per mile, which are .002 and .006 for Greyhound and Gray Coach, respectively. This comparison, too, seems unreasonable in that Greyhound puts more than twice as many miles per year on its buses than Gray Coach does.[102]

In analytic situations for which distance is an inappropriate ratio base, the number of hours in service is often used instead (*e.g.*, tractors in agriculture). With this in mind, we also calculated mechanics per hour: .065 for Greyhound and .145 for Gray Coach. The hours were calculated from the average speeds given by both firms in the exhibits[103] and from total miles. The average speeds reported in the exhibits, however, are quite different from and considerably lower than those which we calculated from the two firm's schedules. Possibly they were calculated on the basis of the drivers' reported hours of driving for payroll purposes or on the basis of the elapsed time buses were out of the garage facilities. At any rate the speeds reported in the exhibits showed more of a difference between the firms than the schedules would indicate should exist.

Interestingly, regardless of the standard of comparison, Gray Coach has more mechanics than Greyhound. There are at least four possible interpretations of this result: (1) the data are incorrect. This possibility cannot easily be dismissed due to the amount of internal arbitrary assignments made by Gray Coach and the TTC; (2) the TTC assigns too many mechanics to Gray Coach; and, related to this point (3) the TTC itself has too many mechanics so that any pro-rationing formula would also automatically assign too many mechanics to Gray Coach. Such a possibility is not inconsistent with the results of other studies of public enterprise which find more than the optimal number of employees for political reasons. Sometimes the jobs are used explicitly for patronage purposes, and sometimes they are used to increase the politician's visibility as large scale job providers, but with no explicit political favouritism shown;[104] and (4) the

---

[101] The Pro Forma Statement, *supra* note 94, submitted by Greyhound in its discussion of comparative efficiencies between Gray Coach and Greyhound, presents a summary of the relevant material in the exhibits and statements from the hearing in Schedule 504.

[102] OHTB Report, *supra* note 50, at 17-A. See also Exhibits 21, 23, 24, 144, 145, and 160 in the appendices to the Report for the data on which the calculations are based.

[103] Pro Forma statement, *supra* note 94, in Schedule 502.

[104] Discussions of these motivations appear in Stigler, *supra* note 68, and Borcherding, ed., *supra* note 62.

TTC has been billing Gray Coach for too many mechanics. This last possibility would be consistent with the argument suggested in the previous section that much of the potential profitability of Gray Coach is redirected to the TTC via charges for repair and maintenance service provided to Gray Coach by the TTC. Aside from the possibility of incorrect data, all three explanations are consistent with our prediction that the TTC-GC managers have strong incentives; (1) to increase the combined sizes of the TTC and Gray Coach; and (2) to do so, in part, by charging Gray Coach for some TTC expenses. And even the first possibility (incorrect data) is consistent with our predictions if the data are conceptually incorrect.

(ii) Maintenance Costs

In its report to the Provincial Cabinet, the Ontario Highway Transport Board asserted that maintenance costs were, ". . . largely independent of route structure".[105] This assertion, without serious qualification, seems incorrect. Short-trip routes with stop-and-go traffic surely create higher maintenance costs per mile than longer express routes. Consequently, if Gray Coach does have more of the shorter, tougher routes, its maintenance costs per mile should be expected to be higher than for Greyhound. In 1975, the maintenance costs per mile were:

Greyhound	12.8¢
National Association of Motor Bus Operators (NAMBO)[106]	16.1¢
Gray Coach	33.5¢

These maintenance costs per mile seem excessively high for Gray Coach relative to other companies, and they make Grey Coach appear to be extremely inefficient. Some of the difference is probably due to differences in route structure, as indicated by the miles per bus in 1975:[107]

	in 000's
Greyhound	132
NAMBO	86
Gray Coach	53

It can be argued that nearly all maintenance costs in the bus passenger industry continue on a calendar basis rather than a mileage basis because the correct basis for comparison must include the hours that buses are in service to correct for the differences in route structure. If so, maintenance costs per bus might be a more meaningful measure.[108]

---

[105] *Supra* note 50, at 28.

[106] The data for NAMBO are based on interstate U.S. carriers.

[107] *Cf.*, note 15. Surely not all of the difference reported here in mileage per bus is due to differences in route structure. As will be indicated later, Gray Coach probably has too many buses for the size of its operation, and this would also contribute to the finding of fewer miles per bus for Gray Coach.

[108] OHTB Report, *supra* note 50, at 28e, ff.

Greyhound	$17,153
Gray Coach	$17,528

These figures are virtually identical, and if the above argument is correct, they considerably dampen the impact of the maintenance costs per mile figures. It is difficult to believe, though, that mileage has no effect on maintenance costs. It is surprising that Gray Coach should have only 40 percent of the Greyhound mileage per bus and yet have slightly higher maintenance costs per bus. One wonders, too, how the maintenance costs per bus can be so similar when Greyhound has .72 maintenance employees per bus as opposed to only .52 for Gray Coach.[109] Gray Coach may have paid higher wages in 1975-76, due in large part to its Toronto location, but they were not 40 percent higher.[110]

Since Gray Coach had more mechanics per bus than Greyhound, and also had fewer maintenance employees per bus, it is possible that the mechanics and other maintenance employees are receiving some of the potential Gray Coach profits. For the TTC-GC managers to allow this to happen is not inconsistent with the broad notions of organizational slack in the theories of managerialism. Also, as Borcherding has pointed out in Chapter 2 in this volume, labour represents one of the many rent-seeking interest groups in the economy, and this group might seek rents via Gray Coach in the form of increased wages and/or employment. We wish to note, though, that the data are also consistent with the idea that the GC-TTC managers have been consistently allocating excess expenses to Gray Coach for maintenance services so that they can expand the size of the combined GC-TTC firm.

There is, however, a potential problem using maintenance costs per bus to examine efficiency: it is quite possible that Gray Coach has an inefficiently large number of buses *and* maintenance costs which are too high as well, so that a ratio of the two would be similar to the bus/maintenance cost ratio for Greyhound.[111] Because Gray Coach is exempt from the Federal income tax, which is essentially a tax on the return to capital, Gray Coach will have an incentive (uniquely different from the Averch-Johnson effect) to be over-capitalized relative to firms which are subject to the Federal tax. This incentive to over-capitalize would result in the use by Gray Coach of more buses than would otherwise be efficient, giving Gray Coach a higher-than-competitive capital-labour ratio. That Greyhound has more maintenance employees per bus than Gray Coach may seem inconsistent with this line of

---

109 Pro Forma Statement, *supra* note 94, at 11-13; *cf.*, Exhibits 11 and 24 in the appendix.

110 OHTB Report, *supra* note 50, at 21a-d, presents data suggesting a wage-rate differential of less than 3%.

111 As noted earlier, the comparison involving mechanics was also least favourable to Gray Coach when buses were used as the basis of comparison. The discussion here applies equally to that comparison.

argument.[112] However, using data on mileage per bus and mileage per driver, we can calculate the ratio of buses per driver for each firm and for NAMBO in 1975:[113]

Greyhound	.45
NAMBO	.58
Gray Coach	.81

Gray Coach has substantially more buses per driver than do the other companies, a result which is consistent with the argument. it seems unlikely that Gray Coach would be able to make much, if any, factor substitution between drivers and buses. If, due to its route structure, Gray Coach needs more buses to solve its scheduling problems, it would likely need more drivers as well. We would be surprised if the production function for inter-city bus passenger service were not one of nearly fixed coefficients for buses and drivers.

The managers of Gray Coach may also wish to have a larger bus fleet to gain additional pay, power, and prestige, in accordance with the managerial theories of firm behaviour. And a further incentive to over-capitalize, in fact to use "too many" of all factors of production, is possibly provided by the desire of the managers to have sufficient quantities of all inputs on hand at all times to assure their offering of more reliable service than would be offered if they were strictly profit-maximizers. Having more of all factors of production ready to be used for unforeseen variations in demand and for peak-load problems will make the managers' jobs easier and increase the size of the firm. The former of these two effects is consistent with Hicks' observation that ". . . the best of all monopoly profits is the quiet life".[114] We have chosen to modernize this theory of managerial behaviour by renaming it, "the Excedrin Theory of Public Enterprise".

Some support for the Excedrin Theory is provided by evidence of fare change applications presented to the OHTB by Gray Coach and other carriers. If the managers of a less closely monitored firm attempt to reduce headaches, one way to do so is to apply less frequently for across-the-board fare increases rather than more often for trip-specific fare increases. Data on the number and type of fare-increase applications indicate Gray Coach behaviour consistent with this line of thought:[115]

---

[112] It need not necessarily be inconsistent, though, if TTC-GC managers can increase their utility more by increasing their use of factors of production other than maintenance employees by more than they could by increasing the number of maintenance employees. This possibility would occur if they can more simply increase the TTC over-billing of Gray Coach for maintenance expenses and increase the size of the TTC system with the proceeds and with the additional provincial/Metro subsidy ensuing from the over-billing. In this way the managers can increase the combined firm size while appearing to respond to political pressure to increase TTC service.

[113] OHTB Report, *supra* note 50, at 17.

[114] Hicks, *supra* note 82.

[115] These data were collected from OHTB files.

Firm	Trip Specific	Across-The-Board
Charterways		
(1975-79)	16	2
Voyageur (1973-79)	12	7
Travelways (1978-79)	11	1
Gray Coach (1974-79)	3	8

As can be readily seen, Gray Coach did indeed seek fewer, across-the-board increases rather than more trip-specific fare incrases.

A final source of support for the Excedrin Theory of Public Enterprise is the fact that Gray Coach uses only two different sizes of buses (43 and 49 passengers) when it might be more efficient to use smaller buses on some of its less well-traveled routes. When we asked about this decision, we were told that it was made to reduce scheduling difficulties. In fairness to Gray Coach managers, it may be more efficient for them to reduce scheduling difficulties than to reduce the asset size of the firm; their decision is, however, also consistent with the Excedrin Theory.

(iii) Support and Overhead Expenses

There is mixed, but fairly strong evidence that Gray Coach has higher support and overhead expenses than other firms. The OHTB Report asserts that Gray Coach had higher administrative costs per mile (9.0¢) in 1975 than Greyhound (4.0¢), but again non-comparabilities in route structure may account for some of this difference.[116] It also reports that for Gray Coach, administrative costs as a percentage of total costs (6.1 percent) were higher than for Greyhound (4.8 percent). Gray Coach has contested this last comparison, claiming that the calculations were done inappropriately.[117] Its own comparison of the ratios of administrative to total costs is

	Greyhound	Gray Coach
1975	7.77%	7.67%
1976	7.64%	7.66%

Although the Gray Coach calculations were probably performed using more comparable data, it must be remembered that if both the total costs and the administrative costs for Gray Coach have been elevated as a result of managerial behaviour or political pressure (to provide more service and/or more jobs), the comparison of such ratios is meaningless.

The last piece of evidence in this section is a comparison of support staff per driver in 1975:[118]

Greyhound	.78
NAMBO	1.05
Gray Coach	1.26

---

116 OHTB Report, *supra* note 50, at 30.
117 Gray Coach petition, *supra* note 40, at 36-37.
118 OHTB Report, *supra* note 50, at 18.

Not only does Gray Coach have more buses per driver, but it also has more support staff per driver than other firms. In sum, there is a fairly convincing case that Gray Coach is over-capitalized and has costs which in general are too high. To some extent these higher costs can be explained by noncomparabilities, but it is doubtful if they can be completely explained away by these factors.

(d) A Model of Inter-City Bus Passenger Service

In this part of Section IV we present a simplified theoretical model of a bus firm. From this model we derive some empirically testable implications about profit or non-profit-oriented behaviour, and then we test these implications with some statistical regressions.

(i) The Model

We assume that the number of people (Q) willing and able to pay to ride a bus for a given distance (D) is a linear function of the fare per mile (F/D). Letting *a, b,* and *m* be constants, we can write the inverse demand function as

(1) $F/D = a - bQ + m/D$

A graph of this demand function is shown in Figure 2, with F/D on the vertical axis and Q on the horizontal axis.

The demand curve depicted indicates that as the fare per mile decreases, more people will want to ride the bus. The slope of the curve, $-b$, captures many of the demographic and geographic variations in demand. Assuming that all potential passengers have similar demand functions for regularly scheduled inter-city bus passenger service, an increase in demand resulting from increased population will *not* have any effect on the intercept of this curve; it will simply change $-b$, the slope, rotating the demand curve outward and making it flatter. Also it will not affect the price elasticity of demand or marginal revenue associated with any given fare per mile.

The intercept of the demand curve shown in Figure 2 is determined by *a* and by *m*/D. Generally speaking, the greater the costs of alternative modes of transportation, the more people will be willing and able to pay for bus service, and the higher will be the intercept of this demand curve. The term *a* will vary as the fare per mile varies for competitive modes; *m*/D will vary as the fixed costs per mile of competitive modes vary. The constant *m* will also indicate the rate at which fare per mile falls as the length of a trip increases.[119]

---

[119] The rate at which fare per mile declines as distance increases is commonly referred to as the fare taper.

FIGURE 2

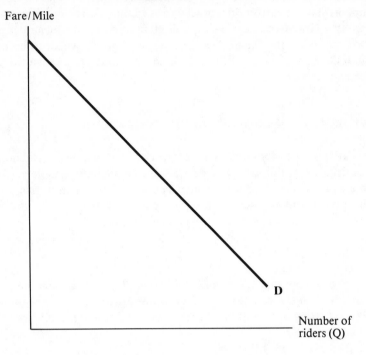

The total costs of providing the bus service in our model are given by

(2) $TC = e + fQD$

where e represents fixed costs, and f represents the incremental costs of carrying an extra passenger an extra mile.

The marginal conditions for profit maximization require that the firm set its fares at

(3) $F^* = (a + f)D/2 + m/2$

and its profit-maximizing fare per mile will be

(4) $(F/D)^* = (a + f)/2 + m/2D$

Another necessary condition for profit maximization is that

(5) $(F/D)^* \geq (e/QD) + f$

If the firm is a profit-maximizing firm, capacity utilization, Q, will not have any direct bearing on its fares, nor will the slope of its demand curve(s). Capacity utilization will affect only the decision concerning whether to operate a bus. The firm will, as a result, engage in a sequential decision-making process of first deciding on the optimal fare for a particular scheduled trip, and then deciding when or if to make the trip. This feature of the model derives from the two quite plausible assumptions of a linear demand curve and constant marginal costs per passenger mile. It also is quite consistent with the structure of decision-making described for us during interviews with the managers of firms included in our study.

As we explained earlier, there are many good reasons why one might not observe profit-maximizing behaviour and fares in the inter-city bus passenger industry. For one thing, the fares in Ontario are regulated by the Ontario Highway Transport Board, though our impression is that the regulatory constraint is not serious and may not be binding. For another, there may be political forces at work encouraging cross-subsidization between different interest groups as emphasized by Borcherding and in Section III. And the managers of these firms, if they are utility-maximizers whose utility functions are not congruent with their firms' profit functions, may also have incentives to engage in some unprofitable behaviour. In all three possible situations, the firms will select F/D for a particular route which differs from (F/D)*, but which still lies on the demand curve.

These differences in objective functions and firm behaviour imply that capacity utilization should be included in a regression model to explain F/D. If its coefficient is not significantly different from zero, we cannot reject the hypothesis that the firm is a profit-maximizer; and if its coefficient is significantly different from zero, we have some strong evidence in support of the non-profit behaviour hypothesis. The regression model to be estimated, then, is

(6) $F/D = A + M/D + BQ + \epsilon$

If the firm maximizes profits, B will equal zero; A will equal the average of the intercept term and the marginal costs, $(a + f)/2$; and M will equal $m/2$. If the firm does not maximize profits, B might not equal zero; A will equal the intercept of the demand curve; a; and M will equal m. Of course, by looking at A and M alone, we will not be able to distinguish between profit and nonprofit maximizing behaviour.

We are interested not only in obtaining evidence as to whether the firms maximize profits; we would also like to know whether the large block of voters in Toronto can directly or indirectly influence fare regulation by the Minister and the OHTB to obtain lower fares for trips originating or ending in Toronto. Alternatively, there may be strong voter support for lower fares to residents living in and travelling between outlying communities, in which case trips to or from Toronto would have higher fares than the others. If there is a type of cross-subsidization practiced by the firms or possibly enforced by the provincial authorities, it is not clear whether the subsidy (and/or tax) would be on a per passenger basis or on a per passenger-mile basis. Including a dummy variable to represent trips to or from Toronto in equation (6) will specify a per passenger mile impact of cross-subsidization; multiplying both sides of equation (6) by distance and using fares as the dependent variable would mean specifying a *per passenger* effect of cross-subsidization if the dummy variable were included (and not multiplied by distance).

Similarly, certain routes may be affected by the existence of train and/or bus competition. Although the provincial government regulates bus fares, if it does so imperfectly, the intercepts of the demand curves will be affected by this competition. We can test for both the strength of fare regulation and the effects of competition by including dummy variables to represent bus and train competition. Once again, depending on whether we use fare per mile or just the fare as our dependent variable, the coefficients of the competition dummy variables will represent per passenger mile or per passenger effects, respectively.

Our basic regression model, then, can be represented by

(7a) $F = AD + M + BQD + \bar{t}T + \bar{b}Bus + \bar{n}Train + e'$ or

(7b) $F/D = A + M/D + BQ + tT + bBus + nTrain + e'$,

where T is a dummy variable representing trips with Toronto as the origin or destination and e' is an error term.[120]

Unfortunately we were not able to obtain capacity utilization data from all of the firms in our sample. Consequently, we were forced to omit the terms involving Q from our multifirm regressions. Our having to do so implies that we are forced to assume that either the firms are all profit maximizers or that their non-profit behaviour follows a pattern which makes it undetectable in the aggregate.

The data for our multifirm regressions were taken from the published regular fares and schedules for the Fall of 1978 of the five major companies operating in southwestern Ontario: Gray Coach, Greyhound, Voyageur, Travelways, and Charterways. We generally collected the data for fares, etc., between cities or towns which were shown in bold print in the published schedules and which lay on a single route (a list of the cities included for each firm is provided in Appendix A at the end of this chapter). We specifically wanted only those cities on single routes so that we could avoid the problems of fare and distance calculations for multipart and interline trips, and we were willing to accept whatever bias this selection procedure might impart to our statistical tests. We realize, too, that by eliminating the smallest towns and villages from our sample, we may be biasing our tests of cross-subsidization; nevertheless, many of the towns included are very small and have little traffic, and so we expect this bias, if any, to be small.

(ii) Empirical Results

a. Multifirm Analysis

The results of the regression for equation (7a) are presented in Table III. Looking down the first column, we see that trips to and from Toronto

---

[120] We experimented with alternative theoretical and economic specifications of the model, including nonlinear (*e.g.*, loglinear and polynomial) demand functions, with less satisfactory results than those reported here. We felt the experimentation was necessary because it was possible that the specification rather than the data was generating the reported results. Alternative specifications, when not plagued with multicollinearity, yielded results not markedly different from those yielded with our more simple specification and often with lower levels of overall significance.

have fares which are 19.6¢ lower than other fares, *cet. par.,* but this result is not statistically significant. On routes along which there is bus competition, the fares are insignificantly higher, by about 28¢ per passenger; and on routes along which there is train competition, the fares are significantly lower, by about 40¢. Also, dummy variables were included for each of the firms, except Gray Coach, to see whether Gray Coach charges fares which differ significantly from those of the other firms. Three of the other four firms do, perhaps, charge lower fares, according to these regression results, but only the coefficient for Travelways is statistically significant, with that of Charterways nearly so. The adjusted R^{-2} is high in this and all the regressions reported in Table III because distance explains a large amount of the variation in fares.

Because of its possible uniqueness, *i.e.*, being owned by the Toronto Transit Commission, Gray Coach may have its own particular incentives to engage in cross-subsidization between passengers on different routes. To test for this possibility, we ran the regression reported in the second column of Table III. This regression form is identical to that used in the first column with the addition of GCTO, a dummy variable identifying scheduled routes to and from Toronto for Gray Coach. With the addition of this variable, the results change somewhat dramatically. Gray Coach passengers to and from Toronto, on the average, appear to pay nearly 92¢ less, *cet. par.*, than do other passengers in southwestern Ontario. Although the coefficients for bus and train competition change slightly in both absolute value and significance, it is difficult to believe that GCTO is picking up the effects of competition since none of the other bus lines appears to charge lower fares to or from Toronto.

Another interesting feature of this regression's results is that now the coefficients for all of the other bus lines are negative, and significantly so for all but Voyageur. In general, it seems that Gray Coach trips to or from Toronto have fares commensurate with those of most of the other firms in the industry, while the remaining Gray Coach trips and most Voyageur trips have fares which are higher.

This conclusion is reasonably well born out in the remaining columns of Table III, which report the results of regressions for individual firms. Once again we see that only Gray Coach has lower fares for trips originating or ending in Toronto. The only anomaly among these regressions which we are at a loss to explain is the positive and significant coefficient for Voyageur trips to or from Toronto.[121]

---

[121] Numerous possible explanations (for which we have no evidence) have been suggested to us: (1) Perhaps, since Voyageur is a Quebec-based firm, it is required by its owners and/or regulators to tax people traveling to Toronto rather than to Montreal. (2) Perhaps, since Voyageur has no Metro Toronto constituency, it must respond more to Ontario provincial pressure via the OHTB to subsidize (relatively speaking) the people living in and traveling between the smaller communities of Ontario. This explanation assumes that such pressures via the OHTB exist for all firms but that for some reason Voyageur responds to them the most while Gray Coach, because of its ownership by the TTC, responds to them the least.

TABLE III
Multifirm Analysis
Dependent Variable is Fare; t's in parentheses

	I Full Sample	II Full Sample	III Gray Coach	IV Greyhound	V Voyageur	VI Charterways	VII Travelways
Constant	.663 (4.49)	.806 (5.25)	.437 (3.58)	-.0403 (-.0489)	1.60 (7.46)	.195 (.561)	.355 (1.04)
Distance	.0413 (80.95)	.0413 (82.04)	.0425 (46.24)	.0430 (47.90)	.0365 (40.10)	.0437 (12.89)	.0372 (10.84)
Bus Competition	.282 (.899)	.387 (1.24)	-.373 (-1.40)	2.49 (2.60)		-2.28 (-2.16)	.618 (1.06)
Train Competition	-.405 (-2.66)	-.382 (-2.54)	.182 (1.37)	-.645 (-.845)	-.439 (-2.04)	-2.38 (-2.25)	-.281 (-.340)
Toronto	-.196 (-1.16)	.206 (.947)	-.733 (-3.59)	-.594 (-1.02)	.882 (3.20)		-.00623 (-1.04)
GCTO		-.919 (-2.87)					

Greyhound	-2.39 (-.967)	-.527 (-2.00)					
Voyageur	.141 (.822)	-.0758 (-.409)					
Charterways	-.374 (-1.73)	-.516 (-2.37)					
Travelways	-.673 (-2.73)	-.971 (-3.68)					
R^2	.973	.974	.968	.990	.962	.824	.922
No. of observations	248	248	86	28	72	38	24
Ave. Fare/Km	.0460	.0460	.0482	.0406	.0472	.0455	.0418
Ave. Distance	159.7	159.7	119.4	315.8	202.3	89.6	114.9
Ave. Speed (Km/hr)	64.9	64.9	66.6	62.8	63.7	67.1	61.1
% Toronto	23.1	23.1	30.2	32.1	18.1	0	37.5
% Bus Competition	4.1	4.1	7.0	10.7	0	2.6	8.3
% Train Competition	40.9	40.9	50.0	82.1	45.8	2.6	4.2

TABLE IV
Multifirm Analysis
Dependent Variable is Fare/Km; t's in parentheses

	I Full Sample	II Full Sample	III Gray Coach	IV Greyhound	V Voyageur	VI Charterways	VII Travelways
Constant	.0414 (27.61)	.0431 (29.96)	.0417 (22.56)	.0417 (15.97)	.0385 (22.90)	.0448 (16.81)	.0410 (6.15)
1/Distance	.478 (9.71)	.455 (9.12)	.487 (8.18)	.108 (.606)	.967 (7.17)	.127 (.981)	.106 (.254)
Bus Competition	-.00805 (-2.79)	-.00199 (-.7456)	-.00336 (-.904)	.00570 (1.71)		-.0346 (-3.63)	.00626 (.864)
Train Competition	-.00058 (-.0446)	-.000534 (-.413)	.00120 (.654)	-.00331 (-1.23)	.000709 (.404)	-.0190 (-1.98)	-1.63 (-.165)
Toronto	.000915 (.664)	.00340 (1.85)	-.00391 (-1.81)	.000954 (.467)	.00518 (2.28)		-.247 (-.441)
GCTO		-.00761 (-2.78)					
Greyhound	-.00419 (-2.13)	-.00584 (-2.68)					
Voyageur	.00200 (1.39)	.000221 (1.36)					
Charterways	-.00333 (-1.83)	-.00504 (-2.67)					
Travelways	-.00564 (-2.71)	-.00785 (-3.43)					
R^2	.343	.334	.510	.142	.423	.293	-.104

Looking next at Table IV, one can see the results of our regressions using equation (7b). Here the dependent variable is fare per kilometer rather than just fare. Hence the coefficients of the competition and Toronto variables will show the effects of these influences per passenger kilometer rather than just per passenger. At a glance, one can see that the results are very similar to those presented in Table III. GCTO has a significantly negative coefficient in the second regression of the full sample; and Toronto has a negative but not significant coefficient in the Gray Coach regression. It appears that fares per kilometer for Gray Coach trips involving Toronto are about the same as the fares per kilometer for the other firms, including Voyageur trips outside of Toronto. Gray Coach trips not involving Toronto have fares per kilometer similar to those for Voyageur on trips involving Toronto.

It is interesting to note that only for Gray Coach and for Voyageur is M, the coefficient of $1/D$, significantly greater than zero, implying a greater fare taper for these firms than for the others. Recalling that M in some sense represents the fixed costs of competitive modes of transportation, it is difficult to believe that these should vary from one firm to another. It is more likely that in this case, M represents some cross-subsidization from passengers taking short trips to passengers taking longer trips on these two bus lines.

As we pointed out in our discussion of the regression equation, if the firm is a profit maximizer, M will equal m/2; but if the firm is not a profit maximizer, M will equal m. M is the constant in the regressions of Table III, and it is the coefficient of $1/D$ in Table IV. In both tables, M is significantly greater than zero only for the full sample, Gray Coach, and Voyageur regressions. These results lend further credence to the theories predicting that the Gray Coach-TTC managers may be pursuing non-profit maximizing goals.

In summary, we see that Gray Coach has a pricing strategy which differs significantly from that of the other firms in southwestern Ontario. Because these other firms are not public enterprises this finding of different pricing strategies, along with the other indications of non-profit-oriented behaviour and performance, provides strong additional support for the theory developed in Section III.

b. Gray Coach

Because of the help and co-operation of Mr. Roy Perrot of Gray Coach, we were able to obtain capacity utilization data for each of their buses run during a one-week period in the fall of 1978. We collected data for the number of people on the bus, the entire distance between selected points and for the number of people on the bus for any portion of the trip between those points. Assuming that, on average, the passengers on the bus for a portion of the trip rode half the distance, we devised a capacity utilization measure that is equal to (a) the number of passengers for the entire trip, plus (b) one-half the number of passengers for a portion of the trip. The averages (a) and (a) + (b) are presented in Appendix B at the end of this chapter.

In this portion of our empirical work, the unit of observation was a single bus trip between two selected points. We have many more observations for some city pairs than for others (unlike the multifirm portion of our empirical work) for two unrelated reasons. First and foremost, there were many more buses run between some cities than between others; second, and less honourable, we simply fatigued of writing down zeros for some trips between small population centres. Nevertheless, we have a very broad sample. For the full sample there are 3,815 observations with a mean capacity utilization of 23.1 (standard deviation = 11.5). In a subsample of all observations with capacity utilization (Q) less than or equal to 20, there are 1,709 observations with a mean of 12.87 and standard deviation of 4.9; and in a subsample for $Q \geq 26$ there are 1,477 observations with a mean of 34.9 and standard deviation of 7.1.

The results of regressing the fare on the independent variables are presented in Table V. Because of multicollinearity between D and $Q \times D$, and because we generally have a preference for discussing effects in per mile terms (as seems reasonable from our results), we will move on to a discussion of these results, which are presented in Table VI. Column 1 shows the results of the regression using our full sample. The constant and coefficients here differ from those in column 3 of Table IV, in part because here distance is measured in miles rather than in kilometers, in part because of the differences in the observations, and, perhaps, in part because of the inclusion of Q. The results for our full sample are presented in the first column: they are fairly similar to those presented in Table IV. The coefficient of $1/D$ is positive and significant; and the coefficient for Toronto is negative and significant. The coefficient for train competition here, however, is significantly negative; and the coefficient for capacity utilization is not significantly different from zero.

We found it difficult to believe (and inconsistent with our theoretical model) that passengers to or from Toronto would pay substantially lower fares per mile and yet the firm would be maximizing profits, as indicated by the insignificant coefficient for Q. Consequently we split the sample of observations into various subsamples and reran the regressions on those subsamples. The results of these additional regressions are reported in the remaining columns of Tables V and VI.

The first subdivision of our sample was between short and long trips (columns 2 and 3). [122] Here we see not only a greater taper in the fare per mile

---

[122] This particular subdivision was suggested to us by members of the industry who see the private auto as providing considerably more competition for short trips than for long trips.

TABLE V
Gray Coach
Dependent Variable is Fare; t's in parentheses

	I Full Sample	II Distance < 70 miles	III Distance ≥ 70 miles	IV Outside Toronto	V To or From Toronto	VI No Train Competition	VII Train Competition	VIII No Bus Competition	IX Bus Competition	X Number of Riders ≤ 20	XI Number of Riders ≥ 26
Constant	.774 (35.46)	.215 (8.70)	1.65 (36.30)	.241 (13.68)	.779 (25.14)	.407 (17.47)	.594 (26.86)	.713 (30.24)	1.04 (40.60)	.681 (26.06)	.855 (19.29)
Distance (in miles)	.0708 (247.6)	.0792 (114.8)	.0675 (177.5)	.0806 (264.8)	.0625 (200.2)	.0762 (168.9)	.0704 (203.7)	.0716 (225.4)	.0645 (345.8)	.0735 (152.2)	.0664 (79.51)
Bus Competition	.0933 (2.08)		.421 (8.16)		.682 (15.75)	.0351 (.889)	-.199 (-2.48)			-.138 (-2.19)	.333 (4.31)
Train Competition	-.227 (-10.28)	-.204 (-13.18)	-.274 (-7.14)	-.213 (-12.14)	-.112 (-3.63)			-.187 (-8.14)		-.262 (10.14)	-.174 (3.75)
Toronto	-.562 (-29.94)	-.362 (-16.91)	-1.22 (-42.47)			-.572 (-20.66)	-.594 (-26.81)	-.580 (-30.06)		-.656 (-26.08)	-.425 (-12.89)
Quantity × Distance	-.0000350 (-3.97)	.0000166 (1.41)	-.0000388 (-3.87)	-.0000719 (-6.58)	-.0000116 (-1.33)	-.0000111 (-.720)	-.0000310 (-3.08)	-.0000498 (-5.00)	-.00000656 (1.18)	-.0000935 (-3.26)	.0000208 (.891)
R^2	.974	.947	.970	.990	.977	.985	.973	.967	.999	.981	.969
No. of Observations	3815	1958	1857	1687	2128	821	2994	3663	182	1709	1477
Average Fare	5.71	3.55	7.99	4.65	6.56	5.09	5.89	5.25	11.10	5.44	5.93
Average Fare/Mile	.0758	.0791	.0723	.0817	.0711	.0822	.0740	.0760	.0726	.0776	.0741
Average Distance	77.6	45.7	111.2	57.7	93.4	64.5	81.2	73.7	155.6	72.44	81.98

TABLE V—*Continued*

	I Full Sample	II Distance < 70 miles	III Distance ≥ 70 miles	IV Out-side Toronto	V To or From Toronto	VI No Train Compe-tition	VII Train Compe-tition	VIII No Bus Compe-tition	IX Bus Compe-tition	X Number of Riders ≤ 20	XI Number of Riders ≥ 26
Average Speed (mph)	41.6	41.2	41.9	39.5	43.2	39.3	42.2	41.4	44.3	40.2	43.4
Average No. of Riders	23.1	22.8	23.4	20.1	25.5	19.7	24.0	23.0	24.1	12.9	34.9
% Toronto	55.8	41.0	71.4	0	100	39.5	60.3	53.6	100	43.1	68.5
% Bus Competition	4.8	0	9.8	0	8.6	14.3	2.2	0	100	4.2	4.9
% Train Competition	78.5	73.9	83.3	70.5	84.8	0	100	80.6	35.7	72.0	85.9

TABLE VI
Gray Coach
Dependent Variable is Fare/mile; t's in parentheses

	I Full Sample	II Distance < 70 miles	III Distance ≥ 70 miles	IV Outside Toronto	V To or From Toronto	VI No Train Competition	VII Train Competition	VIII No Bus Competition	IX Bus Competition	X Number of Riders ≤ 20	XI Number of Riders ≥ 26
Constant	.0825 (193.3)	.0839 (107.5)	.0785 (146.4)	.0860 (136.7)	.0639 (119.8)	.0766 (91.51)	.0791 (202.1)	.0826 (187.6)	.0642 (183.67)	.0846 (125.4)	.0777 (72.00)
1/Distance	.127 (12.07)	.0987 (5.30)	.398 (10.74)	.0886 (6.57)	.601 (22.50)	.404 (18.35)	.00892 (.798)	.127 (11.81)	1.08 (28.69)	.0958 (6.84)	.187 (9.34)
Number of Riders (Q)	.000005 (.501)	.000006 (.406)	-.000017 (-1.75)	-.000058 (-3.29)	.000039 (4.22)	-.000020 (-.799)	-.000006 (-.635)	.000005 (.500)	.0000102 (1.18)	-.0000566 (-1.69)	.0000663 (2.72)
Bus Competition	-.0097 (-1.79)		+.00339 (8.40)			.00332 (3.67)	-.00173 (-2.29)			-.000309 (-.369)	-.00128 (-1.44)
Train Competition	-.00606 (-21.68)	-.00743 (-17.81)	-.00283 (-9.32)	-.00790 (-17.97)	-.00190 (-5.99)			-.00614 (-20.66)		-.00584 (160.4)	-.00634 (-11.40)
Toronto	-.00787 (-29.52)	-.00520 (-10.69)	-.0110 (-46.53)			-.00860 (-12.51)	-.00841 (-31.33)	-.00786 (-28.73)		-.00936 (-24.33)	-.00514 (-11.33)
R^2	.444	.305	.594	.194	.246	.538	.338	.439	.824	.476	.356

for longer trips, but also a greater discount in the fare per mile for trips involving Toronto. The coefficient for bus competition is positive and significant most likely because Greyhound recently selected those routes which were the most profitable to enter, and we have identified an entry decision, not a fare decision, with this variable. In this subdivision, as with the full sample, the coefficient for capacity utilization does not significantly differ from zero. The greater fare taper (*M* from our earlier discussion) and greater discount for Toronto trips, combined with a coefficient on *Q* which *is* significant at the 5 percent level for a one-tailed test, are all suggestive of non-profit-maximization on these longer trips.

The next subdivision of our sample was between trips involving Toronto and other trips. In this subdivision (columns 4 and 5), important differences emerge. The constant is much lower for trips involving Toronto, but this is to be expected because those trips have already been identified as having lower fares per mile. There is also a large difference between the coefficients for $1/D$ indicating that for trips involving Toronto the fare per mile taper is greater. Interpreting the coefficient as a representation of the fare per mile taper, it appears that short-haul passengers to or from Toronto are subsidizing long-haul passengers to or from Toronto. This interpretation is consistent with the coefficients for Toronto trips shown in columns 2 and 3. And following our earlier discussions of this coefficient, the larger *M* for trips involving Toronto implies non-profit fare structures for these routes. Note that the R^{-2}'s are considerably lower for the regressions over this subdivision of the sample than they are for the full sample or for other subdivisions of the sample. These Low R^{-2}'s provide an additional indication that economic variables are not as important relative to non-economic variables in explaining variations in fare per mile within these subdivisions of the sample. Consequently, they provide additional evidence of non-profit-oriented behaviour of the firm, and they highlight the sub-samples of routes among which such behaviour is most prevalent.

On this subdivision of the sample, we see for the first time some additional evidence of non-profit-oriented behaviour on the part of Gray Coach. For trips with both origin and destination outside Toronto, the coefficient for *Q* is significantly negative, while for trips to or from Toronto it is significantly positive. In the former case, the coefficient may indeed be reflecting different price-output configurations along a negatively-sloped demand curve, but it is difficult to accept the notion of a positively-sloped demand curve for trips involving Toronto. Rather, we suspect that this positive coefficient reflects a policy of giving a greater discount to passengers on trips with lower capacity utilization. To anticipate the presentation of our results somewhat, this suspicion is supported by the results presented in columns 10 and 11, where the coefficient for Toronto trips is considerably larger (in absolute value) for trips of low capacity utilization.

The next four columns of Table VI present the results of subdividing our sample by the type of competition facing the firm. Here there are no great surprises so long as it is kept in mind that trips facing bus competition are a subset of trips to or from Toronto, and hence the results for these trips are similar to those for all trips involving Toronto. As a further note, however, it appears that the existence of train competition presents a market force which severely constrains Gray Coach's ability to set fares per mile with a significant distance taper, *i.e.*, it constrains Gray Coach to behave as if it is a profit-maximizing firm along those routes.

The final two columns represent a subdivision of our sample into low and high capacity utilization trips. Once again, we see differences in the distance tapers and also some indication that capacity utilization influences pricing decisions.

In particular, the low capacity routes, like the routes beginning and ending outside Toronto appear to have fares not established according to profit-maximizing criteria. The coefficients seem to be picking up the slope of the demand curve and the amount of the discount offered passengers traveling to or from Toronto. As we noted earlier, the rider to or from Toronto appear to get more of a discount on the low-capacity-utilization routes than on the high-capacity-utilization routes.

In summary, the results presented in the six tables provide considerable support for a number of hypotheses predicting that a public enterprise would not always behave in a profit-maximizing fashion. Gray Coach seems, on balance to charge higher fares than most of the private firms in the industry. Nevertheless, it engages in internal cross-subsidization as well. It clearly offers lower fares to passengers traveling to and from Toronto. But despite these lower fares, some of these trips are sufficiently profitable that the firm can "afford" to use the profits (1) to offer even greater discounts for Toronto trips with low capacity utilization, and (2) to continue to operate routes with low price-cost margins and still be able to meet its profit constraint of "break even plus a bit."

These Gray Coach performance characteristics identified by our regressions results are, for the most part, consistent with the predictions generated by our synthesis of the various theories of public enterprise together with the institutional framework peculiar to the Gray Coach operating environment. Whether consciously or not, the managers of TTC-GC are behaving as if they are reasonably well-insulated from most political forces and are able to maximize their utility by increasing the size of the combined firms. They appear to operate (1) with more than the profit-maximizing rate of utilization of several types of inputs, (2) along many routes which are unprofitable, and (3) with fares which reduce profits on some politically sensitive portions of their route structure. These results can also, however, be interpreted, with careful selection, very generously for the managers of the TTC-GC. Even though they are not politically constrained to do so, it is clear that they are operating Gray Coach along some routes which would otherwise be without commercial transportation services. In this respect, the managers are redistributing wealth from Metro taxpayers (owners of Gray Coach) to other Ontario residents. This effect may very well be consistent with the social goals of the voters in the province. What is not clear, though, is whether the social costs of having Gray Coach (with all of its other apparent market distortions) do so is the socially optimal manner in which to provide a redistribution of wealth to the people living along routes which would not be served if Gray Coach ceased operating along its unprofitable routes. Politically, this method of wealth redistribution is not extremely visible to the voter-taxpayers providing the financial support for it, yet it is highly visible to its beneficiaries. As a result, the method may be politically optimal despite its costs in terms of lost social efficiency and the attendant reduction in social welfare.

V. CONCLUSIONS

In Section IV we presented empirical results consistent with the predictions of our model developed in Section III. We found that Gray Coach, Ltd. is being operated inefficiently, and that the inefficiencies manifest themselves in ways which are consistent with the managers' pursuit of their own self-interest. Because the managers of Gray Coach are also managers of the Toronto Transit Commission, their self-interest affects their decisions concerning both Gray Coach and its interaction with the TTC. Postulating that managerial self-interest includes pay, power, prestige, and job security, and following the literature developed on this topic, we predicted that the GC-TTC managers would seek to increase the joint size of Gray Coach and the TTC. In Section III we demonstrated algebraically how the managers could increase the size of the TTC by expanding Gray Coach beyond its profit-maximizing size. We also pointed out that the pursuit of self-interest by the managers would be constrained to some extent by forces in the political and economic marketplace, thus shaping their decisions about pricing and the manifestation of overexpansion within Gray Coach. In this section we assess the results presented in Section IV relative to competing explanations and with respect to social goals.

(a) Alternative Explanations

(i) Market Failure

There are three categories of market failure which might explain public ownership of Gray Coach and, more importantly for our study, which might explain the performance of Gray Coach. The first market failure we will discuss is externalities, the second is market power, and the third is option demand.

There are two types of externalities which might help to explain the performance behaviour of Gray Coach. The first of these is the negative externality of congestion in Toronto created by commuters from outside Toronto. All Metro taxpayers may be willing to pay higher taxes rather than have Gray Coach maximize profits (and use the profits to reduce the overall level of taxation) if Gray Coach uses these foregone potential profits to encourage commuters to ride the bus rather than drive to and from Toronto. Such a line of reasoning might help to explain the existence of lower fares for Gray Coach trips to or from Toronto. Of course it is unclear that if reduction of congestion is a desired objective then such a subsidy via Gray Coach fare differentials is an efficient or even effective means of attaining the objective. We should point out that nowhere in our research did we read or hear such an argument.

A second type of externality is a positive one, emanating from the increased utility derived by most (or many) people from indirect support of the residents of small rural communities. We are at a loss to explain the phenomenon, but we perceive in political statements as well as in popular writings in magazines and newspapers, that there exists in many people's minds a "yeoman ideal". Many people seem unwilling to exchange their urban standards of living for this yeoman ideal yet they willingly support policies designed to reduce the costs of those who do pursue the more rural life. These people would also be willing to forego possible tax cuts, which they *could* have if Gray Coach maximized profits, in exchange for having Gray Coach provide unprofitable service to smaller rural communities. We are not sure how much wealth people would be willing to forego in order to generate increasing amounts of these positive externalities, but we are confident that most people are presently unaware of the amount they are paying to subsidize this objective.

The second market failure is market power in the bus passenger industry. Due to entry restrictions imposed by the Ontario Highway Transport Board (at least until 1976), Gray Coach had a virtual monopoly on its routes. It may in fact have been attempting to behave as a profit maximizing, price discriminating monopolist by charging lower fares on trips to or from Toronto and by running other trips which did not cover full costs but which did cover incremental costs. If the travelers to or from Toronto have a higher price elasticity of demand than do other Gray Coach passengers, Gray Coach could be price discriminating by charging them lower per-mile fares. Toronto passengers might have a higher price elasticity of demand if they have more, better, and/or lower cost alternatives available to them. These conditions do not seem prevalent, however, for the auto (Gray Coach's major competitor) is available as a competitor on all the routes. Similarly, train service is available on most of the routes as well, limiting Gray Coach's ability to discriminate (see Table V).

Even if Gray Coach were engaging in monopolistic price discrimination, it is clear that their behaviour is *not* profit maximizing discrimination. We base this conclusion on two general results presented in Section IV. The first is that Gray Coach has considerable inefficiencies throughout its operations which reduce its profits, and it seems unlikely that a profit maximizing firm would pursue profit maximization in pricing but not in its dual, cost minimization. The second fact is that Gray Coach has routes which clearly are not covering their incremental costs, another fact inconsistent with the model of profit maximization. And finally, the regression coefficients revealed in Section IV, especially in the subsamples of Table VI, are inconsistent with profit maximization.

The third type of market failure is, in theory, a special type of positive externality—option demand. The availability of regularly scheduled intercity bus passenger service is of value to Metro residents because it acts like an insurance policy, giving them the option of taking the bus should alternatives be temporarily delayed or inconvenient *e.g.*, a person whose car breaks down during a train strike on a foggy night (when planes cannot fly) still has the possibility of taking the bus. And even if that person never actually takes the bus, he or she might value having the option available as insurance against unforeseen risks. Of course many, if not most, people would be unwilling to contribute voluntarily to the provision of the service, preferring instead to be free riders. For this reason passenger transportation is often subsidized with tax revenues or publicly owned. As with the congestion argument, we never read or heard this argument applied to Gray Coach. Furthermore, it seems unlikely that Metro residents would forego possible tax reductions to satisfy the option demands of people traveling between rural communities, the routes which are most heavily subsidized by Gray Coach. In other words, Gray Coach may perform in a fashion which satisfies some option demands, but since these demands are not necessarily those of Metro residents, it does not seem plausible that such a theory can be used to explain the behaviour of the firm.

(ii) Cross Subsidization

One of the arguments put forward consistently by Gray Coach in the Greyhound entry case was that it was offering service at below cost to many rural communities, using the profits from its more heavily traveled routes to effect the cross subsidy. This argument is probably incorrect. Rural communities are indeed being subsidized, but not necessarily by "profits" from the more heavily traveled routes (recall, in fact, that most of these routes involve trips to or from Toronto, routes on which passengers pay *less* than the profit-maximizing fare). More likely these subsidies are coming indirectly from the taxpayers of Metro in the form of foregone Gray Coach profits (and, hence, foregone tax reductions). While the OHTB might informally require cross-subsidization as a condition of a firm's license, we doubt that OHTB pressure has generated the type of behaviour observed in Gray Coach. For one thing, the licensing regulations under the Public Vehicles Act authorize route abandonment upon ten days notice to the OHTB. Presumably, firms need not continue to operate unprofitable routes, at least insofar as the law is concerned. Moreover, Greyhound has consistently operated elsewhere in Ontario without also being required to operate along unprofitable routes. We know that Cabinet did refer the entry case back to the OHTB to study the impact of Greyhound's entry on service to rural communities, but this decision reflects the political pressures on Cabinet and should cast further doubt on the argument that the OHTB has been significantly concerned about cross-subsidization in the inter-city bus passenger industry. And it must be remembered that both Cabinet and the OHTB have province-wide constituencies, while Gray Coach has a municipal constituency. Cabinet and the OHTB might understandably respond to arguments favouring indirect cross-subsidization from Metro taxpayers to rural residents, but surely Metro taxpayers would be less likely to support such a policy.

What emerges from this discussion of alternative explanations is that none provides a satisfactory explanation of the results presented in Section IV. While each possible alternative explanation is consistent with some of the behaviour of Gray Coach, none can explain the entire package of results. Yet the model presented in Section III is consistent with the results presented in Section IV. Cross-subsidization occurs because utility maximizing managers respond to political forces, but they do so in many ways which also increase the size of the combined Gray Coach-TTC firm in order to increase their own pay, power, prestige and job security. The questions now to be addressed are: (1) whether the objectives attained by Gray Coach's performance are actually those desired by (a) its owners, and (b) the province; and (2) whether these objectives might be more efficiently attained via alternative institutional arrangements.

(b) Social Objectives

We have no direct evidence (*e.g.*, survey results) of constituency views concerning the performance of Gray Coach. We would be very surprised, though, if its owners (*i.e.*, the Metro taxpayers) would support the present goals of the firm if they realized the opportunity costs of these goals. Nevertheless, these costs are probably very low on a per household basis, and so the voting taxpayers are unlikely to be able to organize an effective political lobby to change the behaviour of the firm.

The non-Metro residents of the Province of Ontario, especially Southwestern Ontario, derive the greatest net benefit from the policies of Gray Coach and will continue, through their political representatives, to support them. The major concern of Cabinet in the Greyhound entry case was not efficiency, nor was it whether Metro residents were receiving a fair rate of return on their investment. Rather, Cabinet, a body in which non-Metro residents are strongly represented, was concerned with continuing service to rural communities. And the final decision of the OHTB reflected this concern with their finding that rural service would not deteriorate despite the risk of cream-skimming by Greyhound. These concerns and positions by the provincial political decision-makers serve to emphasize the concerns of their constituencies, namely, that rural communities continue to receive service even if that service is unprofitable.

(c) Institutional Design

Given that different political interest groups have different objectives, the design of socially optimal institutional arrangements poses a complex problem. It is difficult at best, and often impossible, to satisfy the mutually exclusive and conflicting goals of different groups. In some ways it seems that the residents of Metro would benefit from the privatization of Gray Coach; tax bills could be reduced and/or the revenue from the sale of the firm could be used for other municipal projects. Yet the existence of Gray Coach as a public enteprise owned by the TTC may enable the TTC system to expand and receive additional provincial subsidies. It appears, then, that a very complex form of two-way cross-subsidization is taking place: (a) from Metro to others through the provision of unprofitable service; and (b) from others to Metro through increased provincial subsidization of the TTC. One might be tempted to conclude incorrectly that the process nets out to zero and that there is no need to consider institutional redesign. This conclusion is incorrect if for no other reason than that the process involves a negative sum game: the arrangements which maintain dual cross-subsidization involve immense administrative costs and the utilization of societal resources which could be used more efficiently elsewhere in the economy. Furthermore, the process provides managerial incentives which encourage inefficient resource use. The only possible justification for a process involving two-way cross-subsidization is that the process, despite its inefficiencies, encourages certain types of production which could not be encouraged under any other politically feasible institutional design. Our concern is that voting constituencies be made aware of the existence of this problem so that other more direct options for subsidization become politically feasible.

APPENDIX A

CITIES INCLUDED IN THE REGRESSION ANALYSIS

Greyhound

Windsor
Chatham
London
Woodstock
Brantford
Hamilton

Toronto
Sudbury
Sault Ste Marie
Thunder Bay
Buffalo

Gray Coach

Toronto
Barrie
Collingwood
Owen Sound
Brampton
Orangeville
Shelbourne
Guelph
Fergus
Durham
St. Catharines
Niagara Falls
Buffalo
Burlington
Schomberg
Beeton

Alliston
Midland
Penetang
Gravenhurst
Port Carling
Pt. Severn
Parry Sound
Sudbury
Orillia
Huntsville
Burk's Falls
North Bay
Kitchener
Stratford
London

Voyageur

Ottawa
Kemptville
Brockville
Kingston
Belleville
Oshawa
Toronto
Montreal
Cornwall
Hawkesbury
Smiths Falls
Perth

Arnprior
Pembroke
Deep River
Mattawa
North Bay
Barry's Bay
Bancroft
Peterborough
Kaladar
Marmora
Winchester

Charterways

London	Sarnia
Dorcester	Windsor
St. Thomas	Amherstburg
Mitchell	Wingham
Listowel	Ipperwash
Exeter	Kitchener
Clinton	Cambridge
Hanover	Brantford
Grand Bend	Simcoe
Goderich	Delhi
Kincardine	Guelph
Owen Sound	

Travelways

Toronto	Port Elgin
Arthur	Port Perry
Clifford	Lindsay
Kincardine	Haliburton
Southampton	Oshawa
Paisley	Beaverton
Owen Sound	Orillia
Tobermory	Peterborough
Walkerton	Cobourg

APPENDIX B

SELECTED CAPACITY UTILIZATION
DATA FOR GRAY COACH

The tables which follow present average capacity utilization data for a one-week sample period in the fall of 1978. Under columns (a), the figures apply to passengers on the bus for the entire distance (or more) between the two-city pairs; under columns (b), the figures are for all of those passengers included in (a) plus one half of the passengers on the bus for part of the distance between the two cities. For each two-city pair, the first figure is the average capacity utilization for the one-week sample period; the second figure (in parentheses) is the sample standard deviation of the capacity utilization; and the third figure is the number of buses run by Gray Coach between the two points during that period.

Destination Origin	Toronto (a)	Toronto (b)	Barrie (a)	Barrie (b)	Orillia (a)	Orillia (b)	Gravenhurst (a)	Gravenhurst (b)	Huntsville (a)	Huntsville (b)	North Bay (a)	North Bay (b)
Toronto			28.77 (12.84) #111	28.77 (12.84) #111	18.21 (11.83) #85	26.18 (10.68) #85	16.09 (12.11) #52	27.39 (11.01) #52	13.54 (10.11) #42	27.53 (9.02) #42	13.21 (9.96) #37	27.55 (10.44) #37
Barrie	26.48 (11.17) #91	26.48 (11.17) #91			21.53 (13.27) #76	21.82 (13.23) #76			15.67 (11.44) #43	25.52 (11.10) #43	12.67 (7.42) #31	27.01 (9.93) #31
Orillia	16.88 (12.07) #71	24.41 (11.12) #71	20.69 (13.43) #71	20.85 (13.43) #71			21.84 (14.53) #52	23.98 (16.59) #52	22.80 (12.77) #31	27.51 (13.36) #31	13.87 (7.48) #31	24.75 (10.78) #31
Gravenhurst	16.34 (12.05) #49	26.72 (10.87) #49	16.47 (12.99) #44	22.73 (12.42) #44					19.25 (14.48) #44	21.00 (14.79) #44		
Huntsville	14.73 (10.45) #42	26.03 (8.80) #42			16.51 (11.75) #41	20.81 (12.52) #41					15.25 (7.84) #31	19.00 (8.78) #31
North Bay	13.00 (8.28) #44	23.72 (10.88) #44	12.30 (7.64) #26	27.67 (9.02) #26	13.66 (8.67) #27	24.44 (9.48) #27			13.96 (8.66) #29	18.13 (8.94) #29		

Origin \ Destination	Toronto (a)	Toronto (b)	Guelph (a)	Guelph (b)	Galt (a)	Galt (b)	Kitchener (a)	Kitchener (b)	Stratford (a)	Stratford (b)	London (a)	London (b)
Toronto			25.62 (11.42) #83	25.62 (11.42) #83	29.73 (9.45) #23	29.73 (9.45) #23	15.57 (11.78) #101	23.70 (9.27) #101	2.35 (2.39) #39	23.61 (6.68) #39	.182 (.501) #22	26.77 (6.02) #22
Guelph	27.45 (12.22) #73	27.45 (12.22) #73					17.40 (10.26) #71	17.62 (10.28) #71	3.88 (2.76) #27	18.14 (6.00) #27	1.70 (1.60) #24	21.41 (6.39) #24
Galt	23.27 (9.96) #22	23.29 (10.00) #22										
Kitchener	15.65 (13.31) #89		17.89 (10.40) #54	18.05 (10.50) #54					9.97 (6.93) #42	12.51 (7.47) #42	6.00 (4.03) #26	15.13 (5.39) #26
Stratford	2.24 (2.76) #33		2.70 (2.64) #30	14.97 (5.63) #30			9.07 (6.32) #41	11.93 (6.67) #41			9.20 (5.17) #25	11.24 (5.35) #25
London	.22 #18	.54	1.63 (1.70) #19	18.02 (6.95) #19			6.76 (5.57) #26	15.11 (5.07) #26	9.16 (4.57) #24	11.70 (4.92) #24		

Origin \ Destination	Toronto (a)	Toronto (b)	Barrie (a)	Barrie (b)	Pt. Sev. Rd. (a)	Pt. Sev. Rd. (b)	Parry Sound (a)	Parry Sound (b)	Sudbury (a)	Sudbury (b)
Toronto			24.9 (9.65) #18	24.9 (9.65) #18	16.1 (7.74) #18	23.1 (9.65) #18	14.2 (8.24) #25	20.08 (9.91) #25	17.1 (14.18) #31	22.56 (17.79) #31
Barrie	23.8 (17.28) #20	23.8 (17.28) #20			20.8 (9.36) #17	22.4 (9.71) #17	17.2 (9.14) #18	20.7 (9.98) #18	8.4 (4.62) #17	18.7 (7.22) #17
Pt. Sev. Rd.	12.2 (7.57) #19	17.6 (8.74) #19	16.2 (9.42) #19	17.4 (9.88) #19			19.5 (9.51) #18	20.3 (9.76) #18	9.5 (6.91) #18	17.5 (7.85) #18
Parry Sound	13.9 (8.13) #25	19.7 (8.51) #25	14.6 (9.01) #19	16.6 (9.57) #19	14.7 (7.64) #20	15.8 (8.51) #20			12.5 (6.75) #16	14.7 (6.92) #16
Sudbury	15.8 (14.07) #34	22.0 (10.73) #34	7.0 (5.45) #15	15.0 (6.87) #15	7.2 (5.32) #15	14.1 (6.99) #15	11.7 (7.21) #21	12.9 (6.52) #21		

Destination Origin	Toronto (a)	Toronto (b)	Brampton (a)	Brampton (b)	Orangeville (a)	Orangeville (b)	Owen Sound (a)	Owen Sound (b)
Toronto					17.34 (9.32) #26	19.92 (10.55) #26	7.27 (5.89) #18	17.02 (7.65) #18
Brampton					22.86 (12.73) #22	23.68 (13.01) #22		
Orangeville	13.36 (6.06) #25	16.02 (6.95) #25	17.39 (7.30) #23	18.15 (7.38) #23				
Owen Sound	7.95 (6.15) #20	15.80 (5.94) #20						

Destination Origin	Toronto (a)	Toronto (b)	Bolton (a)	Bolton (b)	Alliston (a)	Alliston (b)	Barrie (a)	Barrie (b)
Toronto			12.54 (4.29) #11	14.40 (4.39) #11	6.83 (3.37) #6	12.33 (3.77) #6		
Bolton	10.07 (4.51) #13	11.96 (4.16) #13						
Alliston	6.87 (5.59) #8	11.06 (4.56) #8					3.25 (3.30) #4	5.00 (5.71) #4
Barrie	1.00 0 #1	10.50 0 #1			3.50 (2.12) #2	3.75 (1.76) #2		

Destination Origin	Toronto (a)	(b)	Barrie (a)	(b)	Oakview (a)	(b)	Collingwood (a)	(b)	Owen Sound (a)	(b)
Barrie	20.00 0 #2	20.00 0 #2			24.13 (13.66) #16	25.15 (14.31) #16	18.55 (10.19) #18	23.97 (11.82) #18	4.86 (6.04) #15	18.43 (10.11) #15
Oakview	15.00 0 #1	20.00 0 #1	25.33 (10.12) #12	26.12 (10.72) #12						
Collingwood	27.50 (19.09) #2	31.25 (14.49) #2	13.53 (10.17) #15	20.23 (9.06) #15						
Owen Sound			4.14 (6.06) #14	17.71 (7.05) #14						

Destination	Toronto		Barrie		Midland	
Origin	(a)	(b)	(a)	(b)	(a)	(b)
Toronto					43.00 (0) #1	43.00 (0) #1
Barrie					12.23 (5.47) #26	14.00 (6.00) #26
Midland			12.51 (9.42) #27	14.18 (9.45) #27		

Destination Origin	Guelph (a)	(b)	Fergus (a)	(b)	Durham (a)	(b)	Owen Sound (a)	(b)	Mt. Forest (a)	(b)
Guelph			20.88 (12.84) #17	23.29 (13.93) #17	13.42 (9.89) #14	21.03 (12.44) #14	8.92 (6.53) #13	20.26 (9.92) #13	15.06 (11.53) #16	20.59 (13.41) #16
Durham	9.60 (5.77) #15	17.46 (7.39) #15					10.93 (6.25) #15	11.67 (6.25) #15		
Owen Sound	5.35 (4.66) #14	15.96 (6.35) #14								
Mt. Forest	12.47 (7.46) #19	18.34 (8.24) #19					9.21 (6.09) #14	12.92 (7.36) #14		

Destination Origin	Toronto (a)	Toronto (b)	Burlington (a)	Burlington (b)	St. Catharines (a)	St. Catharines (b)	Niagara Falls (a)	Niagara Falls (b)	Buffalo (a)	Buffalo (b)
Toronto					31.05 (9.70) #121	31.39 (9.69) #121	22.18 (12.87) #134	27.40 (10.31) #134	20.10 (13.74) #59	25.00 (12.05) #59
Burlington					34.15 (9.76) #26	34.32 (9.72) #26	21.00 (10.95) #20	28.40 (8.93) #20	18.43 (18.95) #23	26.80 (17.70) #23
St. Catharines	29.30 (10.58) #149	29.55 (10.57) #149	31.13 (9.14) #52	31.34 (9.19) #52						
Buffalo	18.32 (12.53) #58	25.35 (9.65) #58					19.85 (13.64) #34	20.88 (13.58) #34		

CHAPTER 7

WORLD WAR II CROWN CORPORATIONS: THEIR FUNCTIONS AND THEIR FATE

SANDFORD F. BORINS*

I. INTRODUCTION

The theme of this volume is that Crown corporations can be viewed as one possible means by which government pursues its objectives. The essays in this volume attempt to explain the existence of various Crown corporations as a more effective way of achieving certain objectives than alternatives such as either the use of regular government departments or regulation of the private sector. This paper attempts to apply this approach to the Crown corporations which were established during World War II. During the war, the Department of Munitions and Supply, which was responsible for military production, established 28 Crown corporations: a total of 229,000 people, or one-sixth of the entire manufacturing workforce, was employed in government-owned plants.[1] The federal government used Crown corporations as a policy tool more frequently during World War II than in the entire period between Confederation and 1939, a period which includes the war years of 1914 to 1918, when the government's major priority was also military production, but when few Crown corporations were established. Recognizing the difference between peacetime and wartime economic management, this paper will explore the differences and similarities between the uses of Crown corporations in both economic environments.

This paper explores a second theme as well. Upon the conclusion of the war, the government's priority changed to peacetime production, with the result that many wartime Crown corporations were terminated. However, there were a number of Crown corporations which had begun to produce commodities during the war which were also of value in a peacetime economy. In these cases, the government had to decide whether to keep the Crown corporations or whether to sell them off to the private sector.

---

* Faculty of Administrative Studies, York University.

[1] Canada. Department of Reconstruction and Supply. *Disposal and Peacetime Use of Crown Plant Buildings* (Ottawa: King's Printer, 1948) at 11-12.

For those that were retained, the question that arose was how they would be managed. For those that were sold to the private sector or, to use a now-popular term, "privatized" at issue were the terms on which they would be given to the private sector. This paper examines some cases of Crown corporations that were retained and some that were privatized. Some conclusions are drawn from this experience as to the characteristics of successful and unsuccessful privatizations.

The key individual in this story is, of course, C. D. Howe, who served as the Minister of Munitions and Supply, then Minister of Reconstruction, and finally as Minister of Trade and Commerce. Howe was a dynamic and thorough manager and, as the records which are now available in the Public Archives of Canada show, was deeply involved in all the major decisions about Crown corporations. By virtue of his formidable effectiveness as manager of Canada's war production effort, he was very rarely overruled by his Cabinet colleagues. Finally, as the Minister responsible for the Crown corporations, he provided the public explanation for the decisions. Therefore, this paper pays great attention to his statements and actions.

II. THE FUNCTIONS OF CROWN CORPORATIONS DURING THE WAR

During World War II, the federal government had the power, by virtue of the *Department of Munitions and Supply Act* and the *War Measures Act,* to run what was essentially a planned economy. The central planner in that economy was C. D. Howe. The *Department of Munitions and Supply Act* gave the Minister wide powers to compel manufacturers to undertake wartime production on the basis of prices and terms which he considered fair and reasonable. The Minister also could expropriate private sector firms without appeal or delay and incorporate Crown corporations under the *Companies Act.*

The department consisted of three main elements: production branches, controllers, and Crown corporations.[2] Production branches, such as the Ammunition Production Branch or the Defence Projects Construction Branch, were in charge of contracting for and overseeing the production of war materials. Controllers were responsible for rationing, allocating, and setting prices for key materials, such as chemicals, steel, or oil. Crown corporations served a number of functions, as will be discussed below. Finally, there were a number of mechanisms for co-ordinating the entire department, such as the Wartime Industries Control Board, which in-

---

[2] A major source of information about individual wartime Crown corporations and about all aspects of the Department of Munitions and Supply is J. de N. Kennedy, *History of the Department of Munitions and Supply*, 2 vols. (Ottawa: King's Printer, 1950).

cluded the heads of all the production branches as well as Crown corporations engaged in production. Overall co-ordination was the ultimate responsibility of C. D. Howe, who zealously guarded the power to make basic policy decisions.[3] Internally, the department resembled a modern multidivisional corporation. In its relationships with its environment, the department was much more powerful than a corporation, because it had both legal powers and access to tax revenues which together enabled it to expand its domain farther and more easily than any corporation.

The Crown corporations in the Department of Munitions and Supply were less autonomous than present-day Crown corporations. They were created by Order-in-Council under the *Department of Munitions and Supply Act,* as opposed to modern Crown corporations which have their own legislative mandates. World War II Crown corporations returned all revenues to and paid disbursements directly from the Consolidated Revenue Fund, unlike present-day Crown corporations which keep their own accounts. The World War II Crown corporations were tightly integrated into the structure of the department, rather than reporting only to the Minister. C. D. Howe exercised a great deal of control over senior personnel of the Crown corporation, appointing directors and officers and frequently moving people between Crown corporations and branches of the department. In many instances, individuals simultaneously held positions in Crown corporations and in the department.[4]

There are a number of possible ways to classify the wartime Crown corporations. For instance, Howe identified three major functional groups: administrative and supervisory corporations, manufacturing corporations, and corporations that stockpiled raw materials.[5] This paper uses a different classification. Because our concern is with the policy instruments which were the alternatives to Crown corporations, they are classified in two groups that emphasize the choice between Crown corporations and a common alternative for each group. The first group consists of those corporations which produced some good or service, for which the logical alternative would be private sector production under government regulation. The second group consists of administrative Crown corporations, which oversaw the production of goods or services by the private sector. The alternative instrument to these Crown corporations would be public bureaucracies within the Department of Munitions and Supply.

---

[3] R. Bothwell and W. Kilbourn, *C. D. Howe: A Biography* (Toronto: McClelland and Stewart, 1979), at 130.

[4] The most notable case of this was T. Arnold, who was simultaneously Machine Tools Controller and President of three Crown corporations. Kennedy, *supra* note 2, Vol. 1, at 23, 326, 330, 368 and Vol. 2, at 94.

[5] Canada. Parliament. House of Commons. *Debates*, 2nd session of the 20th Parliament, May 14, 1946, at 1512.

TABLE I

Classification of World War II Crown Corporations

Production	*Administrative*
Defence Communications Ltd.	Aero Timber Products Ltd.
Eldorado Mining and Refining	Allied War Supplies Corporation
(1944) Ltd.	Atlas Plant Extension Ltd.
Machinery Service Ltd.	Citadel Merchandising Company
National Railways Munitions Ltd.	Ltd.
Polymer Corporation Ltd.	Cutting Tools and Gauges
Quebec Shipyards Ltd.	Limited
Research Enterprises Ltd.	Fairmont Company Ltd.
Small Arms Ltd..	Federal Aircraft Ltd.
Toronto Shipbuilding Company	Melbourne Merchandising Ltd.
Ltd.	North West Purchasing Ltd.
Turbo Research Ltd.	Park Steamship Company Ltd.
Victory Aircraft Ltd.	Plateau Company Ltd.
	Veneer Log Supply Ltd.
	War Supplies Ltd.
	Wartime Housing Limited
	Wartime Merchant Shipping Ltd.
	Wartime Metals Corporation
	Wartime Oils Ltd.

(a) Public Sector Production

This section of the paper examines the various Crown corporations producing goods and services to develop a number of different rationales that explain the 11 instances where public sector production was preferred to regulated private sector production. Apart from these cases, the vast majority of military production facilities were owned and operated by the private sector under government regulation: Crown corporations were the exception and not the rule. Since many of the rationales applied to a number of corporations, the discussion is arranged in terms of rationales, rather than on a corporation-by-corporation basis.

(i) Secrecy

Research Enterprises was established in early 1940 to produce optical and communications equipment. Very quickly it became involved in the production of radar, then a British military secret, referred to as "Secret RDF (Radio Direction Finding)".[6] Turbo Research was incorporated in

---

[6] Kennedy, *supra* note 2, Vol. 1, at 407-440.

1944 to do research on and ultimately produce jet propulsion engines, also a military secret.[7] The government expropriated Eldorado Mining and Refining to have control over the supply of uranium, which was then being used in the production of the top-secret atomic bomb.[8] In these three cases, a Crown corporation was established because it was felt that government ownership and production would maintain greater secrecy than private production under contract.

(ii) Continuity of Production

The war effort demanded that continuous production be maintained. The Minister of Munitions and Supply had the power immediately to expropriate private firms for this reason. Toronto Shipbuilding was taken over when the principal shareholder was interned[9] and Quebec Shipyards[10] was established because there was a strike at two Quebec City shipyards. In the case of Quebec Shipyards the strike had ethnic overtones, in particular, protest by Francophone workers against Anglophone management, so that the strikes probably could not have been settled simply by higher wages underwritten by the government. After the expropriation, most of the new managers and directors were Francophone. One might ask in both cases why the government did not lease or sell the expropriated shipyards to private sector firms. One reason is that for the expropriated firms to perform effectively, some co-operation from the existing management was required. If, as is quite likely, the private sector purchaser or lessee were competitors in the same industry, the existing management could have been unco-operative. On the other hand, the prospect that the expropriated firms might be returned by the government to the original owners after the war would encourage co-operation.

Expropriation enabled the government to keep the firms in operation, because government-appointed directors and senior managers would be running the plants while negotiating the terms of compensation for the original owners. If the managers were to attempt to sell or lease the expropriated plants they would be involved in a second set of negotiations at the same time, which would undoubtedly have made it more difficult for them to supervise operations. Government ownership of the expropriated firms was a simpler alternative.

---

[7] Kennedy, *supra* note 2, Vol. 1, at 456-460.
[8] Kennedy, *supra* note 2, Vol. 1, at 336-343.
[9] Kennedy, *supra* note 2, Vol. 1, at 454-455.
[10] Kennedy, *supra* note 2, Vol. 1, at 404-406.

(iii) Co-ordination

Polymer Corporation[11] is an example of a Crown corporation being used to co-ordinate a large number of private firms in a complicated project. Due to the shortage of natural rubber after Japan's victories in the Pacific, the government decided to build, as rapidly as possible, an efficient scale synthetic rubber plant. The construction was a massive undertaking, involving a great deal of complicated engineering. The completed plant was managed by a consortium of six companies: Imperial Oil, Dow Chemical, and Canadian Synthetic Rubber Limited, a joint venture of four Canadian rubber processing companies. Given the large number of firms involved in both construction and operation, there was a clear need for central co-ordination: furthermore, the firms involved probably preferred co-ordination by a neutral arbitrator than by one of their own number.

(iv) Unacceptable Risks to the Private Sector

Machinery Service Limited[12] operated a plant in Montreal which serviced machinery used by government contractors. Skilled labour for this activity was in such short supply that the employees of this plant were German prisoners of war. Private sector production was not possible because private sector producers were not willing to take the perceived risk of employing German prisoners. The prisoners were housed in a hostel adjacent to the plant, a function which private sector firms would scarcely have been willing to perform.

(v) Public Sector Origins of the Corporation

In some cases, the impetus for or a crucial input to a wartime production project came from another organization which was in the public sector and which, for its own reasons, preferred that the project be in the public sector. National Railways Munitions built and operated a gun factory located on a vacant section of the CNR yards in downtown Montreal.[13] The CNR was involved in the construction of the factory and in providing senior managers for the operation. After the war, it purchased the factory and converted it into a railroad car repair plant. In a letter to J. de N. Kennedy, the Official Historian of the Department of Munitions and Supply, W. H. Hobbs, CNR Corporate Secretary wrote that "convert[ing the arms fac-

---

11 Kennedy, *supra* note 2, Vol. 1, at 394-403.
12 Kennedy, *supra* note 2, Vol. 1, at 365-368.
13 Kennedy, *supra* note 2, Vol. 1, at 375-378.

tory] into a badly needed freight and passenger car repair plant, of course, was the original intention: the whole conception of this particular Crown company venture would appear to be an example of fruitful cooperation as it met an urgent wartime need with the maximum of economy and efficiency".[14]

At the request of the Department of National Defence, Defence Communications Limited was established to build and operate a communications system in Atlantic Canada. The Department of National Defence, probably for security reasons, preferred that the Department of Munitions and Supply establish a Crown corporation, rather than use private contractors.[15] Similarly, Small Arms Limited was a large arms factory, established in 1939 by the Department of National Defence. As soon as the Department of Munitions and Supply began operating in 1940, the plant was transferred to it.[16]

(vi) To Prevent Inefficiency

Most military production was undertaken by the private sector, operating on government contracts. Competitive bidding was often impossible because the number of bidders was small or because the process of bidding itself would have created too much delay. As a result, the branches of the Department of Munitions and Supply which supervised contracts developed procedures to promote efficiency.[17] Standing behind the regulatory process, as an ultimate threat, was the possibility that if a contractor was excessively inefficient, his operation could be nationalized. In one case, the threat was carried out.

National Steel Car Company was a privately-owned aircraft manufacturer in Malton near Toronto airport. Like a number of other aircraft manufacturers, it was producing Anson trainer aircraft. By comparison with the others, it was clearly operating inefficiently. In November 1942, the company fired its general manager, who was directly responsible for production. C. D. Howe demanded that he be reinstated immediately: when the company refused, the company was expropriated for $4 million and reorganized as Victory Aircraft.[18] Was Victory Aircraft in fact more efficient than National Steel Co.? The Official Historian of the Department

---

[14] Letter from W. H. Hobbs, Corporate Secretary, Canadian National Railways, to J. de N. Kennedy, April 10, 1947. Dept. of Munitions and Supply, RG 28A, Vol. 28. For this and all subsequent departmental and personal papers, Public Archives of Canada classifications are provided.

[15] Kennedy, *supra* note 2, Vol. 1, at 332-335.

[16] Kennedy, *supra* note 2, Vol. 1, at 442-452.

[17] Kennedy, *supra* note 2, Vol. 1, at 217-223 and Vol. 2, at 316-331.

[18] Bothwell and Kilbourn, *supra* note 3, at 130.

of Munitions and Supply claimed that it was—a claim which, standing alone, would be deserving of scepticism. Much more convincing evidence is the fact that two of the Directors of the British aircraft firm of Hawker Siddeley toured all Canadian aircraft plants in late 1943 (one year after Victory Aircraft was established) and were sufficiently enthusiastic about Victory Aircraft that they began to consider Hawker Siddeley purchasing it after the war.[19] This tends to indicate that not only had Victory Aircraft improved relative to private ownership but it was comparable to, if not more efficient than, other aircraft plants in Canada or the U.K.

If the Crown corporations that produced goods and services were efficient—as will be argued in the next section—then they could have been of use in another way in preventing private sector inefficiency. By owning such corporations as Small Arms Limited, National Railways Munitions, Victory Aircraft, and Quebec Shipyards, the government was operating a factory in each of the major wartime industries. Information learned about technology and costs in these plants could be compared to the performance of private-sector plants that were working on contract. In this, these firms operated in a similar way to such present-day "windows on the industry" as Petro-can or Canadian Cellulose (now part of BCRIC). While all of these firms could have been returned to the private sector, their usefulness as windows on the industry was another reason for retaining public ownership.

(vii) Efficiency and Public Sector Production

Armen Alchian and his students have argued that publicly owned firms are not as efficient as privately owned firms because public ownership weakens incentives to efficiency as there is no discrete set of individuals who have property rights in the firm and would therefore benefit from monitoring the firm's managers.[20] This "property rights" school has done a substantial amount of empirical research which seems to support this proposition, with the exception that publicly owned firms which are subject to competitive pressures are comparable in efficiency to private-owned firms.[21] During World War II, all firms, both public and private, producing armaments were not subject to such pressures, since they were working on government contracts. Nevertheless, Victory Aircraft stands as an example of a publicly owned firm which was more efficient under public than private ownership. While a more thorough study of comparative costs for public and private sector operations during the war is beyond the scope of this paper, there are reasons to believe that the Department of Munitions and Supply provided a set of organizational incentives which acted as a sub-

19 J. Dow, *The Arrow* (Toronto: James Lorimer, 1979) at 24-25.
20 This literature is most thoroughly reviewed by Borcherding, Chapter 2, in this volume.
21 *Ibid.*

stitute for the monitoring characteristic of private ownership and which therefore induced managers of other Crown corporations to behave as efficiently as private sector managers.

Many of the managers of Crown corporations were C. D. Howe's "dollar-a-year" men: present or retired corporate executives, the former group being paid by their corporations and the latter living off their retirement incomes. The fact that these executives were not being paid by the government meant that their compensation was unrelated to the size of the operation they were managing. This removed the incentive to empire-building and budget-maximizing which Niskanen claims to typify bureaucratic managers.[22] Because Howe's dollar-a-year men were recruited from private-sector companies operating in similar areas to the Crown corporations, they would have taken with them whatever skills they had built up in managing private enterprise efficiently. Many of the dollar-a-year men were ambitious middle-level executives, generally in their late thirties or early forties.[23] This group was slightly too old to be able to serve in the war effort, and it was probably the case that they felt some guilt over this. They could be expected to assuage their feelings of guilt and serve the country by running public enterprise efficiently.

Organizational structure also supported efficiency. The Crown corporations were not really autonomous organizations but part of a multi-divisional department. Presidents of Crown corporations who performed effectively would be rewarded by impressing Howe himself. This often resulted in being moved to a more challenging job within the department or at least building a reputation as an efficient manager of a public enterprise. The latter would undoubtedly be of benefit in the postwar world.

Managers of Crown corporations had authority delegated to them that was comparable to that of private sector managers. They were as free to hire and fire as the private sector and followed the same collective bargaining practices. They did not have to deal with the peculiarities of public sector collective bargaining and were not required to report to Parliament on their activities. In short, the president of a Crown corporation was like the manager of a division in a multi-divisional corporation: the corporate veil prevented detailed public scrutiny of his activities, but he was completely accountable to corporate management.

(b) Administrative Crown Corporations

This section seeks to explain why in many instances administrative Crown corporations were established with identities separate from the other

---

[22] W. A. Niskanen, *Bureaucracy and Representative Government* (Chicago: Aldine, Atherton, 1971).

[23] Bothwell and Kilbourn, *supra* note 3, at 137.

administrative units of the Department of Munitions and Supply. On many occasions someone in the department, usually the director of a production branch or a controller, wanted to undertake some new initiative, generally involving increased production of some commodity or production of new commodities. These initiatives were often inappropriate for controllers to supervise, since their main concern was prices and distribution, and difficult for production branches to supervise, since their main concern was production of existing goods by existing firms. Futhermore, in many of these cases new production required a high degree of co-operation between government and all of the firms in the industry. Crown corporations were an ideal vehicle for such co-operation because their organizational flexibility permitted employees of private sector firms to serve as directors or work part-time for the Crown corporation. Many of the administrative Crown corporations illustrate this rationale.

The initiative for Aero Timber Products[24] and Veneer Log Supply[25] came from the Timber Controller, due to sharp increases in demand in 1942 for Sitka spruce (produced by Aero Timber) and plywood (produced by Veneer Log Supply) for use in aircraft. The directors of these corporations came from the lumber companies, and the companies provided workers and materials.

The Fairmont Company[26] was established to buy crude rubber, Melbourne Merchandising to buy wool,[27] Plateau[28] to buy silk and Citadel Merchandising to buy machine tools.[29] These companies worked closely with the rubber, clothing, and metal-working industries, respectively. Industry leaders were appointed to their boards of directors and there were agreements on storage and distribution of the crude rubber, raw wool, silk, and machine tools. These companies provided a centralized purchasing service for their respective industries in a period when supply became difficult. The rationale for using a Crown corporation, rather than designating one firm as purchasing agent, is that other firms in the industry would have perceived the latter as favouritism and, therefore, would have been less willing to co-operate. In these cases, the government was playing a co-ordinating role similar to that of co-ordinating the Polymer joint venture.

Over time, the mandates of these corporations changed. When the supply of crude rubber disappeared due to the Japanese conquest of southeast Asia, Fairmont began to store and distribute scrap rubber. When Polymer began production, Fairmont became Polymer's marketing agency

---

24 Kennedy, *supra* note 2, Vol. 1, at 287-289.
25 Kennedy, *supra* note 2, Vol. 1, at 461-467.
26 Kennedy, *supra* note 2, Vol. 1, at 344-350.
27 Kennedy, *supra* note 2, Vol. 1, at 369-374.
28 Kennedy, *supra* note 2, Vol. 1, at 389-393.
29 Kennedy, *supra* note 2, Vol. 1, at 323-327.

and was ultimately integrated into Polymer. In order to achieve economies of scale, Plateau and Melbourne Merchandising merged.

Wartime Oils was established at the initiative of the oil controller in order to expand production rapidly on some marginal sites at the edge of Alberta's Turner Valley, then the major Canadian oil field, which were being ignored by the private sector. Because Canada was not producing much oil at that time, there was no oil production branch in the department to which this task could be given.[30]

Wartime Metals was established at the recommendation of the Metals Controller: working with the mining industry, it funded and supervised construction of a number of new mining projects.[31]

When the General Purchasing Branch had difficulty acquiring gauges and cutting tools, a Gauge and Cutting Tool Production Branch was established, which later became the Crown corporation Cutting Tools and Gauges Limited. The Crown corporation was established to co-ordinate with industry all purchases and production: previously, defence contractors were ordering cutting tools and gauges on their own initiative which created confusion and delay. Once again, the justification for a Crown corporation was that it was a vehicle that accommodated industry participation. When supply caught up with demand in 1944, the Crown corporation was wound up, and the General Purchasing Division resumed the job of purchasing tools and gauges.[32]

North West Purchasing was established in 1943 to deal with economic dislocations caused by the U.S. Army during the construction of the Alaska Highway. The army established procurement branches which were buying supplies wherever they could, at prices frequently higher than Canadian controlled prices. This Crown corporation was established to work with the various commodity controllers to provide supplies for the U.S. Army. In 1944, when the situation stabilized, its duties were taken over by the local purchasing office of the Department of Munitions and Supply.[33] The reason for the initial establishment of a Crown corporation was that it was a more visible, high profile response to the problem than simply assigning it to a local government office.[34]

Wartime Housing was established to build housing for soldiers and war workers. The Crown corporation was responsible for land acquisition, ob-

---

[30] Kennedy, *supra* note 2, Vol. 1, at 519-520. See also letter from G. R. Cottrelle, Oil Controller, to C. D. Howe, May 9, 1944, Dept. of Munitions and Supply (Public Archives classification: RG 28A, Vol. 197).

[31] Kennedy, *supra* note 2, Vol. 1, at 506-518.

[32] Kennedy, *supra* note 2, Vol. 1, at 160-164, 328-331.

[33] Kennedy, *supra* note 2, Vol. 1, at 380-382.

[34] Memo from G. K. Sheils, Deputy Minister of Munitions and Supply, to H. Borden, Coordinator of Controls, November 12, 1943. Dept. of Munitions and Supply, (Public Archives classification: RG 28A, Vol. 196).

taining local government approval, planning and architecture: the actual construction was contracted out to the lowest bidder.[35] It is clear the government had no expertise in housing construction and left that to the private sector. On the other hand, there were economies of scale in land acquisition, planning, and design, all of which support the use of a national program. The Crown corporation structure was chosen over a regular department for two reasons. First, it facilitated co-operation with municipalities, builders and architects. Second, a regular department would probably have been more autonomous from the Department of Munitions and Supply than a Crown corporation, which was undesirable because of the necessity of co-ordinating the construction of war workers' housing with the construction of war plants.

In contrast to the administrative Crown corporations discussed above, there were a number of such corporations which performed functions similar to those of regular branches of the Department, rather than the roles of industry co-ordination and liaison with the government.

Shortly after the Aircraft Production Branch was established to supervise production of a variety of aircraft, it received a mandate to mass produce the Anson trainer. Ralph Bell, the Director-General of Aircraft Production set up a Crown corporation, Federal Aircraft Ltd., to handle the Anson program and for a while was simultaneously Director-General of the Aircraft Production and President of Federal Aircraft. He gave up the latter job because the workload was too onerous. Bell's successor as President of Federal Aircraft, Ray Lawson, did not get along well with Bell, and the Branch and the Crown corporation carried on a long feud over priorities.[36] In 1944, after the Anson program was completed, the Aircraft Production Branch was taken over by Federal Aircraft. This is a case where a Crown corporation and a production branch were performing the same function and fighting jurisdictional battles over it.

Atlas Plant Extension was established early in the war to finance, construct and supervise an extension to the Atlas Steels Ltd. plant in Welland, Ontario. Subsequently, a large number of plant extensions were built elsewhere and were either government or privately owned, but in no case was one project set up as a Crown corporation. Atlas Plant Extension was thus an anomaly which was not repeated but which, once established, remained as a Crown corporation until the end of the war, when the extension was sold to Atlas Steels.[37]

The Naval Shipbuilding Branch in 1941 set up a Crown corporation, Wartime Merchant Shipping, to supervise the building of merchant ships and a Controller of Ship Repairs and Salvage to supervise ship repairs and the building of destroyers.[38] There appears to be no reason why the two

[35] Kennedy, *supra* note 2, Vol. 1, at 480-489.
[36] Bothwell and Kilbourn, *supra* note 3, at 138-144.
[37] Kennedy, *supra* note 2, Vol. 1, at 318-322.
[38] Kennedy, *supra* note 2, Vol. 1, at 238, 490-505.

similar activities were organized differently. In 1942, Park Steamship Company was established to contract out the operations of the merchant ships built under the supervision of Wartime Merchant Shipping.[39] Here it is not clear why Wartime Merchant Shipping could not have retained ownership, nor why Park Steamship Company was set up as a Crown corporation.

At about the same time that War Supplies Limited was set up to seek U.S. purchases of Canadian military products, the United States Purchases Branch of the Department was set up to handle Canadian purchases of U.S. military supplies.[40] One possible explanation for the anomaly is that the President of War Supplies Limited was E. P. Taylor, who felt more comfortable as President of a Crown corporation than Director-General of a branch of the department.

(c) Summary

A key way in which wartime economic management differed from peacetime economic management was that all policy instruments were more effective. The government could regulate private sector producers more closely because it had greater power to inspect records, renegotiate contracts, and threaten immediate expropriation. Crown corporations were more effective because the Department of Munitions and Supply supervised them closely and provided a set of incentives to efficient management. Therefore, the *relative* effectiveness of public and private sector production probably did not change very much from what it had been in a peacetime context. Thus, regulated production by the private sector was the way that most of wartime production was organized. Crown corporations were reserved for the exceptional cases: those involving secrecy, unacceptable risks to the private sector, public sector origins, and finally cases where a managerial problem arose for which no regulatory instrument had been designed. Examples of the latter were Quebec Shipyards' labour-management relations and National Steel Cars' managerial efficiency. Both had deteriorated so badly that external rules or incentives could not improve the situations as rapidly as the government desired. In these instances, public ownership can be seen as something of a last resort: after trying all other possible policy instruments, the government opted for public ownership. This appears to be the case at the present time as well: when such policy instruments as financial incentives or penalties and regulation fail to achieve a government's policy objectives, public ownership is finally considered. A recent example of this is the nationalization of the potash industry by Saskatchewan.

The wartime Crown corporations, especially those that have been classified as administrative, were also used in situations where the co-operation

---

[39] Kennedy, *supra* note 2, Vol. 1, at 383-388.
[40] Kennedy, *supra* note 2, Vol. 1, at 281-283, 474-479.

of a large number of firms was required, such as running a complicated joint venture like Polymer or allocating a scarce resource in very short supply, such as wool, rubber, or silk, or rapidly increasing production of a critical product, such as Sitka spruce. Crown corporations provided a flexible managerial structure which was more open to voluntary and part-time participation by private sector managers than were public bureaucracies. Crown corporations became a major vehicle of co-ordination between government and industry. At the present time, there are still situations which require such co-ordination, but they have been handled by somewhat different organizational mechanisms. The two which come to mind are joint ventures, such as Telesat or Syncrude, where a specific project is involved, and advisory boards, where long-time consultation about a number of issues is involved.

This survey of the functions of Crown corporations in World War II appears to support the utility of the approach taken by Trebilcock and Prichard[41] in searching for factors which explain the choice of Crown corporations as opposed to other policy instruments. The factors presented here have similarities (such as the secrecy motive) and differences (such as the greater efficiency of Crown corporations in wartime and the greater emphasis placed on Crown corporations as a co-ordinating mechanism) with those in the Trebilcock-Prichard schema: however, the instrument-choice approach to the analysis is a fruitful one.

III. PRIVATIZATION—THE POLICY CONTEXT

Trebilcock and Prichard distinguish between two possible motives for privatization.[42] In the first case, Government may abandon the objective for which a Crown corporation was created, or modify its objectives such that the Crown corporation is no longer the most effective way of achieving the new objectives. In the second, the Government's purpose is unchanged but there is change in the characteristics of either the Crown corporation or the alternative instruments such that the relative effectiveness of the Crown corporation as an instrument of intervention has diminished. This approach can be applied to decisions taken on the future use of Crown corporations as the war drew to a close.

At the conclusion of World War II, there was a very clear shift in the Government's major economic policy objective, away from producing military equipment and toward the maintenance of full employment in an economy producing mainly consumer goods. The classic statement of the Government's new objectives was made in the *White Paper on Employment and Income* which C. D. Howe presented to the House of Commons on

---

[41] Trebilcock and Prichard, Chapter 1, in this volume.
[42] *Ibid.*

April 12, 1945, and which became the Liberal Party's program in the 1945 election.

To economists, the most interesting aspect of the White Paper is its clear Keynesian framework. What better statement of the simple Keynesian income-expenditure model can be found than the following?

> Remunerative employment and economy in any economy are provided by the expenditures which are made. These expenditures are best classified according to the channels through which the expenditures flow, viz., (a) export trade, in which the decision to spend is made outside the country; (b) private investment in plant, equipment and other durable goods and goods in stock, in which the decision is governed largely by prospective earnings in relation to cost; (c) consumption expenditures, the level of which is mainly dependent on the level of incomes; (d) public investment in useful works for improving the productiveness of resources, and the welfare and opportunities of the people. . . . In maintaining a high and stable level of employment and income, the Government proposes to use appropriate means to influence expenditures in all channels with particular emphasis on those which are most susceptible of encouragement and control.[43]

The paper then went on to outline a series of policy instruments, other than Crown corporations, which would be used in each area to maintain full employment. To stimulate exports, the government committed itself to support for re-establishment of multi-lateral trade and the reduction of trade barriers. The government planned to support private sector investment by allowing corporations to write off postwar losses and maintenance expenditures against heavily taxed wartime profits. In 1944, the government amended the income tax laws to allow accelerated depreciation for investments undertaken between November 1944 and March 1949. Ultimately, investments of $1.4 billion were approved for accelerated depreciation.[44] The government also committed itself to reducing both expenditures and taxes, so as to facilitate the shift to private sector production and consumption. Consumption would be stimulated by transfer payments such as Family Allowances and Unemployment Insurance payments which would raise the incomes of those temporarily unemployed immediately after the war.

The White Paper saw public investment mainly as a residual source of employment:

> The post-war employment problem is not going to be solved by huge expenditures on "public works." . . . On the other hand, it is the firm intention of the Government to institute a system of managing its capital expenditures so

---

[43] Government of Canada, *White Paper on Employment and Income* (Ottawa: King's Printer, 1948) at 4.

[44] Canada. Department of Reconstruction and Supply. *Encouragement to Industrial Expansion in Canada: Operation of Special Depreciation Provisions* (Ottawa: King's Printer, 1948).

that they may contribute to the maximum to the improvement and stabilization of employment and income.[45]

The public works envisaged were not the ongoing operations of Crown corporations, but projects undertaken by government departments primarily to provide the infrastructure for the private sector. For example, in 1943 R. B. Bryce of the Department of Finance prepared a list of such possible projects, which included aerial mapping, forestry development, health centres in small towns and rural areas, rural electrification, highway modernization, loans for farm and home modernization, airport development, rural community centres, fish hatcheries, construction of public buildings such as replacement of the temporary buildings in Ottawa, drainage, irrigation, flood control, and Northern development.[46] While Bryce suggested initiating studies to prepare the projects, no further plans were made during the war. The White Paper explained this failure due to the preoccupation of the government's engineers with war work. It added that the actual implementation of many projects would depend on Federal-Provincial agreements.

What role could Crown corporations play in the postwar economy? One immediate role was in the disposal of surplus war materials. The War Assets Corporation was established to receive and dispose of materials declared surplus by all other departments and Crown corporations. Disposal was handled on a centralized basis to achieve economies of scale and ensure consistent and thereby equitable policies. By January 1947, all but a few of more than 100 plants had been sold. The total cost of the plants was $73.8 million and total sales revenue was $26.8 million, or 36 percent of cost.[47] From all its sales, the War Assets Corporation ultimately recovered revenues of about $450 million.[48]

Dismantling the planned economy meant dismantling the regulatory structures of the Department of Munitions and Supply. All the administrative Crown corporations which had not already been dismantled were wound up. The assets of all these corporations were ultimately disposed of by the War Assets Corporation. Companies which had been expropriated to assure continuity of production (Quebec Shipyards, Toronto Shipbuilding) were returned to their original owners.

In a number of cases, Crown corporations were retained because the specific objectives for which they were created had not changed. After the detonation of the atomic bomb, security of supply of uranium increased in

---

[45] Government of Canada, *supra* note 43, at 15.

[46] R. B. Bryce, "Rough Check List of Possible Emergency Employment Projects for Immediate Post-War Use", Privy Council papers, (Public Archives Classification: RG 2/18, Vol. 12, file 50-3).

[47] "War Plants Going, Going, Almost Gone," *Financial Post*, January 25, 1947, at 7, col. 1.

[48] "Expect WAC Will Salvage $450 Millions," *Financial Post*, January 4, 1947, at 1, col. 4.

priority and Eldorado Mining and Refining was therefore retained. In a tion to preparedness in the production of nuclear weapons, the government felt it was important to maintain some capacity to produce tactical weapons. Another Crown corporation, Canadian Arsenals Limited, was established, consisting of six munitions plants which were used to produce guns, small arms, ammunition, and explosives. The corporation had both the capacity to produce a limited amount of weaponry itself for peacetime needs and the tools and plans to support a rapid increase in arms production by the private sector, if it were necessary.[49]

Wartime Housing was retained, not because the government had any long-term wish to remain in the housing industry, but because there were acute housing shortages, particularly for returning veterans, and it was felt that equity demanded the government alleviate shortages, rather than simply allow the private market to equilibrate supply and demand. An Interdepartmental Housing Committee of civil servants concluded that the housing problem could be handled more effectively if all the government's policy instruments were merged. Thus Wartime Housing, which was under the control of the Department of Reconstruction and the National Housing Administration and Central Mortgage Bank, which were both part of the Department of Finance, were merged to form a new Crown corporation, the Central Mortgage and Housing Corporation.[50]

C. D. Howe had a number of difficult decisions as to whether or not to retain Crown corporations in the shipping, synthetic rubber, aircraft, and communications equipment industries. The approach he took was one of commercial pragmatism. Regardless of its initial mission, if a Crown corporation could survive economically, without subsidy, in the postwar world, Howe felt it was worth keeping. This approach to privatization can be contrasted with that of present-day governments. Chandler has argued that governments of all ideological persuasions are likely to establish Crown corporations, such as the Cape Breton Development Corporation, to take over the operations of unprofitable private firms and thereby support employment in economically declining regions.[51] On the other hand, governments of the left, such as the NDP or Parti Québécois, are more likely to use Crown corporations to redistribute the profits of economically viable activities than are governments of the centre or right (Liberal, Conservative, Social Credit) which generally would not consider redistribution, in the absence of some other policy objective, to be a legitimate justification

---

[49] "Arsenals Project Assures Canada Won't Again Be Caught Unarmed," *Financial Post*, February 16, 1946, at 3, col. 2.

[50] "Ottawa Moves to End Bottlenecks in Housing," *Financial Post*, January 5, 1946, at 1, col. 2.; Memo from the Interdepartment Housing Committee to J. K. Ilsley and C. D. Howe, October 31, 1945, Dept. of Munitions and Supply Papers (Public Archives classification: RG 28A, Vol. 341).

[51] Chandler, Chapter 3, in this volume.

for public ownership. While Howe, unlike the NDP, had no interest in re-distribution, nevertheless, unlike current Liberals and Conservatives, he had no qualms about government ownership of profitable enterprises even if no specific policy objectives were being served.

Howe was deeply concerned that the profitable wartime Crown corporations remained economically viable. He believed that competition was more likely to control inefficiency in the private sector than in the public sector.

> If a private industry is not well managed—and plenty are not—it will go broke in a short time, be reorganized, and put under more efficient management. Under public operation that usually does not happen. It goes steadily down grade. It is allowed to go down grade, unless it becomes enough of a scandal, when the government is very apt to get rid of it and pass it to private hands.[52]

Howe felt that the best way to instill efficiency in Crown corporations, absent the usual mix of idealism and incentives in the wartime Department of Munitions and Supply, was to subject them to the discipline of the market. This belief appears consistent with a substantial body of research, which indicates that public enterprises which operate in a competitive environment are more likely to be efficient than those which do not.[53] As will be shown in the case of Polymer, Howe generally refused to give it special privileges not accorded private sector firms. On the other hand, Howe did not want to handicap Crown corporations. For instance, he introduced legislation in 1946 to set up pension plans, salary scales, and accounting practices for Crown corporations comparable to those in the private sector. He summed up his position in the debate on that legislation saying:

> Surely no hon. member will suggest that the government should go into the manufacturing business with one hand tied behind its back. No one would suggest that the Polymer Corporation, a $50 million project with a turnover of $40 or $50 million a year would be operated by a man with a civil service salary. The government is going into business on equal terms with private business. It must do so if it expects to have a record which will compare with that of private business.[54]

Through this legislation Howe was moving the Crown corporations out of the Ministry of Munitions and Supply, which itself was being dismantled, and creating the autonomy and distance from the government which characterizes present-day Crown corporations.

Howe applied the logic of commercial pragmatism to the government's

---

[52] Canada. Parliament. House of Commons *Debates*, 5th session of the 19th Parliament, March 27, 1944, at 1899.

[53] Borcherding, *infra,* at pp. 171-172.

[54] Canada. Parliament. House of Commons. *Debates*, 2nd session of the 20th Parliament, June 4, 1946, at 2176.

fleet of merchant vessels owned by Park Steamship Company. By the end of the war, this was the world's third largest merchant marine. However, it was realized that there would be a substantial oversupply of shipping capacity when the war ended. Evidence of this was that by 1945 the British were chartering fewer Canadian ships. It was also felt that Canadian ship construction and operation costs would be higher than those of other nations, particularly the U.K.[55] Therefore, the entire Park Steamship fleet was sold, to both Canadian and foreign purchasers.[56]

(a) Polymer—Public Enterprise Preserved

C. D. Howe was convinced right from the outset that Polymer should remain a Crown corporation after the war. On June 16, 1943, he told the House of Commons, "it is the intention of the government to continue to operate the plant at Sarnia to make rubber for the country at war and the country at peace".[57] The major reason for keeping Polymer was not national security, but economic viability. Howe was proud to point out that its costs were comparable to the largest and most modern U.S. plants. It was a member of a patent pool operated by synthetic rubber manufacturers and therefore would have continued access to new technology. It would have a substantial capacity for export. Finally, even if Polymer was not able to operate at full capacity producing rubber it could sell chemicals profitably. There was no political disagreement with Howe about keeping Polymer. The Conservatives supported it, and the CCF suggested that the government should create many firms like Polymer to ensure the availability of raw materials besides rubber.[58]

After the war, Howe worked behind the scenes to protect Polymer's autonomy. Its managers wanted to terminate their management contract with the consortium of the rubber companies, which Howe supported. Howe interceded to make sure that Polymer's profits were not simply added to the Consolidated Revenue Fund, but were held separately in order to be readily available to the firm. In December 1946, Canadian National Railways complained to Howe because Polymer was shipping its product on the U.S.-owned Père Marquette railroad. Howe refused to direct Polymer to use the CNR, and Howe's executive assistant wrote back to the CNR that

---

[55] Draft Report of the Interdepartmental Committee on Merchant Shipping Policy, March 1944, Dept. of Trade and Commerce papers, (Public Archives classification: RG 20, Vol. 273).

[56] "75 Park Line Vessels Bring $36 Millions," *Financial Post*, June 8, 1946 at 17, col. 5.

[57] Canada. Parliament. House of Commons. *Debates*, 4th session of the 19th Parliament, June 16, 1943, at 3707.

[58] Canada. Parliament. House of Commons. *Debates*, 2nd session of the 20th Parliament, May 27, 1946, at 1921-23. (Alastair Stewart, CCF—Winnipeg North).

"you will appreciate that the Polymer Corporation, with its Board of Directors, is operated on the same basis as a private company, and it is only in matters of major policy that the Minister is consulted".[59] On the other hand, operating like a private company meant being exposed to the discipline of the market. In November 1946, Polymer asked Howe to extend controls on natural rubber, so as to leave the Canadian market open to Polymer. Howe responded that it could expect no more than four additional months of controls.[60]

(b) The Aircraft Industry—Successful Privatization

The success of Canada's aircraft manufacturing industry during the war stimulated hopes for the post-war period. In April 1943, the Department of Munitions and Supply established a Committee on the Post-war Manufacture of Aircraft, on which were represented the Aircraft Production Branch, the aircraft manufacturers, the National Research Council and the airlines.[61] The Committee, as might be expected, concluded that it was in Canada's national interest, for both military and commercial reasons, to encourage the design and development of aircraft in Canada. Thus, it recommended that the Canadian government support an aircraft industry through contracts for at least the next ten years. Initially, Howe was unreceptive to this appeal, reminding the Committee that neither the American nor British governments did this, and that manufacturers traditionally stayed in business by selling aircraft to airlines. Howe angrily wrote to the Committee, "I suggest that the airplane business in the post-war period must not expect to find itself a ward of the Government. In that position it will be no different from any other peacetime industry."[62]

As time passed, Howe changed his mind and became more willing to support the aircraft industry. The reason may be that his participation as a founder of the International Civil Aeronautics Organization convinced him of the industry's potential. Howe came to feel that the key to success in the industry would be strong design and development capability. During the war, the Canadian aircraft industry received American and British designs and technology free of charge. Howe doubted that this would persist after the war and felt it more likely that British and American firms would make

---

59 Letter from T. M. Bryson, Executive Assistant to C. D. Howe, to M. A. Metcalf, Executive Assistant to the President of the CNR, December 6, 1946. This letter and documentation for the other episodes mentioned in this paragraph can be found in C. D. Howe papers (Public Archives classification MG 27 111 B20, Vol. 45).

60 See C. D. Howe papers, *supra* note 59.

61 Dow, *supra* note 19, at 23-24.

62 C. D. Howe memorandum to Ralph Bell, February 12, 1944, Dept. of Munitions and Supply papers (Public Archives classification: RG 28A, Vol. 155).

their technology available only if they could share in the profits of Canadian production. Therefore, a more appropriate instrument for the postwar development of the Canadian aircraft industry would be direct British and American investment. This illustrates Trebilcock and Prichard's second motive for privatization: given an objective of developing a Canadian aircraft industry, the effectiveness of Crown corporations as a policy instrument diminished relative to foreign investment.

In 1945, Roy Dobson, the Hawker Siddeley Director who had been so impressed by his visit to Victory Aircraft two years previously, convinced his company to purchase the Crown corporation. Hawker Siddeley set up a Canadian subsidiary, A.V. Roe Canada (Avro) which leased the Malton plant for seven years. The rental fee would be 50 percent of the subsidiary's gross profits. The British agreed to establish in Canada design and research and development facilities for commercial and military aircraft, engines, and other equipment in which the company specialized.[63] Dobson felt the financial terms were very generous. Howe still remained sceptical of the viability of the company (telling Dobson he had "more guts than brains"), but was willing to give it some support at the outset.[64]

At about this time, the future of Turbo Research Limited was in question. The Crown corporation prepared a five-year plan in which it proposed to continue its research and produce ten aircraft and two non-aircraft gas turbine engines a year. This would have required a staff of 380 people, capital expenditures of about $1 million and operating expenditures of $8 million by 1950.[65] Crawford Gordon, the Director-General of the Industrial Reconversion Branch, and later President of Avro, was sceptical about Turbo's plan. He felt that such a small expenditure would not allow Canada to keep up with aircraft jet engine development being undertaken on a much larger scale in Britain and the U.S. nor with the development of turbines for other purposes, in which Westinghouse, General Electric and Allis Chalmers were investing hundreds of millions of dollars.[66] Gordon concluded that Turbo should be integrated with Avro, thereby making available to it Avro's more substantial resources. Howe concurred. Thus Turbo Research moved from its location in the Toronto suburb of Leaside, adjacent to Research Enterprises, out to Malton.

Through its military acquisitions policy, the government gave Avro strong support. Avro produced the CF-100 Canuck interceptor and the

---

[63] Minutes of the Cabinet Committee on Reconstruction, January 19, 1946, Privy Council papers (Public Archives Classification: RG 2/18, Vol. 59).

[64] Dow, *supra* note 19, at 33.

[65] Turbo Research Ltd., "A Proposed Five-Year Plan on Gas Turbine Development for Turbo Research Limited" August 1945, Dept. of Munitions and Supply papers (Public Archives classification: RG 28A, Vol. 20).

[66] Crawford Gordon, memo to C. D. Howe, December 11, 1945, Dept. of Munitions and Supply papers (Public Archives classification: RG 28A, Vol. 20).

Orenda jet engine, which was used to power both the CF-100 and the F-86 Sabre jet fighter. In 1947, Avro began the development of the Jetliner, a 50-passenger commercial aircraft powered by jet engines, rather than propellers. The Jetliner's first test flights were in 1949, only weeks after those of the Comet, the world's first passenger jet. Howe, as Minister of Trade and Commerce, believed the Jetliner had a good chance of becoming commercially viable, and therefore between 1947 and 1952 the government invested $6.6 million in its development, as compared with the $2.3 million invested by Avro. In fact, the government carried the project: Trans-Canada Airlines, Avro's prospective customer, was very dubious about the Jetliner, would not have supported it on its own, and never agreed to buy even one. In 1952, Howard Hughes offered to purchase 30 Jetliners for use on TWA, a deal which could have made the plane a success. Ironically, the deal was killed by Howe himself who felt that Avro should devote itself entirely to the production of fighter aircraft for use in the Korean war.[67] Despite this setback, the Hawker Siddeley group's Canadian operations prospered. Profits from the CF-100 program were used to support diversification into shipping, steel products, trucks and buses, rolling stock, and electronics.

During the war, the government built an aircraft plant in Montreal which was then operated by Canadian Vickers. In December 1944, the government set up a Crown corporation called Canadair Limited, which took over its operations.[68] Initially, the Crown corporation was busy converting military versions of the DC-3, then the mainstay of civil aviation, to commercial aircraft. Most of these orders were from foreign airlines. In addition, Canadair received an order to develop the North Star, which combined a DC-4 airframe with Rolls Royce engines, for use by Trans-Canada Airlines and the RCAF. While this initial development work kept the company going, the government was looking for a purchaser to ensure its long-run success. In early 1947, Canadair was purchased by the Electric Boat Company, the forerunner of General Dynamics. In the agreement, Electric Boat agreed to lease the plant for 15 years for $200,000 per year, with an option to purchase the plant for $4,000,000 less accrued depreciation. Electric Boat agreed to provide $2,000,000 in working capital and the government placed a firm order for 44 North Stars.[69] Later contracts to produce the F-86 Sabre in the 1950s assured that Canadair would remain a going concern.

To summarize, privatization of the aircraft industry was a success. The policies of importing technology, making Turbo Research available to

---

[67] Dow, *supra* note 19, at 35-58.
[68] D. Moody, "Vickers Earnings Unhurt by Plane Plant Transfer," *Financial Post*, December 9, 1944, at 1, col. 45.
[69] Privy Council Minute 242, January 21, 1947, Privy Council Papers (Public Archives classification: MG 25 J4, Vol. 240, file 2410); Minutes of the Cabinet Committee on Reconstruction, March 11, 1947. Dept. of Finance papers (Public Archives classification: RG 19 E 5(d), Vol. 4014).

Avro, and aircraft purchases and development support had created a viable aircraft industry.

(c) Research Enterprises Limited: "The Atomic Bomb Killed Santa Claus"

Between 1941 and 1946, Research Enterprises Limited manufactured over $220,000,000 worth of optical instruments (binoculars, periscopes, range-finders, etc.) and communications equipment (radios, wireless sets, radar). The research and design work was done primarily by the National Research Council in Ottawa (with some assistance from American and British manufacturers) and the manufacturing in Research Enterprises' complex of buildings in Leaside, a Toronto suburb. C. D. Howe was proud of this Crown corporation. For example, he sent Prime Minister King the hundred thousandth optical instrument manufactured by the company, a pair of binoculars, and wrote to him that "Relations between the management and the 7500 workers are a model for all war plants, the record being that not a day has been lost through labour disputes. The plant itself is recognized among the Allied Nations for its workmanship and production ability."[70] During the middle of the war, Howe was quite undecided about what to do with the company after the war:

> Obviously the manufacture of optical glass should and no doubt will continue after the war. Certain other processes . . . have great peace-time value, such as the adaptation of radar equipment to peace-time purposes, and arrangements may be made to carry on Research Enterprises. I cannot say at this time whether it will operate as a public or private company.[71]

By the end of the war, Howe had made up his mind. Research Enterprises was broken up and its various components sold to the private sector. There were two reasons. The first was Howe's assessment that the peace-time demand for radar and optical instruments could not support the corporations' wartime production level. The second reason derived from Howe's understanding of research. He drew a sharp distinction between research and production and felt that the two operations should be logically, physically, and organizationally separate. As he perceived it, Research Enterprises was simply manufacturing products designed by the National Research Council. Therefore, the two organizations could be separated without any harm to either: the Research Enterprises factories could be used to make other products and the NRC laboratories could continue develop-

---

[70] C. D. Howe to Mackenzie King, June 23, 1944, King papers (Public Archives classification: MG 26 J1, Vol. 361).

[71] Canada. Parliament. House of Commons. *Debates*, 4th session of the 19th Parliament, June 16, 1943, at 3714-15.

ing new products which could be licensed by other manufacturers. Howe presented these views vigorously in the House of Commons debate about the corporation.

> Every article, with very few exceptions, was developed in the form of a proto-type in the laboratories of the National Research Council of Canada and was sent to Toronto for manufacture. That is the function of the plant. . . . All my experience has indicated that such a plant should be one thing or the other, either a research laboratory or a manufacturing plant. . . . We have in store in the plant optical glass to fill any possible requirements of Canada for two years, and we made that in one day. . . . Now here is a great plant the work for which has ended, and the question is, shall we keep the plant for its original purpose? . . . We cannot sell the product unless the government pro-poses to spend $8,000,000 a month to keep the staff employed. Otherwise, I do not know of anything that they can make in quantity which could be used . . . should we [not] use the plant to provide a centre of employment for the same skills that we used here, by turning it over to private enterprise which can manufacture and sell on a scale that will mean real employment?[72]

The decision to dissolve Research Enterprises was indeed a controver-sial one. When it was announced in May 1945, the United Steelworkers of America, who had organized the workforce, immediately protested. When Howe was in Toronto in September at a golf tournament, he was accosted in the clubhouse by four union representatives: he ended the discussion shouting, "All I ask is that you get the hell out of here."[73] In a letter to a friend a few days later, Howe explained his behaviour:

> It is hard for our privileged class in war plants to realize that the atomic bomb killed Santa Claus as far as they are concerned, and they must now go to work. . . . I am convinced that there are jobs for all. After a time, I think that people will become convinced that they must move out of cities and go back to what they were doing before the war. . . . I have never believed that because some unfortunate is a Cabinet Minister he should allow everyone to push him around. . . .[74]

The sale of Research Enterprises was opposed by both the Conser-vatives and the CCF. Speeches urging Howe not to break up Research Enterprises were made by Donald Fleming (PC, Toronto Eglinton), Dr. Harry Bruce (PC, Toronto Parkdale), and Alastair Stewart (CCF, Win-nipeg North). Fleming was concerned about the loss of employment, as would be expected because the plant was located in his constituency. Where

---

[72] Canada. Parliament. House of Commons. *Debates*, 1st session of the 20th Parliament, November 21, 1945 at 2363-64.

[73] "Strike Challenge Leads to Demand That Howe Resign" *Toronto Globe and Mail*, September 5, 1945, at 1, col. 1.

[74] C. D. Howe to J. M. Gilchrist, September 10, 1945, C. D. Howe papers (Public Archives classification: MG 27 111 B20, Vol. 171).

the Conservatives and the CCF differed was in their proposals as to what should be done with Research Enterprises. Dr. Bruce emphasized the importance of keeping alive the expertise developed, in order to give Canada an assured domestic source of supply for radar and optical equipment.

> It should not be necessary to urge the government to maintain a small part of Research Enterprises where this industry [optics] may be continued under government direction and control, perhaps through the National Research Council, and where the employment of a small group of trained personnel may be retained . . . some of the buildings now occupied by Research Enterprises could be retained and have productive facilities in a state of readiness, with a nucleus of trained personnel whose skills could be used on [defence] projects. . . .[75]

Stewart was much more expansive about the potential of Research Enterprises. He suggested that the expertise which had been built up could be used to diversify beyond radar and optical glass and into other fields, such as "measuring instruments, cameras and photographic equipment, motion-picture projectors and high-class hearing-aids, television, . . . surveying instruments, . . . automobile and aero instruments, . . . medical and dental equipment, electronic equipment, control instruments, electrical and radio test equipment, commercial radio and FM sets."[76] Stewart had a keen appreciation of the potential use of radar, predicting that "eventually, with the use of radar, we can expect that the day will come when aircraft will land with all the precision we associate with the movement of railway trains today".[77] By contrast, Howe, the great supporter of aviation, said two days later, "What are the peace-time uses of radar? There are a few limited uses and one will come into being on ships."[78] The irony of these statements is that C. D. Howe was an engineer and Stewart an accountant! What ultimately happened to the components of Research Enterprises? One building, which originally cost $522,000 was sold to Corning Glass for $150,000. Research Enterprises already had links with Corning, which had loaned the corporation two scientists and made some of its technology available. Howe was pleased to bring Corning, a leader in the glass industry, into Canada. Corning began manufacturing Pyrex ovenware at the Leaside plant and planned to export it to Mexico and Australia. However, both Mexico and Australia raised their tariffs and Corning, therefore, decided to produce locally in both places. Corning continued manufacturing Pyrex ovenware for the Canadian market until the early 1950s, when it was decided that exporting from the United States was more profitable.

---

[75] Canada. Parliament. House of Commons. *Debates*, 1st session of the 20th Parliament, October 30, 1945, at 1659.

[76] *Debates, supra* note 72, at 2247.

[77] *Ibid.*

[78] *Ibid.*, at 2363.

Corning still uses the plant as a warehouse: Corning Canada is only a packaging and marketing organization. Furthermore, Corning never had any plans to do research or production of glass for scientific or industrial uses in Canada.[79]

Eighty percent of Research Enterprises' production was radar and communications equipment. Howe ultimately found a purchaser, Rogers Majestic Ltd., a Toronto radio equipment manufacturer. Rogers Majestic had been formed by Edward S. (Ted) Rogers, Sr., who made a very important invention in the early days of radio, a tube which allowed radios to use electric current rather than batteries. In addition, Rogers Majestic had been a major subcontractor for Research Enterprises during the war. Rogers Majestic bought 13 Research Enterprises buildings for $628,000. The company planned to use them to produce radios for both the Canadian and export markets.[80]

At that time, the Canadian Army required $1.7 million worth of radar and the British government had approached the Canadian government for another order. The Defence Committee of Cabinet was undecided as to whether production should be undertaken in the private sector or by Canadian Arsenals and referred the matter to Howe.[81] Howe preferred the private sector because "it would be very expensive to maintain an arsenals organization for the sole purpose of filling occasional peacetime orders for equipment of this type. Canada's defensive position will be strengthened by having private industry trained to carry out such work, since in the event of war private production could be expanded rapidly."[82] The Cabinet concurred. As expected, Rogers Majestic ultimately got the orders.

From this promising start, Rogers Majestic moved in a different direction. Before his death in 1939, Ted Rogers, Sr. became interested in broadcasting, having founded the Toronto radio station CFRB. His successors, particularly his son, Ted Rogers, Jr., concentrated their energies in broadcasting and ultimately cable television, rather than electronics. Given that broadcasting is a regulated industry earning very high rates of return and that competing in the electronics industry meant taking on giants like RCA, General Electric, Philips, and later Sony, Rogers' choice is hardly surprising. Philips wished to establish an electronics manufacturing facility in Canada, and by 1950 had purchased all the former Research Enterprises plants from Rogers Majestic.[83] Philips has remained in Canada, though no

---

79 Interview with Tom Gillan, Former General Manager, Corning Canada (August 19, 1980).

80 "Research Enterprises Plant New Home of Rogers Radios," *Financial Post*, May 11, 1946 at 4, col. 3.

81 Memorandum from J. R. Baldwin to C. D. Howe, March 22, 1946, C. D. Howe papers (Public Archives classification: MG 27 111 B2, Vol. 43).

82 Memorandum from C. D. Howe to J. R. Baldwin, March 23, 1946, Dept. of Munitions and Supply papers (Public Archives classification: RG 2/18, Vol. 196).

83 Interview with Gerry Wright, Assistant to the President, Philips Canada Ltd. (September 24, 1980).

longer in Leaside: they still manufacture but have never done any research and development here.

In retrospect, what is regretable is not that Research Enterprises was privatized, but that the corporation was broken up. Howe failed to recognize that its great strength was the strong interplay between the National Research Council in Ottawa and the manufacturing facility in Toronto. As Herschel Hardin, in *A Nation Unaware*, put it, "Howe did not consider the possibility of scientists attached to the enterprise of developing new products, nor the converse possibility of the enterprise attached to the Council animating new science."[84] Howe also did not recognize that Research Enterprises had become a diversified firm, producing a large number of related products. In the 1950s and beyond, many successful firms adopted strategies of related diversification,[85] which permitted them to grow by avoiding the risk associated with producing only a single product. Howe would have maximized Research Enterprises' chances of success by merging with it the optics and electronics research units at the National Research Council and selling the entire firm *en bloc*. Of course, maximizing the firm's chances of success would have also maximized the return the government received for selling it. It might be argued that this is clear in retrospect, but not at the time of the original decision. However, Stewart's speech indicates that there was at least someone who saw those possibilities. Furthermore, Professor E. F. Burton of the University of Toronto, a director of Research Enterprises, outlined a proposal for developing Research Enterprises, as a research-based company with optical, glass-making, and radio divisions.[86]

In comparing these two privatizations, the sale of the aircraft producers was an example of Trebilcock and Prichard's second motivation (change in the relative effectiveness of Crown corporations) and the sale of Research Enterprises an example of the first (a change in government's objectives). In the case of Research Enterprises, even though the government was unwilling to provide much additional support through contacts, for example, it is clear that the privatization was done in such a way that it was impossible for Research Enterprises to survive as an economic entity. The sum of the disjoint parts was far less than the original whole. Some of the policies that made the aircraft firms viable could have been applied to Research Enterprises. The purchasers could have been required to undertake research and development in Canada. The firm could have been given its research units, in the same way that Avro was given Turbo Research. The

---

[84] H. Hardin, *A Nation Unaware: The Canadian Economic Culture* (Vancouver: J. J. Douglas, 1974) at 288.

[85] See B. Scott, "The Industrial State: Old Myths and New Realities" (1973), 51(2) *Harv. Bus. Rev.* 133-148.

[86] Canada. Parliament. House of Commons. *Debates*, 1st session of the 20th Parliament. November 21, 1945, at 2360-2361. (Quoted by Donald Fleming)

factories could have been leased, rather than sold outright, so that the government would have had some threat to induce good performance.

IV. CONCLUSIONS

The first part of this paper can be viewed as a test of the instrument-choice approach to explaining the existence of Crown corporations. On the whole, it was possible to find systematic factors which explain the origins of most of the production and administrative Crown corporations in World War II.

One very interesting aspect of the World War II experience was the incentive system used by the Department of Munitions and Supply to promote efficient management of its Crown corporations. It has similarities to the multi-divisional corporation or to the Government of Saskatchewan's Crown Investments Corporation and Committee on Crown Corporations. Both are structures designed to oversee Crown corporations, co-ordinate their policies, and induce efficiency. Breton and Wintrobe suggest that the public has no interest in inefficiency and that mechanisms such as the competition for budgetary funds can provide incentives for efficient resource allocation by public corporations.[87] A useful line of research would involve both theoretical and empirical analysis of the utility of such external oversight mechanisms in promoting efficient management of public enterprises.

In addition to external incentives to public enterprise managers, there are also internal incentives. Herschel Hardin put a great deal of emphasis on such incentives in his book, *A Nation Unaware*. He argues that the founders of a number of Crown corporations displayed a missionary zeal in pursuit of their objectives which is reminiscent of the behaviour of the managers of the best wartime Crown corporations. Specifically, Hardin mentioned the dedication of Adam Beck of Ontario Hydro to efficient technology and power at cost, of René Levesque and Hydro-Québec to Francophone technological progressiveness, and of Graham Spry and the CBC to quality programming and national identity.[88] It would be worthwhile for students of the Crown corporation more sceptical than Hardin to see if these cases indeed support Hardin's point. More generally, studies of Crown corporations should put greater emphasis on the entire set of incentives, monetary and non-monetary, external and internal, which influence managers of Crown corporations. This would include analysis of the professional backgrounds of managers of Crown corporations and of the resulting "mind-sets" which characterize Crown corporations. This knowledge will

---

[87] A. Breton and R. S. Wintrobe, "An Economic Analysis of Bureaucratic Efficiency" [Unpublished ms., 1979].

[88] Hardin, *supra* note 84, at 96-140, 254-284.

be useful in enabling us to characterize the set of objectives a Crown corporation is pursuing. This is important because what may appear at first glance to be inefficiency may turn out to be the efficient pursuit of objective set in which the government determines what the factors are which comprise the objective set and the weights applied to each. One practical use of this increased understanding would be that it would enable government to derive indicators (which may be very different from the traditional "bottom line") to measure and motivate performance by the managers of Crown corporations.

The second half of this paper examined the privatization of Crown corporations at the end of the war. Some clear lessons emerge from the contrasting experiences of Federal and Victory Aircraft, on the one hand, and Research Enterprises, on the other. If a Crown corporation is to be privatized, the government should be aware of what the corporation's true sources of strength are, since they may be located somewhere else in the government, such as Research Enterprises' collaboration with the National Research Council. When a Crown corporation is to be privatized, the package that is put together should be one which maximizes the corporation's chance of survival on the private market. Finally, government should be careful not to give up a Crown corporation completely, because it may find that the performance of the private sector owners is inadequate, or that the objectives for which the corporation was originally founded again become relevant. Retention of a minority position, and leasing rather than selling the physical plant are possible ways of doing this.